LANGDON E. LONGSTRETH, Ph.D., University of Iowa, is Associate Professor of Psychology at the University of Southern California. He has also taught at George Peabody College, where he was awarded a Visiting Research Professorship, and at the University of Hawaii, where he was affiliated with the Newborn Psychological Research Laboratory. He has published widely in the areas of learning and motivation in children.

PSYCHOLOGICAL DEVELOPMENT OF THE CHILD

LANGDON E. LONGSTRETH

UNIVERSITY OF SOUTHERN CALIFORNIA

THE RONALD PRESS COMPANY • NEW YORK

Library of Congress Catalog Card Number: 68–21651
PRINTED IN THE UNITED STATES OF AMERICA

Preface

Having taught a university course in child psychology for more than a decade, I have gradually developed a frame of reference concerning what the ideal textbook should present to the student. This book represents my attempt to make that ideal a reality. What, then, are its unique characteristics?

It is, first and foremost, heavily data-bound. There is an attempt to present the student with three sets of data: (1) background data on heredity, learning, and motivation; (2) correlational data describing the stability—the patterns—of psychological development through childhood and into adulthood; and (3) experimental data that provide tests of explanations of these data. The book follows this logical sequence. Chapters 1–6 present the background information, including a detailed discussion of genetic determinants of personality development, determinants of intellectual development, learning, and motivation. Chapters 7–9 present the descriptive information of personality development: the stability of behavior from childhood to adulthood, utilizing facts and striking case histories from the Fels study. The rest of the book, Chapters 10–16, is concerned with explanations of these developmental facts.

A second characteristic of the book is a serious attempt to show the student the importance of the child's environment. The logic is this: First it is shown that personality development is stable—the child's behavior at five is predictive of his behavior at ten, and his behavior at ten is predictive of his behavior at twenty (until recent longitudinal data were made available, the stability of behavior had to be *assumed* rather than demonstrated). Then it is shown that child behavior can be manipulated by environmental events, according to general principles of learning (and bounded by genetic potentialities). It then follows logically that adult behavior is also affected by these events, and hence the importance of childhood is demonstrated. In other words, the student is not asked to take the importance of childhood on faith, but rather is presented with the facts that make the conclusion inevitable.

iii

Third, there is an overall orientation toward S-R learning theory. I make no apologies for this "bias": it is perfectly clear to me that much of human behavior is learned, and is therefore to be explained by *theories* of learning. Social learning and imitation fit easily within this rubric, of course, as well as recent research on curiosity and novelty. Cognitive approaches are not ignored either: Genevan psychology, including both its intellectual and moral components, is described and discussed in detail, with an attempt to integrate it within a learning-theory frame of reference.

I am greatly indebted to Wendell Jeffrey, who read the greater part of the manuscript and made many constructive criticisms. I am also indebted to John Wiley & Sons, Inc., publishers, for making available the Fels Research Institute materials (from *Birth to Maturity* by J. Kagan and H. A. Moss). In addition, I wish to thank my typist, Kathy Kato, who did an excellent job, not only of typing but of editing as well.

Finally, my special thanks go to my wife and children, whose patience and encouragement speeded up my work enormously.

LANGDON E. LONGSTRETH

Los Angeles, California
February, 1968

Contents

PSYCHOLOGICAL
DEVELOPMENT
OF THE CHILD

1

Introduction

This book attempts to describe and explain some of the courses of psychological development from infancy to adulthood. It does not, of course, present all the facts or all the explanations. An author must rely upon his own judgment in selecting the facts and explanations he writes about. His choices are dictated by his beliefs, his "point of view," toward child psychology. In this introductory chapter, I shall try to describe my attitude, for it provides the basic frame of reference for all subsequent chapters.

THE ASSUMPTION OF CAUSALITY

The behavior of man has often occupied a special place, an isolated niche, when the lawfulness of nature is discussed. Most people are willing to accept the idea that all natural phenomena, from the fall of a stone to the output of a high-speed electronic computer, are caused by antecedent events that behave in a regular, lawful way. These cause-effect relationships are used by the scientist to construct theories that explain the phenomena. Theories thus specify the causes of a phenomenon, for that is what an explanation is: it tells *how* and *why*.

All of this is not new as far as the natural sciences go. In colleges and universities, though, the department of psychology is usually not a member of the division of natural sciences, but rather a member of the division of social sciences. This administrative fact is indicative of the special niche occupied by psychology. It is as though there was something *un*natural about the causation of human behavior. Indeed, while most people are willing to believe that all "natural" phenomena at least have a cause, many of them react negatively to the assertion that all human behavior is caused. They act as though such a fact, if true, would remove their "humanity" and leave them indistinguishable from everything else in the universe.

Many people believe that man is something "special"; he has something unique that places him outside the boundaries of natural causation. He has a soul, he lives, he thinks, he feels, and he has free will; he can make decisions all by himself. Do not these characteristics, particularly the last one, prove that he is indeed unique, that he can do as he pleases, rather than remain chained to the mundane regularities of natural causality?

No, I am afraid these characteristics prove no such thing. Whether he has a soul or not is not susceptible to scientific study; it is a matter of belief, not fact. It is true that man lives, thinks, and feels, but these properties are not incompatible with the idea of natural causation. They are simply properties that distinguish man from other objects, just as water is distinguished by its molecular construction and such properties as viscosity, etc., from other substances. Because water evaporates and "disappears," we do not say it is "magical" or not explainable in scientific terms, but rather we explain *why* and *how* it "disappears" in the same way we explain the why and how of anything else—*by reference to scientific theories*. The same is true of "life," "feeling," and the other human characteristics; they are subject to the same kind of scientific explanation as anything else. Recent success in the artificial creation of life in the laboratory should make it clear that there is nothing unnatural about life.

But does not "free will" prove the uniqueness of man? No, for it need only be argued that there are causes that determine what a person "wills" or "decides." But the psychologist cannot prove that, can he? No, but no one can prove the contrary, either. The final argument, and one that cannot be denied, is that the history of science yields an important generalization: *when causes are looked for, they are usually found.* Thus, the evidence is overwhelmingly on the side of causality. "Since science has found orderliness decade after decade and in subject matter after subject matter, the scientist is prone to believe that all events of nature, be they events characteristic of stones, oceans, angleworms, ministers, corpuscles, or nerve tracts, have discoverable correlates" (Underwood, 1957, p. 5). To assume that part or all of behavior occurs with no cause is to assume that behavior is chaotic, unpredictable, and not subject to scientific investigation. Psychology, one of the youngest of the scientific specialties, is already advanced far enough to show in a hundred different ways the error of such a statement.

Therefore, psychologists assume that behavior is caused in the same natural way that everything else is caused. As such, we feel justified in *looking* for the causes. If we meet with failure, as often happens, we cannot explain it by arguing that there must not be a cause, because of the special nature of man. We cannot, in other words, appeal to supernatural causes to explain why a natural cause could not be found. Rather, the conclusion must be that the natural cause still exists but that we could not find it.

CLASSIFICATION OF CAUSES

It is possible to classify the possible causes of behavior in a number of ways. The most frequent way is in terms of past environment, present environment, and heredity; that is, a person's behavior at any time is completely determined (caused) by his past environment, his present environment, and his heredity. This classification is exhaustive; there are no other possible classes of causes that cannot be restated in terms of one of these three classes. While thus providing maximum conceptual coverage, this classification also reveals the complexity of behavioral causes. We do not know all about the past environment of anyone, or all about the present environment, not to mention our ignorance about human heredity. Furthermore, we will never obtain such complete information about anyone in any of these three categories. For instance, to obtain complete information about a person's past environment would require continuous recording of environmental conditions since the moment of birth, or, worse yet, since conception. It is therefore sometimes asserted that psychology is, in principle, an inexact science, since lack of complete knowledge of causative factors will lead to behavioral predictions with a corresponding amount of error.

Without careful analysis, this assertion is misleading. For example, all scientific disciplines deal with error of observation and, in that sense, are inexact. What is meant, rather, is that psychology is more inexact than, say, physics, because the causes of behavior are much more elusive and, therefore, harder to observe. For instance, mass, velocity, and distance of one object from another are easier to determine than what one's mother did at 3:00 P.M. exactly one year ago. But the assertion still needs careful analysis to minimize misinterpretation. For example, one's mother's behavior at a precise moment in the past may be unimportant, in the same sense that the color of a stone is unimportant in predicting its velocity x seconds after dropping it. But the assertion is nevertheless well taken; we know so little about the past or present environment of anyone, or their heredity, that, even under the best of conditions, predictions of behavior are bound to be inexact. While admitting such inexactness, the author would still insist that inexact predictions are better than no predictions at all. Besides, it is not that information about environment and heredity is relatively inaccessible *in principle,* but rather that it is hard to obtain in practice. Therefore, when greater and greater pains are taken to obtain such information, predictions will become more and more accurate.

An alternative classification scheme seems to get around the difficulty of inaccessible data. Let us study the logic of this second point of view. First, everyone agrees that every bit of behavior involves a corresponding physiological event (i.e., a word cannot be spoken or an arm moved without neural and muscular action within the body). Thus, anything that affects behavior must also affect physiological events. To assert that behavior is affected by the individual's past environment is to assert, therefore, that past environmental events affect physiological events. Let us make clear what is meant here. Not all past environmental events affect behavior. My father's scowl whenever I swore on Sundays does not affect my present behavior *if I did not see him* when he scowled. Thus, only some events of the past environment affect present behavior: those that had an impact upon the nervous system. The second point is that any physiological change in the past that affects behavior at the present time must have left a change or trace within the body that is still there at the present time. To conclude otherwise is tantamount to asserting that A can affect B even though B is completely isolated from A. The very word *isolated* means that A cannot affect B. Thus, we must conclude that any event A that affects another event B must be spatially and temporally contiguous with B; otherwise we have "action at a distance," which has never been acceptable to scientists. An illustration of this principle is provided by the case of John, who ate some poison yesterday. The poison will kill him today unless the doctor removes its traces, i.e., unless the doctor removes or stops the processes now in operation that are contiguous with the ingestion of poison yesterday. He may attempt to do just that with a blood transfusion.

The gist of the preceding two points is that all environmental events of the past or present that affect behavior at the present time leave a physiological change or trace that exists at the present time. It is therefore not necessary to look for the environmental event; we need only look for its physiological trace. To understand a person's behavior at the present time no longer requires a search into the past environment. Therefore, a physiological or "inside" approach will lead to more exact predictions than an environmental or "outside" approach. It will lead to more precision because the body at the present time is more accessible than past environmental events that are gone forever.

The new classification therefore consists of just one category—physiological conditions. It is related to the environmental-heredity point of view as indicated in Figure 1.1; it is environment (past and present) and heredity that determine the state of the body at any given time.

Figure 1.1. The relationship between environmental-genetic and physiological classifications of causation.

There are two practical difficulties with the physiological point of view. First, at the present time very little is known about the physiological correlates of behavior. Given a certain physiological condition, a specific behavior pattern usually cannot be predicted. Second, physiological information is as difficult to obtain as information about the environment. There are at least two factors that contribute to this difficulty: (1) most people are quite unwilling to submit themselves as objects of examination for the types of observations required for physiological-behavioral research, and (2) the physiological events that are correlated with day-to-day behavior are apparently very complex and hard to detect, even if people did submit their bodies for examination for the sake of "pure science." In short, the physiological approach faces the same problem as the environmental approach—the inaccessibility of data.

A third classification has also been suggested and deserves consideration. It is often asserted that, to understand a child (or adult), one must put himself in the place of the person to be understood. That is, "you must see things as he sees them"; you must "empathize" with him. According to this point of view, the child's feelings, needs, and perceptions must be known in order to understand his behavior. The difficulty with this point of view is easy to illustrate: how does one determine the feelings and perceptions of someone else? Does one simply ask him? We know better than that, since a person (1) may not be aware of all his feelings or perceptions, (2) he may be aware of them but unable to verbalize them, and (3) he may be aware of them and able to verbalize them, but be unwilling to do so; i.e., he may lie. In other words, a person's inner sensations are his own, and neither the psychologist, psychiatrist, nor anyone else can get at them. They are, *in principle*, inaccessible.

The first classification, environment and heredity, is the most fruitful approach. We probably will never be able to predict a person's day-to-day behavior on the basis of physiological information alone. Certainly, we cannot do so now. Of course, as such information becomes available, it must be incorporated into the scheme of things. It would be unwise to ignore relevant information just because it falls outside of one's general point of view. At the human level, however, most of the known determinants of day-to-day behavior are environmental variables, such as the way one was raised by his parents, or the nature of the peer group he was exposed to as an adolescent. It is these environmental variables that are stressed in this book.

CLASSIFICATION OF BEHAVIOR

There are different ways of classifying behavior just as there are different ways of classifying its causes. It could be described physiologically, for example, since every pattern of overt behavior must have a corresponding physiological pattern. But the psychologist is not interested in the bioelectric characteristics of a person's nervous system; his interest is in what they *do*. Hence, he should use a *behavioral* classification scheme.

There are many such schemes, and an exhaustive list would fill many pages and, further, would be incomplete, as new classifications are forever being introduced. Some examples may suffice to communicate their nature. At the present time, the following classes of behavior are frequently used:

Intelligence	Delinquency
Dependency	Schizophrenia
Aggression	Anxiety
Masculinity	Achievement motivation
Morality	Extroversion
Neurosis	Inhibition

Of course, there are many other classes, since the above are merely a sample. Is one list preferable to another, or is the selection of a list completely arbitrary? A satisfactory answer to this question would be long and complicated, for there is no simple answer. It seems that there are at least two fundamental criteria that should be considered.

First, a classification can be evaluated in terms of its *usefulness.* Some kinds of information are simply more useful than others. *Intelligence*, for example, is a very useful item of information because it is related to a number of other items. It predicts school grades, education of parents, and intelligence of siblings, just to mention three. *Therefore, the greater the number of relationships a classification has with other items of information, the more valuable it becomes, from a predictive point of view.*

Second, a classification can be evaluated in terms of its *theoretical relevance.* Some classifications are "theoretically rich" in the sense that they relate to explanatory concepts that appear in theories of behavior.

Anxiety is such a classification, and so is *extroversion. Intelligence,* on the other hand, is not. There are very few theoretical concepts related to one's IQ score. Thus, a classification can be useful from a predictive point of view but relatively sterile from a theoretical point of view.

But regardless of whether a given classification scheme is "good" or "bad" in terms of the preceding criteria, we are obliged to use those that have actually been used. Fortunately, the "best" are also the most frequently used, simply because they are the best. A sample of those used in this book includes: *love for mother* in infancy, *mother love for infant, intelligence, sex-typing, anxiety, boredom and curiosity, dependency, passivity, aggression, achievement strivings, social anxiety, heterosexuality,* and *morality.*

CLASSIFICATION OF METHODOLOGY

There are different ways of studying behavior and its causes; one can describe methodology in terms of classes just as one can describe classes of behavior and classes of causes. Further, all methods can be classed as correlational or experimental. This distinction is an important one and therefore is discussed in some detail.

Suppose a psychologist is interested in causes of aggression. He suspects that frustration has something to do with it. In fact, he thinks that frustration *causes* aggression, in the sense that children who are frustrated at one time are more likely to be aggressive at another time than children who were not frustrated or who were frustrated less. He wants to determine if his hypothesis is true or false and decides to conduct a study to find out. We shall consider two ways in which he can go about it.

Correlational Study

First, our psychologist secures the cooperation of a group of mothers. They agree to let him visit their homes as frequently as he wishes, and whenever he wishes, so that he can watch and record the ways in which each mother raises her children. Unknown to them, he records all instances of frustration, all instances where the mother prevents the child from doing something he wanted to do. The psychologist is very careful to spend the same amount of time at each home, to record during the same parts of the day in each home, etc. To make sure his recordings are valid, i.e., that the mothers are not putting on an "act" for him, he asks the husbands to rate their wives in terms of how often they frustrate their children. He finds a strong relationship between what the husbands say and what he saw in the home, and thus he concludes, rightly enough, that his recordings were valid. Then he assigns a score that represents the amount of frustration produced by each mother: the higher the score, the greater the frequency of frustrations.

Next, he directs his attention to the children; he needs an "aggression score" for each child. He chooses two methods so that he can check the validity of these measurements. First the psychologist observes each child as he plays during recess at school and records all instances of aggression. Then he counts the number of such responses for each child, thereby computing the aggression score for that child. The higher it is, the more aggressive is the child. Second, he asks the teacher of each child to rate the child on aggression, just as the husbands were asked to rate the mothers on frustration. He then compares his own scores with those provided by the teachers and finds that they are in high agreement. Thus, he concludes that his aggression scores are valid: a reasonable conclusion.

He now moves to the final phase of the study—the analysis. He compares the *frustration score* of each mother with the *aggression score* of each child. He finds that mothers with a high frustration score usually have children with a high aggression score and vice versa. He plots his results on a graph, as in Figure 1.2. Each dot describes the frustration score of a mother and the aggression score of her child. Such a graph is called a *scatter diagram*. Notice how the dots tend to go from the

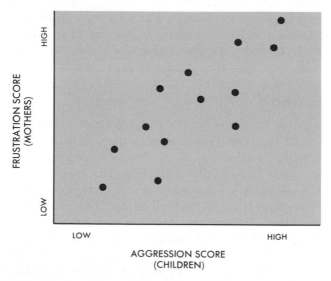

Figure 1.2. Scatter diagram of relationship between maternal frustration and aggression of children.

lower left to the upper right, indicating that high frustration scores are predictive of high aggression scores.

If the relationship were absolutely perfect, with no exceptions, the scatter diagram would yield a straight line, indicating no exceptions to the relationship. On the other hand, if there were no relationship at all, the scatter diagram would yield a random scatter of dots (i.e., they would form no pattern at all and would be of approximately equal density in all parts of the figure). Finally, if the relationship were the *reverse* of the hypothesized one, i.e., if aggression became *less* as maternal frustration became *greater*, the slope of the dots would be the opposite of those shown in Figure 1.2: they would form a pattern from the upper left to the lower right.

It is possible to describe the degree of relationship between the two sets of scores mathematically as well as graphically. There is a numerical index, computed by a simple formula, that describes the exact degree of relationship between two sets of scores. It is the *correlation coefficient*. We are not concerned here with its calculation, but only with its meaning, since it appears a number of times in subsequent chapters.

Referring to Figure 1.2, the actual results of our hypothetical study, our psychologist computes the correlation based on these scores; it turns out to be about .70. If he had found a perfect relationship, indicated by a straight line, the correlation would have been 1.00. If he had found no relationship at all, the correlation would have been near 0. And if he had found the reverse relationship and with about the same strength as what he actually found, the correlation would have been about −.70. If the reverse relationship had been perfect, he would have found a correlation of about −1.00. The correlation coefficient can thus range from −1 to +1. The closer it is to either extreme, the stronger the relationship between the two sets of scores. If the sign is positive, the scores are *directly* related to each other; as one increases, so does the other. If the sign is negative, the scores are *inversely* related to each other; as one increases, the other decreases. The closer the correlation is to 0, the weaker is the relationship (i.e., the greater are the number and magnitude of exceptions).

Our psychologist has found a correlation of .70, a high correlation. Thus, he found a strong relationship between the two scores, as predicted. He concludes that his hypothesis is therefore correct: frustration does produce aggression in children.

Experiment

Suppose another psychologist has exactly the same hypothesis: frustration causes aggression. He goes about investigating its truth value too, but in a different way. First, he secures the cooperation of a group of mothers, much as our previous friend did. He does not request permission to enter the home, however, but merely asks them if they will cooperate in a study he is doing. If they say yes, he takes their name. He continues in this manner until he has, say, 40 names.

Then he divides the names into two groups. He does this in a very special way: he divides them into two *random* groups. He accomplishes this by flipping a coin for each name. If "heads" comes up, the name goes into Group 1; if "tails" comes up, the name goes into Group 2. Since heads and tails come up about an equal number of times, he winds up with about 20 names in each group.

Then he asks all the mothers of Group 1 to do the following: On some weekday evening, before the child is put to bed, the mother is to announce that the next day the whole family is going to an afternoon movie that "children love," and that he can skip school the next day. The next morning, however, it is announced that the child must go to school after all, and that the family cannot go to the movie that day. In other words, these mothers are asked to *frustrate* their children just before they leave for school. Mothers of Group 2 are given no such instructions but are told to act as usual.

On the day that each child is frustrated, our psychologist visits the school and observes the child's behavior during recess. He scores the children's aggression in exactly the same way as our previous friend. Likewise, he asks the teachers to rate it too, and he finds his scores are valid, just as before.

He now proceeds to the analysis. He compares the aggression scores of the children from Group 1 with the aggression scores of the children from Group 2. He finds that the scores in Group 1 are higher than those in Group 2, indicating more aggression. Furthermore, he finds that the relationship between the aggression scores and group membership is of the same strength as our friend found in the first study. In other words, the same degree of relationship between maternal frustration and child aggression is found in both studies. This psychologist concludes, as did the first one, that his hypothesis is supported: frustration does cause aggression.

Comparison of the Two Methods

Speaking intuitively now, which of the two studies is more convincing? Although the results of both are *consistent* with the hypothesis, the second study—the experiment—is much more convincing. Why? (1) The two groups of mothers probably did not differ except as instructed by the investigator; and (2) whether the children were frustrated or not occurred *independent of* and *before* their aggression occurred. Let us reflect upon each of these two assertions, for they describe the crucial differences between a correlational study and an experiment.

The Importance of Randomization

In the correlational study, it was found that mothers scoring high in frustration had children who scored high in aggression at school. Now, why did these mothers frustrate their children so frequently? Surely something caused them to do so. Everything has a cause, including frustrative acts of mothers. *Whatever it was, perhaps it also caused their children to be more aggressive.* The chances are very high, in other words, that mothers who were most frustrative were also different in other unknown ways. Any one of these differences could have been the real cause of aggression in their children, and thus there is a high probability that the investigator arrived at a false conclusion.

Is not the same argument equally applicable to the experiment? Is it not equally probable that the two groups of mothers in that investigation also differed in unknown ways? No, it is not. Remember that the only reason these mothers did or did not frustrate their child that morning was because a coin came up heads or tails. Now, the behavior of the coin was surely not affected by any characteristic of the mothers, known or unknown. Therefore, whether the frustrative act did or did not occur was equally unrelated to any characteristic of the mothers. The chances are very low, then, that the mothers who performed the frustrative act differed in any way from the mothers who did not perform the frustrative act.

Cause-Effect Direction

Let us temporarily ignore the previous criticism by assuming that the mothers who scored high on frustration did not, in fact, differ in any other way from the mothers who scored low on frustration. Are the two sets of results then equally convincing—does the hypothesis receive the same amount of support from both studies? No, the experiment is still much more convincing. *It is more convincing because the direction of the cause-effect relationship is known, whereas it is not known in the correlational study.*

The results of the correlational study could be explained by assuming that *aggressive children caused their mothers to respond with frustrative counterreactions,* just the reverse of the hypothesis. This possibility exists because it is not known which originated first, the frustrative behavior of the mothers or the aggressive behavior of the children. In the experiment, however, it is known that the frustrative act occurred first, and the aggressive behavior later. Therefore, the aggressive behavior of the children could not possibly have affected the preceding frustrative act of the mothers. The possibility of "reverse causation" in the experiment is therefore eliminated, since a cause can never follow its effect.

Let us now compare the merits of correlational studies (hereafter referred to simply as *studies*) and *experiments* more abstractly. In essence, all a *study* consists of is a determination of the relationship between two or more sets of measurements. The emphasis is on finding out if a relationship exists or not. A study is not designed to isolate the cause(s) of the relationship, should one be found. It does not fulfill this function because, fundamentally, *it does not manipulate one variable and observe its consequent effects on another variable.*

There is a fundamental rule in science: if one wants to determine the effect of X on Y, then X and only X must be varied, and measurements made of consequent changes in Y. If, under these conditions, Y changes as X changes, one has as strong an argument for X-to-Y causation as it is possible to get. An experiment attempts to do just this. The variable that is manipulated, X, is called the *independent variable*, since it is manipulated independently of everything else. The variable that is consequently measured, Y, is called the *dependent variable*, since the question is whether or not it "depends" upon (is *affected* by) X.

To vary X, at least two values are required. At the simplest level, X and not-X will do. Thus, many experiments consist of two groups, one in which X is present (the *experimental* group) and one in which it is absent (the *control* group). But X and only X must be varied. This is accomplished by taking pains to insure that the two (or more) groups do not differ in any other way. The most common method is to form the groups by a strictly random procedure, such as by the flipping of a coin. The larger the groups, the less the probability that they are different. Thus, large, randomly selected groups are usually indicative of an experiment where X and only X was manipulated.

Suppose a child sucks his thumb while clutching a teddy bear. The preference for such "security objects" might be caused by thumb-sucking in their presence: the satisfaction derived from thumb-sucking might become transferred to associated objects. If this hypothesis is correct, a way to test it would be to determine if children who have security objects are also thumb-suckers. If the two are indeed correlated, the hypothesis would be supported. But it would be weak support for two reasons: (1) maybe something else, such as too much nursing experience (late weaning), causes *both* of these behavior patterns, and hence they are not causally related at all; or (2) even if they are causally related, maybe it is in reverse—maybe possession of a security object causes thumb-sucking.

Thus, at best, such a study could only show whether thumb-sucking and possession of a security object are correlated or not. It could not tell why. The only way to find support for the original hypothesis is by means of an experiment. Ideally, it would consist of first identifying a group of thumb-suckers who had not yet developed preferences for security objects. This group would be randomly divided into an experimental and a control group. Members of the experimental group would be exposed to some object—e.g., a teddy bear—whenever they sucked their thumbs. Members of the control group would be exposed to the same object equally often, but not necessarily while they were sucking their thumbs. Thus the only difference between the two groups would be whether or not the potential security object was paired with thumb-sucking. Sometime later, the preference of each group for the object would be determined. If the experimental group exhibited a stronger preference, the hypothesis would be confirmed: thumb-sucking in the presence of an object does increase the child's preference for that object.

A correlational study, then, does not establish causation. Underwood (1957) gives an example that makes this point clear. There are two forms to the Stanford-Binet Intelligence Test: Form L and Form M. Scores on one correlate about .95 with scores on the other. Yet no one would argue that the behavior on one form *causes* the behavior on the other form. It is assumed, rather, that some other factor—intelligence—causes the behavior on both forms.

Many studies about children are correlational. One of the most frequent types is similar to the original example in this chapter: scores that describe parental behavior are correlated with scores that describe child behavior. In this way, it is hoped that some idea of the effects of different child-rearing practices on personality development can be obtained. But even if such a correlation is found, we have seen that causation could flow in the opposite direction; it could be the personality of the child that influences his parents' behavior. Indeed, is this not almost a certainty? Coupled with the fact that such studies do not isolate X anyway (unmeasured differences between the parents might be involved), one is forced to conclude that such studies are of questionable value as far as explanation is concerned.

In this book, primary emphasis is therefore directed to experiments rather than to studies. We shall be concerned mainly with those investigations where something is done to one group of children, and where their subsequent behavior is compared to that of another group that has been treated the same in all other respects. When differences are found between the experimental and control groups, we can be fairly sure it was caused by the independent variable, and thus our understanding of child behavior (our knowledge of causes) has been extended.

Experiments and Studies in Combination

Correlational studies will not be completely ignored, however. At least they suggest where profitable experiments might be carried out; that is, it can be argued that the *study* shows the existence of a relationship, and the *experiment* looks for the reason. Another argument, and a better one, is based on the fact that some hypotheses are practically impossible to investigate in a strict experimental sense. In such cases, any information is better than no information at all. The discovery of a correlation between two such variables is at least consistent with the hypothesis, and thereby provides some support. After all, the correlation could fail to materialize, in which case there would be weak evidence against the hypothesis (it would be weak because other contaminating variables might have canceled out and erased a true X-Y relationship).

Such experimentally intractable hypotheses are always prevalent in questions having to do with the causes of human behavior. There are many things we would like to do to people in order to discover their effects, but ethics or practicalities prevent it. Thus, it would be nice to know if psychoses are really inherited, but the necessary experiment—controlled mating between randomly selected psychotics and non-psychotics—is clearly out of the question. The same is true of intelligence: we obviously cannot require men and women to marry each other solely on the basis of their IQ scores. Child-rearing practices are in the same situation: although we may want to know if "tender loving care" (TLC) really affects a child's personality development, we cannot randomly assign one group of babies to "rejecting" mothers and another group to "loving" mothers.

In all these cases, we have to take the evidence as nature presents it to us. This evidence is correlational. For example, we may look for rejecting mothers and loving mothers, and compare the behavior of their children. If there is a relationship between the behavior of the mothers and the behavior of the children, the hypothesis is supported. The support is weak, of course, because of previously discussed reasons. But such evidence is better than none at all. The author has found similar evidence relating smoking and cancer to be convincing enough to give up smoking.

There is a strategy in such cases that this author favors. It consists of buttressing the correlational fact with a "miniature experiment" that is feasible. In regard to TLC, this might involve the experimental manipulation of some mild, short-term type of "love." For example, a randomly selected group of orphanage babies might be intensively cared for by the experimenter for a duration of, say, a month, while another group is exposed to routine institutional care. Assuming that such care involves less

TLC, conditions of X and not-X would have been achieved, if only for a month and if only in "weak" amounts. If a difference is found in the subsequent behavior of the babies, it can be assumed to be the result of the differential treatment—of differences in TLC. If such miniature experimental findings are in the same direction as real-life correlational findings where, say, children of brutal mothers are compared with children of normal mothers after five years of exposure, then it seems that one can have added confidence in his explanation of the original correlational finding; that is, one can be surer that the maternal rejection causes the deviant personality development than, say, the reverse.

Many investigators subscribe to this strategy. For example, the preceding TLC experiment has actually been carried out (Rheingold and Bayley, 1959) and is described in detail in a later chapter. There are many examples of this strategy in succeeding chapters, particularly with respect to hypotheses about effects of various child-rearing practices. Thus, a careful "mixture" of correlational and "miniature" experimental data can minimize the risk of misinterpreting the results of those correlational studies that cannot be completely reproduced in an experimental setting.

PLAN OF THE BOOK

There are five main parts to this book. The first part, "Basic Processes of Development," is concerned with heredity, intelligence, learning, and motivation. The human infant starts life with certain genetically determined potentials for development. One of the most important of these is intelligence, although there are many other kinds of potentials, too. These potentials are not the same for everybody, and hence right from birth there are individual differences in behavior.

Imposed on top of genetically controlled differences are differences caused by the environment, which also vary from infant to infant from the moment of birth, and even before. These environmental differences provide explicit direction to the potentialities locked up in the genes, as demonstrated in Chapter 3, which is concerned with environmental effects upon intelligence. Sometimes the environmental effect is weak, leading us to conclude that heredity plays the major role. Often, however, the environmental effect is strong, as indicated by large personality differences associated with known environmental differences. In these cases, we conclude that environment plays the major role.

Environmental effects are due primarily to *learning*, although sickness and injury are also important. Learning is intimately connected with motivation. An unmotivated organism, human or otherwise, learns very little, if anything. The last two chapters in Part I describe the basic processes of learning and motivation.

Part II, "Patterns of Development," asks if the child is truly father of the man. There is little reason for studying psychological development if this is not so—if no relationship exists between behavior at one age and behavior at a later age. It is often assumed that such continuity exists, that behavior during childhood is predictive of behavior during adulthood. But this is an empirical matter, to be decided by observation, not reason. It is entirely possible that the relationship is minimal, or that some classes of adult behavior are related to child behavior, but not others.

The study of personality stability requires the study of behavior over time. Such *longitudinal* studies are very rare, as compared to the easier, shorter, less expensive *cross-sectional* study, which makes only one observation per child. The only clear way to determine if child behavior is predictive of adult behavior is to study a group of children all the way to adulthood. There are very few such studies. The most definitive was initiated some 30 years ago by the Fels Institute of Yellow Springs, Ohio. Its findings up to the present (the study is still ongoing) are summarized by Kagan and Moss (1962). This book summarizes the psychological development of 89 individuals from birth to young adulthood and provides the subject matter for Part II.

A sample of the kinds of questions that are asked is: Are two-year-old children shown to be highly aggressive also aggressive when they are ten? When they are twenty? Is a shy, withdrawn kindergarten child likely to be shy and withdrawn when he enters high school? When he enters college? Is a six-year-old who works very hard to "get good grades" in the first grade likely to strive equally hard for intellectual achievement in college, or will "fatigue" have set in by then? Does the three-year-old who has frequent temper tantrums become a young adult who easily loses his temper? These questions, and many more like them, are discussed in Part II. It will be found that the relationship between child and adult behavior is complex, depending upon the sex of the child, the type of behavior, its relationship to cultural pressures, etc. There are no simple answers.

Part III, "Parents and Children," and Part IV, "Influence of the Community," take the facts of Part II and ask, "How?" and "Why?" While Part II describes personality development, Parts III and IV inquire about its environmental determinants (genetic determinants were considered in Part I). Parental behavior is probably the most important single determinant, and it is discussed in detail in Part III. Community determinants—the school, the peers—are discussed in Part IV. Knowledge of the environmental causes of personality development is crucial if one wants to control the development of his children. Presumably, all parents are vitally interested in such control. Parts III and IV provide the relevant information; they present the "equations," as it were, that relate the environment to behavior.

The last part, Part V, "Moral Development," consists of just one substantive chapter: "Morality and Parental Responsibility." This author feels that studies of moral development were sadly neglected from 1940 to 1960. With the last half-dozen years or so, interest has reawakened. Part V summarizes current knowledge. The epilogue is concerned with morality, too, the moral responsibilities of parents to their children. But it assumes knowledge of the material in the earlier chapters, the facts and causes of psychological development. Let us begin.

BIBLIOGRAPHY

KAGAN, J., and MOSS, H. A. (1962). *Birth to maturity.* New York: John Wiley & Sons, Inc.

RHEINGOLD, HARRIET L., and BAYLEY, NANCY (1959). The later effects of an experimental modification of mothering. *Child development,* 30, 362–372.

UNDERWOOD, B. J. (1957). *Psychological research.* New York: Appleton-Century-Crofts, Inc.

I

BASIC PROCESSES
OF DEVELOPMENT

2

Genetic Determinants

INTRODUCTION

The greatest intellectual event of the nineteenth century was publication of Charles Darwin's *The Origin of Species* (1859) and *The Descent of Man* (1871). These two books "cured" man of his "superiority complex" over his own origin—that the infinite variety of life on earth was a result of spontaneous, heavenly creation, with no relationship between the various forms other than that of a heavenly origin. While preserving the possibility of a heavenly relationship, Darwin's books presented incontrovertible evidence of a second relationship. All forms of life sprang from a common, *earthly* origin, and they later diverged because of environmental pressures favoring different life forms in the battle for survival. The theory of evolution is therefore quite a step down from a belief that puts man at the very pinnacle of heavenly creation, created not only by God, but in the very image of God. Evolution asks man but to look at life forms as they can be traced back through history, down a "gnarled and twisted family tree through mammals and amphibians to the lowly fish . . ." (Moore, 1964) and on back to a time when the surface of the earth was a hot, bubbling slime, and there he will find his own origin in the chemical reactions of the mud. Such was Darwin's shattering solution to the mystery of the origin of species.

But in solving one problem, Darwin created another, the riddle of heredity. How does evolution occur? What are the laws of inheritance? By what mechanisms are parental characteristics passed on to offspring? The answers to these questions were unknown to Darwin, even though he spent the last years of his life in a futile search for them. The common belief of the day was that the blood of the parents somehow became mixed during the act of procreation, and that the child was thus a

23

"blend" of the parents. Ironically enough, at the very time Darwin's ideas were culminating in his famous books, another man launched the beginning of a series of investigations that was likewise to culminate in a famous publication. In 1856, an obscure Austrian monk, Gregor Johann Mendel, embarked on a series of studies with the common garden pea and reported his results to the Brünn Society for the Study of Natural Science in February, 1865. A monograph was published in the society's proceedings a year later, but apparently no one realized the magnitude of Mendel's discoveries, and he died, unrecognized, in 1884. The riddle of heredity, however, became increasingly painful. Its solution became critical for the final proof of the theory of evolution. In 1900, three different men rediscovered Mendel's monograph and immediately recognized its significance. It was re-presented to the scientific world. The reaction was definite; there was no question but that Mendel had made one of the greatest discoveries in the history of science—the basic laws of heredity.

The nature of these laws and how they operate to affect psychological development are the topics of this chapter. The emphasis upon *psychological* development needs to be made clear. This chapter is concerned with genetic effects upon *behavior patterns*, not with genetic effects upon morphological or structural characteristics; these are matters of embryology and physiology, not psychology. It will be seen, however, that some morphological characteristics indirectly affect behavior through the reactions they elicit from other people. These reactions, and thus their physical antecedents, affect the personality and psychological development of the recipient. In this way, a person's race may have no direct effect upon his personality but may exert a strong *indirect* effect. Such characteristics will thus be considered along with more direct genetic determinants of psychological development.

THE MECHANICS OF HEREDITY

Mendel's Laws

Although Mendel never saw a chromosome, he concluded that heredity occurs as the result of the combinations of independent, inheritable units. How did he come to this remarkable conclusion? He began his work with garden peas and asked the basic question: "Was there some predictable regularity in the characteristics of offspring, given the characteristics of their parents?" For example, he noted that ripe peas were either smooth or wrinkled. After a trial period, he identified one variety that always yielded smooth peas when self-fertilized, and another variety that always yielded wrinkled peas.

He was now ready to ask what would happen if he cross-fertilized, if he took pollen from smooth pea plants and deposited it on the stigmas of wrinkled plants, taking care to prevent self-fertilization by removing the stamens and then tying a paper bag around each cross-fertilized flower. When the pods emerged late in summer, he opened them and found only smooth peas! The wrinkled characteristic had completely disappeared, even though it was the characteristic of one of the two parents. He called the surviving characteristic *dominant* and the vanished characteristic *recessive*. Thus, smoothness was dominant and wrinkledness was recessive.

The following spring Mendel planted his first-generation smooth peas, and now allowed them to *self*-fertilize. When the pods were opened in late summer, both smooth and wrinkled peas were found, side by side within the same pod. The wrinkledness had come back. Carefully counting the number of each kind, Mendel found 5,474 smooth peas and 1,850 wrinkled peas. If 5,474 is divided by 1,850, the answer is 2.96. Thus, there were almost exactly three smooth peas for every wrinkled pea. Exactly the same ratio was found for other characteristics. In each case, self-fertilization of first-generation hybrids resulted in a 3 to 1 ratio; the characteristic that had completely disappeared in the hybrids now reappeared once for every three occurrences of the other (dominant) characteristic. Here was regularity and lawfulness never before observed in heredity.

Mendel next invented a model—a set of assumptions—that, if true, would account for the results of his experiments. Let S stand for the dominant characteristic of smoothness, and w for the recessive characteristic of wrinkledness. Now retrace the experiments. First, plants that produced only smooth peas, and hence had only S hereditary units for form, were crossed with plants that produced only wrinkled peas, and hence had only w hereditary units for form. Assume that each offspring pea received a unit from each parent; i.e., an Sw combination. Since S is dominant over w, all these first generation hybrids would be smooth, as observed. Next, each hybrid was allowed to self-fertilize. Assume that half the pollen is S and half is w, and likewise, that the eggs are half S and half w. In other words, assume that these *germ cells* arising from the Sw hybrid pea do not contain the Sw combination, but only the one genetic unit or the other (we shall later discuss *reduction division* in greater detail). Further, assume that the joining of a particular pollen with a particular egg is a chance affair, so that an S pollen is equally likely to join with either an S or a w egg, and likewise for a w pollen. Thus, four combinations would be equally possible: SS, Sw, wS, and ww. Since S is dominant over w, whenever the unit S is present, smoothness will occur. Wrinkledness will occur only when S is absent, i.e., only when two w units are joined. Of the four possibilities, S occurs in three. Thus, there should be three smooth peas for every wrinkled pea, as found. The assumptions work! The Mendelian laws of inheritance were born.

Now a crucial test: What should happen if the second generation is again allowed to self-fertilize? Look at the problem as Mendel must have seen it. He now had both smooth and wrinkled peas, with three smooth peas for every wrinkled pea. Presumably, the hereditary units were distributed SS, Sw, and wS in the smooth peas, and ww in the wrinkled peas. What is predicted when each of these four kinds of peas is planted, allowed to grow, and then self-fertilized? Obviously, the ww plants can only produce pollen and ova with w units, and when these are joined, a ww combination will occur. Thus, the first test was that self-fertilization of wrinkled plants would produce only wrinkled peas. This is precisely what Mendel found for seven succeeding generations.

Turning to smooth peas, the predictions are of the same type for the SS peas; they would produce only S pollen and S ova, and hence only SS plants. But there was no way of separating the SS peas from the Sw and wS peas; all looked exactly the same. How was the prediction to be tested? The answer was simple. Even though which smooth peas contained only SS combinations was unknown, the assumptions implied that one-third of all smooth peas were of this type. Thus, if all smooth peas were allowed to self-fertilize, one-third of them should produce only smooth peas. This is exactly what Mendel found; a second prediction was confirmed.

Turning finally to the Sw and wS peas, they would constitute the other two-thirds of all smooth peas. When allowed to self-fertilize, four equally likely combinations would occur: SS, Sw, wS, and ww. Three of these combinations would produce only smooth peas, and the fourth, only wrinkled peas. Thus, two-thirds of the smooth peas, when self-fertilized, should produce peas three of which are smooth and one of which is wrinkled. Again, the prediction was confirmed; two-thirds of the smooth plants produced both smooth and wrinkled peas in the ratio of 3 to 1.

A series of further tests allowed for additional refinements of the basic assumptions. These assumptions, Mendel's laws, are paraphrased below.

1. Inherited characteristics are determined by a number of genetic elements that are passed along *unchanged* from one generation to the next. (Later, these elements were given the name *genes,* a word meaning "determiners." Thus, belief in genes long preceded the physical evidence which is now available.

2. These elements are found in pairs, and where the effects of the two are different (i.e., smoothness versus wrinkledness), one produces an

observable effect, while the other does not; i.e., one is dominant over the other. The recessive gene, however, if paired with another like itself, will produce an observable effect of its own. (Thus, an organism's appearance—his *phenotype*—does not necessarily mirror his gene makeup—his *genotype*.)

3. When seeds (germ cells) are formed in an individual, one of each pair goes to each seed, and thus an offspring receives one of the pair, but not both, from each parent. Which member of the pair a given seed will receive is a matter of chance. (Mendel here assumed the process of reduction division.)

4. The separation of one pair of genes into two seeds does not affect the separation of another pair of genes. For *each* pair, separation is independent of all other pairs. Thus, the fact that a seed receives A_1 of the pair A_1A_2 has no effect on whether it will receive B_1 or B_2 of another pair B_1B_2; the probability of either remains fifty-fifty.

These laws constitute the essence of Mendel's assumptions. It is remarkable indeed that they were derived from simple experiments with plants and yet should have generality across the entire living kingdom, and that 100 years of subsequent research have not replaced them with another theory. Not that modifications and refinements have not occurred. The fourth law, for example—the so-called *law of independent assortment*—is modified by the phenomenon of *linkage*, an important enough phenomenon to merit discussion in the next section. It is remarkable, though, that a man working alone, with none of the "brass instruments" of a later age or the computers of a still later "electronic age," had the insight to see in his simple experiments a theory that has proved so durable.

Chromosomes and Genes: The Physical Basis of Heredity

A milestone following the discovering of Mendel's laws was the discovery that genetic units, genes, are not scattered indiscriminately throughout cellular material, but are located in a linear fashion on threadlike bodies called *chromosomes*. When a dividing cell is stained and put under the microscope, colored threads (*chroma*, which have absorbed the dye) appear. In its normal state, a body (somatic) cell shows no evidence of chromosomes. But as it divides, chromosomes appear. They split in two and go to opposite sides of the cell. A wall gradually grows between the two halves, and in an hour or so, two cells exist where before there was one. The chromosomes then disappear and are not detectable until the new cells are about to divide. Then they reappear in exactly the same number as in the parent cells. Clearly, if the chromosomes contained genes, here was the secret of how genes were transferred from one cell to another. They were carried by the chromosomes.

But immediately a problem in arithmetic becomes apparent. When germ cells (gametes) from two parents combine to form a fertilized egg (zygote), the zygote does not have the sum of the number of chromosomes in two body cells, but only half that many. It has, in other words, the same number as a single body cell. Thus, a special kind of chromosome "reduction" must occur in the development of germ cells, such that each possesses only half the number as in a normal body cell. When two germ cells combine to form a zygote, the total number of chromosomes would once more be the same as in a body cell. Microscopic examination confirmed this reasoning, which was predicted by Mendel. In the process of producing germ cells from body cells (gametogenesis), the final cell division is of a special "reduction division" type (meiosis), which is different from that involved in the production of somatic cells (mitosis). Instead of each chromosome splitting in half, the chromosomes do not divide, but migrate as a whole to one side or the other of the dividing cell. Thus, when cell division is complete, each new germ cell has half the original number of chromosomes: 23 instead of 46 for humans. Since meiosis occurs in the production of gametes in both parents, fertilization results in a doubling of the number of chromosomes in each gamete, yielding the original number again (46 for humans).

It is extremely important to note that a random process is apparently involved in meiosis. Of the 46 chromosomes in a human body cell, half are from the father and half from the mother. They form 23 *pairs* of chromosomes, with both members of a pair holding genes that determine the same characteristics. It has been estimated that more than 40,000 genes exist in human chromosomes. During meiosis, one chromosome of each pair migrates to one new cell, and the other member to the other new cell. *Whether it is the maternal or paternal member of a given pair that migrates to a given cell has no effect on the remaining 22 pairs; each pair is assorted independently of the others.* The number of different possible combinations is thus extremely large. Suppose a body cell had only 4 pairs of chromosomes instead of 23. During meiosis, the probability of the maternal member of each pair grouping together is $1/2^4 = 1/16$. Thus, with 4 pairs of chromosomes, 16 different gametes could be created. With 23 pairs, $1/2^{23}$ means that 8,388,608 different combinations are possible. Since the same number is possible from each parent, the possible number of offspring with different combinations is in excess of 64 trillion (64×10^{12}). Thus, the potential for genetic variation is tremendous. Such potentiality for variation is fundamental to the process of evolution and survival.

The fact that hundreds of genes are linearly arranged on a single chromosome introduces a complication for Mendel's law of independent assortment. If genes A, B, and C are all on the same chromosome and are all dominant, then the phenotypes determined by these genes should be linked. Whenever the A phenotype occurs, so should phenotypes B and C. This reasoning leads to the expectation that frequency of some traits should be correlated in the general population. Individuals with phenotype A should also tend to exhibit phenotype B, etc. However, another phenomenon called *crossing over* interferes with linkage. During meiosis, a pair of chromosomes may lay one on top of the other, forming an X. As gametogenesis proceeds and the two strands separate, they may break at the point of contact and "trade halves," thus producing new linked-gene combinations and destroying old combinations. As this process occurs over and over in succeeding generations, up and down the entire length of pairs of chromosomes, ultimately all possible combinations of genes will occur, producing a population distribution of gene combinations close to that required by Mendel's law.

Sex and Sex-linked Genes

There is another type of gene linkage called *sex-linked genes*. But first a discussion of the determination of sex is required. Electron-microscope photographs of human chromosomes reveal a systematic difference between one chromosome of males and females. One of the 23 pairs of male chromosomes does not consist of 2 equal-sized chromosomes, but rather of a long one and a short one. The long one is called the X chromosome and the short one the Y chromosome. The Y chromosome determines maleness. Females do not possess a Y, but rather two X's. During the process of gametogenesis in males, the XY chromosome splits and divides, the X going to one sperm and the Y to another. If the X sperm penetrates an ovum during fertilization, an XX combination results, producing a female. But the chances are just as good that a Y sperm will penetrate the ovum, producing an XY combination, and a male. Thus, it is the sperm, and therefore the father, that determines the sex of offspring.[1]

---

[1] Although the chances are theoretically fifty-fifty that a given zygote will be male or female, the facts indicate that slightly more male babies than female babies are born—perhaps 106 to 100. Just why this small but consistent disproportionality should occur is not completely understood. It used to be thought that males were stronger and more apt to survive from conception to birth, but the opposite is now known to be the case. Males are biologically weaker and less likely to survive. It appears that considerably more males than females are conceived, perhaps 130 to 100 —and that the higher mortality of male fetuses reduces this advantage to 106 to 100 by the time of birth. The higher conception rate of males is perhaps due to physical and/or chemical differences between X and Y sperms, such that a Y sperm has a better chance of penetrating and fertilizing the ovum.

Because the Y chromosome is different from the X chromosome, the XY combination in males results in two sets of genes that determine different characteristics. With other pairs, each chromosome carries a gene for a given characteristic, and the phenotype of that individual depends upon the interaction between the two genes, whether one is dominant and the other recessive, or whether some kind of "averaging" occurs. But with an XY pair, no interaction occurs. The X genes express themselves with no modification from the Y genes. Now consider what is likely to happen if a mother (XX) has inherited a recessive defective gene on both X chromosomes. She will then exhibit the defect herself. Suppose she has a son (XY) and a daughter (XX). The daughter inherits one X chromosome from her mother, carrying the defective gene. The X chromosome from her father is probably normal and thus probably does not carry the same defective gene. Thus, the daughter might exhibit the defect, but the probabilities are quite high that she will not. The son, however, receives only one X chromosome, and that from his mother. Thus, he must exhibit the defect, for he has no normal dominant X gene from his father to counteract the defective maternal gene. This knowledge provides the solution to a long-standing mystery: *certain defects and diseases are transmitted to sons only through their mothers.* Such conditions are called sex-linked defects. They account for the much higher incidence in males of such defects as hemophilia, color blindness, nystagmus, baldness, some forms of progressive muscular dystrophy, some rare forms of albinism and anemia, etc.

Genes Outside the Chromosomes

There is widespread belief, perpetrated by oversimplified accounts of the mechanics of heredity, that all the elemental units of hereditary transmission are in the chromosomes. Yet at about the same time as the relationship between chromosomes and genes was first being entertained, Carl Correns, one of the three who rediscovered Mendel's monograph, described evidence suggesting a *non*-chromosomal gene (cited in Sager, 1965). In 1908, Correns investigated such a possibility in several plant species. But the simultaneous discovery of chromosomal inheritance and the mathematical similarity between chromosomal division and Mendelian ratios (i.e., the 3-to-1 ratio, as well as a number of others) led to such an expanding concentration of research and publications concerned with chromosomal inheritance that non-chromosomal genes were virtually forgotten. Yet such evidence has been known for years, and a recent publication calls for "a new and sharply revised picture of cell heredity" (Sager, 1965). For the present purposes, its major significance is simply one of completeness and accuracy. It is incorrect to assert that

". . . the genes are carried by the chromosomes . . . ," but rather
". . . chromosomal genes account for most hereditary transmission, in accordance with Mendelian principles, but non-chromosomal genes also account for part of it, possibly following a different set of principles." At the present time, these non-Mendelian principles are not fully understood. More research is required before their significance can be confidently assessed.

Genotypes and Phenotypes

It is to be recalled that Mendel's second law asserts that genes are to be found in pairs, one from each parent. In a *homozygous* individual, the two genes are the same or highly similar; both, for example, determine blue eyes. In a *heterozygous* individual, they are different; one may be recessive and determine blue eyes, and the other dominant and a determinant of brown eyes (blue eyes are recessive to all other eye colors except to albino eyes). A person who is homozygotic for a given trait will always express that trait, and thus a 1-to-1 relationship exists between his genotype and phenotype. A heterozygote, however, may not mirror his genotype. Thus, for example, if he carries a recessive blue-eyed gene and a dominant brown-eyed gene, he will be brown-eyed, and if he marries a spouse who also carries a blue-eyed gene, he may produce a blue-eyed offspring, even though neither parent is blue-eyed. It is through one's offspring that one's genotype is thus discovered. The important lesson to be learned is that heredity accounts for *differences* between generations as well as for similarities. The layman usually attributes similarities to heredity and differences to environment, yet both are affected by heredity. Genetically affected personality traits may be similarly determined; lack of a high relationship between personality traits of parents and offspring does not necessarily mean there is no genetic factor involved.

MECHANISMS OF EVOLUTION

The possibility of inheriting heterozygous genotypes rests upon the phenomenon of sexual recombination of genes from one's two parents. Suppose it were otherwise; suppose a body cell could simply divide, following the usual mitotic processes, producing a new individual with each division. Reproduction by simple cell division, or *fission,* is characteristic of protozoans (one-celled organisms). It is obviously a stagnant process, genetically speaking. The maternal genes are always reproduced in exactly the same pattern in each offspring—no genetic variability is added. If the environment changes in such a way as to make it difficult for such an organism to survive, there is no way to inject variability into offspring to give them a better chance. All are equally susceptible to the vicissitudes of the environment, from the first generation to the last. Consequently, it is probable that such an organism will have a last generation and will perish in the battle for survival.

Sexual Recombination

As evolution proceeded from protozoans to metazoans (many-celled organisms), various cells began to specialize, and such specialization gave rise to germ cells, gametes, whose nature made it possible for a new kind of reproduction to take place: for a mixing—a *fusion*—to occur, thus making possible almost infinite genetic variation between organisms —thus making possible genetic individuality. With individuality came adaptability to the environment, for now changes in the environment could be matched with changes in the organism, and changes valuable for survival would automatically be passed on, insuring the survival of the fittest. Sexual recombination, then, is one way in which organismic variation is produced. It is a fundamental mechanism in evolution.

Mutation

A second mechanism is *mutation.* It is possible for a gene to change, and when it does, it is called a mutation. The cause of the mutation is called a *mutagen.* Every one of the thousands of genes carried by an individual has a small chance of changing in the individual's lifetime. If the mutated gene is in a germ cell that combines with another (opposite-sexed) germ cell to form a zygote, the new organism will carry the mutated gene in all his body cells and in half his germ cells. Thus, a number of his offspring will also inherit the gene and, in turn, pass it on to succeeding generations. Now, if it so happens that the gene produces a phenotype that yields some survival advantage to its bearer, it follows that all individuals possessing the gene will have an advantage over others of their kind. Over many succeeding generations, it is apparent that the ratio of these "lucky gene bearers" will increase. In this way, the process of mutation contributes to genetic variability, increasing the adaptability of the organism.

What causes mutations? The complete list is far from known; new mutagens are constantly being discovered. Two main classes are ionizing radiation and certain chemicals. Thus, the advent of the X-ray machine, atomic bombs, and hydrogen bombs undoubtedly has led to unknown increases in the "normal" rate of mutation. And since the vast majority of mutations are detrimental (and recessive, fortunately), there is little question but that modern man is contributing to his own genetic deterioration. One estimate is that 8,000 children are born every year with serious defects caused by atomic radiation (Scheinfeld, 1965). We are therefore well advised to take precautions minimizing this danger, from avoiding X-ray exposures to the genital area—where the germ cells are found—to the problem of world disarmament. It is a sobering thought to realize that the average person is carrying about eight dangerous recessive mutations. Paired with another similar mutation, four are probably fatal, and the other four would probably cause serious abnormalities. Fortunately, these mutations are so varied that it is extremely unlikely that any two parents would possess the same type of defects, and hence the chances are small that an offspring would receive a lethal double dosage. Nevertheless, descendents of the Japanese exposed to atomic radiation in World War II will probably be turning up with abnormally high rates of defects and death for generations to come.

Natural Selection

The third, and final, mechanism of evolutionary change is natural selection. Variability is initiated by sexual recombination of genes and by gene mutations. But not all genetically new organisms survive and multiply. Nature—the environment—makes the final decision. Only those organisms who are genetically fitted to the environment survive and multiply; the rest naturally die out. Thus, adaptation occurs over the generations, leading to new phyla and species, to new breeds and "strains." Thus it was that *Homo sapiens* emerged:

Now that life has made him, man can look back (as Huxley shows) and begin to see just why his actuality rests at every point on this particular evolutionary process and no other. Speech and conceptual thinking, hands and alloplastic evolution, brains and animal societies all rest upon prior necessities. A metazoan organization of cells was needed for size and specialization. Sexuality was necessary for the combining of heredities. The inner and the outer skin of the gutowning coelenterates underlie efficient nutrition. A circulatory system, as in the worms, was a prerequisite for further size. A free-swimming tube like the lancelet rationalized the head-tail axis and the collection of the senses and nervous system. A backbone and an inner skeleton were imperative for the land existence of large animals. Lungs were another need for a land animal large enough to afford a brain, and so are the vertebrate, kidney, and liver.

.   .   .   .

Mammalian reproduction rescued animals from the enormous wastage of their offspring in earlier animals. Tree life preserved primates from the blind alleys of other mammals' specializations, and tree life perfected sight as the greatest of the senses. Fetalization (and big brain) required an arboreal species with singly-born young. Fruit-eating and tropical habitat achieved primate social organization, and size probably drove the anthropoids back to the ground. But only man stands, and man alone has free hands. Climatic catastrophe shaped man to culture—fire, clothing, and meat obtained by weapons—and anthropoid family association further nurtured the fetalization necessary for a prolonged period of learning. Hands emancipated man from autoplastic evolution, and his enormous learning brain gives him alloplastic freedom. And the heightening of all mammalian traits in the anthropoids gave man the closeness of emotional ties which alone can build the human animal.

It takes a long-perspective biological view to see properly why man is the cumulative triumph of animal striving that he unquestionably is. And the argument that man is the best animal there is, can be well defended on the purely technical grounds provided by evolution itself. Until competing intelligences are known from other planets, this is where we must stand. [La Barre, 1955, pp. 159–162.] *

The Doctrine of Inheritance of Acquired Characteristics

At one time, there were proponents of a fourth mechanism of evolutionary change—inheritance of acquired characteristics. According to this doctrine, often labeled Lamarkianism in honor of one of its proponents, it was possible for an organism to genetically pass on to its offspring characteristics that it did not itself inherit, but acquired from the environment. Thus, the long neck of the giraffe originated from short-necked ancestors who acquired a slightly elongated neck in their own lifetimes by stretching to reach leaves in treetops, and then genetically passed this advantage on to their offspring, who, in turn, stretched their own necks a little more, etc. Similarly, a parent who acquires, say, a fear of thunder, may genetically determine a similar fear in his offspring. Or a talented musician, who learned his talent, may produce an offspring who inherits this acquired trait.

Numerous experiments demonstrate quite conclusively that the doctrine is false (e.g., Munn, 1965). Indeed, it is contradicted by one of Mendel's law, which states that genetic elements are passed along *unchanged* from one generation to the next. Ignoring mutations, which are not affected by acquired characteristics anyway, there is nothing a person can do to change the nature of the genetic units in his germ cells. Indeed, a female possesses all her ova at birth. At puberty, they simply "ripen" at regular intervals and proceed down the fallopian tubes. Thus, it must be concluded that we cannot affect our children's genetic potential by what we learn or develop in our own lifetimes. Our acquired characteristics have no genetic counterpart; they have somatic-cell correlates, but not germ-cell correlates.

The Nature-Nurture Issue

Sexuality, mutations, and natural selection—these three mechanisms account for *phylogenetic development,* the generation-to-generation history of genetically controlled characteristics that are common to all members of a phylum or species. They suggest a kind of interaction between heredity and environment that lies at the base of a very old question— that of the relative contributions of heredity (nature) and environmental experiences (nurture) with respect to a given characteristic.

A little thought will make it clear that such a statement as "Characteristic X is determined solely by heredity" has questionable meaning. The same holds true for the opposite kind of statement: "Characteristic Y is determined solely by the environment." The reason is simply that *genes do not exist in a vacuum.* They exist in an environment, *and the environment affects the action of the genes.* ". . . every character that any plant or animal develops has its basis in the genes (without which it would not develop at all) and is to that extent 'inherited'; but because the character is the result of interaction between the genes and the factors of the environment, it is also to that extent 'acquired.' There is no such thing as a character that owes its existence solely to heredity or solely to environment. All that is inherited by any offspring is a packet of genes with the capacity of reacting in various ways to the environment . . ." (de Beer, 1962).

The evidence for nature-nurture interaction exists at both the microscopic and macroscopic levels. Consider events at the cellular level. An advanced metazoan such as man has many different kinds of cells: nerve cells, muscle cells, brain cells, blood cells, germ cells, etc. Yet presumably each cell carries exactly the same set of genes as every other cell (ignoring germ cells). How is it, then, that with precisely the same genetic constituents, cells nevertheless diversify and specialize? Clearly, it must be that the cellular environment differs from cell to cell, and depending upon its nature, gene activity also differs, thus producing different kinds of cells. The mechanism of this environmental control of gene activity has been sought by biologists since the turn of the century and is still largely unknown. Recent evidence suggests that hormones are involved in this "organizing" influence (Davidson, 1965). Whatever the ultimate nature of the "organizer," its function seems to be that of selectively releasing capabilities lying dormant within the cell, locked in the genes. The genes determine the potential of the cell, and the environment cannot modify this potential. What it can do, however, is to select one potential rather than another and see that it becomes a reality. Here is a true interaction between heredity and environment. It is meaningless to conceive of one operating in isolation from the other.

The evidence for interaction at the macroscopic level is overwhelming, and often amazing. Every college student who has been exposed to an introductory course in psychology probably recalls the cases of Vicki and Gua, chimpanzees raised as human infants by their owners, the Hayeses and the Kelloggs (Hayes and Hayes, 1951; Kellogg and Kellogg, 1933). The results of these famous studies show very clearly both environmental selection of genetic potentials and genetic limitations of environmental potentials. Thus, Gua, who was treated in every conceivable way the same as the Kelloggs' real son Donald, developed many "human" behavior patterns, such as walking upright, skipping, drinking from a glass, using a spoon, kissing for forgiveness, responding correctly to commands (about 20), toilet habits, and such personality characteristics as cooperativeness and obedience. These "humanized" traits clearly show the effect of the environment upon psychological development of the chimp. Although Gua's genetic potential was the same as her peers' in the jungle, she was more similar in many ways to her genetically distant "adopted parents." At the same time, however, Gua did not develop many other behavior patterns that were manifested by Donald. It was impossible, for example, to teach her to speak. Vicki, in spite of much training, learned to say only three words: mama, papa, and cup.[2] Thus, heredity sets definite limits that cannot be exceeded, regardless of the beneficence of the environment.

Other studies also show the interaction of heredity and environment, even for those characteristics we often assume are a "complete" result of heredity. For example, vertebrates have possessed two eyes in their heads for approximately 350 million years, and it is a rare person who would not attribute this two-eyed trait to heredity. Yet if a fish embryo is allowed to develop in water to which a small amount of salt has been added, it sometimes develops one eye in the middle of its head, like a mermaid Cyclops. The study of teratology (developmental abnormalities) likewise demonstrates the cruel extent to which environment can bend an organism's genetic potential into freakish organizations.

We are sometimes fooled in the opposite direction as well; we attribute to environment some things that are mainly determined by heredity. In recent years, our knowledge of obesity has apparently revealed such an error. Prior to the 1960's, and excluding causes of obesity determined by known glandular abnormalities, it was believed that obesity was an environmental problem; the person ate too much,

---

[2] Even these words were pronounced with a "monkey accent." Cup, for example, sounded like "cop." Supposedly, while driving to a speaking engagement in Detroit, the Hayeses, with Vicki in the back seat, stopped and asked a policeman for directions. As he stuck his head in the window, he commented on the chimp and asked if it were trained. He received his answer when Vicki pointed at him and said "cop."

and he did so because of his particular environmental past. Perhaps he learned to eat too much because he was raised in a family of "big eaters," where a "clean plate" was mandatory, or perhaps the environment had produced a problem of adjustment entirely unrelated to eating, but which led to compensatory eating as a "defense mechanism." To reduce the amount of intake, it was therefore deemed necessary to change the person's personality. Yet recent research indicates that a metabolic deficiency, perhaps hereditary in nature, is responsible for some cases of obesity. The disorder converts an abnormally large amount of food into stored fat rather than into other substances. Doctors had been inclined to doubt these people when they said they did not eat an unusual amount of food and were following their prescribed diets. Recent research indicates that at least some of these people may have been telling the truth. Whether medical science can correct the underlying disorder or not is as yet an unfinished story.

In summary, it must be recognized that neither genes nor their environment exist isolated in space; it is only through their interaction that the reality of the living organism is achieved. Thus, the nature-nurture question can never be of an either-or variety, but must always be phrased in terms of relativity.

GENETIC DETERMINANTS OF HUMAN BEHAVIOR

Those aspects of heredity that are most germane to the present chapter concern genetic determinants of normal human behavior. Furthermore, major emphasis is directed toward those classes of behavior that have psychological significance. Such behavioral classes consist of genetic effects upon personality characteristics, since the major orientation of this book is toward personality development.

It is convenient to divide the data into three main groups. The first group consists of *genetically affected physical characteristics that influence personality in an indirect manner.* Race was previously mentioned as an example. "Looks" is another; most of the specific characteristics determining "looks" have a heavy genetic component. Since a person's "looks" affects the reactions of other people, and since these reactions affect the personality of the recipient, "looks" becomes a relevant topic. The second group is concerned with *genetic effects upon intelligence.* For many years, intelligence was at the heart of the nature-nurture issue, with opposing camps making assertions at the logical extremes: intelligence was completely determined by heredity versus the position that it had no effect whatsoever. Considerable heat was generated by this controversy, but it has begun to subside, leaving behind a massive amount of data for the modern student. The third group is concerned with *direct genetic effects upon personality.* It is different from the other two in that the first group is indirect in nature and the second considers a concept (intelligence) that is often considered to be separate from personality. The third approach asks such a question as: "Is there any evidence that aggressiveness has a genetic determinant?" There are few investigations of this type, since modern statistical techniques had to become available first.

INDIRECT GENETIC DETERMINANTS OF PERSONALITY

Race

"To separate [Negro children] from others of similar age and qualifications solely because of their race, generates a feeling of inferiority as to their status in the community that may affect their hearts and minds in a way unlikely ever to be undone" (stated by Chief Justice Earl Warren in the 1954 public school desegregation action of the Supreme Court). Common sense alone suggests that a person's race will affect his personality to the extent that racial characteristics evoke correlated responses from others. Nowhere would this seem more true than with the American Negro. In the southern United States, Negroes have been allowed to marry only Negroes and have been treated as social inferiors. Negroes, in other words, have formed a veritable caste system. If race-correlated responses from others affect personality, such effects should surely be found with the American Negro. We shall examine the relevant evidence to test the validity of this argument. If it is found to hold for Negroes, we may assume it holds for any racial characteristic to the extent that people respond differentially to that characteristic.

Just how racial discrimination began in the United States is beyond the scope of this book. It may be noted in passing, however, that a predominant racist argument is clearly incorrect. This argument states that the physical characteristics of Negroes show a genetic inferiority in the sense of greater similarity to our lower primate cousins, the great apes. Caucasian characteristics such as white skin, straight (small-nosed) faces, and blue eyes are "advanced" traits, since our primate cousins are dark skinned, prognathous, and dark eyed. It follows that the dark-skinned, large-nosed, dark-eyed Negro is less of an evolutionary advancement than the Caucasian. But the racist considers only evidence that fits his dogma. He forgets, for example, that the thick lips, frizzly hair, lumbar curve, and large buttocks of many Negroes are signs of "advancement," since lower primates (and whites) tend to possess thin lips, straight hair, a straight back, and small buttocks. La Barre presents the final blow: "We must face the dreadful facts straightforwardly: relatively profuse body hair clearly places the Caucasoids closest of all living races to the lower primates, while Mongoloids and Negroids are more advanced in their humanoid hairlessness" (La Barre, 1955). There is absolutely no evidence that Negroid characteristics are more or less "advanced" than Caucasoid characteristics. Whatever the basis for the Negro caste system, it is not a result of racial inferiority.

Case history material and anecdotal evidence strongly support the previous quotation from Warren. The Los Angeles riots of 1965 and the Detroit riots of 1967, each involving over 30 deaths, furnish stark evidence of the possible ramifications of race-correlated treatment. As one Negro said, "I got this letter from a friend of mine. He's gone to Paris and he says, 'come over here. You need a rest from being a Negro.' I never told him it bothered me, but he's right. I do need a rest from being a Negro" (Karon, 1958).

But anecdotal evidence is not the basis of science. How is one to counter the argument that although the Negro may be just as "advanced" as the Caucasian, he has certain personality differences that are genetically determined and that result in his current problems? One way to investigate this question would be to compare southern and northern Negroes. If personality differences between the races are a primary genetic phenomenon, there should be only slight differences, or none at all. If, on the other hand, they are completely a result of differential treatment, differences should be large, since the northern Negro is exposed to fewer discriminatory actions than the southern Negro.

But the careful thinker will see a flaw in this reasoning. It could be argued that any observed differences between southern Negroes and northern Negroes are because northern Negroes migrated north as a result of certain personality characteristics, rather than the reverse.

This objection is a valid one and makes a simple comparison of southern and northern Negroes of doubtful value. Is there a way of sharpening the study, so that the *selective migration hypotheses* can be separated from the *secondary genetic hypothesis?* One way would be to include a third sample—northern whites. If northern Negroes were found not to differ from northern whites, but both groups were found to differ from southern Negroes, and in the same ways, it would be extremely tenuous to appeal to the selective migration hypothesis. This is because the selective migration hypothesis, while it can explain southern-northern Negro differences, does not say anything about the nature of the differences. Because of the multidimensional nature of personality, there is a myriad of ways northern and southern Negroes could differ. To find that the differences are the same as between northern whites and southern Negroes would be an extremely unlikely coincidence, so unlikely that the selective migration hypothesis would be in serious trouble.

A third hypothesis, however, would predict nothing else. The *caste system hypothesis* (that personality differences between the races are secondary effects of genetic racial differences) would argue that, since the northern Negro is treated more similarly to whites than the southern Negro, his personality structure should also be more similar. It can be seen, then, that a third group consisting of northern whites allows for a way of testing the "truth value" of three different hypotheses concerning racial differences in personality.

But there is still another way to go about it. Consider two groups of northern Negroes, one of which recently arrived from the south, and the second of which was born in the north: first- and second-generation northern Negroes. According to the selective migration hypothesis, the first-generation northern Negro should differ just as much, if not more, from southern Negroes as the second-generation northern Negro, since the personality differences that "pushed" him north were in existence before he moved. The caste system hypothesis predicts just the opposite. The first-generation northern Negro should differ less from southern Negroes than the second generation, since he has not experienced a full lifetime of northern environmental effects.

It would appear, then, that a decisive study of the determinants of racial differences in personality between American Negroes and Caucasians would consist of four groups: northern whites (NW), first-generation northern Negroes (NN1), second-generation northern Negroes (NN2), and southern Negroes (SN). If the difference between SN and NN was found to depend upon length of time spent in the north, such that NN2 was more different from SN than NN1, and at the same time was more *similar* to NW, the caste system hypothesis would be very strongly supported. If, on the other hand, the difference between SN and NN was either not related to length of time in the north or was greater for NN1 than for NN2, the case for the selective migration hypothesis, and hence for the primary genetic hypothesis, would be strong.

Karon carried out just such a study (Karon, 1958). He studied a total of eight groups, but we shall consider just four, the four mentioned above. First, he administered a carefully constructed objective personality test to all the groups. Then he corrected the scores for differences that were due to factors he was not interested in; that is, he found that age and IQ affected the personality scores. Since the groups were not exactly the same on these two factors, the personality differences could have been due to these unwanted effects. Therefore, he corrected each score so that the resulting group means were what would have been obtained had there been no differences in age or IQ. The statistical procedure for this method is regression analysis, and it is a straightforward, frequently used tool.

The corrected means are presented in Table 2.1. They show that the caste system hypothesis, and hence the secondary genetic hypothesis, is strongly supported. Second-generation northern Negroes (NN2) are practically identical to northern whites (NW), first-generation northern Negroes (NN1) are less similar, and southern Negroes (SN) are quite different. There is no support for the selective migration hypothesis, and hence for the primary genetic hypothesis. This study strongly suggests, then, that racial differences in personality are not something the individual is born with, but are acquired as a result of differential treatment.

TABLE 2.1

Mean Personality Scores for Northern Whites (NW), First Generation Northern Negroes (NN1), Second Generation Northern Negroes (NN2), and Southern Negroes (SN)
(Adapted from Karon, 1958)

NW	2.3
NN2	2.1
NN1	2.9
SN	4.5

It is interesting to examine the nature of the personality differences found by Karon. He found that most of the differences were related to the southern Negroes' handling of feelings of anger and hostility. He found that the southern Negro is more likely to feel that people are going out of their way to make trouble for him; he has strong feelings of anger but does not display them directly; he is more likely to delay their expression, or to do so symbolically, such as by doing sloppy work or being chronically late; he tends not to recognize, or to deny to himself, the existence of situations that should make him angry, and along with this he tends to avoid close contact with other men. Finally, he tends to be emotionally "flat"; that is, his emotions are seldom recognized as strong, but rather as dampened.

How should these differences be interpreted? Karon offers the following analysis:

These findings seem to confirm the widely held belief among social scientists that the most serious emotional problems of the Negro concern the handling of aggression.

The reason for the increase in these characteristics would seem simply to be that the caste sanctions are, in fact, ways in which people are making trouble for the Negro; this trouble may mean not only inconvenience, discomfort, or humiliation, but also real physical danger. Against these problems, he may have no defense: any attempt to fight back seems likely to lead to vindictive and inescapable retaliation. He must therefore fight a continuing battle with his own feelings of anger, lest he lose control. [P. 172.]

In a rural deep south area, where the possibility of white retaliation is at a maximum, and where physical security for the Negro is at a minimum, aggressive tendencies seem to be most strongly suppressed. Coincident with the suppression of anger and hostility is emotional flatness:

One of the consequences of choking back one's anger may be a complete deadening of one's emotions. This seems to occur only in the rural sample where the Negro is most insecure. . . . The avoidance of male-male contacts is still another characteristic which showed a more striking increase for the rural sample than for the urban. This supports the notion that close contacts between men are avoided because these contacts are most likely to erupt in physical aggression. [P. 172.]

Karon concludes,

It is striking that, with the exception of labile affect, all of these characteristics are indicators of pathology, that is, they indicate disturbed individuals. This is clearly not an artifact of our procedure, since these characteristics were selected on an empirical basis from among all the possible traits measured by the Picture Arrangement Test—some of which, like these, indicate pathology, others of which indicate strengths, and the majority of which are simply descriptive. What this implies is that the impact of the caste sanctions on human beings is destructive, and the destructiveness varies with the severity of the sanctions.

The implications of these findings are obvious. Any of us who have had honest doubts about whether the caste sanctions hurt Negroes now have an objective answer. Those who have been sincerely convinced that the caste system was good for Negroes, or that, at worst, it did them no harm, are now faced with the unpleasant alternatives of reappraising their view of the situation, or of simply shutting their eyes to the facts. [P. 173.]

A number of other studies are in essential agreement with Karon's conclusions. Many point to the Negro's difficulty in handling feelings of anger, hostility, and rejection; his lack of self-confidence; and his feelings that his fate is more in the hands of others than within himself (e.g., Dreger and Miller, 1960; Katz et al., 1964; Lefcourt and Ladwig, 1965). The close fit of these independent results with those of Karon could hardly be due to chance.

The Negro has been considered in some detail only to serve as a clear example. The basic principle—that other peoples' reactions to purely physical racial characteristics affect the personality characteristics of those people—cannot be doubted. The principle is applicable to any race, or to any ethnic-racial combination. Any member of the Jewish faith subjected to the ugliness of anti-Semitism will feel qualified to suggest a second example.

Facial Characteristics

Some nicknames given to childhood friends such as "Bug-eyes" (someone with protruding eyes), "Red" (a child with bright red hair), and "Greasy" (someone who has extremely oily skin and hair) imply that children are sensitive to the facial characteristics of others. Since the face is usually the first part of a person's body to be observed, since it is the most expressive, and since it sits naked on the top of the neck for all to see, we may inquire into the importance of "looks" as a second physical characteristic that may or may not secondarily affect personality.

It is well established that facial characteristics are determined by a multitude of genes. There is no single gene for "prettiness" and a second for "plainness." Rather, there are groups of genes that determine such characteristics as length of nose, width of nose, size of nostrils, width and shape of lips, presence or absence of dimples, shape and size of teeth, shape of head, and type of hair. It is the pattern formed by all these independent characteristics that determines the "attractiveness" of a face (ignoring differences in cultural standards of beauty). Perhaps the most immediate evidence indicating the genetic control of facial characteristics is the precision and symmetry of opposite sides of the head—the near perfect duality of eyes, ears, nostrils, and teeth. If environment played a major role in the determination of these traits, and if genes did not exert exceedingly minute control over a myriad of details, paired facial features would hardly be such perfect mirror images of each other.

The Nose. Apparently, there are separate genes for the following characteristics: shape, height, and length of bridge of nose; shape, size, and breadth of nostrils; point of nose (small or bulbous); root of nose; and the nature of the junction of the nose with the upper lip. Since each gene tends to separate independently of other genes, all sorts of combinations can and do appear. On the other hand, it often seems as though a child inherits "his father's nose" or "his mother's nose." We may assume in these cases that linkage occurred; many of the relevant genes were on the same chromosome and thus separated as a unit during meiosis. Generally speaking, more extreme nose characteristics, such as a high and narrow bridge (as compared to a low and broad bridge), are dominant over more moderate characteristics. Thus, where the two parents differ in nose types, the chances are greater than half that an offspring will inherit the more extreme characteristics. Often, these genes do not fully assert themselves until maturity or even later, so that an adult's nose may be relatively unpredictable from its childhood version. Perhaps we are more two-faced than we think.

The Mouth. The mouth is exceedingly difficult to analyze. In the first place, its general size and shape are partly determined by genes affecting the underlying teeth, jaw bones, and palate. Furthermore, environment plays a considerable role, depending upon chewing habits and the way the individual has learned to "set" his jaw muscles (for example, whether he tends to breathe with his mouth open or closed). Finally, as with the nose, a number of genes are involved in such characteristics as size and shape of lips, and dimples and their location. Thick lips apparently dominate thin lips, so that if just one parent has thick lips, the chances are greater than half that the child will have thick lips. But the situation is probably a polygenic one, since all degrees of in-betweenness are also observed. A prominent chin dominates a receding chin, and dimples are dominant over smooth skin. Unusually shaped teeth tend to be dominant over more average teeth, and a number of dental abnormalities are genetically controlled.

The Hair. The genetics of hair characteristics are quite well established. Marked racial differences are obvious. Negroid peoples have kinky or woolly hair; Mongolians (Chinese, Japanese, Eskimos, American Indians) have straight, coarse hair; and Caucasians have wavy, curly, or fine straight hair. Within-race matings of different hair forms indicate that kinky genes dominate curly genes, which in turn dominate wavy genes, and straight hair is recessive to all others (except in Mongolians, where it is dominant over woolly hair). Thus, two straight-haired parents may be confident that all their children will have straight hair. Hair color is also controlled by genes, the rule being a relatively simple one: dark colors tend to be dominant over light colors, from black and brown to red to blond. Thus, if one parent is dark-haired, and all his ancestors were also dark-haired, all the children will have dark hair, regardless of the color of the other parent's hair.

The Eyes. Like most facial characteristics, those for the eye are polygenic. There are genes for eye width, eye distance (from each other), shape (straight or one of two kinds of "slantedness": the Cau-casian almond eye or the Mongolian "fold"), length of eyelashes, and even presence or absence of eye "bags" (which are not a valid index of one's dissipation habits). Generally speaking, wide eyes are domi-nant over narrow, "slit" eyes; straight eyes are dominant over almond eyes; but the Mongolian fold is dominant over straight eyes. Long eye-lashes are dominant over short eyelashes, and eye color follows the same general rule as hair color: dark colors tend to dominate over light colors, from black and brown to gray or green to blue to albino.

Personality. Having sampled the facts concerning the genetics of "looks," the effects of facial characteristics on the reactions of other people may be considered. Most people at least believe that others react to their looks. Indeed, a multimillion dollar cosmetics industry spends millions of dollars a year fostering just such a belief. That the money is not entirely wasted is indicated in numerous studies showing that children of all ages are very much concerned with their looks. Jersild, for example, asked children ranging in age from nine to twenty-two what they liked most and least about themselves (Jersild, 1957). Physical characteristics were mentioned more often than either personality or intellectual characteristics, and facial-head features were the most frequently mentioned physical characteristics. Not only do children attach considerable importance to their own looks, but they react to others on the basis of looks too. Boys rank good looks as very important in determining the popularity of a girl, while girls attach less importance to good looks in boys (Horrocks, 1962; Mather, 1934; Taylor, 1938). The familiar feminine complaint that "Men are interested only in looks" appears to have some support.

It is established, then, that (1) facial features are strongly affected by heredity, (2) children consider their own facial features to be of considerable importance, and (3) children react to others partly on the basis of their peers' looks. Do these differential reactions affect the personalities of the recipients? Both common sense and research data say yes. It is well known that good-looking youngsters tend to be more sociable, more popular, and more extroverted than less attractive youngsters (Lippitt, 1941; Pope, 1953; Zander and Van Egmond 1958). Kagan and Moss (1962) found that anxiety about social interactions was related to attractiveness in girls. In their longitudinal study, six girls showed a shift from high social anxiety at ages three to six to low social anxiety in young adulthood. All six blossomed into pretty girls during the intervening years. Three others showed the opposite shift: from low social anxiety during the preschool years to unusually high anxiety as young adults. All three were unattractive as adolescents. Of course, not all pretty girls show a trend similar to that found in this study, nor all plain girls the opposite trend. Yet these studies make it clear that for both sexes, and possibly girls more than boys, facial characteristics do function as a secondary genetic effect upon personality.

The effect is not always one way. Jersild (1957) offers an insightful statement about a complicating possibility:

The extremely pretty girl faces certain hazards and problems her plainer-looking sister does not. Others may try to exploit her or to gain prestige by being associated with her. She may become the object of competition for favor that is not founded on appreciation of her personality but rather on appreciation of the glamour of her looks. [P. 65.]

The author knows of one family with a very pretty thirteen-year-old girl and a plainer seventeen-year-old girl, Freshman and Senior, respectively, in the same school. While the seventeen-year-old has her share of problems in securing dates for school dances, etc., the thirteen-year-old faces an entirely different situation. Her very beauty—an exquisite yet voluptuous beauty—elicits such frequent advances from the opposite sex that she is literally overwhelmed with popularity. She simply has not had time or experience enough to learn how to react appropriately and thus engages in such immature responses as flirting, necking in public, and a certain flaunting of the hips that is as disquieting to her parents as it is inspirational to her admirers. She may not think she has problems, but she does; so do her harassed parents.

Campbell (1966) actually studied the personalities of beautiful women. He administered the Strong Vocational Interest Blank for Women to 100 models from three of the world's top fashion centers: New York, Paris, and Minneapolis. One major pattern differentiating the models from other women was a strong preference for exciting, exhibitionistic activities—those associated with actresses, manikins, professional dancers, chairmen of publicity or entertainment committees, reporters, etc. A second pattern was a dislike for order and routine. The vocations and activities least liked were regular hours for work, author of a technical book, geometry, civil service employee, algebra, cashier, etc. (it is to be noted that activities on the inventory are to be rated as though they all paid the same amount and as though preparation for each was already accomplished).

In terms of special adjustment problems, Campbell (1966) discussed two:

> First, fashion models tend to develop over-exaggerated ideas of their own worth, and this is quite understandable. Anyone who is paid up to $60 to $80 an hour just to stand still, and then has her face and figure, looking their very best, splashed coast-to-coast on the covers of the most prestigious magazines can hardly be expected to keep both feet firmly on the ground. Some of them, to their very great credit, manage to. For others, the problems are great. . . .
> A second major problem for the pretty model is that of growing old. While women in general do not relish the inevitability of this nor men either, for the models it seems to hold a special kind of threat. What they have and what they are is so dependent on the image of youth that they are reluctant to relinquish it. While some of them could easily shade over into posing for the matronly type advertisement, I'm told that many refuse to do this, and the elderly women that you see baking pies for Betty Crocker are usually women who started modeling relatively late in life, perhaps as grandmothers. . . . [Pp. 5–6.]

Physical Growth Rates

Attainment of physical maturity is viewed as an important landmark by our culture. Children themselves adopt this value orientation at a relatively early age. Indeed, the processes of imitation and identification, by which a child tends to adopt the mannerisms, values, and appearances of his liked-sexed parent, begin prior to school age. Thus, a four-year-old boy may compare his physical features with those of his dad, requesting him to "feel my muscle," or, standing on a chair to match his father's height, say, "I'm almost as big as you are now."

But it is not until early adolescence that physical growth embarks on a course that results in dramatic gains toward the adult physique. The very word *puberty,* used to describe the *adolescent growth spurt,* is derived from the Latin word *pubertas: age of manhood.* It is during puberty that the onset of sexual maturity begins. Figure 2.1 indicates the

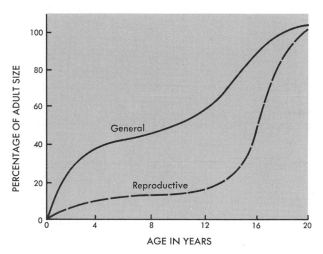

Figure 2.1. Growth curves for general body dimensions and reproductive organs (Scammon, 1930).

general nature of the adolescent growth spurt. The top curve represents general body growth as a whole, in terms of height and weight. The lower curve represents growth of reproductive organs. Observe how both characteristics show a spurt in growth during early adolescence.

There are substantial sex differences in age of puberty. For girls, the onset begins at about age eleven and lasts until thirteen or fourteen, with maximum growth occurring during the twelfth year. For boys, the onset is usually during the thirteenth year, and lasts until fifteen or sixteen, with maximum growth occurring during the fourteenth year. Thus, boys manifest an average lag of two years behind girls before entering the growth spurt. Figure 2.2 illustrates this sex difference.

A much more dramatic way of showing the sex difference is to consider *rates* of growth. Figure 2.3 presents mean increments per year

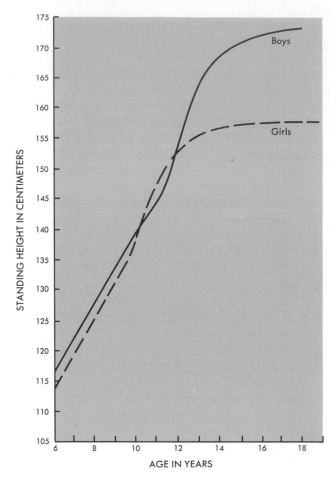

Figure 2.2. Average height of girls and boys at different ages (Shuttle-worth, 1939). Copyright 1939 by The Society for Research in Child Development.

in height for boys and girls, where each sex is grouped in terms of the year of maximum growth (i.e., regardless of whether a girl manifested her maximum growth spurt at age eleven, thirteen, or fifteen, it is plotted at age twelve and a half, the average for all girls). This figure shows that the average girl has increased from about 5 cm. (2 in.) per year to 8 cm. (3+ in.), and has slowed down again to 5 cm. *before the average boy gets started.*

There are also large individual differences within each sex. Considering either boys or girls, there are some children who are "early maturers" and others who are "late maturers." What causes these individual

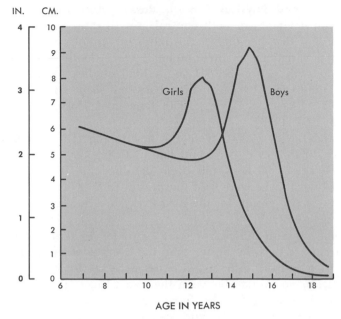

Figure 2.3. Height gains per year for girls and boys (Shuttleworth, 1939). Copyright 1939 by The Society for Research in Child Development.

differences? Heredity and environment are, of course, both involved. It seems certain that heredity is the more important of the two, given the environmental conditions presently prevailing in the United States. For example, if two tall people marry, it is almost certain that all their children will be tall, and if one or both parents are short, the children may be either tall or short. Tallness, in other words, is probably recessive, and shortness dominant. Likewise, broad-chested and early maturing parents are likely to have early maturing children, and vice versa. But environment plays a role too. Maximum height in boys is now attained by the age of eighteen or nineteen, while a few generations ago it was not attained until twenty or twenty-one. A similar trend is evident for girls, who now attain final height at about seventeen, instead of eighteen or nineteen. These trends toward earlier maturing over successive generations are undoubtedly due to environmental factors such as better nutrition and better medical services. A popular misconception is that each generation is getting larger and taller. There is little actual truth to this; one expert estimates less than a half-inch gain in the last century, if that much (Meredith: reported by McCandless, 1967, p. 386). What has occurred is that mature status is reached earlier, not that it is much different from what it used to be.

Personality and Physical Growth Rates. Accepting the fact that heredity and environment both control growth rates and physical characteristics, and that heredity is the more important of the two (given only normal variations in environment), what do these characteristics have to do with personality? Longitudinal studies indicate some remarkable differences in personality between early and late maturers (Jones, 1957; Jones and Bayley, 1950; Jones and Mussen, 1958; Mussen and Jones, 1957, 1958).

Jones and Bayley (1950) were the first to report a careful study of personality differences in early and late maturing boys. They measured the skeletal age of 90 boys and then identified the 16 who were most mature and the 16 who were least mature for further investigation. After studying these two groups for the next five years, they arrived at the following conclusions:

First, the physical differences were extreme. In terms of height, all of the late maturers were shorter than the average of the early maturers at age eleven, and this difference increased to age fourteen, when there was practically no overlap between the two groups (i.e., the tallest late maturer was hardly as tall as the shortest early maturer). The late maturers tended to be long legged and slender at all ages, relatively weak, below average in athletics, and to have less pubic hair and smaller genitals. The early maturers, on the other hand, were usually broad, large, and strong, were good in athletics, and had more pubic hair and larger genitals than average. It may be concluded that these two groups differed widely in physical maturity, in spite of comparable chronological ages.

What were their personalities like? They were rated in three different ways: (1) by observers when the boys were interacting in small, male-only groups; (2) by observers at a social club for both sexes; and (3) by classmates themselves, both girls and boys.

Ratings by observers in male-only situations indicated that the late maturing boys were significantly less physically attractive (as judged by the observers), took less care of their physical appearance, were more animated and active, more "eager" and uninhibited, more "affected," less matter of fact, and less relaxed. In terms of popularity, however, there seemed to be little difference. The authors suggested that the late maturer compensates for some inadequacies—such as attractiveness, strength, and athletic ability—by exaggerating other qualities—such as activity and attention-seeking.

When personalities were rated in a mixed-sex situation, where dancing and social interaction between sexes occurred, marked differences were noted between the two groups for sex-related behavior. The nature of some of these differences is suggested by the following:

At a Saturday graduation party three of the early-maturers came to the party conspicuously late, a mark of sophistication not shown by any of the late-maturers. Three others had Saturday jobs, had been working all day and were eager to talk to adults about their work. Among the observer's comments about the early-maturers were such notations as "he dances well"; "seems to think of himself as an adult"; "acts a bit condescending"; "reserved, little energy output"; "ran and sat in the corner and flirted with Myra"; "cheek-to-cheek dancing"; "gay and assured, tried to cut in."

In contrast, these phrases described some of the boys who were of the same age but were late-maturing: "the first time I've ever seen him with a girl"; "he held his head tensely while dancing"; "didn't dance at all"; "acted extremely silly"; "Ronnie admitted he had been to only three dances before"; "Claude showed a beaming countenance at all times"; "began to wiggle and giggle." [Jones and Bayley, as reported in Kuhlen and Thompson, 1952, p. 47.]

Finally, when personalities were rated by classmates, a number of further differences appeared. As seen by their classmates, late maturers were more attention-seeking, more restless, more talkative, less grown up, more "bossy," and less good looking. In terms of popularity, they were about average until around age thirteen, when they began to drop to a lower status.

How are these differences to be explained? Jones and Bayley suggest the most likely answer:

A general picture emerges from the various ratings and characterization of these two contrasting groups of boys. Those who are physically accelerated are usually accepted and treated by adults and other children as more mature. They appear to have relatively little need to strive for status. From their ranks come the outstanding student body leaders in senior high school. In contrast, the physically retarded boys exhibit many forms of relatively immature behavior: this may be in part because others tend to treat them as the little boys they appear to be. Furthermore, a fair proportion of these boys give evidence of needing to counteract their physical disadvantage in some way—usually by greater activity and striving for attention, although in some cases by withdrawal. [P. 48.]

Mussen and Jones (1957) and Jones and Mussen (1958) studied these same boys with different measurement techniques and found similar personality differences. It may therefore be concluded that the differences were quite reliable.

There have also been studies of groups of early and late maturing girls (Jones and Mussen, 1958). In general, personality differences between the two groups were smaller and less frequent than for boys, suggesting minimal differences. Those that were found, however, tended to be opposite to the direction found for boys. Late maturing girls seemed to enjoy some personality advantages, at least as measured by popularity, whereas early maturing boys had the advantage. Other investigations have suggested a more complicated picture. Faust, for example, found that the relationship between prestige and growth rate varied with chronological age (Faust, 1960). Studying 731 girls in grades 6 through 9, she found that, in the sixth grade, late maturers had more prestige, but the reverse was found in grades 7, 8, and 9: the early maturers had more social prestige. Thus, late maturation was a social advantage at the end of the elementary grades, but a disadvantage in junior high school. Recalling that previous studies found late maturing to be of some advantage during junior and senior high school, it is apparent that the findings are somewhat contradictory for girls.

Heterosexual popularity in both sexes is more affected by physical maturity than same-sexed popularity. We have already seen this to be the case for boys, where the early maturing boy has definite advantages. We would expect the opposite to be the case for girls. The early maturing girl is not only physiologically a year or two out of step with her female classmates, being larger, taller, and heavier—decidedly unfeminine characteristics—but is three or four years out of step with the boys in her class. In Figure 2.4, the dashed line presents the mean height for early maturing girls (whose adolescent growth spurt occurred at age ten and a half), while the solid line presents mean heights for *average* boys (growth spurt occurring at fourteen and a half). Note that at age twelve, the early maturing girls are almost 4 inches taller than average boys of the same age. The picture is about the same with regard to weight. The early maturing twelve-year-old girl weighs 24 pounds more than the average twelve-year-old boy. Thus, the early maturing girl is approaching physiological maturity by the age of twelve, but not psychological maturity. Consequently, she may find herself overextended and at a disadvantage in dating behavior, associating with older boys with more experience and sophistication. The psychological discrepancy may well result in conflicts, fears, and confusions that contribute to the less acceptable personality of some early maturing girls.

The early maturing boy, on the other hand, is at an obvious advantage on two counts. First, he is as large and as interested in girls as the average twelve-year-old girls are in boys. Since most of his male classmates are not yet interested in girls, he has little competition; he is in demand. Second, his rapid development has also endowed him with characteristics admired by his own sex: a good build, strength, height, a beard, and relatively large genitals. Thus, he enjoys increased popularity with boys as well as with girls. It may therefore be concluded that during early adolescence early maturing boys and late maturing girls seem to develop more desirable personalities on the average. Of course, there are many exceptions to this rule (recall the Faust results); *extreme* variations in pubertal onset are likely to be detrimental to *either* sex because of the concern and worry they may elicit. Then, too, some early matur-

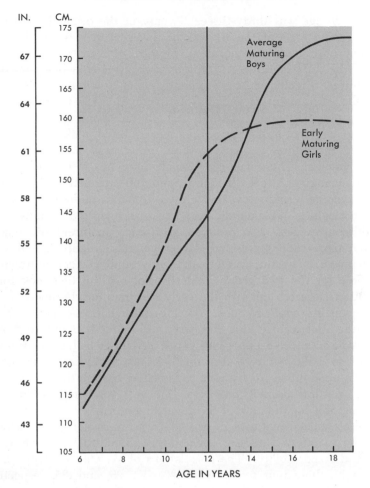

IN.   CM.

AGE IN YEARS

Average Maturing Boys

Early Maturing Girls

Figure 2.4. Growth curves for early maturing girls and average maturing boys (Shuttleworth, 1939). Copyright 1939 by The Society for Research in Child Development.

ing boys may suffer a temporary drop in popularity because of acne and other skin problems characteristic of adolescence. Many other factors may also operate in any one individual to attenuate the generalizations suggested by the research literature.

Adult Differences.   There is also the question of the later, adult personalities of early and late maturers. Do the personality differences of the early teens remain in evidence in adulthood, or do they tend to disappear, just as the physical differences tend to shrink? Jones (1957) conducted a follow-up study of the early and late maturing boys when their average age was thirty-three. Twenty of the original 32 were located. Looking back at the records of these 20 men when they were adolescent boys revealed enormous physical differences: the average height of the early maturers at fourteen was 5 feet 8 inches; that of the late maturers, 5 feet even. A 34-pound average weight difference prevailed: the early maturers weighed an average of 127 pounds; the late maturers only 93 pounds. Ratings of body-build and genital size also varied; the early maturers were of a more solid build, with larger genitals.

By age thirty-three, however, these differences had become considerably smaller. There was only ½-inch difference in height, the early maturers averaging 5 feet 10 inches, and the late maturers, 5 feet 9½ inches. Average weights revealed only a 7-pound difference, with early maturers weighing 172 pounds, and late maturers, 165 pounds. Body-build differences were also reduced, with early maturers still enjoying somewhat more solid builds and larger genitals. Figure 2.5 illustrates the differences in height, weight, and body-build at ages fourteen and thirty-three for the two groups, clearly showing the tendency for the late maturers to catch up with the early maturers in adulthood.

In personality configurations, too, the differences seemed to be less than during adolescence. But they were still marked enough to show up on relatively insensitive paper-and-pencil inventories. Late maturers, as compared to early maturers, did not feel they could create as good an impression upon others, or were as responsible, cooperative, enterprising, sociable, or warm as early maturers. Indeed, "good impression" scores (consisting of a combination of the preceding scores) correlated .50 with the level of skeletal maturity measured 18 years earlier! The early maturers also manifested greater sociability, self-control, dominance over others, and responsibility. The correlations of skeletal maturity (at age fifteen) with these four scores were .40, .31, .26, and .35, respectively. Thus, it would appear that the early maturers tended to carry over into adulthood some of the same personality characteristics that distinguished them in early adolescence. Jones concludes: "The adolescent handicaps and advantages associated with late- or early-maturing appear to carry over into adulthood to some extent, and perhaps to a greater extent in psychological than in physical characteristics" (1957, p. 128).

From an environmental point of view, such a conclusion is not unexpected. Having learned certain habitual ways of responding to others during adolescence, a certain amount of stability for these habits would be expected, even though the conditions under which they were learned had changed. Thus, if the late maturer learned certain compensatory habits that offset real or imagined status problems during adolescence, it would be expected that such habits would continue to control behavior even after the associated physical characteristics had disappeared.

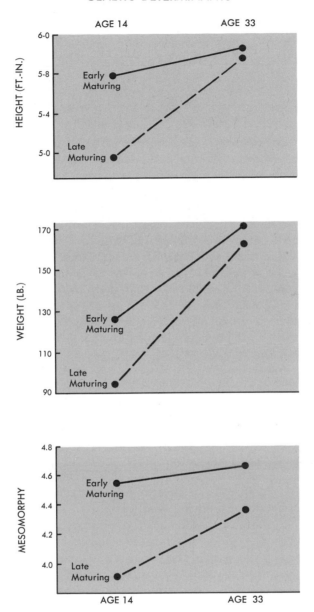

Figure 2.5. Physical changes from adolescence to adulthood for early maturing and late maturing males (Jones, 1957).

There is practically no information available concerning the long-term effects of growth-rate differences upon female personality development. What little there is contrasts with the picture for males, since little evidence of adult differences has been found. Ames (1957) found practically no significant correlations between adolescent skeletal age and adult personality scores. Shipman (1964) also found negative results. He found that age of menarche was not related to personality scores obtained in adulthood. These results, of course, are what would be expected, since few personality differences were found in adolescence between early and late maturing girls.

Heredity or Environment? It has been assumed that personality differences associated with differences in growth rates are only indirectly caused by the physical characteristics themselves. It is the reactions of others to physical characteristics that are assumed to cause the differences in personality. The most obvious evidence for such an environmental assumption, of course, is that personality similarities do not run in families as growth-rate characteristics do. Mussen and Boterline (1964), however, have presented evidence of another kind. They have found that, while American and Italian-American late maturing boys are more likely to feel inferior and inadequate than early maturers, native Italian boys living in Italy were not affected by growth-rate differences. They concluded that such results strongly indicate that it is the *culture's reaction* to growth-rate differences that determines their effects upon personality development.

GENETIC EFFECTS UPON INTELLIGENCE

If *personality* is defined as all those behavior patterns that distinguish one individual from another, then certainly *intelligence* constitutes an important dimension of personality. Surely a "bright" person differs from a "dull" person in many ways: his behavior in school, on the job, and during recreation hours; the nature of his conversation (whether it is stimulating and "full" or boring and "empty"); the handling of his finances; etc. It is because intelligence is so pervasive that it is important.

As previously noted, the nature-nurture controversy reached its climax with respect to intelligence. The child development journals of the 1930's, 1940's, and the early 1950's are full of argument and counterargument, fact and counterfact, and accusation and denial over the relative contributions of heredity and environment. Nor has the question yet been settled. The author is always amused to note that his colleagues in sociology usually conclude that culture plays the dominant role, while his psychological colleagues usually conclude the opposite. What are the facts?

The first blow for heredity was struck by Sir Francis Galton, Darwin's cousin. Possibly impressed by the extent to which his own family had contributed to English science and literature, he was the first to seriously investigate the possible role of heredity. Using both family pedigree information and questionnaires answered by twins, he was impressed with the extent to which prominence ran in families. Studying statesmen, literary men, scientists, commanders, musicians, poets, painters, and even "North Country wrestlers," he concluded that: "Nature prevails enormously over nurture when the differences of nurture do not exceed what is commonly found among persons of the same rank of society and in the same county" (1883, p. 241).

But Galton, undoubtedly a genius himself, was wrong in assuming that such genealogical evidence made a very strong case for heredity. Money also runs in families. If one family member is wealthy, the chances are abnormally high that any one of his siblings and/or descendants will also be wealthy. Yet no one assumes that a gene for "wealthiness" exists; rather, it is obvious that wealthy people give their money to their descendants, thus keeping it in the family. Therefore, it is environment that causes money to run in families—how one family member treats another. Might not the same be true of intelligence? Perhaps the way a person is "treated" affects his intelligence as well as his purse.

Methodological Problems

What kind of evidence is needed to further investigate this question? The basic strategy in any nature-nurture question is so well known it has almost become a cliché: "vary heredity or environment and hold the other constant." What does this rule mean? It means that we should study groups of people who (a) have different environments but the same heredity, or (b) have different heredities but the same environment. Let us consider the logic of each of these strategies.

Suppose we follow (a) and take pairs of people with exactly the same heredity, but who were raised in different environments. Nature is not overly generous in providing a large supply of people with identical heredities—we have seen how fantastically slim the odds are—but she does give us a pair of *identical twins* ever so often, about 1 in every 250 births. Identical twins, of course, have exactly the same heredity and thus fit our needs. But now we must "vary the environment." That means we must find one group of identical twins where the two members of each pair were raised in roughly the same environment, and another group where each pair was separated and the members raised in different environments. In this way, environment has been varied in the two groups; in one group, it is about the same for both members of each twin pair, and in the other group, it is different for the two members of each pair. To the extent that heredity controls intelligence, it should make little difference whether identical twins are reared together or apart; their intelligence scores should be highly similar in either case. If, on the other hand, environment affects intelligence, twins reared apart should have less similar intelligence scores than twins reared together. Such is the logic of strategy (a).

The basic strategy of (b), where heredity is allowed to vary, but environment is held constant, is exemplified with two groups of twins again, but now each pair is raised together, thus holding environmental similarities constant for each pair. But the twins of one group are not as genetically similar as the twins of the other group. Nature has again proved cooperative, furnishing us not only with identical twins but also with *fraternal* twins. Identical twins are *monozygotic*, while fraternal twins are *dizygotic;* that is, identical twins are genetically identical because both members come from one zygote, while fraternal twins are genetically as dissimilar as siblings, since each comes from a different zygote, as is the case with siblings. Consider, then, a group of identical twins, each pair raised together, and a group of fraternal twins, each pair raised together. If it is the case that parents treat fraternal twins as similarly as identical twins, then predictions relevant to the nature-nurture issue are easy to make. For if heredity is the sole determinant of intelligence, then identical twins ought to be more similar than fraternal twins. If environment is the major determinant, however, the similarities ought to be about the same in the two groups.

It is obvious that the logic of strategy (b) depends upon the validity of the assumption that fraternal twins are treated as similarly as identical twins. Since fraternal twins can differ in sex, and identical twins cannot, a group of randomly selected fraternal twins would consist of about 50 per cent same-sex pairs and 50 per cent different-sex pairs. Certainly, a boy and girl of the same age are not treated as similarly as two children of the same sex. Thus, the assumption would certainly be false unless precautions were taken to include only fraternal twins of the same sex. Accepting this precaution, it is usually assumed that same-sex fraternal twins are treated as similarly as (same-sex) identical twins.

Yet recent evidence suggests that they are not. Smith (1965) found a number of differences between the experiences of same-sex fraternal twins that were greater than those between identical twins. For example, parents of female identical twins dressed them alike for a longer period of time than parents of female fraternal twins (there was little difference on this point for boys). Identical twins had the same friends almost twice as often as fraternal twins; they also attended movies and sporting events together more often, studied together more often, etc. Smith concluded, ". . . it seems evident that the assumption of a common environment for MZ and DZ twins is of doubtful validity" (p. 59). For the time being, however, we shall ignore this criticism.

Evidence for Heredity

The type (a) study requires identical twins reared together and identical twins reared apart, and the type (b) study requires identical twins reared together and same-sexed fraternal twins reared together. A total of only three groups is thus required for both studies, since they have one group in common. Three published studies have included all three groups, thus providing six different comparisons for evaluation. The difficulty of obtaining sets of identical twins reared apart is indicated by the fact that the first study (Newman et al., 1937) required 10 years to obtain 19 such pairs. This in spite of public appeals in newspapers and in coast-to-coast radio broadcasts and a booth at the Chicago World's Fair.

The results of all three studies, in terms of the correlations between intelligence scores for the pairs of twins, are presented in Table 2.2. Because identical twins reared apart are so difficult to find, the number obtained in each study is indicated in parenthesis. Note how it increases with the advent of modern communication facilities.

TABLE 2.2

Correlations Between IQ Scores of Three Groups of Twins
for Three Separate Studies

	Newman et al. (1937)	Burt (1958)	Shields (1962)
Identical twins Reared together	.91	.92	.76
Identical twins Reared apart	.67 (N = 19)	.84 (N = 30)	.77 (N = 44)
Fraternal twins Reared together	.64	.53	.51

Table 2.2 provides incontrovertible evidence for the role of heredity in the determination of intelligence. Two comparisons point in this direction. First, identical twins reared together are more similar than fraternal twins reared together. Assuming environmental similarities to be the same, this difference can only be accounted for by heredity. Second, and most convincing, identical twins reared apart are more similar than fraternal twins reared together. In this comparison, it must surely be assumed that identical twins reared apart are treated less similarly

than fraternal twins reared together. Yet a common heredity overcame this differential environment in all three studies, producing greater similarity in identical twins reared apart.

The third possible comparison, between identical twins reared together and apart, provides some support for the role of environment; that is, if the environment had no effect, it should make no difference whether twins were reared together or apart. Yet two of the three studies indicate that it does make a difference, with greater intellectual similarity observed when twins were reared together. (Note, however, that a large difference is shown in only one study, and that no difference is shown in the Shields study.) Thus, Table 2.2 cannot be interpreted to mean that heredity made all the difference, but rather that it definitely made some difference, that environment probably made some difference too, and that the case for heredity seems clearer than the case for environment.

Two further analyses of one of these studies are also of interest. The Newman, Freeman, and Holzinger study provided enough descriptive material on the environments of identical twins reared apart that it was possible to measure the relationship between environmental and intellectual similarities. Two difference scores were computed for each set of twins: first, the difference in IQ scores for the two twins, and, second, the difference in scores representing educational advantages for each twin. Then the correlation between these two sets of difference scores was computed. It was amazingly high: .79. Thus, separated twins afforded similar educational advantages had very similar IQ scores, and twins afforded discrepant educational advantages had discrepant IQ scores. The mean difference in IQ scores for the five sets of twins with the most discrepant educational advantages was 16, with the twin from the more advantageous environment obtaining the higher score in each comparison. The mean difference for the five sets of twins with the most similar educational advantages was only 4. These data present strong evidence for the role of the environment in determining intelligence.

The authors of this study point out, however, that the omission of four extreme cases attenuates this correlation considerably: from .79 to .41. With 15 cases, a correlation of .41 is not statistically significant, and thus it would be concluded that little relationship exists between environmental differences and intellectual differences. One should view the correlation of .79 with some suspicion, then, until it is confirmed with other, independent data.

A second analysis of the Newman, Freeman, and Holzinger study does not agree with the implications from the preceding analysis (Johnson, 1963). Johnson divided the 19 pairs of identical twins reared apart

These three children are triplets. The two on the left are identical, and hence are very similar in intelligence as well as appearance. The child on the right is fraternal (note different colored eyes and hair, and different dentition) and would be expected to differ in intelligence as well as appearance.

(plus 4 more pairs located elsewhere) into one group of 11 and another group of 12 pairs, on the basis of age at separation. The first group was separated at an average age of two months (all were separated prior to six months of age), and the second group at an average of twenty-four months (all were separated after one year or more). It was reasoned that if environment at these early ages affected later IQ scores, then twins in the first group, who were separated at an extremely early age, should be less similar than twins in the second group, who remained together for a longer period. But the opposite was found! The first group had a mean difference of 4.7 IQ points, and the second a mean difference of 9.4. Johnson concludes, "It seems clear, however, that the results do not support the idea that similarity in early environmental enrichment or deprivation is related to later IQ similarity in children" (p. 748).

Finally, a summary paper by Erlenmeyer-Kimling and Jarvik (1963) may be considered. These investigators summarized the results of 52 studies. The results may be presented in terms of the correlations obtained in comparison of IQ scores. These correlations are presented in Figure 2.6. The groups are ordered in terms of genetic similarity, be-

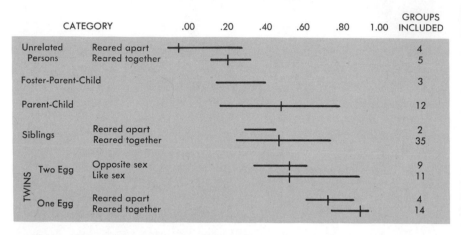

Figure 2.6. Correlations between IQ scores for pairs of individuals according to their genetic relationship (Erlenmeyer-Kimling and Jarvick, 1963). Copyright © 1963 by the American Association for the Advancement of Science.

ginning at the top with unrelated persons (zero genetic similarity) and progressing to identical twins (perfect genetic similarity). The horizontal lines indicate the range of correlations found for each type of comparison, and the short vertical marks indicate the median values. A definite trend toward increasing similarity of IQ scores regardless of environmental similarity is apparent. Thus, siblings reared either together or apart are more similar than unrelated children reared together; fraternal twins, as genetically similar as siblings, are about as similar in IQ scores as siblings, irrespective of a more similar environment (.53 versus .49, median values); and identical twins, reared either together or apart, are more similar than fraternal twins. Considering the fact that the 52 studies used different measures of intelligence; that the investigators had different views and backgrounds regarding the importance of heredity; that the samples varied in size, age structure, ethnic composition, etc.; that data were collected in eight countries; that a time span of 40 years is involved, it is all the more convincing that such a clear genetic picture nevertheless emerges.

On the other hand, there is some evidence for environment in Figure 2.6. Unrelated children reared apart yield a median correlation of about

0, as compared with .22 for unrelated children reared together; siblings reared apart are not as similar as siblings reared together (median correlations of .40 and .49, respectively); and identical twins reared apart are not as similar as identical twins reared together (median correlations of .75 and .87, respectively).

Where do all these studies lead us? Since we are not concerned here with the question of heredity *or* environment, but only whether heredity has any effect, these studies indicate an unqualified "yes." Environment also has an effect, and in the next chapter, this effect is examined in greater detail. But we may say now that the intellectual changes environmental conditions are capable of producing are limited by heredity. As Erlenmeyer-Kimling and Jarvik concluded: "Individual differences in behavioral *potential* reflect genotypic differences: individual differences in behavioral *performance* result from the nonuniform recording of environmental stimuli by intrinsically nonuniform organisms" (1963, p. 1478).

Abnormal Variations in Intelligence

There is another line of evidence that implicates heredity in the determination of intelligence in a much more direct manner than the correlational evidence of the previous section. Reference is made here to the fact that several types of mental deficiency have been shown to have direct chromosomal and metabolic antecedents. Some of these abnormalities are Down's syndrome (Mongolism), cretinism, galactosemia, and phenylketonuria (PKU). We may take Down's syndrome as illustrative of the kinds of genetic breakthroughs that have occurred with amazing rapidity since modern techniques of cytogenetics (preparation and study of cellular genetic material) became available in the late 1950's.

The symptoms of Down's syndrome are well known, including a number of morphological abnormalities (slanting eyes with "Mongolian" folds, fissured tongue, enlarged lower lip, broad stubby hands with abnormal palm lines, etc.) as well as mental retardation. It is now an established fact that all such individuals possess extra chromosomal material in all their body cells (Eichorn, 1963). Modern cytogenetic techniques make it possible to identify pairs of chromosomes by their relative size, with the largest pair numbered 1 and the smallest pair numbered 23. Individuals afflicted with Down's syndrome usually have an extra chromosome with pair 21, and are often referred to as "Trisomy 21." If they are not "Trisomy 21," an elongated chromosome is detectable somewhere else, usually on chromosomes similar in size to Number 21.

The parents of individuals afflicted with this disorder may or may not exhibit abnormal amounts of chromosomal material. Some do and are therefore classified as "carriers." While they are not afflicted with the symptoms of Down's syndrome (although there is evidence that they usually have some minor morphological abnormalities), the probability that one of their offspring will inherit the entire syndrome may range as high as 30 per cent (Jarvik et al., 1964).

If the parents are not carriers, where does the extra chromosomal material in their afflicted offspring come from? It is probably the result of non-disjunction at the time of parental gametogenesis. During meiosis, one of the chromosome pairs does not separate into two autosomes, and both members migrate to the same side of the dividing cell. When fertilization occurs with a normal gamete from the other parent, the resulting zygote has 47 chromosomes rather than 46. What, then, causes non-disjunction? Nobody knows for sure. One clue is that many kinds of non-disjunction increase in frequency the greater the age of the mother, suggesting that maternal gametogenesis is at fault rather than paternal gametogenesis. Further evidence implicating the female is that overripe eggs in the rat often exhibit non-disjunction (Witschi, 1960).

As yet, there is no cure for Down's syndrome. The discovery of trisomy and the discovery that some people are carriers at least allow one to estimate the probability that an offspring will inherit the disorder. If the probability is high, it might be wise to consider adoption. Thus, *prevention* can be facilitated by taking advantage of chromosomal information. The next advance will probably consist of identifying the metabolic disorders produced by the extra chromosomal material. These disorders may involve either an excessive amount of some metabolite, as with diabetes, or a deficiency of some metabolite, as with cretinism, which is produced by thyroid deficiency. When the metabolic disorders have been discovered, it may be possible to prevent Down's syndrome *after conception,* or to cure the affliction with early chemotherapy. Cretinism cannot only be halted by the timely administration of thyroid hormone, but its developmental course can actually be reversed, returning some afflicted individuals to normality. Phenylketonuria and galactosemia are other examples where knowledge of the inherited metabolic errors has led to recent cures.

Viewed against the background of the previously discussed correlational studies of normal variations in intelligence, the genetics of mental deficiency, in some of its forms at least, is seen to be in a far more advanced and specific state, involving as it does the specification of chromosomal and/or metabolic processes. It is somewhat ironic that more is known about the genetics of intellectual subnormality than about the genetics of intellectual superiority.

DIRECT GENETIC EFFECTS UPON PERSONALITY

The effects of heredity upon personality require exactly the same research strategy as was used to investigate intelligence. Thus, twin studies are again of primary importance. Unfortunately, much less personality than intelligence data exist, perhaps because of the questionable reliability and validity of many personality tests.

Newman, Freeman, and Holzinger (1937) collected some personality data along with their intelligence data. They administered the Woodworth-Mathews Personal Data Sheet to their three samples, obtaining a single "adjustment score" for each individual. They also obtained four other personality scores for two of the groups: identical and fraternal twins reared together. The correlations are presented in Table 2.3. Two characteristics stand out: (1) The correlations are much lower than is the case for IQ scores from the same individuals (see Table 2.2), reflecting, in part, the lower reliability of these personality tests. Another interpretation, not incompatible with the preceding one, is that environmental differences had greater effects on these personality scores than on IQ scores, thus producing the lower correlations. (2) With the exception of the Woodworth-Mathews score, fraternal twins are just as similar as identical twins; only powerful environmental effects would be expected to lead to such equality. Thus, both characteristics may be interpreted as indicating minimal genetic effects and strong environmental effects.

TABLE 2.3

Correlations of Personality Test Scores
(Adapted from Newman, Freeman, and Holzinger, 1937)

	Woodworth-Mathews Adjustment Score	Speed of Decision	Finality of Judgment	Motor Inhibition	Coordination of Impulses
Identical twins reared together	.56	.50	.31	.51	.82
Identical twins reared apart	.58				
Fraternal twins reared together	.37	.69	.37	.58	.79

About the same time that Newman *et al.* were collecting and analyzing their extensive data, Carter reported results on 55 pairs of identical twins and 78 pairs of fraternal twins (Carter, 1935). He administered the Bernreuter Inventory, probably a better test than those used by Newman *et al.* His results for six scales of the test are presented in Table 2.4.

TABLE 2.4

Correlations of Personality Test Scores
(Adapted from Carter, 1935)

	Neuroti-cism	Self-Sufficiency	Intraver-sion	Domi-nance	Self-Con-fidence	Socia-bility
Identical twins reared togther	.63	.44	.50	.71	.58	.57
Fraternal twins						
Same sex	.32	−.14	.40	.34	.20	.41
Different sex	.18	.12	.18	.18	.07	.39

Without exception, identical twins are more similar than fraternal twins, which could be the result of either genetic or environmental factors. More revealing is the difference between fraternal twins of the same sex and those of different sexes. When the sexes are different, the correlations are much lower, with only one substantially above zero. Since the genetic relationship is the same regardless of sexual differences, these lower correlations can be accounted for only in terms of less environmental similarity. Since the high correlations of identical twins can also be accounted for in terms of greater environmental similarity, an environmental point of view accounts for all of Carter's results. It may therefore be concluded that Carter's results support those of Newman *et al.:* genetic effects upon personality characteristics appear to be small.

Shields (1962), using modern personality tests, obtained correlations between identical twins reared apart as well as between identical twins and fraternal twins reared together. His results are presented in Table 2.5. These results are contrary to those of the preceding studies, for they suggest a strong genetic effect. Identical twins reared apart are not only just as similar as twins reared together but actually more similar, and fraternal twins are much less similar, hardly departing from a zero correlation.

TABLE 2.5

Correlations of Personality Test Scores
(Adapted from Shields, 1962)

	Extroversion	Neuroticism
Identical twins reared together	.42	.38
Identical twins reared apart	.61	.53
Fraternal twins	−.17	.11

Gottesman (1963) also concluded that heredity has definite effects upon personality. He examined 34 pairs of identical twins and 34 pairs of fraternal twins, all reared together. Each person took two modern personality tests, which yielded a total of 24 different personality scores. Gottesman's conclusion is based primarily on the fact that correlations were usually higher between identical twins than between fraternal twins (18 out of 24 comparisons). On six scales, this difference was statistically significant. Interestingly enough, three of these six scores were related to the dimension of extraversion-introversion, thus corroborating Shields's finding of a genetic determinant for this dimension. On the other hand, it must be kept in mind that the higher correlations for identical twins could have been due to a more similar environment. Gottesman's study, like so many others, lacks the crucial data provided by identical twins reared apart. The most that can be said is that his results can be interpreted in favor of either heredity or environment. The strongest statement about heredity that seems safe is that one broad personality dimension may have sizable genetic determinants: extraversion-introversion.

Other recent studies present a mixed picture. None has included a group of identical twins reared apart. Two found some evidence for a genetic determinant of extraversion-introversion, corroborating the conclusions of Shields and Gottesman (Eysenck, 1956; Vandenberg, 1965). Cattell (1957) administered a large battery of tests to over 600 children between the ages of ten and fifteen. The group included identical and fraternal twins raised together, siblings raised together and apart, unrelated children reared together, and a sample of the general population. Intelligence showed the clearest indication of genetic effects, and only one other dimension was affected more by heredity than by environment: "comention," reflecting a corrigibility-incorrigibility or general rigidity dimension (Cattell indicates that an exact definition of the scale is unknown). Six other dimensions were judged to be influenced primarily by the environment, and three were judged to be affected about equally by heredity and environment (inhibition and cautiousness, carefulness and exactness, and "exuberance," reflecting good immediate memory, verbal fluency, and strong "ego strength").

An entirely different kind of study was reported by Freedman (1965). He reasoned that infants could be profitably studied because (1) imitation between siblings does not begin until far after the first year, and thus differences in environmental similarity between identical and fraternal twins would have little, if any, effects upon infants; and (2) it is difficult even for parents to distinguish between identical and fraternal twins in the first year or so, thus precluding systematic differential treatment. Freedman therefore decided to study the actual behavior of infants, rather than relying on test scores. He and his colleagues intensively studied 20 pairs of twins over the first year of life, making half-day visits to the home each month, at which time tests and motion pictures of each infant were obtained, as well as interview data from the mothers.

After the data had been collected, zygosity was determined by blood tests, with the result that 9 of the twins were found to be identical and 11 fraternal. Note that recording of the data could not have been influenced by possible biases of the investigators, since they did not know the zygosity of the pairs until later. Other elaborate safeguards were also taken. For example, one group of judges rated the filmed behavior of one member of each pair, and another group rated the filmed behavior of the other member of each pair. Since the two groups of judges were unaware of each other's ratings, there was no possibility that identical twins could have received more similar ratings as a result of judges' biases. Incidentally, it is interesting to note that the parents outguessed the obstetricians on zygosity. The obstetricians were correct only 47 per cent of the time, as compared to 70 per cent accuracy for the parents. Of the 20 parental guesses, 17 were "fraternal." Thus, practically all the parents thought they had fraternal twins, and presumably treated their babies accordingly. The author suggests this strong bias for fraternal twins perhaps reflects the social desirability of "individuality" at the time of the study.

Freedman found that personality differences even at this early age were less between identical twins than between fraternal twins. Identical twins were significantly more similar in terms of *responsiveness* to people and toys, *goal directedness, attention span, motor coordination, reactivity* (amount of stimulation required for a reaction), and *fearfulness.* In view of the methodological sophistication employed in this study, it is unlikely that differential environmental similarities can account for these results. The only likely explanation seems to be a genetic one.

Emotional Reactivity and Genetics

Some physiological evidence indicates a genetic determinant of "emotional reactivity." It is well known that a number of autonomically mediated responses are correlated with introspective sensations of anxiety and fear. Such responses as the galvanic skin response (GSR), pulse pressure, pulse rate, respiration rate, and salivary output are often used as indexes of emotionality. In a well-known study, Jost and Sontag (1944) measured all these responses in three groups of children between the ages of six and twelve: 16 pairs of identical twins, 54 pairs of siblings, and over 1,000 pairs of unrelated children. The various scores were combined into a total score of "autonomic balance," and correlations were computed for each of the three sets of pairs. The correlations were .49, .29, and .08, respectively, indicating greatest similarity for identical twins and practically no similarity for unrelated pairs. Although these results may be interpreted in terms of different environmental similarities, they are also consistent with a genetic point of view. Jule-Nielson and Harvold (1958) report that electroencephalograms (also indicative of emotional arousal) are almost indistinguishable for identical twins. And there is a body of evidence indicating a low threshold for physiological arousal in schizophrenics, a psychotic disorder that runs in families (e.g., Mednick and Schulsinger, 1965).

Animal studies also yield both behavioral and physiological suggestions of a genetic role in emotional responses. It is well known that animals can be bred for emotional reactivity. Differences in dog breeds, for example, are obvious by casual observation alone—the nervousness of the fox terrier as compared to the imperturbable aloofness of the basset hound. A number of studies, mostly with rats and mice, have purposely attempted to produce strain differences in emotionality. In one of the earliest and best-known studies, Hall (1938) measured emotionality in rats by frequency of urination and defecation when the animal was suddenly put in a strange environment. The parental generation was divided into high and low scorers, and selective mating was then carried out within each of these subgroups. The next generation was similarly measured and bred, and so on for 12 generations, the most emotional animals always mated together, and, likewise, the least emotional animals always mated together. The mean "emotionality" scores for succeeding generations are presented in Figure 2.7. This figure shows that inbreeding of emotional rats resulted in a dramatic increase in emotionality scores, while inbreeding of non-emotional rats resulted in maintenance of a low score. Other studies have found similar results (see Fuller and Thompson, 1960, for a more complete review of these studies).

Some years later, Hall and Klein (1942) measured the "aggressiveness" of Hall's two strains. Pairs of rats were caged together for a given amount of time, and the number of attacks by each rat was scored. The non-emotional rats initiated 326 attacks as compared to 68 by the emotional rats, thus indicating that rats bred for emotionality (i.e., "fear" or "anxiety") were less aggressive.

Physiological differences in Hall's strains have also been found. Yeakel and Rhoades (1941) weighed adrenal, thyroid, and pituitary glands and found that adrenals and thyroids were larger for emotional males than for non-emotional males, and that pituitaries and thyroids were larger for emotional females. Other investigators have found larger adrenals for wild rats than for tame rats (e.g., Rogers and Rickter, 1948).

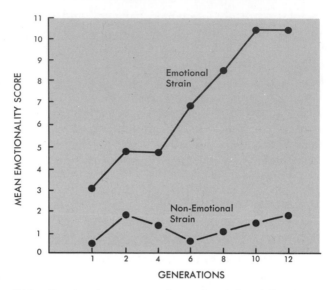

Figure 2.7. Emotionality scores of rats bred for differences in emotionality (Hall, 1938).

Rundquist and Bellis (1933) found basal metabolism rate (BMR) differences between active and inactive strains, with considerably larger BMR's for active rats. Thus, it is clear that behavioral differences as well as physiological differences in emotionality can be influenced by breeding, thereby pointing directly to the role of heredity.

Genetics and Personality: Conclusions

What conclusions seem most justified concerning direct genetic effects upon personality? The author suggests three. In the first place, the conventional view that heredity has but negligible direct effects on personality is being challenged. As more and better research accumulates, the case for heredity grows stronger, not weaker. What the final picture will be is anybody's guess, but it is a foregone conclusion that heredity will be paid greater respect than has been the case in the past.

Second, the dimension of extraversion-introversion has turned up in a number of studies, suggesting that if any personality dimension has a sizable genetic component, this is likely to be it. What is the difference between extraversion and introversion? Basically, the extravert describes himself as outgoing, sociable, lively, prone to direct action rather than reflection (i.e., somewhat impulsive), authoritarian, and tough-minded, while the introvert describes himself as inhibited, meditative, withdrawn from social contacts, cooperative, and sentimental. The dimension is thus an extremely broad one, covering a number of more restricted dimensions. The interested reader is referred to Cattell (1945, 1946) and Cattell and Gruen (1955) for expanded discussions of the dimension. Suffice it to say that because of its broadness, it has been considered to constitute one of three fundamental personality dimensions (the other two are "neuroticism" and "psychoticism"); see Eysenck (1965). If one may thus loosely state that it describes one of the three main personality dimensions, it follows that the genetic component is of considerable magnitude.

Third, the physiological and animal evidence points strongly in the direction of a genetic determinant of emotional reactivity. The effects of such a mechanism may be pervasive. Suppose, for example, that such a mechanism exists for humans as well as for animals; some people are easily upset and bothered by environmental stress, while other people are emotionally calm—"steady" and "cool" in the face of stress. As long as the environment is normal, both groups would be expected to get along all right. But if things become difficult, the reactive people will become more emotional and more anxious. Presumably, anxiety is at the bottom of many kinds of psychopathology, both of neurotic and psychotic varieties. It follows that the reactive person would be more likely to develop symptoms of maladjustment than the calm person. The genetic factor would not directly produce the symptoms but would "set the stage" for a variety of possible symptoms. In other words, a genetically determined predisposition to psychopathology would exist. Just such a mechanism has long been assumed by a number of investigators (see Meehl, 1962, for an elaborate discussion). The studies reviewed in this section indicate the bases for such an assumption.

SUMMARY

Heredity determines the developmental potential of all living organisms. Without it, a dog would be as likely to father a chicken, a snake, or a "blob" as another dog; there would be no continuity from one generation to the next. But heredity does much more than merely insure phylogenetic similarity. It also insures slow phylogenetic change, in keeping with Darwin's doctrine of survival of the fittest. Thus, man evolved as he did because of his ancestors; their characteristics kept them alive to reproduce others of their kind, and because genetically controlled modifications were eliminated by nature if they did not contribute to survival. Man is thus the heir to all the tested and proved characteristics of animal forms that preceded him. He would not be as he is if other forms had been completely successful in the battle for existence. He is a direct result of the interaction between genetic potential and environ-mental selection.

The chromosomes and the genes are the carriers of the chemical sub-stances through which heredity manifests itself. Through sexual re-combination of parental genes, a tremendous variety of genetic potential is made possible. No two people are genetically identical (except identi-cal twins, who are produced not by independent genic combinations that just "happened" to be identical, but from a "split" from a *single* zygote). Since the environment is also unique for each individual (including iden-tical twins), it follows that the combination is also unique, probably never to be repeated again.

For any given characteristic, the question therefore arises as to the relative "contributions" of heredity and environment—the nature-nurture question. The word "contributions" may easily be misinterpreted. It does not imply that heredity or environment can ever singly determine a characteristic, any more than water can be singly determined by hydro-gen *or* oxygen. Obviously, both are required. The word "contributions" refers, rather, to the amount of variability in a characteristic from one person to another that can be accounted for by genotypic variability on the one hand and environmental variability on the other.

Indirect genetic effects upon personality denote physical characteris-tics that affect the reactions of other people, which in turn affect the personality of the person in question. Three examples of such effects are *race, facial characteristics*, and *physical growth rates*. In each case, research indicates that personality is indeed affected. As an example of race, American southern Negroes appear to have problems coping with feelings of anger and aggression. In the case of "looks," good-looking people tend to be more sociable, more extraverted, more popular—and yet may suffer from unique problems of adjustment as well. Finally, early maturing boys tend to have psychological advantages over late maturers, with the opposite tending to be the case for girls.

Intelligence is very definitely a personality characteristic, yet it occu-pies a place removed from the other dimensions, perhaps because of its greater generality. It is directly affected by heredity. Sir Francis Galton was very close to the truth when he wrote: "Nature prevails enormously over nurture when the differences of nurture do not exceed what is com-monly found. . . ." Note that such a conclusion does not deny environ-ment its due, but states that environmental conditions must be somewhat extreme before correlated intellectual variability appears.

Other personality dimensions have also been examined for direct ge-netic determinants. Until recently, the common assumption was nega-tive; it was assumed that direct genetic effects on personality dimensions other than intelligence were minimal. That is no longer the case. The evidence for heredity grows stronger, and where it will lead nobody knows. There is strong evidence that the broad dimension of *extraversion-introversion* has a genetic component, and that *emotional reactivity* also is affected by heredity. Beyond these two dimensions, little can be asserted with confidence at the present time.

BIBLIOGRAPHY

AMES, R. (1957). Physical maturing among boys as related to adult social behavior: a longitudinal study. *California journal of educational research*, 8, 69–75.

BURT, C. (1958). The inheritance of mental ability. *American psychologist*, 13 (1), 1–15.

CAMPBELL, D. P. (1966). The vocational interests of beautiful women. Paper read at Midwestern Psychological Association, Chicago.

CARTER, H. D. (1935). Twin similarities in emotional traits. *Character & personality*, 4, 61–78.

CATTELL, R. B. (1945). The description of personality. Principles and findings in a factor analysis. *American journal of psychology*, 58, 69–90.

CATTELL, R. B. (1946). *The description and measurement of personality.* New York: Harcourt, Brace & World, Inc.

CATTELL, R. B., and GRUEN, W. (1955). The primary personality factors in eleven year old children by objective tests. *Journal of personality*, 23, 460–478.

CATTELL, R. B., STICE, G. F., and KRISTY, N. F. (1957). A first approximation to nature-nurture ratios for eleven primary personality factors in objective tests. *Journal of abnormal and social psychology*, 54, 143–159.

DARWIN, C. (1859). *The origin of species.* London: J. John Murray, Publishers, Ltd.

DARWIN, C. (1871). *The descent of man.* London: J. John Murray, Publishers, Ltd.

DAVIDSON, E. H. (1965). Hormones and genes. *Scientific American*, 212 (6), 36–45.

DE BEER, SIR GAVIN (1962). Mankind evolving: the evolution of the human species, by Theodosius Dobshansky: a review. *Scientific American*, 207 (3), 265–272, at p. 266.

DREGER, R. M., and MILLER, K. S. (1960). Comparative psychological studies of Negroes and whites in the United States. *Psychological bulletin*, 57, 361–402.

EICHORN, DOROTHY H. (1963). Biological correlates of behavior. In W. STEVENSON (Ed.), *Child psychology.* Chicago: University of Chicago Press. Pp. 4–61.

ERLENMEYER-KIMLING, L., and JARVIK, L. F. (1963). Genetics and intelligence: a review. *Science*, 142 (3598), 1477–1479.

EYSENCK, H. J. (1956). The inheritance of extraversion-introversion. *Acta psychologica*, 12, 95–110.

EYSENCK, H. J. (1965). Factor theory psychology: a dimensional approach to personality. In W. S. SAHAKIAN (Ed.), *Psychology of personality.* Chicago: Rand McNally & Co. Pp. 415–436.

FAUST, MARGARET S. (1960). Developmental maturity as a determinant in prestige of adolescent girls. *Child development*, 31, 173–184.

FREEDMAN, D. (1965). An ethnological approach to the genetical study of human behavior. In S. G. VANDENBERG (Ed.), *Methods and goals in human behavior genetics.* New York: Academic Press, Inc. Pp. 141–162.

FREEDMAN, D., and KELLER, B. (1963). Inheritance of behavior in infants. *Science*, 140, 196–198.

FULLER, J. L., and THOMPSON, W. R. (1960). *Behavior genetics.* New York: John Wiley & Sons, Inc.

GALTON, F. (1883). *Inquiries into human faculty and its development.* London: Macmillan & Co., Ltd.

GOTTESMAN, I. I. (1963). Heritability of personality: a demonstration. *Psychological monographs,* 77 (9).

HALL, C. S. (1938). The inheritance of emotionality. *Sigma xi quarterly,* 26, 17–27.

HALL, C. S., and KLEIN, S. J. (1942). Individual differences in aggressiveness in rats. *Journal of comparative psychology,* 33, 371–383.

HAYES, K. J., and HAYES, C. (1951). The intellectual development of a home-raised chimpanzee. *Proceedings of American philosophical society,* 95, 105–109.

HORROCKS, J. F. (1962). *The psychology of adolescence.* Boston: Houghton Mifflin Co.

JARVIK, L. F., FALEK, A., and PIERSON, W. P. (1964). Down's syndrome (Mongolism): the heritable aspects. *Psychological bulletin,* 61, 388–398.

JERSILD, A. T. (1957). *The psychology of adolescence.* New York: The Macmillan Co.

JOHNSON, R. C. (1963). Similarity in intelligence of separated identical twins as related to length of time spent in the same environment. *Child development,* 34, 745–747.

JONES, MARY C. (1957). The later careers of boys who were early- or late-maturing. *Child development,* 28, 113–128.

JONES, MARY C., and BAYLEY, NANCY (1950). Physical maturing among boys as related to behavior. *Journal of educational psychology,* 41, 129–148.

JONES, MARY C., and MUSSEN, P. H. (1958). Self-conceptions, motivations, and interpersonal attitudes of early- and late-maturing girls. *Child development,* 29, 491–501.

JOST, H., and SONTAG, L. W. (1944). The genetic factor in autonomic nervous system function. *Psychosomatic medicine,* 6, 308–310.

JULE-NIELSON, N., and HARVOLD, B. (1958). The electroencephalogram in univolar twins brought up apart. *Acta genetica,* 8, 57–64.

KAGAN, J., and MOSS, H. A. (1962). *Birth to maturity.* New York: John Wiley & Sons, Inc.

KARON, B. P. (1958). *The Negro personality.* New York: Springer Publishing Co., Inc.

KATZ, I., ROBINSON, J. M., EPPS, E. G., and WALY, PATRICIA (1964). The influence of race of the experimenter and instructions upon the expression of hostility by Negro boys. *Journal of sociological issues,* 20 (2), 54–59.

KELLOGG, W. N., and KELLOGG, LUELLA A. (1933). *The ape and the child.* New York: McGraw-Hill Book Co.

KUHLEN, R. G., and THOMPSON, G. G. (1952). *Psychological studies of human development.* New York: Appleton-Century-Crofts, Inc.

LA BARRE, W. (1955). *The human animal.* Chicago: Phoenix Books, University of Chicago Press.

LEFCOURT, H. M., and LADWIG, C. W. (1965). The American Negro: a problem in expectancies. *Journal of personality & social psychology,* 1 (4), 377–380.

LIPPITT, ROSEMARY (1941). Popularity among preschool children. *Child development,* 12, 305–332.

McCANDLESS, B. R. (1967). *Children: behavior and development.* (2d ed.) New York: Holt, Rinehart & Winston, Inc.

MATHER, W. G. (1934). The courtship ideals of high school youth. *Sociological research,* 19, 166–172.

MEDNICK, S. A., and SCHULSINGER, F. (1965). A longitudinal study of children with a high risk for schizophrenia: a preliminary report. In S. G. VANDENBERG (Ed.), *Methods and goals in human behavior genetics.* New York: Academic Press, Inc. Pp. 255–296.

MEEHL, P. E. (1962). Schizotaxia, schizotypy, schizophrenia. *American psychologist,* 17 (12), 827–838.

MOORE, RUTH (1964). *Evolution.* New York: Time, Inc.

MUNN, N. L. (1965). *The evolution and growth of human behavior.* (2d ed.) Boston: Houghton Mifflin Co.

Mussen, P. H., and Boterline, Y. H. (1964). Relationships between rate of physical maturing and personality among boys of Italian descent. *Vita humana*, 7 (3–4), 196–200.

Mussen, P. H., and Jones, Mary C. (1957). Self conceptions of early and late maturing boys. *Child development*, 28, 242–256.

Mussen, P. H., and Jones, Mary C. (1958). The behavior inferred motivations of late and early maturing boys. *Child development*, 29, 61–67.

Newman, H. H., Freeman, F. N., and Holzinger, K. J. (1937). *Twins: a study of heredity and environment*. Chicago: University of Chicago Press.

Pope, B. (1953). Socio-economic contrasts in children's peer culture prestige values. *Genetic psychological monographs*, 48, 157–220.

Rogers, P. V., and Richter, C. P. (1948). Anatomical comparison between the adrenal glands of wild Norway, wild Alexandrine, and domestic Norway rats. *Endocrinology*, 42, 46–55.

Rundquist, E. A., and Bellis, C. J. (1933). Respiratory metabolism of active and inactive rats. *American journal of physiology*, 106, 670–675.

Sager, Ruth (1965). Genes outside the chromosomes. *Scientific American*, 212 (1), 70–81.

Scammon, R. E. (1930). *The measurement of man*. Minneapolis: University of Minnesota Press.

Scheinfeld, A. (1965). *Your heredity and environment*. Philadelphia: J. B. Lippincott Co.

Shields, J. (1962). *Monozygotic twins*. London: Oxford University Press.

Shipman, W. G. (1964). Age of menarche and adult personality. *Archives of general psychology*, 10 (2), 155–159.

Shuttleworth, F. K. (1937). Sexual maturation and the physical growth of girls age 6 to 19. *Monographs of society for research in child development*, II.

Shuttleworth, F. K. (1939). The physical and mental growth of girls and boys age 6 to 19 in relation to age at maximum growth. *Monographs of society for research in child development*, IV.

Smith, R. T. (1965). A comparison of socioenvironmental factors in monozygotic and dizygotic twins, testing an assumption. In S. G. Vandenberg (Ed.), *Methods and goals in human behavior genetics*. New York: Academic Press, Inc. Pp. 45–61.

Taylor, K. W. (1938). *Do adolescents need parents?* New York: Appleton-Century-Crofts, Inc.

Vandenberg, S. G. (Ed.) (1965). *Methods and goals in human behavior genetics*. New York: Academic Press, Inc.

Witschi, E. (1960). Sex reversals in animals and man. *American scientist*, 48, 399–414.

Yeakel, E. H., and Rhoades, R. P. (1941). A comparison of the body and endocrine gland (adrenal, thyroid-pituitary) weights of emotional and non-emotional rats. *Endocrinology*, 28, 337–340.

Zander, A., and Van Egmond, E. (1958). Relationship of intelligence and social power to the interpersonal behavior of children. *Journal of educational psychology*, 49, 257–268.

3

Environment and Intelligence

INTRODUCTION

In the previous chapter, evidence for a genetic relationship to intelligence was evaluated, and it was concluded that such evidence clearly exists. The present chapter considers the other side of the coin; it evaluates the evidence for an environmental effect. It is divided into two main parts: studies with animal subjects and studies with human subjects. Both groups of studies will show that the coin truly has two sides: the environment also affects intelligence.

ANIMAL STUDIES

Behavioral Studies

Prior to the 1950's, investigations of determinants of intelligence in animals were primarily aimed at demonstrating the importance of heredity. The work of Tryon (1940, 1942) is probably best known. He spent a lifetime studying the inheritance of intelligence in rats. Rats were selectively bred according to performance on an "automatic" maze, brightest rats (e.g., fastest learners) bred with brightest rats and dullest with dullest. The results were clear cut, as indicated in Figure 3.1, which shows number of errors for the first eight generations, separately for bright and dull rats. Divergence is clearly observable by the second generation, and continues to practically no overlap by the seventh and eighth generations.

Beginning in the 1950's, evidence began accumulating which indicated that environment also plays a role. Experimenters began to impose various kinds of "stimulus deprivation" on experimental animals, and compared their performance with that of normally raised control animals. A learning deficit was usually found: deprived animals did not solve problems as quickly as non-deprived animals.

Thompson and Heron (1954) carried out one of the more dramatic studies. They divided 26 Scottish terriers, all descendants of the same original litter, into two groups of 13 each. One group, the controls, were reared as pets, in private homes or laboratories, until they were about eight months of age, at which time they were put into ordinary dog cages and received the ordinary amount of exercise and handling. Experimental animals had it drastically different. Two were exposed to *severe* isolation, each maintained in a small cage 30 by 40 by 60 inches, with solid walls to prevent visual exploration of the outside. Each day they were transferred to another cage by entering through a sliding door, with no handling. The following day the original cage was again entered. One of the two cages was kept in darkness; thus every other day these dogs were in darkness, and they were always alone.

Eight other dogs were *moderately* restricted: two or three lived together in ordinary (e.g., larger) dog cages. The sides remained covered so they could not see outside, and light entered from the uncovered top. They were handled about 10 minutes a day while the cages were cleaned. Three other dogs were *slightly* restricted. They were treated like the preceding group except that the cardboard sides were absent from the front of the cages, allowing more visual exploration of the outside. At the end of eight months, all these experimental animals were treated like control animals; that is, they were put into ordinary dog cages and given ordinary amounts of exercise and handling.

There were noticeable differences between the two groups as a result of these deprivation conditions. Some were noticeable from the outset, as soon as the experimental animals were treated normally. They were hyperactive, for example, running around the room during exercise periods and often jumping at the walls. They also manifested a strange approach-avoidance conflict toward the experimenter, tending to suddenly dash away but finally licking his hands in a compulsive, excited manner. These behavior patterns were more or less permanent, observable a year after the end of restriction. In terms of other response patterns, however, there were no systematic differences between the two groups in their day-to-day behavior, so that the experimenters felt justified in attributing differences in learning performance (to be described subsequently) to differences in learning capacity (intelligence) rather than to, say, differences in emotionality or motivation.

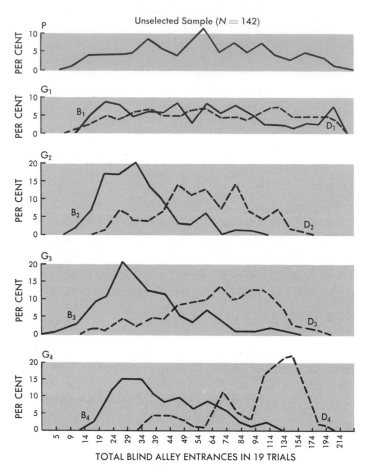

Figure 3.1. Selection for maze brightness and maze dullness in rats (Tryon, 1942).

Four learning tests were administered, two "orientation" and two "barrier" tests. All four tests were carried out in the same 8- by 10-foot room. Call the four corners A, B, C, and D, as in Figure 3.2a. In the first orientation test, each dog was first given ten training trials of running from D to A for food. All dogs easily learned this response. Then, in full view of the dog, the food pan was moved 90 degrees to C, so that it was now along the left wall instead of the right wall. The pan was banged on the floor and the food was held up for the dog to see, to make sure that the changed position was noticed. Five trials were then given. Then the food pan was moved to another corner, and then another, until a total of 14 test trials had been given. A correct response was defined as choosing a direct path to the food pan.

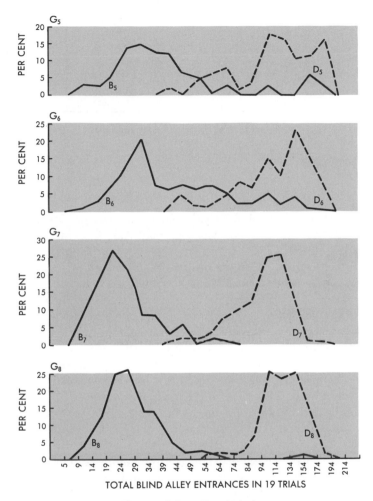

Figure 3.1. Continued.

The control dogs performed almost perfectly, with an average of 13.7 correct responses. The experimental dogs showed a large decrement, with an average of only 5.9 correct responses. The poorest control dog did better than the best experimental dog. There was no overlap at all. The nature of the errors is revealing. They consisted almost entirely of going to the previously correct location, wherever that might have been. It wasn't that the experimental dogs did not notice the food pan location—the experimenters had made sure of that—but rather that they were not able to "take advantage" of this information—they were "stupid."

The second orientation test consisted of placing the dog within a starting box and the starting box in the middle of the room facing wall *AB*.

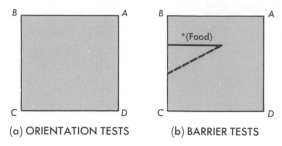

(a) ORIENTATION TESTS   (b) BARRIER TESTS

Figure 3.2. Test conditions in the Thompson and Heron experiment.

Food was placed at A and the dog was given ten trials of locomoting from the starting box to A for food. Then the starting box was rotated so that its door faced, in turn, wall BC, wall AD, and wall CD, etc., for a total of eight test trials. A correct response was defined as before: a direct run to the food. Control dogs responded correctly an average of 5.1 times, while experimental dogs achieved an average score of 2.7. Thus, control dogs were twice as accurate as experimental dogs. Errors were of the same nature as before: the dogs persevered with responses which were previously correct but were no longer so.

The barrier tests consisted of first teaching the dogs a particular path to food, and then inserting a barrier—a fence—between the dog and the food. In the first test, the dog initially learned to run from C to B, as indicated in Figure 3.2b. Then a barrier was inserted in front of the food, as indicated by the solid line. An "error zone" was marked off on the floor (dotted line). If the dog got to the food without entering the error zone, the response was scored correct; otherwise an error was recorded. Ten trials were given. The average number of correct responses for control dogs was 6.8, and for experimental dogs, 2.4. Restricted dogs thus made almost three times as many errors. They consisted, for the most part, of runs directly at the food instead of around the barrier.

The second barrier test was more difficult, requiring the dog to turn his back on the food in order to get around the barrier. In this test, time to get to the food was measured instead of number of correct responses. Five trials were given. Control dogs required an average of 29.4 seconds to obtain the food, and experimental dogs, 72.1 seconds—about two and one-half times longer.

Still other tests were administered: a delayed-reaction test and a maze-learning test, but the results were monotonously the same. In each case control dogs performed much better than experimental dogs. Some of the tests were administered a year after removal from restriction; the differences appeared to be more or less permanent. The investigators concluded that early restriction of perceptual experience had a definite and fairly permanent retarding effect on the dogs' intelligence. Numerous other studies show similar results. Gibson and Walk (1956), for example, reared "enriched" and "deprived" rats, differentiated by amount of visual stimulation in the home cages. Cages of enriched rats had metal triangles and circles hanging from the walls, while cages of deprived rats were bare, as is customary for laboratory rats. At ninety days of age both groups were presented with a discrimination problem: choosing one of the two geometric forms to obtain food. Rats from the enriched environment learned the problem much faster than deprived rats. Thus, we may take it as well established that deprived animals behave in a "less intelligent" manner.

Physiological Studies

It is even possible to detect physiological effects of environmental deprivation. It has been known for some time, for example, that sense organs require exercise in order to develop normally. Such evidence has been most clearly shown for the visual system, where keeping animals in darkness results in easily detectable changes in the retina, and in corresponding retardation in the ability to solve visual problems (much of this research is summarized by Riesen, 1961). Likewise, biological discoveries of neurobiotaxis and transneuronal degeneration indicate that neuronal stimulation is necessary for normal growth of the nervous system.

More recent physiological data, however, were quite unexpected; they came in two forms: in terms of chemical changes within the brain itself, and in terms of changes in RNA concentration in nerve cells. Let us summarize what is known in each of these research areas.

Krech, Rosenzweig, and Bennett, at the University of California (Berkeley), have discovered chemical brain modifications associated with degrees of stimulus deprivation (e.g., Bennett, Krech, and Rosenzweig, 1964; Rosenzweig, Bennett, and Krech, 1964; Krech, Rosenzweig, and Bennett, 1960, 1962). Until recently, it was widely assumed that brain size was not correlated with intelligence. Yet the California group discovered that (1) rats raised in enriched environments developed heavier and thicker cortexes, resulting in total greater brain weight, and (2) they learned maze problems faster than control rats. The first discovery came as a complete surprise, most experts having resigned themselves long ago to the assumption that so gross a measure as brain weight could not possibly be related to intelligence. But the relationship has now been replicated a dozen times or so, leaving little doubt as to its reality. Associated with the increased brain weight are chemical changes which are of the nature predicted by neurological information. Hilgard and Bower summarize this information as follows:

Nerve cells may be thought of as telephone transmission lines that connect with one another functionally at junctures known as synapses. Line A connects to line B across a synapse, and the synapse is responsible for transmitting to B any nerve impulse (signal) traveling down line A. It is believed that this transmission is largely a matter of biochemistry. An impulse in line A, releases, literally squirts out at its end, a small amount of a substance called acetylcholine (ACh); this goes across the tiny gap between A and B, and is absorbed by nerve B, causing an electrical impulse to be generated and propagated down B. ACh is called the *transmitter* substance because of its essential role in this process. Following the firing of B, the enzyme cholinesterase (ChE) comes into play at the synapse. This enzyme works by hydrolizing (neutralizing) the ACh released at the synapse during transmission. In this manner, the ACh is cleared away and the synapse is returned to its prior state, making it ready to conduct further signals. The biochemical reactions here are extremely fast requiring but a few milliseconds, and the interplay of the ACh and ChE systems are in a synchronized and delicate balance at a normal synapse. Small changes in the availability or speed of access to one or the other chemical could result in malfunctioning, or at least reduced efficiency in transmission of finely modulated, temporal patterns of neural impulses across the synapse. [1966, pp. 461–462.]

The California group has concentrated on measurements of ChE, since ACh is more difficult to assay. The measurement they have found to be most sensitive is the ratio of total cortical ChE to total subcortical ChE, called the cortical/subcortical (C/S) ratio. They found that descendants of Tyron's maze-bright rats had a lower C/S ratio than the maze-dull rats. Roderick (1960) actually bred for C/S ratios and was able to develop one strain of rats with a high ratio and another strain with a low ratio, with little overlap between the two distributions. Thus biochemical brain differences were shown to be subject to genetic selection, a necessary requirement for a physiological correlate of intelligence. But most surprising of all, lower C/S ratios could also be manipulated by environmental deprivation conditions, and rats with environmentally produced low C/S ratios learned maze problems faster than rats with high C/S ratios. Even individual differences in learning scores—differences between one rat and another—were correlated with individual differences in C/S ratios. And the correlations were about as high as those obtained between learning scores and IQ scores for human subjects. For rats raised in the enriched environment, the correlation was .81, and for rats raised in sensory isolation, .53. These are indeed strong correlations between learning ability and brain chemistry.

The second line of research, concerned with the role of RNA (ribonucleic acid) in learning, has turned up equally surprising discoveries. It will be recalled that DNA (deoxyribonucleic acid) is the gene-carrying material found in chromosomes. RNA is very similar to DNA and is believed to play a "messenger" role, carrying "instructions" from DNA to all parts of the cell, thereby establishing a line of communication between DNA and the cell. There is good reason to believe that RNA changes its concentration and molecular structure as a result of learning experiences. For example, it is found in copious amounts in neural cells and brain cells, suggesting a role in nervous system functioning. Its concentration first increases and then decreases with age, much as do IQ scores. More directly, RNA concentration fed to aged persons has been reported to improve their immediate memory.

Assuming, then, that presence of RNA makes a neural cell able to "store" information from preceding electrical inputs from adjacent cells, it is highly significant to note that repetitive stimulation of a neural cell increases the concentration of RNA, thereby better equipping the cell to profit from subsequent learning experiences. Since stimulation of a neuron is greater (more frequent) in an enriched environment, it would follow that an enriched environment would lead to the development of a nervous system better able to modify itself (e.g., to learn) as a result of experience.

Not only is the amount of RNA increased by stimulation, but the nature of the stimulation affects the nature of RNA *structural* changes as well, providing fairly direct evidence of its role as a memory mechanism. Hydén and Egyházi (1962) trained rats to walk up an inclined rope to obtain food. These rats had to learn not only where to go, but also the balancing habits necessary to remain on the "tight-rope." The vestibular nucleus contains nerve fibers which relay signals to the brain from the semicircular canals, which in turn are receptor organs involved in the maintenance of balance. It was therefore hypothesized that RNA in these cells might have "recorded" the new balancing information, so that the rats could, in fact, learn. RNA in the vestibular nucleus was not only increased as a result of the training, but was different from that of control rats who had also been subjected to stimulation of their semicircular canals, but not by exposure to rope climbing.

Even more dramatic evidence involves the transfer of RNA from a trained organism to an untrained organism. If the transferred RNA can find its way to the proper neurons, one might expect the untrained organism to suddenly become "trained," in the absence of learning experiences. McConnell (1962) was one of the first to carry out experiments of this type. A primitive flatworm, the planaria, was conditioned to contract to a light (conditioned stimulus) as a result of pairing the light with a mild shock (unconditioned stimulus). Then the worms were cut up and served as food to untrained flatworms. The fed flatworms then responded to the light with contraction! Control worms, which were presented with unpaired exposures of the light and shock, and thus had no opportunity to develop a conditioned contraction to the light, were also cut up and fed to a second group of cannibals. This second group did not respond to the light as often as the first group, indicating that the right "diet" was essential: "trained" food had to be eaten, not just any food.

It is not difficult to imagine the public reaction to such results. Newspaper and magazine articles appeared over the country contemplating the horrible implications for human learning: brains of geniuses should perhaps be fed to others, perhaps as "brain pills" or "IQ tablets." Television ads would compete for the market, with pill X being advertised as coming from smarter corpses or as less likely to cause stomach upset.

Scientists, however, were less gullible than the public or the press. They began to repeat the original experiments with minor variations here and there, and the results were disturbing. For every study reporting a positive result, another could be found reporting negative results (e.g., Bennett and Calvin, 1964). The flatworm studies are thus in a state of controversy at the time of this writing, and no definite conclusions are warranted.

Biological transfer effects have also been reported with rats. Jacobson et al. (1965) trained one group of rats to approach a food cup to the sound of a click, and a second group to approach a food cup to a flashing light. After training, RNA was removed from the brains of these rats and injected into naive rats, one group being injected with the "click" RNA and the other group with the "flashing light" RNA. Each of the recipient rats was then given 50 test trials, 25 with the click and 25 with the flashing light. The average number of approach responses for each group is presented in Table 3.1. It shows that subjects injected with "click" RNA responded more to the click than to the light, and subjects injected with "flashing light" RNA responded more to the light than to the click.

TABLE 3.1

Mean Number of Approaches to Click and Light
(Adapted from Jacobson et al., 1965)

	Click	Flashing Light
"Click" RNA recipients	5.75	1.87
"Flashing light" RNA recipients	1.00	3.75

In another, similar study (Jacobson et al., 1966), rats were trained to turn either left or right in a T-maze for food, and after reaching a given criterion of correct responses, RNA was extracted and injected into recipients. The recipients were then given 25 test trials in the maze, with no food reward for either response. The experiment was run "blind": the testers did not know whether the donor of a given rat had been trained to respond to the left or to the right. Twenty-two donors had been trained to turn left, and twenty to turn right. The behavior of the 42 recipients is presented in Table 3.2. It indicates the preference of each recipient for left or right turns during the 25 test trials. There is obviously a decided tendency for recipients of left-trained donors to turn left (15 out of 22), and vice-versa for right-trained donors (14 out of 21).

TABLE 3.2

Number of Subjects with Left- and Right-Turn Preferences
(Adapted from Jacobson et al., 1966)

Test Preference of Recipient	Training of Donor	
	Left	Right
Left	15	7
Right	6	14

But controversy has arisen about the rat results as well as the flatworm results. Gross and Carey (1965) and Luttges et al. (1966) have been unable to find RNA transfer effects in rats. Part of the inconsistency is undoubtedly due to poor methodology, and part is due to hasty conclusions on the part of the pioneer investigators. Thus, in Jacobson's first study, involving approach responses to a click or flashing light, there were only eight rats in each of the two recipient groups—a rather small number of subjects when percentage figures are involved. In his second study, although recipient rats indicated an apparently strong tendency to turn in the same direction as donors, and although more subjects were involved (42), absolute preferences were very small. The mean number of responses in the predicted direction was 13.1. Since 25 test trials were given, an average of 12.5 would be expected by chance alone. The difference of 0.6 is so small as to suggest that nothing at all was demonstrated. Jacobson et al. (1965) did not test the statistical significance of the difference between 12.5 and 13.1. (The author did, and it falls far short of significance [$p > .10$].) Thus, according to current rules of statistical evidence, it would have been concluded, had the test been carried out, that nothing indeed *had* happened.

Putting together the flatworm and rat RNA research, then, we find that the transfer effects have not yet been convincingly demonstrated.

Maybe they never will. It seems incredible that things could be so simple and easy to demonstrate. All that can be said with certainty is that there are neurophysiological correlates of intelligence, that it looks as though some of them are being discovered, and that they seem to be subject to environmental influences. Recognizing the evolutionary continuity from rat to man, one is tempted to speculate that the same will prove to be true of human beings.

Hebb's Phase Sequences

Let us conclude this discussion of animal intelligence with brief mention of a neurophysiological model which helps to suggest just how the environment can have such a pervasive effect. Imagine a person, blind from birth, who suddenly acquires normal vision at adulthood. Assume this person to be of normal intelligence and to enjoy normal health, e.g., to be entirely normal except for his history of blindness. Now suppose he is confronted for the first time in his life with two figures, a square and a triangle. He has handled such forms many times in the past, but now he sees them for the first time. Without letting him touch them, he is told which is which, and then is asked to point, say, to the square. What will happen? We would expect him to immediately point to the correct form, since he has normal vision, he has handled similar objects and heard their names many times in the past, and he has just been told their names. Yet, he will make many errors, and weeks of practice will be required before he can point to one of the objects and say correctly, "This is a square." The task will be immensely difficult, and learning will be very slow. When he does start to make correct responses, they will be based upon a crude kind of comparative process. He will count the corners one by one, and determine which object has three corners and which has four corners. It will be some time before he can tell the difference by a mere glance.

These facts have been documented by appropriate experiments with people who actually did gain their vision for the first time as adults (Hebb, 1949). What do they mean? They mean that simple perceptual processes require experience for normal development. They mean a person *learns* to use his senses in even the most simple kinds of discriminations. Hebb has presented a most provocative theory of how experience contributes to such perceptual learning.

The first time the previously blind adult looks at a triangle, according to Hebb, he tends to fixate on one of the corners. A particular set of brain cells is fired as a result of this stimulation, and as a result of this neural activity, the person "sees an angle." Then he moves his eye along a straight line until another angle is encountered: *B* rather than *A* in Figure 3.3. Now a new set of brain cells is fired, and he "sees" angle *B* instead of angle *A*. Call these two neuronal patterns *A* and *B*, respectively. Assume that they lie proximate to each other, and indeed have common neurons linking them together. Suppose that at first the

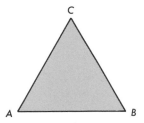

Figure 3.3. In first looking at a triangle, a person fixates one angle, say *A*, and then another, say *B*, and perceives the angles as isolated events.

synaptic resistance between *A* and *B* is fairly strong, so that electrical impulses set in motion in *A* do not fire *B*, but rather take some other terminal pathway, say *X*, until they die out. Figure 3.4 illustrates this situation, with the solid line indicating the initial path.

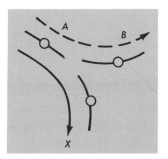

Figure 3.4. A hypothetical group of cells, with the solid arrow indicating the original electrical pathway and the dotted arrow the final pathway, following a number of simultaneous firings.

As the person shifts his gaze rapidly from angle *A* to angle *B*, cell group *B* is fired soon after the firing of cell group *A*. Hebb now makes a long-respected neurological assumption, namely, that *when adjacent groups of neuronal cells are fired simultaneously or in close temporal sequence, the synaptic resistance between them will change to a lower level.* The result is that activating one of the two cell groups will have a greater probability of automatically activating the other cell group. The dotted line in Figure 3.4 indicates this subsequent state of affairs, with impulses from *A* now activating *B*. Subjectively, the person now "sees both *A* and *B*" while looking only at *A*. In Hebb's terminology, cell group *A* has "recruited" cell group *B*, and a "phase sequence" has resulted. With further experience, angles *A*, *B*, and *C* all become integrated into a phase sequence, so that stimulation of any part sets off the entire neural network. At this point, the individual can recognize a triangle at a glance, for a glance is all that is required to start the sequence.

Thus it is that one learns to use his senses. Environmental stimulation is absolutely essential to the building of complex neural phase sequences, so that what was once experienced as unrelated parts comes to be experienced as a whole. Although the example was confined to vision, it is presumed to hold for all the senses.

Hebb's theory is largely conceptual rather than factual, but the important point to recognize in the present context is that it suggests an interesting neuro-physiological mechanism for the behavioral and physiological data this chapter has summarized. Consider the notion of "recruitment"—that repeated firings of adjacent neurons lower the synaptic resistance between them. One basis for this could be the build-up of RNA, which we have seen is increased by environmental stimulation. If so, then injections of RNA should create a nervous system more able to profit from learning experiences. Research has supported this prediction. Rats injected with RNA perform better in learning tasks than control rats injected with a placebo (e.g., Cook *et al.*, 1963; Salzom *et al.*, 1966). RNA may thus have two different roles: it may facilitate the cell's ability to store information, or it may facilitate the cell's access to information by reducing resistance with adjacent cells. As previously noted, cholinesterase (ChE) plays a similar role, preparing the synapse to react to oncoming signals. Hebb's theory has thus been very influential in synthesizing many of the facts we have touched upon so far in this chapter. We shall now consider human studies, where Hebb's theory may be equally applicable.

HUMAN STUDIES

In order to provide some structure for the large number of human studies concerned with environmental determinants of intelligence, the studies are grouped into three types, according to the amount of control over extraneous factors which complicate interpretations of the results.

Considered first are *isolated group studies*. These studies examine the intelligence of groups of people who for one reason or another have endured unusual deprivation from normal environmental events. Usually, no control groups are available for comparative purposes, and hence unambiguous interpretations are difficult. At a more refined level are *self-sorting studies*, where a group of individuals by "chance" forms two subgroups, an "experimental" group and a "control" group. Finally, there are genuine *experimental studies*, where one randomly selected group is deprived of some sort of normal stimulation, and another randomly selected group is not so deprived. These studies are methodologically "clean" in the sense that randomization minimizes the probability that group differences observed at the end of the experiment are due to factors other than the deprivation conditions.

Isolated-Group Studies

A number of isolated-group studies appeared in the 1920's and 1930's. Gordon (1923) measured the intelligence of English canal-boat children. The home environment of most of these children provided little in the way of "intellectual" stimulation; many of the parents were illiterate, contacts with persons outside the family were rare, the children were exposed to very little formal education (attending school only when the boat docked for loading or unloading), etc. The mean Stanford-Binet IQ of the 76 children was 69.9, suggesting borderline mental deficiency. Now, of course, a *selective genetic hypothesis* could account for these results: perhaps only dull people lived on these boats, and their children were dull as a result of inheritance. If this argument is correct, age of the children should make no difference: young and old children alike should average out to the same low IQ, since the same genetic probabilities apply to each child. But Gordon found that IQ scores dropped off with increasing age: the average IQ of four- to six-year olds was 87, while that of the oldest group (twelve to twenty-two years) *within the same families* was 60. The correlation between age and IQ was a startling −.76. The selective genetic interpretation is therefore strongly contradicted. It appears instead that environmental deprivation was cumulative in its effects, taking a greater and greater toll the longer the children were exposed to it.

Another interpretation is that as the children became older, the brighter ones left the boat, leaving only dull older children behind. Such an interpretation would allow the selective genetic interpretation to account for all the facts. Unfortunately, Gordon gives no information on the intactness of the family unit as the children grew up. The situation is therefore ambiguous. *Either* nature or nurture could account for the results.

In another part of the same study, Gordon reports similar results for 82 gypsy children. Again, exposure to normal educational opportunities was extremely limited. The children attended school an average of 35 per cent of the total number of actual school days. Social conditions were also inadequate, involving a limited contact with the outside world and more or less decrepit, unsanitary living conditions. But, as Gordon puts it, conditions could have been still worse:

> I should say that they washed rather more than the average East-end hop-picker or pea-picker would. They are a more cleanly class than those that one sees hop-picking who are East-enders. [P. 47.]

The average IQ of this group of children was 74.5, and again IQ scores decreased with age, the correlation being −.45. That the age decrement is not as great as for canal-boat children can be accounted for in terms of better school attendance for the gypsy children, as well as relatively more social contacts with the outside world. While the decrement with age is again suggestive of cumulative environmental effects upon intelligence, one cannot rule out the possibility that brighter older children tended to leave their gypsy families, leaving only dull children behind.

A number of American studies of isolated mountain children corroborate Gordon's results. For example, Sherman and Key (1932) obtained IQ scores from 183 mountain children, 102 living in isolated hollows in the Blue Ridge Mountains, approximately 100 miles from Washington, D.C., and 81 living in a small village at the foot of the Blue Ridge. It was possible to rank the four hollows and one village in terms of degree of isolation and lack of educational opportunities. Colvin Hollow was the worst off, with hardly any schooling available (an average of about one and one-half months per year), and no roads leading into the hollow from the outside. The families lived in scattered mud-plastered log huts. With three exceptions the adults were illiterate. Many of the younger children did not even know their last names, identifying themselves as "Sadie's Benny" or "Dicy's Willie." The accompanying photograph shows a Colvin Hollow family in their front yard. As one proceeded down the mountains from Colvin Hollow, things gradually improved: roads leading in and out became visible (first just rocky paths, then graded roads), schools were maintained more regularly and for longer periods of time, illiteracy decreased, etc. Finally, at Briarsville, the village at the entrance to the hollows, a veritable metropolis existed in comparison to the hollows: there was a modern school, a general store, telephones, newspapers, etc.

Grouping the IQ scores by hollows, an interesting pattern emerged. As one progressed from Briarsville back into the hollows, IQ scores be-

(Photograph courtesy of Cora B. Key)

A Colvin Hollow family in their front yard.

came lower and lower, reaching the lowest point at Colvin Hollow. Table 3.3 presents the percentage of children at each of the five communities who scored higher than the average for the four hollows combined. As a number of different IQ tests were administered, several comparisons are possible. Table 3.3 presents the results from five different tests. Note that the progression is just as obvious for tests with a high *performance* content (the Goodenough Draw-a-Man test and the two performance tests) as for tests with a high *verbal* content (such as the Stanford-Binet). For all tests the pattern is the same: lower IQ scores as one proceeds from Briarsville to Colvin Hollow.

A second important finding was that the older the children, the lower their IQ scores. Table 3.4 presents the results for the Goodenough Draw-a-Man test, separately for the four hollows combined and for Briarsville. For the hollows, the average IQ of six- to eight-year-olds was 80, as compared to 49 for fourteen- to sixteen-year-olds. In Briarsville, the six- to eight-year-olds were near normal (93), but at older ages a low of 70 was reached.

TABLE 3.3

Percentage of Children Scoring Higher Than the Average of the Four Hollows
(Adapted from Sherman and Key, 1932)

	Briars-ville	Rigby	Oakton	Needles	Colvin
Stanford-Binet	*	75	50	36	16
Pinter-Cunningham	81	78	50	34	34
Goodenough Draw-a-Man	53	71	40	37	0
Year scale performance test	90	53	75	41	30
Med. M. A. performance test	100	54	38	53	20

* Stanford-Binets were not given in the village because of scheduling problems with the school.

TABLE 3.4

Average IQ Scores as a Function of Age
(Adapted from Sherman and Key, 1932)

Chronological Age	Goodenough Draw-a-Man IQ	
	Hollows	Briarsville
6–8	80	93
8–10	66	82
10–12	71	69
12–14	69	73
14–16	49	70

Sherman and Key concluded, "The only plausible explanation . . . is that children develop only as the environment demands development" (p. 289). Unfortunately, the same criticism as that leveled at the Gordon studies is applicable here too: the brighter children may have tended to wind their way down the hollows to the village and beyond as they got older, leaving only duller older children behind. Of course, it is doubtful if much "desertion" occurred during the first 16 years of life, so that this interpretation is rather farfetched. Yet its mere possibility is enough to mitigate the environmental interpretation.

Results from other studies are quite consistent with those of Gordon and Sherman et al., including studies of hollow folk in Kentucky (Asher, 1935; Hirsch, 1928), Georgia (Edwards and Jones, 1938), and Tennessee (Chapanis and Williams, 1945; Wheeler, 1932, 1942). Wheeler's Tennessee results are especially interesting. In 1930 and again in 1940 group intelligence tests were administered to over 3,000 children in 40 rural schools. During the intervening years there was a considerable economic, educational, and social improvement in the area. Paralleling these environmental improvements, IQ scores increased in the years from 1930 to 1940, from a median of 82 to a median of 92. Similar results were reported by a study carried out in Hawaii, involving a 14-year interval during which educational facilities were much improved (Smith, 1942).

Finally, it should be noted that IQ decrements at older ages are not confined to isolated groups. They have been observed in other situations as well, including a number of environments with minimal educational facilities (Jordan, 1933; Lichtenstein and Brown, 1938; Skeels and Fillmore, 1937). They have been observed in rural-urban group differences, where lower IQ scores for rural groups are almost always found. Table 3.5 presents results from the 1942 standardization sample of the Stanford-Binet (McNemar, 1942). Prior to the age of schooling, the average difference between rural and urban children is 5.7 points (ages two to five and a half), but it increases to 12.2 points by ages fifteen to eighteen. Similar results are reported by Baldwin *et al.* (1930).

TABLE 3.5

Mean Stanford-Binet IQ Scores of Urban and Rural Children
(Adapted from McNemar, 1942)

	Age Range in Years		
	2–5½	6–14	15–18
Urban	106.3	105.8	107.9
Rural	100.6	95.4	95.7

It is unlikely that all these negative correlations between age and IQ in deprived environments can be accounted for in terms of selective migration of brighter children at the older age levels. Even if selective migration occurred in all these studies, it is subject to an environmental interpretation. It need only be argued that it was superior environmental conditions which produced higher IQ's in the first place. One is thus forced to choose the more parsimonious interpretation, which would seem to be that a stimulating environment is conducive to greater intelligence.

Self-sorting Studies

Self-sorting studies are those in which "natural" experimental and control groups have been formed by the exigencies of life, upon which the investigator capitalizes. Such studies are always frequent in research areas where ethics or practicalities prevent the investigator from forming the groups himself. The effects of environmental deprivation obviously fit this category.

Nursery-School Experience. One group of such studies has been concerned with the effects of nursery-school experience on intelligence: Anastasi (1958) estimates that over 50 such investigations have been reported. Interest in this topic reached a peak as a result of a series of studies reported from the State University of Iowa in the 1930's and 1940's (e.g., Wellman, 1932). In one of these publications, Wellman analyzed the IQ scores of 652 children who had attended university nursery schools or kindergarten. The children were tested at the beginning and the end of each year they attended the school. An average gain of 6.6 IQ points was found as a result of the first year's attendance, and further but smaller gains were found for the second and third years. In order to determine if these gains were, in fact, due to the schools, a control group of non-school children was required. Wellman matched 34 nursery-school children with 34 non-school children on both chronological age and initial IQ scores. A year later the nursery-school children had gained an average of 7.0 points, while the control children had lost 3.9 points. The difference of almost 11 points was statistically significant, and in view of the fact that there was no initial difference, it was attributed to the nursery-school experience.

Protest arose over this interpretation, resulting in an exchange of charges and countercharges in the published literature (e.g., Goodenough, 1940; McNemar, 1940; Wellman et al., 1940). In the first place, Wellman could find no significant correlation between amount of IQ gain and actual number of days in school. Those children attending as few as 37 days gained about the same amount as those attending 148 days—surely an unexpected result if school exposure was the crucial factor. Then again, the nursery-school children sometimes were tested more frequently than control children. Since it is well known that *test sophistication* and *practice effects* result in IQ gains, the differences could be explained on this basis. And again, it is probably the case that nursery-school children are more used to interacting with adults (in the Iowa University Nursery School, there is one adult for every four or five children) and thus feel more "at home" with them. Thus, they may be better adjusted to the test situation, thereby performing more efficiently. Unless it can be assumed that different individuals are equally motivated, adjusted, and healthy, IQ *score* differences do not necessarily reflect *intellectual* differences.

There were more serious criticisms. Consider how the two matched groups of 34 children were formed. They were "natural" groups and were not assigned randomly from the same population of children. Those who attended nursery school probably differed from the non-attenders in a number of respects. Since the two groups were matched on CA and IQ, these two factors can presumably be ruled out. But a number of other possibilities exist: it would be reasonable to assume that the parents of nursery-school attenders were *more interested in their children,* perhaps more concerned with their intellectual achievements. There is evidence that such parents actually do have children who manifest greater IQ gains than children with parents less interested in their achievements (Kagan and Moss, 1959). If this concern became manifest at about the same time the children started nursery school, the IQ gains could be explained with no reference at all to nursery school per se. Finally, there is the argument that although the two groups did not initially differ in IQ *scores,* they probably did differ in *intelligence.* This argument is based on the fact that nursery-school children usually are brighter than the average non-school child, even before the beginning of school attendance. Thus, in finding non-school children with the *same* high IQ (*scores*), one would be likely to locate a number of children who scored too high on the intelligence test and, if the test were to be given again, would score lower. In other words, these children, because of the unreliability of the test, scored higher than they deserved. On the second test, given at the end of the year, they would be likely to score lower, thus producing a net gain for the school attenders. This phenomenon is known as *regression to the mean,* and the reader is referred to Anastasi (1958) for a fuller discussion.

Finally, other university nursery schools have not always been able to replicate the Iowa results (Anderson, 1940; Bird, 1940; Goodenough and Maurer, 1940; Jones and Jorgensen, 1940). Thus, the empirical facts themselves are open to question, ignoring the methodological shortcomings. On the other hand, there are nursery schools and there are nursery schools, and nobody assumes they are all equally stimulating. To find IQ gains in *all* nursery schools would certainly be unexpected.

McCandless (1961) summarizes a number of defenses of the Iowa results: the gains are not transitory, but persist over long periods of time; academic performance is related to the "new" scores rather than to the "old" scores, suggesting that more than mere *score* changes were involved; gains are not observed over the summer months when school is not in session, and therefore practice effects are obviously not important, as they would lead to gains from spring to fall as well as from fall to spring; control subjects had the same number of tests as experimental subjects in some of the studies, etc. Thus, one cannot perfunctorily dismiss the Iowa results as without value—they are most intriguing. On the other hand, they must be interpreted with a good deal of caution. There are a number of plausible interpretations, environmental stimulation being only one.

Adult Self-sorting Studies.   There are some similar results with adults. IQ tests administered to U.S. service personnel during World Wars I and II showed high correlations with amount of schooling: .73 and .74 (United States Army, 1945; Yerkes, 1921). These findings do little to clarify the picture, however, since they could be due to either environmental effects upon intelligence or to selective education, the brighter men tending to seek more education than the duller men.

There are some long-term longitudinal studies which come under the category of self-sorting studies. We may view the nursery-school studies as *short-term* longitudinal studies—only a year or two is involved from pretest to posttest. Perhaps with longer time intervals, stronger environmental effects would show up. Husén (1951) obtained IQ scores from 722 Swedish boys when they were in the third grade and again when they were examined for military service, approximately ten years later. He divided them into five groups on the basis of amount of education they had received beyond the third grade. The group with least education lost an average of 1.2 IQ points, and the other groups gained 2.1, 3.0, 3.2, and 11.0 points as amount of education increased. Owens (1953) conducted a similar study in the United States with similar results. Unlike the U.S. Army studies described in the preceding paragraph, these results cannot be explained in terms of selective education, since we are talking here about *gains*, not just one-shot scores. But a criticism made in regard to the nursery-school studies is equally appropriate here, as it is to *all* self-sorting studies: there were reasons in the Husén and Owens studies that some individuals exposed themselves to considerable education and others to very little. Whatever the nature of these unknown causes, they might have influenced the second IQ score as well as the decision to obtain more education. It is clearly impossible to measure all such possible factors, and thus uncontrolled effects are always possible in the self-sorting study.

The Skeels Study.   Back in the 1930's, Skeels carried out a short-term study on the effects of an enriched environment on the development of orphanage children. The reason for the experiment can best be described in Skeels's own words:

Early in the service aspects of the program, two baby girls, neglected by their feebleminded mothers, ignored by their inadequate relatives, malnourished and frail, were legally committed to the orphanage. The youngsters were pitiful little creatures. They were tearful, had runny noses, and sparse, stringy, and colorless hair; they were emaciated, undersized, and lacked muscle tonus or responsiveness. Sad and inactive, the two spent their days rocking and whining.

The psychological examinations showed developmental levels of 6 and 7 months, respectively, for the two girls, although they were then 13 and 16 months old chronologically. This serious delay in mental growth was confirmed by observations of their behavior in the nursery and by reports of the superintendent of nurses, as well as by the pediatrician's examination. There was no evidence of physiological or organic defect, or of birth injury or glandular dysfunction.

The two children were considered unplaceable, and transfer to a school for the mentally retarded was recommended with a high degree of confidence. Accordingly, they were transferred to an institution for the mentally retarded at the next available vacancy, when they were aged 15 and 18 months, respectively.

In the meantime, the author's professional responsibilities had been increased to include itinerant psychological services to the two state institutions for the mentally retarded. Six months after the transfer of the two children, he was visiting the wards at an institution for the mentally retarded and noticed two outstanding little girls. They were alert, smiling, running about, responding to the playful attention of adults, and generally behaving and looking like any other toddlers. He scarcely recognized them as the two little girls with the hopeless prognosis, and thereupon tested them again. Although the results indicated that the two were approaching normal mental development for age, the author was skeptical of the validity or permanence of the improvement and no change was instituted in the lives of the children. Twelve months later they were re-examined, and then again when they were 40 and 43 months old. Each examination gave unmistakable evidence of mental development well within the normal range for age.

There was no question that the initial evaluations gave a true picture of the children's functioning level at the time they were tested. It appeared equally evident that later appraisals showed normal mental growth accompanied by parallel changes in social growth, emotional maturity, communication skills, and general behavior. In order to find a possible explanation for the changes that had occurred, the nature of the children's life space was reviewed.

The two girls had been placed on one of the wards of older, brighter girls and women, ranging in age from 18 to 50 years and in mental age from 5 to 9 years, where they were the only children of preschool age, except for a few hopeless bed patients with gross physical defects. An older girl on the ward had "adopted" each of the two girls, and other older girls served as adoring aunts. Attendants and nurses also showed affection to the two, spending time with them, taking them along on their days off for automobile rides and shopping excursions, and purchasing toys, picture books, and play materials for them in great abundance. The setting seemed to be a homelike one, abundant in affection, rich in wholesome and interesting experiences, and geared to a preschool level of development. [Skeels, 1966, pp. 5–6.] *

On the basis of this serendipitous observation, Skeels secured the cooperation of the orphanage in a study which was indeed radical at the time. It was decided that children who were so retarded that adoption was out of the question should be removed from the orphanage and placed in the institution for the mentally retarded, each assigned to a ward and cared for by the inmates of that ward. Accordingly, 13 chil-

* Copyright © 1966 by The Society for Research in Child Development.

dren, all less than three years of age, were eventually transferred to the mental retardation institution as "house guests." Their average IQ was 64, with a range from 35 to 89. In the institution they were treated much as the two little girls previously described. The attendants became very fond of "their children," playing, talking to and training them, bringing them gifts, taking them on excursions around the grounds, etc. In almost every case, one attendant developed an especially close, one-to-one relationship with the child, which was supplemented by interactions with the other inmates of the ward. Thus the total environment for these 13 young children could be described as stimulating, relatively rich, and emotionally warm.

A control group was formed by going back through the records after the study was over. Twelve children were selected who were about the same age as the experimental children, who had IQ scores available, and who had remained in the relatively unstimulating environment of the orphanage during the time the experimental children were "guests" at the institution. The orphanage environment is described by Skeels as follows:

The orphanage in which the children were placed occupied, with a few exceptions, buildings that had first served as a hospital and barracks during the Civil War. The institution was overcrowded and understaffed. By present standards, diet, sanitation, general care, and basic philosophy of operation was censurable. At the time of the study, however, the discrepancies between conditions in the institution and in the general community were not so great and were not always to the disadvantage of the institution. Over the past 30 years, administrative and physical changes have occurred that reflect the economic and social gains of our society. The description of conditions in the institution in the 1930's, therefore, does not apply to the present.

and

Overcrowding of living facilities was characteristic. Too many children had to be accommodated in the available space and there were too few adults to guide them. . . . Thirty to thirty-five children of the same sex under six years of age live in a "cottage" in charge of one matron and three or four entirely untrained and often reluctant girls of thirteen to fifteen years of age. The waking and sleeping hours of these children were spent (except during meal times and a little time on a grass plot) in an average-size room (approximately fifteen feet square), a sunporch of similar size, a cloakroom, . . . and a single dormitory. The latter was occupied only during sleeping hours. The meals for all children in the orphanage were served in a central building in a single large dining room.

The duties falling to the lot of the matron were not only those involved in the care of the children but those related to clothing and cottage maintenance, in other words, cleaning, mending, and so forth. . . . With so much responsibility centered in one adult the result was a necessary regimentation. The children sat down, stood up, and did many things in rows and in unison. They spent considerable time sitting on chairs, for in addition to the number

of children and the matron's limited time there was the misfortune of inadequate equipment. . . .
No child had any property which belonged exclusively to him except, perhaps, his tooth brush. Even his clothing, including shoes, was selected and put on him according to size. [Pp. 3 and 4.]

The average IQ of the control children was 87 at the time the experimental children were moved from the orphanage to the mental retardation institution. Thus the controls started the study with a 23-point advantage in intelligence.

At the end of approximately a year and a half, follow-up IQ tests were administered to all children, and again approximately two years later. Thus three IQ scores are available for each child: the initial score, obtained at the start of the study; a second obtained at the end of the special treatment period (one and one-half years later); and a third two years after the second one. When the study started, the experimental children averaged 64, but at the end they averaged 92, an amazing 28-point gain. The controls changed from 87 to 61, manifesting a *drop* of 26 points. Thus the initial 23-point advantage of the control children was not only completely lost, but the relative standing was reversed, with the experimental children now 31 points ahead. Two years later, when the third test was given, the experimental children, 11 of whom had been adopted by then (remember that they were originally picked because of their "unsuitability" for adoption), maintained their gains, averaging 96, as compared to 66 for the control children.

In 1966, Skeels reported a final follow-up study on these two groups, who were then adults. By diligent effort, every single person was located, except one control child who died at the age of 15. Because of the dangers of awakening curiosity about their pasts, IQ tests were not administered. Instead, an attempt was made to get an all-round picture of the life adjustment of each member in each group.

The differences were striking. All 13 of the experimental group were self-supporting, and none was a ward of any institution, public or private. The occupations were: one staff sergeant, one real estate salesman, and one vocational counselor (males); six housewives, a nursing instructor (registered nurse), waitress, gift-shop saleslady, and domestic servant (females). In the control group, on the other hand, five of the eleven were still institutionalized. Of the remaining six, three were dishwashers in nursing homes and small restaurants, a fourth lived with her mother and worked in a cafeteria where she folded napkins around silverware (on paydays, her mother picked up her check and deposited it in the bank for her), a fifth was an unskilled transient laborer who had traveled from coast to coast supporting himself with such jobs as chicken plucking, dishwashing, etc., and the sixth is the surprise in the group: he became a compositor and typesetter in a city of 300,000, was married and had four normal children, and made more money than the other ten control persons combined. The income for the experimental group averaged $4,800, which was actually a little higher than the average for all employed males in the area at that time (1959). The controls averaged $1,200.

Educational differences were also extreme. Eight of the thirteen experimental children had completed high school, and five of these went on to college, one obtaining a B.A. and another graduating from a business college. The average amount of education was equivalent to the second semester of the 11th grade. In the control group, only one child had progressed beyond the eighth grade, this man continuing until he finished one semester of college (the compositor-typesetter). The average amount of education for all 11 control subjects was equivalent to the fourth grade.

Eleven of the 13 experimental subjects had married, and only one was subsequently divorced. As far as could be determined by interviews, the remaining 10 marriages seemed stable and normal. The 11 marriages produced 28 children, with IQ scores ranging from 86 to 125, with a mean of 104. *In no case was there any evidence of mental retardation.* In the control group, only two had married. One marriage, which subsequently terminated in divorce, produced one child with clear mental retardation, the IQ estimated at 66, and with signs of possible brain damage. The other marriage involved the compositor-typesetter whose four children ranged in intelligence from 103 to 119.

Thus, in every conceivable way the experimental subjects, who started the study with a 23-point disadvantage in intelligence, out-performed the control subjects. The monetary savings to the state were large: Skeels estimated that custodial care for the control group had cost the state five times the cost of the experimental group, and for at least four control subjects the state would continue to pay $200 a month each for another 20 to 40 years. Skeels concluded:

At the beginning of the study, the 11 children in the experimental group evidenced marked mental retardation. The developmental trend was reversed through planned intervention during the experimental period. The program of nurturance and cognitive stimulation was followed by placement in adoptive homes that provided love and affection and normal life experiences. The normal, average intellectual level attained by the subjects in early or middle childhood was maintained into adulthood.

It can be postulated that if the children in the contrast (control) group had been placed in suitable adoptive homes or given some other appropriate equivalent in early infancy, most or all of them would have achieved within the normal range of development, as did the experimental subjects.

It seems obvious that under present-day conditions there are still countless

infants born with sound biological constitutions and potentialities for development well within the normal range who will become mentally retarded and
noncontributing members of society unless appropriate intervention occurs.
It is suggested by the findings of this study and others published in the past
20 years that sufficient knowledge is available to design programs of intervention to counteract the devastating effects of poverty, sociocultural deprivation, and maternal deprivation. [P. 56.]

It is difficult to quarrel with Skeels's conclusions. Although it is possible that initial, unknown differences between the two groups existed,
such differences would have more likely favored the control group instead of the experimental group, since the control group started the
study with a distinct intellectual advantage. The results document what
most students of mental deficiency have felt for some time: with borderline retardates having no demonstrable brain damage, improvements in
the environment are often associated with dramatic rises in IQ. The
contrary has also been argued for some time: confinement of such individuals to institutions results in progressive deterioration the longer the
confinement.

Experimental Studies

Considered next is a small group of true experimental studies, similar to the Skeels study except that the experimenter decided who would
be in the experimental and control groups.

Taken in chronological order, the first experiment was reported by
Wellman and Pegram (1944). Within the environs of an orphanage,
Wellman established a preschool for experimental subjects, while control
subjects, matched for IQ, age, sex, nutritional status, and length of orphanage residence, were not allowed to enroll. All of the children were
below average in intelligence, and the orphanage provided little in the
way of stimulation. Experimental subjects who attended the preschool
at least 50 per cent of the time over a three-year period showed a mean
gain of 6.8 IQ points, significantly more than control subjects, who
showed practically no change at all.

Kirk (1958) reported a similar study with mentally retarded children
between the ages of three and six. In one institution the children were
enrolled in a preschool if their IQ score was between 40 and 80. In
another institution in the same state, children within the same age and
IQ ranges served as controls, with no preschool experience. There were
15 children in the experimental group and 12 in the control group. They
were administered the Stanford-Binet at three different times—before enrollment of experimental subjects, directly afterwards (two years later),
and a year later. The mean scores for the experimental group were 61,
73, and 71, and the control group, 57, 50, and 51. Thus, the experimen-

tal group showed a 10-point gain, while the control group showed a 6-point loss. All but one of the 15 experimental subjects gained in IQ scores, whereas only two of the 12 control subjects gained. Additionally, six of the experimental subjects were eventually released from the institution, while none of the control children was released.

Finally, there is a study by Gray, which is still ongoing (Gray and Klaus, 1965). Beginning in the 1960's large sums of federal money were made available for research on mental retardation, cultural deprivation, and accelerated schooling. A series of research programs was initiated which just now is beginning to bear fruit. Gray's project is one of these. The subjects are described as follows:

The Ss (subjects) are 60 children in a city of 25,000 in the upper South, plus an additional group of 27 children in a nearby town who serve as a distal control group. These children were selected on the basis of father's or mother's occupation, education, housing conditions, and income. Parent's incomes at the beginning of the study were well below the present $3,000 cutting point for poverty; their occupations are unskilled or semiskilled, with some additional mothers on aid to dependent children; their educational level is eighth grade or below; their housing conditions are poor. Most of them have television sets, but no books or magazines, and little in the way of toys for the children. The median number of children is five; in nearly half of the homes there is no father present. The children were all born in 1958 and entered school in September, 1964. These children are Negro. At the time we began our study the schools of the city were segregated. Because of this it seemed wise to work with either Negro or white children. We had reason to believe that in the particular setting our chances of success were greater with the Negro children and therefore chose them. [P. 888.] *

The 60 children were randomly divided into two experimental groups and one control group, with the experimental groups exposed to summer preschool training. An interesting control problem soon arose: some of the parents of control children knew some of the parents of experimental children. After discovering that the experimental children were attending school, these control mothers thought they were "missing something," and began to *personally* enrich their children's home life. In order to measure these possible "diffusion effects," a second control group was formed from families in another nearby town, who did not know the experimental families. This second control group constitutes the distal control group.

The general philosophy and typical activities in the preschool are suggested by the following excerpts:

The general programs and the actual day-by-day activities provided for children in the project centered around two classes of variables. The first of these was that of attitudes toward achievement. We were particularly concerned

* Copyright © 1965 by The Society for Research in Child Development.

with achievement motivation, especially as it related to the kinds of activities expected in school, with persistence, with ability to delay gratification, and with general interest in the use of typical school materials such as books, crayons, puzzles, and the like. These approaches grew out of research such as that of Rosen and Andrade (1950) and of Strodtbeck (1959) on achievement motivation, and of Mischel (1961) on delay of gratification. We attempted to translate these variables into certain operational procedures for the teachers and assistants who worked directly with the children. We were also interested in the parent's attitude toward achievement, particularly as it related to aspirations for their children and concern with the children's schooling in relation to these aspirations. Our work with parents has been carried on largely through a home visitor program in which a specially trained preschool teacher has met weekly with each mother and attempted to develop in her more awareness of the instrumental acts involved in her child's attaining these aspirations.

Each of the two experimental groups had a specially trained head teacher and four teaching assistants who worked with groups of four to six children. The teaching staff was about equally divided as to sex and as to racial composition. The teaching assistants were either college students or trainees in a doctoral-school psychology program. The low ratio of children to adults had several major purposes. One was to change the motivational patterns of the children. With only four to six children to each adult, it was possible to reinforce children immediately for any desired behavior. It was also possible to individualize types of reinforcement and scheduling to fit a given child's level in the program. The adults also served as identification figures for the children, important particularly for the boys, who in general lacked appropriate achieving-role models in the home. The low ratio also made possible a large amount of verbal interaction between adult and child.

  ·   ·   ·   ·   ·   ·   ·   ·   ·   ·

Books were of course our mainstay. We attempted to build up as wide a collection as possible of attractive picture books on subjects that would be appropriate to these children from the standpoint of their home experiences and their interests. We made considerable use of duplicate copies of certain books, so that children could learn to follow by pictures as a story was read to them. Looking at pictures promoted ability to discriminate forms and colors. Obviously books were of prime importance in terms of language development. It seemed to us in the first summer that the children with whom we were working could not pick up the meaning of a picture as adequately as middle-class children, probably more familiar with deriving meaning from two-dimensional surfaces. We read to the children several times each day; we encouraged the children to look at pictures as we read, to talk about what they were reading, to tell what would happen next in the story, and, as time went on, to dramatize some of the familiar folk tales such as *Cinderella* or *Three Little Pigs*. Children were given small, inexpensive books as rewards for performance; the home visitor ran a small circulating library during the year.

One experimental group was exposed to three summer preschool sessions prior to entrance into the first grade. The second experimental group, begun a year later, was exposed to two summer preschool sessions. In addition, the continuity of the summer preschool was preserved by weekly visits during the year to each home. With entrance into the first grade, all experimental treatment stopped, and experimental subjects were treated the same as control subjects: no summer preschools and no weekly visits.

Intelligence tests were administered to all four groups at periodic intervals. Figure 3.5 presents the mean scores for seven administrations. The numbers interrupting the curves for the experimental groups indicate when the summer preschool sessions intervened. Note that the last two IQ tests were administered following the end of the experiment and coincident with entrance into the public schools.

Two interesting trends are shown in Figure 3.5. First, the special treatment of the experimental subjects had beneficial effects on intellectual development. By August, 1964, following the last summer preschool session, experimental groups showed an average gain of about

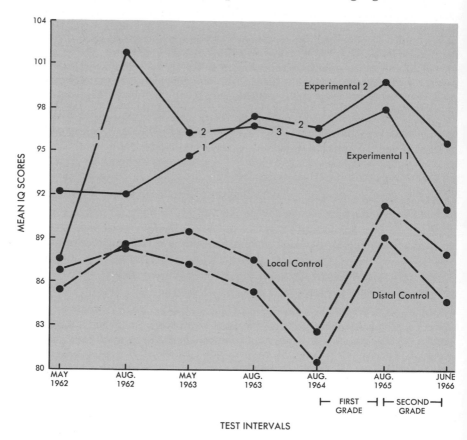

Figure 3.5. IQ scores for experimental and control groups (Gray, personal communication).

7 points, while control groups showed an average loss of about 4 points, yielding a relative gain of 11 points for the experimental groups.

Second, termination of the treatment and entrance of all groups into the public schools led to a closing of the gap. The investigators interpret this as suggesting that the homes and schools must follow up the special treatment provided by the experimental program if the gains are to be maintained into the school years. They write:

. . . it is folly to hope that such a program can continue to offset inadequate schools in later years. Our findings . . . make us hopeful that intervention programs can have long lasting effects that go beyond the immediate children with whom one may be working. Such programs, however, cannot be expected to carry the whole burden of providing adequate schooling for children from deprived circumstances; they can only provide a basis for future progress in schools and homes that can build upon this early intervention. [Gray and Klaus, 1966.]

A final experimental study, carried out at a younger age level, is reported by Irwin (1967). He persuaded 55 mothers of one-year-olds to read aloud to them for at least 10 minutes a day. Of course, a one-year-old cannot read at all and understands precious little of what is read to him. Nevertheless, by the time these children were twenty months old, their speech development was measurably ahead of that of a control group, who had not been read to by their mothers. The experimental mothers were as surprised as the experimenter: "You asked us to read 10 minutes a day, but I can't get away from that kid. He wants me to read to him all the time" (McCandless, 1961, p. 260). In view of the positive correlations between speech development and intelligence, the implications of this study are obvious.

The experimental studies just reviewed consistently show IQ gains for retardates and underprivileged children as a result of enriched environments. They are in contradiction to the university nursery-school studies, which, ignoring the poorer methodology, showed inconsistent effects. What is the reason for the contradictory outcomes from these two groups of studies? The answer probably lies in two factors: the initial IQ's of the children, and the relative amounts of stimulation received at home. The nursery-school studies, conducted as they were in college towns, enrolled children with higher than average IQ's. Indeed, many of the children came from the homes of professors. With high IQ's to begin with, there was simply less room for improvement than for children with lower IQ's, such as retardates and underprivileged children. In addition, the nursery-school children were probably already receiving considerable intellectual stimulation at home, and thus the nursery school did not offer much improvement. Both in terms of IQ and stimulation, then, there was not as much room for improvement in the one group of studies as in the other. Therefore, there is probably no *funda-mental* disagreement between them: in retrospect, one would not predict much improvement for the nursery-school children.

Miscellaneous Studies

Finally, we may consider some studies which are difficult to fit into the classification system of this chapter. Intelligence is related to socioeconomic class, with about a 20-point spread between children raised in the highest and lowest S-E levels and a resulting correlation of IQ with socioeconomic level of about .40. The relationship is not due entirely to biased tests which penalize the lower socioeconomic child, since "culture-fair" tests have not been able to erase the difference (e.g., Haggard, 1954; Lesser *et al.*, 1965; see Anastasi, 1960, for a review of these studies). Two explanations of the IQ–socioeconomic status relationship are the following: (1) a genetic interpretation, to the effect that parents in the upper socioeconomic levels endow their children with greater intelligence, and (2) an environmental interpretation, to the effect that the environmental characteristics of an upper-class home are conducive to the development of a higher level of intelligence. Consider the second interpretation in more detail. One item supporting it comes from studies of adopted children, who are usually adopted by parents from a higher socioeconomic level than the true parents. According to the environmental interpretation, the IQ scores of these adopted children should eventually become higher than the scores of their true parents, because of the enriched environment provided by their higher-status foster parents. According to the genetic interpretation, their IQ scores should not rise above the average of their true parents, since the foster environment should have no effect on intelligence. What are the facts?

A number of studies have shown that the elevation predicted by the environmental interpretation actually occurs (e.g., Skodak and Skeels, 1949; Skeels and Harms, 1948). In fact, the IQ scores of adopted children in these studies exceed those of their true parents by an average of 20 to 30 points. At the same time, however, a correlation with the IQ scores of the true parents remains. How can both facts be true simultaneously? The answer is simply that the rank order of the children's scores remains the same, whether they are adopted or not. All that adoption does is to raise all the scores by the same amount, leaving the order unchanged. Thus while the brightest adopted child is 20 points brighter than his true parent, and the dullest adopted child is also 20 points brighter than his parent, brighter true parents still have brighter children than duller true parents. Figure 3.6 illustrates the point graphi-

CHILDREN'S IQ
IF RAISED BY
TRUE PARENTS

TRUE PARENTS'
IQ

CHILDREN'S IQ
IF RAISED BY
FOSTER-PARENTS

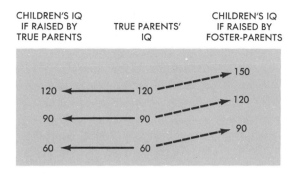

Figure 3.6. The relationship between children's IQ scores and that of their true parents, depending upon whether they are adopted or not.

cally. When the adopted-child studies are thus looked at in their entirety, it appears that there is evidence for both genetic and environmental positions. In the previous chapter, these studies were scrutinized only in terms of their support for the genetic point of view, it being argued that adoption does not remove the correlation with the intelligence of the true parents. There is a moral here: look at *all* the data before jumping to conclusions.

A second item supporting the environmetal interpretation of socioeconomic differences in intelligence comes from a study by Wolf (1963). He asked, what *is* it about a high socioeconomic environment that produces a high IQ? He hypothesized 13 characteristics which might be important. These are listed in Table 3.6.

Using these 13 characteristics as a guide, Wolf devised 60 interview questions to serve as probes in order to obtain the desired information from parents. He then interviewed 60 mothers of fifth-grade children, scoring the interviews in terms of how closely the home environment approximated the hypothesized 13 characteristics. The correlation between these interview scores and the children's IQ scores was a surprising .76, suggesting a strong relationship between the home environment and children's IQ scores. Wolf reports a number of other studies which report correlations of a similar magnitude, indicating that the relationship is a reliable one (Wolf, 1964). It thus appears that at least one determinant of the socioeconomic class–IQ relationship is the home environment associated with different socioeconomic levels. It would have been even more interesting if Wolf had ruled out the effects of heredity by computing a *partial* correlation between the interview scores and children's IQ scores, holding parental IQ constant. One would then have a purer index of the environmental contribution to the socioeco-

TABLE 3.6

Wolf's Hypothesized 13 Characteristics of High Socioeconomic Families
That Produce High-IQ Children
(Adapted from Bloom, 1964)

A. Press for Achievement Motivation
   1. Nature of intellectual expectations of child
   2. Nature of intellectual aspirations for child
   3. Amount of information about child's intellectual development
   4. Nature of rewards for intellectual development
B. Press for Language Development
   5. Emphasis on use of language in a variety of situations
   6. Opportunities provided for enlarging vocabulary
   7. Emphasis on correctness of usage
   8. Quality of language models available
C. Provisions for General Learning
   9. Opportunities provided for learning in the home
   10. Opportunities provided for learning outside the home (excluding school)
   11. Availability of learning supplies
   12. Availability of books (including reference works), periodicals, and library facilities
   13. Nature and amount of assistance provided to facilitate learning in a variety of situations

nomic class–IQ relationship. But in any case, it is clear that the correlation of .76 is considerably higher than .40, the usual socioeconomic class–IQ correlation, indicating the importance of environmental factors.

Bloom (1964) reports an interesting correlation. It is well known that the longer the time interval between the administration of two IQ tests to the same individuals, the lower the correlation between the two sets of scores. Further, the discrepancies between first and last scores are not always random, but often reveal a systematic trend for a given individual, either steadily increasing or steadily decreasing. If these changes are due to the impact of environmental events during the intervening time period, knowledge of these events should allow one to compute an even higher correlation between test-retest IQ scores. Bloom tested this notion. He noted that in one developmental study of intelligence, the Harvard Growth Study (Anderson, 1939), the correlation between IQ scores obtained at ages 7.4 and 16.4 was .58. He recalculated this correlation, taking into account the educational level of the parents, his reasoning being that educational level would serve as a crude index of how the children were treated between the two tests. The resulting multiple correlation was .92, indicating the importance of the intervening environmental events. Bloom was led to the conclusion that the correlation between any two sets of IQ scores, regardless of the time interval separating them, would be close to 1.00 if intervening environmental conditions were taken into account.

The Fels longitudinal study presents some more relevant data. One of the five main personality constellations measured in the Fels study was "achievement and recognition behavior," reflecting intensity of involvement in intellectual mastery strivings. Such behavior was highly correlated with the children's intelligence (correlations in the .60's for both boys and girls). Thus, it is likely that parental practices which affect intellectual achievement strivings also affected intelligence. The most important such practice was "acceleration"—the extent to which the mother was concerned with and reinforced achievement of all kinds, from age of walking to school grades. Such behavior correlated .57 with achievement strivings in boys at ages six to ten, and .49 in girls. Interestingly enough, such parental "pushing" was ineffective and even detrimental if carried out within a hostile context. "Maternal hostility" was *negatively* correlated with achievement strivings.

In a further analysis of these data, Kagan and Moss (1959) found that maternal acceleration was correlated with IQ *gains*. They found that maternal acceleration in the first three years of life correlated .37 with IQ gains in girls at ages six to ten. For boys, however, the correlation was essentially zero. The investigators speculated that the weaker identification between boys and mothers might account for this result. It is too bad paternal acceleration was not also measured.

In another, related study, Kagan investigated possible personality correlates of IQ changes (Kagan et al., 1958). Seventy boys and seventy girls with the necessary information were selected. They were divided into the 25 per cent with the greatest gains in IQ (from age six to ten) and the 25 per cent with the greatest losses. The average gain for the former group was 17 points, while the latter group averaged a 5-point loss. The two groups had comparable IQ scores to begin with, 116 and 119 respectively. Both groups were administered selected Rorschach and TAT pictures and asked to tell a story about each one. These stories were scored for signs of achievement concern, the scorer not knowing to which group they belonged. Nineteen per cent of the "gainers" told achievement-related stories to at least two pictures, while no "loser" did so. To the single picture eliciting most such stories, 41 per cent of the gainers told an achievement-related story, as compared to 19 per cent of the losers. There was thus a measurable tendency of IQ gainers to be oriented toward achievement and mastery, as compared to IQ losers.

SUMMARY

In this chapter a large group of studies concerned with possible environmental effects upon intelligence has been summarized. Beginning with animal studies, both behavioral and physiological evidence is quite clear: an extremely deprived environment, defined in terms of monotonous regularity of stimuli and a corresponding lack of things to *experience* and *do*, leads to a retarded problem-solving ability as well as to abnormal chemical accumulations in the brain. At the human level, results seem to be equally clear. Whether the effects of a relatively unstimulating and undemanding environment are measured in terms of isolated groups such as English canal and gypsy children or U.S. hollow folk, or in terms of self-sorting groups such as those involved in amount of schooling, or in terms of actual experiments purposely designed to "enrich" one group relative to another, the results are the same: children exposed to a more stimulating, challenging environment perform at a higher intellectual level.

The overwhelming evidence for an environmental effect on intelligence must come as something of a surprise after reading the previous chapter. Overwhelming evidence was presented there for *genetic* effects. It was concluded that Galton's statement of a century ago was not far off the mark: "Nature prevails enormously over nurture when the differences of nurture do not exceed what is commonly found among persons of the same rank of society and in the same county." *There is really no contradiction other than an apparent one between the two chapters.* Galton's conclusion, if read carefully, states that environmental conditions must be fairly extreme before intelligence is strongly affected. The present chapter does not contradict that statement. Most of the studies in this chapter did involve extreme environmental conditions. Look again at the photograph on page 91, showing a U.S. hollow family. There is nothing "minor" about the differences between that environment and the environment of an urban city dweller with a white-collar job. Nor are many functional retardates and culturally disadvantaged individuals much better off. The environments in which these people live are often pathetic when compared to the "American dream." McCandless (1961) gives a list of some of these conditions: (1) stark poverty, (2) abandonment by parents, (3) social humiliation, rejection, and defeat, (4) parental drunkenness, feeblemindedness, and psychosis, (5) failure at school and rejection by peers, increasing with age, (6) malnutrition, (7) cultural barrenness of the home, (8) parental indifference, (9) poor health. These are the conditions which are encountered with increasing frequency as one visits the dregs of the socioeconomic ladder, the minority-group ghettos, and the isolated coal miners in the hollows.

Studies which have not sampled such extreme conditions are the very ones which do not find consistent or strong environmental effects upon intelligence. The university nursery-school studies, involving children who were far from deprived to begin with, did not find consistent or large differences between school attenders and non-attenders. In Galton's words, the control children were "from the same rank" as the experimental children, and hence little difference was to be expected.

Just how an "enriched environment" increases intelligence is a difficult question to answer. This chapter mentioned Hebb's theory as an example of what such a theory might be like. While Hebb's notions seem applicable to the results of the animal studies, the author doubts if they have much relevance to the human studies. There are three reasons for this reservation. First, the animal studies involved degrees of environmental deprivation far in excess of those encountered in the human studies. It may be that the neurological retardation assumed in the animal studies would not occur in an environment more comparable to, say, that of an institutionalized mental retardate. While the retardate may satisfy Galton's meaning of a "different rank," he is not locked up in a box with absolutely no objects to look at or handle, or nobody to communicate or interact with, or no opportunity to observe the behavior of others. On the contrary, he is in a ward with a number of other people with whom he talks and interacts; he usually has a TV set to watch, as well as picture magazines to peruse; he has grounds to wander on in nice weather, usually equipped with swings, etc.; he has a diet with at least some variation to anticipate and enjoy; his institution observes holidays with decorations, special meals, and other novel preparations; etc. Clearly, he exists in an infinitely more complex environment than the experimental rat in a darkened 8- × 8- × 8-inch cage.

Second, it may not be so much the *amount* of environmental stimulation which is important as it is the *quality*. In terms of amount of stimulation, there may be little difference between the environments of a hollow child and a New York lawyer's child. The quality, however, is tremendously different. Hebb's theory and the neurological evidence regarding RNA and the C/S ratio seem to be more concerned with quantity than with quality, thereby leading to reservations concerning their applicability to the human studies. There is also the fact that although quality may be as important as quantity, very little is known about it. Until the specifics are discovered, detailed theorizing is probably premature.

Finally, there is an alternative interpretation as applicable to the animal data as to the human data. It may be that emotional factors are involved in all these studies. A deprived rat may be "upset" when first exposed to squares and triangles (more technically, he may react with anxiety and avoidance to these novel stimuli), and his poorer performance in responding to these stimuli may be merely a reflection of emotionality rather than a reflection of lack of capacity to learn. It will be recalled from the Thompson and Heron study that the deprived dogs exhibited unusual behavior patterns a year after the end of deprivation. Although the authors felt these responses did not interfere with performance in the test situations, their assumption was a matter of faith, not fact.

Similar considerations apply to many of the human studies. Take the isolated group studies, where not only were lower-than-average IQ's found, but also a cumulative deterioration with age. Now certainly it is possible that cumulative *emotional* effects of such cultural deprivation could account for the results as easily as cumulative *intellectual* effects. Not that such adjustment problems would show up as psychoneuroses or psychoses, but as a *lack of acculturation*—a lack of the mannerisms, habits, attitudes, interests, and values that help to define a given social class. To the extent such characteristics affect test performance, one could account for the low IQ scores of deprived groups in these terms rather than in terms of low intelligence.

On the other hand, test constructors have not been successful in creating an intelligence test which is free of such cultural variables—"culture-fair" tests do not eliminate the socioeconomic differential. Thus, it is tempting to argue that it is meaningless to talk about intelligence as independent of acculturation. The two are inextricably interwoven, and to be deviant in one means to be deviant in the other. From this point of view, the "emotional adjustment" interpretation is fallacious, and one is forced back to the conclusion that it is intelligence (defined as including acculturation) which is changed in the environmental deprivation studies. From the author's point of view, this is probably the correct interpretation. It seems extremely unlikely that all the results covered in the present chapter, plus other similar results not mentioned, could be due to emotional adjustment problems. A direct effect on intelligence seems more likely.

BIBLIOGRAPHY

ANASTASI, ANNE (1958). *Differential psychology*. New York: The Macmillan Co.
ANASTASI, ANNE (1960). Cultural differences. In C. W. HARRIS (Ed.), *Encyclopedia of educational research*. New York: The Macmillan Co. Pp. 350–358.
ANDERSON, J. E. (1939). The limitations of infant and pre-school tests in the measurement of intelligence. *Journal of psychology*, 8, 351–379.
ANDERSON, L. D. (1940). A longitudinal study of the effects of nursery-school training on successive intelligence-test ratings. *National society for studies in education, 39th yearbook*. Part II, 3–10.
ASHER, E. J. (1935). The inadequacy of current intelligence tests for testing Kentucky mountain children. *Journal of genetic psychology*, 46, 480–486.
BALDWIN, B. T., FILLMORE, EVA, and HADLEY, I. (1930). *Farm children*. New York: Appleton-Century-Crofts, Inc.
BENNETT, E. L., and CALVIN, M. (1964). Failure to train planarians reliably. *Neurosciences research program bulletin*, 2, 467.

BENNETT, E. L., KRECH, D., and ROSENZWEIG, M. R. (1964). Reliability and regional specificity of cerebral effects of environmental complexity and training. *Journal of comparative and physiological psychology*, 57, 440–441.

BIRD, GRACE E. (1940). The effect of nursery-school attendance upon mental growth of children. *National society for studies in education, 39th yearbook*. Part II, 81–84.

BLOOM, B. S. (1964). *Stability and change in human characteristics*. New York: John Wiley & Sons, Inc.

CHAPANIS, A., and WILLIAMS, W. C. (1945). Results of a mental survey with the Kuhlman-Anderson intelligence tests in Williamson County, Tennessee. *Journal of genetic psychology*, 67, 27–55.

COOK, L., DAVIDSON, A. B., DAVIS, D. J., GREEN, H., and FELLOWS, E. J. (1963). Ribonucleic acid: effect on conditioned behavior in rats. *Science*, 141, 268–269.

EDWARDS, A. S., and JONES, L. (1938). An experimental and field study of North Georgia mountaineers. *Journal of social psychology*, 9, 317–333.

GIBSON, ELEANOR J., and WALK, R. D. (1956). The effect of prolonged exposure to visually presented patterns on learning to discriminate them. *Journal of comparative and physiological psychology*, 49, 239–242.

GOODENOUGH, FLORENCE L. (1940). Some special problems of nature-nurture research. *National society for studies in education, 39th yearbook*. Part I, 367–384.

GOODENOUGH, FLORENCE L., and MAURER, KATHERINE M. (1940). The mental development of nursery-school children compared with that of nonnursery-school children. *National society for studies in education, 39th yearbook*. Part II, 161–178.

GORDON, H. (1923). *Mental and scholastic tests among retarded children*. Educational pamphlet no. 44. London: Board of Education.

GRAY, SUSAN W., and KLAUS, R. A. (1965). An experimental preschool program for culturally deprived children. *Child development*, 36 (4), 887–898.

GRAY, SUSAN W., and KLAUS, R. A. (1966). Deprivation, development, and diffusion. Presidential Address, Division of School Psychologists, American Psychological Association meetings.

GROSS, C. H., and CAREY, F. M. (1965). Transfer of a learned response by RNA injection: failure of attempts to replicate. *Science*, 150, 1749.

HAGGARD, E. A. (1954). Social status and intelligence: an experimental study of certain cultural determinants of measured intelligence. *Genetic psychological monographs*, 49, 141–186.

HEBB, D. O. (1949). *The organization of behavior*. New York: John Wiley & Sons, Inc.

HILGARD, E. R., and BOWER, G. H. (1966). *Theories of learning*. New York: Appleton-Century-Crofts, Inc.

HIRSCH, N. D. M. (1928). An experimental study of the East Kentucky mountaineers. *Genetic psychology monographs*, 3, 183–244.

HUSÉN, T. (1951). The influence of schooling upon IQ. *Theoria*, 17, 61–88.

HYDÉN, H., and EGYHÁZI, E. (1962). Nuclear RNA changes of nerve cells during a learning experiment in rats. *Proceedings of the national academy of science in the United States*, 48, 1366–1373.

IRWIN, O. C. (1967). Acceleration of infant speech by story-reading. In YVONNE BRACKBILL and G. G. THOMPSON (Eds.), *Behavior in infancy and early childhood*. New York: The Free Press of Glencoe, Inc. Pp. 299–303.

JACOBSON, A. L., BABICH, F. R., BUBASH, S., and GOREN, C. (1966). Maze preferences in naïve rats produced by injection of ribonucleic acid from trained rats. *Psychonomic science, 1966*, 4, 3–4.

JACOBSON, A. L., BABICH, F. R., BUBASH, S., and JACOBSON, A. (1965). Differential approach tendencies produced by injection of ribonucleic acid from trained rats. *Science*, 150, 636–637.

JONES, H. E., and JORGENSEN, ADA P. (1940). Mental growth as related to nursery-school attendance. *National society for studies in education, 39th yearbook.* Part II, 207–222.

JORDAN, A. M. (1933). Parental occupation and children's intelligence scores. *Journal of applied psychology*, 17, 103–119.

KAGAN, J., and MOSS, H. A. (1959). Stability and validity of achievement fantasy. *Journal of abnormal and social psychology*, 58, 357–364.

KAGAN, J., SONTAG, L. W., BAKER, C. T., and NELSON, VIRGINIA L. (1958). Personality and IQ change. *Journal of abnormal and social psychology*, 56, 261–266.

KIRK, S. A. (1958). *Early education of the mentally retarded.* Chicago: University of Chicago Press.

KRECH, D., ROSENZWEIG, M., and BENNETT, E. L. (1960). Effects of environmental complexity and training on brain chemistry. *Journal of comparative and physiological psychology*, 53, 509–519.

KRECH, D., ROSENZWEIG, M., and BENNETT, E. L. (1962). Relations between brain chemistry and problem-solving among rats raised in enriched and impoverished environments. *Journal of comparative and physiological psychology*, 55, 801–807.

LESSER, G. S., FIFER, G., and CLARK, D. H. (1965). Mental abilities of children from different social-class and cultural groups. *Monographs of the society for research in child development*, 30 (4).

LICHTENSTEIN, M., and BROWN, A. W. (1938). Intelligence and achievement of children in a delinquency area. *Journal of juvenile research*, 22, 1–25.

LUTTGES, M., JOHNSON, T., BUCK, C., HOLLAND, J., and McGAUGH, J. (1966). An examination of "transfer of learning" by nucleic acids. *Science*, 151, 834–837.

McCANDLESS, B. R. (1961). *Children and adolescents.* New York: Holt, Rinehart & Winston, Inc.

McCONNELL, J. V. (1962). Memory transfer through cannibalism in planarians. *Journal of neuropsychiatry*, 3, 542.

McNEMAR, Q. (1940). A critical examination of the university of Iowa studies of environmental influences upon the IQ. *Psychological bulletin*, 37, 63–92.

McNEMAR, Q. (1942). *The revision of the S-B scale.* Boston: Houghton Mifflin Co.

OWENS, W. A., JR. (1953). Age and mental abilities: a longitudinal study. *Genetic psychology monographs*, 48, 3–54.

RIESEN, A. H. (1961). Stimulation as a requirement for growth and function in behavioral development. In W. FISKE and S. R. MADDI (Eds.), *Functions of varied experience.* Homewood, Ill.: The Dorsey Press, Inc. Pp. 57–80.

RODERICK, T. H. (1960). Selection for cholinesterase activity in the cerebral cortex of the rat. *Genetics*, 45, 1123.

ROSENZWEIG, M. R., BENNETT, E. L., and KRECH, D. (1964). Cerebral effects of environmental complexity and training among adult rats. *Journal of comparative and physiological psychology*, 57, 438–439.

SALZOM, L., BEAULIEU, C., and HILDEGARD, E. E. (1966). The effect of RNA on the operant conditioned behavior of white rats. *Psychonomic science*, 6 (7), 341–342.

SHERMAN, M., and KEY, CORA B. (1932). The intelligence of isolated mountain children. *Child development*, 3, 279–290.

SKEELS, H. M. (1966). Adult status of children with contrasting early life experience. *Monographs of the society for research in child development*, 31 (3).

SKEELS, H. M., and FILLMORE, EVA A. (1937). Mental development of children from under-privileged homes. *Journal of genetic psychology*, 50, 427–439.

SKEELS, H. M., and HARMS, IRENE E. (1948). Children with inferior social histories: their mental development in adoptive homes. *Journal of genetic psychology*, 72, 283–294.

SKODAK, MARIE, and SKEELS, H. M. (1949). A final follow-up study of one hundred adopted children. *Journal of genetic psychology*, 75, 85–125.

SMITH, S. (1942). Language and non-verbal test performance of racial groups in Honolulu before and after a 14-year interval. *Journal of genetic psychology*, 26, 51–93.

THOMPSON, W. R., and HERON, W. (1954). The effects of restricting early experience on the problem-solving capacity of dogs. *Canadian journal of psychology*, 8, 17–31.

TRYON, R. C. (1940). Genetic differences in maze-learning ability in rats. *National society for studies in education, 39th yearbook*. Part I, 111–119.

TRYON, R. C. (1942). Individual differences. In F. A. Moss (Ed.), *Comparative psychology*. Englewood Cliffs, N.J.: Prentice-Hall, Inc. Ch. 12.

UNITED STATES ARMY, THE ADJUTANT GENERAL'S OFFICE, PERSONNEL RESEARCH SECTION (1945). The army general classification test. *Psychological bulletin*, 42, 760–768.

WELLMAN, BETH L. (1932–1933). The effect of preschool attendance upon the IQ. *Journal of experimental education*, 1, 48–69.

WELLMAN, BETH L., and PEGRAM, EDNA L. (1944). Binet IQ changes of orphanage preschool children: a re-analysis. *Journal of genetic psychology*, 65, 239–263.

WELLMAN, BETH L., SKEELS, H. M., and SKODAK, MARIE (1940). Review of McNemar's critical examination of Iowa studies. *Psychological bulletin*, 37, 93–111.

WHEELER, L. R. (1932). The intelligence of East Tennessee mountain children. *Journal of educational psychology*, 23, 351–370.

WHEELER, L. R. (1942). A comparative study of the intelligence of East Tennessee mountain children. *Journal of educational psychology*, 33, 321–334.

WOLF, R. M. (1963). The identification and measurement of environmental process variables related to intelligence. Unpublished Ph.D. dissertation, University of Chicago.

WOLF, R. M. (1964). *The measurement of environments*. Princeton, N.J.: Educational Testing Service.

YERKES, R. M. (Ed.) (1921). Psychological examining in the United States army. *National academy of science*, 15.

4

Nature of Intelligence

INTRODUCTION

In Chapter 2, we considered the genetic determinants of intelligence. In Chapter 3, we considered its environmental determinants. The present chapter completes the picture; it asks, "What *is* intelligence?"

Three approaches to the answer are considered. The first half of this chapter describes the Western approaches: *factor analysis* and studies of *thinking*. The factor analysis approach attempts to discover the components of intelligence: Is an "intelligent" person intelligent in all things, doing well in all intellectual activities, or can he be intelligent in different ways—one person by virtue of "numerical" intelligence, another by virtue of "spatial" intelligence, another by virtue of "logical" intelligence, etc.? How many such components are there? Factor analysis is used to find the answer.

Studies of thinking ask a different question. They are oriented toward discovering what a person *does* when he intellectualizes. There is general agreement that thinking consists of symbolization. Language is the dominant system of symbols used by humans. Thus, much of the research on thinking has to do with the acquisition and functions of language.

The second half of this chapter describes an approach that originated in Europe—in Geneva, Switzerland. It is the research and theory of *Jean Piaget*. It is quite different from the Western approaches, although the nature of its differences cannot be described in a sentence or two. Suffice it to mention two characteristics at this time: it is "cognitive" rather than "associative," and "developmental" rather than "static." We shall see in due time what these characteristics mean. But first, the Western approaches.

116

THE FACTOR ANALYSIS APPROACH

We have treated intelligence as a unitary thing, like water; a person has so much of it—more or less than another person—and it affects his behavior in a rather pervasive way. Such a point of view is an over-simplification, used for communicative and pedagogical reasons. From the very beginning, it was recognized that intelligence is not unitary, but rather a combination of an unknown number of *kinds* of intelligence. In describing the first intelligence test, Binet wrote:

This scale properly speaking does not permit the measure of *the* intelligence, because intellectual qualities are not superposable, and therefore cannot be measured as linear surfaces are measured, but are on the contrary, a classification, a hierarchy among diverse intelligences; and for the necessities of practice this classification is equivalent to a measure. [Italics added.]

and:

Every child has his individuality; one succeeds best in item "A" and fails in item "B"; another, of the same age, fails in "A" and on the other hand succeeds in "B". How shall we account for these individual differences in the experimental results? We do not know exactly; it is probable that the mental faculties involved in the tests are different, and of unequal development in the children. ["Item" has been substituted for "test" in this quotation.] [Binet and Simon, 1905, pp. 37, 45.]

The analytic tools for identifying the components of intelligence were not available to Binet, but since then a great deal of research has accumulated that attempts to isolate these components. The method of analysis has been a complex statistical procedure known as *factor analysis*. The basic procedure is as follows: Answers to different test items are correlated with each other, indicating the degree to which correct answers to one item are related to correct answers to all other items. Groups of items are then identified according to the extent to which a correct answer to one predicts a correct answer to others within the group. It is possible to arrange the groups so that each group is minimally related to all other groups. Suppose, for example, that people who answer item 1 correctly usually answer items 7 and 9 correctly; answers to the three items are correlated. It is then possible to substitute one score for all three. Suppose that answers to these three items are not related to answers to items 4, 5, and 8, but that if 4 is answered correctly, so are 5 and 8. We then have evidence that items 1, 7, and 9 measure one kind of intelligence, and items 4, 5, and 8 another, unrelated kind.

How many such "primary factors" are there, and what is the nature of each? Thurstone (1938) was the pioneer in attempting to answer this question. Using almost 60 different tests of intelligence, he ultimately identified seven such factors: verbal comprehension, word fluency, numerical ability, space visualization, memory, perceptual ability, and reasoning. He then constructed a separate test for each factor—seven "pure" tests, each measuring only a single factor. But when he administered the tests to new samples, he suffered an unwelcome surprise. The seven scores were correlated with each other, such that a high score on one test usually meant a high score on all the tests, and vice versa. Thus, a general, unified type of intelligence was suggested, as well as overlapping specific types. Spearman (1904) had anticipated Thurstone's results 30 years earlier, when he had suggested just such a "two-factor" theory of intelligence.

Thurstone thus did not succeed in developing uncorrelated tests, and whether or not there was such a thing as general intelligence, in addition to specific types, continued to inspire factor-analytic research. Perhaps Thurstone's failure was due not to a general intellectual factor but to more than seven factors, some of which overlapped from one test to another, thus producing positive correlations. The question was still an open one.

By far the most elaborate analysis of intelligence into its possible components has been the work of Guilford (1967) and his associates. Guilford has developed a model of intelligence that hypothesizes an astounding 120 factors. They are organized along three dimensions. First is the *content* of the required intellectual behavior. Some types of information, for example, are "figural"—concrete things we see, hear, or feel. Another type of content has to do with the meaning of words—"semantic" content. Another is "symbolic," such as mathematics or logic. A fourth is "behavioral," where the information to be dealt with is the behavior of other people.

These four types of information (figural, semantic, symbolic, and behavioral) can be presented to us in different ways—as different products, the second main dimension. A "unit" is one such form: a word is a semantic unit, a number is a symbolic unit, etc. Units form "classes": classes of words and classes of numbers—verbs and prime numbers, for example. Sometimes we must think in terms of "relations": Y is higher than Z, X is greater than A, etc. Altogether, there are six types of products: units, classes, relations, systems, transformations, and implications. A given content can be expressed in any one of these six products, making a total of 24 possible combinations (4×6).

Finally, we may consider what a person does with a particular content expressed as a particular product—the type of mental operation called into play. Perhaps the information is merely "memorized." Or perhaps it must be "evaluated" as correct or incorrect, good or bad, etc. Or perhaps new information must be generated from that given. Guilford suggests two kinds: "divergent" and "convergent" production. Finally, perhaps the individual is required to comprehend or understand the information; Guilford calls it "cognition." There are thus five kinds of possible mental operations: memory, evaluation, divergent production, convergent production, and cognition.

As any given mental operation can be performed on a given content-product combination, there are 5 × 24 = 120 possible combinations in the model. Figure 4.1 presents the model as a three-dimensional cube, with the interconnecting lines forming 120 smaller cubes, one for each three-way combination. As of 1967, about 80 of the 120 factors had been isolated.

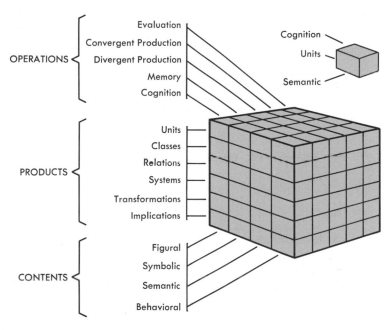

Figure 4.1. Guilford's model of human intelligence: the structure of intellect (Guilford, 1961).

Different Points of View

Where has factor analysis led us? In the author's opinion, its major contribution has been to provide some empirical support for what everybody already "knew" anyway; after all, we all know people who are "good at numbers" but "bad at reasoning," etc. But the *number* of independent factors remains in question. Most of Guilford's factors, like Thurstone's, are positively correlated with each other. Whether this suggests a general intelligence or simply "impure" tests is a moot question. There is a certain amount of subjectivity inherent in the factor-analytic procedure, depending upon the original items used, the type of rotation used, the population of subjects, etc. These considerations practically preclude an entirely objective analysis. As Humphreys wrote, ". . . test behavior can almost endlessly be made more specific, . . . factors can almost endlessly be fractionated or splintered" (1962, p. 475). Indeed, when Thurstone first reported that he could not find a general factor in his data, Spearman reanalyzed the same data and did find a general factor.

McNemar, in his 1964 presidential address to the American Psychological Association, carefully evaluated dozens of studies purporting to have identified the components of intelligence. He observed: "The structure of intellect that requires 120 factors may very well lead the British, and some of the rest of us, to regard our fractionalization and fragmentation of ability, into more and more factors of less and less importance, as indicative of scatterbrainedness" (p. 872). He concluded: "It has been the thesis of this paper that the concept of general intelligence, despite being maligned by a few, regarded as a second-order function by some, and discarded or ignored by others, still has a rightful place in the science of psychology and in the practical affairs of man" (p. 880).

A year later, Vernon (1965) made the same point:

> Despite Thurstone's and Guilford's assurance that general intelligence is too vague and heterogeneous a construct to be worth measuring—we should break it down into its components and measure each individual's profile of factors—most practicing psychologists in schools, clinics, and industry happily go on using the familiar group or individual tests of intelligence. The main concessions they make to the factorists are to obtain separate linguistic and quantitative scores in some academic aptitude tests, and separate verbal and performance scores in the Wechsler scales. When I visited some military psychological establishments in 1957, I was told more than once that military psychologists could not ignore g. Try as they would to find differential tests for different army trades, intercorrelations were always so high that recruits appeared to be differentiated more by all-around level of ability than by type of ability, that is to say, by g rather than by factor profile. . . . A general intelligence factor seems unavoidable since substantial positive intercorrelations are found when any cognitive tests are applied to a fairly representative population. [P. 724.]

Vernon's conception of intelligence consists of a general intellectual factor, g, which pervades all intellectual behavior. When its effects are statistically removed, two main subgroups remain: a "verbal education" group, and a "spatial-practical-mechanical" group. As he says, this conception

. . . gives the best indication I can manage of the factors that emerge most consistently when large and varied tests batteries are applied to representative samples of adolescents or young adults. I admit, of course, that there is no one final structure, since so much depends on the population tested, its heterogeneity and educational background, the particular tests chosen, and the techniques of factorization and rotation employed. [P. 726.]

Considering all points of view, then, factor analysis has failed to come up with a set of well-defined, independent, and replicable components of intelligence, nor has it ruled out a general factor. The verbal-spatial groups often appear, but they are correlated with each other. The safest statement would seem to be similar to Vernon's: There is a general intellectual ability, which permeates several more specific types. Figure 4.2 represents this state of affairs, with g being present in each of

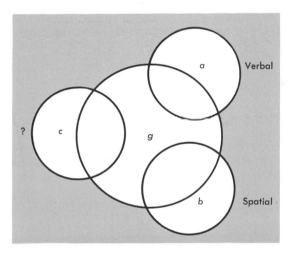

Figure 4.2. A compromise model of human intelligence.

the more specific factors a, b, and c, and yet each specific factor being different from the others. Two of these are labeled verbal and spatial, in keeping with the conclusions of Vernon, and the third is left unspecified to indicate the lack of certainty of the final story. Improved methodology applied to future studies can be expected to clarify the picture.

THINKING

While factor analysis can suggest what kinds of questions "go together," it does not reveal what a person does in order to arrive at an answer. A person is presented with a problem, be it a real-life problem or a question on an intelligence test. An answer is ultimately generated, right or wrong. Between these two events—the question and the answer—a process occurs. It is in this process that intelligence is "used," and the answer is the result of the process. Bright people must use different processes than dull people, for they generate different answers. To understand intelligence, then, this process—*thought*—must be analyzed. Such is the logic for including thinking as an integral part, perhaps the crucial part, of intelligence.

But thinking is largely covert. As Glucksberg (1966) observed, Rodin's statue, the *Thinker*, is not hopping about—he is depicted in an immobile position. How can a process so unobservable and private as thinking be studied? The answer is that it is studied indirectly, in the same way that the physicist studies electricity indirectly. The physicist does not *see* electricity, but by observing its effects—the swing of an ammeter needle, a change in magnetic flux—he constructs a theory as to its nature and behavior. The same is true of thinking; by observing the individual's overt processes, theories are constructed about his covert processes.

Definition of Thinking

Consider a deceptively simple question: What is thinking? It is often asserted that the great qualitative distinction between man and animals is that man can think; animals cannot. It is easy enough to find a person who agrees with this assertion, but nine times out of ten, he will not be able to come up with an articulate definition of thinking. Thus, his distinction between man and animals is a superficial one—just a verbal, "lip-service" one—he does not really know what he means. The assertion that man can think and animals cannot is true or false, *depending upon what is meant by thinking.* Let us seek a definition that makes the statement true, for then thinking will be identified with high intelligence (man *is* more intelligent than animals), and thereby a study of thinking will reveal something about intelligence.

The usual definition of thinking is that it consists of *symbolic activity.* According to this definition, both man and animals can think. A rat, for example, can be taught to "alternate" in a two-choice T-maze: to turn left on one trial, right on the next, in an alternating fashion. The rat can learn this *even though the maze is exactly the same on each trial.* Since no environmental cues are thus available to "inform" the rat that the last turn was, say, to the left, it follows that the rat must provide the information itself; it must be able to present to itself a symbol representing the fact that the last turn was to the left. The nature of this symbol need not concern us, although it is a matter of some concern in theories of learning. The important point is recognition of the fact that animals can symbolize, and can react to their symbols in a systematic fashion.

Typical human thinking involves much more than merely producing symbols and reacting systematically to them. *What all (normal) humans can do, and what no animal can do, is to arrange a set of symbols into a new pattern and react meaningfully to the pattern upon its very first occurrence.* A corollary is that only humans can react meaningfully to a set of symbols produced by someone else, never having experienced the pattern before.

Reflect for a moment on this distinction between man and animals, for it is a crucial one. A parrot can be taught dozens of words, and even whole phrases, such as "Polly wants a cracker." But no parrot has ever been observed to recombine the words into a novel combination *with any evidence that the parrot "understood" the new combination.* Such recombinations are "random," and we say the parrot has made a "mistake." But with humans, the story is different. Mowrer writes:

Up to this point the speech learning of birds and babies seems to be virtually identical; but before long, somewhere around 18 months or two years of age, human infants begin to do something of which birds, even the most talented of them, are incapable. It is always a big event for the rest of the family (and probably for the baby, too!) when a baby begins to "put words together," i.e., to make original, functional sentences. [1960, p. 81.]

Mowrer describes such an occasion with his own little girl:

The author will never forget when his own first child, a little girl, met him at the door one evening and excitedly exclaimed: "Pammy-kitty! Pammy-kitty!" He knew that his daughter had visited a little neighbor, Pammy, that afternoon. Therefore, "Pammy-kitty" clearly said, "Pammy (has a) kitten," and the enthusiasm which accompanied the statement also implied the qualifying clause, "which is really quite wonderful." [P. 135.]

Imagine how strange it would be to witness such behavior in even the world's most brilliant parrot. To be sure, it could be taught to say "kitty," and perhaps could be taught to say it only when a kitten was in sight. Likewise, it could be taught to say "Pammy" whenever Pammy was in sight. But after seeing Pammy with a kitten, would it greet its owner in the evening with "Pammy-kitty"? Not on your life.

We conclude, then, that man alone can produce sequences of symbols whose patterns are novel, and yet invariably meaningful both to himself and to others. With this definition of thinking, it can be truthfully asserted that only man can think.

Functions of Language

It is words that man rearranges into new combinations. Hence, the study of language has always been intimately associated with the study of thinking. Let us begin by briefly considering the functions of language—how language helps us to cope with the world. We will then consider how it is acquired.

Representation. The most general function of language, upon which all other functions are dependent, is representation of the "not here—not now." To think about something, one must have something to think with. Words fill that need. Helen Keller wrote poignantly about her discovery of this function of words:

One day, while I was playing with my new doll, Miss Sullivan put my big rag doll into my lap also, spelled "d-o-l-l" and tried to make me understand that "d-o-l-l" applied to both. Earlier in the day we had had a tussle over the words "m-u-g" and "w-a-t-e-r." Miss Sullivan had tried to impress it upon me that "m-u-g" is *mug* and that "w-a-t-e-r" is *water*, but I persisted in confounding the two. In despair she had dropped the subject for the time, only to renew it at the first opportunity. I became impatient at her repeated attempts and, seizing the new doll, I dashed it upon the floor. I was keenly delighted when I felt the fragments of the broken doll at my feet. Neither sorrow nor regret followed my passionate outburst. I had not loved the doll. In the still, dark world in which I lived there was no strong sentiment or tenderness. I felt my teacher sweep the fragments to one side of the hearth, and I had a sense of satisfaction that the cause of my discomfort was removed. She brought me my hat, and I knew I was going out into the warm sunshine. This thought, if a wordless sensation may be called a thought, made me skip with pleasure.

We walked down the path to the well-house, attracted by the fragrance of the honeysuckle with which it was covered. Some one was drawing water and my teacher placed my hand under the spout. As the cool stream gushed over one hand she spelled into the other the word water, first slowly, then rapidly. I stood still, my whole attention fixed upon the motions of her fingers. Suddenly I felt a misty consciousness as of something forgotten—a thrill of returning thought; and somehow the mystery of language was revealed to me. I knew then that "w-a-t-e-r" meant the wonderful cool something that was flowing over my hand. That living word awakened my soul, gave it light, hope, joy, set it free! There were barriers still, it is true, but barriers that could in time be swept away.

I left the well-house eager to learn. Everything had a name, and each name gave birth to a new thought. As we returned to the house every object which I touched seemed to quiver with life. That was because I saw everything with the strange, new sight that had come to me. On entering the door I remembered the doll I had broken. I felt my way to the hearth and picked up the pieces. I tried vainly to put them together. Then my eyes filled with tears; for I realized what I had done, and for the first time I felt repentance and sorrow.

I learned a great many new words that day. I do not remember what they all were; but I do know that *mother, father, sister, teacher* were among them—words that were to make the world blossom for me, "like Aaron's rod, with flowers." It would have been difficult to find a happier child than I was as I lay in my crib at the close of that eventful day and lived over the joys it had brought me, and for the first time longed for a new day to come. [1917, pp. 22–24.]

A simple experiment by Spiker (1956) illustrates very nicely this representational function of language. One group of preschool children was taught a name for each of two stimuli, a card with five concentric circles and a second card with seven concentric circles. These cards were presented side by side, sometimes "7" and "5," sometimes "7" and "7," etc., with the subject being asked to name each card on each presentation. The usual names were "five" and "seven," although some subjects used other words: "larger" (7) and "smaller" (5), "darker" and "lighter," etc. This training was continued until the subject gave the same correct responses for twelve successive trials. Control children were given exactly the same training except that names were not required; they simply had to state whether each pair was the "same" (e.g., 7 and 7, 5 and 5) or "different" (e.g., 7 and 5, 5 and 7).

Following training, each subject was told there was a different "game to play." A phonograph turntable was displayed, with two boxes mounted on opposite sides from the center. The tops of the boxes were hinged so that they could be opened. On top of one box was the five-circle card, and on top of the other box was the seven-circle card. The subject was told that the experimenter would put a toy coin into one of the boxes while the subject was watching, that the turntable would then be spun to make the boxes disappear, and that when it stopped the subject was to point to the box with the coin in it. If enough coins were won, they could be used to "buy a prize."

Six such trials were given to each subject. The experimenter put the coin into one of the boxes while the subject watched, then turned the turntable on for 25 seconds, during which time it rotated so fast that the boxes could no longer be seen, then stopped it and waited for the subject's choice. Now, the question is: How many correct responses were given by each group, experimental and control? By chance, three correct responses could occur, since there were only two possible answers. The experimental group, which had learned a name for each box, averaged 4.8 correct responses, and the control group, 2.9. Thus, the experimental group averaged about one error, while the control group performed almost exactly at chance level. The difference was highly significant.

How is this difference to be explained? What the subject had to do was to remember the correct box for 25 seconds. Presumably, the remembering was accomplished by "thinking" about the correct box during the delay period. Thus, an experimental subject might have said to himself, "The coin is in box 7," or simply "Box 7," or "He put it in the darker box," etc. What could a control subject say to himself? He could say, "The coin is in . . . ," but then what could he say? If he had no symbol for a particular box, he could not represent it in isolation. If he said "box," and by this he meant either box, such a representation would not "steer" him to the correct box after the delay interval. With no symbol for a specific box, the possibility of thinking about that specific box was theoretically precluded. And, indeed, the subjects behaved as though they had not thought at all; they would have done just as well if they had been blindfolded.

A number of other studies report similar results (Cantor, 1955; Gagné and Baker, 1950; Goss, 1953; Rossman and Goss, 1951). They all point to the fundamental importance of symbols—words—to think with. Of course, not all symbols are words. There are also *images* that can be used, as well as *muscular movements* of one kind or another, such as those used by the deaf. Indeed, many such movements are so minute they are not observable at all and can be detected only by measuring electrical activity of the muscles in question—electromyographs (EMG's). But *words* are the most important and the most frequently used, either alone or in combination with other symbols.

Mediation.   Under the rubric of representation, there are many more specific functions of language. A very important one is *mediation*. Mowrer (1960) gives an interesting example. Suppose someone says to you, "Tom is a thief." If you understand the meaning of this sentence, it will affect your behavior in subsequent interactions with Tom. You might be more careful to padlock your locker if it is next to Tom's, or to not loan him books, etc. How did this string of words elicit these responses? Presumably, the next time you see Tom, you will be reminded of his name, "Tom." The name will serve to remind you of the words with which it was previously associated: "thief." "Thief" will elicit responses consistent with your definition of "thief," e.g., padlocking your locker, etc. "Thief," in other words, will serve as a bridge—a mediator—between Tom and your reactions to him.

Animals cannot behave in this way. A mother dog cannot tell her puppies to stay off the street because she has no symbols for the street. Each dog must therefore experience the actual situation anew; he must gradually build up a fear of the street by experiencing the street and its associated perils. Each dog—each generation—must start from scratch; there is no "acculturalization" across generations, or even within generations.

Bloomfield (1933), a linguist, gives another example of the mediational function:

Suppose that Jack and Jill are walking down a lane. Jill is hungry. She sees an apple in a tree. She makes a noise with her larynx, tongue, and lips. Jack vaults the fence, climbs the tree, takes the apple, brings it to Jill, and places it in her hand. Jill eats the apple.

This succession of events could be studied in many ways, but we, who are studying language, will naturally distinguish between the *act of speech* and the other occurrences, which we call *practical events*. Viewed in this way, the incident consists of three parts, in order of time:

A. Practical events preceding the act of speech.
B. Speech.
C. Practical events following the act of speech.

After elaborating on A and C, Bloomfield goes on:

If Jill had been alone, she might have been just as hungry and thirsty and might have seen the same apple. If she had sufficient strength and skill to get over the fence and climb the tree, she could get hold of the apple and eat it; if not, she would have to stay hungry. The lone Jill is in much the same position as the speechless animal. If the animal is hungry and sees or smells food, it moves toward the food; whether the animal succeeds in getting the food, depends upon its strength and skill. The state of hunger and the sight or smell of the food are the *stimulus* (which we symbolize by S) and the movements toward the food are the *reaction* (which we symbolize as R). The lone Jill and the speechless animal act in only one way, namely

$$S \longrightarrow R.$$

If this works, they get the food; if it does not work—if they are not strong or skillful enough to get the food by the reactions R—they must stay hungry. [Pp. 23–24.]

Bloomfield then goes on to point out what *being human* means. The stimulus situation elicits a *verbal* response, r, from Jill: $S \longrightarrow r$. The verbal response becomes a stimulus, s, for Jack, who responds to it, R, by vaulting the fence and getting the apple for Jill. With language, the situation is changed from $S \longrightarrow R$ to:

$$\overset{\text{(Jill)}}{S} \longrightarrow r \ . \quad . \quad . \quad . \quad . \quad . \quad . \quad . \quad . \quad s \overset{\text{(Jack)}}{\longrightarrow} R$$

Bloomfield writes:

The difference between the two types [of stimulus-response sequences] is evident. The speechless reaction occurs always in the same person as does the stimulus; the person who gets the stimulus is the only one who can make the response. The response, accordingly, is limited to whatever actions the receiver of the stimulus can make. In contrast with this, the reaction mediated by speech may occur in a person who did not get the practical stimulus; the person who gets a stimulus can prompt another person to make a response, and this other person may be able to do things which the speaker cannot. The [solid] arrows in our diagrams represent the sequence of events within one person's body—a sequence of events which we think is due to some property of the nervous system. Therefore the speechless reaction can take place only in the body which received the stimulus. In the reaction mediated by speech, on the other hand, there is the link, represented by a dotted line, which consists of sound-waves in the air: the reaction mediated by speech can take place in the body of any person who hears the speech; the possibilities of reaction are enormously increased, since different hearers may be capable of a tremendous variety of acts. [P. 26.]

Planning. Another, related, function of speech is that it makes *planning* possible. It allows us to represent a possible future stimulus situation and to "program" a response. Mowrer gives the following interesting example:

A few weeks ago, I took home to my seven-year-old son a box of small blocks and other scrap lumber from our departmental machine shop. I knew the box, after the blocks were taken out, ought to be returned to the shop and so took it back to the psychology building; but, at the time, the shop was locked so I put the box in a storage room—and, then, forgot about it for several days. Later, at home, I remembered the box and thought, "Machine-shop door, box. Machine-shop door, box." In more elaborate terms I was, I suppose, saying to myself something like this: "The next time I pass the *machine-shop door* I must remember to get and return that *box* to the shop." Later, when walking down the hall on the way to my office, I passed the door, was reminded of the box, got it, and returned it to its accustomed place.

What I had done, evidently, was to *condition myself in advance* to the door, by using a symbol thereof, so that it would cue off the reaction of getting and returning the box. I had, in other words, in the absence of the door (and the box too for that matter)—i.e., in the realm of the "not here—not now"—conditioned myself so that the door, on the basis of generalization from symbol to thing, would bring to mind, or remind me, that I ought to do a particular thing. In effect, I had "talked to myself" and produced a result apparently quite comparable to that which we have here made the basic criterion of objective sentence formation and interpersonal communication. [1960, pp. 223–224.]

We use symbols, Mowrer is saying, to condition ourselves to objects or events *that are not present.* Animals cannot do this. Referring to the dog-street example again, if a dog wished to make her puppy afraid of the street, she could accomplish it only by *putting him in the street,* and then, say, by nipping him or growling at him. The fear elicited by the nip or growl might then become conditioned to accompanying stimuli—to the street. But a human can learn fear of the street in the complete absence of the street. All children are exposed to such learning when mother says: "You mustn't play in the street or a car might hit you." Humans thus have a tremendous capacity for learning responses to objects or events before they are experienced, and thereby to accumulate a myriad of habit tendencies infinitely larger and more varied than that of the brightest animal.

Concept Formation. A final example of language functions is that of *abstraction*, or *concept formation*. A concept is a symbol that represents a class of objects or events. "Dog," "house," "tree," "man," and "woman" are concepts, and so are "number," "force," "life," "instinct," and "sound." The importance of forming concepts is that *once an object or event has been assigned to a concept, we then bring to bear on that object or event all the habit tendencies elicited by the concept.* For example, suppose we hear a loud "boom!" If we decide it is an instance of "thunder," we seek shelter; if we decide it is an instance of a "sonic boom," we ignore it; if we decide it is an instance of an "earthquake," we might tremble with fear. In other words, we react not only to the specific external stimulus situation—the "S," in Bloomfield's terminology—but also to the concept to which we assign it. Thus, we extrapolate; we react to not only what actually occurred but also to where we "categorize" it—to where we "place" it in our conceptual scheme of things. Bruner (1964) says we "go beyond the information given." He explains:

> The first form of "going beyond," then, is to go beyond sense data to the class identity of the object being perceived. This is the more remarkable an achievement when the new object encountered differs from in more respects than it resembles other exemplars of the class that have been previously encountered. A speck on the horizon surmounted by a plume of smoke is identified as a ship, so too a towering transatlantic liner at its dock, so too a few schematic lines in a drawing. Given the presence of a few defining properties or cues, we go beyond them to the inference of identity. Having done so, we infer that the instance so categorized or identified has the other properties characteristic of membership in a category. Given the presence of certain cues of shape, size, and texture, we infer that the thing before us is an apple: *ergo*, it can be eaten, cut with a knife, it relates by certain principles of classification to other kinds of fruit, and so on. The act of rendering some given event equivalent with a class of other things, placing it in an identity class, provides then one of the most primitive forms of going beyond information given. [P. 295.]

Not only do different objects acquire equivalence by assignment to the same class concept, but similar objects acquire distinctiveness by assignment to different class concepts. In the former case, one speaks of the *acquired equivalence* of stimuli, and in the other case, of the *acquired distinctiveness* of stimuli. Bruner's discussion of different stimuli all being assigned to the class "ship" is an example of acquired equivalence. Consider an example of acquired distinctiveness:

Suppose a man is "flocking" some Christmas trees, spraying them with a white fluffy substance to create the illusion of snow, on an outdoor lot. A little boy scoops up a handful of the "snow" and starts to make a snowball when the worker says, "Hey, that's poison!" The boy quickly drops the ball and does not play with it again. By assigning the substance to the class "poison," the worker elicited a dramatic change in the boy's behavior; the boy learned to react quite differently to two very similar substances, snow and flock, by having them assigned to different categories. *And he learned this without experiencing the effects of the poison; the worker's words alone accomplished the distinction.* Language thus allows equivalence or distinctiveness to be learned without direct experience with the bases of the classification. It is language that labels the concept, and it is language that allows the classification to occur in the absence of the objects being classified; the functions of representation and abstraction occur simultaneously.

The Learning of Language: What Is Learned

Language acquisition has been measured in a number of different ways. One way is to count the number of different words used during a given time interval of free play; an hour is often used. Another way is to count the length of, say, 50 consecutive sentences and calculate the average number of words per sentence. Another way is to count the number of words in a written essay on some common subject. By these and other methods, language norms have been developed, and by comparing a given child's score to the average score for his age, his relative standing can be determined. Table 4.1 presents such norms as collected by eight different investigators and gives the reader some idea of what is normal at different ages.

TABLE 4.1

Norms for Early Speech Behavior

(As reported in eight major studies, summarized by McCarthy, 1954)

Behavior	Age
Coos and babbles	2–3 months
Vocalizes at sight of a person	4–6 months
Imitates sounds	6–8 months
Repeats syllables, such as *ma-ma, da-da*	7–9 months
Says one word	12 months
Says two words, separately and not knowing their meaning	12–14 months
Says five words (not together)	16–18 months
Says two words together, knowing the meaning, such as *ma-ma go*	20–24 months
Names familiar objects, like key, spoon, etc.	22–26 months

Tables 4.2 and 4.3 present some norms for *sentence length* at different ages. In general, it can be seen that the eighteen-month-old child is still

in the one-word stage, while a year later two- and three-word sentences are typical. By the time first grade is entered, five or six words per sentence is normal. At later ages, written sentences instead of oral sentences have been used to collect norms. By ten years of age, nine to twelve words comprise an average written sentence, and this number increases to about twenty at adulthood.

TABLE 4.2

Mean Length (Number of Words) of Spoken Sentence as Sampled in One-Hour
Conversations in Play Situations
(Adapted from McCarthy, 1954)

Group	Age								
	1½	2	2½	3	3½	4	4½	5	5½
Boys	1.2	1.5	2.4	3.3	4.3	4.4	5.0	4.9	5.4
Girls	1.3	2.0	2.6	3.8	4.2	4.7	4.9	5.0	4.7

TABLE 4.3

Mean Length (Number of Words) of Written Sentences in Compositions
(Adapted from McCarthy, 1954)

Age	Mean Length
9	11.1
11	12.0
13	15.2
15	17.8
17	19.8
College freshmen	19.9
College upper classmen	21.5

Children learn the *rules of grammar* too. Although a six-year-old may not be able to tell you any such rules—that a noun comes before its verb, for example—his speech gives him away. Thus, he may learn "daddy" and "go," and suddenly one day says "daddy go" as daddy leaves the house, and after learning "car," he may suddenly say "car go" as a car drives by. Braine (1963) demonstrated experimentally that children learn the positions of words in a sentence. Children were introduced to a "word game" in which they were exposed to sequences of two nonsense syllables, such as "Kiv Fuj" and "Juf Mub." "Kiv" and "Juf" always occurred first; "Fuj" and "Mub," second. To determine if the children had learned the positions of the words, they were later presented with a new word and asked to choose one of two old words and to place it sometimes before, sometimes after, the new word. Thus, the new word "Yag" was presented, along with the two old words "Kiv" and "Mub." The children were asked to pick the word that should go before "Yag." In 78 per cent of these problems, the children filled the vacancy with the word that had occupied that position in the initial learning.

Thus, children get some idea of whether a new word is, say, a noun or a verb by the position it occupies in a sentence they hear. If they are told that "Dogs tunk all the time," they are likely to assume the existence of a verb "to tunk," and to accept as meaningful a sentence such as "Cats tunk too." By a similar process, children learn the correct use of connectives, adjectives, and modifiers. They learn to say, for example, "The man" rather than "Man the," since "The" usually occurs before the first noun in a sentence.

Prefixes and suffices are learned by a similar process. Brown (1965) describes an experiment where a child is shown a picture of a small animal and is told, "This is a wug." Then he is shown a picture of two such animals, and the experimenter says, "Now there are two of them. There are two _____." The child usually finishes the sentence by saying "wugs," indicating knowledge of a rule for changing singulars to plurals. It is not until later, of course, that he makes all the necessary refinements and discriminations characteristic of adult speech. Thus, he may say "sheeps" and "gooses," indicating overgeneralization of the rule. Other word endings undergo a similar developmental history. A child is shown a picture of a man and is told, "This man knows how to gling. He glings every day. Today he glings. Yesterday he _____." Brown finds that adults are torn between four possibilities: glinged, glang, glung, and glought. But children know fewer possibilities and reply with "glinged."

In summary, then, what is learned is a complicated business when it comes to language, involving as it does meanings, pronunciations, word orders and endings, not to mention proper inflections, pauses, intonations, etc. Unquestionably, the most important single thing that is learned are the *rules of grammar,* for it is only by following the rules of grammar that novel sentences become intelligible. There are far too many possible sentences to ever learn them all by sheer rote memory. Miller (1965) estimates there are 10^{20} sentences 20 words long, which, you will recall, is the average length of a written sentence by adults. That is 100,000,000,000,000,000,000 sentences. ". . . if a child was to learn only these it would take him something on the order of 1,000 times the estimated age of the earth just to listen to them" (Miller, 1965, p. 19). Thus, it would be absurd to argue that language is learned by simple exposure to sentences, followed by a selection of the correct ones for a given circumstance. People make up their own sentences, having never heard them before. These sentences are meaningful because people have learned the rules of grammar—of sentence construction. The rules of grammar, then, make possible the type of thought that distinguishes man from other animals—the putting together of novel and meaningful strings of symbols.

How Language Is Learned

Now that we have some idea of what is learned, let us consider how language is learned. First of all, there is a distinction between the *meaning* of words and the *reproduction* of words. The two are probably learned differently.

Meaning of Words. Meanings of words, spoken or written, are probably learned as a result of pairing; the word is paired with the thing it represents. Thus, the spoken word "tree" is paired with the object tree, and the child learns the equivalence of the two. Later, when he enters first grade and is taught the meaning of written words, the process is the same; the written word "tree" is paired with a picture of a tree. The child's attention is directed to the picture and he is asked, "What is that?" He says, "A tree." Then the teacher points to the word below the picture and says, "This word is *tree*." Then the child is asked to say "tree" as he looks at the picture and the written word. Meaning is established by the pairing of the object and the word that names it—pairing of referent and symbol. In the next chapter, we shall see that such learning is an example of classical conditioning; a neutral stimulus (the written word "tree") is paired with a second stimulus (picture of a tree), which elicits a response ("tree"). After a few such sequences, the response is elicited by the previously neutral stimulus; the child responds to the written word with the verbalization, "tree."

Reproduction of Words. A word can be understood without the child being able to pronounce the word. A one-year-old may be able to say just three or four words, but he may understand twenty-five different words. When mother says, "Daddy is coming home now," he toddles to the front door; when she says, "Let's eat now," he smacks his lips and tries to climb into the high chair; when she says, "It's time to go to bed now," he cries; when she says, "Stop that," he inhibits ongoing activity; etc. Yet all he can say is "da-da" and "ma-ma."

One explanation of how word reproduction is learned has been called the "babble-luck" theory (Mowrer, 1960). Based on conventional learning theory, it assumes that in the course of babbling, the infant occasionally has the "luck" of making a sound that resembles a word. If the parents hear it, the child is rewarded in a variety of ways: the parents smile at him, pick him up, pat his head, and in general create a most enjoyable state of affairs. The child gradually develops a habit of making this particular sound, since it is rewarded. Thus, the first words are born.

The trouble with this theory is that it does not fit the facts very well. Parents do not sit around waiting for the child to talk to them. On the contrary, it is the parents who talk to the child. Eventually, the child *imitates* their sounds, and thus the spoken language is born.

But why do children imitate sounds? Mowrer says they do for the same basic reason they imitate their parents' actions and gestures and appearance, for the same reason that "identification" occurs; that is, the imitative act reproduces a part of the beloved parent and thus serves to make the child "feel good" in the same way that the beloved parent himself makes them feel good. The child, in other words, provides his own reward by "re-creating" a part of the beloved parent, and by then responding with pleasant emotional reactions the same as if the parent were in fact there. The autistic nature of the process has led Mowrer to call it *autism theory*. He studied language acquisition in "talking birds" for several years in order to understand the nature of the process. He writes:

Operationally, the first step in teaching a bird to talk is to make a "pet" of it, which is to say, tame, care for, and "baby" it in such a way as to deflect the interests and emotional attachments of the bird away from members of its own species to another species, namely *homo sapiens*. This is commonly done by isolating the bird from its own kind and making it dependent for food, water, and social attention and diversion upon its human caretakers.

But there is another step involved which only a few species of birds—and apparently no mammal save man—can make. As one cares for and plays with these creatures, one makes certain characteristic noises. These may or may not be parts of conventional speech; any kind of a noise will do—be it a word or phrase, a whistled or sung fragment of a tune, a nonsense vocalization, or even a mechanical sound like the creaking of a door or the opening of a food box—anything so long as it is intimately and consistently associated with the trainer and his care-taking activities. As a result of the association of these sounds with basic satisfactions for the bird, they become positively conditioned, i.e., they become *good sounds;* and in the course of its own, at first largely random vocalizations, the bird will eventually make somewhat similar sounds. By the principle of generalization, some of the derived satisfaction or pleasure which has become attached to the trainer's sounds will now be experienced when the bird itself makes and hears like sounds; and when this begins to happen the stage is set for the bird's learning to "talk."

In terms of learning theory, what has happened is that initially neutral sounds, by virtue of their occurrence in temporal contiguity with primary reinforcements, have acquired secondary reinforcing properties. When the bird itself happens to make somewhat similar sounds, it is now secondarily rewarded for having done so and tries to perfect these sounds so as to make them the maximum of pleasure and comfort. [Mowrer, 1960, pp. 79–80.]

But autism processes do not work alone; there are other processes that also contribute to language reproduction. One of these is *instrumental conditioning*, described more completely in Chapter 5. Once the child begins to produce words, he gradually is exposed to their usefulness in controlling the behavior of others. Instead of going hungry, he finds that "Me hungry" or "Cookie" influences mother so as to reduce his hunger. He thus receives powerful rewards for using words in a utilitarian sense, and thus he continues to do so with increasing frequency.

Finally, one cannot escape the fact that humans are simply "built to talk." Regardless of what parents do, their children will learn to talk. There is undoubtedly a strong genetic contribution to the infant's proclivity to babble, and thus to set in motion the processes described by the autism theory and instrumental conditioning.

Evidence for the Three Theories.   What is the evidence for each of the three theories? In truth, the evidence is exceedingly fragmentary, and we must perforce consider the three theories as no more than hypotheses concerning the true state of affairs. Consider the autism theory.

First, deaf babies become seriously retarded in sound production after the first few months; their babbling does not keep up with that of a hearing child. Since they cannot hear their beloved parents, sounds do not "remind" them of anything and thus are not reinforcing. The autism theory would thus predict retardation, as found. Second, there is evidence that warm, loving mothers rear children with a larger vocabulary than children of colder, more rejecting mothers. Milner (1951) studied the home environments of two groups of first-grade Negro children who differed widely in language development. Striking differences were found. "High scorers" had more affectionate and praise-giving mothers; ate breakfast and dinner with their families more often, thus engaging in more two-way conversation; and described themselves as happier, remembering more "happier" situations in the past. Autism theory would clearly predict more vocal imitation of loving, verbal mothers than of colder, non-verbal mothers. A related finding reported by Irwin was mentioned in the previous chapter. One group of mothers was instructed to read to their children 10 minutes a day, while control mothers did not. After 18 months of such treatment, the experimental infants babbled and talked significantly more than controls. Assuming both groups of mothers to be equally loving, the autism theory would predict more vocal imitation of the more vocal mothers, as found.

It is a well-established fact that girls are more verbal than boys. Note the longer sentences uttered by girls than by boys in Table 4.2, for example. The autism theory can easily account for this sex difference by first noting the qualitative difference between the average mother's voice and the average father's voice. A mother's voice is much higher in pitch, and smoother, and is thus more similar to the child's voice. Thus, it is easier for a child to imitate his mother's voice than to imitate his father's voice. Realize, too, that mothers are around more often to be listened to than fathers. Assuming that girls identify more with mothers, and boys more with fathers, it follows that girls should be more verbal; their model—mother—is easier to imitate and is heard more.

Then there is the fact that the firstborn and the only child usually are exceptionally verbal, as compared to later-borns and multiple-birth children (twins, triplets, etc.). The firstborn and the only child have two factors working to facilitate speech reproduction, according to the autism theory. First, they receive more parental attention, and thus fall more deeply in love with their parents, and thus are more likely to imitate them. Second, they are exposed to adult speech more consistently than, say, a multiple-birth child (who is exposed to the babblings of his sibling) and thus have a better verbal model to imitate. On both counts, they should be more verbal, as found. If there is a wide age separation between firstborns and second-borns, the second factor is mitigated, since the older firstborn may provide as good a verbal model for the second-born as his parents did for him at the same age. It is when the siblings are close together in age that the firstborn has the advantage.

Turning now to the second hypothesized process—instrumental conditioning—Rheingold (1959) has provided direct experimental evidence. Experimental infants were given adult attention whenever they emitted a sound, while control babies were not. In a very short period of time, the experimental infants were vocalizing significantly more, and this rate returned to that of the control infants when the social reinforcement was withdrawn. Thus, when vocalizations influenced the behavior of others so as to provide reinforcement, they were strengthened, and when the reinforcement no longer appeared, they were weakened (extinguished).

A second fact implicating the same process is that parental overprotection is often associated with retarded verbal behavior (McCarthy, 1954); that is, where the parents are overattentive, anticipating and satisfying every real and imagined need of the child before a normal request for aid is made, the child has less "need" for language. He gets along without making verbal demands. His reinforcements come without a contingency relationship to speech, and thus speech is retarded.

A third, related, finding is that speech retardation is often associated with an elaborate system of gestures. Presumably, the gestures are so well understood by adults that no further reinforcement is gained by learning a *verbal* communication system. If this reasoning is correct; that is, if the gestures have become substitutes for verbalizations, then non-reinforcement of gestural requests should facilitate the acquisition of language. McCarthy writes that just this actually occurs:

> If, in a particular case, it can be shown that such is the cause of linguistic retardation, a refusal on the part of the adults in the environment to understand and respond to the child's gesture-language is usually effective in bringing about the emergence of true language. [P. 597.]

Turning to the third and final suggested factor—the nature of the human beast to vocalize—there is no direct evidence that can be cited. It simply seems to be the case than human infants babble more than other species no matter what, and this tendency must be attributed to the evolutionary history of the species—to heredity. Babies begin to babble at about two months of age, in spite of everything; even deaf babies babble normally at this age, and it is not until later that a deficiency is noted (Ervin and Miller, 1963).

Excluding humans, the animal world is rather silent, except in times of great danger or pain. It is interesting to speculate why. Perhaps "noisy" animals tended to die out because they gave away their where-abouts to predators. Only the "safe" animals developed a tendency to vocalize. Trees and flight provided such safety, and it is probably not coincidental that arboreal creatures are the vocalizers: the arboreal primates (but not ground-loving apes) and birds. Some anthropologists have thus speculated that it was partly because of spending a protracted period of time "in the trees" that man's ancestors developed a sound-producing proclivity. Whatever the reason, one must not ignore the biological uniqueness of man in the understanding of language development. As always, heredity and environment interact, and it is the product of the two that leads to language.

JEAN PIAGET AND GENEVAN INTELLIGENCE

The last half of this chapter is devoted to one man: Jean Piaget. He was born on August 9, 1896, in Neuchâtel, Switzerland. In 1921, he was offered the position of Director of Studies at the Institute J. J. Rousseau in Geneva, where he embarked on a series of studies that was to make him famous before the age of thirty. He has remained at Geneva, having established the Centre International d'Epistemologie Genetique in 1955, where he is at the time of this writing. He has devoted his entire life to the study of intelligence. Out of his truly prodigious efforts, a theory has evolved that, just recently, is beginning to exert a tremendous influence on conceptualizations of the nature of intelligence. It is an entirely different conceptualization than those produced by Western thought. Some have claimed, for example, that it is the only theory of intellectual development in existence. Because of this unique claim, because of its novelty, and because of the brilliance of Piaget, we shall consider it in some detail.

This is no small undertaking. Piaget's theory is extremely rich in illustrations and complex in organization and is presented in over 30 books and over 200 articles (in French). Thus, it must be admitted at the outset that the present treatment is oversimplified and brief. Nevertheless, an attempt will be made to give the reader at least an idea of what the theory is like. The serious student will be motivated to read Flavell (1963) and then Piaget for a more thorough understanding.

In trying to grasp the nature of intellectual development, Piaget partitioned it into stages—*periods*—of growth. The periods do not exist in reality, of course, but are merely arbitrary divisions of the continuous flow of developmental change. They provide a convenient way of conceptualizing the nature of the changes over time. There are four such periods: the *sensorimotor* period (ages zero to two, approximately), the *preoperational representation* period (approximately two to seven), the *concrete operational* period (seven to eleven), and the period of *formal operations* (eleven to fifteen). We shall consider each in turn.

The Sensorimotor Period

During the first two years of life, the child is a sensing-acting sort of creature, with little *thought* occurring. Thus, very little "intelligent" behavior appears until the end of this period, when symbolization makes its appearance. Yet much is taking place intellectually, according to Piaget. The notion of *object constancy* illustrates this point.

Development of Object Constancy. Consider what an adult conceives an "object" to be. The idea of an object is so taken for granted that it is difficult to put it into words, in the same way that an artist cannot verbalize how he paints a masterpiece—he just does it. We can capture the conception of an object, however, by observing a person's behavior toward objects in different situations.

If a person takes a pen with his hand and holds it up and twists it around, it presents an ever-changing panorama of tactile and visual sensations. By holding it against his palm with the thumb, parallel to his face, a certain pattern of pressure on various parts of his hand is detectable. Visually, he sees an object about 5 inches long. Now if he

Development of object constancy. By viewing the stone from different perspectives and seeing parts of it disappear under the sand, only to reappear, this child learns about the stone "out there."

holds it as he would a dart, with one end pointing directly away from his face, there is a completely different tactile pressure pattern, consisting of pressure on the thumb and forefinger. Visually, no longer does he see a 5-inch object, but rather a round dot about 3/8 inch in diameter. Yet, in spite of these completely different sensations, he still sees and feels the "same pen." He does not assume the pen has changed from a stick to a dot! He assumes that the shape of the pen is constant, in spite of changes in sensations. This is called "shape constancy." If he holds the pen parallel to his face again, but at arm's length, he will still judge it to be about 5 inches long, even though it occupies a much smaller distance on his retina than when he held it up close—about one-third the former distance. Even if he sees it across the room lying on a table, it still seems to be about 5 inches long, although it then occupies about one-twentieth of the distance on his retina as before. This is "size constancy." Regardless of the distance of the object from the eyes—regardless of the size of the retinal image—a person automatically "corrects" for this and thus assumes the size of the object to remain constant.

If the person accidentally drops the pen on the floor, and it rolls under a desk and out of sight, it presents no tactile or visual sensations at all; it is phenomenally "gone" and no longer exists in his senses. Yet he bends down to retrieve it, behaving as though he sensed it all the time. He is greatly surprised if it is not there and looks again. Similarly, if the pen disappears from the desk about the same time as someone walks by, he again behaves as though it were affecting his senses, even though he did not see the theft and does not see the pen. He goes to the other person and demands the pen back. In other words, he behaves as though the object existed *quite independently of whether he is around to sense it or not.* He behaves as though its existence is independent of him, which, of course, it is. In short, he believes objects have *permanence.*

Size constancy, shape constancy, permanence—these are some of the attributes an adult assigns to objects, whether he knows it or not. Objects have a continuity in time and space; they do not exist one moment and cease to exist another moment; they do not mysteriously reconstitute themselves in different places, but rather always travel a continuous spatio-temporal route from one location to another. To put it more succinctly, objects have properties—weight, volume, area, color, etc.—that are *conserved* through changes in position, distance, illumination, time, etc.

Did we always react to objects in ways that imply these beliefs? It would seem that the answer must be sought in the behavior of very young children—of infants. Piaget observed his own three children. What did he find?

He found that infants do not behave as though they believe objects were constant and permanent, with an existence independent of the observer, but rather as if objects were nothing more than sensations. In the first few months, there seems to be no distinction between the object and the sensations it creates; the sensations are reality, and there is nothing beyond. When the sensations change or cease, the infant behaves as though the object has changed or ceased. When a three-month-old infant accidentally pushes his rattle over the side of the crib and it falls out of sight to the floor, he does not lean over to look for it (although he is physically capable of such a response), but stares at the place where he last saw it as though by repeating his last response to the rattle, he can re-create it.

When Piaget's daughter, Jacqueline, was playing with an object in her crib, Piaget moved it just out of reach but still in sight. Jacqueline immediately reached for it and retrieved it. But when Piaget covered the object with his hand, Jacqueline abandoned the object at once, as though it no longer existed. At seven months, her behavior was still similar:

. . . Jacqueline tries to grasp a celluloid duck on top of her quilt. She almost catches it, shakes herself, and the duck slides down beside her. It falls very close to her hand but behind a fold in the sheet. Jacqueline's eyes have followed the movement, she has even followed it with her outstretched hand. But as soon as the duck has disappeared—nothing more! It does not occur to her to search behind the fold of the sheet, which would be very easy to do (she twists it mechanically without searching at all). . . . I then take the duck from its hiding-place and place it near her hand three times. All three times she tries to grasp it, but when she is about to touch it I replace it very obviously under the sheet. Jacqueline immediately withdraws her hand and gives up. The second and third times I make her grasp the duck through the sheet and she shakes it for a brief moment but it does not occur to her to raise the cloth. [Flavell, 1963, p. 132.]

A little later—a couple of months or so—the first hints of an emerging object permanency become apparent:

. . . Jacqueline is seated on a mattress without anything to disturb or distract her (no coverlets, etc.). I take her parrot from her hands and hide it twice in succession under the mattress, on her left, in A. Both times Jacqueline looks for the object immediately and grabs it. Then I take it from her hands and move it very slowly before her eyes to the corresponding place on her right, under the mattress, in B. Jacqueline watches this movement very attentively, but at the moment when the parrot disappears in B she turns to her left and looks where it was before, in A.
During the next four attempts I hide the parrot in B every time without having first placed it in A. Every time Jacqueline watches me attentively. Nevertheless each time she immediately tries to rediscover the object in A; she turns the mattress over and examines it conscientiously. During the last two attempts, however, the search tapers off. [Flavell, 1963, p. 133.]

Although Jacqueline, in this example, behaves as though she has a belief in object existence independent of her sensations (e.g., she looked for the parrot when it was hidden), it is an immature kind of belief, as indicated by the fact that, when the parrot is hidden in a second place, Jacqueline continues to look at the first place, as though the way to regain a hidden object is always the same, regardless of where the object is hidden. A little later, the child looks only at the last place the object was seen, and even infers a hiding place in the absence of witnessing the actual hiding:

. . . Jacqueline watches me when I put a coin in my hand, then put my hand under a coverlet, I withdraw my hand closed; Jacqueline opens it, then searches under the coverlet until she finds the object. I take back the coin at once, put it in my hand and then slip my closed hand under a cushion situated at the other side (on her left and no longer on her right); Jacqueline immediately searches for the object under the cushion. I repeat the experiment by hiding the coin under a jacket; Jacqueline finds it without hesitation.

II. I complicate the test as follows: I place the coin in my hand, then my hand under the cushion. I bring it forth closed and immediately hide it under the coverlet. Finally I withdraw it and hold it out, closed, to Jacqueline. Jacqueline then pushes my hand aside without opening it (she guesses that there is nothing in it, which is new), she looks under the cushion, then directly under the coverlet where she finds the object.

During a second series (cushion and jacket) she behaves in the same way.

I then try a series of three displacements: I put the coin in my hand and move my closed hand sequentially from A to B and from B to C; Jacqueline sets my hand aside, then searches in A, in B, and finally in C. [Flavell, 1963, p. 134.]

Thus, sometime during the second year, a fairly mature notion of an object apparently develops. It seems incredible that approximately a year and a half is required for the child to develop a notion so primitive and so taken for granted by the adult that it is difficult to imagine what behavior would be like without the concept. Yet Piaget convincingly argues that the concept of object constancy—the mere fact of the substantiality of objects independent of the self's experience—is learned during the sensorimotor period. The period is so named because of the infant's behavior prior to acquisition of the concept of object constancy —his confusion of his sensations and motor responses with the whole of reality.

Other Developments. Other things are also going on during this period. One of the most important is that, toward the end of the period, the child acquires rudimentary techniques of representing the world; symbolism makes its appearance. At first, the symbolic responses are purely gestural, as we previously noted with respect to language development. These gestures have an imitative quality, as Piaget illustrates in the following example:

Then I put the chain inside an empty matchbox (where the matches belong), then close the box leaving an opening of 10 mm. Lucienne begins by turning the whole thing over, then tries to grasp the chain through the opening. Not succeeding, she simply puts her index finger into the slit and so succeeds in getting out a small fragment of the chain; she then pulls it until she has completely solved the problem.

Here begins the experiment which we want to emphasize. I put the chain back into the box and reduce the opening to 3 mm. It is understood that Lucienne is not aware of the functioning of the opening and closing of the matchbox and has not seen me prepare the experiment. She only possesses the two preceding schemata: turning the box over in order to empty it of its contents, and sliding her finger into the slit to make the chain come out. It is of course this last procedure that she tries first: she puts her finger inside and gropes to reach the chain, but fails completely. A pause follows during which Lucienne manifests a very curious reaction bearing witness not only to the fact that she tries to think out the situation and to represent to herself through mental combination the operations to be performed, but also to the role played by imitation in the genesis of representations. Lucienne mimics the widening of the slit.

She looks at the slit with great attention; then, several times in succession, she opens and shuts her mouth, at first slightly, then wider and wider! Apparently Lucienne understands the existence of a cavity subjacent to the slit and wishes to enlarge that cavity. The attempt at representation which she thus furnishes is expressed plastically, that is to say, due to inability to think out the situation in words or clear visual images she uses a simple motor indication as "signifier" or symbol. [Flavell, 1963, pp. 119–120.]

Piaget feels that during this latter part of the sensorimotor period, the child, through his use of gestural-imitative responses, takes an extremely important developmental step. *He is now able to represent (some) objects and events not perceptually present*—he is able to think about them. Soon these imitative responses move "inside" and become implicit rather than explicit. Piaget believes the original explicit responses are the precursors to *imagery;* that is, their outer manifestations drop out, and all that is left is a certain neurological activity—the image.

With the advent of symbolic representation, the sensorimotor period comes to a close. The child's intellectual development has been considerable. He now distinguishes the world from himself and acts as though he is merely one object in the world and as though there are other objects as well, which exist independently of him. He is able to represent some of these objects, albeit in a crude, gestural-imitative sort of way. He even has some rudimentary concepts of *causality* and *time.*

Concerning causality, he acts as though he knows that one event might lead to another event *under the appropriate circumstances.* At a younger age—six months or so—he tended to ignore the circumstances; contiguity alone seemed sufficient. If he should happen to say "da" as his carriage moves, he says "da" again when it stops and waits for it to move again. Later he acts differently, as though he knows there must be physical contact between two objects before one can affect the other. When his carriage unexpectedly moves, he looks behind, suggesting that he knows a force must be applied to move it. Piaget gives an interesting example:

. . . Laurent is seated in his carriage and I am on a chair beside him. While reading and without seeming to pay any attention to him, I put my foot under the carriage and move it slowly. Without hesitation Laurent leans over the edge and looks for the cause in the direction of the wheels. As soon as he perceives the position of my foot he is satisfied and smiles. [Flavell, 1963, p. 146.]

Intimately bound up with a developing concept of causality is that of time. By innumerable repetitions, the child gradually becomes aware that first something happens (he pushes a ball; he sees a bottle; he sees his mother), and then other things happen (the ball moves; he obtains milk; he is picked up). At first, he is aware only of his own actions and their effects; his idea of time is "subjective," to be comprehended only in terms of his own actions and reactions. Gradually, toward the end of the sensorimotor period, his time concept becomes more objective; he acts as though, *quite independently of his own behavior,* other persons and objects behave in a time medium, just as they do in a space medium:

. . . Jacqueline, on the terrace of a mountain chalet, locates the people I name, taking into account their recent displacements. "Where is Mother?" She points to the chalet. "Where is Grandpa?" She points down to the plain where her grandfather went two days before. "Where is the boy?" She points to the chalet. "Where is Vivianne?" She points to the woods where Vivianne went for a walk. And so on. [Flavell, 1963, p. 148.]

The Preoperational Representation Period

The second great period of intellectual development is from ages two to seven, approximately. It is subdivided into two phases: a *preconceptual* phase (two to four), and an *intuitive* phase (four to seven). What are the most important characteristics of this period and its two phases? The most important characteristic of the preconceptual phase is the increasing perfection of a symbolic system of representation—language. The most important characteristic of the intuitive phase is the appearance of certain mental "operations"—thinking in terms of classes, numbers, and relationships. Permeating both phases is a characteristic that defines the preoperational nature of both phases. *The child does not perform a given mental operation as part of a system of other, related possible operations, but rather as an isolated event that has no bearing on other possible operations.* It is because his mental operations are not related to each other that the period is called preoperational. The ensuing discussion will make this characteristic more clear. But first, let us consider symbolization.

As we have noted, the origins of symbolization are in the sensorimotor period. The child first represents an object or event by imitating it, and gradually the overt manifestations of the imitation disappear, and a central act alone suffices—the image, we may call it. Thus, thought—representation—occurs before language, instead of the reverse. Piaget treats language as merely a symptom of the child's increasing capacity for symbolization—as the *result* of symbolization, rather than its cause. There is a reflexive effect, of course. Once language is acquired, it adds tremendously to the underlying symbolization process; it has far greater generality than imitative symbolization. The important point to note, however, is its dependence upon a prior, sensorimotor type of symboliza-

Learning about causality and time. This boy undoubtedly learned that first you hit your thumb . . .

tion. Piaget's theory is a *stage* theory: intellectual abilities at one level always emerge from the accomplishments at a previous level. Language illustrates this principle; it is preceded by non-language thinking through the use of imitative responses.

During the preconceptual phase, the child gains enormously in language ability. His statements increase from the one- and two-word stage at age two to the four- and five-word stage at age four (see Table 4.2). According to Piaget, this increase in the use of language results in a number of intellectual gains, similar to those previously discussed under *thinking*. First of all, language frees the child from the here and now, from the momentary phenomenalism of an instant's sensation, and gives him access to the past and the future in a way that is impossible without symbolism. Language symbolism does a far better job of this

. . . and then it hurts!

(Wide World Photos)

than the former imitative symbolism. That symbolism was cumbersome and restricted to only a few imitable objects and events. Language is fast, versatile, and infinite in its applicability; as Helen Keller suddenly realized, everything has a name. Furthermore, language is public, while the earlier gestural symbolism was largely private in the sense that only the child knew what it meant. With language, he not only profits from his own thoughts *but also from the (verbalized) thoughts of others.* By listening to others, he can tap into their experiences—their pasts and their futures—as well as his own. Thus, his world becomes infinitely larger and richer, and he begins to learn "second hand," not by doing something and observing its effect, as he did in the sensorimotor period, but by hearing about something and its effect from the words of others. At two he could ask, "Where Daddy?" But he could hardly be told, "Daddy is working at his desk now and doesn't want to be bothered." He would have had to find that out for himself—by bothering daddy and suffering the consequences. At four he simply nods his head to the verbal answer, thus acting "intelligently"; he saves himself effort and avoids the consequences of bothering daddy at the wrong time.

In the last half of the preoperational period—the intuitive phase—new mental behaviors make their appearance for the first time—thinking in terms of classes, numbers, and relationships. His behavior is intuitive because, although he can respond on these bases, he cannot verbalize the reasons for so responding; he is unaware of the rules that guide his own behavior. We have already noted this phenomenon with respect to language usage. The child says, "Daddy come," not "Come Daddy"; "I hungry," not "Hungry I." He puts words in the right order without being able to explain why. He thus has a *noun* class and a *verb* class, as well as a *singular* class and a *plural* class. His ability to classify words allows him to create new and meaningful sentences and to understand new sentences uttered by others. Sometimes he creates sentences he himself does not understand, but since language rules are followed, the sentence is understood by others.

The four- to seven-year-old also understands simple relationships: Daddy is *Momma's husband,* the dog is *larger than* the cat, he is *smaller than* Daddy, etc. And he can respond to the relationship of numerosity; he can sort things in terms of the number involved, such as knowing that two hands have more fingers than one hand (without counting). He can count and thus can produce a sum. If you tell a five-year-old to hold up seven fingers, he will count off five on one hand and two on the other and hold up the seven.

But in spite of these sophisticated conceptual processes, there is one thing he cannot do, and that brings us back to the fundamental characteristic of the preoperational period. He cannot perform these mental operations as part of a larger system of possible operations. Consider some examples of this limitation. While he understands that Daddy is Momma's husband, he does not understand that Daddy is also Cousin John's uncle; Daddy belongs to Momma, and that is all there is to it. He cannot understand that *husband* is just one of many relationships descriptive of Daddy—that a whole system of such relationships exists. Or again, show the six-year-old two rows of 10 pennies each. Make the two rows exactly the same length, with the same space between adjacent coins within each row. Ask the child how many are in each row. Let him count them and discover there are 10 in each, or let him pair them off until he discovers there are none left over. When he is convinced there is the same number in each row, stretch one row out before his eyes, so that it is longer. Ask him which row has more pennies, or if they both have the same number. He will likely answer by either pointing to the longer row, judging only by *length,* or by pointing to the shorter row, judging only by *density*. He is apparently unable to consider both relationships at once, to be aware that as length increases, density decreases, so that the two cancel each other out, leaving the number unchanged. In other words, he does not react to length and density as though both were part of a larger, integrated system, but responds to them in isolation, one dimension at a time.

Piaget carried out some dramatic illustrations of this point. Let us consider one of the best known. A five-year-old is shown a lump of clay and is asked to "make two piles of clay with the same amount in each"; to make "two equal hunks of clay"; to "divide the clay into two parts that are the same." He tears the clay apart into two piles. Then he is asked, "Which is larger?" If he points to one, a little is taken away and added to the other, and he is asked again. This process is continued until he says, "They're the same" or some equivalent answer. After getting his judgment of equality, the experimenter picks up one of the piles and, in front of him, rolls it in his palms until it becomes a long, thin sausage. Then he lays it down in its previous spot and asks again, "Which is larger?" Amazingly, the child does not say they are the same. Instead, he examines them for a moment, or even minutely, and then picks one or the other and says it is larger. Some children pick the sausage, apparently judging on the basis of length. Others pick the hunk, judging by width. As with the pennies, the child cannot consider relationships between concepts, but thinks about them in isolation, one at a time. He does not know that length and width are related by a more comprehensive system of coordinates, such that changes in the one are compensated for by changes in the other, leaving amount (volume) unchanged.

But perhaps the phenomenon is unique with clay or pennies. Try it with something else—say, liquids. Seat the child at a table with three tumblers in front of him: two short and equal ones, and one longer and thinner one. Fill up the two short tumblers (T-1 and T-2) with the same amount of water, so that they are at exactly the same height. Ask the child if they have the same amount of water, or if one has more than the other. Depending upon his answer, pour water from one into the other, just a few drops, until he says they are the same. Then perform the test. Pick up one of the tumblers and empty the water into the long, narrow tumbler (T-3). Then ask him the following questions: "How much water is there here (pointing to T-3)? Does it have the same amount as here (pointing to T-1), or does it have less, or does it have more?" He will answer with either "More" or "Less," but not with "The same." If he says, "More," and you ask him why, he will say, "Because it is higher in this one (pointing to the water level in T-3) than in this one (pointing to the water level in T-1)." If he says, "Less," it is because, "It is smaller here (pointing to the width of the neck in T-3) than here (pointing to the width of the neck in T-1)." But maybe he does not understand. Ask him what will happen if the water is poured back into T-2 from T-3—how high will it go? He will now point to a level that is higher than the water level in T-1, suggesting that he really thinks there is more water. As with the clay, he responds to one concept (height or width) independently of its relationship to the other concept, and thus makes an error. Piaget says the preoperational child does not "decenter"; that is, he "centers" attention on one concept or dimension at a time and ignores other, related dimensions, and thus is led to distorted reasoning.

Another, closely related characteristic of the preoperational child is that he pays attention to the successive states of a changing sensation—like the fact that the row of pennies was first *short* and then *long*—but he ignores the process by which the change occurred. Piaget likens his thinking to that of successive "stills" of a motion picture; each frame is an isolated event by itself, and the process by which it changes from the preceding frame is ignored. Thus, the child ignores how the row of pennies got longer—that the experimenter simply increased the distance between the same number of coins—and notes only that one row is longer than the other; therefore, it must have more coins. This inability to think of *transformations* can be well illustrated by asking a five-year-old to draw (or to pick out the correct illustrations from a set of illustrations) the successive movements of a ruler as it is placed on one end and then allowed to fall over. Preoperational children find it very difficult to reconstruct the successive transformations of the ruler from a vertical to a horizontal position (Flavell, 1963, p. 158).

But the single most important characteristic of preoperational thought, according to Piaget, is its *irreversibility*. Piaget means that the preoperational child tends to think of an aspect of reality only in terms of the sequence in which it actually occurred. If ice is taken from the refrigerator and put on the stove and melts, the child can think about the two-stage event: ice, refrigerator—water, stove. But he tends not to think about the reverse process (water, stove—ice, refrigerator) unless he experiences it too. He does not symbolize the process—the transformation—that makes it possible to conceive of the stages moving in the opposite direction—that presence or absence of heat is the transformation by which ice is changed to water, *or water to ice*. He thinks only in the direction he observes and does not symbolize to himself the reverse. Piaget believes this irreversible nature of preoperational thinking is fundamental, since it impedes the development of logical thinking and substitutes egocentric (austistic) thought instead. We can best capture the flavor of this argument by moving on to the next period.

The Concrete Operational Period

Imagine a nine-year-old child presented with the same water tumbler problem as previously described: T-1 and T-2 are filled to the same height, and then T-2 is poured into T-3, a higher and narrower tumbler. How does the nine-year-old differ from the five-year-old? First, when asked if there is the same amount, or more or less, in T-3 as in T-1, the nine-year-old does not minutely examine the tumblers, peering carefully at the water in each. On the contrary, he hardly looks at them at all; he merely glances at them. Second, he promptly gives the right answer: "The same." If the experiment is repeated with other tumblers, he grows impatient and says, "They're the same—they're always the same." He performs in the same manner with the clay and coin problems. In each case, he hardly bothers to examine the objects at all, and he gives the right answer. As Brown says, "The correct answer appears to have a necessity in it that removes it from the sphere of matters requiring empirical verification" (1965, p. 201).

Now how did this remarkable change in behavior come about? Piaget believes it is because the nine-year-old child can think in terms of reversibility. If you ask him why T-1 and T-3 have the same amount of water, he may say, "Because if you pour it back (from T-3 to T-2), it will be the same as before" (i.e., the same as when he said they were equal). The clay sausage could likewise be balled up to resemble its original hunklike appearance, and the long row of pennies could be shortened again to equal its previous length. *For each sequence, the child is able to think of a transformation that would reverse the sequence.* Because the original condition can be restored, he arrives at the conclusion that something has remained unchanged, that quantity or numerosity has been conserved through the witnessed transformations.

It thus appears as though the nine-year-old is thinking logically. If A can be changed to B, and B back to A again, it follows that there is something alike in A and B—quantity, numerosity, area, volume, etc., as the case may be. It is because of this indication of logicality in his thought processes that Piaget attaches such importance to the attainment of reversibility.

Why should this be so? What is so important about logical thinking? Almost anybody is willing to admit that it is "better" than illogical thinking, but if you ask for a specific reason why, you are apt to get stony silence. We shall try to answer the question, and then we will be in a better position to understand Piaget. Concisely, the answer is this: *Given a set of premises from which one derives a consequence, if the derivation is a logical one, the consequence is every bit as certain as the premises. If, on the other hand, the derivation is not logical, the con-*

sequence may be false even though the premises are true. That is the heart of logic. To put it another way, if a set of statements is true, and another statement is logically derived from these, it also is true. It would be a waste of time to check its truthfulness; it has to be true. Logical reasoning thus allows one to obtain new truths from old truths, and therein lies its great value. It allows one to "go beyond the information given," and thus to behave in a more intelligent manner.

The seven- to eleven-year-old begins to occasionally think in this way. Because he is able to consider a number of logical possibilities, all interrelated to each other, he is "operational." But he still suffers from one great weakness; he can think logically only about concrete objects and events, not about abstract possibilities having no particular content. Hence, the title for this period: "the concrete operational period." In thinking about the tumbler problem, the child can think about a whole system of transformations in the shape of the water, from T-1 to T-3, and also to hypothetical, non-existent tumblers: T-1 to T-4, T-1 to T-5, etc. He can think about the reverse sequences too: T-5 to T-1, T-4 to T-1, etc. It is because of this whole, infinite set of possible reversible transformations that he is able to impatiently say, "It's *always* the same." But what he has difficulty with is in thinking only in terms of the logic of the situation, devoid of concrete instances. He can reason that if stick *A* is longer than stick *B*, and stick *B* is longer than stick *C*, then stick *A* is longer than stick *C*. But he cannot reason that, for any relationship *Rx* and for any objects *A*, *B*, and *C*, if *A Rx B* and *B Rx C*, then it follows that *A Rx C*. To reason purely at the abstract or formal level is beyond him. Such behavior does not occur until the fourth great period—the formal operational period.

The Period of Formal Operations

The fundamental difference between the concrete operational period and the formal operational period has to do with the *real* and the *possible*. The seven- to eleven-year-old has begun to deal logically with concrete, real problems. He organizes what is real into a logical system, and even "goes beyond" to logical implications. Given the three sticks *A*, *B*, and *C*, with *A* longer than *B* and *B* longer than *C* (e.g., $A > B > C$), he can not only deduce that $A > C$, but he may even imagine smaller and smaller sticks such that $A > B > C > D > E$ . . . But the non-existent possible relationships are a secondary, fleeting sort of thing, stumbled upon accidentally as the child ponders what *is*. The *possible* is a special case of the *real*, so to speak, and is not given systematic importance by the concrete operational child.

The adolescent behaves in a dramatically different way. He first considers all possibilities of a problem, and then attempts to discover where the *real* fits into this larger schema. To him, the *real* is merely a special case—an instance—of the *possible,* rather than the other way around.

Let us contrast these two ways of approaching a problem. Piaget presented the following problem to children of different ages. Four similar flasks are presented, all containing a colorless, odorless liquid that appears identical. Call these four flasks 1, 2, 3, and 4. A fifth, smaller bottle, *b,* is also presented, with a dropper in it. The experimenter now produces two more flasks containing liquid that looks the same as that in the first four flasks. He takes the dropper from the small bottle *b* and adds a few drops of the liquid in *b* to each of the two flasks. The liquid in one now turns to yellow, while the other retains its previous appearance. He then says to the child, "Now you produce the yellow color—do whatever you want." He gives the child flasks 1, 2, 3, and 4, and bottle *b,* and sits back and watches. Figure 4.3 summarizes the problem.

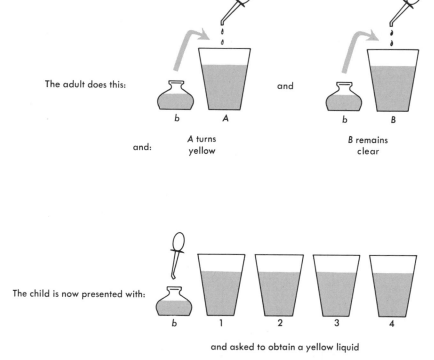

Figure 4.3. Piaget's yellow-liquid problem.

Consider the typical reaction to this problem at each of the four great intellectual periods. The sensorimotor child (ages zero to two) must be ignored, of course, since there is no problem for him; he does not understand the words of the experimenter. The preoperational child (ages two to seven) does better, depending upon how old he is. The five-year-old, generally speaking, makes a mess of things. He puts some of b in 1 (e.g., $1 + b$), then in 4 ($4 + b$), then pours 2 into 3 ($2 + 3$), and gives no indication that he has considered all the possibilities, that he is keeping track of what he has done, or that a plan has been considered. If he stumbles across the right combination ($1 + 3 + b$) and is asked to do it again, he cannot do so, but must start over again in a new random manner. There is no evidence of logical thinking at all.

The concrete-operational child (ages seven to eleven) proceeds much more systematically. First, he puts a few drops of b in 1, then in 2, then in 3, and then in 4 ($1 + b, 2 + b, 3 + b$, and $4 + b$). It appears that he has thought about some possible combinations, and then carries them out, one by one, in an orderly manner. But none of them work, and now he may abandon a logical procedure. He may say, "I tried them all and it didn't work—it doesn't work anymore," thus indicating that, although he considered some of the possible operations, he did not consider them all. It does not occur to him, for example, to try combinations of two flasks plus b at a time, such as $1 + 2 + b$. If it does occur to him (and here Piaget might prompt him with, "You took each bottle separately—what else could you do?"), he carries out the combinations in a haphazard manner, perhaps first $1 + 2 + b$ and then $4 + 3 + b$, then all together $1 + 2 + 3 + 4 + b$, and so on, in a non-systematic order.

The formal-operational thirteen-year-old presents a different picture. Here is an excerpt from Piaget's description of a thirteen-year-old.

"You have to try all the bottles. I'll begin with the one at the end [and he goes through $(1 + b)$, $(2 + b)$, $(3 + b)$, and $(4 + b)$]. It doesn't work anymore. Maybe you have to mix them [he tries $(1 + 2 + b)$ and $(1 + 3 + b)$, the latter turning yellow]. It turned yellow. But are there other solutions? I'll try [and he combines $(1 + 4 + b)$, $(2 + 3 + b)$, $(2 + 4 + b)$, and $(3 + 4 + b)$, and says] It doesn't work. It only works with $[1 + 3 + b]$." [Flavell, 1963, p. 207.]

Study carefully what the thirteen-year-old has done. First, he systematically tried out all one-bottle possibilities, and then all two-bottle possibilities, and he even continued with fresh combinations after solving the problem. Clearly, he seemed disposed right from the start to think in terms of all possible combinations, and they were investigated systematically until the problem was solved. This is the *sine qua non* of the formal operational period: the tendency to logically arrange the problem in terms of all possibilities and then to proceed to the actual solution by investigating the possibilities one at a time—to go from the *possible* to the *real* in an exhaustive, logical fashion.

Thus, the adolescent approaches his day-to-day experiences with the beginnings of an integrated cognitive system. Events that to a younger child were unrelated are now cognized as parts, not only of the *real whole*, but also as parts of a larger, *possible whole*. Everything must fall into place in this structure, and thus the adolescent develops a picture of the world that is tightly bound together by all kinds of inter-relationships and transformations. This tendency to seek order permeates all his activities, including moral convictions. Behavior that at one time was categorically "good" *or* "bad," not both, is now "iffy"; it is "good" *if* certain other conditions hold, and "bad" *if* other conditions hold. He can transform a "good" act into a "bad" act, and can reverse the two back again by considering the possible circumstances that may be related. Out of an earlier moral absolutism has emerged moral relativism. We shall have considerably more to say about Genevan morality in a later chapter.

Piaget's Theoretical Foundations: Assimilation and Accommodation

Two key concepts in Piaget's theory are *assimilation* and *accommodation*. The various periods of intellectual development are manifestations of the child's tendency to "assimilate" and to "accommodate" to his environment. By considering the meaning of these two concepts, it is possible to take a fresh look at Piaget's theory and to understand it better.

To Piaget, intelligence is intimately related to the living organism in a biological sense; a nervous system is a prerequisite for intellectual activity. Indeed, intellectual behavior is just a special kind of biological functioning, just as reproduction is another and nutrition is still another. In all biological activities, assimilation and accommodation are constantly at work. Let us see what these concepts mean in a strict biological context. We shall begin with nutrition.

A fundamental property of living matter is that of incorporating into its body life-giving nutrients from the outside world. Two phases of this process are distinguished by Piaget. First, the organism transforms an aspect of the outside world into a form that allows for its incorporation within the body. If the food is a solid, it is first chewed and thereby transformed into a pulpy, formless mass suitable for swallowing. In the stomach and intestines, various further changes occur as it is slowly digested and broken apart into its chemical constituents, until ultimately it loses its original identity and assumes that of its host: a muscle cell, a blood cell, a nerve cell, or some other part of the host. Piaget calls this process, changing the environment in such a way that it becomes part of the organism, *assimilation;* i.e., the material is assimilated to the organism.

But the process of assimilation involves a second process, whereby the organism adapts to the demands of the environment. Considering nutrition, first the mouth must open, then chewing and salivation must occur, followed by swallowing. Later, certain combinations of digestive juices must be discharged, depending upon the chemical properties of the nutrient. Just as the nutrient is transformed—changed—to become part of the existing organism, so the organism changes according to the demands of the nutrient. This adjustment of the organism Piaget calls *accommodation;* i.e., the organism accommodates itself to the peculiarities of the object it is assimilating.

Adaptation of any kind consists of an interweaving of assimilation and accommodation. The two are inextricably bound together in all adaptive interchanges between the organism and its environment; the environment is changed to the demands of the organism, and the organism is changed to the demands of the environment.

As these complementary processes complete one cycle and start another, the organism reaps the benefits. It evolves—*grows*—into a more complicated structure, with a different organization of its parts and an ever-changing set of adaptive responses called forth by environmental realities. Referring again to nutrition, as the organism develops, it assimilates the same object in different ways, each successive way being a product of past assimilations and accommodations. Thus, the one-week-old infant can assimilate only liquids; it cannot accommodate to solid foods as the six-month-old child can. Instead of smacking and swallowing, the neonate drools, spits, and vomits. With time, new accommodative responses gradually emerge, leading to assimilations that were not previously possible. The two-year-old can assimilate a piece of steak because it has developed the necessary accommodative adaptations. It tears the meat apart with its incisors, grinds it with its molars, and swallows it efficiently. At a later age, still new accommodations will appear: use of silverware to assist in the tearing process, less smacking, etc. Thus, assimilative responses change as the organism grows, the growth always being dependent upon past assimilations and accommodations.

Now consider intelligence. In terms of assimilation, intellectual development consists of *fitting an experience into the cognitive structure existing at that moment.* Thus, in looking at a ring, and grasping it and sucking it, the infant interrelates various aspects of the ring—visual, tactile, frictional—with his pre-existing organization of the world defined in those terms. For example, the infant learns that the ring, like a nipple, can be sucked, and thus the ring is made to fit into the pre-existing cognitive structure exemplifying sucking; a new part of the world, the ring, is assimilated into a relationship with a nipple—both can be sucked. In a similar manner, the ring is made to fit into his primitive coordinates of sight (the ring, like mother, can be seen), movement (like the bottle, the ring can be moved), etc. The ring becomes identified—*known*—in terms of its relationships to pre-existing "knowns."

As the ring is thus assimilated, the infant also accommodates to it. He learns that a ring is grasped and sucked differently from a nipple, that it looks different and feels different. Thus, his repertoire of responses changes and becomes more differentiated, and we say that he "recognizes" the ring; he treats it differently from the nipple. As these new accommodative reactions are developed, the infant also tries them out on other objects, and thus new accommodations to old objects emerge. As a result, the old objects are reclassified and reidentified into new, more complex conceptual coordinates—*schemas*, as Piaget calls them—making possible still another level of assimilation. The cycle repeats itself endlessly, leading to ever-increasing complexity in the child's cognitive structure.

Throughout development, assimilation and accommodation serve to create an organized relationship between man's intellect and the environment. At each developmental period, it is the assimilations and accommodations of previous periods that make possible the next step. Piaget's theory is thus a stage theory, as a previously noted; intellectual development is dependent upon what happened before, and the order is thus invariant. The exact ages may vary, depending upon the opportunities for assimilation and accommodation, but the order remains the same.

Commentary on Piaget's Theory

Piaget's theory of intellectual development has been considered in some detail. One may well ask why. As previously noted, there is no other comparable theory of intellectual development. Let us consider, in this final section, the truth status of the theory. It should be recognized from the outset that Piaget accomplished a truly monumental task; the absence of competing theories attests to this. Some have ranked Piaget second only to Freud in terms of his contribution to psychology. Ironically, his theory has had, until recently, very little impact upon psychology. This has been for several reasons, all of them in one way or another connected with the assumed truth status of the theory.

In many ways, Piaget's methodology invites questions. Psychology, at the time Piaget was making his first observations, in the 1920's and 1930's, was very self-conscious about its methodology. This was partly a reaction to its philosophical background, an era more distinguished by speculation than facts. The new psychology, however, proclaimed a different set of rules, patterned after those in the natural sciences, particularly physics. Measurements had to be objective and reproducible, so that the findings could be confirmed or disconfirmed by others. One was supposed to sort out causes and effects, and ultimately construct theories to explain them. The theoretical concepts had to be operationally defined, clear and unambiguous in definition, so that others would know exactly what was meant. Subjects had to be representative, and large groups of subjects were advisable, in order to balance out peculiarities in individuals that were not related to the hypothesis under test.

In all these ways, Piaget fell short. There was little objective measurement to speak of—just conclusions by Piaget as to whether a mental process was or was not manifested at a given age, with no specific criteria laid down. No causes were sought. Piaget did not ask what caused the six-year-old to behave as he did, nor did he ask if the processes could be speeded up or slowed down by certain experiences, nor did he experiment to find out. Thus, he did not have an explanatory theory, but "merely" a descriptive theory—a theory of what *was*, but not *why*. And even at that, his theoretical concepts were exceedingly vague and ill-defined, with few attempts at operational definitions. One must read all his works (over 30 books and over 200 articles) to be exposed to the entire theory. Today, a theory that cannot be succinctly stated within the covers of a single book, or better yet, within a single article, is by that fact alone judged to be "rambling" and "not well worked out." Finally, his first subjects were his own three children—hardly a representative group.

Why, then, with all these shortcomings, is Piaget's theory enjoying a "rebirth" so powerful that entire "Centers of Cognitive Development" are now in existence? There seem to be four reasons. First and foremost, there are no other comparable theories of intellectual development. For all the methodological and philosophical sophistication of modern psychology, for all its self-proclaimed similarity to the great natural sciences with its emphasis upon the "scientific method" and "objective observation," the fact remains that it has not come up with a theory of intellectual development. Piaget's theory thus fills a great void that modern psychology has chosen to ignore. It is as though psychologists believed the *method* assumed priority over the *problem:* If you cannot do it perfectly, do not do it at all. Unfortunately, the proper method often does not become obvious until after some "improper" methodology has been used to open the door. Piaget's great strength was in forging ahead alone, and in laying out some rough maps of intellectual development that would get the research going.

Second, the theoretical concepts used by Piaget to summarize his voluminous observations seem to possess a great deal of generality. The notion of *conservation of properties across irrelevant changes,* for example, covers almost an infinite number of instances. This notion was discussed with respect to *object permanency,* an extremely general concept itself, as well as with respect to specific types of conservation: quantity, weight, volume, number, color, etc. To be able to classify all these behavioral reactions in all these different contexts under a single concept is no mean achievement. The notion of *reversibility* is another example, explaining, as it does, various types of conservation and logical thought. One recognizes the generality of these concepts when he reads about a specific experiment of Piaget's and then suddenly thinks, "Oh! that's another example of _____!" One is continually rediscovering Piaget's concepts in this manner. Such generality is important, for it allows for a great deal of theoretical economy; only a few concepts are required to classify a large amount of data. Such parsimony is an essential part of any theory.

Third, there is the remarkable fact that the order of intellectual development described by Piaget's theory—from sensorimotor to formal operational—has held up in other, independent investigations (see Baldwin, 1967; Flavell, 1963; Siegel, 1964; and Wallach, 1963, for reviews of these studies). In summarizing a large number of European and American replications, for example, Wallach concludes: "But the same general developmental sequences have, on the whole, been obtained by such work" (p. 247). This is all the more amazing when it is recognized that the original studies were carried out in the Swiss culture—many of them with Piaget's own children—and hence one would expect large cultural artifacts to appear when cross-cultural comparisons were made. Of course, the age ranges *do* vary from sample to sample, but the invariance of the order is the important thing. It suggests a fundamental pervasiveness of Genevan processes that is common to much of the human race, independent of specific environments.

Fourth, *the appearance of the developmental periods is not greatly affected by special training.* In general, a child cannot be taught a particular intellectual operation unless he has already attained the level of development wherein that operation is naturally acquired. Smedslund (1961) provides an example. He attempted to teach the principle of weight conservation by the following procedure: The child was exposed to two plasticine hunks that he agreed were equal in weight. Then one was deformed before his eyes, and he was asked about the weight of both forms again. Then the two hunks were put on a balance to prove equality of weight. While the children did learn to conserve weight in this situation, Smedslund felt it was somehow different from that acquired "naturally." For example, when the experimenter "cheated" by secretly removing a piece from one of the hunks before weighing it against its pair, children who had acquired the concept *naturally* behaved differently from those who learned it as a result of *training*. The latter children abandoned their newly learned principle of weight conservation when confronted with the unbalanced scales. They reasoned that the deformation changed the weight, since the deformed plasticine now obviously weighed more. Children who had acquired the concept naturally, however, did not abandon it, but suggested other factors that might have produced the observed results. For example, some insisted that a piece must have fallen on the floor, and they looked for it. Even in the face of direct contradictory evidence, these children did not give up the concept, but rather suggested mitigating circumstances—which, of course, were close to the truth of the matter. In Piaget's terms, they did not abandon their previously developed cognitive schemata in order to accommodate the new "facts," but rather deduced new facts by use of the very concept apparently contradicted, and then assimilated the whole phenomenon into their existing cognitive structure.

Other studies confirm Smedslund's results: specific training has negligible effects on the attainment of Genevan intellectual concepts. What does this mean? It means that Genevan intelligence is stable in the face of environmental variations, just as the invariance of its order across cultures would suggest. It means that it is not dependent upon transitory experiences that occur on a random basis, experienced by some children, but not by others. Whatever its causes, they are extremely pervasive and general. To quote Flavell:

> The implication is that there is a deep developmental reality about these structures, and in this sense the learning studies confer a degree of backhanded validity to Piaget's previous assertions that they are, in fact, real existents which exert weight in the young child's intellectual life. Thus, these experiments tend to argue against the view that such structures are entirely artifacts of verbal confusion and misunderstanding, nothing but the momentary and fragile vagaries of an immature and unstable organism. To put it another way, if you cannot get rid of a way of thinking, it must really be there in force. [1963, p. 377.]

SUMMARY

What is intelligence? This chapter considered three approaches to the question: factor analysis, studies of thinking, and the theory of Piaget. What is the answer of each?

Binet himself knew that intelligence was not like length, that it could not be completely described with a single number. It is multidimensional, requiring a separate number for each dimension, just as a three-dimensional cube needs a separate number for length, width, and height. Factor analysis is a complex statistical procedure that seems made to order for this problem, for it is a method by which the independent dimensions may be discovered. Spearman, Thurstone, and Guilford are the big organizers. Spearman thought there was an all-round general factor (e.g., that intelligence did possess some unity) as well as more specific factors, all influenced by the general factor. Thurstone thought there were five independent factors. Guilford believes there may be 120. The picture is obviously in a state of flux. Factor analysis has not yet identified *the* components of intelligence. There are those—Humphreys, McNemar, Vernon—who believe it never will, that it is too subjective to ever provide a basis of agreement. At the present time, according to these critics, there is as much evidence suggesting the unity of intelligence as there is suggesting its fractionization. Perhaps the safest assumption is similar to Spearman's original guess 50 years ago: there is a general factor as well as a few more specific factors, the number of which is open to question, and perhaps which is unanswerable by the factorial technique. Other research strategies are called for.

Research on thinking asks different questions. It asks: "What goes on during intellectual behavior—what is the nature of the process?" What occurs when one thinks? Definitions of thinking, like all definitions, are arbitrary. A good strategy is to choose a definition of thinking that is related to intelligence. Such a definition is that thinking consists of *the rearrangement of symbols into new, meaningful combinations.* Apparently, only man can do this.

Language provides the symbols to be rearranged. The rearrangement of words into meaningful combinations allows many intellectual functions to be carried out; for example, *mediation, planning,* and *concept formation.* Granted, then, the importance of language, how is it learned? How is meaning learned and how is language reproduction learned? Meaning is probably learned in a simple way, analogous to classical conditioning. Reproduction is more complicated. There are at least three factors that must be considered: the autistic consequences of sound imitation, the rewards gained from controlling others by sound, and the biological propensity of man to verbalize. All three are important.

Finally, there is the approach of Piaget. With no formal training in psychology at all, his work is undoubtedly the most influential at the present time. It is not simple, consisting of detailed *assimilations* and *accommodations* of the organism to his environment, with ever new levels of cognitive integration—*schemas*—emerging. The cycle is repeated over and over again as the child progresses through the four great periods of intellectual development: sensorimotor (ages zero to two), preoperational (two to seven), concrete operational (seven to eleven), and formal operational (eleven to fifteen).

BIBLIOGRAPHY

BALDWIN, A. (1967). *Theories of child development.* New York: John Wiley & Sons, Inc.

BINET, A., and SIMON, TH. (1905). Methodes nouvelles pour le diagnostic du niveau intellectuel des anormaux. *L'Année Psychologique*, 11, 191–244.

BLOOMFIELD, L. (1933). *Language.* New York: Holt, Rinehart & Winston, Inc.

BRAINE, M. D. S. (1963). On learning the grammatical order of words. *Psychological review*, 70, 323–348.

BROWN, R. (1965). *Social psychology.* New York: The Free Press of Glencoe, Inc.

BRUNER, J. S. (1964). On going beyond the information given. In R. J. C. HARPER, C. C. ANDERSON, C. M. CHRISTENSEN, and S. M. HUNKA (Eds.), *The cognitive processes.* Englewood Cliffs, N.J.: Prentice-Hall, Inc. Pp. 293–310.

CANTOR, G. N. (1955). The effects of three types of pretraining on discrimination learning in preschool children. *Journal of experimental psychology*, 49, 339–342.

ERVIN, SUSAN, and MILLER, W. R. (1963). Language development. In H. W. STEVENSON, J. KAGAN, and C. C. SPIKER (Eds.), *Child psychology.* Chicago: University of Chicago Press. Pp. 108–143.

FLAVELL, J. H. (1963). *The developmental psychology of Jean Piaget.* Princeton, N.J.: D. Van Nostrand Co., Inc.

GAGNÉ, R. M., and BAKER, K. E. (1950). Stimulus pre-differentiation as a factor in the transfer of training. *Journal of experimental psychology*, 40, 430–451.

GLUCKSBERG, S. (1966). *Symbolic processes.* Dubuque, Iowa: W. C. Brown Co.

GOSS, A. E. (1953). Transfer as a function of the type and amount of preliminary experience with task stimuli. *Journal of experimental psychology*, 46, 419–428.

GUILFORD, J. P. (1967). *The nature of human intelligence.* New York: McGraw-Hill Book Co.

HUMPHREYS, L. G. (1962). The organization of human abilities. *American psychologist*, 17 (7), 475–483.

KELLER, HELEN (1917). *The story of my life.* New York: Doubleday & Co., Inc.

McCARTHY, DOROTHEA (1954). Language development in children. In L. CARMICHAEL (Ed.), *Manual of child psychology.* New York: John Wiley & Sons, Inc. Pp. 492–630.

McNEMAR, Q. (1964). Lost: our intelligence? Why? *American psychologist*, 19 (12), 871–882.

MILLER, G. A. (1965). Some preliminaries to psycholinguistics. *American psychologist.* 20 (1), 15–20.

MILNER, E. (1951). A study of the relationships between reading readiness in grade one school children and patterns of parent-child interaction. *Child development*, 22, 95–112.

MOWRER, O. H. (1960). *Learning theory and the symbolic processes.* New York: John Wiley & Sons, Inc.

PIAGET, J. (1966). *The origins of intelligence in children.* New York: International Universities Press, Inc.

RHEINGOLD, HARRIET, GEWIRTZ, J. L., and NELSON, HELEN W. (1959). Social conditioning. *Journal of comparative and physiological psychology*, 57, 68–73.

ROSSMAN, I. L., and GOSS, A. E. (1951). The acquired distinctiveness of cues: the role of discriminative verbal responses in facilitating the acquisition of discriminative motor responses. *Journal of experimental psychology,* 42, 173–182.

SIEGEL, I. E. (1964). The attainment of concepts. In M. L. HOFFMAN and LOIS W. HOFFMAN (Eds.), *Review of child development research.* Vol. 1. New York: Russell Sage Foundation. Pp. 209–248.

SMEDSLUND, J. (1961). The acquisition of conservation of substance and weight in children. *Journal of Scandinavian psychology,* 2, 71–87.

SPEARMAN, C. (1904). "General intelligence" objectively determined and measured. *American journal of psychology,* 15, 201–293.

SPIKER, C. C. (1956). Stimulus pretraining and subsequent performance in the delayed reaction experiment. *Journal of experimental psychology,* 52, 107–111.

THURSTONE, L. L. (1938). Primary mental abilities. *Psychometric monographs,* No. 1.

VERNON, P. E. (1965). Ability factors and environmental influences. *American psychologist,* 20 (9), 723–733.

WALLACH, M. A. (1963). Research on children's thinking. In H. W. STEVENSON (Ed.), *Child psychology.* Chicago: University of Chicago Press. Pp. 236–276.

5

Learning

In Chapter 2, numerous examples of genetic effects upon behavior were documented. In spite of this fact, however, it is nevertheless the case that learning is probably even more important. The reader can test this assertion in the following way: Make two lists, one naming all the day-to-day behavioral patterns manifested by a normal adult that would occur if he had spent his first 20 years in complete isolation, and the other list naming all those patterns that would occur only if the individual had been exposed to normal cultural influences. The first list would name those patterns determined primarily by heredity, while the second list would name those patterns determined primarily by learning.

A few moments of reflection will convince the reader that the second list would grow prohibitively long in a very short time. Thus, it might be better to begin with the first list, and then conclude that everything else belongs by necessity in the second list. What behavior patterns of a normally behaving adult, then, are determined primarily by heredity? One might start with intelligence, as implied in Chapter 2, although one would then be ignoring the environmental effects on intelligence described in Chapter 3. Even so, it is clear that all that is inherited is a *capacity to learn;* what is learned is controlled by the environment. Thus, a person can act stupidly even though he is very intelligent, because of a lack of learning opportunities. Personality traits fare even worse. Evidence was presented in Chapter 2 that most personality traits do not have a strong genetic component. And even where evidence for a genetic component was presented, the possibility of an even stronger environmental component was not thereby excluded. For example, it is

163

the environment that determines to *what* a person will be emotionally reactive—only the predisposition toward emotionality has a genetic component, not the manifestation itself.

Surely it cannot be denied that sexual behavior is genetically controlled. It is an established fact that lower animals will engage in full-blown sexual behavior upon reaching maturity, even in the absence of opportunity to learn such responses. But this statement is not completely true. Harlow (1962) found that monkeys need considerable social experience if normal mating is to occur. Indeed, he found it almost impossible to successfully mate monkeys who had been isolated, even after considerable "social therapy." The fact is, as one ascends the phylogenetic scale, less and less of sexual behavior remains instinctive. Man, it turns out, is more dependent upon learning in this regard than any other organism.

About the only responses that are controlled primarily by heredity are the simple reflexes: sneezing, sucking, the patellar reflex, the Babinski reflex, blinking, breathing, defecating, etc. If we exclude the simple reflexes, which one would hardly mention in the first place, it is very difficult to name normal human behavior patterns that are not heavily influenced by learning.

We turn, then, to an examination of the facts of learning. The primary question is not *what* is learned but rather what are the *conditions* for learning. At this point, it is well to recall the discussion of causation in Chapter 1. It was emphasized that the search for causation requires experimental control. Applying that rule to the present situation has important implications about the most appropriate research strategy. Suppose it is hypothesized that motivation is necessary for learning. The test of this hypothesis requires that everything be held constant except motivation. If a relationship is then found between amount of motivation and subsequent amount of learning, the hypothesis is confirmed. But holding everything else constant is easier said than done. In order to accomplish it, a very simple situation is selected. And this is the very point where the student of a scientific endeavor encounters a stumbling block: the simple situation designed by the scientist is very different from any real-life situation, and it is the real-life situation the student is interested in. One is tempted to ask: "Why not study real life if it is real life one wants to understand?" The answer by now should be clear to the reader. *The real-life situation leaves too many variables uncontrolled,* thereby precluding a careful cause-effect analysis.

. . . in the instances we have from other sciences of successful development of comprehensive systems of knowledge, analysis and investigation of simple situations under artificial, controlled conditions quite remote from reality have played a decisive role. Thus the physicists' laws of dynamics do not deal directly with real bodies behaving in the real world, but with such abstractions as mass points, frictionless rolling balls, a perfect vacuum, and so on. It is my personal belief that if psychologists are ever to attain a comparable level of synthesis of behavior phenomena they too will have to formulate such abstract concepts and laws.

These statements were made by a well-known experimental psychologist prominent in the area of learning (Spence, 1956, p. 23).

Many of the studies considered in this chapter, and the next, are therefore far removed from ordinary learning situations, and the student should be prepared for the abstract nature of these investigations. Science always involves such abstractions, for experimental control of extraneous variables is otherwise impossible.

THE FUNDAMENTALS OF LEARNING

Many learning theorists would argue that all of the thousands of learning experiences in an individual's lifetime are reducible to a handful of fundamental forms. Many would argue that there are only two kinds of learning that stand out as fundamentally different; all specific instances fit into the one pattern or the other. We shall accept this argument; everyone agrees, at least, that *most* learning experiences can be reduced to one of these two forms. If they are understood, a powerful tool is available to analyze and understand a large number of superficially unrelated learning situations. These two learning processes are called *classical conditioning* and *instrumental conditioning*, although some people prefer the terms "respondent" and "operant" conditioning, respectively. We shall use the former terms.

Classical Conditioning

Classical conditioning is the simplest of all learning situations. It is "classical" because it is the kind of process studied in detail by one of the first men to scientifically study any kind of learning: Ivan Pavlov, a Russian physiologist. It consists, essentially, of the presentation of two stimuli, one after the other, with the second stimulus eliciting any kind of reliable and observable response from the learner. Call the first stimulus S_1, the second stimulus S_2, and the response it elicits, R_2. Classical conditioning can then be described as *any process of the type* $S_1 \longrightarrow S_2 \longrightarrow R_2$. After a number of repetitions of this sequence, the first stimulus begins to elicit parts of the response originally elicited only by the second stimulus: R_2 begins to be elicited by S_1. The result of such conditioning can be diagrammed as $S_1 \mathrel{-\!-\!-\!\rightarrow} R_2$, the dashed line indicating what is learned.

Pavlov, experimenting with dogs, employed the sound of a metronome as S_1, and followed its onset by the presentation of food (S_2) a few seconds later. The food elicited salivation, chewing, swallowing, tail-wagging, etc., the whole pattern symbolized by R_2. The part of it that Pavlov measured was salivation. A tube attached to the dog's salivary glands through a fistula in the cheek delivered saliva to a measuring instrument where the amount of saliva was recorded. After a few trials (exposures to the sequence $S_1 \longrightarrow S_2$), the metronome alone began to elicit a few drops of saliva *before* the food was presented; $S_1 - - \rightarrow R_2$ conditioning had occurred.

Consider another example. During the human infant's first year or so of life, the sequence *mother-nipple* occurs a number of times. The infant makes a reliable response to the insertion of the nipple in its mouth; the sucking reflex is elicited. Thus, the conditions of classical conditioning are satisfied—*mother-nipple-sucking reflex*: $S_1 \longrightarrow S_2 \longrightarrow R_2$. Assuming only three feedings a day (an underestimate), and counting only the first year of life (another underestimate), a total of 1,095 trials is derived. Pavlov found conditioning after 20 or 30 trials. Is it any wonder, then, that the baby begins to smack his lips when he sees and hears mommy?

It is not necessary that the response be "reinforced" in order to become conditioned to S_1. Lipsitt and Kaye (1964) conditioned a sucking reflex in infants to a tone even though the bottle to which the nipple was attached was empty. All that is necessary for conditioning to occur is that S_1 and S_2 be paired together temporally, and that S_2 reliably elicit the response that is to be conditioned to S_1. Classical conditioning is thus often said to be dependent solely upon contiguity between S_1 and S_2, and this assumption is called the basis of "contiguity theory," in as much as some theorists believe that *all* learning is a matter of contiguity between stimuli. We shall see that this is probably not the case for instrumental conditioning.

The time interval between S_1 and S_2 is, of course, of crucial importance. Generally speaking, the greater its duration, the less the amount of conditioning. To put it another way, the greater the duration, the greater the number of trials required before any conditioning takes place. For every response, there is probably some optimal $S_1 \longrightarrow S_2$ interval that leads to the most rapid conditioning. Except for the eyelid response (blinking) and the galvanic skin response (a change in the electrical resistance of the skin), these optimal values are unknown. They are probably quite small, however, since the optimal interval for the eyelid response is about half a second, and the optimal interval for the galvanic skin response is somewhere in the neighborhood of just a few seconds. If several minutes pass between S_1 and S_2, and if the individual pays attention to other stimuli in the meantime, it is unlikely that any conditioning to S_1 will occur.

In the last chapter, learning to read words was discussed as an example of classical conditioning. We shall now be more specific. As mentioned previously, when the child enters the first grade, the teacher attempts to instill a basic vocabulary of written words by pairing the to-be-learned word with the object or picture it represents. Thus, the *word* dog is paired with the *picture* dog. The child does not "understand" the word; he makes no response to it. But he knows what the *picture* is, and he says, "Dog!" The sequence is *word* dog $\longrightarrow$ *picture* dog $\longrightarrow$ "Dog": $S_1 \longrightarrow S_2 \longrightarrow R_2$. After enough trials, the *word* dog alone elicits the response: $S_1 \dashrightarrow R_2$. Classical conditioning has occurred. It should now be clear why it was asserted in the previous chapter that a child's basic reading vocabulary is probably learned as the result of classical conditioning.

Classical Conditioning of Emotions. One of the most important aspects of classical conditioning is that it is probably responsible for most of the emotional responses a person makes to various people, objects, and ideas in his environment. Emotions, of course, are hard to observe. Yet they do occur; they are always present during our waking hours, to a greater or lesser degree, in a positive or negative direction. And, of course, they influence what we do as well as how we feel. We tend to repeat those responses that result in pleasant emotional feelings, and to avoid those responses that result in aversive emotional feelings. Thus, from either a hedonistic or behavioral point of view, emotional reactions are of great importance.

There is considerable evidence that emotional responses can be classically conditioned, and that such conditioning can occur in a very few trials—even in a single trial. All that is required is a stimulus that already elicits a reliable emotional response (S_2), and any other stimulus (S_1) to pair with it. In experiments of this type, shock is often used as S_2, since its intensity and duration can be carefully controlled, and since it elicits a reliable emotional response—fear. Solomon, Kamin, and Wynne describe in vivid terms what happens when a dog is subjected to such conditioning:

When a typical, normal, mongrel dog is put into a small compartment with a steel grid floor, he will usually exhibit persistent exploratory behavior. Thus confined, he will sniff at the grid bars and the corners of the compartment, walk back and forth, intermittently stand up on his hind legs with forepaws against the walls of the compartment, occasionally look over the head-high barrier which separates him from another compartment. . . . If this dog is suddenly stimulated through the steel grid floor by a high-voltage electric shock, of an intensity just below the tetanizing level, the dog will immediately exhibit an intense fear reaction. If the shock is left on during the time the dog remains in the compartment, this intense fear reaction will typically contain these components: The dog will scramble rapidly and vigorously around the compartment, slamming into walls, perhaps, or leaping up against them; he will simultaneously emit a high-pitched screech, will salivate profusely, will urinate and defecate in a manner which could be called "projectile elimination," and will roll his eyes rapidly and jerkily; in addition, his pupils will dilate, portions of his hair will stand on end, small muscle groups all over his body will tremble, and his breathing will consist of short, irregular gasps. Sooner or later the dog's vigorous scrambling movements result in his getting over the barrier into the other compartment, to safety. If the shock is repeated at a later time, the same fear responses will occur again. [1953, p. 1.]

These investigators go on to point out that, after only a few trials—all dogs received fewer than ten shocks—*the dog begins to behave in a similar manner to the compartment itself.* Even after a long series of subsequent "therapy" placements in the compartment without shock—after hundreds of "extinction" trials—the dog still exhibits all the old fear manifestations if he is confined in the compartment and not allowed to escape.

There have been many demonstrations of such emotional conditioning in humans too. Nature has built man in such a way that it is relatively easy to detect the emotion of fear or anxiety—if the experimenter knows about nature's peculiarities. One measurement is the galvanic skin response (GSR), previously mentioned. When a person is exposed to an unexpected or painful stimulus, there is a minute drop in the electrical resistance on the surface of his skin. Modern amplification and recording systems can record this resistance change. Indeed, the GSR is one of the most important responses measured in the "lie detector" test used in criminal investigations.

All that is required to demonstrate classical conditioning of fear is to pair a mild shock with a preceding neutral stimulus and to record the GSR. First, the GSR is elicited only by the shock (although a weak response might be elicited by the neutral stimulus too, because of the novelty of its first few presentations). After a few trials, the GSR response to S_1 increases, indicating that conditioning has begun to occur. Figure 5.1 presents the actual results of such an experiment. In this study, children were presented with two stimuli: a tone and a light. One of the stimuli (a tone for half the children; a light for the other half) was always followed by a brief shock to the arm five seconds later. This stimulus was called the *test* stimulus. The other stimulus, the *control* stimulus, was never followed by shock. Figure 5.1 shows the mean GSR responses to the two stimuli prior to conditioning trials (adaptation) and for 16 conditioning trials. Note how the subjects begin the experiment with equal emotional responses to both stimuli and then gradually be-

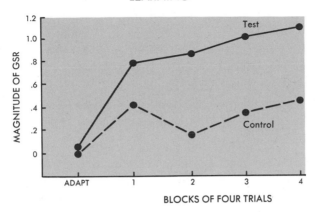

Figure 5.1. Mean GSR responses to a test stimulus paired with shock and a control stimulus not paired with shock (Grings *et al.*, 1962).

come fearful of the test stimulus; it elicits a larger and larger GSR. Responses to the control stimulus remain at about the same magnitude throughout the experiment, showing that it was the pairing of shock with the test stimulus that made the difference.

Positive emotional responses are undoubtedly learned in a similar way, although there is little data to support this assumption. The trouble is that nature has cloaked man's pleasant emotions in a veil of secrecy; there is no known response analogous to the GSR that reflects pleasure the same way the GSR reflects fear. It seems logical, however, that, if pairing a neutral cue with an aversive stimulus results in the conditioning of *negative* emotional responses, then pairing a neutral cue with a positive stimulus should result in the converse—in the conditioning of *pleasant* emotional responses.

There is certainly plenty of anecdotal evidence for such an assumption. Dogs fed food from the refrigerator soon begin to wag their tails whenever the refrigerator door is opened, and cats begin to rub against it and purr; a six-month-old infant will laugh when mother says, "gitchie gitchie goo" and pretends to tickle the infant (in the past, the verbal phrase served as S_1 and actual tickling as S_2); an older child will laugh hysterically when father grabs a foot and says he is going to tickle it; the words "Let's go to a movie" elicit all sorts of pleasant emotional manifestations from children who "understand" the sentence (e.g., have had the sentence, or its equivalent, paired with attendance at enjoyable movies in the past); and so on.

The Importance of Emotional Conditioning. Emotional conditioning is important because the feeling component plays such an important role in day-to-day living. As suggested previously, both the hedonic and behavioral-guidance aspects of emotional responses are important. Concerning the former, imagine what life would be like with no feelings of exhilaration, happiness, love, fear, anger, or hate. It is an interesting philosophical question as to whether it would be worth living at all in the absence of emotional feelings. Unfortunately, no experimental evidence can be cited in support of this argument; that is why it is a *philosophical* argument.

The behavioral-guidance function of emotions—repeating responses that lead to pleasant emotions and avoiding those leading to aversive emotions—is just as important and will be discussed more specifically in the next section. Its importance, though, can be demonstrated by reconsidering the *mother-nipple-sucking reflex* sequence previously discussed. That sequence was described as being very similar to the sequence studied so extensively by Pavlov: *metronome-food-salivation.* It was concluded that the sucking reflex becomes conditioned to mother just as the dog's salivary reflex becomes conditioned to the metronome. Experimental evidence was cited that supports this prediction (e.g., Lipsitt and Kaye, 1964).

What is important is that, just as Pavlov's dogs exhibited other, unrecorded responses that no doubt were also conditioned to the metronome, such as tail-wagging, panting, and whining, so are responses other than sucking conditioned to the human infant's mother. They would include relaxation, cooing, lip-smacking, plus a whole pattern of unobserved physiological responses. *With both the dog and the infant, these responses form a pattern that is the very pattern we label as "loving" or "affectionate." Thus, classical conditioning of emotional responses is no doubt very intimately involved in the origins of the infant-mother affectional bond.* In Chapter 10, we shall examine a considerable amount of objective evidence supporting this assertion. We shall see evidence of another type too: *the mother is also conditioned during the feeding situation,* in a way that may be for better or for worse, in a psychological sense.

It does not take too much imagination to realize that the conditioning of aversive emotional responses can also occur between mother and infant, just as between Solomon's dogs and the shock compartment. Even the feeding situation, which certainly seems to be one heavily dominated by pleasant emotional responses, may not always be so. We shall see evidence of this too in Chapter 10. It is not difficult to see that a tense, nervous mother, who perhaps does not want "another mouth to feed," might handle her infant in a rough manner, with quick movements, bumps, rapid insertions and removals of the nipple, etc., and that the infant begins not to feed very well, because he has been conditioned to fear his mother. Thus, the feeding situation might result in the classical conditioning of aversive emotional responses to the mother and in the development of an infant who is cold and withdrawn. Years later, the mother might be heard to say, ". . . he always was distant. . . ."

Instrumental Conditioning

Instrumental conditioning is often referred to as trial-and-error learning, and therein lies its major difference from classical conditioning. In Pavlovian conditioning, the dog did not have to "earn" the food; the food was actually put directly into his mouth by the experimenter, quite independently of anything the dog might have been doing. Suppose that it was decided that the dog must say "please" before getting the food. The metronome is turned on, *but no food is presented until the dog barks*. If it does not bark within a preselected time period, say one minute, the metronome is turned off, and some time later another trial is started. Only if the dog barks within the one-minute time period does it get the food.

This kind of conditioning is called "instrumental conditioning" because the second stimulus is received only if the animal makes a particular response, or one of a particular class of responses; the response is *instrumental* in obtaining the second stimulus. Of course, the animal does not "know what the rules are" on the first trial and engages in a wide variety of behavior that is not followed by food. The dog may wag its tail (R_a), paw the experimenter (R_b), pant (R_c), scratch its ear (R_d), until ultimately it barks. The first trial may thus be diagrammed as follows: $S_1 \longrightarrow R_a \longrightarrow R_b \longrightarrow R_c \longrightarrow R_d \longrightarrow R_{bark} \longrightarrow S_2 \longrightarrow R_2$. Notice that the sequence is identical to classical conditioning except for the insertion of the response sequence R_a–R_{bark}.

After more trials, the response R_{bark} begins to occur sooner and sooner after the presentation of S_1, and the other responses R_a–R_d simultaneously begin to disappear. Ultimately, the presentation of S_1 elicits a prompt bark, which is followed promptly by S_2, to which the dog responds by eating, R_2. When conditioning is complete, then, the situation may be diagrammed as follows: $S_1 \longrightarrow R_{bark} \longrightarrow S_2 \longrightarrow R_2$.

As an example of instrumental conditioning with children, consider a four-year-old child somewhat large and well coordinated for his age and therefore capable of enforcing his wishes against the possible objections of his smaller playmates. Suppose that he wants a toy truck that belongs to his friend. He may ask for it, and if this does not work (and it is not likely to work with four-year-olds), he may cry. He may then run inside and ask the boy's mother if he can have the truck. She is likely to tell him to play with something else; the truck belongs to her son. Finally, he simply grabs it with one hand while pushing his friend back with the other hand and proceeds to play with it. The sequence of events can be diagrammed as follows: S_1 (friend with desired toy) $\longrightarrow$ Ra (asks for it) $\longrightarrow$ Rb (cries) $\longrightarrow$ Rc (asks mother) $\longrightarrow$ Rd (pushes friend and takes toy) $\longrightarrow$ S_2 (toy) $\longrightarrow$ R_2 (plays with toy).

Now suppose that, over a period of time, similar episodes occur, not only with this one little playmate, but with most of his other playmates as well: a toy or ball or some other object is wanted, or a turn at the swing is desired, etc. Because of his size, our subject always, or at least usually, gets his wish when he uses force. It is not a surprising outcome if this little boy develops into a "bully." The end product may be diagrammed as follows:

S_1 (friend with desired object) $---\rightarrow$ R (object taken by force) $\longrightarrow$

S_2 (possession of object) $\longrightarrow$ R_2 (object played with)

The Role of Reinforcement in Instrumental Conditioning.   Two factors seem to be required in order to produce instrumental conditioning. First, the to-be-learned response must occur soon after S_1. This requirement is actually the same as the contiguity requirement in classical conditioning, although there it was stated that two stimuli, S_1 and S_2, must be contiguous, whereas now it is stated that a stimulus and a response must be contiguous. But since S_2 promptly elicits R_2 in classical conditioning, it can be seen that S_1–S_2 contiguity leads to S_1–R_2 contiguity, and thus stimulus-response contiguity is required in both kinds of learning.

Second, the to-be-learned response must be followed promptly by a reward, S_2. In the first example, in which the dog was taught to say "please," if the bark had not been followed by food (S_2), the dog would no more have learned to bark than to make any of the other responses that went unrewarded. It is this second contiguity requirement that is the essence of the difference between classical and instrumental conditioning. In classical conditioning, the dog gets its reward (food) regardless of what it does; the reward is always presented a fixed temporal interval after presentation of S_1. In instrumental conditioning, on the other hand, this interval may vary from a few seconds to infinity, depending upon how long it takes the organism to make the to-be-learned response. Instrumental conditioning thus requires the presence of a reward. This fact serves as the basis of "reinforcement theory," which stresses the fundamental fact that *responses followed by reinforcement tend to be learned, while responses followed by non-reinforcement tend not to be learned.*

Instrumental Conditioning of Voluntary (Skeletal) Responses.   While emotional responses are largely involuntary (one cannot *will* oneself to be happy or sad), responses involving general bodily movement, such as reaching, bending, running, and talking, are largely voluntary. We "decide" what we are going to do (see Chapter 1 for a discussion of free will). Such "skeletal" responses, involving as they do muscles attached to the skeleton, seem to be learned primarily as a result of instrumental conditioning. The dichotomy, however, is not perfect. We have seen how the basic reading vocabulary can be learned as a result of classical conditioning, even though it involves voluntary responding. Nevertheless, it is generally true that, while involuntary emotional responses are learned primarily as a result of classical conditioning, voluntary skeletal responses are learned primarily as a result of instrumental conditioning.

What this means is that most of the overt behavior patterns we see in other people are learned instrumentally. This is a far-reaching statement, since it includes personality patterns as well as other, more specific responses. After all, what is a "personality pattern" other than a combination of particular responses that remain relatively stable over time and across situations? A person who has an "aggressive personality" is one who responds aggressively in many different situations. Aggressiveness and other personality characteristics, such as dependency, social withdrawal, masculinity, and competitiveness, are probably learned as the result of instrumental conditioning. Instrumental conditioning of aggressiveness was described in the hypothetical example of the little boy who learned to be a "bully" because it "worked"; aggressiveness was reinforced by subsequent possession of the desired object, and hence such behavior presumably became well established. In subsequent chapters, we shall see evidence for such a process in the development of many different behavior patterns.

Classical and Instrumental Conditioning in Combination

It is probable that, whenever an instrumental response is learned, a classically conditioned response is also learned. Such a state of affairs is implied by the similarity between the two sequences as discussed on page 171; the sequence $S_1 \longrightarrow S_2 \longrightarrow R_2$ is involved in both paradigms.

In the case of the dog learning to say "please," suppose that a number of trials have occurred, and the dog is beginning to perform as desired. When the metronome is turned on, the dog barks within a few seconds, receives food, and eats. The sequence can be diagrammed: $S_1 \longrightarrow R_{bark} \longrightarrow S_2 \longrightarrow R_2$. According to classical conditioning theory, whenever the sequence $S_1 \longrightarrow S_2 \longrightarrow R_2$ is experienced, there will be a tendency for R_2 to become conditioned to S_1. Since the sequence under discussion is of this type, it would be predicted that not only would the dog learn to bark in response to the metronome (instrumental conditioning) but it should also learn to respond with R_2 in its presence; the dog should begin to salivate, wag its tail, etc. (classical conditioning). If we were to engage in a bit of anthropomorphizing, we might say that the dog "expects food" when it hears the metronome.

It is well established that such conditioning of R_2 to S_1 actually occurs (e.g., see Shapiro and Miller, 1965; Williams, 1965). When rats are instrumentally conditioned to run down an alley (S_1) by giving them water (S_2) at the end of the alley, they not only learn to run but to also lick their lips as they approach the end of the alley. When dogs are instrumentally conditioned to press a lever in order to obtain food, they also learn to salivate as they press the lever.

The importance of this relationship is that occurrence of the instrumental response is apparently facilitated by occurrence of the classically conditioned response. Shapiro's dogs, for example, did not press the lever unless they salivated, and if they did salivate, they almost always pressed the lever. What does this relationship mean? It means that "expectations of reward" serve to motivate the organism to perform the instrumental response. Hence, the "expectation" is said to provide incentive motivation for the performance of the instrumental response.

There are two logical types of incentive motivation, corresponding to anticipation of pleasant events (as in the preceding examples) and anticipation of aversive events. The latter type is of particular interest because it seems to be involved in a good deal of pathological behavior.

The Paradox of Instrumental Avoidance Conditioning

Suppose a dog is trained to jump over a hurdle to get food. It is deprived of food for, say, 24 hours and is then presented with the hurdle. If the dog jumps the hurdle within 10 seconds, it receives a small amount of food. If it does not, the hurdle is removed, the dog gets no food, and later another trial is begun. It would not be long before the dog promptly jumped the hurdle when it was presented.

Now, what would happen if the dog were allowed to eat to satiation and then were presented with the hurdle? There would be a rather dramatic weakening of its tendency to jump the hurdle. The dog might yawn and go to sleep instead. We might be tempted to anthropomorphize that "the dog is not motivated anymore." We would be right, for *one way of quickly weakening a response is to remove its source of motivation.* We shall see later that this is a general rule applicable to almost all situations.

With this rule in mind, the paradox of instrumental avoidance conditioning can now be described. Suppose the dog is trained to jump the hurdle by a different method. The dog is presented with the hurdle, and if it does not jump in 10 seconds, it is given a powerful electric shock, and the shock is not turned off until the dog jumps the hurdle. Thus, the *pain of shock* takes the place of the *hunger of food deprivation*, and *termination of the pain* takes the place of food (*termination of the hunger*).   all other respects, the experiment is the same as before. At first, of course, the dog would not jump the hurdle, just as it did not do so on the first few trials when hungry. But after escaping the shock a few times, the dog would soon begin to jump the hurdle promptly, within the 10-second time interval, and would thus avoid the shock.

Suppose we then apply the just-discussed rule of lowered motivation. We present the hurdle *but do not follow it with shock, whether the dog jumps it or not.* Having removed the painful source of motivation, the response should quickly weaken. But it does not! The dog keeps right on jumping *as though it were still being shocked.* Furthermore, the dog may go on in this fashion almost indefinitely. Figure 5.2 presents the

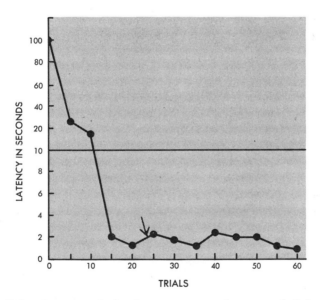

Figure 5.2. Latency of the jump response for one of Solomon's dogs (Turner and Solomon, 1962).

actual behavior of one such dog. The horizontal line drawn at 10 seconds indicates which responses were preceded by shock and which were not. All responses above the line (requiring more than 10 seconds) were preceded by shock, while all responses below the line (requiring less than 10 seconds) were not shocked. This dog never received a shock after the 14th trial, and, in fact, the shock was permanently turned off 10 trials later (indicated by the arrow in the figure). After the 24th trial, in other words, the dog could have "loitered" as long as it pleased, and no shock would have been forthcoming. Yet at the end of 60 trials, this dog was jumping more promptly than ever, in less than two seconds.

Solomon, Kamin, and Wynne (1953) treated 13 dogs in this manner. Figure 5.3 shows the average response latency (time required for the jump response to occur after presentation of the hurdle) for all 13 dogs for 200 trials after the shock was permanently turned off. There is absolutely no sign of response weakening. Rather, the response becomes stronger and stronger, a most peculiar state of affairs, considering the effort of the response (jumping a shoulder-high hurdle).

The paradox of instrumental avoidance conditioning is now clear. *When the painful stimulus that motivated the response in the first place is removed, the response does not necessarily weaken, but may continue unabated for an indefinite number of occurrences.* This paradox is not restricted to dogs; it has been demonstrated many times with other animals (e.g., Miller, 1948) and even with human subjects (Turner and Solomon, 1962). The learning theorist, if he is to explain the strong *resistance to extinction* of an instrumental avoidance response, would seem to be forced to abandon the rule that is applicable in all other learning situations—that when motivation for a response is removed, the response is immediately weakened. Indeed, this theoretical problem plagued learning theorists for some time before Miller offered the solution in 1948.

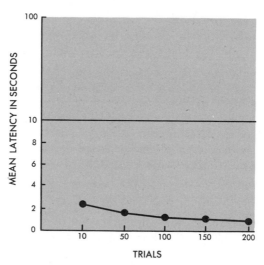

Figure 5.3. Mean latency of jump response for 13 dogs for 200 trials after shock was turned off (Solomon *et al.,* 1953).

Solution of the Paradox

The solution of the paradox is that removal of the shock does not remove all the motivation for the avoidance response. In fact, it does not remove any of the motivation. This can be seen to be the case on logical grounds alone. If the animal makes the avoidance response (by which we mean it jumps the hurdle before the shock is presented), the pain from the shock did not exist on that trial and hence could not possibly have been the motivation for any response. Likewise, pain reduction following the jump response could not possibly have been the reinforcement, since there was no pain to reduce. What does motivate avoidance behavior, then, and what reinforces it? It is fear that motivates avoidance behavior, not pain from the aversive stimulus. The fear that was initially elicited by the aversive stimulus becomes classically conditioned to accompanying stimuli—to the compartment itself. Thus, when the dog is replaced in the compartment, conditioned fear is elicited, and it goads the dog into activity. When the dog jumps the hurdle, the feared compartment is gone, and hence the dog's fear subsides. It is thus the reduction in conditioned fear that provides the reinforcement.

The behavior of Solomon's dogs no longer appears so mysterious. It does not violate the reduced motivation–reduced response rule after all, since shock was not the motivation to begin with. While it is true that shock was the initial source of motivation during those early trials when the dog delayed too long, on later avoidance trials it was fear, not shock, that provided the motivation, and fear reduction, not shock reduction, that provided the reinforcement.

Such avoidance behavior thus forms a vicious circle: the more the organism avoids the feared (but harmless) stimulus, the more likely it will do so in the future, since each such response is reinforced by fear reduction. Such a process often leads to a "fixation"—a response that occurs over and over with no obvious reinforcement or source of motivation. It is because fear is not directly observable that the behavior appears to be a fixation—to be strange and inappropriate to the situation.

Fixations in Children

These same principles apply to children (and adults) as well as to animals. Dollard and Miller (1950) describe the case of a four-year-old boy who manifested a sudden going-to-bed problem.

He protested at having to leave his toys, asked for extra bedtime stories, came down repeatedly for drinks of water, was found sitting at the head of the stairs, expressed various fears of the bedroom that were hard for the parents to understand, and had to be put back to bed as many as fifteen or twenty times in a single night. [P. 159.] *

As the parents applied greater and greater force in an attempt to curb the behavior of their son, he engaged in increasingly strange behavior; he was often found sleeping at the top of the stairs, in the hall, and even at the threshold to his bedroom. Sometimes he had on two or three pairs of pants in spite of the hot summer weather.

Finally, the baffled and perturbed parents gave up and went to a clinic for help. There the following story was gradually reconstructed. The mother had decided to be quite permissive about childhood masturbation because of the strict way her own brother had been handled in this regard by her parents. So she gradually developed an understanding in her son that this behavior was to occur only in the privacy of his own home. But a new maid had at least twice punished him, once when she found him masturbating, at which time she slapped him and told him he was nasty, and once when she saw him fingering his penis, at which time she told him again that he was nasty. The going-to-bed problem developed soon after these episodes.

The clinic advised the mother to require the maid to apologize to the boy and admit she should not have said he was nasty for masturbating, and to make it clear to both the maid and the boy that there was to be no punishment for masturbation. After these steps were taken, the boy's strange behavior quickly disappeared, along with an improvement in his general attitude and spontaneity.

Dollard and Miller's acute analysis of this situation follows:

In this case it seems fairly evident that punishment and disapproval from the maid had attached fear to the response of masturbation. The child seems to have been more strongly tempted to masturbate when he was alone in bed. Thus the fear was aroused in bed. (It is also possible that some of the punishments were administered in bed, but unfortunately we have no evidence on this point.) Whenever the child approached the bed or was told to go to bed, his fear was increased; any response that took him away from bed was reinforced by a reduction in the strength of this fear. He learned a variety of such responses. Putting on the two pairs of pants probably also tended to reduce the fear of masturbation in bed, not by physical escape but by covering up the penis. When the fear of masturbation was reduced, the motivation to perform all of these responses (i.e., symptoms) was removed. Freedom from this source of anxiety and conflict also improved the child's general mood. [P. 160.]

The similarity between this boy's fixated behavior and the behavior of Solomon's dogs is obvious: (1) The dogs were punished in the compartment, and the resulting fear became classically conditioned to the

* From *Personality and Psychotherapy* by J. Dollard and N. E. Miller. Copyright 1950 McGraw-Hill, Inc. Used by permission of McGraw-Hill Book Company.

compartment; the boy was punished while engaging in autoerotic behavior, and the resulting fear became classically conditioned to such behavior. (2) The fear motivated the dogs to be active, and when their activity resulted in a hurdle jump, the compartment was "gone," and fear was reduced; the fear motivated the boy to be active, and when his activity resulted in avoidance of autoerotic temptations (e.g., avoidance of the bedroom), autoerotic inclinations were "gone," and the fear was reduced. (3) The fear reduction reinforced the hurdle-jumping of the dogs, and hence they continued to make the response whenever they were presented with the hurdle; the fear reduction reinforced the bedroom-avoidance and other symptomatic responses of the boy, and hence he continued to make these responses at bedtime.

It can thus be seen that strong parental punishment constitutes a risky child-rearing technique. Involving as it does strong negative emotional responses, subsequent fixated responses may appear that are extremely resistant to ameliorative efforts. It is not coincidental that strong parental punishment frequently appears in the case histories of maladjusted adults. Maladjustment almost always involves persistent response patterns that are inappropriate to the situation, that appear "out of place" to the observer. Such fixations are often the result of avoidance conditioning motivated by strong fears that were learned as the result of classical conditioning.

EXTINCTION

Responses are "unlearned" or weakened as well as learned. The behavior of a ten-year-old is considerably different from his behavior five years previously. Much of his earlier behavior has disappeared, and only remnants remain. Other aspects of his earlier behavior have been so changed that their historical antecedents are completely untraceable. Some of these changes were "accidental" in the sense that the parents took no active, preplanned role in modifying the learning situations. In other behavioral areas, parents are more conscious of their desires and wishes concerning their offsprings' behavior and purposely attempt to weaken undesirable traits as well as to strengthen more acceptable traits. Thus, we must consider the fundamental conditions by which learned behavior is weakened, or "extinguished," to use a more technical word. There are at least five basic ways learned behavior may be weakened: (1) withholding reinforcement (non-reinforcement), (2) teaching a new response to replace the old (counterconditioning), (3) removing or weakening the motivation that energizes a given bit of behavior, (4) punishing the response that is to be weakened, and (5) "habituating" or "adapting out" the response to be weakened.

Non-Reinforcement

An obvious way to weaken a learned response is to remove any reinforcement that usually follows the response. Sometimes this is easy to do. A child who formerly liked to play with his next-door neighbor may become "disinterested" if his playmate ceases to supply the usual social rewards or, perhaps, is forbidden to invite friends over to his swimming pool. Often, however, the removal of reinforcement is difficult: the source of reinforcement is often unknown, and hence its elimination becomes a matter of guesswork. Consider a child who is shy and withdrawn: what is the reinforcement for such behavior? It could come from any one of many different sources. In the author's opinion, treatment of adjustment problems is often a matter of identifying the reinforcement for the "abnormal" behavior. Once it is identified, a "cure" is forthrightly begun by its removal.

Counterconditioning

A second way to weaken undesirable behavior is to replace it with new behavior. The new response thus "counters" the old. An amusing example of counterconditioning in animals is described by Guthrie (1935):

> Two small country boys who lived before the day of the rural use of motor cars had their Friday afternoons made dreary by the regular visit of their pastor, whose horse they were supposed to unharness, groom, feed and water, and then harness again on the departure. Their gloom was lightened finally by a course of action which one of them conceived. They took to spending the afternoon of the visit re-training the horse. One of them stood behind the horse with a hay-fork and periodically shouted "Whoa" and followed this with a sharp jab with the fork. Unfortunately no exact records of this experiment were preserved save that the boys were quite satisfied with the results. [P. 48.]

In this example, the horse's old learned behavior consisted of *stopping* when presented with the auditory stimulus, "Whoa." It was weakened by conditioning a new, different response to the same stimulus: *leaping forward*. Application of the fork was necessary to initially elicit the leaping-forward response, an example of classical conditioning.

Counterconditioning is an extremely important way of weakening fears, in either man or beast. It can be illustrated with a famous three-year-old boy, Peter. Peter is famous because his experience was the first published account of the use of counterconditioning to eliminate a strong fear in a human being (Jones, 1924).

Peter was attending a nursery school where a psychologist noticed that he reacted with strong fear to a white rat and a rabbit. Although the origins of these fears were unknown, it was decided to attempt to weaken them by counterconditioning. The rabbit was chosen as the fear stimulus, and the following procedure was adopted. Every day Peter and three other children were brought to a special room to play together. The three other children were chosen because of their complete absence of fear of the rabbit. While the children played each day, the rabbit was introduced into the room, first for a short period of time, and gradually for longer periods of time. Occasionally, Peter and the rabbit were brought together alone, in order to measure his fear of the rabbit. Over a period of months, the following notes were recorded:

A. Rabbit anywhere in the room in a cage causes fear reactions.
B. Rabbit 12 feet away in cage tolerated.
C. Rabbit 4 feet away in cage tolerated.
D. Rabbit 3 feet away in cage tolerated.
E. Rabbit close in cage tolerated.
F. Rabbit free in room tolerated.
G. Rabbit touched when experimenter holds it.
H. Rabbit touched when free in room.
I. Rabbit defied by spitting at it, throwing things at it, imitating it.
J. Rabbit allowed on tray of high chair.
K. Squats in defenseless position beside rabbit.
L. Helps experimenter to carry rabbit to its cage.
M. Holds rabbit on lap.
N. Stays alone in room with rabbit.
O. Allows rabbit in play pen with him.
P. Fondles rabbit affectionately.
Q. Lets rabbit nibble his fingers.

What actually happened to Peter? According to the notion of counterconditioning, the presence of the three children who not only played with Peter but also showed no fear of the rabbit was essential. These children, by virtue of their playful interactions with Peter, elicited relaxation, laughing, and other behavior we may summarize by the word *happiness*. By initially presenting the rabbit for short periods of time and at a distance, happiness occurred in the rabbit's presence, thus interfering with and suppressing Peter's fear of the rabbit. As Peter learned to relax with the rabbit at a distance, it could be brought closer and closer for longer periods of time, until ultimately no trace of the previous fear remained.

The secret, then, is to get the organism to relax in the presence of the fear stimulus. Relaxation and fear cannot occur simultaneously, and hence relaxation will prevent the fear from occurring. The difficulty, however, is in finding a stimulus that elicits relaxation in the presence of the fear stimulus. In Peter's case, three happy little children (with no rabbit fears) constituted the relaxation stimulus. But it was important that the rabbit was presented at a distance to begin with. Other-

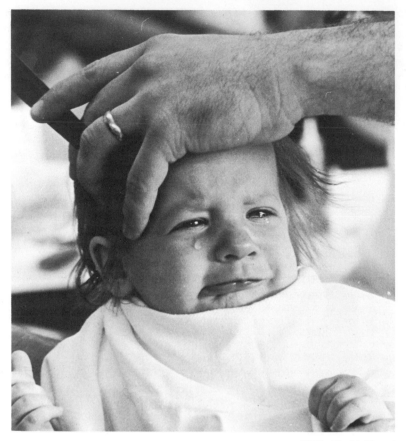

This little boy is experiencing his first haircut. The situation elicits considerable fear. With gentle treatment from the barber, and perhaps a lollypop afterward, fear of the barbershop will be weakened by counterconditioning.

wise, a most unfortunate consequence may have followed. If the rabbit had been brought near enough to elicit strong fear reactions (crying and screaming) in the presence of the three little children, and if such a sequence had been repeated a few times, it is highly probable that Peter would have learned *to fear the children.* Counterconditioning would have still occurred, but it would have been the opposite of the experimenter's intentions. Fear would have countered relaxation in the presence of the children, rather than relaxation countering fear in the presence of the rabbit.

Removing or Weakening Motivation

Reduction of motivation, like counterconditioning, is an extremely important way of controlling human behavior. An example of it has already been described. Recall the case of the four-year-old boy with a going-to-bed problem. His strange behaviors were motivated by a strong fear of the bedroom, which in turn was brought about by a strong fear of autoerotic activities, because of punishment for such behavior by a new maid. His bizarre behaviors disappeared soon after the maid apologized, and it was made clear that autoerotic behavior was acceptable. Why did such treatment result in the weakening of the bedroom-avoidance behavior? Simply because the boy learned not to be afraid of autoerotic tendencies, and hence there was no point (motivation) in avoiding the bedroom. The fear had been removed by counterconditioning (apology of the maid and reassurance of parents, both of which presumably elicited relaxation), and with the motivation thus reduced, behavior motivated by it also disappeared.

Many learning theorists hold that the removal of fear is the fundamental solution to the many kinds of neurotic behavior exhibited by humans. Neurotic behavior is driven by fear, and hence reduction of the appropriate fears and anxieties is held to result in the reduction of the neurotic symptoms. The following case history of a little boy with a strong school phobia describes many ways in which his fear of school was weakened, and hence his avoidance behavior weakened too.

When he was referred for therapy Paul, age 9, had been absent from school for 3 weeks. The summer vacation had ended 6 weeks previously, and on entering the fourth grade, Paul avoided the classroom situation. He was often found hiding in the cloakroom, and subsequently began spending less time at school each day. Thereafter, neither threats, bribes, nor punishments could induce him to re-enter school.

Paul's history revealed a series of similar episodes. During his first day of kindergarten he succeeded in climbing over an extremely high wall and fled home. His first-grade teacher considered him to be "disturbed." Serious difficulties regarding school attendance were first exhibited when Paul entered the second grade of a parochial school. It was alleged that the second-grade teacher who, according to Paul, "looked like a witch," generally intimidated the children and was very free with physical punishment.* Paul retrospectively informed his parents that he felt as though "the devil was in the classroom." At this stage he became progressively more reluctant to enter the school and finally refused entirely. A psychiatrist was consulted and is reported to have advised the parents to use coercion, whereupon Paul was literally dragged screaming to school by a truant officer. Paul was especially bitter

* Vehement complaints from many parents finally led to the dismissal of this teacher.

about his experience with the psychiatrist. "All we did was talk and then the truant officer came." In the third grade Paul was transferred to the neighborhood public school where he spent a trouble-free year at the hands of an exceedingly kind teacher.

. . . .
Following his entry into the fourth grade, the sudden death of a 12-year-old girl, who had been a close friend of his elder sister, profoundly affected the entire family. It is also noteworthy that Paul's father experienced personal stress in his work situation during the child's turbulent second grade, as well as immediately preceding fourth grade. Finally, Paul seemed to have been intimidated by a warning from his eldest sister that fourth grade school work was particularly difficult.

Therapeutic Procedure

. . . .
     The school was situated two and one half blocks away from the home. The routine was for Paul to leave for school at 8:30 A.M. in order to arrive by 8:40. The first recess was from 10:00–10:30; lunch break from 12:00–1:00; and classes ended at 3:30 P.M. At the time when therapy was initiated, the boy was extremely surly and dejected in the mornings (as reported by the parents), refused breakfast, rarely dressed himself, and became noticeably more fearful toward 8:30. Parental attempts at reassurance, coaxing, or coercion elicited only sobbing and further withdrawal.
     Accordingly, the boy was exposed to the following increasingly difficult steps along the main dimensions of his school phobia:

     1. On a Sunday afternoon, accompanied by the therapists, he walked from his house to the school. The therapists were able to allay Paul's anxiety by means of distraction and humor, so that his initial exposure was relatively pleasant.
     2. On the next 2 days at 8:30 A.M., accompanied by one of the therapists, he walked from his house into the schoolyard. Again, Paul's feelings of anxiety were reduced by means of coaxing, encouragement, relaxation, and the use of "emotive imagery" (i.e., the deliberate picturing of subjectively pleasant images such as Christmas and a visit to Disneyland, while relating them to the school situation); . . . Approximately 15 minutes were spent roaming around the school grounds, after which Paul returned home.
     3. After school was over for the day, the therapist was able to persuade the boy to enter the classroom and sit down at his desk. Part of the normal school routine was then playfully enacted.
     4. On the following three mornings, the therapist accompanied the boy into the classroom with the other children. They chatted with the teacher, and left immediately after the opening exercises.
     5. A week after beginning this program, Paul spent the entire morning in class. The therapist sat in the classroom and smiled approvingly at Paul whenever he interacted with his classmates or the teacher. After eating his lunch he participated in an active ball game, and returned to his house with the therapist at 12:30. (Since parent-teacher conferences were held during that entire week, afternoon classes were discontinued.)
     6. Two days later when Paul and the therapist arrived at school, the boy lined up with the other children and allowed the therapist to wait for him in-

side the classroom. This was the first time that Paul had not insisted on having the therapist in constant view.

7. Thereafter, the therapist sat in the school library adjoining the classroom.

8. It was then agreed that the therapist would leave at 2:30 P.M. while Paul remained for the last hour of school.

9. On the following day, Paul remained alone at school from 1:45 P.M. until 2:45 P.M. (Earlier that day, the therapist had unsuccessfully attempted to leave the boy alone from 10 until noon.)

10. Instead of fetching the boy at his home, the therapist arranged to meet him at the school gate at 8:30 A.M. Paul also agreed to remain alone at school from 10:45 A.M. until noon provided that the therapist return to eat lunch with him. At 1:45 P.M. the therapist left again with the promise that if the boy remained until school ended (3:30 P.M.) he would visit Paul that evening and play the guitar for him.

11. Occasional setbacks made it necessary to instruct the lad's mother not to allow the boy into the house during school hours. In addition, the teacher was asked to provide special jobs for the boy so as to increase his active participation and make school more attractive.

12. The family doctor was asked to prescribe a mild tranquilizer for the boy to take on awakening so as to reduce his anticipatory anxieties.

13. After meeting the boy in the mornings, the therapist gradually left him alone at school for progressively longer periods of time. After 6 days of this procedure, the therapist was able to leave at 10 A.M.

14. The boy was assured that the therapist would be in the faculty room until 10 A.M., if needed. Thus, he came to school knowing the therapist was present, but not actually seeing him.

15. With Paul's consent the therapist arrived at school shortly after the boy entered the classroom at 8:40 A.M.

16. School attendance independent of the therapist's presence was achieved by means of specific rewards (a comic book, and variously colored tokens which would eventually procure a baseball glove) contingent upon his entering school and remaining there alone. He was at liberty to telephone the therapist in the morning if he wanted him at school, in which event he would forfeit his rewards for that day.

17. Since the therapist's presence seemed to have at least as much reward value as the comic books and tokens, it was necessary to enlist the mother's cooperation to effect the therapist's final withdrawal. The overall diminution of the boy's anxieties, together with general gains which had accrued to his home situation, made it therapeutically feasible for the mother to emphasize the fact that school attendance was compulsory, and that social agencies beyond the control of both therapists and parents would enforce this requirement eventually.

18. Approximately 3 weeks later, Paul had accumulated enough tokens to procure his baseball glove. He then agreed with his parents that rewards of this kind were no longer necessary. [Lazarus et al., 1965, pp. 226–227.]

Steps 1 through 15 were all geared toward reducing Paul's fear of school by associating school a little at a time with more pleasant experiences. Once this fear was reduced, there should have been a reduction in his school-avoidance behavior, for there should have been little motivation, and little reinforcement, to maintain the responses. That this actually occurred is indicated by the fact that a one-year follow-up revealed that Paul had not only continued going to school with the same regularity as at the end of treatment but had actually improved beyond that level.

Punishing the Response To Be Weakened

A fourth way that behavior may be weakened is to punish the response, i.e., to present an aversive, painful stimulus after the undesired response has occurred. Several such pairings should result in a form of conditioning the reader is now acquainted with; the fear elicited originally by the punishment will become conditioned to the undesired response. Hence, whenever the response begins to occur, fear will be elicited; when the response ceases, the associated fear will also cease. Thus, the organism will be reinforced for stopping the response. It was just such a process that was hypothesized to explain the four-year-old's going-to-bed problem. His fear of going to bed was reduced when he stayed up, and hence he effectively stopped going to bed. Unfortunately, going to bed was not "undesired" in this case, so that other steps had to be taken (weakening of the fear response) in order to strengthen the going-to-bed response again.

Thus, fear may either strengthen or weaken a response, depending upon its temporal relationship to the response. If it occurs before the response, and is reduced afterwards, the response will be strengthened. If it occurs after the response, the response will be weakened. When parents consistently spank a two-year-old toddler after it has wandered off the sidewalk onto the road, the toddler eventually abandons such behavior. It is abandoned because cessation of "road walking" is reinforced by fear reduction. It is not that the punishment directly weakens the preceding behavior; rather, it indirectly weakens it by strengthening a new behavior pattern—the response-fear pattern.

While we have seen that severe punishment, or "trauma," may lead to serious fixation responses, one should not jump to the conclusion that punishment is always undesirable. Applied judiciously, with careful attempts to attach the resulting emotional responses to the right cues—to the forbidden response itself—punishment can and does have beneficial effects. The following case history, while extreme, is a case in point. It describes a therapeutic program devised for a six-year-old boy with a serious school phobia as well as other "acting out" behavior problems. His parents were helpless. He disobeyed them at will, stole money from his father's wallet, turned off all the lights in the house by breaking into the padlocked fuse box, broke out of his room when locked in, etc. He was finally taken to a psychologist.

While a secretary watched Rusty to prevent his slipping away—he made one half-hearted attempt to walk off down the hall—his parents were told that what they needed most in order to prevent such misbehavior from continuing was courage. They were instructed to buy a screen door latch for Rusty's bedroom door to use, when necessary, to keep him in his room when he had been sent there as a disciplinary measure. Spankings were suggested as appropriate only if they produced the desired results—they had been ineffective up to that point. We pointed out that, unless they literally imprisoned Rusty in his room, he had the power to run away at any time he chose. That since it was impractical from every point of view to make Rusty a permanent prisoner, they must admit to his ability to leave the home or the school, but that they should make the consequences of such behavior so drastic that he would decide for himself to be cooperative. We instructed them to tell Rusty that, if he ran away, he would be locked out of the house and would not be let in until he apologized and promised to behave. We further instructed them to refuse to give Rusty his meals while he misbehaved if it became necessary to do so in order to impress upon him that he could not flaunt authority and enjoy family privileges. They were urged to report regularly by telephone on the progress of their efforts.

Such a regimen appears harsh, but it has a distinct advantage. It is highly unlikely that a parent would not have ambivalent feelings toward a child manifesting a severe behavior disorder. With verbal or other symbolic forms of discipline, ambivalence may be expressed to a degree which seriously reduces or even reverses the intended effect of parental action. When reward and punishment are kept on a more basic physical level, there is a much higher degree of efficiency in the learning situation. Both the child *and* the parents understand the rewards and punishments, and are able to recognize and profit from positive changes when they occur.

We spoke to Rusty for only a few minutes. He at first acted the part of a frightened, mistreated, misunderstood child, backing into a corner, hiding his face in his arms, and whimpering. He would not talk. (This was less than 3 hours after he had successfully manipulated a strange housewife and a police officer to suit his purposes.) We pulled him onto our knee and began by commenting that he must be very angry to act the way he had, and that we would guess that he was mad at his mother. We then suggested that his misbehavior was a lot of trouble for him and that it probably wasn't worth the effort. At this point he slid off our lap and began to talk in a very unconcerned manner about something trivial which had happened the day before. We terminated the interview and the family left. His mother reported that as soon as they were in their car, Rusty commented to his parents that they must be pretty mixed up to need to go to a doctor to find out how to make him behave. No attempt had been made to elicit important content during the few minutes spent with Rusty, but it was concluded that this child's ability to shift his behavior and expressions of affect so rapidly and dramatically indicated a minimal loss of emotional control and a good potential for learning from direct interaction with his parents. His mother's account continues.

Wednesday morning Rusty attempted to run away from home, but his father caught him and locked him in his room. He proceeded to try to rip out the window screen and escape. All implements which he could use for this purpose were removed from his room, but he continued to work at the screen with his belt buckle. In later morning, he was let out so that he could be fed and dressed for school. He immediately darted into the bathroom and locked the door, where he stayed for about an hour before the door could be opened. He refused lunch and was dressed by force and carried by his father to school, kicking and screaming, and deposited in the classroom.

The teacher closed the door and Rusty jumped out of the window and left school. He remained away from home just as before until after 3 o'clock. He was locked out of the house because of this until after 5:30 that evening.

At 5:30 he came to the door and apologized. He was let in, fed, and allowed to follow a normal routine through the evening.

Thursday and Friday he stayed in school. Then Friday, after supper (he ate a very large meal) Rusty asked if he could go out and play. When told he couldn't, he left anyway. When he came back and found the door locked (which he had been told before he left would happen) he became pretty upset. He beat on the door with a broom, rang the doorbell, and when he found out this did him no good, he went to the fuse box and proceeded to push all the trippers, thereby turning off all the lights except the one in the garage, where he began playing. He also pushed down the lever which turned off the air conditioner. (His mother telephoned during this period and was quite upset. She was advised to take the other children and leave home for an hour, but she could not bring herself to do so.) He finally went to a neighbor's house and asked to use the phone. He called his daddy at work and told him that he was locked out. His daddy advised him to come apologize, and when he did he was let back into the house.

Saturday (This was Rusty's sixth birthday. His party and presents had been cancelled because of his bad behavior. His mother first greeted him in the morning by singing "Happy Birthday to You." This obviously ambivalent act threw Rusty into a violent fit of anger and precipitated a behavioral crisis which was the turning point in his relationship with his mother.) I told him he had to stay in his room. I locked him in, so he then cut his screen and was going to get out a window. I told him if he wanted out I would let him out the front door, but that he could not get back in. He started to walk away from the house (without socks and shoes). In about 5 minutes he was back to get his bicycle, but I locked the garage so he couldn't get it. So, he went and turned off the air conditioner at the fuse box. (The box had been padlocked, but he broke the lock.) When I told him I didn't care, he then said that he was going to climb the pole and cut the wires at the pole. He then climbed on the roof and remained there while I got in the car with the other children and drove off. When we returned about an hour later, he was playing in the backyard. (At noon his mother called and reported that she could not go on. Her husband was contacted and told that he was to go home at once and back up his wife. He was instructed to take his wife's side in the battle and to tell Rusty that any more destruction of property would be met by him with extremely severe punishment. Rusty did not come in during the 3 hours his father was at home, but neither did he make a pest of himself. At this point he had missed breakfast and lunch.) He had been given two deadlines—to come in by 12 o'clock in order to receive his lunch and 4 o'clock in order to receive his supper. He was also told by his father that when he came in he would have to spend the rest of the day in his room. He chose to stay outside until 6:15 P.M. at which time it began to rain. When he came in, he was spanked, bathed, and put in bed without supper.

This was putting it mildly. After her husband returned to work, Rusty's mother began to feel really angry for the first time. Whether she was most angry at Rusty, her husband, or the author is a moot question, but when Rusty finally came in she exploded, and he got the whipping of his life. This episode, 4 days after the family's consultation, was the turning point in overcoming Rusty's misbehavior. His mother was learning that she was capable of continuing disciplinary pressure long enough to force Rusty to choose to cooperate, but that she must not initiate hostile, rejecting behavior or it would drive him to further rebellion. Rusty was learning that rebellion, while exciting, was too costly in terms of creature comforts when he went beyond certain limits. The effectiveness of the change in relationship between Rusty and his mother is seen in her final account.

Rusty was an angel all day Sunday and most of Monday. Monday evening while at the dinner table, Rusty and his sister began to get rather wild—giggling and talking—everything except eating. So, they were warned that if they weren't finished by a certain time, their dinner would be thrown out and they would get nothing until breakfast. They continued to misbehave, so the food was thrown out. Well, Rusty was furious. He pushed the table, and in doing so turned over some coffee. He was told to go to his room. Instead he ran and locked himself in the bathroom. He was ignored. In about 15 minutes he came out and went to his room. A few minutes later when I checked on him, I found him sound asleep on the floor.

This was Rusty's final gesture of rebellion. It occurred 6 days after the family's consultation. During the following 11 months, Rusty has remained a spirited but not a rebellious boy. He was tested with the Wechsler Intelligence Scale for Children and found to be of bright-normal intelligence.
A procedure such as this produces rapid results—or none at all. In properly selected cases the probability of success is high, and the major risk involved lies in the assumption that the parent or parents are capable of initiative, rapid learning, and insight when faced with the responsibility for all of the actions required for repairing the relationship with their child. Many parents deserve such a vote of confidence. [Boardman, 1962, pp. 295–297.]

Habituating the Undesired Response

The phenomenon of *habituation* has been known for a long time. It consists of the gradual weakening of a response merely as a result of its continued elicitation by a given stimulus. Habituation is most likely to occur when a new or novel stimulus elicits general exploratory behavior; the exploratory behavior gradually weakens as the novel stimulus becomes old. What parent is not aware of a child's insatiable appetite for new toys, and what children's TV program does not try to take advantage of it?

Habituation is somewhat of a temporary phenomenon, tending to disappear in time. Thus, a child may play with an old toy that has been lost and out of sight for a long time, and an adult may read a book a second time after a long delay interval. But habituation is likely to occur sooner the second or third time around, and to last longer. Thus, it is not to be passed over lightly. It is an easy, painless way to weaken a response. Indeed, it often becomes a nuisance in experiments involving avoidance conditioning: the fear response elicited by the shock weakens with successive exposures to the shock, resulting in reduced motivation for the instrumental response. To compensate for this habituation, the shock is often increased in intensity with each successive exposure, up to some maximum amount.

SUMMARY

The human organism is probably more plastic than any other form of life. It is probably more modifiable by the environment than any other organism.

Behavioral modification as a result of past experience is called learning. Two fundamental types of learning are classical conditioning and instrumental conditioning. Classical conditioning is defined as a result of the sequence $S_1 \longrightarrow S_2 \longrightarrow R_2$. Repetitive exposure to any such sequence results in an increasing tendency for R_2 to become conditioned to S_1. It is difficult to conceptualize a simpler type of learning, and therein lies its importance. Individuals are exposed to such sequences every day of their lives, and, accordingly, they learn every day of their lives. Such learning has been documented in the first few days of life, in a sequence all infants are systematically exposed to: mother $\longrightarrow$ nipple in mouth $\longrightarrow$ sucking reflex.

One important kind of classical conditioning is the learning of emotional responses. Such conditioning can be of either a positive or negative kind, depending upon whether the emotional response is pleasant or aversive. There is evidence that aversive emotional responses can be conditioned very quickly, even in a single trial if the emotional response is intense enough. Such conditioning is extremely important, because emotions not only contribute to feelings of joy and misery, but they also influence the more overt responses a person makes in a given situation. Responses leading to pleasant emotions tend to be repeated, while responses leading to unpleasant emotions tend not to be repeated.

The second fundamental type of learning is instrumental conditioning. It is similar to classical conditioning in that the same sequence is involved. It is different in that a fourth element enters the sequence: S_2 does not occur unless a specific kind of response precedes it. If S_2 is a reward, the response that precedes it becomes conditioned to S_1; if S_2 is not a reward, the preceding response is not learned. Thus, reinforcement, as well as $S_1 \longrightarrow R$ contiguity, seems to be important in instrumental conditioning, while only the latter seems crucial in classical conditioning.

Voluntary skeletal responses are learned primarily as a result of instrumental conditioning. If the parent manipulates rewards in an appropriate manner, he has a powerful tool to guide the personality development of the child. This consists essentially of reinforcing those response patterns the parent wants to strengthen, and not reinforcing contradictory responses. It is through the operation of reinforcements, controlled consciously and unconsciously by parents, teachers, peers, and others—by the child's culture—that personality is formed. These overt responses, in combination with emotional responses that have been learned as a result of classical conditioning, form the total personality constellation—the emotional as well as the behavioral.

The two fundamental kinds of learning are not independent; wherever instrumental conditioning occurs, classical conditioning occurs too. One important result of this complexity is the learning of incentive motivation, reward anticipations that serve to motivate the performance of instrumental responses leading to the reward—or avoidance responses leading away from a feared situation.

A peculiarity of the latter case, called instrumental avoidance conditioning, is that the avoidance response often perseveres long after the original cause of the fear has disappeared. Such "fixations" are perplexing to the observer, since he usually is unaware of the original "traumatic" event(s), and hence feels the behavior is strange and inappropriate. Such conditioning is often seen in the backgrounds of adults with personality disorders.

Just as there are fundamental ways of learning a response, there are fundamental ways of weakening (extinguishing) a response. Five of these ways are (1) non-reinforcement, (2) counterconditioning, (3) removing the source of motivation, (4) punishment, and (5) habituation. Non-reinforcement is most appropriate for the extinction of instrumental responses; counterconditioning is most appropriate for the extinction of classically conditioned responses; the remaining three can be employed in either situation, although habituation would seem to be most appropriate in situations involving novelty and curiosity.

BIBLIOGRAPHY

BOARDMAN, W. K. (1962). Rusty: a brief behavior disorder. *Journal of consulting psychology*, 26, 293–297.
DOLLARD, J., and MILLER, N. E. (1950). *Personality and psychotherapy*. New York: McGraw-Hill Book Co.

192   BASIC PROCESSES OF DEVELOPMENT

Grings, W. W., Lockhart, R. A., and Dameron, L. E. (1962). Conditioning autonomic responses of mentally subnormal individuals. *Psychological monographs,*
76 (39).
Guthrie, E. R. (1935). *The psychology of learning.* New York: Harper & Row.
Harlow, H. F. (1962). The heterosexual affectional system in monkeys. *American
psychologist,* 17, 1–9.
Jones, Mary C. (1924). A laboratory study of fear: the case of Peter. *Journal of
genetic psychology,* 31, 308–315.
Lazarus, A. A., Davison, G. C., and Palefca, D. A. (1965). Classical and operant
factors in the treatment of a school phobia. *Journal of abnormal psychology,* 70,
225–229.
Lipsitt, L. P., and Kaye, H. (1964). Conditioned sucking in the human newborn.
Psychonomic science, 1, 25–26.
Miller, N. E. (1948). Studies of fear as an acquirable drive: I. Fear as motivation
and fear-reduction as reinforcement in the learning of new responses. *Journal of
experimental psychology,* 38, 89–101.
Shapiro, M. M., and Miller, T. M. (1965). On the relationship between conditioned
and discriminative stimuli and between instrumental and consummatory responses.
In W. F. Prokasy (Ed.), *Classical conditioning.* New York: Appleton-Century-
Crofts, Inc. Pp. 269–301.
Solomon, R. L., Kamin, L. J., and Wynne, L. C. (1953). Traumatic avoidance
learning: the outcomes of several extinction procedures with dogs. *Journal of ab-
normal and social psychology,* 48, 291–302.
Solomon, R. L., and Wynne, L. C. (1953). Traumatic avoidance learning: acquisi-
tion in normal dogs. *Psychological monographs,* 67 (4).
Spence, K. W. (1956). *Behavior theory and conditioning.* New Haven, Conn.:
Yale University Press.
Turner, Lucille H., and Solomon, R. L. (1962). Human traumatic avoidance
learning. *Psychological monographs,* 76 (40).
Williams, D. R. (1965). Classical conditioning and incentive motivation. In W. F.
Prokasy (Ed.), *Classical conditioning.* New York: Appleton-Century-Crofts, Inc.
Pp. 340–357.

6

Motivation

INTRODUCTION

In the preceding chapter, an important aspect of behavior, instinctive as well as learned behavior, was purposefully slighted for pedagogical reasons. Its importance can be illustrated by reconsidering one of the learning examples. In the first example of instrumental conditioning, where a dog is taught to say "please" when the metronome is turned on, the procedure involved turning on the metronome, waiting for the dog to bark, and then promptly rewarding it with a bit of food.

Now, what if the dog simply does not bark? What if he yawns and goes to sleep? With such a "stubborn" dog, it would be impossible to reward the response of barking, because it does not occur. Thus, the dog would not be taught to "speak." There is a general rule implied in this reasoning: *a response must occur in order to be strengthened (learned).*

Is there a way out of this problem? Yes. Make sure the dog is hungry when the metronome is turned on. If hungry, the dog will not fall asleep. Hunger will keep it awake and active. Hunger will energize a variety of different responses: looking, sniffing, locomoting, tail-wagging, whining—and barking. Any condition that energizes a wide variety of responses in this manner is called a source of *motivation* or *drive*. Hunger is thus one source of drive, and it is objectively defined in terms of number of hours of food deprivation. It thus ranges from low motivation (0 hours' food deprivation) to moderate motivation (say, 10 hours' food deprivation) to high motivation (say, 24 hours' food deprivation).

If the dog is hungry, it will not only be more likely to bark than if it

193

is not hungry, it will also be more likely to consume the reward—to eat the food. Indeed, if the dog has just been fed to satiation (zero hours' food deprivation), it is unlikely that the dog will eat the food, and hence it will be impossible to reinforce the dog for barking. Thus, hunger serves two essential roles: it goads the dog into activity, and it insures that the reward will be consumed—that it will be a reward.

Now, since hunger is called a source of motivation, and since the eating of food reduces hunger, it seems natural to say that *a reward is something that reduces motivation.* It seems natural to ask, then, are there any rewards that do not reduce motivation? Let us explore this question by asking what procedures other than the hunger-food sequence could be used to teach the dog to bark.

Surely, thirst could be used just as effectively as hunger, and water could be used as the reward. What else could be used? We could shock the dog if it does not bark within 10 seconds after the onset of the metronome, just as Solomon's dogs were shocked for not jumping over the hurdle in 10 seconds. As soon as a bark occurs, the shock could be turned off. If the dog barks before it is time to be shocked, and thus avoids the shock, we would reward it. How? By turning off the metronome, which the dog has learned to fear. Thus, a shock–bark–no shock or a fear–bark–no fear sequence could be used.

What else? The reader should use his imagination to invent some other possibilities. The point is he will find it difficult to think of a reward that does not reduce some source of motivation. It is for this reason that a *drive-reduction theory* becomes tempting—to assume that all rewards involve a reduction in drive. Such a theory has its advocates, although there are others who feel it is a bit out of favor at the moment. We shall leave the question open, since it is more the concern of learning theory than of child psychology. It is worth noting, however, that of the thousands of animal experiments concerned with learning, hunger, thirst, and pain are used most often as sources of motivation, and food, water, and pain reduction are used most often as rewards. The reason they are used so frequently is simple: they work better than most other methods.

Motivation is just as important in classical conditioning as it is in instrumental conditioning, although reinforcement is of less importance. Pavlov himself noted that it was difficult to condition a dog to salivate if it were not hungry. The reason is that the dog tended not to respond with salivation to the food, and since R_2 did not occur, it could not be conditioned to the metronome. Thus, motivation is as essential in classical conditioning as in instrumental conditioning. In both situations, something is required to goad the animal into activity, thus making it possible for the correct response to occur.

THE PROBLEM OF HUMAN MOTIVATION

Humans too must be motivated if they are to be active, if they are to learn. Since they suffer from the same pangs of hunger and thirst, and the same pain of bodily insult, as do other animals, it would seem that a list of the same drives that motivate most of animal behavior would also account for human behavior. But it does not. When the variety of circumstances under which the occurrence of human activity and learning is considered, it becomes manifestly apparent that such a list would not do. For example, children spend a good part of each day playing. Usually, this behavior occurs in the absence of such deprivations. Thus, children eat a hearty breakfast, drink a large glass of orange juice, go to the toilet, and then run outside and engage in vigorous play activity. They are not hungry, thirsty, or prodded by painful stimuli. Where does the motivation for such activity lie? Adults, too, spend a good deal of time engaged in behavior apparently not motivated or reinforced by such conditions. Witness the research scientist who abandons more profitable activities (i.e., activities that would earn him more money to spend on food, shelter, etc.) to pursue a line of inquiry that nets him little, and often imperils his health, who "exists" rather than "lives," according to his perplexed fellow man. At a less extreme level, consider the common-place adult activities of an evening's poker game, a morning's walk, a tennis match, or reading a book. These activities also occur in the relative absence of the drives and reinforcements previously considered.

Such "motivationless" behavior patterns have perplexed psychologists for a long time. Harlow, a prominent student of motivation, wrote as follows:

> Motivationally, man is a strange, if not bizarre, creature: he is the only known organism to arise in the morning before he is awake, work all day without resting, continue his activities after the diurnal and even the crepuscular organisms have retired to rest, and then take narcotics to induce an inadequate period of troubled sleep. But lest we decry man's motivational mechanisms, we should point out that without them we would not have the steam engine, the electric light, the automobile, Beethoven's Fifth Symphony, Leonardo da Vinci's undigested 'Last Supper," gastric ulcers, coronary thrombosis, and clinical psychologists. Indeed, we might well regard this aggregate as the human motivation syndrome. [1953, p. 24.]

Another prominent psychologist, Berlyne, writes in a similar vein:

> The cases that raise the most acute motivational problems, however, . . . are those in which perceptual or intellectual activities are engaged in for their own sake. . . . In these cases, none of the more conspicuous kinds of motivation and reward may be in evidence. . . . The result is what we normally classify as play or, to use a more technical and comprehensive term, "ludic behavior" (Latin *ludare*, to play).

and:

> In human beings, ludic behavior includes everything that is classified as recreation, entertainment, or "idle curiosity," as well as art, philosophy, and pure (as distinct from applied) science. To gauge the strength of the motivations to which these activities respond, one has only to think of the immense industries that have grown up to cater to them and consider the economic resources that are devoted to them by advanced societies, i.e., those that have self-preservative necessities most firmly under control. [1960, pp. 4, 5.] *

What do these quotations imply? Simply that our notions of motivation, based on careful animal experimentation, tend to not explain a good portion of human behavior. At the present time, human motivation is but poorly understood. Too much behavior appears to occur in the absence of motivation, and to be learned in the absence of drive reduction. But some gain has been made in recent years, and this chapter will survey this recent work. The reader will be sorely disappointed if he expects a unified, articulate theory of human motivation to be presented, for such a theory does not exist. Rather, a few new sources of motivation have been tentatively identified, and it is to these we now turn.

IMPORTANT HUMAN DRIVES

Boredom and Curiosity

One of the motivation-reward pairs the reader probably did not think of in the previous discussion is related to a concept that was presented in Chapter 3—stimulus deprivation. It was shown there that stimulus deprivation is associated with intellectual impairment, both in animals and man. There is another line of evidence, though, which shows that *stimulus deprivation is highly motivating if the organism is in his wakefulness cycle.* In other words, if the animal has just finished a good night's sleep and is wide awake, stimulus deprivation is "boring" and unpleasant. Like other unpleasant feelings, the organism is goaded into activity until the unpleasant feeling is removed. Responses that are successful tend to be learned. Thus, boredom is reduced by novel stimuli, and the boredom-novelty duo takes its place alongside the other drive-reward duos previously discussed.

Recent evidence indicates that stimulus deprivation becomes a more and more important source of motivation as one moves up the phylogenetic scale to man. It is difficult to imagine a worm becoming bored with his subterranean environment, but easier to imagine a dog or cat becom-

---

* From *Conflict, Arousal, and Curiosity* by D. E. Berlyne. Copyright © 1960 McGraw-Hill, Inc. Used by permission of McGraw-Hill Book Company.

ing "sick" of a cage, and very easy to imagine a chimpanzee or monkey as reacting with boredom to a deprived environment. Indeed, Köhler, while studying apes enclosed inside a wooden pen, peeked through a hole to observe them and was somewhat surprised to find one peeking out at him.

A systematic study of boredom in monkeys was reported by Butler (1957). He put monkeys one at a time into an aluminum box about 2½ feet square, which they could not see out of. By pushing a panel mounted on one wall, a window was opened for 12 seconds, allowing a view of a monkey colony outside the box. Two questions were asked: (1) Would the monkeys learn to push the panel when the only obvious reinforcement was the 12-second view of the monkey colony outside? (2) Could the number of panel pushes be varied by varying the preceding amount of visual deprivation?

The answer to both questions was yes. Not only did the monkeys learn to push the panel, but after having learned it, the number of responses was successfully varied by manipulating the amount of preceding confinement with the window shut. Monkeys were confined in the box with the window shut for zero, two, four, or eight hours, after which the panel was made available, and the number of responses occurring in the next test hour counted. These data were compared with the number of responses occurring in a test hour that was preceded by no confinement, although even then there was confinement during the test hour itself in between the 12-second intervals when the window was open.

Figure 6.1 presents the relationship between the number of hours of visual deprivation and the subsequent panel-pushing behavior. As the deprivation time increased, so did the number of subsequent panel pushes, rising from an average of about 380 with just a few seconds of deprivation to over 500 with eight hours of deprivation. Thus, stimulus deprivation is seen to function the same way as food or water deprivation: the greater the deprivation, the higher the motivation of the animal, and the more active it becomes.

A recent exploratory study with human infants confirms these inferences. Rheingold (1963) asked if a normal six-month-old infant could be taught a response if the only reinforcement was boredom reduction. The infant was seated in a "baby seat" with a rubber ball mounted on a firm stem within easy reach, as indicated in the accompanying photograph. Each time the infant touched the ball, a movie projector was automatically turned on, displaying colored patterns slowly moving against a dark background.

An initial 10-minute session was used to determine the infant's tendency to touch the ball with no subsequent increase in visual stimulation; that is, the projector remained off for the entire session. In the

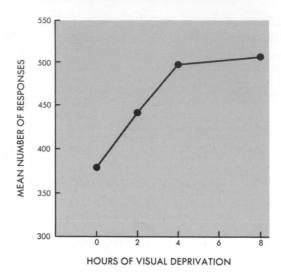

Figure 6.1. Mean number of responses as a function of visual deprivation (Butler, 1957).

second 10-minute session a week later, the projector was turned on for a second and a half every 2½ seconds, quite independent of the infant's behavior. In a third weekly session, the projector was turned on for 1½ seconds only if the infant touched the ball.

If we analyze these three conditions in terms of boredom and boredom reduction, as defined by stimulus deprivation and stimulus variation, respectively, it becomes possible to order the conditions in terms of the predicted amount of ball touching. Let us therefore assume that, if the projector is off, boredom is greater than if it is on, and that motivation is therefore greater when the projector is off. Likewise, onset of the projector is reinforcing, since it reduces boredom.

Condition one, with the projector off for the full 10 minutes, would thus involve relatively high motivation because of stimulus deprivation, but no reinforcement for ball touching. Condition two, with the projector turned on every 2½ seconds, would result in lower motivation, since there is a periodic increase in visual stimulation, but would produce little reinforcement for ball touching, since activation of the projector is not contingent upon the infant's behavior. Thus, conditions one and two are about equal in terms of reinforcement for ball touching, and condition one provides more motivation than condition two. We would thus expect activity to be greater in condition one, and therefore would expect more ball touching in condition one than in condition two. Condition three, with the projector off until ball touching occurs, and then on for

A subject in the Rheingold experiment. Pushing the ball results in colors appearing on the wall in front of the infant.

1½ seconds, provides high motivation prior to ball touching and reinforcement after ball touching. Thus, condition three, with both high motivation and reinforcement, should result in the greatest amount of such behavior.

The number of responses in conditions one, two, and three was 65, 39, and 215, respectively. The predictions are confirmed. The difference in behavior between conditions one and two was apparently produced by motivational differences determined, in turn, by stimulus deprivation measured in minutes (each session was only 10 minutes long). Likewise, the tremendous increase in ball handling during session three was due to reinforcements consisting of stimulus variation for 1½ seconds. It thus appears that stimulus deprivation and stimulus variation may be of extremely short duration and yet provide significant amounts of motivation and reinforcement.

Longer durations have been studied. These investigations, receiving some of their impetus from Korean attempts to brainwash G.I.'s during the Korean War, have produced extreme deprivation conditions for long periods of time. One of the pioneer investigators describes his studies as follows:

> In our experiments, the subject is suspended with the body and all but the top of the head immersed in a tank containing slowly flowing water at 34.5 C. (94.5 F.), wears a blacked-out mask (enclosing the whole head) for breathing, and wears nothing else. The water temperature is such that the subject feels neither hot nor cold. The experience is such that one actually feels the supports and the mask, but not much else; a large fraction of the usual pressures on the body caused by gravity are lacking. The sound level is low; one hears only one's own breathing and some faint water sounds from the piping; the water-air interface does not transmit air-borne sounds very efficiently. It is one of the most even and monotonous environments I have experienced. After the initial training period, no observer is present.

and:

> In the tank, the following stages have been experienced:
> (1) For about the first three-quarters of an hour, the day's residues are predominant. One is aware of the surroundings, recent problems, etc.
> (2) Gradually, one begins to relax and more or less enjoy the experience. The feeling of being isolated in space and having nothing to do is restful and relaxing at this stage.
> (3) But slowly, during the next hour, a tension develops which can be called a "stimulus-action" hunger; hidden methods of self-stimulation develop; twitching muscles, slow swimming movements (which cause sensations as the water flows by the skin), stroking one finger with another, etc. If one can inhibit such maneuvers long enough, intense satisfaction is derived from later self-stimulations.
> (4) If inhibition can win out, the tension may ultimately develop to the point of forcing the subject to leave the tank.
> (5) Meanwhile, the attention is drawn powerfully to any residual stimulus: the mask, the suspension, each come in for their share of concentration. Such residual stimuli become the whole content of consciousness to an almost unbearable degree. [Lilly, 1956, p. 4.]

Even more dramatic effects have been observed in such experiments, including the appearance of hallucinations and other reality-unreality confusions symptomatic of psychotic disorders. Fiske and Maddi (1961) have presented a review of this research. We may take it as an established fact that stimulus deprivation may have profound effects upon human behavior and, depending upon its duration, may be experienced as an extremely unpleasant situation.

What implications does such research have for the understanding of child behavior? It is probable that a good deal of child behavior is motivated by stimulus deprivation, and that a good deal of learning occurs as the result of reinforcement provided by stimulus variation. Sequences of TV programs are recalled; plots of books and stories are remembered; school lessons are learned; games are learned and replayed (but not too often lest they become boring); tunes are learned, whistled, and sung; and a host of other behavior patterns are learned, partly because such responses have been followed by boredom reduction in the past.

Certain developmental trends may also be partly caused by reactions to stimulus deprivation. The author suspects that children have an extremely low threshold for boredom, that much less stimulus deprivation is required to produce boredom in a child than in an adult. He also suspects that children are much more dependent upon overt, physical activity in order to reduce boredom than adults. Adults have recourse to a large storehouse of *symbols* that can be used to produce memories, fantasies, and ideas, thus substituting *mental* variation for variation in the physical world. Such an assumption would account for the greater amount of physical play behavior observed in children than in adults, as well as for the common observation that highly intelligent children are often physically sedentary as compared to children with a less generous endowment. The shorter attention span of children would also be accounted for, since it would be simply a manifestation of a low boredom threshold.

Most important, however, the notion of stimulus deprivation as a source of motivation helps to explain why human beings, adults as well as children, must be *doing something* when they are awake, quite independent of hunger, thirst, and the other sources of motivation considered previously. Indeed, there is perhaps no greater punishment than solitary confinement, at either the adult level (e.g., imprisonment) or the child level (e.g., standing in a corner).

Frustration and Conflict

Frustration is conventionally used to denote a situation wherein a behavioral sequence is blocked by an external condition, i.e., is prevented from "unfolding" in its normal sequence by an obstacle in the environment. Thus, a flat tire is frustrating if one is in a hurry, since the normal sequence of driving to the destination is temporarily blocked. *Conflict* is a special case of frustration, since a response sequence is again blocked, but the source of the blocking is from within the organism rather than from without. The blocking of one response sequence is provided by the simultaneous elicitation of a second, incompatible response. The 1964 Surgeon General's report on the linkage between

A study in frustration. This little girl was all ready to go outside to play when it started to rain.

cigarette smoking and cancer was undoubtedly the source of much conflict, since the response sequence involved in smoking was blocked to some extent by a simultaneous tendency not to smoke.

There seems to be little doubt that frustration and conflict have one characteristic in common with hunger, thirst, pain, boredom, etc.: they result in activity. Because of their energizing effect, they qualify as additional sources of motivation. Like the other sources, they are phylogenetically pervasive; they are not limited to *Homo sapiens*, but occur in lower organisms as well.

Frustration. An experiment by Adelman and Maatsch (1956) can be used to demonstrate frustration in animals. A common way of providing frustration is to remove a reinforcement from its customary spatio-temporal location. Thus, if a rat is fed in a particular goal box whenever

it runs down an alley, encountering an empty goal box following a subsequent run would be defined as a frustrating situation, since the consummatory response would be blocked by the absence of food. Adelman
and Maatsch gave 23-hour food-deprived rats 37 trials down a runway
to a goal box with food, where they were allowed 20 seconds to consume
the food. On subsequent trials, the goal box was empty, thereby providing a frustrating situation. To determine if such frustration was
motivating enough to serve as the basis for further learning, these rats
were allowed 5 minutes to climb out of the empty goal box to a surrounding ledge. It was reasoned that, if the frustrating goal box increased motivation, then any response followed by escape from the goal
box, such as ledge climbing, should be learned as a result of the reinforcement provided by a reduction in frustration. This group, motivated
by hunger plus frustration, and reinforced for ledge climbing by frustration reduction (but not hunger reduction), was called the *frustration*
group.

A second group was not given 37 runs to food in the goal box. Instead, the goal box was empty for each of the 37 trials. These rats were
then given 5 minutes to climb out of the goal box onto the surrounding
ledge, just like the former group. This group found food on the ledge
and was allowed to eat it. Thus, the second group was motivated by
hunger but not by frustration, and ledge climbing was reinforced by
hunger reduction instead of by frustration reduction. This group was
therefore called the *food* group.

A third group was treated exactly like the food group except that
ledge climbing was not followed by food. Instead, the ledge was empty,
and after remaining on it for as long as the other groups, these rats were
removed to await the next trial. Thus, this group was hungry just as the
food group, but food reinforcement was withheld following the ledge-
climbing response. It was called the *control* group, since it allowed for
a measurement of the effects of food reinforcement.

Figure 6.2 presents the results of the 30 test trials (opportunities for
ledge climbing) in terms of the median time required for the ledge-
climbing response in blocks of 5 trials. It indicates that the frustration
and food groups manifested about equally rapid learning, while the control group manifested variable behavior and no evidence that the ledge-
climbing response was strengthened. These results are unequivocal and
dramatic: *frustration and frustration reduction resulted in learning that
was actually faster than that produced by the more conventional procedure—hunger and hunger reduction.* We may thus conclude, for rats
at least, that frustration is indeed a source of motivation, and, likewise,
that frustration reduction is reinforcing.

The motivational property of frustration has been demonstrated with

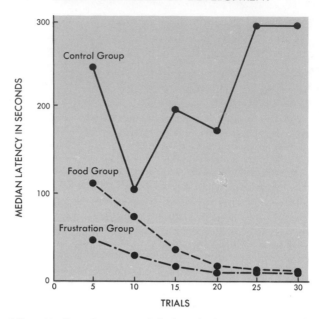

Figure 6.2. Median latency of ledge-climbing response for frustration group, food group, and control group (Adelman and Maatsch, 1956).

children a number of times (Haner and Brown, 1955; Holton, 1961; Longstreth, 1966a, b). As with rats, it has frequently been defined in terms of absence of reinforcement from its customary spatio-temporal location. Haner and Brown, for example, taught elementary school children a game in which they had to place 36 marbles into 36 holes in a box. They were told that, if they could complete this task four times in the limited time allowed, they would win a prize. Unknown to them, the experimenter could press a secret button that caused whatever marbles already placed in the holes to drop through to the box below. Whenever this frustration occurred, a buzzer sounded, and the subject was instructed to depress a spring-loaded plunger to turn off the buzzer before starting the marble task again. The energizing property of frustration was measured in terms of the distance the plunger was displaced on frustration trials.

Each subject was frustrated at four distances from the goal. The marbles disappeared and the buzzer sounded after 9, 18, 27, and 32 marbles had been placed. After the goal had been reached (all 36 holes filled), the buzzer sounded again, eliciting the plunger-press response. Obviously, no frustration was involved on these latter trials, since a goal had just been reached rather than lost.

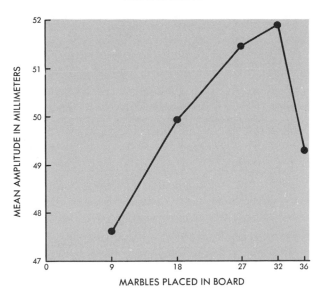

Figure 6.3. Mean amplitude of plunger press as a function of nearness to goal when frustrated (Haner and Brown, 1955).

Figure 6.3 shows the results of this study in terms of mean amplitude of the plunger-press response as a function of distance from the goal. It shows that the response increased in strength the nearer the subject was to the goal at the time of frustration, and then dropped precipitously after the goal of 36 filled holes was reached. This study thus not only demonstrates the motivating property of frustration in children, but also shows that the amount of frustration-produced motivation increases as the frustration point moves nearer and nearer to the goal. Studies by the author (Longstreth, 1966a, b) as well as by others (e.g., Holton, 1961) completely confirm these findings with children. They lead to the generalization that *the aversive motivational property of frustration is maximized if it occurs at just that point in time when the child's expectations of reinforcement are maximal.* This generalization is completely consistent with everyday observations. Absence of a reinforcement "is not missed" if the individual did not "expect" it in the first place. "What you do not expect will not be missed" summarizes the notion quite well.

The author found similar results (Longstreth, 1966b). Forty children learned to push a joy-stick response handle upon signal from a light, which then went off and turned on again four seconds later. The light progressed from bright (B) to dim (D) for half the subjects, and from D to B for the other half. At the end of each four-light sequence, a marble was automatically ejected, which was placed on a marble board. When the marble board was filled, the subject could trade the marbles for a present situated at the end of the board.

The children soon learned to anticipate the marble at the end of each sequence of four trials. This was revealed in different ways by different subjects. Some put their hand under the marble delivery tube to catch the marble; others looked at the tube just before marble delivery; etc. The most common indication, however, was intensity of the joy-stick response (intensity was automatically recorded on a polygraph on each trial). Figure 6.4 presents the actual recording from a representative subject for 12 trials. The top line shows when the light came on (downward stroke) and when it was terminated by a joy-stick response (up-

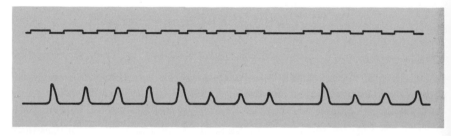

Figure 6.4. Amplitude of joy-stick response. A marble followed every fourth response. (Read from right to left.) (Longstreth, 1966a.)

ward stroke). The bottom line shows response intensity: the higher the tracing, the harder the subject pushed the response handle. Notice how every fourth response, which was followed by a marble, was harder than the previous three responses, clearly showing that the subject attached particular importance to that light intensity.

Sixty-three marbles were required to fill the marble board. After 61 had been earned, frustration was introduced; the last two marbles were not delivered. Furthermore, half the subjects found themselves "stalled" at the beginning of the sequence. When they turned off the first light intensity, it came back on again, instead of progressing to the next intensity as it previously had done. This light was presented over and over until the subjects stopped responding. The other subjects continued to be exposed to the entire sequence, and they too were allowed to extinguish. It was predicted that the first group, presented only with S_1, would be less frustrated than the second group, which was presented with S_1–S_4, since S_4 elicited stronger reward anticipations than S_1. This prediction was confirmed. Figure 6.5 shows response intensity for the

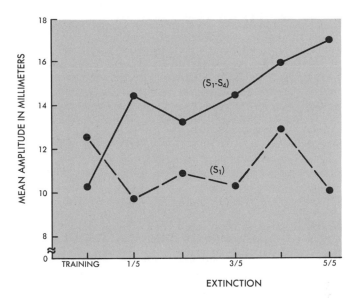

Figure 6.5. Mean amplitude of joy-stick response at end of training and during fifths of extinction (Longstreth, 1966b).

two groups at the end of training and during fifths of extinction. Although Group S_1–S_4 was responding with slightly less intensity at the end of training, it responded with considerably more intensity during extinction. The motivating property of frustration was thus demonstrated, as well as its relationship to goal anticipations.

That frustration-produced motivation is aversive was also demonstrated in this study. Group S_1–S_4 extinguished sooner than Group S_1. They responded an average of 122 times as compared to an average of 237 for Group S_1, thus indicating that they found the situation more unpleasant.

Conditioned Frustration. Frustration increases motivation presumably because it makes a person emotional. Thus, blood pressure, a commonly used index of emotionality, rises sharply when a person is frustrated (Hokanson *et al.*, 1963). Now suppose that the emotional response could be classically conditioned to a neutral stimulus in the same way that fear is conditioned. Then *conditioned frustration* would be demonstrated. The author suspects that frustration is indeed conditionable in this sense, and that it is a rather pervasive source of human motivation. Consider an example.

Suppose that Jean, a six-year-old girl, exhibits a curiosity about the piano in the living room, and so mother decides that she may take lessons if she so desires. The weekly lessons with the piano teacher go along nicely at first, and Jean practices 15 or 20 minutes on her own every day until boredom sets in and she seeks a change in stimulation. Meanwhile, mother observes that five-year-old Van next door plays much better than Jean, so she begins to insist that Jean practice one-half hour each day. Soon, she observes that Jean not only tries to avoid playing the extra 10 to 15 minutes but also tries to avoid playing at all. Her interest in piano playing mysteriously disappears. How is this situation to be understood?

In terms of previous reasoning, the extra practice demanded by Jean's mother created a frustrating situation. Jean wanted to leave the piano after 15 minutes of practice but was blocked from doing so by her mother. The emotionality resulting from the response blockage gradually became conditioned to correlated cues. Since the voluntary practice during the first 15 minutes, as well as the piano itself, was invariably paired with the frustration resulting from the second 15 minutes, the emotional responses became conditioned to these cues. Jean began to feel uneasy as soon as she sat down at the piano, because she "knew" she was soon going to feel even worse. She felt frustrated before the frustration actually occurred; in other words, it became hooked to other cues.

Music teachers, although not necessarily aware of frustration theory, have long known that children should not be required to practice long beyond the time when they would voluntarily quit, lest they gradually quit practicing altogether. Speaking more generally, it would appear that any kind of "forcing" creates some frustration, and it is therefore well to be aware of the possible consequences.

Wagner (1963) presented evidence that conditioned frustration can be learned in rats, and Longstreth (1965) demonstrated that children can be so conditioned. Using the same joy-stick apparatus as before, a buzzer was paired with frustration (non-delivery of an expected marble) for experimental subjects but not for control subjects. Subsequent presentation of the buzzer alone resulted in an increase in response intensity for experimental subjects, but not for control subjects. Experimental subjects, in other words, responded to the buzzer the same way they had previously responded to frustration; frustration had been *conditioned* to the buzzer.

Conflict. Everything that has been said of frustration is applicable to conflict as well, since conflict is merely a special case of frustration. It is conventional to describe three basic kinds of conflict: approach-approach, avoidance-avoidance, and approach-avoidance. As these paradigms are described in almost all introductory psychology textbooks, they need not be dwelled upon here. Instead, an experiment will be described that illustrates rather dramatically the thesis that conflict, as well as frustration, elicits emotional responses.

The experiment, titled *Behavioral Study of Obedience* (Milgram, 1963), was concerned with factors influencing obedience in adult human beings. The subjects were 40 males between the ages of twenty and fifty, drawn from all walks of life in the New Haven area via a newspaper advertisement. As soon as they arrived at the appropriate place (on the campus of Yale University), they were paid $4.50 and were informed that the money was theirs for merely showing up, and that they could keep it regardless of what happened thereafter.

They were told that the experimenter wished to study the effects of punishment on learning. They were to be the "teacher," and another subject would be the "learner." Both "teacher" and "learner" (the "learner" was really an accomplice working with the experimenter) were then taken to an adjacent room where the learner was strapped into an "electric chair." Electrodes, coated with paste, were fastened to his wrist with the explanation that the paste was applied to "avoid blisters and burns." It was also made clear that the electrodes were attached to a shock generator in an adjoining room. In order to improve credibility of the experiment still more, the experimenter declared, in response to a question by the "learner": "Although the shocks can be extremely painful, they cause no permanent tissue damage."

The "teacher" (the real subject) was then taken into the control room, and the procedure was explained to him. He was to teach the learner to respond with the correct word when the teacher presented him with a stimulus word. If the response was incorrect, the teacher was to give him a short electric shock. For this purpose, a "shock generator" was used. The following quotation describes it:

The instrument panel consists of 30 lever switches set in a horizontal line. Each switch is clearly labeled with a voltage designation that ranges from 15 to 450 volts. There is a 15-volt increment from one switch to the next going from left to right. In addition, the following verbal designations are clearly indicated for groups of four switches going from left to right: Slight Shock, Moderate Shock, Strong Shock, Very Strong Shock, Intense Shock, Extreme Intensity Shock, Danger: Severe Shock. (Two switches after this last designation are simply marked XXX.)

Upon depressing a switch: a pilot light corresponding to each switch is illuminated in bright red; an electric buzzing is heard, an electric blue light, labeled "voltage energizer," flashes; the dial on the voltage meter swings to the right; various relay clicks are sounded. [P. 373.]

The teacher was instructed to increase the shock by 15 volts each time the learner made an error. The entire setting was so realistic that not a single subject indicated any suspicion that everything was not genuine.

The victim (the "learner") gave standard, prearranged responses to the supposed shocks. No sign of protest was given until the shock level reached 300 volts. At that point, ". . . the learner pounds on the wall of the room in which he is bound to the electric chair. The pounding can be heard by the subject. From this point on, the learner's answers no longer appear. . . ." That is, as far as the teacher knew, the learner was paralyzed, unconscious, or worse!

At this point, the teacher (subject) usually turned to the experimenter for additional instructions, expressing concern as to whether he should go on. The experimenter responded with prearranged standardized answers, using four different replies:

1. "Please continue" or "Please go on."
2. "The experiment requires that you continue."
3. "It is absolutely essential that you continue."
4. "You have no other choice, you *must* continue."

These replies were always in sequence, and if the subject refused to go on after the fourth reply, the experiment was terminated.

It is apparent that the experimental situation created a powerful conflict between two incompatible response patterns: (1) the tendency to avoid hurting a fellow human being against his will, which would involve refusing to go on with the experiment; and (2) the tendency to obtain the approval of the scientist from Yale University, which would involve continuation of the experiment to the end.

How many subjects went all the way—i.e., how many depressed the last switch, supposedly administering 450 volts to a fellow human being strapped in an electric chair? All subjects went up to 300 volts, at which point the learner pounded on the wall and then was heard from no more. Five refused to go beyond 300 volts, but 26 went all the way (the remaining 9 quit after 300 but before 450 volts). The experimenters were amazed that so many continued to the end. Subjects gave signs of extreme emotionality but continued to deliver the shocks. The following paragraphs describe the manifestations of emotionality:

Many subjects showed signs of nervousness in the experimental situation, and especially upon administering the more powerful shocks. In a large number of cases the degree of tension reached extremes that are rarely seen in sociopsychological laboratory studies. Subjects were observed to sweat, tremble, stutter, bite their lips, groan, and dig their fingernails into their flesh. These were characteristic rather than exceptional responses to the experiment.

One sign of tension was the regular occurrence of nervous laughing fits. Fourteen of the 40 subjects showed definite signs of nervous laughter and smiling. The laughter seemed entirely out of place, even bizarre. Full-blown, uncontrollable seizures were observed for three subjects. On one occasion we observed a seizure so violently convulsive that it was necessary to call a halt to the experiment. The subject, a 46-year-old encyclopedia salesman, was seriously embarrassed by his untoward and uncontrollable behavior. In the post-experimental interviews subjects took pains to point out that they were not sadistic types, and that the laughter did not mean they enjoyed shocking the victim. [P. 375.]

and

I observed a mature and initially poised businessman enter the laboratory smiling and confident. Within 20 minutes he was reduced to a twitching, stuttering wreck, who was rapidly approaching a point of nervous collapse. He constantly pulled on his earlobe, and twisted his hands. At one point he pushed his fist into his forehead and muttered: "Oh God, let's stop it." And yet he continued to respond to every word of the experimenter, and obeyed to the end. [P. 377.]

Thus, it is clear that strong competing response tendencies elicit strong emotional responses. Such conflict-produced emotionality increases the level of motivation and thus provides energy (and subsequent reinforcement) for responses that reduce or terminate the conflict. We shall see later that the American culture sets the stage for several powerful conflicts that are difficult to resolve, but that must be resolved to some extent if normal adult "maturity" is to be reached. A basic knowledge of how conflicts in general affect behavior through their motivating and reinforcing properties will assist in the understanding of these more specific conflicts.

Anxiety as a Basis for Assumed "Human Needs"

Man has more sources of motivation attributed to him than all other organisms combined. An introductory psychology textbook has the following passage:

Biological drives have a direct physiological basis. They are fundamental. But obviously there are many other forms of human motivation. What is the relationship between physiological needs and such motives as man's curiosity about the world, his political and religious beliefs, his capacity to hate and to love, his patriotism, and his ambitions to make money and gain prestige? In many ways these complex psychological and social motives are more significant to man than his biological drives. [Ruch, 1963, p. 158.]

Following are some of the motivational sources attributed to humans (Mussen et al., 1963): hostility ("This motive refers to the desire to hurt, injure, destroy, or cause pain to an individual or object," p. 141); dominance ("This is the desire to influence or control others and to resist the demands of other people," p. 141); affiliation ("This motive is the

desire to form friendships and associations with other people," p. 141);
and so on for a number of other "motives." Mussen *et al.* conclude:
"This list, although incomplete, includes some of the major motives that,
in the opinion of many psychologists, direct much of the child's behavior" (pp. 141–142).

Travers (1963) lists a number of motives, of which the following constitute a sample: *acquisition* ("the need to gain possession," p. 158);
order ("the need to arrange, to be precise, to be orderly," p. 158); *con-
trarience* ("a need to be different from others," p. 158); etc. Travers
concludes the list by stating: "The list refers to what are supposed to
be the common needs of man, but this does not mean that all individuals
manifest these needs" (p. 159).

The author is tempted to suggest one more human "need": *needance*
(the need to assign needs to others). These various lists of human needs
suffer from several important deficiencies. For example, many of them
overlap so completely that it is difficult to tell them apart. The most
important criticism, however, has to do with the way they are defined.
*They are usually defined in terms of the very behavior they are supposed
to explain,* and thus they explain nothing. Suppose, for example, it is
observed that two-year-olds have a greater tendency to cry when away
from mother than children of any other age. On the basis of this fact,
a "dependency motive" is defined: two-year-olds have a strong "need
for mother." Mary Contrary is then observed to cry when her mother
leaves the room, and an observer asks, "Why does Mary cry?" Our
need-inventor answers, "Because two-year-olds have a strong dependency
need." How does he know that? Because they cry when mother is
absent. Crying is used to explain crying. Holt (1931), in criticizing
such circular reasoning with respect to instincts, wrote:

> For instance, man is impelled to action, it is said, by his instincts. If he goes
> with his fellows, it is the "herd instinct" which activates him; if he walks alone,
> it is the "anti-social instinct"; if he fights, it is the instinct of "pugnacity"; if
> he defers to another, it is the instinct of "self-abasement"; . . . Thus every-
> thing is explained with the facility of magic . . . word magic. [From Hall,
> 1961, p. 13.]

What is an alternative way of accounting for the diversity of human
behavior? Let us begin by recognizing that a specific bit of behavior
does not necessarily pinpoint the motivation behind it. For example, a
rat may be observed to consistently turn left at a choice point in a maze,
but ". . . what is apparently seldom said is that the rat has a strong left-
alley-seeking drive" (Brown, 1953, p. 10). The reason a left-alley-seek-
ing drive is not assumed is that it is known that such behavior can be
motivated by a variety of sources. The animal may be deprived of food,
or water, or stimulus variation; it may be receiving shock and can escape

it only by turning left; etc. Note that, in each of these latter cases, the motivation is defined in terms of *antecedent events* that are independent of the present behavior. Since a cause must precede its effect, the identification of the relevant antecedent conditions makes possible a respectable (i.e., non-circular) cause-effect explanation.

The same logic applies to human behavior. To assert that Mary has a strong dependency need is to do nothing more than replace the word *crying* with *dependency.* *It appears likely that many human behavior patterns previously "explained" by word magic are, in fact, all energized by one and the same source of motivation—anxiety.* We shall analyze two of the more dominant human "needs" in these terms. The two "needs" have been referred to by a variety of names, but the most common names are (1) the need for social approval, and (2) the need for achievement.

Emotions and the Need for Social Approval. There is no doubt that an immense segment of human behavior is controlled by the social approval of others. The author considers social approval as second to nothing in terms of its importance in the control of human behavior. The "need for social approval" appears in practically all listings of human "needs." What is it and what are its antecedents?

The assertion that a need for social approval exists is based on the almost infinite number of incidences in which people, adults as well as children, learn behavior that is followed by social approval and abandon behavior that is not followed by social approval. Fashion fads are a notorious example. Working for academic grades is another: a ten-year-old will work hard to "get 100 per cent" on a weekly spelling quiz, although all he obtains for such performance is a nod of approval from the teacher (and parents). Similarly, many college professors work long hours, and on weekends, in order to "carry out research," the culmination of which is a publication in a scholarly journal. But the journal is not eaten, drunk, or anything else. About all it is "worth" is a mere sound from a colleague, "Congratulations."

How does social approval gain its tremendous power? All it consists of is words, gestures, and facial expressions, and these do not satisfy any of the motivational sources we have considered thus far. Perhaps it is because of this very enigma that a *need* for social approval was suggested, since it could then be stated that the *need* for social approval was reduced by social approval. As we have seen, however, such an approach begs the question. A more acceptable answer is suggested by learning theory.

How do children learn the meaning of social *dis*approval? That is, how do they learn to understand what mother means when she says,

"No no, bad boy, naughty naughty," or when she employs a facial expression we may summarize as a frown? It is likely that such examples of social disapproval acquire meaning as a result of their association with other parental responses, such as a spanking, a cuff, or merely a loud voice. These latter events elicit anxiety and fear, and thus we have the conditions required for classical conditioning of negative emotional responses: social disapproval $\longrightarrow$ spanking $\longrightarrow$ fear. Soon, the fear becomes conditioned to the social disapproval itself, and then we say the child "understands."

Classical conditioning of *positive* emotional responses is probably also involved. Associated with infant reinforcements are the sights and sounds of mother, so that the relaxation, giggling, cooing, and other manifestations of pleasant emotional responses should become conditioned to mother. Now, these sights and sounds of mother do not consist of a topsy-turvy combination of all possible mother images, but of certain combinations that occur more frequently than others. Thus, mother is usually smiling rather than frowning, singing rather than crying, and saying "Momma's sweetheart" in a soft voice rather than "Momma's brat!" in a loud voice. Eventually, we would expect the child to respond with pleasure to these particular cues: cues we call "social approval." They are cues of approval only because they have been, and continue to be, associated with reinforcement.

Once such classical conditioning has occurred, the stage is set for the control of behavior by social approval. Behavior followed by social approval will be strengthened because of the positive emotional reactions that follow, as well as by reductions in anxiety elicited by previous social disapproval. In either case, there is no necessity to invent a "need for social approval." Simple emotional conditioning provides a much better explanation.

Emotions and the Need for Achievement.   The "need for achievement" may be analyzed in a similar fashion. If children are punished by their parents, teachers, uncles, and aunts whenever they do not succeed in a task, we would expect failure to elicit anxiety, and the termination of failure (i.e., *success*) to result in anxiety reduction. Thus, such a child would be motivated to persevere in a task until the stimuli denoting failure disappear; i.e., until he succeeds.

Middle-class children seem to have a much stronger "need for academic achievement" than working-class children. There is nothing mysterious about this. Middle-class parents are simply more likely to punish their children or socially disapprove of academic failure than working-class parents. Thus, middle-class children are more anxious about academic failure, and thus they possess greater motivation to achieve, as well as experiencing greater reinforcement (anxiety reduction) when they do achieve.

The analysis of the so-called human needs in terms of anxiety should now be clear. *A child or adult will appear to have a "need" for something (call it "X") to (1) the extent that the absence of X has been associated with anxiety, and (2) to the extent that the presence of X has been associated with reduction in anxiety and other pleasant emotional responses.* It becomes apparent, then, that parents play a major role in the determination of the "needs" their children have, since it is the parents who can control the stimuli that are paired with emotionally arousing events.

HABITS AND MOTIVATION IN COMBINATION

It is easy to demonstrate that, even though a response is strongly conditioned to a particular stimulus, presentation of that stimulus is no guarantee that the response will occur. The neighborhood children, for example, have a strong habit of asking for a dime when they hear the tune emanating from the Good Humor ice cream truck. This habit, *melody X* ⟶ *dime request*, must be strong because the request often occurs so promptly after the melody is heard. But it does not always occur; sometimes the melody is completely ignored. On such occasions, we do not assume that the *melody X* ⟶ *dime-request* connection has mysteriously disappeared, or that it has even weakened. If we did, we would have difficulty explaining the subsequent occurrence of "May I have a dime" in the absence of intervening reinforcements. Rather, omissions of the dime-request response tend to occur when the melody is heard after a meal, or when the child is sick, or when a snack has just been consumed. In other words, when motivation is low, the response tends not to occur. Thus, we assume that the *habit* is as strong as ever; i.e., the child has not forgotten how to ask for a dime, nor has the response extinguished, since on a subsequent occasion it occurs. It is simply that motivation is low.

It is also easy to demonstrate that strong motivation does not always lead to appropriate behavior, i.e., behavior that results in reinforcement. For example, no matter how anxious a child may be to obtain the social approval of his teacher, if the correct habits are "not there," he will not behave in those ways that elicit social approval. In other words, if he has not learned how to obtain social approval, high motivation will be to little avail.

Thus, correct habits and high motivation would both appear to be necessary before correct behavior will occur. This notion can be expressed mathematically by letting M stand for motivation, Hc for a correct habit, and Rc for a correct response:

$$Rc = +f(M \times Hc)$$

Verbally, this equation states that the strength of a correct response is some positive function of the product of motivation and strength of the habit to perform that response. If either is zero, the product will also be zero, and hence Rc will not occur. An additive relationship would not do, since then Rc could occur in the complete absence of either motivation or learning, an unlikely state of affairs. Thus, the multiplicative relationship between M and Hc fits the facts better and, indeed, is the cornerstone of one very important theory of behavior (Hull, 1943, 1952; Spence, 1956).

The dependence of behavior upon both habits and motivation has many ramifications for the understanding of child behavior. We shall consider just one of the more important implications. Suppose a child has learned a wrong habit in the eyes of his parents. For example, many first-grade children have considerable difficulty learning to print the letters of the alphabet because they often develop a family of incorrect habits of printing some of the letters backwards. It is somewhat distressing to observe one's child printing both the letters of his name as well as the order of the letters backwards. Suppose a parent, exasperated by the backward printing of a "backward" offspring, stops him and shouts, "No no, you're doing it all wrong—now do it again!" What is likely to be the immediate outcome of this understandable outburst?

Social disapproval is likely to elicit fear, which, in turn, will increase motivation. The increased motivation will multiply the incorrect habit, *Hi, with the result that backward printing is likely to be increased.* Stating it another way, frightening a child or making him anxious while he is doing something wrong is likely to make his immediate performance worse instead of better. Numerous experiments have actually demonstrated this point (Castaneda, 1956, 1961; Chiles, 1958; Glucksberg, 1962; Palermo, 1957; Standish and Champion, 1960). These studies have experimentally taught wrong habits to human subjects, and then varied motivation. Half the subjects were subjected to conditions that increased motivation, or were picked because they were already highly motivated; the other half were not subjected to these conditions, or were picked because their motivation was low. These studies found that subjects under high motivation did worse on the task than those under lower motivation. These studies also showed that high motivation resulted in improved behavior if the correct habits had been learned.

A general rule, then, is the following: *If the habits a person possesses for a particular task are correct habits, moderate increases in motivation are likely to improve performance still more, but if the habits are mostly incorrect, an increase in motivation is likely to result in an immediate decrement in performance.* Thus, the assumption that high motivation is always beneficial is wrong. Whether it is beneficial or not depends upon the correctness of the habits involved.

It is thus not always wise to increase a child's anxiety level by the use of social disapproval (i.e., scoldings) when he is having trouble learning a task. It is wiser to calm him down, to get him to relax as much as possible. The effect of this decrease in motivation will be to weaken the incorrect responses, and thus to "make room" for the appearance of correct responses. Teachers are well aware of this technique, not because of acquaintance with the theory involved, but because they have seen it work. College students, too, have experienced its effects. Reference is made here to the phenomenon of "blocking" on final exam day, wherein the ill-prepared student, anxious because he knows he is ill prepared, does even worse than he expected to do. He is probably correct when he belatedly tells the instructor that he knew more than his test performance indicated, but his high level of anxiety at test time, multiplying mostly incorrect habits, resulted in still poorer performance than anticipated. The road to good test performance would thus seem to include *calmness* when one knows mostly wrong answers (i.e., possesses mostly incorrect habits), and *excitement* when one knows mostly the correct answers (i.e., possesses mostly correct habits). Unfortunately, the opposite situation almost always prevails.

SUMMARY

The only unmotivated organism is a dead one or one fast asleep. Drives, in other words, make an organism active—they make him respond to his environment. Since a response cannot be learned unless it occurs, motivation becomes a necessary condition for learning. It has a second kind of necessity too, related specifically to instrumental conditioning. To the extent reinforcements consist of reductions in drive, a response cannot be rewarded unless there is some motivation to reduce.

The drives that energize animal behavior consist primarily of hunger, thirst, and pain. These decrease in importance as one moves up the phylogenetic scale to man. But new sources of motivation begin to appear, including boredom, frustration and conflict, and anxiety. Boredom is produced by stimulus (sensory) deprivation when one is wide awake, and makes itself manifest in terms of exploratory activity usually called *curiosity*. *Frustration* is defined in terms of response blockage, as is *conflict*, the difference being that conflict involves blockage from within, while frustration involves blockage from without.

Anxiety is also an important human motivation. It probably is the basis for many so-called human "needs," such as the "need for social approval" and the "need for achievement." Since anxiety can be elicited or terminated by the behavior of parents (as well as by the behavior of other people), parents, because of their close association with their children, undoubtedly play a major role in the "needs" their children manifest, both as children and as adults.

Behavior is dependent upon the presence of both motivation and habits. If either is absent, no behavior will occur. Thus, a *multiplicative relationship* exists between motivation and habits in the determination of behavior. One of the implications of this principle is that high motivation is not always beneficial; sometimes a reduction in motivation results in better, more adequate, behavior. It is impossible to predict whether behavior will be improved or impeded by consideration of motivation alone. The effects of shifts in motivational level depend upon the habits involved.

BIBLIOGRAPHY

ADELMAN, H. M., and MAATSCH, J. L. (1956). Learning and extinction based upon frustration, food reward, and exploratory tendency. *Journal of experimental psychology*, 52, 311–315.

BERLYNE, D. E. (1960). *Conflict, arousal, and curiosity*. New York: McGraw-Hill Book Co.

BROWN, J. S. (1953). Problems presented by the concept of acquired drives. In *Current theory and research in motivation: a symposium*. Lincoln: University of Nebraska Press. Pp. 1–21.

BUTLER, R. A. (1957). The effect of deprivation of visual incentives on visual exploration motivation in monkeys. *Journal of comparative and physiological psychology*, 50, 177–179.

CASTANEDA, A. (1956). Effects of stress on complex learning and performance. *Journal of experimental psychology*, 52, 9–12.

CASTANEDA, A. (1961). Supplementary report: differential position habits and anxiety in children as determinants of performance in learning. *Journal of experimental psychology*, 61, 257–258.

CHILES, W. D. (1958). Effects of shock-induced stress on verbal performance. *Journal of experimental psychology*, 56, 159–165.

FISKE, D. W., and MADDI, S. R. (1961). *Functions of varied experience*. Homewood, Ill.: The Dorsey Press, Inc.

GLUCKSBERG, S. (1962). The influence of strength of drive on functional fixedness and perceptual recognition. *Journal of experimental psychology*, 63, 36–41.

HALL, J. F. (1961). *Psychology of motivation*. Philadelphia: J. B. Lippincott Co.

HANER, C. F., and BROWN, P. A. (1955). Clarification of the instigation to action concept in the frustration-aggression hypothesis. *Journal of abnormal and social psychology*, 51, 204–206.

HARLOW, H. F. (1953). Motivation as a factor in the acquisition of new responses. In *Current theory and research in motivation: a symposium*. Lincoln: University of Nebraska Press. Pp. 24–49.

HOKANSON, J. E., BURGESS, M., and COHEN, M. F. (1963). Effects of displaced aggression on systolic blood pressure. *Journal of abnormal and social psychology*, 67, 214–218.

HOLT, E. B. (1931). *Animal drive and the learning process, an essay toward radical empiricism.* New York: Holt, Rinehart & Winston, Inc.

HOLTON, RUTH B. (1961). Amplitude of an instrumental response following the cessation of reward. *Child development,* 32, 107–116.

HULL, C. L. (1943). *Principles of behavior.* New York: Appleton-Century-Crofts, Inc.

HULL, C. L. (1952). *A behavior system.* New Haven, Conn.: Yale University Press.

LILLY, J. C. (1956). Mental effects of reduction of ordinary levels of physical stimuli on intact, healthy persons. *Psychiatric research reports,* 5, 1–9.

LONGSTRETH, L. E. (1965). Unconditioned and conditioned frustration in retardates. *American psychological association proceedings,* 1, 1–2.

LONGSTRETH, L. E. (1966a). Distance to goal and reinforcement schedule as determinants of human instrumental behavior. *American psychological association proceedings,* 2, 39–40.

LONGSTRETH, L. E. (1966b). Frustration and secondary reinforcement concepts as applied to human instrumental conditioning and extinction. *Psychological monographs,* 80 (11).

MILGRAM, S. (1963). Behavioral study of obedience. *Journal of abnormal and social psychology,* 67, 371–378.

MUSSEN, P. H., CONGER, J. J., and KAGAN, J. (1963). *Child development and personality.* New York: Harper & Row.

PALERMO, D. S. (1957). Proactive interference and facilitation as a function of amount of training and stress. *Journal of experimental psychology,* 53, 293–296.

RHEINGOLD, HARRIET L. (1963). Controlling the infant's exploratory behavior. In B. F. Foss (Ed.), *Determinants of infant behavior.* Vol. 2. New York: John Wiley & Sons, Inc. Pp. 171–175.

RUCH, F. L. (1963). *Psychology and life.* (6th ed.) Chicago: Scott, Foresman & Co.

SPENCE, K. W. (1956). *Behavior theory and conditioning.* New Haven, Conn.: Yale University Press.

STANDISH, R. R., and CHAMPION, R. A. (1960). Task difficulty and drive in verbal learning. *Journal of experimental psychology,* 59, 361–365.

TRAVERS, R. M. W. (1963). *Essentials of learning.* New York: The Macmillan Co.

WAGNER, A. R. (1963). Conditioned frustration as a learned drive. *Journal of experimental psychology,* 66, 142–148.

II

PATTERNS
OF DEVELOPMENT

7

Behavioral Stability
in Childhood

INTRODUCTION

In the fall of 1929, the Fels Research Institute at Yellow Springs, Ohio, launched a massive longitudinal study of human development. A summary of the major findings discovered during the first 30 years was ultimately published in book form (Kagan and Moss, 1962). This work summarizes the personality development of 89 individuals from birth through early adulthood. There is no other study of development that is comparable to this one in terms of number of individuals studied, duration of the study (it is still in progress), or breadth of behavior observed and recorded. Thus, the Fels study has been selected to provide the reader with the facts of personality development on a broad scale—broad in terms of time, for the Fels study covers over 20 years of development, and broad in terms of *descriptive concepts*, for minute classifications of behavior are as out of place in a study of this breadth as inches are out of place in the measurement of distances between cities.

THE SAMPLE

The Fels study enrolled 89 individuals (45 girls and 44 boys) for observation and study during the period 1929 to 1939. Most of these individuals were enrolled before they were born; the mother's permission and cooperation were secured while she was still pregnant.

Sixty-three different families were involved, with 7 families supplying three children each, 12 families supplying two children, and 44 families supplying one child. Religious background was predominantly Protestant; 53 families had a Protestant background, 9 a Catholic background, and 1 a Jewish background. All families were living in or near Yellow Springs, Ohio. Occupations of the fathers are reported as "equally distributed" among the following groups: professional, white collar, small businessman, farmer, and laborer. The education of the fathers may be summarized as follows: about 70 per cent graduated from high school, and about 38 per cent graduated from college.

There were three divorces among the 63 families during the course of the study, and only 8 of the 89 children were separated from either natural parent prior to the age of voluntary emancipation (i.e., eighteen years of age). A final pertinent fact is that almost all the children in the sample attended an experimental nursery school run by the Fels Institute during ages two and a half to five, and attended a summer "day camp," also run by the Fels Institute, during ages six to ten.

The reason for giving all these facts concerning the nature of the sample is that they allow one to obtain some idea as to the *representativeness* of the sample. Representativeness, in turn, informs us of the population to which one may *generalize*. In other words, if these 89 individuals are representative of all children in the United States, then one may take the findings of the Fels study and generalize them to any and all U.S. children, with the confidence that the generalization will be correct most of the time; i.e., that the generalization is plausible. If, on the other hand, the sample is not representative of such a large population, what smaller population, if any, does it represent?

First of all, the sample is obviously not representative of all children in the United States in either a geographic or a temporal sense; that is, the entire sample was situated in or around Yellow Springs, Ohio, and thus is geographically unrepresentative of all U.S. children. Second, the sample was formed from children born between 1929 and 1939, and thus is unrepresentative of all other U.S. children who were born during some other time period. At the very best, the sample is possibly representative of all children born near Yellow Springs, Ohio, in the decade 1929–1939.

But even such a restricted population is overstating the case. It is almost redundant to point out that the sample consisted only of families willing to permit such an intensive and long-term study. Certainly, not all families in the vicinity of Yellow Springs were so cooperative. What were some of the characteristics of these cooperative families? (1) Approximately 20 per cent of the families had a father whose vocation was labeled "professional" (in the 1930 census, 3.1 per cent of employed males in the United States were so labeled); (2) about 38 per cent of the fathers graduated from college (this was *much* higher than the national average for men at that time); (3) there were three divorces among the 63 families—about 5 per cent (the national average in 1930 was about 17 per cent, and in 1950 it was about 23 per cent).

These facts and comparisons with national trends lead to the conclusion that families willing to cooperate with such a project are not quite representative of families in general. Is there an economical way the nature of the discrepancies might be summarized? Yes. The concept of *socioeconomic status* seems made to order.

Socioeconomic status is usually defined in terms of one or more of the following four items of information about a family: occupation of father, income of father, education of father and mother, and physical condition of the home. The "higher" the occupation of the father ("professional" is highest; "unskilled laborer" is lowest), the greater his income; the greater the parental education (measured in terms of degrees or years of education) and the better the home condition ("better" refers to such things as size of lot, multiple- or single-family dwelling, etc.), the higher the socioeconomic status of the family. Thus, it must be concluded that the Fels sample is unrepresentative with respect to socioeconomic status; the average socioeconomic status in the United States is lower than that of the Fels sample. In addition, the distribution of socioeconomic status in the sample is unrepresentative. There are too many upper-class families and too few lower-class families.

In Chapter 1, it was pointed out that one classification system may be used in place of another because of its usefulness in predicting other relationships. Socioeconomic status is such a system. A family's socioeconomic status is predictive of a large number of other facts about the family. Since the Fels sample is roughly upper middle-class in socioeconomic status, it would be expected, for example, that (1) mean IQ of the Fels sample, parents as well as children, would be higher than the national average; (2) interest in education would be disproportionately high; (3) interest in physical activities would be disproportionately low; (4) heterosexual behavior of the children during adolescence and adulthood would be more inhibited than one would expect from a more representative sample of U.S. families; (5) hostility would be too often expressed verbally rather than physically; and so on for a number of other characteristics.

If the Fels sample is so unrepresentative of families in the United States, or even of families in Ohio, the reader may be tempted to ask, "Of what value is it?" His reasoning might be that, since the sample is so unrepresentative of U.S. families in so many ways, it would be very risky to generalize any of the findings to this larger population.

There are at least two important answers to this justifiable apprehension. First, the stability of development from birth to adulthood may be quite independent of socioeconomic status. For example, the probability of a physically aggressive five-year-old boy developing into a twenty-year-old physically aggressive man might be quite independent of socioeconomic status, even though it is nevertheless true that lower socioeconomic people are physically more aggressive than upper middle-class people. In other words, *stability* of behavior is different from *amount* or *intensity* of that behavior. If amount or intensity of some bit of behavior is related to socioeconomic status, it does not follow that stability of that behavior is also related to socioeconomic status.

Second, not *all* families in the Fels sample were upper middle-class; e.g., there were 20 per cent laborers. Thus, the lack of socioeconomic representativeness is one of degree rather than a matter of yes or no. The representativeness of the Fels sample could have been much worse. What if no laborers had been represented? Since the greater part of the socioeconomic range is represented, but certain groups disproportionately represented, one may still generalize to the entire socioeconomic range but must remember that the generalizations are a little more plausible when directed to the upper middle-class.

Another implication of the second point is that it is possible to analyze the results of the Fels study separately for each major socioeconomic level in order to *find out* if socioeconomic status is related to the stability of specified personality characteristics. If not, then socioeconomic status may be ignored.

Thus, the problem of representativeness of the Fels sample is not as serious as might be suspected. One must keep in mind the complexity of the study and the frequent impositions made on the sample members over a long period of time. A general principle is that the greater the demands put upon a research sample, the less representative the sample becomes. With this principle in mind, the representativeness of the Fels sample is perhaps to be admired rather than questioned.

METHODS OF MEASUREMENT DURING CHILDHOOD

The information obtained about each child varied somewhat from child to child, but the following description is typical.

Half-day visits with mother and child at home. These visits were made at least twice a year from birth to six years of age, and annually from six to twelve. Each visit was made by a professional worker with some psychological training. The same visitor continued to visit a particular family as long as that visitor remained with the Fels Institute. Thus, visitors often became well acquainted with their assigned families, which led to a relaxed atmosphere and good rapport. Results of the three- to four-hour visit were written up in narrative fashion after the visitor returned to the Institute.

Interviews with mothers. Each year, the mother of each sample member was interviewed at the Fels Institute. These interviews occurred until the child reached adolescence, i.e., until he was thirteen or fourteen. The interviews were concerned with both the behavior of the child and the mother's reactions and general attitudes toward the child. (It should be pointed out that most studies of mother-child interactions consist of a single visit with the mother and no observation of her interactions with the child. Perhaps the reader will now understand more clearly what is meant when the Fels study is described as "massive".)

Observation of child in nursery school from ages two and a half to five. Almost all children in the sample attended the Fels nursery school between the ages of two and a half and five. A trained observer summarized each child's behavior in the nursery school twice a year. These summaries were written up in narrative style after each observation period was over.

Observation of child in day camp from ages six to ten. The Fels day camp, open a few weeks each summer, provided a source of observational data as the child became older. Each child was observed once a year at the day camp between the ages of six and ten, and a narrative summary of the observation was made afterwards.

Half-day observations of child in school from first to eighth grades. For the 90 per cent of the children who attended public schools, an observer visited the classroom for half a day twice a year and wrote a summary of his observations. These visits thus provided a source of observational data for years six to fourteen.

Interview with child. Each child was interviewed annually at the Fels Institute from the age of six to the age of fourteen. The interviewers were known to the children, which provided a relaxed, informal atmosphere. Narrative summaries of the interviews were placed in each child's file.

Mental testing. Each child was administered an intelligence test more than once a year from birth through fourteen years of age. He was tested again at seventeen. As development of intelligence is not of major concern in the present context, a detailed description of the tests will not be provided.

Personality testing. Each child was administered four different personality tests between the ages of eight and seventeen. Two of these were administered four times each, at three-year intervals, and the other two were administered once each. As these data were only minimally used, a more detailed description will not be provided.

The home visits with mother and child, the interviews with mothers, the interviews with children, and the observations of the children in nursery school, day school, and public school provided a large pool of information about each sample member over the first fourteen years of life. On the basis of this information, a psychologist made ratings on 7-point scales of 48 behavior (personality) characteristics. A separate rating was made at each of four age periods: zero to three, three to six, six to ten, and ten to fourteen. That is, all the information covering the first three years of a given child's life was separated and studied. On the basis of that information alone, the psychologist rated the child on all of the 48 variables for which there was adequate information. Then all the information for another child over the first three years was similarly rated. After all children had been so rated over these years, the psychologist did the whole thing again, this time using only information gathered while the child was between the ages of three and six. Two more ratings were then done for age periods six to ten and ten to fourteen, providing a total of four ratings per child on most of the 48 variables.

Perhaps it is a good idea to pause at this point to obtain a clearer picture of the Fels study as described thus far. It is a study of the stability of child behavior. Yet the results are described in terms of correlations between ratings. What is the path from child behavior to ratings on 7-point scales? Figure 7.1 presents a summary of this path.

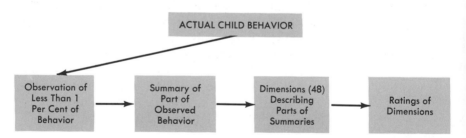

Figure 7.1. The data reduction of child behavior information in the Fels study.

It shows, first of all, that only a small fraction of all the child's behavior was actually observed by a representative of the Fels study. These observations were then translated into summaries. The summaries did not communicate all the observations of the observer, but only those he (1) recalled and (2) considered important. These condensations of recalled observations then served as the basis for information about dimensions of behavior. The 48 dimensions did not cover all the information in the summaries, but only certain parts of it. Finally, the ratings transformed the child's position on a dimension to a number on a scale. This number is related to behavior only through the intervening chain of events and is no more or less meaningful than those events. Thus, it can be seen that, although the Fels study is "massive" compared to other studies of human development, it is based on extremely small samples of behavior. Figure 7.1 also illustrates a typical *data-reduction* procedure, by which the initial observations are transformed and reduced to a form suitable for analysis. All such studies must go through a similar process.

Methodological Questions About Childhood Measurement Procedures

At this point, some questions about the Fels study will be raised concerning its methods. Consideration of these questions will serve two purposes. First, it will bring to attention some aspects of the Fels study that are of great importance when the time comes to interpret the results of the study. Second, these methodological questions are common to most, if not all, longitudinal studies and therefore provide a critical frame of reference from which other studies may be evaluated.

Suppose it is found that children rated as highly aggressive during years zero to three are also rated as highly aggressive at years three to six, six to ten, and ten to fourteen. In other words, ratings of aggression for the four age periods are found to be positively correlated with each other. Is one then justified in concluding that aggression is a relatively stable personality characteristic during childhood? The answer is *no*, not on the basis of such information alone. Why?

Recall that the same psychologist made all four sets of ratings. Consider two possible ways he could have done it: (*a*) After rating child A for years zero to three, child A is rated for years three to six, then for years six to ten, and then for years ten to fourteen. Then child B is rated for zero to three, then three to six, etc. In other words, a single child is rated for all four age periods before another child is rated. (*b*) After rating child A for zero to three, child B is rated for zero to three, then child C, etc. After all children have been rated for years zero to three, the rater starts over again with child A for years three to six, and so on, until the last child has been rated for years ten to fourteen.

Which method, (*a*) or (*b*), is the better method? It is (*b*). Why? Because (*a*) makes it quite possible that ratings of child A at zero to three would influence ratings of child A at years three to six as a result of recall. Thus, suppose that child A is being rated on aggression at years three to six and the rater recalls that he was rated high on aggression for years zero to three. It is unlikely that the rater would rate him low on aggression for years three to six, unless the evidence was very convincing. Most people assume there is some stability to behavior, and on the basis of this assumption, the rater would be likely to rate child A as high on aggression for years three to six whether he was or not. Thus, purely in terms of the effect of recall of previous ratings, one would expect to find positive correlations between ratings of different time periods. It is absolutely crucial, therefore, that such "recall effects" be reduced to a bare minimum. Method (b) comes much closer to this than method (a). It is extremely unlikely that child A's aggression rating for zero to three would be recalled when he is rated for aggression at three to six if 88 other children were rated on 48 personality characteristics in between. Fortunately, method (b) was employed in the Fels study rather than method (a). Approximately 4,224 ratings (88 times 48), requiring six to eight months to perform, intervened between the rating of any one child for two different age periods. We may therefore conclude that it is extremely unlikely there were any recall effects, and that positive correlations of ratings between age groups thus reflect behavioral stability rather than methodological shortcomings.

A second, related, methodological problem is the following: Suppose it is found that children rated high on aggression are also rated high on disobedience to adults. Knowing that method (b) was used, are we justified in concluding that aggressive children also tend to be disobedient children? The answer is *no*. Why? Since each child was rated on all 48 personality characteristics before another child was rated, it is probable that some ratings were recalled while making others. Since everybody has assumptions about what personality characteristics "go together," these assumptions would influence opinions (and ratings) about people. Thus, we must conclude that the correlations of the 48 variables with each other within a single age period are suspect. They are probably contaminated by recall effects.

How might this methodological shortcoming have been avoided? By rating only one of the 48 variables per child at a time. More specifically, after rating child A on aggression for period zero to three, then rate child B on aggression for period zero to three, then child C, etc. After rating all 89 children on aggression for this period, start with child A again and rate him on a second one of the 48 variables. Such a procedure would have produced 88 ratings between any two ratings for the same individual, and thus would have materially reduced recall effects.

It is easy to understand why such a procedure was not followed. All the information of a given age period pertaining to aggression was not localized at one spot in the child's files. Rather, it was spread over all the material for that age period. Intermixed with it was information pertaining to the other 47 variables. Thus, it would have been relatively fruitless to adopt the suggested procedure, since the rater would still have been forced to study the information relevant to aggression while searching for information relevant to some other variable. It is interesting to try and think of methods by which this recall effect could have been reduced. This question is left as a stimulant to the reader's ingenuity, but it is predicted that whatever he comes up with (and there are solutions), it would have been prohibitively expensive and/or time consuming.

There is, finally, a third methodological question. Suppose it is found that aggression during period zero to three had absolutely no relationship with aggression during period three to six; i.e., the two sets of ratings are not correlated. Suppose further that we had strongly expected a positive correlation. The investigators therefore conclude that we are wrong since no relationship was found. But we reply, "No, we are not necessarily wrong. Your rater did a very poor job of rating, and that is why no relationship was found. If any other psychologist had done the ratings, a positive relationship would have been found." The methodological question is, can the investigators protect themselves against an accusation of this sort? The answer is *yes*, by simply obtaining a set of ratings from a second psychologist who was not aware of the ratings of the first psychologist. If the two sets of ratings do not correlate with each other, then the accusation of poor work, or, more technically, of *unreliability*, is tenable. If, on the other hand, the two sets of ratings correlate positively with each other, the accusation of unreliability is untenable. In the Fels study, a second psychologist rated 50 or 60 of the 89 children for each of the four age periods, and his ratings were compared with the ratings of the first psychologist. Of the 48 sets of ratings for each age period, the median correlation coefficients were .68, .76, .85, and .83, for periods zero to three, three to six, six to ten, and ten to fourteen, respectively. These correlations are high enough to render the possible accusation of unreliability as not tenable.

METHODS OF MEASUREMENT DURING ADULTHOOD

Sample members were contacted by the Fels Institute when they were approximately twenty-four years old (range: nineteen to twenty-nine), and arrangements were begun that culminated in a five- to six-hour tape-recorded interview. This interview constituted the primary source of data concerning adult behavior. Thus, information about adult behavior was less direct than information about child behavior; the behavior of children was *observed,* while the adult behavior was *inferred* from the self-descriptions of the sample members. While the more direct method is to be preferred, adults are much harder to observe than children, thus justifying, to some extent, the use of the interview technique. It should be pointed out that, by this time, the sample members had spent over 20 years in association with the Fels Institute. This long-standing relationship with staff members would be expected to contribute toward a friendly, cooperative attitude, which, in turn, would be expected to promulgate an honest, frank relationship in the interview situation.

These expectations are borne out by the report that, of all 89 individuals, only 2 refused to be interviewed. This is all the more amazing in view of the fact that no payment was offered for cooperating with the interviewer. Another 16 lived too far away to make it feasible for them to come to the Institute, leaving a total of 71 who were actually interviewed. Of these, it is stated: "The subjects were interested in the purpose of the research and were willing and, in some cases, eager to talk honestly about their goals, fears, resentments, and conflicts" (Kagan and Moss, 1962, p. 31).

The interview was divided into two or three sessions. After it was completed, the interviewer studied his notes and the recordings and then made ratings of 59 personality characteristics. Fifteen of these were subsequently eliminated because of insufficient information, leaving 44.

Let us now pause once again to consider the adult information in perspective. Figure 7.2 presents the "path" from actual behavior to ratings on 7-point scales. It will be observed that this path is longer and different from the data-reduction sequence for child behavior. The major difference is that ratings of adult behavior were completely dependent upon verbalizations of the adults. No overt adult behavior was actually observed. Figure 7.2 serves to remind the reader of the meaning of the ratings. In the present case, it can be stated that the ratings are of dimensions taken from recordings *of verbalizations of recalled self-behavior.*

Methodological Questions About Adult Measurement Procedures

It is clear from Figure 7.2 that the adult information is more indirect than the child information. It is an interesting exercise to search for a better method—one that does not rely so heavily on self-reports. It would be impossible, of course, to actually observe the adults with the same accuracy with which the children were observed. Adults are too *mobile*. It would take a Herculean effort to follow one around

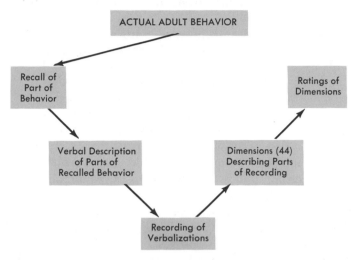

Figure 7.2. The data reduction of adult behavior information in the Fels study.

from sunrise to sunset. Even more important, adults are undoubtedly more sophisticated than children and would be more apt to successfully mislead the observer much of the time.

What other alternatives are there? One possibility would be to interview two or three best friends, including the spouse. These informants would be less likely to cover up negative or embarrassing information than the adult himself (the spouse might be an exception). An added advantage would be that unreliable information—data on which the informants could not agree—could be identified and discarded. When just the adult himself is utilized, there is no way to check the reliability of his reports, except to note contradictions between different parts of the interview.

Keeping in mind the dangers of self-reports, let us briefly consider the same three methodological questions that were previously discussed with respect to the childhood information. The first two questions were about the recall effect. The first of these was concerned with the possibility that ratings of behavior for one time period might be influenced by recall of that individual's behavior at an earlier time period. Fortunately, the psychologist who rated the adult interview data was not only different from the person who rated the child data but knew absolutely nothing about any of the child data. Thus, the child and adult ratings are completely independent of each other. Use of the word "fortunately" is not to be construed as implying that it was an accident; nothing could be further from the truth. It was planned in advance that such would be the case.

The second question was concerned with the effect of knowledge (recall) of one personality characteristic while rating another. As with the child data, since the same person rated all the adult personality variables and did so at one sitting, it is probable that these ratings were affected to some unknown extent by recall of other ratings.

The third question was concerned with rater reliability. A second psychologist rated 32 tape-recorded interviews with no knowledge of the ratings of the first psychologist. Fifteen of the 44 personality characteristics were found to be quite unreliable, *and were therefore abandoned.* The preceding phrase is italicized to communicate to the reader the importance of reliability; without it, the ratings are absolutely useless. The median correlation between the two ratings of the remaining 29 variables was .81, providing evidence of acceptable reliability for these dimensions.

A battery of tests was also administered to the sample, but since little use was made of it, it is not described.

THE PERSONALITY CHARACTERISTICS

The 48 personality characteristics rated during childhood and the 29 characteristics rated during early adulthood provided information about 13 *patterns* of behavior about which there was both childhood and adult information. A *pattern*, as used here, means several personality characteristics grouped together because of their similarity. Thus, aggressive behavior and competitive behavior might be considered together because they are similar in the sense of implying struggles with other people. These 13 patterns of behavior were then combined into five larger patterns and four smaller patterns. We shall be concerned with the five larger patterns. They are called (1) *passivity and dependency,* (2) *aggression,* (3) *achievement and recognition strivings,* (4) *sexuality,* and (5) *social interaction anxiety.*

The next two chapters describe the stability of these patterns of behavior. *Passivity and dependency* and *aggression* are considered in Chapter 8, since they appear to be on opposite ends of a single broad dimension that runs from inactivity to activity. The remaining three patterns are described in Chapter 9.

The discussion of each of these five behavior patterns is oriented around four questions. First, just what is meant by the names used to describe these patterns? That is, what is meant by "passivity" and "dependency"? To communicate fully what is meant by such terms means to describe how they were measured. The descriptions of the operations involved in such measurements are called *operational definitions*. Concepts and terms that are operationally defined are *unambiguously* defined, and that is why scientific concepts are almost always operationally defined.

Second, what is the stability of a specified behavior pattern during childhood? The answer to this question is in terms of tables of correlation coefficients. These correlations describe the relationship between ratings of behavior characteristics at any two of the four age periods: zero to three, three to six, six to ten, and ten to fourteen. An abbreviation is sometimes used: $_3r_6$ (agg) means the correlation between aggression ratings as determined from data of periods zero to three and three to six; $_3r_{14}$ (dep) means the correlation between dependency as rated during periods zero to three and ten to fourteen; etc. Thus, if $_3r_{10}$ (agg) = .50, it will be concluded that aggression was relatively stable from period zero to three to period six to ten.

The third question is concerned with the relationship of various behavior characteristics and patterns within a single age period. For example, what is the ten-year-old aggressive boy like, other than aggressive? Once again, the answer is in terms of correlation coefficients. Thus, if it is found that aggression in the ten-year-old boy is correlated with competitiveness, with $_ar_c$ = .50, it will be concluded that such a boy is also usually competitive.

The fourth question is concerned with the stability of behavior patterns from childhood to adulthood. As with questions two and three, it is answered with correlation coefficients. Thus, a correlation of .50 between aggression during period ten to fourteen and anger-outbursts in young adulthood will lead to the conclusion that aggression is relatively stable between fourteen and twenty-four, particularly if other indexes of adult aggression indicate a similar relationship.

SUMMARY

In terms of sample size, duration of study, and breadth of measurements, the Fels study stands alone as an investigation of behavioral stability. The sample consisted of 89 children who were followed from birth to young adulthood. These 89 children from 63 families were all from the state of Ohio and born between 1929 and 1939, leading to the question of representativeness. Other information, such as fathers' education and vocation, divorce rate for the 63 families, etc., suggests that they were not completely representative of American families, at least in terms of socioeconomic status. But since behavioral stability might be independent of socioeconomic status, even though the magnitude of a given personality characteristic is not, and since most of the socioeconomic range *was* represented, and since it is therefore possible to determine effects of socioeconomic status on personality stability, the lack of socioeconomic representativeness is not as serious as it might have been.

Measurement methods during childhood and adulthood ranged from observation to interview. Child behavior was much more completely observed and recorded than adult behavior. As a matter of fact, adult behavior was not observed at all, but was inferred from interview data. Even in childhood, only a very minute part of all the child's behavior ever found its way to a record. At best, long-term longitudinal studies of human development are very selective; any other approach is impractical.

The massive amount of information eventually collected was rated on 7-point scales of various personality dimensions. A separate set of four ratings, one for each of the four childhood age periods, and a fifth set based upon the adult interviews formed the basis for the determination of personality stability.

The valid measurement of stability demands that the sets of ratings made at different age periods be independent of each other. The requirement of rater reliability is also demanded. Both requirements were reasonably well met in the Fels study. Ratings of different personality characteristics within a single age period, however, were probably not independent and are, therefore, to be interpreted with extra caution.

Five major patterns of personality finally emerged from the ratings of 48 childhood variables and 29 adulthood variables. These are passivity and dependency, aggression, achievement and recognition strivings, sexuality, and social interaction anxiety. The next two chapters are concerned with the stability of these patterns from birth to maturity.

BIBLIOGRAPHY

KAGAN, J., and Moss, H. A. (1962). *Birth to maturity.* New York: John Wiley & Sons, Inc.

8

Passivity-Dependency and Aggression

PASSIVITY AND DEPENDENCY

Passivity and dependency constituted one broad pattern of behavior studied in the Fels investigation. Before its stability can be considered, the pattern must be defined.

Definition

Passivity measured the degree to which an individual gave up or withdrew in the face of difficult situations or frustration. During the early years, it was measured in terms of (1) retreat when in conflict with a sibling, (2) absence of an active reaction when a goal object (e.g., a toy) was lost, (3) withdrawal when an environmental obstacle prevented attainment of a goal, and (4) withdrawal from mildly noxious or potentially dangerous situations (e.g., withdrawal from a friendly wrestling match). During the school years, passivity was measured in terms of (1) withdrawal when socially rejected, and (2) withdrawal from difficult and frustrating tasks. Passivity was rated during each of the four age periods: zero to three, three to six, six to ten, and ten to fourteen.

Dependency measured the tendency for individuals to seek affection and aid from adults. The mother was the most relevant adult in early childhood, with teachers and other adults becoming more important in later childhood. In early adulthood, dependency was also measured in terms of reluctance to be separated from the mother.

Three scales of dependency were, in fact, rated. *Dependency on mother* (dependency 1) was rated for periods zero to three and three to six, since such behavior was relatively infrequent at later age periods. *Seeking of affection from adults in general* (dependency 2) and *seeking of aid when in problem situations from adults* (dependency 3) were more frequent at later ages, and hence were rated for periods six to ten and ten to fourteen. Two other scales were also used but are not reported here for the sake of brevity, and also because they add very little information to what is offered by the preceding scales.

Stability in Childhood

Table 8.1 presents the stability of these ratings during childhood. A number of subsequent tables are organized in precisely the same fashion, so this first table will be discussed in some detail.

TABLE 8.1

Stability of Passivity and Dependency During Childhood

Dimension	Short-Term Stability		Long-Term Stability	
	0–3 to 3–6	6–10 to 10–14	3–6 to 10–14	0–3 to 10–14
Passivity				
Boys	.67	.60	.24	.00
Girls	.58	.76	.51	.44
Dependency 1 and 2	(Dep. 1)	(Dep. 2)		
Boys	.58	.41	−.03	.66
Girls	.64	.34	.26	.17
Dependency 1 and 3	(Dep. 1)	(Dep. 3)		
Boys	*	.56	−.13	.04
Girls	*	.34	.24	.23

* Not measured.

The column titles indicate what age periods are being compared, while the row titles indicate what scales are being compared. The entries within the tables are the correlation coefficients resulting from each comparison. The order of the column titles is arranged as it is for a special reason. The first two columns are concerned with comparisons of two adjacent age periods: zero to three with three to six (column 1) and six to ten with ten to fourteen (column 2). These two columns are concerned with relatively *short-term stability*, both in early childhood (column 1) and in late childhood (column 2). Columns 3 and 4 are concerned with comparisons between non-adjacent age periods; i.e., they are concerned with long-term stability. One age period is skipped in column 3 and two periods are skipped in column 4. There is thus a dimension of duration involved as one reads from column 1 to column 4.

The first correlation, .67, thus indicates that ratings of passivity for boys during the first three years of life correlated .67 with the ratings made during years three to six. This correlation is high and therefore indicates considerable stability of passivity during the first six years. The corresponding correlation for girls, .58, is a little lower, but the two are similar enough to lead to a similar conclusion. The correlations of .60 (boys) and .76 (girls) from years six to ten to years ten to fourteen are of a similar magnitude and lead to the conclusion that stability of passivity from six to fourteen was also high.

Long-term stability of passivity is described by the four correlations in the upper right corner of the table: .24 and .00 for boys and .51 and .44 for girls. These correlations indicate that passivity in boys became less stable as longer durations were considered, culminating in a correlation of zero when the longest time span is considered. In other words, there was no relationship at all between passivity at these two age periods for boys. For girls, the correlations are much higher, although not as strong as short-term stability. Considering passivity over the entire age range, one would therefore conclude that there was short-term stability for both sexes, but long-term stability only for girls.

The second main row, "Dependency 1 and 2," describes the stability of these two ratings of dependency. Recall that dependency 1 (dependency on mother) was rated only during periods zero to three and three to six, since it became too infrequent to rate at the later age periods. Thus, its stability can be described only from periods zero to three to three to six (column 1), resulting in correlations of .58 (boys) and .64 (girls). Dependency 2 (seeking of affection) was rated only during the last two age periods, six to ten and ten to fourteen, and thus its stability can be described only between those age periods, resulting in correlations of .41 and .34. Long-term stability of these two ratings was determined by correlating one against the other. The correlation of −.03 is therefore between dependency 1 at ages three to six and dependency 2 at ages ten to fourteen, and the same is true of the correlation of .26. The other two correlations, .66 and .17, are to be interpreted in a similar fashion, except that ratings of dependency 1 are from years zero to three rather than from three to six.

The last main row, "Dependency 1 and 3," is to be interpreted in the same manner. Since dependency 3 was not measured during periods zero to three and three to six, these spaces are empty.

Interpretation. It is obviously impossible to attempt to memorize tables like Table 8.1. A more economical way of expressing the major findings of such tables is needed. A short interpretation of each table in this chapter is therefore presented, in an attempt to point out the major features of each one. After reading the interpretations of a few tables, the student will begin to understand and might wish to make his own interpretations. He is encouraged to do so, and to match his interpretations against those of the author. The greater the number of such "trials," the closer the two interpretations should become. In order to facilitate accurate interpretations, a few guidelines are offered.

First, for a sample of this size, a correlation of less than ±.30 has little significance. Suppose, for instance, that it is found that $_3r_{14}$(agg) = .25. To assert that a correlation of this size has little significance is to assert that it is still quite possible that the correlation in the *population* of which the Fels group is a *sample* is zero. To put it another way, a sample correlation of at least ±.30 is needed in order to make *plausible* a generalization to the population.

Second, *patterns* of correlations modify the first rule. Refer again to Table 8.1. The long-term stability of dependency in girls is described by the four correlations .26, .17, .24, and .23. None of these correlations reaches .30, and thus we might conclude, according to the first rule, that the stability is probably near zero in the population to which we wish to generalize (all girls aged zero to fourteen). Yet all four are positive. On the basis of this *pattern,* it can be concluded that, although long-term stability is low, it is not non-existent. If population stability were zero, we would expect the sample correlations to be distributed around zero, so that a correlation of .30 is balanced by a correlation near −.30. But such is not the case. All four correlations are above zero, suggesting that the population correlation is also above zero. For boys, on the other hand, the correlations cluster much closer to zero, with two negative correlations and two positive correlations. The one high correlation (.66) seems to be "out of place," since one would expect the others to be of a similar magnitude if there were really "something there," if such stability actually existed in the population of boys to which we wish to generalize.

With these two rules in mind, the most reasonable interpretation of Table 8.1 would seem to be as follows: (1) short-term stability of passivity and dependency was strong for both sexes: a passive two-year-old tended to be a passive six-year-old (and likewise, a non-passive two-year-old tended to be a non-passive six-year-old); a dependent eight-year-old tended to be a dependent twelve-year-old (and an independent eight-year-old tended to be an independent twelve-year-old); etc. (2) Long-term stability was very weak for boys and stronger for girls (i.e., all six correlations for girls were above zero with two above .30). Thus, for girls, one could predict with some accuracy passivity or dependency in early adolescence from similar behavior during the first six years of life. This was not the case for boys. Kagan and Moss (1962) report that a number of boys shifted from passivity in early childhood to assertiveness in later childhood. We shall later see a case history of such a shift.

Relation of Passivity and Dependency to Other Personality Variables

What is a passive and/or dependent child like, other than passive and/or dependent? First of all, passivity and dependency were correlated with each other. For example, the correlations between passivity and dependency 1 during period three to six, and between passivity and dependency 3 during period six to ten, are presented in Table 8.2.

TABLE 8.2

Correlations Between Passivity and Dependency

	Boys	Girls
Passivity and dependency 1 (3–6)	.61	.73
Passivity and dependency 3 (6–10)	.48	.66

Since passivity and dependency were highly correlated with each other, correlations between passivity and other personality variables will approximate the correlations between dependency and those other variables. Thus, for the sake of economy, only the former correlations are presented. Table 8.3 presents the correlations between passivity and other childhood personality variables for period six to ten separately for boys and girls.

TABLE 8.3

Correlations Between Passivity and Other Personality Variables

Other Personality Variables	Boys (6–10)	Girls (6–10)
Indirect aggression to peers	—.74	—.39
Competitiveness	—.58	—.56
Dominance of peers	—.67	—.40
Social withdrawal	.45	.46
Hyperkinesis	—.66	—.32
Conformity to adults	.78	.39

Interpretation. Although the variables in Table 8.3 have not yet been defined, little error will result if they are assigned their everyday meanings. The only variable that may appear completely mystifying is "hyperkinesis." Hyperkinesis refers to physical restlessness and is descriptive of those children who could not or did not inhibit motor discharge, who dashed around in the nursery school, or at home for that matter, with an aimless discharge of energy. The opposite of the hyperkinetic child is the lethargic child who engages in little physical action.

One may conclude that a passive and dependent child also tended to be (1) non-aggressive and non-competitive, (2) submissive to peers (i.e., non-dominant), (3) socially withdrawn, (4) inactive (i.e., not hyperkinetic), and (5) obedient to adult requests. Thus, the concepts of passivity and dependency are very useful concepts in the description of children's behavior; that is, knowledge of either of these two variables is informative about a number of other characteristics of the child in question. It is this total set of interrelationships that defines the *pattern* of passivity and dependency.

Stability of Passivity and Dependency from Childhood to Adulthood

Four adult personality characteristics inferred from the interview data appear to be clear manifestations of passivity and dependency. They are defined as follows:

Adult Behavior	*How It Was Measured*
Dependency on parents	Measured in terms of frequent visits, phone calls, requests for advice on choice of career or choice of college or major purchases, and a reluctance to move away from the parents
Dependency on love object	Measured in terms of apprehension about decisions without consulting spouse or sweetheart; viewing love object as more stable and wiser and, in general, heavy reliance on spouse or sweetheart
Withdrawal from stressful situations	Measured in terms of avoidance of positions of responsibility, postponing challenging or difficult tasks or decisions, changing vocational preparation because of anticipated failure, etc.
Concern with financial security	Measured in terms of avoidance of risk in occupational choice, wife's preference for husband to take a more secure but less promising one, etc.

The relationships between childhood passivity and dependency and these four adult variables are presented in Tables 8.4 and 8.5, separately for the two sexes. Not all possible correlations are shown; passivity dur-

ng periods zero to three, three to six, and six to ten and dependency on
nother (dependency 1), which was rated during periods zero to three
ind three to six, are not represented for the sake of economy. The cor-
·elations between these early childhood ratings and adult behavior were
3enerally low and non-significant.

Interpretation. Compare Tables 8.4 and 8.5 with each other. The
:orrelations for females seem to be mainly in the .30's and .40's, while
:he correlations for males are mainly in the .10's and .20's. Thus, the
most general conclusion is that childhood passivity and dependency dur-
ng ages ten to fourteen were predictive of similar behavior in young
idulthood for women but not for men. This conclusion is consistent with
:he fact that such behavior was not very stable for boys even during
:hildhood, much less from childhood to adulthood. In fact, ratings of
>ehavior for girls at ages six to ten were as predictive of adult behavior
is those at ages ten to fourteen. The stability for girls, then, reached
:ar back into childhood and extended into adulthood.

TABLE 8.4

3tability of Passivity and Dependency from Childhood to Adulthood for Males

Child Behavior at Ages 10–14	Adult Behavior			
	Dependency on Parents	Dependency on Love Object	Avoidance of Stress	Concern with Financial Security
Passivity	.01	.26	.36	.22
Dependency 2	.03	.25	−.24	.08
Dependency 3	.17	.09	−.17	.07

TABLE 8.5

3tability of Passivity and Dependency from Childhood to Adulthood for Females

Child Behavior at Ages 10–14	Adult Behavior			
	Dependency on Parents	Dependency on Love Object	Avoidance of Stress	Concern with Financial Security
Passivity	.47	.23	.67	.54
Dependency 2	.47	.24	.18	.13
Dependency 3	.46	.25	.43	.30

Two case histories are now provided as examples of the correlations
in these tables. The first one is illustrative of the stability of passivity

and dependency in women from childhood to adulthood, and the second
is illustrative of their instability in men.

A Case History—Subject 1173: Stability of Passivity and Dependency in Females

Age 3 years, 4 months: summary of Fels Nursery School observations.

S seems to be able to control and channel her behavior so that she got done
just what she wanted to get done. In this activity she was very independent
and capable. She was very social but also had a streak of aloof self-sufficiency,
and she always made her individuality felt. She was what might be called a
strong personality; often very intense, quite stubborn. . . . Her most outstanding characteristic was her consistent independence and integrity. In spite of
the fact that she imitated and followed certain boys, she seemed to do this very
much from her own choice and never lost the flavor of her individuality. She
was capable of being social and seemed to enjoy contacts, but at all times she
was her own master. She would often withdraw from play and go on in her
own direction at any time that she wished. . . . She was independent with
adults and, at times, negativistic just to be devilish. She seemed somewhat
self-conscious and had some cute little tricks. . . . In all, she could be characterized best by being called "tough minded." She shows determination and
will, originality and spark, curiosity and interest in factual detail. She likes to
quibble and argue, to verbalize, to construct, to accomplish. She is an indi-
vidualist, independent and stubborn.

Age 5 years, 4 months: Fels Nursery School observation.

S seems to be a vigorous, ruthless, competitive, highly sensual young woman,
but one felt quite often that antagonism toward others was simply a direct response to their behavior. . . . She has grown far more social and also popular
with an increasingly large crowd of special friends in a gang. She could be,
when she chose, quite a successful leader, forging ahead and organizing a group
on a hike, directing them and arranging things, and particularly keeping order
in a fair sharing of the tools in the carpenter shop. . . . Many of S's conflicts
with the adult world seemed a direct imitation of a certain boy. She needed
a chance to grumble, would scornfully refuse any adult suggestions or orders,
would usually go officially ahead to carry them out. She was quite demanding,
often shouting an order to an assistant. . . . With her other work the same
drive for strong achievement was also evident, sticking to anything until it was
finished, whatever the group stimuli.

Age 7 years: observation in Fels Day Camp.

S came accompanied by one friend. S did not seem overwhelmed by the
large proportion of adults around, but in her sturdy self-sufficient manner went
ahead with her own activities. Her friend was at first rather shy and withdrawn, and S, with her usual confident bullying and bossing of the adults,
tended to take the girl under her wing and make sure she had a good time. S
remains an exceptionally eager, imperturbable young woman. On a number
of small issues she did insist on her own way, on just how long she would stay
in the gym and play before lunch, but was quite reasonable about making compromises. She chose a rather difficult necklace to make and got quite mad

when it didn't work out well. She kept doggedly with it, very self-sufficient and continuing all on her own after getting some initial advice. . . . Her major effort was put on self-appointed tasks, to be able to master jumping over the horse at the gym where she took numerous tumbles until she succeeded. In spite of her distractability and preference for the apparatus, she did set to learning the new skills required there.

Age 9 years: report from teacher.

S is one of the most responsible children in the group. . . . She is self-reliant, independent, and knows how to plan her time well. She enters all games with enthusiasm, is very well coordinated. She is full of personality and "joie de vivre."

Adolescent behavior.

As an adolescent S was self-sufficient and sought roles that allowed her to nurture peers and have power over them. An independent approach to problems characterized much of her behavior, and this predisposition was as clear at age 3 as it was in young adulthood.

Adult behavior.

S is a 21-year-old unmarried woman who was in her senior year in college and one of the most independent women in the sample. As an adult, she had a strong need for recognition by others, combined with a striving for achievement-related goals. She liked to nurture others and often sought out situations in which she could give advice, support, and encouragement to peers. She was trying to sever any semblance of a dependent relation with her mother and derogated the latter because the mother seemed to be dependent upon her for companionship. Her relationship with men was consistent with the above pattern. She avoided men who attempted to place her in a passive role and she was having difficulty establishing a satisfactory heterosexual relationship. [Kagan and Moss, 1962, pp. 61–63.]

A Case History—Subject 2313: Instability of Passivity and Dependency in Males

One of the boys who showed a marked shift from dependence to independence had a father who placed unusually high values on autonomy of action for himself and his sons. As the boy approached preadolescence he experienced direct familial pressures for independence. The change in his behavior is apparent in the following excerpts.

At 2½ years of age he was described as unusually passive and cautious.

"S spent an unhappy week at nursery school. He cried a great deal and looked ready to cry even when he was not actually doing it. He drew away when other children approached him, and he seemed afraid of them. Usually he stood around and looked lost."

At 4½ years of age passivity was still a prepotent response.

"S was one of the group's most isolated members. He was non-competitive, unassertive, and sedentary. He shrank from actual physical contact with others and his relationships with peers were mild, long-distance verbal ones. S was petrified at rough handling. When he was verbally rebuffed or teased he smiled weakly and put his hands behind his back. S was the most eclipsed member of the group because of his apprehension, shyness, and inhibition."

By age 8 some shift toward independent behavior had occurred. There was a forced independence and swagger, and S had learned to use his intellectual skills as a weapon of power over others. He lectured and bragged to his peers, and the fear and apprehension that were manifest at age 4 were more disguised. S became less dependent on his family and more committed to an intellectual life.

As a late adolescent, the conflict associated with withdrawal from stress had swelled in intensity. S's internal standards did not permit retreat from potential failure situations. At age 16, for example, he realized that he was still afraid of dating girls and decided that there was only one effective way to conquer this fear. He invited to a dance the most popular girl in the school even though he had never been with her before. The primary reason for inviting her was to test his ability to conquer his fears.

As an adult he derogated dependent behavior and dependent people.

E: "Did you ever go to your family for advice with any problems?"

S: "My father was not approachable, and I didn't go to him for advice—in fact—he used to tell me to solve my own problems by myself, and I felt uneasy about going to him for help—ah—my mother—she wouldn't know what to tell me anyway."

His conflict was revealed in his perceptual interpretation of the picture of the man on his knees. On the first exposure, he reported:

"A woman in her thirties—holding a boy 8 or 9—she was comforting him."

On the second exposure:

"A woman in her early thirties with a little boy—she was cheering him up—comforting him or something—perhaps comforting him because something happened to him."

On the third exposure he said:

"A relatively young woman—the man in the foreground has been badly hurt and she was leaning over him—she was trying to pick him up—to get some kind of medical attention."

On the fourth exposure he retreated to his earlier perception and replied:

"A woman in her middle twenties in front of a younger boy—13 or 14—she's trying to pat him on the head—and that's figuratively and not literally—to cheer him up—or something." [Kagan and Moss, 1962, pp. 72–74.]

Adult Derivatives of Passivity and Dependency

Tables 8.4 and 8.5 and the case histories describe the relationship between childhood passivity and dependency, on the one hand, and similar adult behavior, on the other hand. It is possible, however, that adult behavior dissimilar to childhood passivity and dependency was nevertheless related to them. In such cases, we may speak of such adult behavior as being *derivatives* of the earlier, dissimilar behavior. Such derivatives will be presented when it appears they are not due to chance; i.e., when the correlations are above .30 and when the patterns are consistent.

Such happens to be the case with the following four adult variables: competitiveness, avoidance of initiation of heterosexual behavior, anxiety in social situations, and non-masculine interests. First, a short descriptions of these four adult variables is offered:

Adult Behavior	How It Was Measured
Competitiveness	Measured in terms of the adult's strivings for superiority over others in athletics, business, and intellectual pursuits; an orientation toward defeating other people
Avoidance of initiation of heterosexual behavior	Measured in terms of the adult's hesitancy in initiating heterosexual relationships, and the degree of inhibition of erotic behavior (necking, petting, and coitus)
Anxiety in social situations	Measured in terms of the degree to which an individual expressed anxiety and expectations of rejection when interacting with strangers: the general degree of tension when interacting in social situations
Non-masculine interests	Hobbies or spare-time activities such as gardening, reading, music, and cooking (as opposed to athletics, cars, hunting, gambling, etc.)

Table 8.6 presents the correlations between childhood passivity and these four adult variables. Only large correlations are presented in order to clarify the pattern. Correlations with childhood dependency are not presented; they were quite low.

TABLE 8.6

Adult Derivatives of Passivity and Dependency

Adult Behavior	Competitiveness		Avoidance of Heterosexual Behavior		Social Anxiety		Non-Masculine Interests	
	Boys	Girls	Boys	Girls	Boys	Girls	Boys	Girls
Child behavior								
Passivity (3–6)			.44		.41		.51	
Passivity (6–10)	−.58	−.58	.57		.46		.45	.36

Interpretation. Boys who were passive during the first 10 years of life became young adults who (1) behaved in a feminine way, (2) were non-competitive, and (3) avoided heterosexual behavior, as well as interactions with strangers. Childhood passivity in girls was not so systematically related to these derivatives, although it was predictive of feminine interests and non-competitiveness. The lack of a relationship with initiation of heterosexual behavior would be expected in women, since the *initiation* of such behavior is predominantly a male activity.

Summary and Interpretation of the Stability of Passivity and Dependency

Although the present chapter is concerned primarily with the description of personality development, the facts become much easier to remember if there is some kind of theoretical frame to hang them on. It is sometimes asserted that such "thought economy" is the primary function of theory. A short consideration of the theoretical aspects of passivity and dependency will therefore prove useful in remembering the facts. A later chapter will attempt to do more justice to theory.

First, how may we summarize the facts about the stability of passivity and dependency? It appears that one fundamental fact emerges: passivity and dependency were relatively stable in females and relatively unstable in males, both throughout childhood (zero to fourteen) and from middle childhood to early adulthood (i.e., from six to fourteen, to twenty-five). A second, less important, generalization concerns adult derivative behavior, where childhood passivity (but not dependency) in boys was predictive of non-competitiveness, avoidance of heterosexuality, social anxiety, and adult feminine interests.

Kagan and Moss suggest a reasonable explanation of the sex difference in stability of passivity and dependency. The American culture is quite permissive with respect to such behavior in girls; either dependent and passive behavior or independent and energetic behavior is acceptable, the former possibly because of its femininity and the latter possibly because of its *achievement* connotations. In boys, on the other hand, dependency and passivity are not generally acceptable, precisely because of their feminine connotations. Boys are expected to be masculine, and masculinity implies independence and "drive." Thus, the culture, consisting primarily of the home, peers, and the school, punishes, or at least does not reward, dependent and passive behavior in boys and rewards opposite kinds of behavior (unless they get too far out of line). In other words, the culture tries to prevent the dependent and passive boy from developing into a dependent, passive man. It fights such stability, and to the extent it is successful, there will be a low correlation between childhood and adult manifestations of such patterns. The adult man will tend to be independent and energetic regardless of what he was as a child.

AGGRESSION

Aggression is the second pattern of behavior discussed by Kagan and Moss. It was measured by seven different personality characteristics. We shall sample five of these. The definitions of these five are presented first.

Definition

(1) *Physical aggression to peers:* This scale was rated in terms of unprovoked, physical attacks on peers. It was not measured during period ten to fourteen because of its infrequent occurrence at that age interval. (2) *Indirect aggression to peers:* This scale was rated in terms of verbal threats, taunts, and teasing, as well as in terms of destruction or the taking of a peer's property. It was measured at all ages. (3) *Dominance of peers:* Measured in terms of attempts to control and direct the behavior of peers. "Leadership attempts" or "bossiness" might be similar terms. It was not measured during period zero to three because of the minimal amount of social interaction at those years. (4) *Behavioral disorganization:* This scale was rated during the early years in terms of frequency and intensity of crying and temper tantrums. In later years, it was rated in terms of uncontrolled anger outburst and rages, as well as tantrums. (5) *Competitiveness:* Measured in terms of how often the child became involved in games or tasks that involved winning or losing. Also measured in terms of the child's tendency to interpret social interaction in terms of competition for superiority. It was not measured during period zero to three because of its low frequency of occurrence during those years.

Stability in Childhood

Table 8.7 describes the stability of four of these five ratings during childhood. "Physical aggression" is not represented because it was not measured during period ten to fourteen. It was highly stable for both sexes during the first 10 years, with correlations in the .60 to .80 range.

Interpretation. Stability was high and about the same for both sexes, although there is a slight tendency for it to be higher for boys than for girls. Behavioral disorganization during the first three years showed no relationship to similar behavior at later ages. However, when it was observed in the preschool years (three to six) or at elementary school years (six to ten), it was predictive of similar behavior in adolescence for boys, but not for girls.

TABLE 8.7

Stability of Aggression During Childhood

Dimension	Short-Term Stability		Long-Term Stability	
	0–3 to 3–6	6–10 to 10–14	3–6 to 10–14	0–3 to 10–14
Indirect aggression to peers				
Boys	.59	.71	.64	*
Girls	.44	.60	.56	.53
Dominance of peers				
Boys		.84	.72	
Girls		.56	.59	
Behavioral disorganization				
Boys	.11	.67	.52	.35
Girls	.14	.25	−.03	−.02
Competitiveness				
Boys		.75	*	
Girls		.64	.73	

* Not enough ratings.

Thus, the appearance in the first five years of life of a pattern of behavior characterized as aggressive was prognostic of similar behavior during the elementary school years and during the high school years for both sexes. Aggression was quite stable during childhood.

Relation of Aggression to Other Childhood Personality Variables

We now ask, what was an aggressive child like, other than aggressive? If the correlations among the characteristics defining the pattern of aggression are first considered, one can determine if it is justifiable to let one of these characteristics represent the entire pattern when attempting to correlate the pattern with other, non-aggressive characteristics. Table 8.8. presents the correlations among some of the aggressive characteristics for ages six to ten. These correlations are very high for both sexes, suggesting that a physically aggressive child is also indirectly aggressive, as well as both dominating and competitive. Thus, any one of these characteristics can represent all four.

Table 8.9 presents the correlations between indirect aggression and other personality variables. Two of the variables probably require some clarification. *Nurturance to others* refers to a helpful and sympathetic attitude toward others, i.e., concern for the welfare of others. *Recognition behavior* refers to the child's strivings for status and approval from others.

TABLE 8.8

Interrelationships Among Different Kinds of Aggression for Ages Six to Ten

Kinds of Aggression	Boys	Girls
Physical and indirect aggression	.88	.67
Indirect aggression and dominance	.81	.89
Indirect aggression and competitiveness	.69	.55
Dominance and competitiveness	.70	.53

TABLE 8.9

Correlations Between Indirect Aggression and Other Personality Variables

	Boys		Girls	
Dimension	3–6	6–10	3–6	6–10
1. Passivity	—.78	—.74	—.76	—.39
2. Hyperkinesis	.34	.60	.26	.44
3. Conformity to adults	—.84	—.80	—.33	—.59
4. Nurturance to others	*	—.48	*	—.63
5. Recognition behavior	*	.45	*	.49

* Insufficient data.

Interpretation. Aggressive, dominant, and competitive children were also energetic (variable 1), active (2), did not highly conform to the wishes of adults (3), were unsympathetic with the problems of peers (4), and sought recognition for academic and athletic powers (5). As with passivity, these traits are consistent with what one would expect on the basis of everyday experience and indicate that aggressiveness is an important childhood personality pattern, allowing one to predict a good deal of other behavior from a knowledge of aggressive behavior alone.

Stability of Aggression from Childhood to Adulthood

Three adult personality characteristics appear to be similar to childhood aggression. Their definitions follow:

Adult Behavior	*How It Was Measured*
Aggressive retaliation	Measured in terms of the adult's tendency to respond to social frustration with direct verbal aggression or undisguised resistance, i.e., to blow up easily at others, and to let them know it
Ease of anger arousal	Measured in terms of how much it took to make the individual angry, irrespective of whether he expressed retaliation or not
Competitive behavior	Measured in terms of the adult's strivings for superiority over others in athletics, business, and intellectual pursuits; an orientation toward defeating other people

Tables 8.10 and 8.11 present the correlations between childhood aggression during period ten to fourteen and these three adult characteristics of aggression. "Physical aggression" is not presented in these tables because it was not rated during period ten to fourteen.

TABLE 8.10

Stability of Aggression from Childhood to Adulthood for Males

Child Behavior at Ages 10–14	Aggressive Retaliation	Ease of Anger Arousal	Competitiveness
Indirect aggression to peers	.31	.16	.45
Dominance of peers	.48	.47	.36
Behavioral disorganization	.51	.52	.59
Competitiveness	.34	.25	.39

TABLE 8.11

Stability of Aggression from Childhood to Adulthood for Females

Child Behavior at Ages 10–14	Aggressive Retaliation	Ease of Anger Arousal	Competitiveness
Indirect aggression to peers	.15	.24	−.03
Dominance of peers	.17	.09	.00
Behavioral disorganization	.09	.08	−.39
Competitiveness	−.24	−.08	.08

Interpretation. The correlations in Tables 8.10 and 8.11 present a remarkably clear picture. *Aggression was stable from childhood to adulthood for males, but not for females.* Only 2 of the 12 correlations for males are less than .30, while 11 of the 12 for females are less than .30.

Two case histories are now provided. The first illustrates stability of aggression in males, and the second illustrates instability in females.

A Case History—Subject 2610: Stability of Aggression in Males

Age seven years, six months: summary of day-camp observer.

"An impetuous, irresponsible child with lack of judgment and often purposely mean and malicious. He likes to bust up constructive activities of others with destructive and violent acts. He was noisy most of the time and, in any group, would disrupt its organization. He was rather infantile in these destructive activities. He cried easily, was easily frustrated, and would kick up a crying tantrum when he didn't get his way."

The mother felt that S was much too aggressive, and he was unpopular with his peers because of this behavior. On the other hand, she was somewhat fatalistic and remarked, "S is much like his father, nervous and a fighter. All the _____ are fighters."

After a visit to the Institute when S was 10 years old, the observer wrote: "S came in with his customary whoop. He dashed cars across the bridge, knocking down portions of it, building it up again with much noise and thumping. During the course of the morning, he managed to demolish the bridge with much pleasure. He bombed the Tinker-Toy parts, and, in all, his play was quite destructive. He painted several muddy-brown pictures, one of a girl and one of three faces, Japanese, German, and one unidentified, with bombs bursting around them, torpedoes exploding, and a rather colorful battleship under full steam. Later in the afternoon he raced around in the snow with Mary. He evidently teased her, since she came in very indignantly. Left alone, S amused himself by throwing snowballs at passing college students. . . .

"At the Institute, S ransacked the house while he was looking for the underground railway passage that presumably had been under the house. He was uncontrolled and heedless of property or person in his play. He had to be coaxed to endure the test session, and this response seemed to be a hostile reaction to adult authority. His moods were changeable. Happy one minute, sullen the next, and these moods were rather unpredictable as to their occurrence."

An excerpt from a report of a visit to S's school when he was 10 years old was similar in tone.

"S clumped loudly whenever he walked and needled the teacher a great deal in annoying ways. Whenever she spoke to him for talking out loud, his reply was a blank stare and a 'What?' S was almost insolent in his manner to the teacher. During the spelling test he drew airplanes on the blackboard. He erased them at the teacher's request, but wrote his spelling downhill. The teacher reproved him, and he erased it and did the same thing all over again. He made flip remarks to the class and was generally a nuisance throughout the morning. S was rather smug and sarcastic. One girl sighed at the arithmetic test and said, 'It was very hard.' S replied, 'It's easy as pie, just use your brain—what brain?' During the visit he disturbed the whole room twice by noisy trips to the pencil sharpener in a defiant, sullen, cross, and cocky attitude."

At 11 years old, the following summary was written after an annual day-camp session.

"S's play was of a blustering, aggressive sort with little quiet persistence in it. He liked active games, easy activities with quick success, lots of noise and action. He appeared to like 'baiting' the adults; he liked daring authorities by a slim balance more than the actual end product. He liked to run wild in the yard and did this most of the time with an abandoned sort of violent physical effort. S has a loud voice, which he likes to throw around a lot. He loved strange and anal-sounding grunts and groans and sings at the top of his voice. He has no real group cooperative play. He showed off, clowned a lot, and initiated a lot of aggressive play with other boys."

During the adult interview, when S was 27, he indicated a low threshold for anger and frequent retaliations to personal attack.

E: "Can you remember the last time you were mildly irritated at anyone?"

S: "I get irritated at drivers every day. I'm driving in traffic—there's usually some idiot that wants to pull out in front of you or something like that. I'm inclined to get too upset about things like that and be criticized for blowing-up like that."

E: "Do you tend to blow-up if somebody makes an error?"

S: "Yeh—I swear sometimes. Let's see, this morning or last night some character pulled out of the filling station right in the path of a gasoline truck, and he came swerving over into my lane, wasn't very close, but I said a few things under my breath. I get kinda excited about a lot of things. I blow off a lot of steam verbally, and don't do much else—."

E: "What do you tend to do if you come home at night and your wife is irritated with you?"

S: "Well—that depends on the mood I'm in. Sometimes I'll blow-up. Generally, I get too obnoxious and get to feeling guilty and try to smooth things over."

E: "Is there any issue that tends to cause most friction between you and your wife?"

S: "Nothing in particular; well, she criticizes my sloppy habits, like saying I should hang up my coat or something."

E: "And what do you say to this?"

S: "Well, I don't remember exactly. I think I got angry the other night; it wasn't so much. I mean I realize I should have hung my coat up; it was the way she said it. I forget just how it was."

E: "What do you tend to do when someone insults you?"

S: "If somebody gets to insulting me, I insult them right back." [Kagan and Moss, 1962, pp. 96–98.]

A Case History—Subject 121: Instability of Aggression in Females

At 2 years of age S's nursery-school behavior was often punctuated with aggressive outbursts.

"S seldom talks or shows any outward sign of emotion. She is by far the most physically bold child, doing much jumping and climbing. She often reacts to other children destructively, pushing them down, pulling out hair, and absconding with toys."

At home her behavior was similar to that shown in the nursery school. The home observer wrote:

"S often treats her younger sister roughly, pinching and pushing her. The mother thinks it is more a matter of curiosity than of meanness or resentment of the baby's presence. S is the same way with other people, adults and children, attacking them and pushing them over, and standing back to see the effect."

Two years later, at 4 years of age, S's nursery-school behavior was clearly competitive and aggressive.

"S was habitually aggressive, but she was not a successful leader. She was very competitive and seized every opportunity to equal or excel the feats of the other children. She liked to tease, and she had great sport with Mary and Peter, both of whom would yell or whine when she plagued them. Occasionally she played cooperatively with others, but more often she put herself in the role of a rival. S complied with adult requests at times, but at other times resisted with all her might. She needed to be reminded to take turns and to respect property rights. It was not because she did not know about these nursery-school principles, but rather because she could get such a rise out of other children by pushing in front of them or by snatching at their toys."

When S visited day camp at 6½, the predisposition toward unprovoked aggression was still clearly present.

"S was somewhat shy and wary in social situations and made few social advances. She was almost eager in her response when others made advances to her. She seemed to expect that she might not be accepted and was surprised and pleased when other children were nice to her. S was very easy to have around when she was busy. Sometimes in free moments she went a little wild. The other children complained that she pushed them, knocked their sand constructions down, or poked her finger in their clay work. These outbursts were over in a flash. She needed no provocation other than idleness to start her off. She never made excuses for her behavior or even admitted anything about it. S was out for her own advancement and was sort of a lone wolf. She seemed to feel no deep identification with the group or with any of its members."

During the early school years S was independent, and verbally rebellious and attacking. She was competitive with peers and began to gain some peer respect because of her daring, verbal skills and athletic prowess. By age 10 a dramatic shift occurred in her behavior. She became interested in her attractiveness to boys, and this new motive was accompanied by a sharp decrease in overt aggression. At age 10 the day-camp observer wrote:

"There has been a good deal of change in S's appearance: straightened posture, hair washed clean with French braids, and frilly, nice clothes. The big thing seems to be the big shift in S herself. She no longer needs to express her hostility and alienation toward the world. She has the possibilities of becoming a very attractive little girl. Socially S has loosened up a great deal. Though no one in this group was congenial with her, she was much more outgoing than in previous years. At the races she got to the tomboy state, loudly boasting and jeering at one girl for being so awkward. Most of the time she had a quiet, almost demure, air about her, listening to what others had to say and smiling in a friendly fashion."

At 10½ S was interviewed at the Institute and reported a dream sequence that disclosed the essence of her conflict. She has a strong need for power over others, but wanted to retain a feminine identification. Thus blatant forms of aggression were replaced with more subtle methods. The psychologist's notes of the interview follow:

"S is having a number of dreams. They do not seem to be of the nightmare variety, but are obsessional, and she wakes up with a heavy sense of despondency. Last night she had a wish-fulfillment dream in which she was so beautiful that every man fell immediately in love with her and she could have whatever she wanted. The emphasis in the dream seemed to be on the sense of power that this physical attractiveness gave her. A policeman tried to arrest her, and she seduced him into letting her go. She went up to the store with expensive goods and got the manager to give them to her. As S related this dream, she began acting it out, half laughing at herself as she did so.

"Later in the talk, as we got on the S's plans for the future, she said, 'I'd like to be a housewife and a pianist.' Asked what she would do if she were a man, she said, 'She would still play piano and have kids,' and then she suddenly burst out with the wish that she were a boy. Men have so much more fun, they play soccer and baseball, and do not have to be dainty. S hates daintiness, high heels, and having to daintily trip-along. If she were a boy, she could have her hair cut in a crew-cut, never have to bother about it. She says her younger sister also wishes she were a boy and that her mother puts no pressure on them to be dainty. *It is just the outside world that does.* Her mother doesn't care about appearances at all herself, and as a girl, she was one of the best fighters in the neighborhood."

The perception of a cultural pressure to adopt traditional feminine traits is clearly verbalized by this insightful girl. We have repeatedly referred to this process in order to explain many of our results. The cultural prescription of sex-appropriate behaviors forms a limiting wall that the child finds difficult to scale. These cultural rules set definite limits on the external form of every child's overt behavior pattern.

By 12½ years this girl had adopted more completely the traditional feminine-role behaviors. The home visitor wrote:

"S has passed conspicuously into adolescence. Since the last time I saw her, her breasts have developed noticeably, and she has a very pretty figure and is becoming quite attractive. The mother told me privately that S had bought a new bathing suit, a one-piece affair, and when she tried it on for the family, her older brother gave a long, low whistle, which embarrassed her terribly. Mother shows considerable interest in S's appearance and in helping her to become attractive. She mentioned today that before school starts, she plans to take S to a hair stylist for a special cut. She also remarked that S says she wants to grow up and marry and have children, 'so that's what we're getting ready for'."

S did very well academically in high school and college and decided to go to graduate school. On first impression S appeared quiet, reserved, and neither competitive nor aggressive. She became conflicted over an intellectual career because the required competition in graduate school threatened the self-image she was trying so hard to retain. She was sufficiently insecure about her conception of herself as a woman that intense involvement in an intellectually aggressive atmosphere made her uncomfortable. During the adult interview she tried to explain why she withdrew from graduate school.

S: "I have the feeling that if you're going to do something so weird and peculiar, you at least have to feel thoroughly right about it."

E: "And you didn't feel right about it?"

S: "No. Everything didn't quite fit somehow. I mean, a woman who really has a good motivation in her field and—and is also secure in her own values and relationships, feels pretty much at home there (in graduate school) I think."

E: "What kind of woman do you feel would have felt secure in that situation?"

S: "What kind of woman would have?"

E: "Yes."

S: "Well, like there were one or two people there, they had either a real—well, one of them worked and she knew that—ah—that she wanted to be an engineer, and she wanted a degree, and she was very happily married. I had the feeling she—felt secure in her personal life, and secure in what she was doing, and she was pretty. She knew that there were discriminations against her. She didn't have the feeling 'Do I really belong here,' and that kind of thing."

E: "But you did have these thoughts?"

S: "You're never—it was sort of a lonely position, in a way, because—you can't go with them—I mean, men are more groupy and women are more groupy, and it's sort of hard for one woman to be a part of a men's group. You know, eating lunch together and that kind of thing. They were very—the guys were nice. They were understanding and friendly, by and large, but I never quite felt as though you really were a part of things, such as in a really mixed group."

E: "So, in part, you felt that this was primarily a masculine situation, and this was a threat to your concept of yourself as a woman?"

S: "Yes, I think so, 'Are you really a woman or are you a man' type?"

E: "That could have been involved then?"

S: "Yes. I think it was. Quite definitely. The feeling of not—of wanting to establish myself as a person rather than—if you realized that the pressure was going to be like that, you could go to a school, at least, like—well, the University of _____, which I think has more fraternities and sororities. But when you don't even take that into consideration as a factor, well, then you're stuck with it. There you are—and it hits you."

E: "You had no idea this would happen?"

S: "No. Most people don't though. They say, 'Oh, boy—what fun! All those men!' It doesn't work that way. It is nice in a way; it's just not enough."

When the interviewer asked about S's reaction to frustrating situations, she indicated a reluctance to retaliate, even though she might have felt angry.

E: "When you are annoyed, what do you do?"

S: "What do I do? Nothing. Just keep a straight face. One time I was so concentrated on controlling myself that I could hardly move. The girl said, 'Do you have a stiff neck?' I was just so rigid. When I'm annoyed, it's usually not what they're doing that I'm annoyed at as much as the position it puts me in. If someone does something, and I'm mad, that is, completely at cross-purposes with what I happen to want to do in the situation, it doesn't annoy me unless it throws me out of kilter. I always figure rather than get annoyed and start that whole thing up, so that they realize I'm annoyed, I might as well do what I have to do to make what I want to out of the situation, so I won't be annoyed anymore."

E: "You're only annoyed when the behavior of another person, in some way, interferes with what you want to do?"

S: "Interferes and when I can't—umm—when I haven't made peace with that interference somehow, you know. It doesn't matter if it interferes, you know, if I want to plan something, and somebody comes in and says, 'Will you do something else,' or if I—you know, I think, 'Well, that's my job.' You know."

E: "Besides your boss, who else, as you think of it, is more apt to annoy and irritate you by the things they do?"

S: "My boss and the two people that give me work—that I'm not sure is necessary, sometimes."

E: "Are these men or women?"

S: "One of them is a woman and one is a man. I get annoyed sometimes—let's see—there's one guy that, whenever I go anywhere and he's there, he's sort of a nice guy, but he really does annoy me. He's just sort of a hangdog type of guy. And, gee whiz, I guess it's because, to a certain extent, I react against it because—being lonely, you know, not having a decent relationship built, it's a temptation to sort of take him up on the implied offer. I suppose it's partly rationale that I don't just sort of move away and forget it, you know."

E: "In general, when at the moment you are deeply angry at someone, a friend, boy or girl friend, are you more likely to express it verbally at the time or not say anything?"

S: "Do nothing."

E: "Not say anything? Because you don't want to alienate them?"

S: "Yes, I suppose that's it. I don't know why I don't. The only person that I've ever gotten in the hang of really expressing what I felt was my roommate last year. She was brilliant, temperamental, and a strong-minded person and I finally—we would just flare up at each other—just because it was so murderous not to. With her I would get so mad that I just couldn't—just go off and cool down. I'd stay mad at her."

E: "What kind of thing did she do?"

S: "Oh, the precipitating things were—were not very simple, I suppose. We had different ways of life. She had no concern with neatness and order at all. I didn't mind our room, I didn't mind doing her laundry, I didn't mind emptying the trash all the time—most of the time. But sometimes, you know, it's her turn to wash the dishes, and two days later, they're still not washed, you get mad. I don't think that would have bothered me if we had had a basic understanding, but I guess—umm—there was some antagonism between us that I've never really pinned down. Partly, I guess, on my part. I realized this fall when I was listening to some music that we used to play last year and the feeling came back to me, all of a sudden, of this enviousness of her freedom. She would do what she felt like doing. All the time she was buying the food that she felt like eating. It didn't matter how expensive. She could afford it. She was on a Woodrow-Wilson scholarship, which helped. She would study till all hours and sleep till all hours. Her room was in a constant chaos—piles of books. And it just hit me then—how I envied her—her freedom."

E: "Would you say, in general, that you are easily irritated or not?"

S: "I would say sort of medium."

E: "Medium?"

S: "Yes."

E: "When you're in an argument with someone and they start getting very excited and there is a note of anger present, are you apt to persist in your argument or not?"

S: "I like to try to get out of it, I guess. Because I can get involved too. And I know that when I do that, the first thing it indicates is how insecure I feel about what I'm saying. The only time I used to really get into this was when I went with a certain guy last year. The feeling that he was just as right as I was was what really threw me for a loop or that I had nothing to take hold of to say why I felt the way I did. *So, in general, I just try to back out of it if people get me angry or if I think I'm going to get angry.*"

S's preference for withdrawal from situations where she might be tempted into aggression was in sharp contrast to the destruction and aggression that characterized her childhood behavior.

Suppression of aggression in order to maintain a feminine sex-role identification was probably one of the major reasons for the minimal continuity of overt aggression in the present sample of women. [Kagan and Moss, 1962, pp. 112–118.]

Adult Derivatives of Aggression

What adult characteristics other than those defining aggression were associated with childhood aggression? Taking indirect aggression as representative of all childhood aggression characteristics, Table 8.12 presents its correlations with four derivative adult characteristics: avoidance of initiation of heterosexual behavior, sex anxiety, repression of sex, and anxiety in social situations. The first and last of these characteristics were previously defined. Sex anxiety was intended to measure anxiety elicited by thoughts of anticipated or committed sexual behavior; repression of sex was intended to measure denial of sexual thoughts, and the refusal to show any concern about gratification of sexual needs.

TABLE 8.12

Adult Derivatives of Aggression

Adult Behavior	Child Behavior Indirect Agression (6–10)	
	Boys	Girls
Avoidance of heterosexual behavior	−.47	−.49
Sexual anxiety	−.36	−.51
Repression of sexuality		−.67
Social anxiety	−.36	

Interpretation. Boys and girls who were aggressive at ages six to ten were sexually active as adults and had little anxiety about sexual behavior. Aggressive girls, as adults, were frank and open about sexual behavior, rather than defensive (i.e., rather than repressing sexual thoughts). Thus, childhood aggression not only predicted adult aggression (in males) but also was somewhat successful in predicting adult sexual behavior in both sexes.

It will be recalled that childhood behavioral disorganization showed no high relationships with aggressive adult behavior in women, although it did with men (Tables 8.10 and 8.11). Table 8.13 shows that behavioral disorganization in girls was predictive of another pattern of adult behavior. The eight-year-old girl who engaged in frequent temper tantrums became a young woman who was involved with achievement and recognition strivings, and was in conflict about her dependency upon other adults.

TABLE 8.13

Adult Derivatives of Behavioral Disorganization in Women

Adult Behavior	Child Behavior Behavioral Disorganization (6–10)
Recognition Behavior	.45
Achievement Behavior	.45
Intellectual Behavior	.61
Dependency Conflict	.39

Summary of the Stability of Aggression

As with passivity and dependency, an attempt will be made to ease the burden of remembering the major facts about aggression by offering a tentative theoretical guide. But first, what are the basic facts?

Once again, there seems to be only one fundamental, dominant fact: aggression was relatively stable in males and relatively unstable in females. This generalization must be qualified. Aggression was stable for both sexes during childhood, but was predictive of similar adult behavior only for males. A second main fact has to do with derivative behavior. Childhood aggression was predictive of adult sexual initiativeness, frankness, and lack of anxiety in both sexes. In addition, childhood behavioral disorganization was predictive of adult recognition, achievement, and mastery strivings in women.

Consider the first main generalization: aggressive behavior was stable in males from childhood to adulthood, but not in females. Recall that passivity and dependency behavior showed an opposite pattern; it was stable from childhood to adulthood in females but not in males. This latter fact was accounted for in terms of cultural pressures that are different for the two sexes; males are pushed toward independent, non-passive behavior as they get older, while women are not. Kagan and Moss present the same general notion to account for the differential stability of aggression for the two sexes; that is, aggressive behavior is acceptable in the male, but less so in the female. The female is pushed away from direct manifestations of aggression as she gets older; the ten-year-old tomboy is tolerated, but the sixteen-year-old is supposed to be a "sweet sixteen."

This point of view not only accounts for the main fact of sex differences in aggressive stability but also does a reasonable job of accounting for the findings of adult derivative behavior. Recall the findings with respect to passivity. Childhood passivity did not predict adult passivity in men, but it did predict the derivatives of non-competitiveness, avoidance of sex, social anxiety, and non-masculine interests. These male adult characteristics are perhaps more acceptable than passivity, and tendencies toward passivity thus follow the line of *least cultural resistance:*

Thus passivity, which is unacceptable to the male, did not predict adult passivity or dependence but did predict theoretically reasonable derivatives (noncompetitiveness, nonmasculine interests, social anxiety, and avoidance of sexuality). Passivity among women, which is congruent with female sex-role standards, had positive associations with the phenotypically similar adult responses of withdrawal and dependency.

Behavioral disorganization showed the reverse pattern. Rage reactions and low frustration tolerance, which are congruent with traditional masculine sex-role standards, were primarily associated with aggressive behavior in adult men —a phenotypically similar class of behaviors. Behavioral disorganization more clearly conflicts with acceptable behavior for women and was associated with the theoretically reasonable derivatives of intellectual mastery, status striving, and conflict over dependency.

The differential sequelae of passivity and disorganization for men and women suggest an hypothesis related to one formulated previously. *When a behavior is congruent with the traditional definition of sex-appropriate behavior, it is likely to be predictive of phenotypically similar behavior in adulthood. When it conflicts with traditional sex-role standards, the relevant motive is more likely to find behavioral expression in derivative or substitute responses that are socially more acceptable.* [Kagan and Moss, 1962, p. 200.]

This argument makes good sense in terms of learning theory. If we rename "cultural acceptability" *reinforcement* and "cultural unacceptability" *non-reinforcement,* then the results for both passivity and dependency and aggression are seen to fall into line. We need merely restate the italicized conclusion as follows: *When a behavior is reinforced, it is likely to be stable from childhood to adulthood. When it is non-reinforced, it is likely to be extinguished and replaced by behaviors that are reinforced.* It seems amazing that, if we had seriously applied the principle of reinforcement to the concepts of passivity and dependency and aggression, and had taken into account known cultural practices in the application of the principle, we could have predicted the main results of this entire chapter in advance.

SUMMARY

Passivity and dependency constituted one broad behavior pattern whose stability was measured in the Fels study. During childhood, it was defined in terms of degrees of withdrawal and inactivity (passivity) and degrees of affection-seeking and aid-seeking from parents and other adults (dependency). In adulthood, it was defined in terms of degrees of withdrawal from stress and reliance on parents and spouse.

The main finding was that passivity and dependency were reasonably stable in females, both during childhood and from childhood to adulthood. Stability in males was considerably lower, with few correlations exceeding .30. Passivity and dependency were predictive, however, of a derivative pattern of behavior in males: passive and dependent boys tended to be feminine as young adults.

Aggression constituted a second broad behavior pattern. It was defined in terms of direct and indirect aggression to peers, dominance and competitiveness toward peers, and frequency of uncontrolled anger outbursts. In adulthood, it was defined in terms of similar responses: competitiveness in business, ease of anger arousal, etc.

There were three main findings. First, aggression was stable for both sexes during childhood. Second, it was stable from childhood to adulthood in males but not in females. Third, adult heterosexuality was a derivative of childhood aggression in both sexes. A subsidiary finding was that females tended to be strongly oriented toward intellectual achievement if they had been aggressive as children.

Both passivity–dependency and aggression seem to follow the principle of least cultural resistance. According to this notion, a behavior pattern remains stable to the extent it is congruent with cultural expectations. Thus, passivity and dependency, acceptable in females but not in males, manifested greater stability in females. Aggression, more acceptable in males than in females, manifested more stability in males. The principle of least cultural resistance seems to follow directly from the principle of reinforcement, and thus learning theory is seen to play a central role in the understanding of personality development.

BIBLIOGRAPHY

KAGAN, J., and Moss, H. A. (1962). *Birth to maturity*. New York: John Wiley & Sons, Inc.

9

Achievement, Sexuality, and Anxiety

ACHIEVEMENT AND RECOGNITION BEHAVIOR

Strivings for achievement and recognition are behavioral characteristics that can be seen every day: e.g., the child who runs to mother and says, "Look at the picture I made"; and the man who twirls his Phi Beta Kappa key as he walks down the street. Such *recognition* behavior is to be distinguished from *achievement* behavior, which Kagan and Moss define in terms of behavior aimed at ". . . satisfaction of an internal standard of excellence" (1962, p. 120). The goal of recognition behavior is other-approval, while the goal of achievement behavior is self-approval. Keppler's struggle of two decades to discover the laws of planetary motion and Newton's hesitation in publishing the law of gravitation because of doubt were primarily achievement behaviors and only secondly recognition behaviors. Unfortunately, it is difficult to separate the two. A bit of behavior that gives one internal satisfaction is usually approved of by others.

Definition and Stability in Childhood

Achievement behavior was measured by several scales and recognition behavior by only one, as follows: (1) *General achievement:* This scale attempted to provide an overall measurement of achievement in all areas of behavior. It was measured in all periods except for ages ten to fourteen, where more specific achievement behaviors were measured. In the first three years, it was defined in terms of persistence in block building, coloring, and other motor activities. In later years, it was defined in terms of persistence and interest in intellectual and physical activities of one sort or another. (2) *Intellectual achievement:* Measured only in period ten to fourteen, it was defined in terms of the child's attempts to learn and master language and numbers, amount of time spent reading, and his involvement in general pursuit of knowledge. (3) *Athletic achievement:* Measured in period ten to fourteen, it was defined in terms of interest and involvement in athletic skills and the amount of time spent in such activities. (4) *Competitiveness:* As indicated previously, it measured the child's attempt at superiority over others. It was measured in all periods except zero to three. (5) *Expectancy of task failure:* This scale was defined in terms of anticipations of future failures, as indicated by statements to that effect and avoidance of achievement-type behaviors. It was measured in periods six to ten and ten to fourteen. (6) *Recognition behavior:* Measured in periods six to ten and ten to fourteen, it was defined in terms of the child's strivings for status and social approval from others.

Table 9.1 describes the stability of these behavior characteristics during childhood.

Interpretation.   Table 9.1 is to be read in the same way as the tables in Chapter 8. The second and third rows might present some difficulty, since two dimensions are correlated against each other. Thus, the correlation of .81 represents the relationship between general achievement behavior at ages six to ten and intellectual achievement behavior at ages ten to fourteen for boys. Likewise, the correlation of .39 represents the relationship between these same two dimensions except that the general achievement ratings were taken from years three to six.

Look first at the first and last columns. These columns present the correlations between general achievement behavior in the first three years of life with similar behavior at later years. None of the six correlations reach .30, and four are negative while two are positive. The first general conclusion, therefore, is that *general achievement behavior in the first three years was not predictive of similar behavior later on.* The two-year-old who industriously built block structures, persisted in attempts to put simple puzzles together, or patiently put beads on a shoelace was ". . . neither the third grade's scholar nor the eighth grade's creative scientist" (Kagan and Moss, 1962, p. 123). This finding is consistent with the fact that IQ scores obtained during the first two years show only a negligible correlation with later IQ scores.

Now cover up these two columns and glance at the rest of the table. The remaining correlations are quite high and positive with the exception of those concerned with athletic achievement. Ignoring these, *all*

TABLE 9.1

Stability of Achievement and Recognition Behavior During Childhood

Dimension	Short-Term Stability		Long-Term Stability	
	0–3 to 3–6	6–10 to 10–14	3–6 to 10–14	0–3 to 10–14
General achievement				
Boys	−.28			
Girls	−.14			
General achievement and intellectual achievement at 10–14				
Boys		.81	.39	−.19
Girls		.76	.68	−.18
General achievement and athletic achievement at 10–14				
Boys		−.26	−.41	.27
Girls		.30	.16	.15
Competitiveness				
Boys		.75	*	
Girls		.64	.73	
Expectancy of task failure				
Boys		.58		
Girls		.66		
Recognition strivings				
Boys		.77		
Girls		.47		

* Not enough ratings.

the correlations are above .30, and 8 of the 11 are above .60. The second general conclusion, therefore, is that, ignoring the first three years and ignoring athletic achievement, *general achievement and intellectual strivings, competitiveness, expectations of success or failure, and recognition strivings were all exceedingly stable from ages three to fourteen.* The four-year-old nursery-school child, or the six-year-old first-grader who was competitively striving to paint the best picture, who worked hard and expected to do well, and who frequently asked the teacher to look at his picture was engaging in similar achievement and recognition strivings in junior high and senior high school.

The only correlations not yet accounted for are those between general achievement behavior and athletic achievement at ages ten to fourteen. These correlations are generally low, suggesting a weak relationship between the two dimensions. The two negative correlations for boys indicate that *there was some tendency for boys who were manifesting academic achievement behavior from the age of three on to avoid ath-*

letics and not to be interested in sports. For girls, this was not true. There was a slight *positive* tendency for academically oriented girls to also be interested in athletics.

Relation of Achievement and Recognition Behavior to Other Childhood Personality Variables

Achievement and recognition behavior was highly correlated with IQ scores obtained at age six and beyond. For example, IQ scores obtained at age six correlated .60 (boys) and .76 (girls), with intellectual achievement strivings at ages six to ten. Thus, it may be concluded that a characteristic of children with high IQ scores was an orientation toward intellectual achievement. The two probably influenced each other; i.e., a high IQ score may cause one to orient toward intellectual achievement behavior, and such behavior might raise one's IQ score, as we saw in Chapter 3.

IQ scores correlated negatively with athletic achievement behavior in boys. The correlation between IQ scores obtained at age six and athletic achievement behavior at ages ten to fourteen was −.58 for boys. Thus, in this sample, boys tended to choose intellectual or athletic achievement, but not both. Those who chose intellectual achievement scored higher on IQ tests and were generally incompetent in athletics and avoided them. Boys who emphasized athletics were poorly motivated intellectually and academically and obtained lower IQ scores. This sharp division did not occur for girls.

Socioeconomic status was correlated with intellectual and athletic achievement behavior for boys, but not for girls. The correlations between intellectual and athletic achievement behavior and fathers' educational level are presented in Table 9.2. This table shows that the higher the educational level of the father, the greater the intellectual achievement strivings of the son, and the less his athletic involvement. These findings are consistent with the general tendency for upper socioeconomic levels to be more interested in *symbolic* activity and lower socioeconomic levels to be more interested in *physical* activity.

TABLE 9.2

Correlations of Intellectual and Athletic Achievement Behavior with Fathers' Educational Level

Behavior at Ages 10–14	Boys	Girls
Intellectual achievement behavior correlated with fathers' educational level	.71	.09
Athletic achievement behavior correlated with fathers' educational level	−.22	.09

Stability of Achievement and Recognition Behavior from Childhood to Adulthood

Adult behavior that was similar to childhood achievement and recognition behavior is described below.

Adult Behavior	How It Was Measured
Achievement behavior	Measured in terms of strivings for intellectual mastery; athletic achievement behavior in adulthood was minimal—few adults were very interested in this kind of achievement
Recognition behavior	Measured in terms of desire and attempts to obtain status and social recognition, usually in terms of academic honors, positions of leadership, and vocations having high status (e.g., doctor, lawyer, scientist)
Concern with intellectual competence	Measured in terms of the adult's response to a question concerned with the *importance* of education and knowledge
Fear of failure, and withdrawal from potential failure situations: withdrawal from stressful situations	Measured in terms of apprehension about college work, choosing an easier major or vocation because of fear of failure, etc.

Tables 9.3 and 9.4 present the correlations between childhood achievement and recognition behavior and these four adult characteristics, separately for males and females.

TABLE 9.3

Stability of Achievement and Recognition Behavior from Childhood to Adulthood for Males

Child Behavior	Adult Behavior			
	Achievement Behavior	Recognition Behavior	Concern with Intellectual Competence	Fear of Failure
General achievement behavior (6–10)	.46	.57	.68	−.31
Intellectual achievement strivings (10–14)	.40	.60	.66	−.21
Athletic achievement strivings (10–14)	−.18	−.17	−.47	.00
Competitiveness (10–14)	.05	.27	.06	−.01
Expectancy of failure (10–14)	−.34	−.62	−.51	.31
Recognition strivings (10–14)	.25	.36	.24	−.22

TABLE 9.4

Stability of Achievement and Recognition Behavior from Childhood to Adulthood for Females

	Adult Behavior			
Child Behavior	Achievement Behavior	Recognition Behavior	Concern with Intellectual Competence	Fear of Failure
General achievement behavior (6–10)	.38	.51	.49	−.34
Intellectual achievement strivings (10–14)	.42	.56	.49	−.44
Athletic achievement strivings (10–14)	.01	−.09	.02	.04
Competitiveness (10–14)	.00	.06	.24	−.07
Expectancy of failure (10–14)	−.29	−.40	−.40	.37
Recognition strivings (10–14)	.20	.39	.40	−.08

Interpretation. Tables 9.3 and 9.4 indicate considerable stability from childhood to early adulthood for general and intellectual achievement behavior, expectations of success and failure, and recognition strivings. This general trend is true for both sexes. The negative correlations in the last column (adult fear of failure) are, of course, consistent with this trend. Children who were oriented toward achievement developed into young adults who were not afraid of failure. The only exception to the general picture of child-adult stability is with respect to competitiveness. Although this dimension was quite stable during childhood (see Table 9.1), it was not predictive of similar behavior in adulthood. This unexpected result is probably a sampling error, since competitiveness at ages six to ten (not shown) was predictive of similar adult behavior.

Athletic achievement behavior during ages ten to fourteen was, in general, not highly correlated with adult achievement behavior, which is consistent with the finding that it was not highly correlated with general achievement behavior at ages zero to three and three to six. There is a suggestion, however, that adolescent boys not involved in athletic achievement became young men who were rated high on intellectual achievement behavior. Note the correlations of −.18, −.17, and −.47 in Table 9.3. They are low in general but are consistent with the correlations of −.26 and −.41 in Table 9.1, which summarizes the relationship between general achievement at ages three to six and six to ten and athletic achievement, respectively. These five negative correlations out of six suggest the following generalization. Boys who were not involved or who avoided athletics were boys with strong intellectual achievement strivings, and developed into young men with a strong orientation toward intellectual competence; and, vice versa, boys strongly involved in athletics were boys with weak strivings toward intellectual achievement, and developed into young men with little concern about intellectual competence.

Two case histories are now provided. The first illustrates the stability of achievement behavior from childhood to adulthood in males, as well as the negative correlation with athletic achievement in boys. The second illustrates stability in females, but without the avoidance of physical interests as manifested by males.

A Case History—Subject 2313: Stability of Achievement Behavior and Avoidance of Physical Activity in Males

At 2½ years of age the nursery-school observer wrote:

"S was one of the group's most isolated members. At no time did he ever play an aggressive role in relationship to the other children. He was noncompetitive, nonassertive, and his play was puttering and sedentary. He did make a few approaches to others in which he offered a toy to children, but he usually shrank from actual physical contact with other playmates. His relationships with others were mild long-distanced, verbal ones. S was petrified at rough handling. If he were verbally rebuffed or teased, he smiled weakly, put his hands behind his back, and verbalized about what he would do or had once done. He quite frequently refused friendly offers from other children, as if he were apprehensive of new experiences. S appears to enjoy himself as long as direct pressure is not brought to bear on him. The most salient thing about S is a binding inhibition and apprehension. He moves tentatively and quaveringly like an old man on an icy day. His whole posture exudes timidity. He is drawn in at the knees and elbows, hunched at the shoulders, his head is poked forward, his hands, often rabbit-fashion, hanging limply from wrists, tucked together at his chest. In any swirl of noise or rough play he becomes terrified and rigid, holding himself away stiffly. In any excitement of his own he constrains himself and draws in tighter and tighter. When excited or afraid he is wound up so rigid that his posture and expression become taut. He had extreme physical fears, and when threatened by falling, precarious situations, or bullying, he was totally unable to control the situation. He was petrified by any physical threat and verbalized this emotion. He had no positive anger to show, and it was almost impossible to rouse him to any aggression."

At 5½ years of age he was similarly described.

"While S's almost total lack of aggression was very striking, it was not at all clear how much of it was because of a deep emotional taboo against aggression and how much he lacked the emotional courage to try it. Several staff members feel that S's fear of being hurt in physical encounters is extreme."

At 8 years of age, fears of harm and feelings of guilt were strong. After an interview at the Institute, the interviewer wrote:

"After we talked for a long time about airplanes and magic, he turned to me and said in a miserable voice, 'My brain is full of too much.' With some urging this 'too much' turned out to be bad words of which he had learned four or five in school but did not want to say them. He says they keep coming up and bothering him. I suggested that perhaps if he wrote them out on a blackboard and erased them, it might help him to get rid of them. He eagerly accepted this technique and, in a straggling hand, printed a few of the more common smutty words on the board. He erased each before printing the next. He breathed hard for a few minutes after this process and carefully wiped all the chalk dust off his hands.

"He also made many references to a fear of being hurt and a concern about colds and germs. He said he wouldn't like to live in a city because of all the noise, which might keep him awake at night. His current ambition is to be a doctor. 'To see the things I want to—like what tonsils look like—and disease.' He seems definitely ambivalent about expressing emotions, but he can't help it at times when, 'Somebody is talking bad to me.' He doesn't show his anger much because, 'The only way you show it is by fighting, and I don't fight.' "

S's fear of bodily harm and expectation of injury from the environment gradually led to strong needs for power over the social and physical environment. S sought to obtain this power through intellectual competence. In an interview at 9 years of age S expressed these feelings to the staff psychologist.

"S is getting along very well in school, making all 'A's' and 'B's' in the fifth grade. He never gets into any fights and says, 'The teacher makes us stay in if there's a fight, so no one wants to fight.' When asked what he wants to do when he grows up, S said, 'Well, I want to be a scientist.' I asked him what he liked about science and he said, 'Well I like element study in geology, I have a collection of crystals that I find.' S goes to bed at 8:00 P.M. and has a room by himself. He says, 'It takes me about an hour to go to sleep; I think about various things that keep you from getting excited and keep you calm. I try to say the Psalms, but the only one I can remember all the way through is the 23rd Psalm. I also say a few prayers. After a while, my mind gets to scattering, and I think about everything. I think of almost everything: being great, being President, and at other times I think of being a genius, and all kinds of things.' When he said this, I asked, 'Do you think you will be a genius someday?' S replied, 'Oh, I suppose so, scientific, of course.' When asked if there were any things that frighten him, he replied, 'Only at night, something, some unexpected noises. I am used to the pitter-patter of mice, but an unexpected noise like hearing a window break scares me a little. I'm not so awfully scared of the dark.' "

S went through elementary and high school with exceptionally high grades and was an outstanding student in college. As a young adult, the desire for intellectual excellence and social recognition was unusually strong. However, the feeling of isolation from peers and fear of attack from the physical environment were still present. [Kagan and Moss, 1962, pp. 140–142.]

A Case History—Subject 375: Stability of Achievement Behavior in Females

At one year of age the home visitor noted:

"S is pushed rather vigorously toward developing useful skills and independence by both parents. For example, when the father was given the responsibility of feeding S in the morning, he promptly trained her to feed herself to save him the trouble. The mother is nonchalant and lets S toddle about with minimal protectiveness. The mother fails to bat an eye when S tumbles and crys. S straightens herself out after a perfunctory whimper. S can say half a dozen words and is friendly with all strangers. She is unusually independent and active."

Both of S's parents gave her an unusual degree of autonomy, and she seemed to thrive in this atmosphere. She was active, nonfearful, and curious about her environment. Her speech development was advanced, and her peer interactions had an aggressive flavor. At 4½ years of age, S was described as follows:

"S's body is strong and well coordinated, and there is a great push behind everything she did. She had an exceptionally clear voice, and every word of her amazingly large vocabulary was sharply and distinctly enunciated. Her habitual tone was a bellowing shout, but she could modulate it to fit the particular role she was playing. S was one of the group leaders. Her energy, fund of ideas, and verbal manipulation of the world gave her great skills and dominance of peers. S would occasionally attack others if they stood in the way of an object she wanted. She would vary between a diplomatic explanation of, 'Well I need it' to simply snatching the toy.

"S seemed to seek attention and revel in it. She was as pleased when a crowd was around to witness her battles as when someone admired her art work. S's play always had an element of physical energy. The major part of S's activity was concern with ideas, using her own body and voice for the stage in which she acted out things. She would use dolls as props in her play. Another favorite game was being pregnant. She would wear a doll in her sweater and bring it out with a dramatic pop. S was well aware of her special talent in music and openly compared her superiority with others. For S every relationship was structured in terms of competition, and she was aware of the impact of her behavior on others at all times. S loves to use words, both for show-off value as well as for the pleasure involved in using long words and sentences. S seems to get delight from mouthing sounds and enjoys puns, rhymes, and alliterations for their own sake. S loved aggression. She would often select a dramatic role in which aggression was necessary. She would play the role of an alligator, a dragon, or a bear who was the head of a bear tribe. S would then terrorize the children by telling them what was going to happen to them. Although S always wanted audience attention, her method of trying to acquire knowledge often seemed free of self-consciousness or status drives. Rather, there was a great excitement in wanting to know things. S would give respect to any person if he had a particular art technique which she wanted to learn. She would stand and watch him, even ask him to show her how to do it and work hard until she had mastered it."

This intense need to know and the persistent desire for mastery, which were present as early as 4 years of age, remained a salient aspect of S's personality throughout the school years. At 6 years of age the Fels' observer wrote:

"S has learned to read and vitally enjoys it. She has long, silent periods of concentration and was often enraptured by the story she was reading. She loved trips to the Glen and reveled in the space; sure-footed as a mountain goat and fearless to all danger."

The intellectual challenges provided by the school situation were met and conquered with zeal. She was admired by her peers, for she had a vivid and lively imagination. She enjoyed a battle and adopted a competitive and rivalrous attitude with boys as well as girls.

At 15 years of age her story to Card 17BM of the TAT (picture of a man on a rope) captures her preoccupation with status and mastery goals.

"This is one of the greatest sportsmen of all times, who has broken the record, the speed record for rope climbing. It's the world's record. He is shown going up the rope on one of his latest records that he made."

To Card 14 (silhouette of a person in a window), S verbalized a concern with the acquisition of knowledge.

"This is a high school boy who is interested in studying for stars, but his high school didn't offer the proper education for astronomy, so at night he just stands by the window and wishes with all his might that he could have had the proper education so that he could go on and study things he wanted to study."

S graduated second in her high school class. She was involved in almost all the school activities and devoted special energy to music and athletics.

Subject 375 was the most achievement-oriented woman in the entire sample. She was single at the time of the interview and in her last year at college. She viewed the world as a source of challenges and was involved in activities that ranged from inventions of kitchen gadgets to guitar playing. She was doing well academically and was entertaining thoughts of becoming a writer on graduation from college. When asked to name the three people she admired most, S listed three former teachers:

"I admired Mrs. _____, for she gave me a sense of values and was a good model for me. I admired Mr. _____. He has wide interests and knows so much about the world; he's a vital man. And Mrs. _____ because she's a thinking person."

A striving for mastery, a counterphobic and confident attitude to problems, and the parental encouragement of these behaviors were all apparent from the earliest observations on this girl. [Kagan and Moss, 1962, pp. 143–145.]

Adult Derivatives of Achievement and Recognition Behavior

Childhood achievement and recognition behavior was, in general, related only to similar behavior in adulthood, and not to derivative behavior. The only exception is a sex-linked one. High-achievement-oriented girls, most of whom developed into high-achievement-oriented young women, were also competitive women, had masculine interests, were confident and sure of themselves, and did not withdraw in the face of difficult or stressful situations. This pattern of behavior was illustrated in the preceding case history.

Summary of the Stability of Achievement and Recognition Behavior

What are the basic facts about the stability of achievement and recognition strivings? The most general fact would seem to be that intellectual achievement and recognition strivings were stable throughout childhood (omitting years zero to three), that they were stable from childhood to young adulthood, and that they were equally stable for both sexes.

Two more specific generalizations are: (1) boys who were not oriented toward athletic achievement tended to be oriented toward intellectual achievement; and (2) girls oriented toward intellectual achievement and recognition not only developed into young women with similar orientations but also were competitive, confident, and somewhat masculine in adult interests (e.g., interested in inventions, science, etc.).

These trends fit reasonably well with the theoretical point of view suggested by Kagan and Moss as described previously; that is, achievement and recognition behavior is socially acceptable in both sexes, unlike passivity and dependency (unacceptable in males) and aggression (unacceptable in females). Thus, unlike passivity and dependency, or aggression, achievement and recognition behavior would be predicted to be stable in both sexes as found. Few derivative behaviors would also be predicted, as found.

The negative relationship between intellectual strivings and athletic strivings in males is open to several interpretations. Kagan and Moss comment as follows:

Athletic competence is one of the trio of traits—courage, independence, and athletic prowess—that defines the culture's version of the ideal American male. The boy who is identified with this idealized role tends to reject the passivity and nonpragmatic character associated with the acquisition of knowledge. Thus involvement in athletics for some boys involves a rejection of intellectuality. For girls there is less inconsistency between athletic competence and intellectual motivations. Both are viewed by the adolescent girl as appropriate mastery areas. [P. 136.]

A compensatory process may be operative too; those who are athletically incompetent may turn to other kinds of achievement, and vice versa.

SEXUALITY

The achievement of adequate and mature sexual behavior is unquestionably of considerable significance in the American culture, if only because sexuality is highly emphasized by the current culture. Kagan and Moss suggest that there are two main aspects to sexuality: its *hetero-*

sexual aspect and its *role* aspect. The first refers to relationships with the opposite sex of a sexual nature, while the second refers to culturally expected non-sexual behavior by the two sexes; i.e., a man is expected to behave much differently from a woman in areas other than sexual behavior, as we shall see in a later chapter. The Fels study provided one scale for each of these two aspects.

Definition and Stability in Childhood

(1) *Heterosexual interaction:* This scale attempted to measure the frequency and quality of interaction with the opposite sex. Since the main interest was concerned with heterosexual interaction of a *sexual* nature, the quality of the interaction had to involve the partner as some sort of love object, as in dating behavior. For this reason, heterosexual interaction was rated only for periods six to ten and ten to fourteen.

(2) *Opposite-sex interests:* This scale attempted to measure sex-role identification. It was defined in terms of interests and practices traditionally associated with the opposite sex. Athletics, mechanical interests, and *active* activities are usually considered masculine; music, reading, cooking, art, and *sedentary* activities are usually considered feminine.

Table 9.5 describes the stability of the two scales defining sexuality.

TABLE 9.5

Stability of Sexuality During Childhood

	Short-Term Stability		Long-Term Stability	
Dimension	3–6 to 6–10	6–10 to 10–14	3–6 to 10–14	0–3 10–14
Heterosexual interest				
Boys		.40		
Girls		.21		
Opposite-sex interests				
Boys	.79	.82	.38	
Girls	.71	.56	.38	

Interpretation. Heterosexual interaction was fairly stable in boys from the latency period (six to ten) to early adolescence (ten to fourteen), and not very stable in girls ($r = .21$). One would expect more stability in boys, since girls are more restricted in such behavior because of opportunity, i.e., upon being asked by a boy to participate in such behavior. It should also be observed that both correlations are probably underestimates of the stability of heterosexuality during childhood because of the time periods involved. Neither sex engages in much amorous behavior during ages six to ten, and hence low correlations with such behavior at later age periods would be expected. Opposite-sex activities were very stable in both sexes. The six-year-old child who preferred reading and music to wrestling and climbing tended to maintain this disposition into adolescence. Adolescent opposite-sex activities were even predictable from similar behavior of the three- or four-year-old ($r = .38$). These correlations imply, of course, that same-sex activities (behavior appropriate for a given sex) were equally stable.

Relation of Sexuality to Other Childhood Personality Characteristics

Heterosexual interaction and opposite-sex interests were not highly correlated with each other for either of the two periods in which both were measured (six to ten and ten to fourteen). Thus, we are not justified in using one of these scales to represent both; the twelve-year-old boy with feminine interests such as reading and music was not necessarily uninterested in girls as love objects. Therefore, we must consider the relationship of each of these two scales with other childhood personality characteristics separately.

Heterosexual interaction was more adequately measured during period ten to fourteen than during period six to ten because of its relative infrequency at the earlier age period. Therefore, consider the question, what was the twelve-year-old child like who was strongly involved in heterosexual behavior? Table 9.6 provides the answer.

TABLE 9.6

Correlations Between Heterosexual Interaction and Other Childhood Personality Variables for Ages Ten to Fourteen

Child Behavior	Boys	Girls
Conformity to adults	−.41	.04
Social spontaneity	.47	.36
Hyperkinesis	.37	.20
Dominance of peers	.37	.02
Competitiveness	.44	.27
Athletic achievement	.57	.44
Withdrawal from task failure	−.32	−.18
Expectancy of task failure	−.42	−.12

Table 9.7 presents the correlations between opposite-sex interests and other personality characteristics, ages ten to fourteen.

TABLE 9.7

Correlations Between Opposite-Sex Interests and Other Childhood
Personality Variables for Ages Ten to Fourteen

Child Behavior	Boys	Girls
Conformity to adults	.49	−.34
Social spontaneity	−.42	.34
Hyperkinesis	−.39	.38
Dominance of peers	−.32	.38
Competitiveness	−.33	.38
Avoidance of dangerous activities	.60	−.55
Intellectual achievement strivings	.36	.08
Athletic achievement strivings	−.66	.83

Interpretation. Table 9.6 indicates that boys who manifested considerable heterosexual interaction were also non-conforming to adults, active and spontaneous, dominating and competitive with peers, athletically inclined, and confident of success in anticipated tasks. In short, such boys were similar to the stereotype of Jack Armstrong, the red-blooded, all-American boy.

Heterosexually active girls were also spontaneous and active (but not necessarily non-conforming), somewhat competitive (but not dominating), and athletically inclined.

The highest correlations for both boys and girls are with athletic achievement strivings. If we assume that such behavior at ages ten to fourteen is positively correlated with rapid physical development and the reaching of puberty, and that puberty brings about physical changes that precipitate amorous interests in the opposite sex, then the relationship between heterosexual interests and athletic involvement is understandable. We have observed the results of other studies that indicate that early maturing boys are dominant, competitive, socially spontaneous, and heterosexually active. In summary, then, the pattern of correlations in Table 9.6 is probably best understood in terms of early maturers versus late maturers.

Table 9.7 indicates that adolescent boys with feminine interests tend to be obedient, ill at ease with peers, inactive and non-competitive, followers rather than leaders, oriented away from dangerous activities and athletics, and oriented toward intellectual achievement. Girls with masculine interests tended to be the opposite, i.e., non-conforming, at ease with peers, active and competitive, dominant, etc. Although these relationships appear to be about what one would expect on the basis of day-to-day experience, it is well to be reminded again that the ratings of these variables were not completely independent of each other, and that these correlations are therefore probably inflated to some unknown degree.

Stability of Sexuality from Childhood to Adulthood

Two adult variables highly similar in overt appearance to childhood heterosexuality and opposite-sex interests were *avoidance of premarital sexuality* and *opposite-sex interests,* respectively. Their definitions follow.

Adult Behavior	*How It Was Measured*
Avoidance of premarital sexuality	Measured in terms of hesitancy in initiating heterosexual relationships and the degree of inhibition of erotic behavior (necking, petting, and coitus)
Opposite-sex interests	Measured the same way as in childhood, except for the substitution of adult behaviors for child behaviors, examples of adult masculine interests being hunting, fishing, gambling, and concern with power roles

Table 9.8 presents the correlations between childhood sexuality and these two indexes of adult sexuality.

TABLE 9.8

Stability of Sexuality from Childhood to Adulthood

	Adult Behavior			
	Avoidance of Premarital Sex		Opposite-Sex Interests	
Child Behavior	Male	Female	Male	Female
Heterosexual interests (10–14)	—.47	—.06	—.05	—.32
Opposite-sex interests (3–6)	.49	—.14	.54	.10
(6–10)	.65	.13	.63	.44
(10–14)	.35	.22	.57	.10

Interpretation. In general, adult female sexuality was not highly related to childhood behavior. For boys, however, the picture is different. Boys who were heterosexually active in junior high school (ages ten to fourteen) were heterosexually active as young adults. Even more dramatic, four-year-old boys with feminine sex interests were heterosexually inactive as young adults ($r = .49$) and engaged in feminine activities ($r = .54$). The reverse also holds; i.e., the four-year-old boys with masculine interests became young men who maximized heterosexual behavior and engaged in masculine activities. Thus, sexuality was dramatically stable in males.

Two case histories are now provided. The first illustrates the stability of masculinity in males, and the second illustrates the stability of femininity in males.

A Case History—Subject 2283: Stability of Sex Role (Masculinity) in Males

"In the nursery school S was extremely energetic. Even when he was pushing small cars around the floor he seemed to be putting the greatest possible force into it. He talked loudly and accompanied his car and train play with plenty of imitations of engine noises and whistles. Outside he ran around furiously some of the time and played fearlessly on the apparatus. He also played construction games in the sandpile. In the house, he built garages, roads, and usually used blocks in connection with cars or trains. He was interested in small locomotor toys and did the best building of any of the children. S was definitely the leader of the group. He was bright, original, and full of ideas."

Three years later a description of S was similar in flavor.

"S was strong, vigorous, agile, and quite capable on all the apparatus. He rode his bike, used the sand, the swings, and jungle gym in very dramatic play and competition. During routines S was independent and capable. With adults he usually tried to get his own way, and he required supervision when some desire was inconsistent with the requirements of adults. S was outstandingly curious, alert, and vocal. He could not stand to be out of anything and had to know, to run, to see, to examine, to question. He was impetuous and unrestrained in his vocalizations, interrupting others and arguing right through a peer's explanation. He indulged in a lot of competitive word-games in which he compared ability, possessions, hurled insults, challenges, experiences, and stories. Often he directed the best building and dramatic play that went on, and there was a strong interest and concern with construction of different sorts. To others in the group S appeared as aggressive, dominating, and rejecting. He had a tremendous drive to boss, to get things done his own way, and to tell everyone how to act."

When he was 7 years old he was observed at his elementary school.

"S is a well-built, attractive looking youngster; a real little boy. When I saw him, he was building a barracks with blocks. There was a good deal of give and take between the children. S had built the barracks, and another boy built a torpedo boat. This quite naturally led to war-play. In a very short time all the children in the room were machine-gunning each other. S yelled to another boy, 'I'm the Japs and you're the Germans. No, what I mean is him and me are the Japs and you're the Americans. All guns turn this way.'"

At age 7½ his day-camp behavior combined the aggressiveness, dominance, and competitive gross-motor activity that characterize traditional male-role behavior.

"For S everything he does is excitable and highly competitive. He has a fund of physical energy. Bouncing, rushing around, wanting to do things, and a great deal of talk about his own abilities. For the races, he announced before hand that he was not going to do them and, yet, strained himself to the limit to try to win. He loves to play and exert himself physically but does not like to lose. His honesty in competitive situations is sketchy, not listening to the directions and seeing how much he can get away with. There is much compensatory clowning and bravado, and S might say, 'I let him beat me because I thought there would be more races and I could have beat him in there if I had wanted to.' While S is a terrific *alibi ike*, he would argue over every score he received. S would be a much better athlete if he did not try so very hard to win."

S started dating about age 12 and did an average amount of dating during high school. At 16 he began to go steady. He dated one girl frequently and consistently during his last two years of high school, and there were episodes of erotic activity. When S went to college, dating increased, and there were frequent occurrences of coital activity. Some of his comments during the interview follow.

E: "Can you tell me a little bit about your dating history?"

S: "I can give you almost a complete history, down to how many girls I have taken out."

E: "What about dating during college?"

S: "In my sophomore year I went on a rampage I guess—I mean, I went out every weekend. For a while, different girls, then I would take out one girl for 3 or 4 weeks and then another girl, usually for a semester once a week or sometimes twice a week if I was dating two girls at the same time."

E: "Did you neck with them?"

S: "Oh yes, a little bit, depending on the girl."

E: "Any intercourse?"

S: "Some. Do you mean on dates, premeditated dates? There weren't many girls I took out on a premeditated date that I didn't know I couldn't lay before I took them out. Some girls I know go; some girls I'm not sure about. Some girls I know don't. Those I wasn't sure about, I didn't—very few of them I ever laid."

E: "Did you try?"

S: "Well, most of the time I didn't try."

E: "This first group that you knew would lay, you took them out occasionally?"

S: "I would take them out to get laid."

E: "Only for that reason?"

S: "Yeh, but not very often, 'cause that's not my philosophy. I was, I can name about 60 girls that I have taken out on a premeditated basis."

E: "By premeditated you mean what?"

S: "I mean I've called them up in the middle of the week and said, 'Let's go out on Saturday night.' That's what I mean. I mean like when you walk into a bar and walk up to somebody and start dancing with them; now, that to me is not premeditated; that's what I mean."

E: "Have your intercourse experiences been with girls whom you always took out for this one purpose, or are there some girls whom you like and didn't take out specifically for sex?"

S: "Most of the girls that I have had intercourse with I have taken out purely for that purpose."

E: "Have there been exceptions?"

S: "Yes, there have been exceptions, a couple."

At the time of the interview S felt that he was in love with a girl he had known for several years. He was ambivalent about becoming engaged because his schooling was not completed. [Kagan and Moss, 1962, pp. 161–163.]

A Case History—Subject 2373: Stability of Sex Role (Femininity) in Males

At 3 years of age S's nursery-school summary read:

"S is a pale, bleached-out looking child with blond hair, light blue eyes, and very little color in his face. He is tall, thin, and stoop-shouldered. He lacks compactness and sturdiness of muscle or body build. He gave the general impression of being gangling, and this was accentuated by the fact that he did not have good control over his body. During the entire nursery-school period S was uneasy. He was not relaxed and very dissatisfied. He showed tension in many ways. He has many mannerisms and nervous habits. In his use of materials, and in his approach to other children, S was almost constantly on edge. Whenever he was stimulated, he overreacted. His body tensed, his face showed some strain, and there were many excess movements. S sometimes would fall into a very deep lassitude and almost collapse. He would drop in a chair or swing inertly and become very difficult to arouse. He was not very purposeful or creative in his play, and he used materials socially."

At age 4 these traits were more firmly established.

"During this nursery-school period S was thin, tall, and stringy looking. He was rather wooden in his movements, resembling an unfinished marionette during his inactive periods. He seemed weary and empty of animation, like a child who lived perpetually indoors. He was an overly dressed boy, always very trim, and never approaching the usual group dishevelment at the end of the day. S was also able to sustain a thoroughly fatuous smile for long periods of time. S seemed to be on the sedentary side, and in most activities he showed no vigor."

At age 6 he was described as:

"Pasty-skinned, skinny, a loiterer, a slumper, and given either to frozen periods or taking queer gangly or stiff poses. He seemed less like a nursery-school child than a miniature caricature of an adolescent with self-consciousness and emotional difficulties getting in the way of whatever motor controls he might have. S was picked on a good deal, and much of his behavior invited teasing. When someone turned on him, he became helpless, cried, ran to an adult, or sat with a mute grin. He seemed to have no resistance against verbal attacks. S often commented that there was no reason for him to make anything because the other kids would break it. S did not seem to quite fit into the group. He was much like a 2-year-old in his reaction to pain and was helpless when someone else was hurt. In contrast to the interest of most boys in athletics and construction, S became interested in flowers. He was very careful as he picked them so that the stems wouldn't be hurt, sorting out a bunch of beautifully contrasting colors and making up names for the flowers. Hyacinths, for example, were 'those sparkling, purply flowers.' He quickly caught on to the use of the magnifying glass and eagerly brought in specimens of flowers to examine. Occasionally he took delight in the dolls or tiny dishes when he thought no one was looking at him."

At 9 years of age he was interviewed, and the staff psychologist wrote the following summary:

"Throughout the interview S was in constant motion, sliding about in his chair, moving arms and legs, peering about the room. I asked him how he was doing in school and he said he had an 'A', 'B', 'C', and two 'F's.' S shows a preoccupation with threats at night and still shows much fear. Ever since Christmas he has taken several animals to bed: a bear, a chicken, and a panda. S said, 'Sometimes I get scared because everyone is asleep. I get up and turn on the light and go to the bathroom. Sometimes I think there's a man in the house and every night I close the venetian blinds.'"

The isolation from peers, the lack of interest in competitive sports, and the fear of peer aggression were apparent in the description of S at 11 years of age. The summary was written after a visit to S's school and talking with S's teacher.

"S has plenty of ability but does not use it. He has to be pressured all the time and does not volunteer very much. He is slow and seems to have no pep, steam, or temper. He fools around a great deal in class, fiddling with a little car, comic book, or daydreaming. S does not participate at all on the playground with the other boys. The teachers often find him in the schoolroom when he should be out on the playground with his peers. He does not seem to care about being active and would rather be by himself. He has become more interested in reading lately, and he likes books."

As an adult of 20 years, S was tall, thin, and very tense. He was in college but was unsure about a career because of excessive doubts over his intellectual ability. He reported much tension and anxiety with girls and a strong reluctance to initiate erotic activity with them. He was afraid that a girl would reject him if he were to initiate any romance. He never petted with a girl or experienced sexual intercourse. He disliked competitive situations and was thinking of teaching as a vocation. [Kagan and Moss, 1962, pp. 163–165.]

Adult Derivatives of Sexuality

Derivative behaviors of sexuality are not presented or discussed by Kagan and Moss. Socioeconomic status and adult vocational choice are discussed because of their interesting relationships to sexuality. Table 9.9 presents the correlations between the socioeconomic status of parents and adult sexuality of offspring.

TABLE 9.9

Relationship Between the Socioeconomic Status of Parents and Adult Sexuality

Adult Behavior	Correlations with Socioeconomic Status of Parents	
	Men	Women
Avoidance of premarital sexuality	.36	.06
Opposite-sex interests	.33	.46

Boys whose parents were members of the upper-middle or upper socioeconomic classes became young men who tended to avoid sexual behavior with women and who adopted feminine interests. Girls whose parents were members of the upper-middle or upper socioeconomic classes became young women with masculine interests. Note that heterosexual behavior in women was not related to socioeconomic level of parents. As suggested by Kagan and Moss, this is probably due to the importance of *opportunity* for such behavior in women.

Adult vocational choice in men was highly related to sex-related interests in childhood. The vocational choices of the 10 men who were most masculine at ages three to six were compared with the vocational choices of the 7 men who manifested most feminine interests at ages three to six. All 10 chose relatively non-intellectual vocations in adulthood (3 businessmen, 2 farmers, 2 athletic coaches, 1 carpenter, 1 machinist, and 1 engineer). Of the 7 boys with most feminine interests at ages three to six, all chose an intellectual vocation in adulthood (3 secondary school teachers, 1 chemist, 1 biologist, 1 physicist, and 1 psychiatrist). Adult recreational interests showed that men with masculine vocations built amplifiers, worked with machines, or engaged in athletics, while men who chose an intellectual vocation engaged in art, music, and reading.

Summary of the Stability of Sexuality

The main fact concerning stability of sexuality would appear to be its stability in males, both during childhood and from childhood to adulthood. The lack of stability in females can at least partly be accounted for in terms of the greater importance of opportunity for heterosexual behavior in females than in males. This reasoning is supported by the fact that opposite-sex interests, which are less affected by opportunity factors, were about equally stable for girls and boys during childhood. They were not, however, very stable from childhood to adulthood in females.

A meaningful cluster of other childhood personality variables was found to be associated with childhood sexuality in both sexes. Socioeconomic status and vocational choice were associated with adult sexuality, the latter in men only, since few women ever made a vocational choice. In general, these relationships suggest sexuality to be an important pattern of behavior in both sexes.

SOCIAL INTERACTION ANXIETY

The fifth (and last) personality pattern is social interaction anxiety. It refers to the tendency to be tense, inhibited, and ill at ease in social situations, as opposed to tendencies to be relaxed and spontaneous, i.e., to be "one's self." It was measured in five ways during childhood.

Definition and Stability in Childhood

(1) *Anxiety with home visitor:* This scale reflected the amount of crying and avoidance behavior elicited when the Fels home visitor made his call to the home of the sample member. It was measured during periods zero to three and three to six. (2) *Anxiety in novel situations:* Measured during periods zero to three and three to six, it reflected the amount of crying and other signs of distress when the child was exposed to a new or novel situation, such as initial visits to the nursery school and entrance into kindergarten. (3) *Social spontaneity:* Measured in all four periods (zero to fourteen), it reflected the ease and lack of inhibition when interacting with peers and adults. (4) *Expectancy of peer rejection:* This scale reflected the individual's expectation of not being accepted or liked by peers. It was measured during periods six to ten and ten to fourteen. (5) *Withdrawal from social interaction:* Measured only during period ten to fourteen, it reflected the child's reluctance to attend social functions and his tendency to be a "wallflower" in group situations.

The stability of these five characteristics during childhood is described in Table 9.10.

TABLE 9.10

Stability of Social Interaction Anxiety During Childhood

Dimension	Short-Term Stability		Long-Term Stability	
	3–6 to 6–10	6–10 to 10–14	3–6 to 10–14	0–3 to 10–14
Anxiety with home visitor				
Boys	.44			
Girls	.05			
Anxiety in novel situations				
Boys	.60			
Girls	.20			
Social spontaneity				
Boys	.59	.57	.00	−.45
Girls	.47	.53	.00	.12
Expectations of peer rejection				
Boys		.54		
Girls		.47		

NOTE: "Withdrawal from social interaction" was measured only during period ten to fourteen, and thus is not represented.

Interpretation. Table 9.10 indicates that boys were stable on all dimensions for adjacent ages (i.e., short-term stability). Thus, a socially spontaneous or socially inhibited five-year-old boy behaved similarly at ten, and his behavior at fourteen was related to his behavior at ten. Girls were only a little less stable for the short term, with surprisingly low correlations for the first two dimensions. Note, though, that all short-term correlations are positive. The simplest conclusion would thus seem to be that social interaction anxiety was stable over the short term for both sexes.

Long-term stability presents a different picture. There is no stability at all from period three to six to period ten to fourteen, and boys showed a curious inversion from period zero to three to period ten to fourteen. Spontaneous two-year-olds tended to be inhibited twelve-year-olds, and vice versa. This unexpected inverse relationship is probably a reflection of no underlying population relationship at all, as suggested by the other long-term correlations.

Relation of Social Interaction Anxiety to Other Childhood Personality Variables

How were the various scales defining the pattern of social interaction anxiety related to each other? Since long-term stability tended to be low, and since only the last three variables were measured during period ten to fourteen, only the correlations of these variables with each other at this age period are considered. The correlations of social spontaneity with expectancy of peer rejection and withdrawal from social interaction during period ten to fourteen are presented in Table 9.11.

TABLE 9.11

Correlations Between Social Spontaneity and Other Variables Defining Social Interaction Anxiety for Ages Ten to Fourteen

Child Behavior	Boys	Girls
Expectancy of peer rejection	—.63	—.71
Withdrawal from social interaction	—.37	—.59

These correlations show the three variables to be related to each other in the expected direction (i.e., social spontaneity is negatively associated with high expectations of peer rejection and withdrawal from social interactions). Therefore, let social spontaneity represent the entire pattern. The question of immediate concern then becomes, what is the relationship between social interaction anxiety (as represented by social spontaneity) and other child behavior characteristics? Table 9.12 presents the answer for period ten to fourteen (a similar pattern holds for earlier ages, too).

TABLE 9.12

Correlations Between Social Spontaneity and Other Childhood Personality
Characteristics for Ages Ten to Fourteen

Child Behavior	Boys	Girls
Passivity	—.69	—.55
Dominance of peers	.45	.45
Competitiveness	.58	.13
Withdrawal from expected task failure	—.39	—.38
Avoidance of dangerous acts	—.60	—.25
Opposite sex interests	—.42	.34

Interpretation. The socially spontaneous child was also aggressive
(first three variables in Table 9.12), stubborn in the face of difficult
tasks, unafraid of dangerous activities, and had sex-appropriate interests
(i.e., did not have opposite sex interests)—except for girls, who had
masculine interests. These relationships were true for both sexes, perhaps slightly stronger for males than for females.

Stability of Social Interaction Anxiety
from Childhood to Adulthood

Adult social inhibition and anxiety was measured in terms of one
scale—how often the individual expressed such feelings in the adult
interview. Its relationship to childhood social interaction anxiety, as
measured by the five variables already discussed, is summarized in
Table 9.13.

TABLE 9.13

Stability of Social Interaction Anxiety from Childhood to Adulthood

Child Behavior	Adult Social Interaction Anxiety	
	Males	Females
Anxiety with home visitor (3–6)	.30	.25
Anxiety in novel situations (3–6)	.53	.02
Social spontaneity (3–6)	—.27	.09
(6–10)	—.41	—.30
(10–14)	—.50	—.56
Expected peer rejection (6–10)	.18	.09
(10–14)	.41	.48
Withdrawal from social interaction (10–14)	.65	.54

Interpretation. A lack of social spontaneity, an expectancy of peer rejection, and withdrawal from social interaction during early adolescence (ages ten to fourteen) were predictable of social interaction anxiety in young adulthood for both sexes. Such behavior was highly stable between the ages of twelve and twenty-four.

There is a suggestion that the roots of social interaction anxiety in men reach farther back into childhood than is the case for women; note the correlations of .30, .53, −.27, −.41, and .18 between adult behavior and child behavior at ages three to six and six to ten for men, as contrasted to correlations of .25, .02, .09, −.30, and .09 for women. Kagan and Moss suggest an explanation that is somewhat as follows: The bases of social acceptance (and hence low social interaction anxiety) emerge later in life for girls than for boys. Thus, physical attractiveness, presumably so important in female interpersonal relationships and peer popularity during adolescence, is not so highly correlated with popularity *prior* to adolescence. With boys, on the other hand, the bases of popularity remain more constant from the elementary school years to high school to adulthood. Thus, physical fitness and strength are important both before and after puberty. It should therefore be easier to predict adult social interaction anxiety from early childhood for boys than for girls, as found. Kagan and Moss report data that bear this speculation out:

The bases for social acceptance among girls on the other hand, are more varied and do not emerge until late childhood. Attractiveness or intelligence facilitates popularity and leads to confidence in interpersonal relations. These characteristics do not emerge as clear assets until the school years. Thus it should be more difficult to predict adolescent and adult social anxiety from preschool interaction patterns for women. A study of those girls who showed marked shifts in level of social anxiety from Period II (3–6) to adulthood confirms this hypothesis. *There were six girls who showed a major shift from high anxiety during age 3 to 6 to low anxiety during adulthood. All of them were quite attractive as adults, and five of the six had better than average academic records in high school and college. Three girls shifted from minimal anxiety during preschool years to unusually high social inhibition as adults. All three were unattractive as adolescents and adults. One of them had recently left college in an acute anxiety attack; the remaining two did poorly in high school and felt intellectually inadequate.* [Pp. 182–183; italics added.]

An example of the continuity and stability of social anxiety is illustrated in the following case history.

A Case History—Subject 045: Stability of Social Anxiety in Males

S was the second-born child of a lower middle-class family. He usually showed distinct signs of fear when he came to Fels for a physical or mental examination, or for the nursery-school sessions. When he came for his examination at 2 years of age, the following summary was written.

"S gave the appearance of being frightened at first. When taken downstairs for the physical examination following the mental test, S would not allow the doctor to take his hand to guide him. He was shy and remained very timid throughout the procedure. He cried when the examination began and cried at new items in the procedure. He was suggestible and responded to distraction. He recovered quickly from his tears, was attentive to the toys given him, and was interested in their construction. Although the mother was present during the mental test that preceded the physical exam, S was shy and apprehensive."

At 4 years of age S attended the Fels nursery school for the first time. His initial reactions to this new setting were characterized by timidity and caution. The following notes were written after the three-week period.

"This was S's first visit to the nursery school and probably his first time away from home for any length of time. It took the entire period for S to make the adjustment. S was very apprehensive and insecure during his first days. He cried a lot and stood about looking sad in the interim between his howls. Initially he did not enter into any of the play but was entirely concerned with his unhappiness. He objected to coming and cried in the car. Once at the school he stood about weeping or sobbing and followed the teacher around for comfort. He was not in a tantrum of anger, but appeared to be showing fear and apprehension. For the first two weeks S made no attempts to get into any of the groups. He was shy with the older children and timid with the new equipment.

"During the period he was highly emotional and did not try to control his fears at all. He was somewhat sober and depressed most of the time, although he got friendly and happy toward the very end. He showed no anger, little jealousy, and no excitement. With adults he was very conforming and obedient. Even though unhappy, he was not especially rebellious."

One year later, at 5 years of age, S again attended the nursery school for a three-week period. His behavior continued to reflect caution and apprehension.

"S was one of the gentlest creatures of the group. He seemed to be like a delicate plant in the vivid world of the nursery school, meekly and solemnly acquiescing to whatever other children or adults suggested. He would often stand on the edge of the group with wide eyes watching the others. Only as the group dispersed would he get to the front and examine the object the group might have been playing with. At times S would stand helplessly crying and shielding his face while he was pelted with snowballs. S spoke in an exceedingly low voice, barely above a whisper, and never really laughed outright or came near a shout. The words he spoke were spaced with long pauses, and the last words of the sentence were even softer than the first, sometimes drifting into silence. His crying was soft too, with heavy sobs in his chest. S's behavior was much more characteristic of a 2- or 3-year-old, showing immense ranges over the month. He went from tears and hiding in the corner in the beginning of the nursery-school period to a gradual staring and sideline participation. Shyness is a word that really seems to fit him; he has vulnerability to any contact with new people. He would hang his head and edge off when any strange adult was present or give apprehensive glances toward the children in the other groups. He was slow to warm up to the materials and would look at them from a distance, gradually finger them, and when the sanction for their use was established, he would then use them with some gusto. S was the only one in his group to react, as the younger children frequently do, to a change of cars or to a change of drivers. He would cry and resist going in the car until an older girl led him. His hard crying occurred only the first day, but tears came sporadically during the whole first week of nursery-school attendance. His reliance on a familiar person to carry through an unfamiliar situation showed in the car episodes and in any experimental situations. During one experimental session, when he was taken from the room, he came back and saw the nursery-school room deserted. He began to cry, but once I got him playing contentedly with me, he came up willingly again to the experimental room. He was not frightened as long as I was with him. S was quietly and consistently conforming, never laying down the law for others or being shocked at the transgressions of other peers. He did what was expected of him immediately and without supervision. Sometimes with adults there was a quality of extra politeness in his obedience."

When he entered school at 6 years of age, there was occasional crying during the first half-year. His older sister was attending the same school, and he followed her about during the initial month of school. The following notes were written after a visit to the home soon after S had started school.

"The mother says that S would rather be at home than with people, and his shyness is very slow to wear off. Last spring at a big family picnic at the school, where all the children and families had attended, the mother suddenly recognized that S was gone and couldn't find him. They finally discovered that he had gone home, changed his clothes, and was quietly playing in his own yard."

When S visited Fels for an examination at 7 years of age, he was still socially apprehensive.

"S was still on the subdued side, although a less shadowy person than he had been at nursery school the year before. His voice is more audible than it was and his movements less limp. In the morning he cried a little, with the subdued swallowing of tears that he often shows in a new situation. The mental tester reported that he was quite pleasant and cheerful. When he was tested in psychophysiology, he was a little stiff. He lay flat on his bed, quite silent, rolling his big brown eyes. When he was downstairs playing, he just stood around for the first 10 minutes, looking over the familiar rooms but touching nothing. When he went to lunch with another child and a staff member, he didn't know what he wanted to eat but ate what was put in front of him."

During subsequent observations in the following year at home, in the nursery school, and in his public school setting, S seemed afraid of interaction with other boys. During a recess period at school, S typically stayed inside and played with the girls while the rest of the boys were outside running around. When called on to recite, the observer noted, "his wee, small voice could scarcely be heard; he missed so many words, he was asked to reread the last half of the page."

At 8 years of age S attended the Fels day camp.

"S is still a shrinking violet, avoiding any situations where he might be hurt, by physical contact with others, hard objects, high places, etc. He seems to show a social diffidence and an unsureness, and these two things reinforce each other. The first morning S disappeared from the group and was discovered all alone in the front yard quietly sobbing to himself. He explained his presence there in terms of a sore foot, and while he had, in fact, hurt his foot, his generalized discomfort at the newness of the day-camp situation probably reinforced the pain and reduced him to tears. He was continually ignored or shoved around by the more energetic and outspoken children. In any close contact situation, such as a crowded car, S completely withdrew and became self-effacing."

When S was 10 years old, he was interviewed by a staff psychologist, who wrote the following summary.

"S was very quiet and very cooperative during the physical examination and hardly said a word. He warmed up a little afterwards and talked in a friendly way but still without much spontaneity. He talked about school and had a bright smile when he mentioned his teacher, whom he likes very much. He prefers English the best and has a desire to become a school teacher. His general behavior during the interview was placid and rather feminine."

At 16 years of age S was again interviewed.

E: "What are some ways in which you would like to be different from the way you are now, some of the things you would change about yourself?"

S: "I'd like to be more forward, I mean, to be able to meet people and talk."

E: "Any other ways that you would like to change?"

S: "I'd like to feel like I could take on responsibilities which I don't. I don't feel like—I don't feel self-confident. *That's it in a nutshell*, self-confidence."

S was 20 years old when he was seen for the adult interview. He was thin and slight of build, with a bony, pale face. He looked more like an adolescent than a young adult. He spoke in a very low, high-pitched voice, and he was uneasy and tense during the three interviews. He was restless and very eager to please and to cooperate with the interviewer. At the time of the interview he had completed several years of college. As he indicated during preadolescence, he was still interested in becoming a teacher. He had made few friends at college, and he habitually expected rejection and aloofness from authority figures as well as peers. He was tense in his interactions with others, and he had intense feelings of personal inadequacy. Excerpts from the adult interview reveal his extreme social anxiety.

E: "Did you tend to be afraid of your boss on the job when he came around?"

S: "Yeah, I was kinda afraid of him."

E: "What about this fellow you are working with now? Do you feel relaxed with him, or tense?"

S: "No, I don't feel relaxed with him. I just as leave he's not around."

E: "You feel tense when he's around?"

S: "I'm not afraid of him, see; I just don't like to have him around. That other guy down there; at first I couldn't talk to him, ah—not at all, but it's getting a little bit better now."

E: "What about Dr. _____; the man that you worked for in college? Did you feel tense when you were with him?"

S: "It's a funny thing; I wasn't exactly at ease with him, but he was nice and I really liked him and I still do. I think I am in awe with him. You know, he was a big professor, something that I'd like to be, and I was really never friendly with professors. Well, I was really never friendly with any school teachers."

E: "Did you talk much in classes?"

S: "Well, that all depends on the professor. In Dr. _____ class I always had my mouth open, but in other classes—I never said a word."

E: "Why was that? Because you had no questions or because you just didn't want to say anything?"

S: "I don't know, I just didn't want to talk. In history I never said a word unless he asked me."

E: "If you ever had any questions, did you go up after class or during office hours to ask professors about your work."

S: "I didn't do that. I don't know if I could do it yet or not."

E: "Have you ever thought about doing it and decided not too?"

S: "Yeah."

E: "Why did you not go?"

S: "I don't think I would. I never knew professors, any professors that you would say personally, except Dr. _____. Well, of course, I asked him things 'cause I worked with him, but, ah—not any of the others, like Dr. _____. I wanted to talk to him, and I think if I had talked to him, my problems would have been solved."

E: "Why didn't you talk to him?"

S: "I don't know; I couldn't. He had such a way about him that I couldn't get my point across. He would persuade his opinion on me. He would, and I don't want his opinion. I mean he would try to tell me that he was right and I'm wrong and believe me he's right. He had a way about him that my opinion had no value. It was like going in and talking to a blank wall. He would have such a better argument than I would that I would lose, that's what I thought anyway."

E: "Who do you feel more comfortable with, more relaxed with, men or women?"

S: "Older women I don't like, older men, ah—too. Because, you know, they don't talk about the same things I do. Older women don't either—I—I couldn't go in a room with an older woman and talk to her."

E: "How about people your own age? With whom do you feel more comfortable, boys or girls?"

S: "Boys. I don't talk to girls much. I mean, I couldn't go up to a strange girl and talk to her as well as I could a strange boy. But if I know the girl, then I can talk to her."

E: "Can you tell me about your friends, the kind of friendships you have?"

S: "Well, you know, I don't think I have any close friends. When I came home from college, any friends I had in high school were gone, and—ah—I didn't have any people that were more than acquaintances, they weren't close friends. A couple of people that I work with are classified as friends more than acquaintances, but not what I would call a close friend. When I was in school I had, oh, three real close friends and a lot of acquaintances, _____ was a very close friend."

E: "What made you and _____ such close friends?"

S: "Like I said before, he's like me. Neither one of us was very good in sports and it seemed like everyone else was, and I envied them."

E: "You say you envied these other people and he didn't?"

S: "He did. Oh, I don't know if he did or not; I don't know if he cared. But I did. I mean, I'd like to have been good sportswise, but, ah, he wasn't either. You see, we had to go someplace else. I couldn't go with the gang of boys and talk about sports and, ah, there didn't seem to be so many places to go, and I like to talk about books that I've read that other people have read and, ah, argue about 'em. But I couldn't do that with very many people. That's the way I like to talk."

E: "Could you do that with _____?"

S: "No, he didn't read books, but there were a few more people on campus that I could argue with. But, yet he would listen to me and give me his ideas if he had read the book. But we could talk about serious things."

E: "Was there something else about him personally, another reason that might account for the fact that you and he were close friends?"

S: "Well, in the first place, when I first got to know him, we both didn't know any people. It was hard for us to get to know any people, and I sat beside him in class, see, and that's how I got to know him. We didn't know anyone, and it was hard for both of us to get to know people. I think it was even harder—more hard for him to get to know people than it was even for me. Because he lived off campus and it's extra hard then. He didn't know many people and I didn't know anyone and—so we just sorta went together."

E: "In college were you the kind of person who actively sought to make a lot of friends?"

S: "No, I didn't make a lot of friends."

E: "Was that out of choice or because of no time?"

S: "It's probably cause I didn't know how; I couldn't. In the dorm we were in sections and I was in section 5. I lived with these guys, and I know all of them real well, but I was hardly on speaking terms with some of them in the other sections. I have to be with people a long time before I get to know them. I just couldn't go up to a person and enter into a conversation with him, even if I knew him."

E: "Why not?"

S: "I don't know."

E: "Would you say that you feel uncomfortable in this sort of situation?"

S: "I wouldn't have been if I had known all of them. If I had known all of them, I could have gone up to them. If there were several that I didn't know and they wanted to talk, then I did."

E: "What would you be thinking or feeling that would prevent you from doing this?"

S: "Um (pause) I think mostly it was—(long pause) you know, I think it was mostly that maybe I kept thinking that they didn't want me in their group."

E: "You anticipated that they didn't want you?"

S: "Uh-huh."

E: "To join them?"

S: "I think that was it. You know I always thought that someone should ask me to do something instead of me offering to do it. You know like, if they had asked me to come in the group, I'd have gone willingly. But I wouldn't have just gone up by myself."

E: "Are you still like that today?"

S: "Same way. I try to change, but I can't. I mean, I'd like to go up and be able to talk to people that I don't even know, but I can't."

E: "You feel uncomfortable when you're with strange people?"

S: "I think it's because I try too hard to think of what to say. They say that you don't, but you've got to say something—you can't stand there like an ox. People talk to me about me and say how much I talk. But I talk only when I know the people real well. Then I can—you know, but not with strangers, with strangers I don't talk at all. Same way with eating in the cafeteria. If I would have to sit at a table with no one I knew well, I wouldn't say a word. Last year I worked in the cafeteria and—uh—so I got down there on Thursday night on the third shift, and I saved the whole table for my friends. They all came there to sit and they'd wait for me. Maybe I should've got out and met other people, but I liked it that way."

E: "Did you ever look forward to meeting new people or are you rather indifferent?"

S: "Now, you know, I have such mixed emotions about that. Now, I want to meet them, but it's difficult to meet them. And sometimes I'd rather avoid it."

These excerpts capture the chronic social anxiety this man feels in interpersonal interactions. The enduring social inhibition exhibited by this particular man provides some flesh to the correlation of .53 between anxiety in novel situations during age 3 to 6 and social anxiety in adulthood. [Kagan and Moss, 1962, pp. 175–182.]

Adult Derivatives of Social Interaction Anxiety

Possible adult derivatives of childhood social interaction anxiety are not discussed by Kagan and Moss. However, an idea of what an adult was like who was rated high on social anxiety can be obtained from Table 9.14, which presents correlations between adult social interaction anxiety and other adult personality characteristics.

TABLE 9.14

Relationships Between Adult Social Interaction Anxiety and Other Adult Personality Characteristics

Adult Behavior	Men	Women
Dependency on love object	.26	.28
Dependency on parents	.15	.33
Competitiveness	−.51	−.60
Ease of anger arousal	−.34	−.36
Anxiety about aggression	.47	.45
Repression of aggressive thoughts	.25	.48
Withdrawal from anticipated failure	.77	.72
Recognition strivings	−.37	−.51
Achievement strivings	−.48	−.54
Opposite-sex interests	.50	−.33

Interpretation. Table 9.14 indicates that adult social interaction anxiety was associated with dependent behavior, a lack of competitive or aggressive behavior, anxiety about and repression of aggressive thoughts and impulses, as well as withdrawal from stressful situations, low achievement, and low recognition strivings, along with high fear of failure and feminine interests. If Table 9.14 is compared with Table 9.12, a remarkable similarity is discovered. The entire pattern of characteristics described in Table 9.14 took form in early childhood. This adult pattern of widespread withdrawal and femininity, and associated social anxiety, had its roots far back into childhood, and manifested considerable stability from childhood to adulthood.

Summary of the Stability of Social Interaction Anxiety

There would appear to be three main trends suggested by the social anxiety data. First, childhood stability was high for both sexes for ages six to fourteen. Long-term stability from earlier ages was low in both sexes. Second, adult social anxiety was predictable from similar behavior at ages ten to fourteen in both sexes; social anxiety was highly stable from ages twelve to twenty-four. Third, adult social anxiety in men was predictable from similar behavior at ages three to six and six to ten, suggesting stability over a longer period of time for males than for females. Kagan and Moss speculate that the bases of social acceptance for girls are more varied from one age to another than for boys.

SUMMARY

Strivings for recognition and achievement constituted a third broad personality pattern measured in the Fels study. Recognition strivings were defined in terms of attention-seeking and approval-seeking from others. Achievement strivings were defined in terms of interest and involvement in learning, competitiveness, and lack of anticipation of failure. In adulthood, similar definitions were used.

The main finding was that recognition and achievement strivings were stable for both sexes, from childhood to adulthood as well as during childhood itself. One qualification is that such behavior in the first three years of life was not predictive of later similar behavior: stability did not begin until ages three to six. A second subsidiary finding was that boys were oriented toward either intellectual or athletic achievement, but not both.

A fourth personality pattern was sexuality, defined in terms of two independent dimensions: erotic relationships with the opposite sex (heterosexuality) and sex-role identification (masculinity and femininity). Heterosexuality was stable in males, both during childhood (six to fourteen) and from childhood to adulthood. It was not stable in females. Sex-role identification was stable in both sexes during childhood, and was stable in males from childhood to adulthood. Indeed, a relationship was found between degree of masculinity at ages three to six and vocational choice in adulthood, with the more masculine boys choosing less intellectual vocations 20 years later.

The fifth personality pattern measured was social interaction anxiety. In childhood, it was defined in terms of avoidance of social situations, inhibition of behavior when in the presence of others, and anticipations of rejection. In adulthood, it was defined in similar terms. Social interaction anxiety was stable for short periods during childhood but was not stable from early childhood to adolescence. However, it was stable from adolescence to adulthood in both sexes, with suggestions that its roots reached further back into childhood for males than for females.

"The child is father to the man." "As the twig is bent, so grows the tree." Many such sayings attest to the common assumption that continuity exists between child and adult behavior. The last two chapters summarized a study that warrants the substitution of the word "fact" for "assumption." It is a *fact* that human behavior exhibits continuity from childhood to adulthood, that adult patterns of behavior can be predicted from a knowledge of childhood behavior patterns. Of course, the accuracy of the prediction varies with such considerations as sex of child, age, and cultural expectations. But the basic fact remains: much of adult behavior is an extension of child behavior.

Stability means that adult behavior is predictable from child behavior. If it is assumed that child behavior is predictable from parental behavior, and from the behavior of teachers, peers, and so on—in short, if it is assumed that child behavior is predictable from environmental events— then the importance of the child's environment in the determination of adult personality is seen to be a logical certainty. The entire remainder of this book documents that certainty.

BIBLIOGRAPHY

KAGAN, J., and Moss, H. A. (1962). *Birth to maturity.* New York: John Wiley & Sons, Inc.

III

PARENTS
AND CHILDREN

10

Infancy

INTRODUCTION

In this chapter we inquire about the earliest environmental determinants of psychological development. As such, we shall take a careful look at studies which varied one aspect or another of the infant's environment in the first year or two of life. There is an infinite number of aspects which could be varied. Investigators did not proceed blindly, studying all possible conditions they could lay their hands on, but, on the contrary, were guided by theoretical notions with various degrees of sophistication.

What notions are these? Learning theory, as summarized in Chapters 5 and 6, provides the initial clues. We discussed two basic kinds of learning in those chapters—classical conditioning of emotional responses and instrumental conditioning of skeletal responses. Regarding the former, we arrived at the generalization that *neutral stimuli consistently paired with strong emotional responses are likely to become conditioned stimuli for those responses, purely as a result of the temporal contiguity involved.* Regarding the latter, we arrived at the generalization that *skeletal responses occurring in the presence of strong motivation and followed by a reduction in motivation (reinforcement) are likely to become conditioned to accompanying stimuli.*

Both generalizations involve strong motivation and drives. Children, and particularly infants, appear to be unusually vulnerable to strong drives, and hence strong habits should be developed early in life. Dollard and Miller state this point of view in compelling terms:

Because of their physical, mental, and emotional helplessness, children are particularly vulnerable to harsh or confusing patterns of training. They have few skills at evading the effects of unfavorable circumstances. . . . Children

297

cannot understand the world and cannot control their emotional reactions. Therefore young children can be subject to more extreme conditions than adults endure, except perhaps when adults are exposed to combat situations in time of war. In combat and in infancy the extremes of hunger, fear, helplessness, confusion, and timeless strain are reproduced. Only in childhood and in combat are the individual's own capacities to control his life so meager and ineffectual.

It is not surprising, then, that acute emotional conflicts occur in childhood. The infant has not learned to wait, not knowing the world's inescapable routines; to hope, and thus to assure itself that the good moment will return and that the evil occasion will pass; to reason and plan, and thus to escape present disorder by constructing the future in a controlled way. Rather, the child is urgently, hopelessly, planlessly impelled, living by moments in eternal pain and then suddenly finding itself bathed in endless bliss. The young child is necessarily disoriented, confused, deluded, and hallucinated—in short, has just those symptoms that we recognize as a psychosis in the adult. Infancy, indeed, may be viewed as a period of transitory psychosis. Savage drives within the infant impel to action. These drives are unmodified by hope or concept of time. The higher mental processes (the Ego) cannot do their benign work of comforting, directing effort, and binding the world into a planful sequence. What is gone may never return. The present pain may never fade. [1950, p. 130.] *

These "savage drives" should, first, lead to the conditioning of emotional reactions to accompanying stimuli, and second, should reinforce preceding responses when they are reduced. We ask, then, (1) *what conditions are likely to lead to strong emotional responses,* and (2) *in what conditions are strong reinforcements systematically experienced?*

It would seem that the infant would be most likely to build up strong drives and emotional responses as a result of irresponsible caretaking. When he is allowed to cry for hours before he gets his bottle, or when mother is not there to unplug a clogged nipple, when his buttocks are allowed to become chapped and sore from prolonged contact with soiled diapers, when his clothes are not changed or bedcovers varied to compensate for temperature variations, when his position is not changed for hours at a time and muscles get sore, when he is left alone with nothing to look at or hear, and boredom gets unendurable—these conditions should be conducive to the conditioning of strong emotional responses. We shall therefore take a careful look at studies of *maternal deprivation,* where such conditions reach their extremes. There is a long line of such studies.

Most of the reinforcements in infancy consist of the reverse of the above conditions, and thus often occur in the presence of the mother: she is present when the infant is fed, changed, dressed, cuddled, and "entertained." Instrumental conditioning, as well as classical conditioning, should occur in such situations. We shall therefore take a careful

* From *Personality and Psychotherapy* by J. Dollard and N. E. Miller. Copyright 1950 McGraw-Hill, Inc. Used by permission of McGraw-Hill Book Company.

look at the *feeding situation, provisions of warmth and comfort,* and *provisions of novelty.*

The latter situations are considered first since they seem to be conditions which are necessarily present almost from the moment of birth.

EARLY LEARNING IN THE FEEDING SITUATION

Infant Learning

Very important learning may occur in the feeding situation, both for the mother and for the infant. Consider the following quotation from Gunther, a British obstetrician:

> My job for some years has been to observe mothers feeding their babies from the breast. While watching them it became apparent that the total number of patterns of babies' responses was limited. First I noticed that one can predict from the shape of the breast whether the baby would feed easily or not. The prediction was not simply whether the baby would obtain milk or not but whether he would be vigorous or not when taking. The shape of the breast was so effective that where the breast was marginal in design the baby could be positioned better so that he got a better hold and from then on he would feed vigorously. Sometimes this moment of first feeding vigorously had not been reached until the second or third day when I had come to help the baby's position. The mothers would often say to me, "My baby has always known how to feed since you came." For the first years I thought this was flattery, but after a while the inference of it came to me and I became certain that it was true. I then measured breasts to see what length of hold they gave and predicted their effectiveness in inducing feeding from them. The correlation between shape and effectiveness was complete. . . .
> . . . The third thing we wanted to show was a quite separate line of thought, a common behaviour of a baby in which it fights the mother. It does this with its fists. This is a typical action of a baby when it is in anoxia. These babies protest as soon as you put them to the breast—once they have experienced something—and this one experience seems to be obstruction of the airway either by the upper lip going up over the nostrils or by the breast covering the nostrils. The curious thing is that no mother or nurse apparently looks to see what this part of the lip is doing or to notice if it blocks the airway; so when a baby who has experienced nasal obstruction is put to the breast, it cries and boxes itself off. Then the attendant midwife shoves a bit harder to get the baby on and it boxes even more. You have only got to have this fight two or three times and from then on the baby cries as you turn it towards the mother. I have even known babies reach a stage by the fifth day, so that if you turn them on their side they start crying from the expectation that they will be put on the breast. Usually the whole thing has developed by the second or third day; you can sometimes get them out of it up to the fourth day, but generally speaking this is a situation which no mother can endure. It is literally frightful for the mother. Mothers who have endured it lose all wish to feed the baby because they cannot bear being so rejected by the baby. [1961, pp. 37–38.]

Maternal Learning

Successful breast feeding is not only dependent upon a proper sucking reflex in the baby, and a proper orientation to the breast, but also upon maternal reflexes. Two important such reflexes are the nipple-erection reflex and the let-down reflex. The nipple-erection reflex makes the nipple easy for the baby to grasp and suck and usually occurs automatically when sucking begins. The let-down reflex releases the stored milk from small alveoli in the breasts to larger ducts where it is made available to the baby's sucking. If a strong let-down reflex occurs, the mother feels it: there is a tingling or drawing of the breasts, and they feel heavy and ready for sucking. If the breasts are very full, milk may flow freely from the unused nipple as the baby nurses at the other breast. More than enough milk is thus made available for the baby.

As dairy farmers have known for a long time, the let-down reflex in cattle can be inhibited, facilitated, and conditioned by environmental events. The cow must "cooperate" if she is to be successfully milked. If she is frightened or upset, the let-down reflex does not occur, and even with a modern milking machine, little of her milk is released. Ely and Peterson (1941) have demonstrated this experimentally. They popped paper bags in the cows' ears and put cats on their backs when they were to be milked. The cows did not release their milk.

Human mothers are subject to similar influences. The Newtons (1948, 1958) were able to inhibit the let-down reflex in a mother by such tactics as pulling her big toes, putting her feet in ice water, administering an electric shock if she did not answer arithmetic questions correctly, etc. They pointed out that if the let-down reflex is inhibited—by worry, anxiety, or tension of one kind or another—the feeding situation can be frustrating to both mother and infant. It is frustrating to the baby because he is hungry, he has learned that food comes from the breast when he sucks, he sucks, and little or none is forthcoming. He storms and fusses with rage, kicking his arms and legs violently. The mother then becomes more upset, even less milk is made available, and a cycle is begun which gathers momentum with each succeeding response from mother or infant. The mother may thus become conditioned to expecting an unpleasant nursing situation and thereby as a result of her own anxieties, create the very situation she dreads. Note, too, how an unpleasant marital situation could contribute to an unpleasant nursing situation.

Maternal expectations of pleasant nursing experiences should have an opposite effect: assuming that such expectations elicit relaxation, the mother should exhibit a strong let-down reflex, the baby should relax as a result of sufficient food, the mother should respond to the baby's relaxation with further relaxation and contentment of her own, and an entirely different chain of events should ensue. Newton reports that such conditioning not only occurs but that the let-down reflex itself becomes conditioned. He describes one mother who was always served a cool glass of milk just before nursing time at the hospital. When she returned home, she discovered her let-down reflex had been conditioned: when she saw a glass of milk, she started dripping milk. Other mothers start dripping milk when they think of their babies about the time of a regular breast feeding, and some mothers begin dripping in the middle of the night, at the time they usually administer a night feeding to their babies. It is unlikely that such conditioning would occur in a mother who has learned to dread the nursing experience.

A relaxed, loving mother who can let-down her milk not only enjoys the pleasurable effects of a contented baby, and the pleasant experiences of relief from heavy breasts, but also another type of sensual experience: the let-down reflex elicits uterine contractions which have been objectively recorded (Moir, 1934). These uterine contractions may last for 20 minutes or more after the breast feeding. Spence, a British pediatrician, is quoted by Newton as describing relaxed breast-feeding mothers as having a look of "lascivious content" during the feeding sessions (Spence, 1938).

A child who is breast-fed from such a mother has hundreds of mother–nourishment pairings, and the mother has hundreds of infant–"lascivious content" pairings. Thus, both mother and infant experience direct biological sources of reinforcement during the (successful) nursing session. According to learning theory, the accompanying pleasant emotional responses of the infant should thus become conditioned to the mother per se, and likewise the pleasant emotional responses of the mother should become conditioned to the baby per se, whether he is nursing or not. Thus the successful feeding situation probably makes a substantial contribution not only to the development of infant love for mother, but of mother love for the infant.

What support do these predictions from learning theory have in fact? Other than anecdotal observations of the type reported by Gunther, and the facts summarized by Newton, there is little information available from human infants. But convincing information has been gathered at the animal level. This material is presented in the next section.

Animal Experiments of Learning in the Feeding Situation

Harlow carried out some pioneer experiments with monkeys concerned with the origins of infant love for mother (Harlow, 1958). He built two surrogate (imitation) monkey mothers as follows:

We produced a perfectly proportioned, streamlined body stripped of unnecessary bulges and appendices. Redundancy in the surrogate mother's system was avoided by reducing the number of breasts from two to one and placing this unibreast in an upper-thoracic, sagittal position, thus maximizing the natural and known perceptual-motor capabilities of the infant operator. The surrogate was made from a block of wood, covered with sponge rubber, and sheathed in tan cotton terry cloth. A light bulb behind her radiated heat. The result was a mother, soft, warm, and tender, a mother with infinite patience, a mother available twenty-four hours a day, a mother that never scolded her infant and never struck or bit her baby in anger. Furthermore, we designed a mother-machine with maximal maintenance efficiency since failure of any system or function could be resolved by the simple substitution of black boxes and new component parts. It is our opinion that we engineered a very superior monkey mother, although this position is not held universally by the monkey fathers. [Pp. 675–676.]

Two such mothers were built, the only differences being that they had different faces and one was green, the other tan. Each of four infant monkeys had such a pair of surrogate mothers available in its cage 24 hours a day. Whenever it climbed on one mother or the other, a clock was automatically started which stopped when the monkey left the mother. It was thus possible to measure the amount of time spent on each mother.

For two of the four infants, only the tan mother provided nourishment (provided by the periodic insertion of a nippled bottle into her thoracic region), and for the other two infants, only the green mother nursed. The question was this: would the infants display a greater "love" for the nursing mother than for the non-nursing mother as revealed by time spent on each mother?

The answer is provided in Figure 10.1, in terms of the average number of hours per day spent on each mother. Presumably time spent feeding on the lactating mother was subtracted from total time on her, thus allowing quantification of non-nutritional time-on-mother for each mother.

This figure shows that a preference for the nourishing mother was quickly developed, although the crossover at the end of the figure is difficult to interpret. Perhaps the monkeys generalized their emotional responses from the nourishing mother to the non-nourishing mother, explaining the gradual convergence of the curves. It is unfortunate that the study was ended at this crucial moment.

Igel and Calvin (1960) carried out a similar experiment with dogs. Two surrogate mothers were made from wooden blocks covered with foam rubber and surfaced with terry cloth. Leather heads, from toy stick horses, were attached at one end to simulate real dogs. The surrogates were rectangular in form, allowing the puppy to crawl on top and "snuggle" the mother. Two groups of puppies each had a surrogate mother present in their cages at all times. One group was fed from the mother

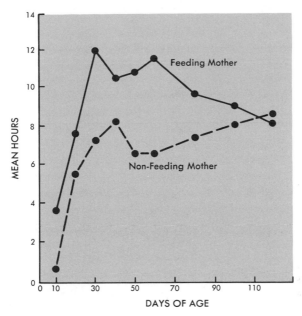

Figure 10.1. Time spent on feeding and non-feeding surrogate mothers (Harlow, 1961).

by a protruding nipple, while the other group was hand-fed by the experimenter. The average amount of time spent on the mother was automatically recorded, and is presented in Figure 10.2, in minutes per day. Time spent feeding was subtracted, so that the curves represent non-feeding contact for both groups. As with the Harlow data, a preference for the nourishing mother soon developed, and unlike the Harlow data, it remained stable to the end of the study.

Animal studies thus provide data which are consistent with learning theory predictions: mothers closely associated with relaxation and contentment produced by feeding have infants who spend more time with the mother—who develop a greater "love" for her. The contentment initially elicited by feeding becomes conditioned to the mother.

The Lu Study

Lu (1967) demonstrated that human infants will develop a visual preference for cues paired with feeding. The cue she used was not the mother, but simply a red light. Ten infants, average age five months, were first tested for length of fixation on a red light located above the crib. Then the mothers of half the infants were instructed to turn on a

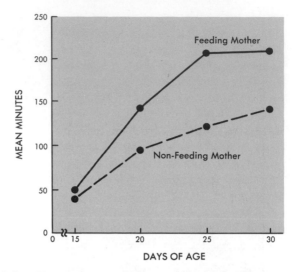

Figure 10.2. Time spent on feeding and non-feeding surrogate mothers (Igel and Calvin, 1960).

red light, and to wear a red blouse or smock at all feedings. The other mothers were given no special instructions. Some time later, all babies were returned to the laboratory for a second visual preference test, the same as before. The experimental babies now showed an increased fixation time on the red light, as compared to the control babies. Presumably the red light now made them feel good, just as the feedings with which it had been paired had done. The response of looking at it was thus reinforced. A similar preference presumably develops for the mother herself under normal circumstances. Thus a baby learns to enjoy looking at his mother, and she interprets it, rightly enough, as love.

MOTHER-INFANT PHYSICAL CONTACT AS A FACTOR INFLUENCING INFANTILE LEARNING

Just as the nursing situation provides obvious nutritional reinforcement, so does mere physical contact between mother and child provide reinforcement of another kind. In the first place, picking up the baby results in changes in the contraction and flexion of various muscle groups, thus resulting in greater relaxation. Second, the "colicky" baby, with gas in its stomach which was swallowed along with the milk from its last feeding, is relieved from the pains of stomach distension when it burps. Holding the baby over mother's shoulder induces such burps and, indeed, is referred to as "burping" the baby. Third, the rhythmic movements most mothers engage in while holding the baby are apparently relaxing, since it is reported that such movements are quite successful in inducing sleep. Fourth, the body heat of the mother provides warmth for the infant, particularly if it is breast-fed and thus comes into contact with a large area of mother's warm skin. Fifth, and perhaps most important, the mother is soft, gentle, and pliable, thus providing sheer comfort for the helpless infant. All these various components probably combine to make close, intimate, physical contact with mother a most reinforcing state of affairs. Such reinforcement should strengthen the infant's tie to its mother in much the same way as maternal nutrition does, as manifested in a loving infant.

On the other hand, a cold rejecting mother might have quite a different effect. Handling the baby a minimum, she may lift and hold it with relatively quick, jerky movements, thus eliciting tension and startle responses rather than relaxation—it is known that sudden changes in movement elicit such behavior in infants. While holding it she may be insensitive to the pinning of an arm between her body and the infant's own body, and insensitive to various bumps and flesh-to-flesh collisions as she quickly moves the infant to a new position. I am reminded of an anecdote concerning a Russian baby who had a "neurosis": he would not nurse without first hitting himself on the nose with his fist. It turned out that he had somehow come to "expect" such a stimulus prior to nursing since his rough mother usually bumped his nose before orienting him optimally to her breast.

Such a lack of reinforcement associated with mother-infant physical interactions would not be expected to lead to the conditioning of infantile relaxation and "pleasure" responses to the sight and sound of mother. Since her handling does not elicit much relaxation, gurgling, or cooing in the infant, there is no opportunity for such responses to become conditioned to her per se. In short, the infant would have difficulty in learning to love such a mother.

Ribble (1943) was among the first to call attention to the probable importance of contact comfort. An M.D., she observed 600 infants as they interacted with their mothers in hospitals and at home. She writes:

> The newborn child gets kinaesthetic satisfaction from being held, moved about, and fondled by the mother. The satisfaction derived from these forms of stimulation are registered in improved breathing, and when observation can be made over a prolonged period, it shows in improved digestion . . . Those who are not held in the arms sufficiently, particularly if they are bottle-fed babies, also develop gastrointestinal disorders. They become air swallowers and frequently develop what is popularly known as colic. They may have trouble with defecation, or they may vomit frequently. . . . Thus, the touch of the mother (or her substitute) has a definite biological implication in the regulation of the reflexes connected with breathing and nutritive functions.

The sense of body position is acute in the infant at birth. It constitutes a second aspect of kinaesthetic experience that is important in establishing the affective tie between mother and child . . . If the body of the newborn infant is not well supported by wrappings or if the child is picked up suddenly or moved about rapidly or violently, it reacts immediately with a startle. This innate sensitivity, or fear of falling as it has been called, tends normally to be overcome through gentle motion or rocking. The old-fashioned cradle and rocking chair have considerable value in the first months of life and they could well be returned to modern nurseries, although the baby carriage may also supply this need.

. . . .

With the distance receptors the child develops the ability to orientate himself more and more through sight and sound. The eyes focus well and can follow the mother about, the ears function well and can differentiate the sound she makes. Sound of her or sight of her produces the positive emotional responses formerly obtained only from contact, and consist of appropriate smiling and even genuine outbursts of joy. From this time on actual physical contact is no longer necessary for fairly prolonged periods just so long as the child can hear the mother's voice or see her while he is awake. [Pp. 631–632, 643.]

Ribble has been severely criticized for lack of objective evidence to support her conclusions (Pinneau, 1950). Yet she may have been more right than wrong. Anyone who has watched either animal or human infants as they are cuddled must be impressed with the obvious signs of contentment: tail-wagging, whining, and face-licking in dogs, purring in kittens, and cooing in human infants.

Animal Experiments

Harlow performed some ingenious experiments with monkeys which dramatically illustrate the importance of contact comfort in the development of love-for-mother (Harlow, 1958, 1962). Along with his previously described terry cloth mother, who was ". . . soft, warm, and tender . . . ," he built a second surrogate mother with less pleasant qualities, a mother made of wire rather than of terry cloth.

Each of eight infant monkeys had access to both imitation mothers 24 hours a day, with the time spent on each automatically recorded. Half the monkeys were fed only by the soft "loving" mother, and half only by the hard "rejecting" mother. It was thus possible not only to measure the importance of contact comfort but to compare it with the importance of nursing. The effects of the two kinds of mothers were measured not only in terms of (a) the amount of time spent on each, but in two other ways as well: (b) to which mother the infant monkey ran when frightened by presentation of an unusual stimulus (a novel object such as a wind-up toy bear was placed into the monkey's cage and his subsequent behavior recorded in terms of which mother he approached); and (c) by a "love machine," which consisted of a dimly

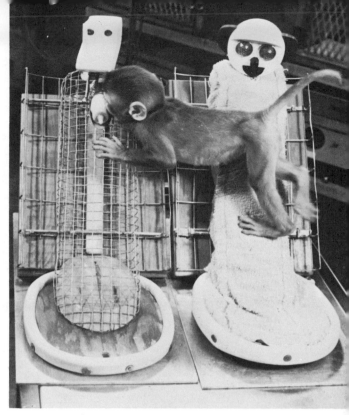

A monkey obtaining contact comfort *and* milk in the Harlow studies.

(Harlow, 1961)

illuminated box with one blocked window which could be automatically opened by pressing a lever. Harlow measured the frequency with which the monkeys pressed the lever depending upon what they saw when the window was open—the "loving" mother or the "rejecting" mother.

The average amount of time spent on each mother per day for the two groups of monkeys, one fed from the soft mother and one from the hard mother, is presented in Figure 10.3. It shows that the infant monkeys spent between 12 and 18 hours per day on the cloth mother, and one hour or so on the wire mother, *regardless of who fed them.* Contact comfort, then, was of overpowering significance in determining which mother the infant interacted with and in addition almost completely overshadowed source of nutrition. The accompanying photograph shows one monkey simultaneously affected by both variables.

Test (*b*) measured which mother the infant monkey ran to when frightened by a novel object. Figure 10.4 indicates the percentage of responses to each mother by each of the two groups. It is clear that the soft mother was chosen most of the time, regardless of which mother had provided nourishment. It seems that these results are particularly convincing. Not only did these monkeys spend more time on the soft mother, they went to her more often when frightened. The soft mother

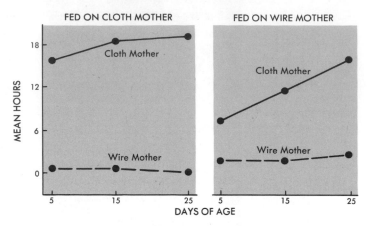

Figure 10.3. Mean time spent on cloth and wire surrogate mothers (Harlow, 1958).

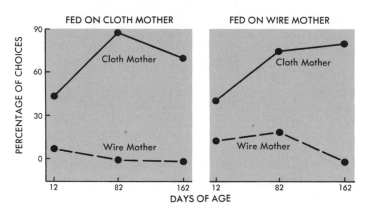

Figure 10.4. Percentage of responses to cloth and wire mothers when frightened (Harlow, 1961).

evidently acquired the capacity to reduce fear as well as to provide contact comfort.

Test (c) measured the number of times each monkey pressed the lever to open the window, and thus provided a test of Ribble's assertion that ultimately sights or sounds alone of mother would provide reinforcement with contact comfort no longer being necessary. Figure 10.5 presents the mean number of lever presses depending upon whether the open window revealed another monkey, the cloth mother, the wire mother, or nothing at all. As can be seen, many more responses were made when they were followed by a brief glimpse of the cloth mother, and the wire

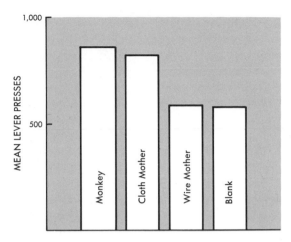

Figure 10.5. Number of lever presses in "love machine" (Harlow, 1958).

mother seemed to be no more attractive than nothing at all. As Harlow concluded, "We can be certain that not all love is blind" (1958, p. 61).

It is important that the reader understand just how learning theory accounts for these results. It is not contact comfort which directly caused the monkeys to push more frequently to see the soft mother than to see the wire mother, since they did not come into physical contact with either mother while in the love machine. Rather, seeing her must have elicited some of the same responses physical contact previously elicited: *conditioned* relaxation and contentment. These conditioned responses, occurring as they did immediately after the lever press, provided reinforcement for the response, thereby insuring that it would occur again. The sight of the mother, instead of her contact, provided the reinforcement. This is what Ribble meant when she wrote, "From this time on actual physical contact is no longer necessary for fairly prolonged periods just so long as the child can hear the mother's voice or see her while he is awake." The learned emotional responses, elicited by sights and sounds, take the place of the "primary" reinforcements provided by direct contact with the mother.

Igel and Calvin verified Harlow's results with dogs. They too built a wire mother. One group of puppies was exposed only to a cloth mother, who also supplied nourishment. Another group was exposed only to a wire mother who supplied nourishment. With nourishment the same for both mothers, differences in the amount of time spent on each presumably reflected the effects of differences in contact comfort. The results, presented in Figure 10.6, show more non-nourishment time spent on the cloth mother.

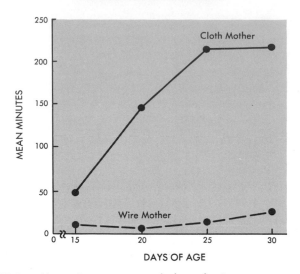

Figure 10.6.   Mean time spent on cloth and wire surrogate mothers (Igel and Calvin, 1960).

A Critical Comment.   Harlow's work, although of a pioneering kind, suffers from certain methodological difficulties. The reader is reminded once again of the fundamental rule: X and only X may be varied if the effects of X are to be unambiguously determined. Presumably Harlow's two mothers varied only in amount of contact comfort, and thus differences in the behavior of the infant monkeys were attributed to differences in comfort afforded by these two mothers. They varied, however, in a number of other ways as well. For example, they looked different, with the wire monkey being transparent while the cloth mother was, of course, opaque. In addition, the faces were different, with the cloth mother possessing a face more similar to a real monkey face than that of the wire mother. Both of these factors resulted in a greater degree of similarity between the cloth monkey and real monkeys and thus could account for the differences in behavior. That these considerations are not unimportant is suggested by Harlow himself, who points out the significance of the face:

> . . . one notes increasing responsiveness to the mother's face and head, beginning at about 45 days of age. . . . thus, *there is every reason to believe that vision, at a particular maturational stage, becomes an important variable underlying the development of the affectional responses to the mother.* [1961, p. 81; italics added.]

In view of this consideration, it is unfortunate that more care was not taken to equate visual differences between the two surrogate mothers.

Parenthetically, the work of Igel and Calvin suffers from the same problem: their wire mother was also less doglike than the terry cloth mother.

One final comment about Harlow's work. The reader must not get the impression that monkeys "raised" by the cloth surrogate mother developed into entirely normal monkeys. Follow-up studies (Harlow, 1962) indicated that their behavior with other monkeys was far from normal. A description of all the behavioral deviations observed is not relevant at the present time, but perhaps a final quotation from Harlow will serve to suggest their general nature: "Month after month female monkeys that never know a real mother, themselves become mothers—helpless, hopeless, heartless mothers devoid, or almost devoid, of any maternal feeling" (1962, p. 9). In other words, these monkeys did not exhibit normal maternal behavior themselves and, indeed, also exhibited considerable sexual deviancy, with Harlow reporting great difficulty in breeding them.

Physical Contact and Visual Experience

Recent research (Korner and Grobstein, 1967) suggests an unexpected consequence of physical contact. Korner and Grobstein noticed a tendency for neonates not only to stop crying when picked up but to become visually alert and to scan the environment. If true, this observation becomes an important finding, for it suggests that the development of early visual-motor schemata, as described by Piaget, may be facilitated by handling.

To determine the validity of this incidental observation, the investigators carried out a simple experiment. Visual scanning of 12 neonates, forty-five to seventy-nine hours of age, was recorded under four conditions: (1) when the neonate was crying but not handled, (2) when crying and then moved to a sitting position, (3) when crying and placed upright on the adult's right shoulder, and (4) when crying and placed upright on the adult's left shoulder. Recordings were made by two observers, whose records were in agreement about 97 per cent of the time.

The results indicated that when left to cry unattended, or when simply moved to a sitting position, the neonates opened their eyes in the following 30 seconds about 25 per cent of the time. When picked up and placed against the adult's shoulder, however, a dramatic change occurred: they opened their eyes about 90 per cent of the time. Thus, being picked up resulted in a profound increase in the infant's visual sampling of the environment. Since other data clearly show that the infant of even this tender age can discriminate between various visual cues (Fantz, 1961, 1963; Lu, 1967), it follows that physical contact of this type is quite likely to lead to accelerated familiarity with the visual environment.

The baby who is frequently handled by a loving mother, who is not left to cry unattended in his crib, who is often carried and rocked on his mother's shoulder, is thus exposed not only to the pleasant kinaesthetic stimuli of soft body contact, but to a much richer visual environment, too. He thereby enjoys all the pleasant surprises of visual novelty—the changing shapes and forms, the different colors as his scanning sweeps the room, the changing perspective of height as he is raised and lowered—which coalesce over time into visual schemata: "expectations" concerning the nature of the visual world. These schemata lay the groundwork for later cognitive structuring of a more complicated variety, according to Piaget, and thus prepare the infant for subsequent intellectual development. Perhaps the handling-visual scanning relationship is one of the factors contributing to the intellectual retardation of children subjected to maternal deprivation (see pages 320 to 325).

NOVELTY

Evidence was presented in a previous chapter indicating that stimulus deprivation produced boredom in an awake individual, and that the consequent boredom-produced motivation is reducible by stimulus variation. A study by Harriet Rheingold with three- to six-month-old infants was summarized, indicating that even such young infants could be taught to press a ball if such behavior was followed by a change in the environment (display of colored lights for two or three seconds).

What are some of the characteristics of a novel object, e.g., an object capable of reducing the pangs of boredom? Common sense and past experience suggest several important categories: *movement* (a moving object is probably more interesting than a stationary object, everything else equal); *brightness differences* (an object that "stands out" from the surrounding environment in terms of a difference in shade is more likely to attract attention); *sound; color;* a certain amount of *unpredictability* (the perfectly predictable movements and sounds of a mechanical dog are nowhere near as interesting as the more variable movements and sounds of a real dog); and perhaps most important, *contingency* (an object *that is available whenever the individual becomes bored*—a novel object which is not there can hardly reduce boredom).

A little reflection will suggest that one object possessing all these characteristics in abundance is the caretaker. The author is aware of only one study, however, specifically concerned with the novelty aspects of motherhood. Friedlander (1967) reports a study in which he investigated the novelty aspects of parents' voices. The instrumentation was clever. He attached two "toys" and a loudspeaker to the sides of the infant's playpen. Inside the "toys" were switches such that whenever the infant exerted more than 2 ounces pressure, the switch closed a circuit which turned on a continuous loop tape-recording for as long as the pressure was maintained. Duration of each response was automatically recorded for later analysis. Two tapes were prepared, one for each switch. One, the "high novelty" tape, consisted of a 120-second recording of a spirited conversation between the infant's mother, father, and a family friend. The other, "low novelty" tape, consisted of a 40-second segment of the same tape. The high novelty tape was thus less repetitious than the low novelty tape.

The eleven-month infant was exposed to the "toys" each day for 16 days, whenever the mother put him in the playpen for his daily play-time. Figure 10.7 presents the amount of time he pressed each lever in each daily session. It reveals an initial preference for the more repetitious tape, followed by a reversal to the more novel tape, which persevered to the end of the experiment. In the last 4 days, the infant spent more than an hour pressing the switch controlling this tape.

Friedlander suggests that the infant first listened to the repetitious tape because it was easier to recognize his parents' voices: there were

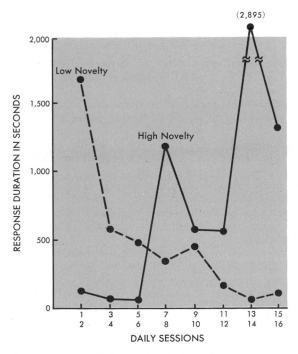

Figure 10.7. Response duration for high and low novelty parental voices (Friedlander, 1967).

more repetitions of each phrase. After recognizing and becoming satiated (bored) with this tape, he then gradually turned to the more novel one, and thus held his boredom to a minimum level. This experiment provides a clear example of the reinforcing properties of novel parental behavior. Assuming that such novelty is reinforcing because of the pleasant emotional responses it elicits, it is easy to see that the pleasant unpredictability of a parent's behavior, nonverbal as well as verbal, contributes to the development of *conditioned* emotional reactions to the parent. These, in turn, are not only manifested as the infant's "love" for his parent, but also serve as reinforcers for any responses which increase the proximity of the parent.

Rheingold and Schaffer have both given serious thought to the importance of parental novelty. Rheingold writes:

. . . the human infant by three months of age is no passive creature. When awake, he is alert, attentive, active and responsive. He occupies himself continually. Especially is this clear in the institution where there is so little interference and where he is left so much to his own entertaining. Already there are developed both a *responsiveness* to stimuli in the environment and a *searching* of the environment for stimulation.

Most prominent among the infant's waking activities is looking. His eyes move freely and often, as he fixates on one object after another. Hearing a sound, he moves his head until his eyes locate the source. When his hands close on an object, he looks *to* the object. When he is placed in the prone position, he moves his head freely, and looks. Picked up, his first activity is to look around him. At this age, before he can reach out and grasp an object with any kind of facility, he is already picking up the physical environment, but, as Gessel said, "with eyes alone."

Intent and fixed visual regard is accompanied by a cessation of physical activity. The infant is showing the orienting reflex of Pavlov, as if asking "what is it?" On occasion, however, there follows the responses I have already enumerated, the brightening of the face, the smiles, the marked increase in total bodily activity, and the vocalizations, a sequence which is often repeated again and again.

The simple enumeration of the components of the response, however, omits what is so striking, but so obvious as to be ignored, that the infant is displaying what seem to be the emotions of delight and glee. Parenthetically, as Bowlby has pointed out, it is just these emotions that his responses evoke in the adult beholder.

Among all the objects of the infant's environment the most interesting, I suggest, is the social object. If one analyzes the social object, the human being, as though it were any other object, one is struck by its extraordinarily high stimulating properties. I can think of no other object with which it can compare. Visually, the human face is bright, parts of it shine, it has contour and complexity. It moves almost constantly, bringing stimulus change with every movement. It produces sound. The human body offers tactile stimulation on occasion. Above all, the social object moves *in response* to the infant's own movements. If he smiles, it smiles. If he vocalizes, it vocalizes in turn. [Rheingold, 1961, pp. 166–168.]

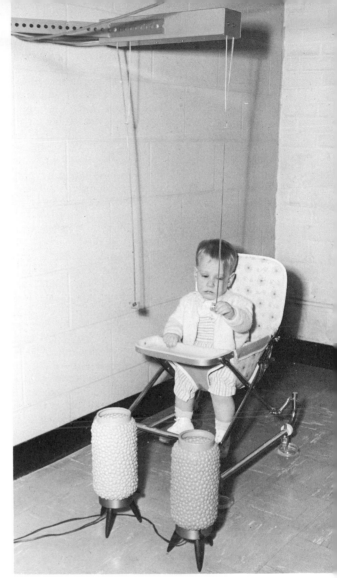

An experimental investigation of novelty in young children. When the correct cord is pulled, the lamps light up, producing stimulus variation for the child.

(Photograph courtesy of Lewis P. Lipsitt)

Schaffer, after studying Rheingold's thoughts, wrote as follows one year later,

It is not only (as Rheingold has rightly pointed out) that human beings in themselves form the most stimulating part of the infant's environment, but also that the supply of non-social stimulation too is usually dependent on the adult. The young infant's motor equipment does not at first enable him to produce all those interesting sights and sounds which he needs to relieve his boredom, for in the early months he cannot even effect a change in position in order to bring about a change in visual perspective. When, therefore, the adult disappears and leaves him to his own devices the infant will have only very limited means at his disposal to produce some form of entertainment, and under these circumstances his natural reaction is to cry. The three-month-old baby, left in the garden facing a blank wall, will begin to cry within a fairly short time; if he is then put under a tree where he can watch the leaves moving about in the wind peace will reign once more. Stimulation-producing devices such as this are in fact commonly employed by mothers in order to stop or prevent their babies' crying, and in the course of our investigation we have come across quite a large number of these. The provision of toys is perhaps the most common example but there are others of a less usual character. One of our mothers, for example, found the most effective way of keeping her baby quiet was to switch on her vacuum cleaner, while another claimed that her infant would only settle in his cot if the radiogram was on. Still another mother used a tape-recorder: at first it was sufficient for the infant merely to watch it going round and round, but after a while he became bored with this and the sound had to be switched on. Several of our infants were said to cry unless the television set was on—with the advertisements acting as particularly effective eyecatchers!

.   .   .   .

. . . as Harriet Rheingold (1961) has pointed out so clearly, the infant soon learns that social objects have a much higher stimulating value than the inanimate part of the environment, that they are both more interesting and more responsive and thus much more satisfying. Herein, I suggest, lie the origins of attachment behavior: having learned of the special stimulating properties inherent in his human partners, the infant begins to distinguish them as a class in their own right, seeks their physical proximity in order to be exposed to their relatively high (but also accommodating) arousal value, and protests when he is prevented from achieving this end. [Schaffer, 1963, pp. 192–194, 196.]

The probability is high, then, that an infant learns to love its mother not only because she has been paired with nutrition, pain reduction, and contact comfort, but also because she has been paired with (indeed, is the embodiment of) boredom reduction. Novelty thus takes its place with these other reinforcers as a determinant of infant love.

FEEDING, PHYSICAL CONTACT, AND NOVELTY IN COMBINATION: THE RHEINGOLD STUDY

The studies thus far have considered the separate contributions of the feeding situation, contact comfort, and novelty. Each was found to have a significant effect on infant learning. Let us now put the components together in a more natural situation. Does a mother who provides frequent feedings in pleasant situations, who affords frequent contact comfort, and who provides stimulus novelty by frequent social interactions with her infant, affect the infant's behavior in a different way from a mother who scores "low" on all three components? Harriet Rheingold carried out a careful experiment which attempts to answer this question (Rheingold, 1956).

Sixteen infants about six months of age who lived in a combined maternity-orphanage served as subjects. Two identical experiments were carried out, with eight infants in each one. Each experiment consisted of an experimental group of four infants and a control group of four infants. The control infants were given no special treatment—they were cared for in the usual manner established as routine by the institution. An idea of their general treatment is provided by the following quotation:

The babies were cared for by students in a one-year child-care course, by supervisors who were graduates of the course, and by volunteers. The volunteers were women from the community who came for a few hours of the day, usually from 9 A.M. to 12:30 P.M. During this period they were the ones who fed, bathed, and generally cared for the babies. The volunteers came on only a personally-fixed schedule, usually once a week. No volunteer came every day or even every other day. The number of volunteers varied from day to day, and from week to week. In their absence the students and their supervisors cared for the babies. Thus, a baby would ordinarily not be cared for by the same person from one time to the next. [Rheingold, 1956, p. 8.] *

The experimental infants were treated differently: Rheingold herself cared for them 7½ hours a day, 5 days a week, for 8 weeks—a total of 300 hours. She writes:

The experimenter cared for, "mothered," the four subjects who were assigned to the experimental condition in each experiment. These babies lived in one room with their cribs side by side along one wall of the room. The experimenter fed, bathed, diapered, soothed, held, talked to, and played with these four babies for seven and one-half hours a day, from 7:30 A.M. to 3:00 P.M., five days a week, for eight weeks, a total of 300 hours. During these hours no one else cared for these babies, although at times other people were in the room, the nurse, the doctor, visitors, or the student nurses who made the beds. After 3 P.M. the experimental babies were cared for according to the hospital routine described earlier under *Institution*. The same routine was followed on Saturdays and Sundays, except that the experimenter was present on Saturdays for the tests to be described shortly.
The experimenter deliberately and consistently tried to adapt her care to the individual needs of each baby as these were apparent to her, limited only by hospital routines and by the demands of caring for four babies at once. Every effort was made to prevent a child's crying or to placate him if he did cry. The babies were out of their cribs often, being held or seated in chairs. The experimenter put toys in their hands and played with the children. She held each child on her lap for some period of every day. She smiled and talked to the babies, and tried to miss no opportunity to respond to their smiles and vocalizations. The goal was to give the children maximal gratification. [Rheingold, 1956, pp. 10–11.]

Rheingold very carefully measured many of the environmental differences between experimental and control infants. She did this by use of a *time-sampling* technique. Another person, the *observer*, visited experimental and control infants according to a time schedule and recorded what was going on during the visit. She recorded for 10-minute periods between 7:30 A.M. to 3:00 P.M. (not continuously on any one day), alternating between experimental and control rooms so that both groups would be observed during similar times of the day.

The major differences between experimental and control infants produced as a result of Rheingold's intensive care were these: (1) The average control baby was cared for by 13 different persons in a 24-hour day, the average experimental baby by six (7½ hours by Rheingold and the remainder of the day by 5 others); (2) the control babies were alone in the room, without an adult, on about 70 per cent of the observations (64 per cent in the first experiment, 74 per cent in the second), while experimental infants were alone on only about 25 per cent of the observations; (3) caretaking acts were actually being performed for control babies on 7 per cent of the observations, and these were divided among 14 or more different persons, while such acts were being carried out for experimental infants on about 22 per cent of the observations, all by Rheingold; (4) control children were being talked to, or held in arms, on about 1 per cent of the observations, while experimental infants were so engaged on about 8 per cent of the observations (about 12 per cent for talking, 5 per cent for holding); and (5) control infants were out of their individual cribs on only 1 observation out of 10 (10 per cent), while experimental infants were out 4 observations out of 10 (40 per cent).

It is clear, then, that the experimental infants received much more reinforcement of all sorts than control infants, and that a large number of these were paired with a single adult, the experimenter. Learning theory would thus clearly predict that positive emotional responses should become conditioned to the experimenter.

The effects of the eight-week intensive interaction were evaluated by administration of a battery of four tests to all the infants, controls as well as experimentals, one week prior to the beginning of the experiment and every other week thereafter, continuing until two or three weeks after the end of the experiment. The following quotation is worthy of note:

> The experimenter gave none of the tests because it was anticipated she might acquire certain biases by her knowledge of the hypotheses to be tested and by her intimate contact with the experimental subjects.
> All tests throughout both experiments were administered by another person (not the observer), hereafter called the examiner. The examiner was a graduate student, trained by the experimenter, *whom we tried to keep in ignorance of the experimental design.* [Rheingold, 1956, p. 14; italics added.]

This was accomplished by mixing experimental and control infants in the same room on testing days, and not identifying to which group each belonged. The position of a given infant in a given room was also varied from one testing session to another. Would that all investigators took such pains to insulate their experimental results from their own biases and expectations.

The four test batteries consisted of an infant intelligence test (the Cattell Infant Intelligence Scale), a finger dexterity test (cube manipulation), a postural development test, and a test of social responsiveness.

Since our present concern is with the infants' social behavior and since no significant differences were found on the other three tests, we shall consider only the test for social responsiveness. The examiner recorded each infant's behavior when another adult (half the time the examiner herself, and half the time the experimenter, Rheingold) stimulated it according to a strict procedure. These stimulations consisted of attempts to "socialize" with the infant: the adult would lean over the crib and smile, say, "How are you?", pick the infant up, etc. The examiner recorded what the infant did when so stimulated, noting such items as looking, reaching, smiling, vocalizing, etc. There were few instances of negative responses (crying). Of 527 scores, only 36 indicated whimpering or crying. Thus, about 95 per cent of the infant responses were positive.

Figures 10.8 and 10.9 present the mean scores of social responsiveness for successive test sessions, Figure 10.8 showing responsiveness to the experimenter (Rheingold) and Figure 10.9, responsiveness to the examiner,

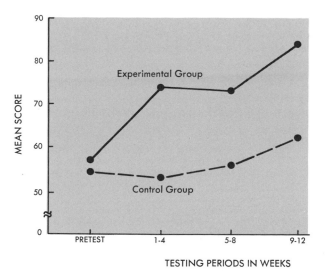

Figure 10.8. Social responsiveness to experimenter (Rheingold, 1956). Copyright © 1956 by The Society for Research in Child Development.

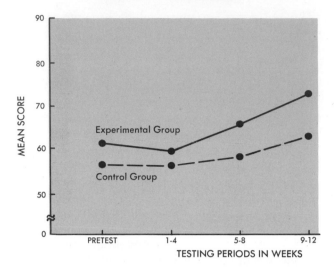

Figure 10.9. Social responsiveness to examiner (Rheingold, 1956). Copyright © 1956 by The Society for Research in Child Development.

a relative stranger. *These data indicate that the experimental infants were more responsive than control infants not only to Rheingold, but also, to a lesser extent, to the examiner.* If we define a loving infant as one who looks, reaches, smiles, and coos when an adult stimulates him, then we must conclude that Rheingold's interaction with the experimental infants over the eight-week period increased their love for her, that this love persisted for at least three weeks following the end of the experiment (but not for a year—see Rheingold and Bayley, 1959), and that it generalized to a relative stranger. The results are consistent with learning theory predictions.

MATERNAL DEPRIVATION

The previous discussion was concerned with infantile sources of reinforcement. The theoretical analysis presented in the introduction also asked about sources of nonreinforcement. It predicted that the ensuing negative emotional responses should become conditioned to cues systematically paired with strong drives and strong aversive emotionality. It was reasoned that the neglecting mother, who does not promptly respond to the nutritional, physical, and novelty needs of her infant, should create an excess of such unfortunate experiences. Thus, studies of maternal deprivation became our immediate concern.

These studies usually follow the same pattern. Infants temporarily deprived of a close relationship with a mother or mother-substitute are compared to infants from more normal environments. Since such studies cannot *purposely* be carried out, the strategy is to *seek* such infants wherever they can be found. Orphanages are therefore the logical target. What we find, then, are comparisons of the "adjustment" of orphanage children with non-orphanage children. There have been dozens of such studies. What do they tell us?

Lowrey (1940) published one of the earliest papers, and it was eventually followed by scores of similar studies, among the better known being those of Bowlby (1952), Goldfarb (1944, 1945), and Spitz (1945, 1946). Let us take a look at these studies. Lowrey, a psychiatrist, studied 28 children who were referred to him when they were between three and five years of age. They had entered an orphanage when less than a year of age, and were subsequently adopted. Lowrey concluded that after leaving the institution, they had caught more diseases than would be expected, were negativistic and hard to get along with, suffered from speech defects, had unusually low IQ scores, etc. He attributed these deficiencies to institutional living, and suggested that such children be provided with a consistent, continuing, intimate mother figure in order to counteract the detrimental effects of maternal deprivation.

Goldfarb published a series of papers in the middle 1940's concerned with the same question. Partly because his studies were methodologically much better than previous ones, and partly because they were published with some frequency, they received considerable attention from child psychologists. Goldfarb studied children who had been institutionalized until about age three and then adopted. He compared them to a control group consisting of children who had also been adopted soon after birth, but had spent no time, or very little, in an institution. Goldfarb administered personality and IQ tests to these groups when they were older: seven, nine, and twelve. He found large differences in favor of the non-institutionalized children, with the institutionalized children showing IQ scores of around 70 (as compared to an average of about 100 for the control group), and manifesting a rather willy-nilly collection of behavioral abnormalities, such as insecurity, isolation, apathy, but also, strangely enough, restlessness, hyperactivity, excessive craving for attention, etc. Aside from the apparent inconsistencies in some of these behavior patterns, it is clear that the institutionalized children wound up at the bottom of the adjustment totem pole. Goldfarb concluded that institutionalization, with its associated maternal deprivation, made the difference.

The most dramatic studies of all, however, are those of Spitz. He studied two groups of institutionalized children, and compared them not only with each other but with "control" children raised by their natural parents. One institution, the *Foundling Home*, was apparently deficient in a number of respects: (1) babies were somewhat isolated from much sensory stimulation by the practice of hanging extra sheets over the sides of the cribs, thus restricting visual stimulation to the ceiling; (2) the babies were pretty much confined to these cell-like beds for the first 15 months of life, seldom being removed except for caretaking; and (3) each nurse was responsible for about 8–10 babies, thus resulting in little adult-infant interaction other than care-taking activities. In the other institution, the *Nursery*, things were different: (1) the babies could see trees, landscape, other babies, etc.; i.e., there were no sheets hanging over the sides of their cribs; (2) they were frequently out of their cribs after the first six months, playing with other infants, etc.; and (3) each infant had the *full-time* care of its *own mother* (*Nursery* was part of a penal institution for delinquent girls—often pregnant when institutionalized).

In most other respects, the two institutions were reported to be comparable: food, clothing, and medical attention, for example, were supposedly very adequate, even "excellent," at both institutions.

The children, 61 in *Foundling Home* and 69 in *Nursery*, were given a number of tests, and motion picture samples of their behavior were made. One of the more dramatic findings was the progressive trend of the developmental quotient (a score representing more or less a combination of physical and intellectual development).

Infants from the *Nursery*, which provided more stimulation, and where the babies were cared for by their own mothers, showed little change over time. *Foundling Home* infants, on the other hand, manifested a drop to 72 by the end of the first year of life, and dropped to an unbelievable low of 45 by the end of the second year of life. As Spitz wrote, "By the end of the second year, the Developmental Quotient sinks to 45, which corresponds to a mental age of approximately 10 months, and would qualify these children as imbeciles" (1945, p. 70). Other data supported these dramatic findings. Of the *Foundling Home* infants 26 per cent died of a measles epidemic, while none died in *Nursery*. By the time the remaining infants were between two and four years of age (a total of 21), only five could walk (average age of walking is around 15 months, with a very small proportion not able to walk by 20 months). Only nine could eat alone with a spoon, only ten had over a three-word vocabulary (as compared to an average of over 100), etc.

It seems clear, then, that maternal deprivation had appallingly detrimental effects on normal development of these infants. Spitz's findings have been cited more widely than any other study as demonstrating the importance of maternal stimulation and love for normal development

Bowlby wrote a review and summary of studies concerned with maternal deprivation in 1952. He cited dozens of studies in addition to those by Lowrey, Goldfarb, and Spitz and concluded that they all pointed in the same direction: maternal deprivation during the first year of life is likely to have long-lasting detrimental effects.

Critique of Maternal Deprivation Studies

It is hard to evaluate these studies for a number of reasons. The most important reason is that they are not *experiments,* and thus subjects were not assigned randomly to the institutionalized and non-institutionalized conditions. Rather, they were taken as found. The risk in such a procedure is obvious. Institutionalized infants may have differed from non-institutionalized infants in a number of ways other than mere institutionalization. Genetic backgrounds are likely to have been different, for example, with the institutionalized infants on the short end of the stick. Likewise, much goes on within an institution besides simple neglect (which itself must vary from time to time and from institution to institution): exposure to maladjusted and low-IQ peers, poor nutrition, poor medical treatment, *stimulus* deprivation as well as maternal deprivation, loss of parents (as independent from *absence* of parents from birth), etc. Where should one put the finger of causation? Any or all of these factors could account for the results. It thus becomes impossible to sort out maternal deprivation as the crucial variable.

Four reviews of these studies have been written since 1960. They speak as one voice. Casler (1961) wrote as follows:

. . . Lowrey's work also requires an additional word of comment. Most striking is the fact that more than half of the children who had been maternally deprived before the age of six months may have suffered from hereditary taints. In one case the father was described as a "moron" while the mother was "dull," in another case the mother was schizophrenic, etc. Thus, the reported ill effects cannot be attributed with any degree of certainty to the loss of maternal ministration. [Pp. 5–6.] [*]

Concerning Goldfarb's studies, he writes:

Within certain limits, Goldfarb's studies were conducted with unusual rigor and thoroughness, and the test differences between the institutional and non-institutional samples were almost overwhelmingly in favor of the latter. While it may be legitimate to discount the significance of these findings because the institution is neither identified nor adequately described, it is only fair to assess the value these studies would have if the institution(s) should turn out to be of top caliber. First, it should be made clear that at least five of the nine studies are descriptions of the same group of 15 institutionalized children and 15 controls. This would not be objectionable if the criteria for selection were

[*] Copyright © 1961 The Society for Research in Child Development, Inc.

made clear; but they are not. Also, three of the studies have to do with Rorschach data gathered and interpreted, apparently, by Goldfarb himself. Such a procedure is, to say the least, inelegant. [P. 6.]

In other words, Goldfarb did not really do nine different studies which were independent of each other, since the same sample was used in five of them, and it was a small sample at that; we know little about the institutions involved, and Goldfarb may have been biased in his scoring of the Rorschach scores. A better procedure would have been to arrange for someone else to interpret them without knowing to which group the children belonged. Finally, in a footnote Casler points out the questionable validity of the Rorschach:

> Levitt has reported that most of the Rorschach anxiety indicators used by Goldfarb are invalid when scores on the Children's Manifest Anxiety Scale are the criterion or when the responses of a large group of normal children are compared to those of children known to be emotionally disturbed. [P. 5.]

Concerning Spitz, a number of critical comments have been published, the severest by Pinneau (1955). For example, the deterioration of the infants in *Foundling Home* was certainly not entirely due to the environment of that institution alone. Spitz commented that a number of children left the institution at one time or another as they were adopted into private homes. Common sense alone tells us that parents would adopt that child who is most appealing to them; i.e., a bright, active infant rather than a slow, dull one. Thus, the remaining infants would be those who were dull from the outset and who were not adopted for this reason. Thus, the lowered IQ may reflect simply the gradual loss of the brighter infants from the institution, resulting in more weight for the score of each remaining dull infant. A number of institutional studies suffer from this same defect. Casler wrote:

> By far the most influential publications cited by Bowlby were those by Ribble and Spitz. It is rather surprising that these studies are still referred to with such frequency by other investigators and by textbook authors, since there is now ample evidence that the studies are, at best, inconclusive. [P. 8.]

After carefully reviewing most of the 45 studies cited by Bowlby as supporting the notion of the detrimental effects of maternal deprivation, Casler concludes:

> Certainly the studies mentioned by Bowlby—and we may assume that he selected those which he felt would most strongly support his thesis—do not give us the persuasive evidence he thought they would. . . . Still, one may argue that, although not one of these reports can, alone, be regarded as definitive, the fact that they all point in the same direction lends them some sort of credence. This position is untenable, however, for there are a number of authors who not only fail to support the maternal deprivation hypothesis, but

also suggest, either directly or indirectly, that the hypothesis is incorrect. [P. 12.]

Casler then goes on to summarize a large number of these negative results.

We thus find that not only are there all sorts of methodological difficulties with these studies but that the results are not consistent. A number of studies, seldom cited, find no detrimental effects of institutionalization. The other reviews since 1960 make the same criticisms (Maccoby, 1964; Rheingold & Stanley, 1963; Yarrow, 1961). It must therefore be concluded that maternal deprivation during infancy has not been isolated in these studies and that its effects are unknown.

Certainly one would expect *prolonged* neglect and isolation at *any* age to have detrimental effects. The studies concerned with environmental deprivation and intelligence, for example, showed a clear and consistent effect (recall the dramatic results of Skeels's 30-year follow-up), but in these studies isolation was prolonged, lasting for years. In the present group of studies, isolation and maternal deprivation were *eliminated* by adoption at an early age (and in the Spitz study this completely confounded the results). These studies were thus concerned with *temporary* institutionalization, and they do not show that it was necessarily detrimental. They are not relevant, nor are we here concerned with prolonged institutionalization.

The reader may well ask why these studies were discussed at all, if the only conclusion is a question mark. They were discussed because of the frequent references to them as "proving" the importance of "mother love" during infancy. *There is no convincing evidence that temporary maternal deprivation during infancy cannot be overcome by normal experiences at a later age.*

WEANING, TOILET TRAINING, AND THUMBSUCKING

Parents express a good deal of concern and anxiety about the best practices associated with feeding, scheduling, and toilet training during the first two years of life. Much of this concern stems from the writings of Sigmund Freud and his followers. Noting that the first year of life is heavily involved with oral stimulation, Freud called it the "oral stage" of development, and speculated that abnormal experiences during this period resulted in "fixation" at the oral level, resulting in the "oral personality"—stinginess, competitiveness, and impulsiveness, to mention a few of the hypothesized characteristics. Likewise, the "anal stage" occurred in the second year of life because of the child's concern with elimination processes. The "anal personality," resulting from abnormal childhood experiences associated with toilet training, was said to be compulsively neat and stubborn if training had been too severe and too early, and sloppy and over-generous if training had been too lax.

Breast-feeding, Weaning, and Scheduling Practices

Every mother has to make decisions about breast- or bottle-feeding, self-demand or time scheduling, early or late weaning to solid foods, and whether the transition should be sudden or gradual. There is a long list of studies concerned with variations in these factors and their effects upon the infant. Consider breast- versus bottle-feeding. Many persons feel that breast-feeding, being the "natural" way to nourish the infant, is therefore the "best" way. They are suspicious of mothers who bottle-feed their infants. Don't they love their children? Don't they know their children will turn out "abnormal" if they are not fed the way God intended?

The straightforward way to investigate this question would seem to involve a simple experiment. Newborns in a hospital would be randomly divided into two groups. Mothers of one group would breast-feed their babies for the first three months (a representative duration), and mothers of the other group would bottle-feed their babies for the same period of time. Since mothers were randomly assigned to one group or the other, we could be reasonably sure that all other mother-infant differences were balanced out in the two groups, and that observed differences in the subsequent behavior of the infants would be due to the fact that one group obtained all nourishment during the first three months of life from the breast, and the other group from the bottle.

Such experiments have not been done. As an illustration of what has been done, consider a study by Sewell and Mussen (1952). These investigators interviewed 162 mothers of five- and six-year-old children in rural Wisconsin. Three specific items of information obtained from mothers were as follows:

1. Whether the baby was breast-fed or bottle-fed in early infancy.
2. Whether the baby was fed on a time or demand schedule.
3. Whether the infant was weaned gradually (i.e., ". . . the child was fed soft food over a period of weeks or months before he was removed completely from bottle or breast") (p. 189), or abruptly (no attempt to shift gradually from one type of feeding to another).

Three sources of information were used to obtain indexes of adjustment of the children at the time of the interview:

1. The interview itself included 13 specific questions concerned with the child's adjustment, such as amount of stuttering, nailbiting, temper tantrums, etc.

2. Each child was administered a standardized personality test during the first school year (California Test of Personality, Primary Form A), which yields a number of adjustment scores, such as Self-reliance, Personal Worth, Freedom from Withdrawing Tendencies, etc. (nine such scores were used).

3. The children's teachers rated children on four behavior patterns (acceptance of authority, reaction to frustration, self-assertiveness, and emotional adjustment).

There were totals, then, of 26 adjustment scores for each child. To determine if breast-feeding or bottle-feeding in infancy made a difference in later adjustment, mothers who breast-fed only were identified, as were mothers who bottle-fed only. There were 60 mothers of the former type and 43 of the latter type (the remaining 59 used both breast and bottle). The scores of the children of these two groups of mothers were then compared on each of the 26 adjustment scores. The two groups of children did not differ significantly from each other on any of the 26 scores!

The mothers were next separated into those who fed on time and those who fed on demand schedules. Fifty-two mothers described themselves as having adhered to a regular schedule, while the remaining 110 said they fed their baby whenever it "demanded" food. The two corresponding groups of children differed significantly on only one of the 26 adjustment scores, and this difference indicated better adjustment for those fed on a time schedule.

Finally, mothers were divided into those who said they weaned their child gradually (139) and those who said they weaned their child abruptly (23). Again the adjustment scores for the two corresponding groups of children were compared. They were different on only one of the 26 scores, this difference indicating poorer adjustment for those children abruptly weaned.

One obvious conclusion is that these maternal variations had little or no effect on child adjustment as it was measured in this study. A more subtle, but more important conclusion, is that even if the children of the various groups had differed significantly on all 26 adjustment scores, such differences could not confidently be attributed to the differences in feeding practices described by the mothers.

Such a conclusion would involve the assumption that the two groups of mothers were alike in all other characteristics. It is much more reasonable to assume that breast- or bottle-feeding is one manifestation of *general* attitudes mothers possess about themselves and their offspring, and that these differences in attitudes between one mother and another manifest themselves in many *other* ways as well. Research bears this assumption out. It has been found, for example, that some mothers who did not wish to breast-feed were unusually anxious about sexuality (Sears *et al.*, 1957). In another study (Klatskin *et al.*, 1950) prospective mothers were interviewed and asked two questions relevant to the present discussion: (1) Would the mothers prefer to "room in" with their babies, or let the hospital nursery care for them? (Under the former procedure, mother and baby share the same room soon after birth, and mother cares for the baby herself as much as she is able to. Under the more conventional nursery-care plan, newborns are kept in the hospital nursery except for feeding sessions with mother.) (2) Did the mothers plan to breast-feed or bottle-feed their babies?

Table 10.1 presents the number of women who answered one way or the other to each of these two questions. Of those who planned to breast-feed, most preferred the rooming-in arrangement, and of those who planned to bottle-feed, most preferred the nursery arrangements.

TABLE 10.1

Relationship Between Feeding Practice and Preferred Plan of Infant Care

	Preferred Care Plan	
Feeding Plan	Rooming-In	Hospital Nursery
Breast	438	138
Bottle	194	235

In other words, there was a clear correlation between feeding plans and baby-care plans. If breast-fed babies were subsequently found to be "better adjusted," one would not know whether to attribute it to feeding method, baby-care method, or to some *other* unknown variable(s) associated with breast-feeding. The picture clearly would be hopeless as far as any cause-effect conclusion is concerned.

Orlansky in 1949 published a careful review of these studies:

It can be concluded that social scientists have failed to produce a definitive answer to the question of the relation between infant disciplines and character development, because of a general lack of historical and cultural sophistication, the difficulty of establishing the validity of the personality measurements employed, *and the difficulty of isolating single factors for study.* It is hard to see how the last obstacle, in particular, can be overcome. Social phenomena cannot readily be subjected to the type of crucial experiment which enables the scientist to support or discredit an hypothesis. One has the feeling that social science theory, therefore, often moves in cycles like fads or persists like customs, for historical reasons, rather than progressing firmly in one direction because certain truths have been established by objective tests and can be built upon by the exercise of reason. [Pp. 38–39; italics added.]

Fads in Feeding Recommendations. Orlansky's "feeling" about the conclusions of scientists in this area stemming from cyclic fads and customs more than from facts leads to a prediction which was dramatically confirmed a few years later. Conclusions based on facts change slowly, while conclusions based on "half-facts" change more rapidly. In 1951, two years after the publication of Orlansky's critical review and conclusions, Vincent published a summary of recommendations in specific child-rearing disciplines as published in 644 articles from 1890 to 1949 (Vincent, 1951). He also presented the results of a similar study published by Stendler in 1950. Table 10.2 presents the percentage of articles from three women's magazines recommending one of three possible types of feeding schedules: a strict, tight schedule, letting the baby cry between feedings; a looser schedule, but still with some mother-imposed regularity; and a self-regulation schedule, which conforms to the infant's needs.

TABLE 10.2

Percentage of Recommended Methods of Infant Feeding Schedules Appearing in Three Women's Magazines from 1890 to 1948
(Adapted from Vincent, 1951) *

Year	Strict Schedule	Loose Schedule	Self-Demand Schedule
1890	0	100	0
1900	22	78	0
1910	77	23	0
1920	100	0	0
1930	75	0	25
1940	33	0	66
1948	0	0	100

* Copyright 1951 The Society for Research in Child Development, Inc.

It is clear that such complete shifts in recommendations as indicated in Table 10.2 could not possibly be based upon hard, cold facts. Rather, they appear to be based upon the dominant "theories" of the time. Thus, behaviorism, founded by John B. Watson in the early 1900's, was strongly committed to a conditioning point of view, and implied that all interactions with children should be analyzed in terms of the S-R "bonds" most likely to result. Babying and mothering were not recommended, because the child might learn to be over-dependent, i.e., to be "spoiled." In 1928, Watson wrote, "There is a sensible way of treating children. . . . Let your behavior always be objective and kindly firm. Never hug and kiss them, never let them sit in your lap. If you must, kiss them once on the forehead when they say goodnight. Shake hands with them in the morning" (from Vincent, 1951, p. 206). The dominance of this movement in the twenties is reflected in Table 10.2 in the fact that all of the sampled articles in the decade 1920 to 1930 recommended a "Watsonian" upbringing, i.e., a strict schedule. The fallacy, of course, was that behaviorism, although correctly emphasizing the role of learning in behavior, had not yet even begun to determine details of the process. It now appears that "babying and mothering," far from "spoiling" a child, may be responsible for the learning of a basic love and trust for the mother, as described earlier.

In summary, there is no convincing evidence that maternal variations in feeding practices have much of an effect upon child behavior. It is not so much that careful studies have *found* no effect as it is that careful studies have not been done. As Orlansky concluded, such studies are almost impossible to carry out: mothers are not likely to depart from what they think is "best" merely to please an investigator. Furthermore, it is rather unlikely that any *single* maternal practice of such a short duration as a few months will have any pronounced effect upon child behavior. It is much more probable that a large constellation of maternal behavior —*the general pattern* of her behavior—is the important consideration. Thus, a basically loving mother may express her love in an infinite number of ways. The important thing is probably that a loving pattern exist, regardless of its details.

Thumbsucking: A Special Problem

Mothers generally have a negative feeling about thumbsucking, vaguely associating it with abnormality of one kind or another. Freudian speculations may have instigated some of these feelings, since oral interests in middle childhood and later were held to be indicative of adverse environmental events in the first year of life—oral "fixation." A second source of anxiety may be the obvious possibility that prolonged thumbsucking, done as it is with the thumb pressing against the upper surfaces of the mouth, may force the upper teeth outward, thus causing malocclusion, as well as adversely affecting the aesthetic appearance of the face.

There is little to indicate that thumbsucking is an indication of abnormality. Merely in terms of frequency, it must be considered a normal manifestation of early childhood development. Yarrow (1954), for example, found that 64 per cent of 66 children were thumbsuckers at some time or other in the first eight years. Half of the thumbsuckers were still sucking their thumbs by the age of four years (i.e., about 35 per cent of the entire sample), and one-fourth of them were still sucking by six years of age. Macfarlane *et al.* (1955) found slightly lower percentages, but still substantial enough to indicate that thumbsucking is frequent in early childhood. In the author's opinion, thumbsucking considered alone is of little significance as far as the "adjustment" of the child is concerned. An obviously contented, happy, six-year-old who sucks his thumb while watching TV, or while playing with his peers, should be no cause for worry. It is only if other more important signs point to adjustment difficulties that parents should become concerned.

There is some evidence that thumbsucking does affect occlusion. Four studies with humans indicate the general conclusion that thumbsucking adversely affects occlusion of both deciduous and permanent teeth if (1) a bad bite exists to begin with, and (2) sucking still occurs regularly when the permanent teeth are erupting (Johnson, 1939; Lewis, 1930, 1931; Sillman, 1951). Studies with monkeys, where sucking was carefully measured, confirm these results (Benjamin, 1962a, b).

Finally, consider causation of thumbsucking. Some psychologists feel that causation of thumbsucking is of considerable *theoretical* importance. The argument, apparently, is that Freudian theory and learning theory yield opposite predictions concerning causations of non-nutritive sucking, of which thumbsucking is one manifestation. Thus identification of the true cause will result in the confirmation of one theory and in the disconfirmation of the other. According to Freudian theory, the infant is born with an innate need for oral stimulation, and inadequate nutritive sucking experience, not satisfying this need, will lead to more non-nutritive sucking. Thus Freudian theory predicts that the lesser the amount of nutritive sucking, the greater the amount of non-nutritive sucking.

Learning theory, it is argued, predicts quite the opposite. Nutritive sucking results in the pairing of sucking responses with reinforcement (milk). The pleasant sensations produced by ingestion should therefore become conditioned to sucking per se, so that non-nutritive sucking should increase the greater the amount of nutritive sucking there is. This prediction is exactly the opposite of the Freudian prediction.

There have been about a dozen reports in the psychological literature purporting to test this "issue." Some were carried out with animals (Benjamin, 1961; Levy, 1934; Ross, 1951a, b) and some with human infants (Bernstein, 1955; Brodbeck, 1950; Davis et al., 1948; Levy, 1928; Roberts, 1944; Sears and Wise, 1950; Yarrow, 1954). The results have been completely contradictory, and no general conclusion is possible. *So far as is known, there is no consistent relationship between feeding practices and thumbsucking.*

Toilet Training

As with feeding practices, eliminative processes received strong "theoretical" emphasis from Freud. According to him, stimulation of the anal region becomes an important source of pleasure sometime during the second year of life, and hence we have the "anal stage" of development following on the heels of the "oral stage." As previously mentioned, improper parental handling of toilet training is supposed to result later in the "anal" personality, with characteristics dependent upon whether training had been too lenient or too severe.

Unfortunately, research concerned with the effects of variations in toilet training methods is every bit as inconclusive as that concerned with variations in feeding methods. The reason is the same. It is practically impossible to experimentally isolate toilet training methods from other parental practices, and hence it becomes largely a matter of guesswork when certain behavioral effects are assigned to toilet training methods rather than to other, *correlated* parental practices. This problem was discussed in sufficient detail in the preceding section that it is only necessary to point out its existence with respect to toilet training. It turns out that severe toilet training is probably associated with severity *in general,* i.e., with strictness concerning a wide collection of behaviors other than elimination, such as table manners, achievement, or illness, etc. (Sears *et al.,* 1957). The impossibility of pinpointing severity of toilet training as a cause of a particular bit of child behavior is obvious.

SUMMARY

Learning theory suggests that infancy may be a time of important learning. The infant is helpless: it cannot control its environment, nor can it communicate with its caretakers in an effective way. Under such conditions drives run rampant, thereby providing the motivating conditions which lead to rapid learning. The infant may learn to respond with emotionality to the cues which have been paired with strong drives, and it may learn to respond with relaxation and contentment to cues which have been paired with reduction of drives.

The mother is thus seen to play a central role, since it is her absence which is paired with strong drives, and her presence, if she is a loving mother, which is paired with drive reduction. Experiments concerned with the feeding situation, physical contact, and the provision of novelty all show that the infant is likely to respond with "love" to a mother, terry cloth or flesh, to the extent she is paired with the reinforcement inherent in such situations. Thus love-for-mother is learned. It is not the inevitable by-product of birth. Mothers (and fathers) are responsible for the emotional conditioning of their infants, for better or for worse.

Love-for-mother is important for two reasons. First, its manifestations serve as a powerful control of maternal behavior. A loving infant provides deep sources of satisfaction and comfort for a parent and elicits similar behavior in return. A rejecting, "fussy" infant, being harder to love, fails to elicit the same amount or intensity of "TLC" from the mother. Thus, a cyclic effect may be set in motion which bit by bit, imperceptible step by imperceptible step, leads to a cumulative effect over the months and years which may be either salutory or tragic, for *both* parent and child.

Second, love-for-mother should generalize to other people. Although there is a rocky road of "fear of strangers" which rears its head in the second six months of life, and although the three-year-old is sometimes infatuated with the novelty of a "fickle stranger," by and large a child who feels good about interactions with his parents should also feel good about interactions with other people. Rheingold's study demonstrated the generalization of social responsiveness from the (substitute) mother to a stranger. The pay-off of such behavior, of course, is that it controls the behavior of others, just as mother's behavior is controlled. Experimental evidence of such give and take is presented in a later chapter.

The cyclic interactions between mother and child may thus be viewed as precursors of later interactions between the individual and society. We earn the respect and friendship of others by our own behavior. Our own behavior is continuous with previous behavior. Who indeed would doubt that the line of continuity extends back to the earliest expressions of emotion between the infant and his mother?

BIBLIOGRAPHY

BENJAMIN, LORNA S. (1961). The effect of bottle and cup feeding on the non-nutritive sucking of the infant rhesus monkey. *Journal of comparative and physiological psychology*, 54, 230–237.

BENJAMIN, LORNA S. (1962a). Nonnutritive sucking and dental malocclusion in the deciduous and permanent teeth of the rhesus monkey. *Child development*, 33, 29–35.

BENJAMIN, LORNA S. (1962b). Nonnutritive sucking and the development of malocclusion in the deciduous teeth of the infant rhesus monkey. *Child development*, 33, 57–64.

BERNSTEIN, A. (1955). Some relations between techniques of feeding and training during infancy and certain behavior in children. *Genetic psychological monographs*, 51, 3–44.

BOWLBY, J. (1952). *Maternal care and mental health*. Geneva, Switzerland: World Health Organization. Monograph series.

BRODBECK, A. J. (1950). The effect of three feeding variables on the nonnutritive sucking of new-born infants. *American psychologist*, 5, 292–293.

CASLER, L. (1961). Maternal deprivation: a critical review of the literature. *Monographs of the society for research in child development*, 26, 1–64.

DAVIS, H. V., SEARS, R. R., MILLER, H. C., and BRODBECK, A. J. (1948). Effects of cup-, bottle-, and breast-feeding on oral activities of newborn infants. *Pediatrics*, 3, 549–558.

DOLLARD, J., and MILLER, N. E. (1950). *Personality and psychotherapy*. New York: McGraw-Hill Book Co.

ELY, F., and PETERSEN, W. E. (1941). Factors involved in the ejection of milk. *Journal of dairy science*, 24, 221 ff. (Reported in NEWTON, 1958.)

FANTZ, R. L. (1961). The origin of form perception. *Scientific American*, 204, 66–72.

FANTZ, R. L. (1963). Pattern vision in newborn infants. *Science*, 140, 296–297.

FRIEDLANDER, B. Z. (1967). The effect of speaker identity, voice inflection, vocabulary, and message redundancy on infants' selection of vocal reinforcement. Paper presented at biennial meetings of Society for Research in Child Development, New York.

GOLDFARB, W. (1944). Infant-rearing as a factor in foster home placement. *American journal of orthopsychiatry*, 14, 162–167.

GOLDFARB, W. (1945). Effects of psychological deprivation in infancy and subsequent stimulation. *American journal of psychiatry*, 102, 18–33.

GUNTHER, M. (1961). Infant behavior at the breast. In B. M. Foss (Ed.), *Determinants of infant behavior*. New York: John Wiley & Sons, Inc. Pp. 37–38.

HARLOW, H. F. (1958). The nature of love. *American psychologist*, 13, 673–685.

HARLOW, H. F. (1961). The development of affectional patterns in infant monkeys. In B. M. Foss (Ed.), *Determinants of infant behavior*. New York: John Wiley & Sons, Inc. Pp. 75–88.

HARLOW, H. F. (1962). The heterosexual affectional system in monkeys. *American psychologist*, 17, 1–9.

IGEL, G. J., and CALVIN, A. D. (1960). The development of affectional responses in infant dogs. *Journal of comparative and physiological psychology*, 53, 302–35.

JOHNSON, L. R. (1939). The status of thumbsucking and finger-sucking. *Journal of American dental association*, 26, 1245–1254.

KLATSKIN, ETHELYN H., LETHIN, A. G., and JACKSON, EDITH B. (1950). Choice of rooming-in or newborn nursery. *Pediatrics*, 6, 878–889.

KORNER, ANNELIESE F., and GROBSTEIN, ROSE (1967). Visual alertness as related to soothing in neonates: implications for maternal stimulation and early deprivation. *Child development*, 37, 867–876.

LEVY, D. M. (1928). Fingersucking and accessory movements in early infancy: an etiological study. *American journal of psychiatry*, 7, 881–918.

LEVY, D. M. (1934). Experiments on the sucking reflex and social behavior in dogs. *American journal of orthopsychiatry*, 4, 203–224.

LEWIS, S. J. (1930). Thumb-sucking: a cause of malocclusion in the deciduous teeth. *Journal of the American dental association*, 17, 1060–1072.

LEWIS, S. J. (1931). Undesirable habits influencing the deciduous dentition. *Journal of the American dental association*, 18, 1766–1778.

LOWREY, L. G. (1940). Personality distortion and early institutional care. *American journal of orthopsychiatry*, 10, 576–585.

LU, ELSIE G. (1967). Early conditioning of perceptual preference. *Child development*, 38, 415–524.

MACCOBY, ELEANOR E. (1964). Developmental psychology. In P. R. FARNSWORTH (Ed.), *Annual review of psychology*. Palo Alto, Calif.: Annual Review, Inc. Pp. 203–250.

MACFARLANE, JEAN W., ALLEN, LUCILE, and HONZIK, MARJORIE (1955). *A developmental study of the behavior problems of normal children between 21 months and 14 years*. Berkeley: University of California Press.

MOIR, C. (1934). Recording the contractions of the human pregnant and nonpregnant uterus. *Transactions Edinburgh obstetrical society*, 54, 93 ff. (Reported in Newton, 1958.)

NEWTON, NILES (1958). The influence of the let-down reflex in breast feeding on the mother-child relationship. *Marriage and family living*, 20, 18–20.

NEWTON, M., and NEWTON, NILES (1948). The let-down reflex in human lactation. *Journal of pediatrics*, 33, 698 ff. (Reported in Newton, 1958.)

ORLANSKY, H. (1949). Infant care and personality. *Psychological bulletin*, 46, 1–48.

PINNEAU, S. R. (1950). A critique of the article by Margaret Ribble. *Child development*, 21, 203–228.

PINNEAU, S. R. (1955). The infantile disorders of hospitalism and anaclitic depression. *Psychological bulletin*, 52, 429–452.

RHEINGOLD, HARRIET L. (1956). The modification of social responsiveness in institutional babies. *Monographs of the society for research in child development*, 21 (2).

RHEINGOLD, HARRIET L. (1961). The effect of environmental stimulation upon social and exploratory behavior in the human infant. In B. M. Foss (Ed.), *Determinants of infant behavior*. John Wiley & Sons, Inc. Pp. 143–170.

RHEINGOLD, HARRIET L., and BAYLEY, NANCY (1959). The later effects of an experimental modification of mothering. *Child development*, 30, 362–372.

RHEINGOLD, HARRIET L., and STANLEY, W. C. (1963). Developmental psychology. In P. R. FARNSWORTH (Ed.), *Annual review of psychology*. Palo Alto, Calif.: Annual Review, Inc. Pp. 1–28.

RIBBLE, MARGARET (1943). *The rights of infants*. New York: Columbia University Press.

ROBERTS, E. (1944). Thumb- and finger-sucking in relation to feeding in early infancy. *American journal of disturbed children*, 68, 7–8.

Ross, S. (1951a). Effects of early weaning on sucking behavior in cocker spaniel puppies. *Anatomical record*, 111, 492.

Ross, S. (1951b). Sucking behavior in neonatal dogs. *Journal of abnormal and social psychology*, 46, 142–149.

SCHAFFER, H. R. (1963). Some issues for research in the study of attachment behavior. In B. M. Foss (Ed.), *Determinants of infant behavior*. Vol. 2. New York: John Wiley & Sons, Inc. Pp. 179–198.

SEARS, R. R., MACCOBY, ELEANOR E., and LEVIN, H. (1957). *Patterns of child-rearing*. New York: Harper & Row.

SEARS, R. R., and WISE, G. (1950). Relation of cup feeding in infancy to thumbsucking and the oral drive. *American journal of orthopsychiatry*, 20, 123–138.

SEWELL, W. H., and MUSSEN, P. H. (1952). The effects of feeding, weaning, and scheduling procedures on childhood adjustment and the formation of oral symptoms. *Child development*, 23, 185–191.

SILLMAN, J. H. (1951). Thumbsucking and the dentition. A serial study from birth to 13 years of age. *New York dental journal*, 17, 493–502.

SPENCE, J. C. (1938). The modern decline of breast-feeding. *British medical journal*, 2, 729 ff. (Reported in Newton, 1958.)

SPITZ, R. A. (1945). Hospitalism: an inquiry into the genesis of psychiatric conditions in early childhood. In O. FENICHEL et al. (Eds.), *The psychoanalytic study of the child*. Vol. 1. New York: International Universities Press, Inc. Pp. 53–74.

SPITZ, R. A. (1946). Hospitalism: a follow-up report on investigation described in Vol. 1, 1945. In O. FENICHEL et al. (Eds.), *The psychoanalytic study of the child*. Vol. 2. New York: International Universities Press, Inc. Pp. 113–117.

STENDLER, CELIA (1950). Sixty years of child training practices. *Journal of pediatrics*, 36, 122–134.

VINCENT, C. E. (1951). Trends in infant care ideas. *Child development*, 22, 199–209.

WATSON, R. I. (1961). *Psychology of the child*. New York: John Wiley & Sons, Inc.

YARROW, L. J. (1954). The relationship between nutritive sucking experiences in infancy and nonnutritive sucking in childhood. *Journal of genetic psychology*, 84, 149–162.

YARROW, L. J. (1961). Maternal deprivation: toward an empirical and conceptual re-evaluation. *Psychological bulletin*, 58, 459–490.

11

Early Childhood

INTRODUCTION

Child A

He has not even fully attained the upright posture. He walks on a broad base, feet wide apart; he runs with a stiff, propulsive flat gait. He squats a great deal; his abdomen is rather prominent; his arms extend out bi-laterally from the body, almost like flippers.

He has only about a dozen words at his command. He relies on a more abundant vocabulary of expressive gestures and odd little clucking sounds. . . . He responds to a few simple verbal directions, but he must be managed chiefly through things rather than words.

With such an action system, and with such very elementary insight into time and space, we do not expect elaborate or refined interpersonal relations. It is doubtful whether he even perceives other run-about children as persons like himself. He pulls, pinches, pushes, and strokes them as though they were objects for manipulation. He is quite content with solitary play, back to back with one of his contemporaries. [Gesell and Ilg, 1943, pp. 142–143.]

Child B

He is ripe for enlarged community experience. Home is not quite enough. He is already well domesticated; indeed almost self-dependent in the every-day personal duties of washing, dressing, eating, toilet, sleep, errands, and simple household tasks. He wants to go to school; he is anxious to be on time when he does go; he glows with pride when he brings home his drawings and handicraft for admiration. He is proud of his possessions, proud of his clothes. . . . All told, he presents a remarkable equilibrium of qualities and patterns, of self-sufficiency and sociality; of self-reliance and cultural conformance; of serenity and seriousness; of carefulness and conclusiveness; of politeness and insouciance; of friendliness and self-containedness. If not a super-man, he is at least a super-infant!

. . . He presents in his person a rather complete diagram of his constitutional make-up. The dynamic traits of his durable individuality are evident. He is the father of the man he is to be. [Gesell and Ilg, 1943, pp. 247–248, 251.]

These two descriptions are summaries of normal children, based on a lifetime of observations by Gesell and Ilg. Child A is a typical eighteen-month-old, and Child B a typical five-year-old. Their behavioral differences are dramatic. Child A has little in the way of a *personality*, while Child B has a complex, well-defined one. The early childhood years, two to five, are important ones, then, because they are the years when many of the complexities of the adult personality emerge.

Beginning with "toddlerhood," the young child acquires mobility, and with it his parents are confronted with a new, more demanding task than was required during infancy: behavioral control. The eighteen-month-old child is like a car without a driver; he goes, but his direction is unpredictable. This is the age of bumps and bruises and cuts, of scattered playthings, pulled out drawers, and tipped-over wastepaper baskets. The child, having learned to walk, and apparently fascinated by his new-found ability, has not yet learned the other habits that will give him self-control over his mobility. He has difficulty turning and stopping, and will have to double his age before he can even stand on one leg. By three, he cannot only stand on one leg, but can also ride and pedal his tricycle. Now his hands hang by his side when he walks, instead of extending out in front of him or out from his sides. On the other hand, he cannot yet swing himself or catch a ball (unless it is so large it cannot pass through his outstretched arms), nor can he throw one overhand with more than chance accuracy. He cannot control his hands enough to draw or cut on a line with a pair of scissors. By four, all these responses, and many others, become possible; and by five, his behavioral self-control is well established.

As his motor behavior becomes more complex, so does his personality; clear hints of sex-typing, dependency and independency, assertiveness, social dominance, anxiety, and withdrawal make their appearance. His parents form their first impressions of how he is "turning out," and they extrapolate. They ask themselves: "Is this the kind of adult I want to produce?" With little other information to go on, they make the reasonable assumption of behavioral continuity from childhood to adulthood. The question of behavioral control then becomes of paramount importance, not merely in terms of control of the child's mobility, but in terms of *personality* control. The parents wonder: "How do I make him less nervous? How do I make him want to share his toys with his little friends? How do I make him happy and self-sufficient instead of a dependent crybaby? Is talking the 'right' way to teach him to tell the truth, or should I spank him when he lies?" The question of how to pro-

Motor control? These twins, less than two years of age, illustrate the lack of motor control which is characteristic of the early preschool years.

duce an "adjusted" offspring thus looms high in importance to the parents of the preschooler.

In this chapter, we shall consider a mixture of experimental and correlational studies of personality control in early childhood. The emphasis is on experimental studies, where single variables are isolated and the cause-effect direction can be determined. In the next chapter, correlational studies of actual parental behavior will be examined, thus approaching the real-life situation more closely.

We begin by considering the emergence of very fundamental and general patterns of behavior variously labeled sex-typing, identification, and imitation. We then consider the emergence of more specific behavior patterns: dependency, aggression, and achievement strivings—three of the five Fels dimensions discussed in Chapters 7 to 9.

SEX DIFFERENCES IN PERSONALITY

"Through genetic accident, it is determined whether a person be born a male or a female. The massive and far-reaching consequences of this accident can hardly be overstated" (Krech et al., 1962, p. 500).

The behavioral differences between the sexes are enormous. Let us consider, for a moment, some of the more obvious differences between the behavior of the adult male and female.

A number of studies indicate that males are more aggressive than females. Terman and Miles (1936), for example, studied hundreds of men and women, assessing their attitudes and personalities with a variety of measurement techniques. They concluded:

The males directly or indirectly manifest the greater self-assertion and aggressiveness; they express more hardihood and fearlessness, and more roughness of manner, language, and sentiments. The females express themselves as more compassionate and sympathetic, more timid, more fastidious and esthetically sensitive, more emotional in general (or at least more expressive of the four emotions considered), severer moralists, yet admit in themselves weaknesses in emotional control and (less noticeably) in physique. [From Krech et al., 1962, p. 500.] *

Second, and not entirely unrelated to aggression, the adult male is more independent and non-conforming than the female. A number of studies show that females are generally more conforming than males (Applezweig and Moeller, 1958; Asch, 1956; Beloff, 1958; Crutchfield, 1955; Hovland, Janis, et al., 1953; Kagan and Moss, 1962; McCandless et al., 1961; Sears et al., 1953; Siegel et al., 1959). Crutchfield, for example, has carried out a number of experiments of the following nature:

* From *Individual in Society* by D. Krech, R. S. Crutchfield, and E. L. Ballachey. Copyright © 1962 McGraw-Hill, Inc. Used by permission of McGraw-Hill Book Company.

Five subjects at a time are seated side by side in individual booths, screened from one another. Each booth has a panel with a row of numbered switches which the person uses to signal his judgments on items presented on slides projected on the wall in front of the group. Also displayed on his panel are signal lights which indicate what judgments the other four members are giving to the item. The booths are designated by letters, A, B, C, D, and E, and the subjects are instructed to respond one at a time in that order. They are not permitted to talk during the session.

Although this is the way the subjects are led to understand the situation, they are in fact being grossly deceived by the experimenter. There are really no electrical connections among the five individual panels; the signals are actually delivered by the experimenter from a master control panel in such a way that pre-established sequences of lights appear in the same way on all five individual panels. Moreover, all five booths are really labeled E, so that *each* subject sees the sequence of judgments allegedly emanating from persons A, B, C, and D before he makes his own judgment. On those critical items where the experimenter wishes to impose group pressure, he makes it appear that all four members—A through D—agree on an answer which is clearly at variance with the correct answer. In this way all five subjects are confronted with the same conflict between their own judgment and the bogus consensus. They may resolve the conflict either by giving the same judgment as the group's, thus conforming, or by giving their own answer, thus remaining independent. [Krech *et al.*, 1962, p. 509.]

Crutchfield usually found, in these studies, that females conform more to group pressure than males. He also found that higher-conforming females are more acceptant of the conventional feminine role, and that females who resist the pressure of the group, i.e., who are independent, are in greater conflict about their acceptance of the conventional feminine role.

Third, the adult male is less *nurturant and affiliative* than the female; that is, the adult male is less likely to express concern or sympathy, or to offer solace and help to others (Goodenough, 1957; Hildreth, 1945; Lansky *et al.*, 1961; Terman and Miles, 1936; Whitehouse, 1959; Winker, 1949). This sex difference even extends to the treatment of animals. Women are usually more sympathetic to the plight of animals than men; the female sports hunter is something of a rarity.

As a final example, the adult male engages in quite *different occupations* than the employed female. These differences are easily detectable in college enrollment figures for various majors. There are few females in physics, chemistry, or mathematics, and relatively few males in home economics, education, or fine arts. Males, in short, are disproportionately represented in the sciences. Looking beyond college, there are few female doctors, ministers, engineers, and few male elementary school teachers, nurses, or secretaries. Indeed, the lack of male elementary school teachers has recently elicited national concern among educators, and is a topic we shall have occasion to discuss again.

Thus, it is possible to form some impressions of an individual's personality *merely by knowing the person's sex.* To be sure, knowledge of sex alone will lead to many errors of personality prediction; not all males are aggressive and non-nurturant, nor are all females dependent and conforming—there are wide variations within each sex. Nevertheless, knowledge of sex is of some help, since lack of all knowledge about an individual would lead to personality predictions with no accuracy at all. We may therefore consider these sex-related patterns of behavior the most general personality configurations we will ever encounter. Such configurations are the result of *sex-typing:* the adoption of beliefs and behaviors defined by one's culture as appropriate for a given sex. We shall now inquire into the origins and determinants of sex-typing.

SEX-TYPING

Sex-typing undoubtedly has its origin in early childhood. For example, if three- to five-year-olds are presented with a series of pictures representing toys and activities appropriate to children of this age, and are asked to indicate their preferences, clear sex differences are observed. Boys pick guns, trucks, and Indian-cowboy games, while girls pick dolls, toy stoves, pots and pans, and mother-baby games (Brown, 1956; Fauls and Smith, 1956; Hartup and Zook, 1960).

The simplest causative statement that can be made is that sex-typing is largely a result of learning. There appear to be four mechanisms by which such learning occurs: *identification, imitation, direct control of habits,* and *awareness of similarity to same-sex parent.* The first two are discussed together because of their similarity.

Identification and Imitation

The term *identification* has become so commonplace that it is almost a member of the layman's vocabulary. In the process of popularization, its meaning has changed so that, as used by most people, it possesses only *some* relationship to its original definition. The term was introduced by Sigmund Freud (1949). He differentiated between two kinds of identification: primary and secondary. Primary identification referred to the infant's supposed inability to distinguish between himself and the external world, while secondary identification referred to a more complex process presumably instigated by anxieties associated with sexual love for the opposite-sexed parent and fear, jealousy, and hate of the same-sexed parent (the Oedipus complex in boys, the Electra complex in girls). Neither of these original meanings has much relevance to the present discussion, since primary identification, if it occurs at all, occurs

A highly developed sense of femininity. This two-and-a-half-year-old girl was photographed while making a pie, curling her hair, "phoning" the grocer, and "sweeping" the rug. *(Wide World Photos)*

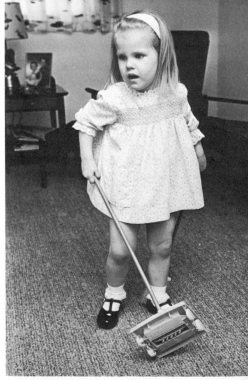

during the first few months of life and is therefore prior to and independent of sex-typing two years later. Secondary identification presumes processes of sexuality, love, hate, and fear, which modern psychologists are hesitant to accept as characteristic of all children, or even of a majority.

The meaning that is most relevant is the more popular one to the effect that *a child incorporates into his behavior patterns those of others with whom he associates.* He acts as though he were they; he "identifies" with them. Such a definition makes "identification" very similar to "imitation," since we, the observers, know that Johnny is identified with his father only because we see Johnny imitate his father. Some would say, however, that the popular definition of identification implies an emotional attachment that imitation does not. It is perfectly conceivable, according to this argument, that a child might imitate certain aspects of his father's behavior without loving him; indeed, he might even hate him, and yet imitate him to achieve some desired goal. This point is well taken. When the child imitates his father's *emotional* behavior as well as aspects of his motor behavior, then imitation seems to be equivalent to identification. If Johnny loves his father, he will laugh when his father laughs, feel sad when his father feels sad, etc. Thus, if both kinds of imitation occur, the two terms become equivalent. When they are to be distinguished, it will be so noted.

What are the environmental determinants of identification? Learning theory would imply that a child might first learn to love a person and then to imitate his motor behavior. As explained previously, an organism learns to love those objects paired with reinforcement. This principle was used in the last chapter to explain the infant's love of mother. The mother, having been paired hundreds of times with food, warmth, contact comfort, novelty, pain reduction, etc., gradually begins to elicit the responses originally elicited by those reinforcers: relaxation, cooing, smiling, and other indications of a pleasant emotional state. When such positive emotionality is conditioned to the appearance and sound of mother, we say the infant has learned to "love" her.

Once this positive classical conditioning has occurred, any reminder of mother should tend to elicit fractional emotional responses, depending upon the similarity between the "reminder" and mother; that is, stimulus generalization should occur from "mother" to the "reminder." Thus, the sound of mother's voice from another room might be sufficiently similar to the sound of her voice when she is near the child to elicit a measurable amount of relaxation and contentment. In a similar manner, characteristic activities of mother might also elicit a sizable amount of contentment, even when performed by someone else. Thus, a baby-sitter who reads a bedtime story to the child, as mother does when she is home, elicits relaxation and contentment not only from the story content per se but, perhaps more important, by the similarity between her behavior and the behavior of the real mother.

Autism Theory. Some parental behaviors can be reproduced by the child himself. To the extent the child successfully reproduces characteristic aspects of his parent's behavior, he will respond with relaxation and contentment to these self-produced cues. The positive emotional responses will reinforce the preceding imitative behavior; thus, imitation should tend to recur. The child who loves his parent will imitate that parent because it "feels good" when he does. Mowrer (1950) was the first psychologist to offer this "autistic" explanation of identification —"autistic" because the child himself provides the reinforcement for imitation. Mowrer cites Anna Freud in giving a poignant example of this process in an institutionalized boy:

> After one of the father's visits, Tony did his best to keep his image alive by imitating him. He developed a morning cough because his father had coughed in the morning. At breakfast he stirred his corn flakes with a spoon for a long time saying: "My daddy did this when we had breakfast together. All the children should do it like my daddy." [Mowrer, 1950, p. 590.]

By imitation, Tony reproduced part of the characteristic behavior of his father and thereby experienced some of the well-being previously elicited by the presence of his father.

Bandura has recently put this autism theory to careful experimental test (Bandura and Huston, 1961). His reasoning was this: If the adult is affectionate and provides plenty of contentment for the child, i.e., if the adult is loving, the child should imitate this adult more than another who is less affectionate.

To test this prediction, nursery school children were subdivided into reward and nonreward experimental conditions.

In the *nonreward* condition a female, who played the role of the model, brought the child to the experimental room. After instructing him to play with the toys that were spread on the floor, she busied herself with paper work at a desk in the far corner of the room.

With children in the *reward* condition, in contrast, the model sat on the floor close to the child, she responded readily to the child's bids for help, approval and attention, and in general was positively demonstrative and rewarding to the child.

The test of imitative learning was conducted immediately following the second social interaction session. The experimenter entered the room and instructed the model and the child that they were going to play a game, the object of which was to guess which of two boxes contained a picture sticker. On each trial the experimenter loaded one of the two identical boxes with two stickers; the model always had the first turn, and in each instance chose the correct box. During the model's trial, the child remained at the starting point at the opposite end of the room from which he could observe the model's behavior. In executing each trial the model exhibited relatively novel verbal, motor, and aggressive responses that were totally irrelevant to the discrimination problem, which was employed primarily as an orienting or diverting task, and to which the child's attention was directed. At the starting point, for example, the model made a verbal response and then marched slowly toward the appropriate box repeating "March, march, march." On the lid of each box was a rubber doll which the model knocked off aggressively. She then paused briefly, emitted additional verbal responses as she raised the lid of the container, removed one sticker, and pasted it on a pastoral scene that hung on the wall immediately behind the boxes. The child then took his turn and the number of the model's responses he reproduced was recorded. This procedure was continued for a number of trials.

The predicted facilitating effect of positive conditioning on imitation was clearly confirmed. Except for aggressive responses, which were readily imitated regardless of the nature of the prior conditioning, children who experienced the rewarding interaction with the model marched and verbalized imitatively, and reproduced other responses resembling those of the model to a substantially greater extent than did children who were in the nonreward condition. [Bandura, 1962, p. 220.]

Table 11.1 presents the results of the study in terms of the number of children in each of the two groups who reproduced various aspects of the model's behavior. Thus, 13 of the children exposed to the "loving" model imitated her marching behavior, while only 5 of those exposed to the "non-loving" model imitated her marching behavior. Bandura also reports incidental data that supported the hypothesis:

Some additional evidence that the model's behavior may have taken on secondary reinforcing qualities and was reproduced by the children for its intrinsically rewarding value is provided by the fact that children in the reward group, unlike those in the nonreward condition, not only marched to the discrimination boxes but also marched in and out of the experimental room, and marched about the anteroom repeating, "March, march, march," while waiting for the experimenter to load the boxes between trials. [Pp. 220–221.]

TABLE 11.1

Differences in Imitative Behavior by Children Exposed
to "Loving" and "Non-loving" Models
(Adapted from Bandura and Huston, 1961)

Response Category	"Loving" Model ($N = 20$)	"Non-loving" Model ($N = 20$)
Non-aggressive behavior	15	7
Marching	13	5
Verbal responses	9	2
Other responses	6	1
Aggressive behavior	20	16
Partially imitative verbal responses	12	5

Further evidence in support of the autism history is provided in a study by Sears et al. (1953). Although not strictly an *experiment*, the study provides data that are unusually objective, and so is mentioned at this time. The investigators tape-recorded a two-hour home interview with the mothers of 379 kindergarten children—a massive undertaking indeed. On the basis of this information, over 200 scales descriptive of child-rearing dimensions were developed. Some had to do with the warmth and affection of the parents as they interacted with their children.

Each of the children, 202 boys and 177 girls, were subsequently exposed to two "doll-play" sessions. We must now digress for a moment and explain the logic and procedure of doll-play sessions as used by the psychologist. In these sessions, the child is exposed to an assortment of dolls representing a family, consisting of a mother and father doll, and at least one child doll the same sex as the subject. In addition, a doll house is usually available, with furniture, etc. The child is invited to "play house" with the experimenter, who maintains a non-directive, passive role, thus giving the child maximum freedom to play as he wishes. Concealed observers record the child's behavior in terms of various scoring schemes: aggressive to daddy doll (e.g., the doll has an "accident"), amount of sex-typing (e.g., the amount of time boys play with the daddy doll and girls with the momma doll), etc. The strategy and logic are that the child might exhibit behavior toward the dolls he would be afraid to exhibit toward the people the dolls represent. Doll-play is thus a projective technique used to detect response tendencies in children that are often inhibited in day-to-day interactions with others.

Sears found that sex-typing for both boys and girls was related to the warmth and affection of the same-sexed parent. Boys with loving fathers played more with the father doll than boys with cold, relatively rejecting fathers; and likewise for girls and mothers. Furthermore, boys with (a) an affectionate mother, (b) a cold father, and (c) a mother who was critical of her husband engaged in feminine doll-play behavior. This finding is precisely in line with autism theory, since it predicts that the combination of (b) and (c) would result in little reinforcement for father imitation, while (a) would result in reinforcement for mother imitation.

Power Theory. A second explanation of identification is "power" theory. According to this explanation, the child observes that his parents can do many things he would like to do but cannot, because he either is physically incapable (e.g., his mother plays the piano) or his parents will not let him (e.g., he is not allowed to stay up after 8:30). He longs to do these things his parents have the power to do. What parent has not heard the four-year-old's request to "stay up as long as you do"?

Observing that a parent has the power to obtain these imagined pleasures, and observing the discrepancy between his own behavior and that of the parent, the child concludes, rightly enough, that, if he were a grownup, he could also indulge in the coveted activities. He then tries to be a grownup; he imitates. The reinforcement is either his own perception of a similarity between his behavior and that of his parent or his being told that such a similarity exists; most parents are aware of the reinforcing value of a comment such as, "You're doing that just like a grownup," or "That's the same way daddy (mommy) does it." Often, the child will ask if he is doing it the "right" way; a four-year-old girl washing her dolly will ask her mother, "Is this how you used to wash me?"

There is experimental evidence supporting the power theory of identification. Bandura, Ross, and Ross (1962) exposed children to two adults, one with power and one without power. Power was defined in terms of control of reinforcements; the powerful adult dispensed toys, cookies, juice, and verbal praise to either the other adult or to the child. Following this exposure, the two adults and the child were invited to play a "game" with the experimenter. The two adults played first, and in so doing exhibited specific sitting positions, verbalizations, and other behaviors observable to the child but entirely irrelevant to the game. After taking their turns, the adults left and the child was allowed to play. A record was kept of the number of imitations of each of the two adults, and the total "imitation score" for each adult was determined.

According to autism theory, the child should imitate the adult who gave reinforcements to him more than the adult who gave reinforcements to the other adult. According to the power theory, it should make no difference, since in both cases it is clear who has the power. Both theories predict that the powerless, non-reinforcing adult should not be imitated.

The results were clear cut; the children imitated the "powerful" adult regardless of whether he gave reinforcements to the child or to the other adult. Power theory was thus supported more than autism theory.

Mussen and Distler (1959) reported an entirely different kind of study that also supports power theory. They first measured the amount of masculine sex-typing in 38 kindergarten boys. This was accomplished by showing the children a picture of a human figure whose sex was not indicated; the figure was referred to as "It." Then the children were shown a series of pictures of toys, games, and activities commonly associated with masculine or feminine behavior. The child was asked to choose what "It" would like. The assumption was that the child would reveal his own preferences since he did not know whether "It" was male or female. The possible range of scores on the "It-test" was from 0 (choices exclusive of feminine toys and activities) to 84 (an exclusively masculine score).

The 10 boys with the highest scores (a range of 79 to 84, with a mean of 83) and the 10 with the lowest scores (a range of 30 to 63, with a mean of 53) were chosen for the second part of the study. This part involved a doll-play session designed to determine how the child perceived each of his parents in terms of their nurturance and punitiveness. Nine stories were told by the investigator. They were incomplete, and the child was asked to finish them by acting out the end of the story with a mother, father, and boy doll. Each story was so structured that the child could describe either or both parents as affectionate or punitive. Two of the stories follow:

> (a) The child wants a certain toy. He can't reach it. He goes into the living room to get help. Both Mommy and Daddy are busy reading. What happens?
>
> (b) Let's pretend the little boy had a bad dream. Now the little boy wakes up from his bad dream, screaming. He calls for Mommy or Daddy. Which one does he call for, Mommy or Daddy? Then what happens? [P. 352.]

The entire doll-play session was tape-recorded. A scorer rated the tape-recorded data in terms of the affection and punitiveness of each parent. He was not aware of the It-test score of the 20 children, and hence his ratings were not influenced by any factor other than what he heard on the recordings.

The results indicated that the 10 boys scoring high on masculine sex-typing on the It-test described their fathers as both more affectionate *and* more punitive than the boys scoring low. Descriptions of mothers did not differ significantly for the two groups. Thus, boys with *powerful* fathers, defined in terms of control of both rewards and punishments, were more masculine. In a subsequent, more elaborate study, these findings were replicated, not only for boys, but in reverse for girls (Mussen and Rutherford, 1963); that is, highly feminine girls described their mothers as more affectionate *and* more punitive than girls scoring low in femininity. Interviews with the mothers also yielded evidence of the father's role in the sex-typing of daughters, a seriously neglected research question. Fathers of feminine daughters were described by mothers as encouraging sex-appropriate play activities more often than fathers of less feminine daughters.

Summary of Autism and Power Theories. According to autism theory, a child acts like a parent because he loves the parent, and acting like him (her) "reminds" the child of the parent and elicits pleasant emotional responses. These responses reinforce the preceding behavior, insuring its repetition. According to power theory, the child wants the same privileges the parent has. He thus tries to be a parent—he acts like one—in the belief he will then be more likely to attain the same privileges.

The two theories are not necessarily incompatible; a powerful parent can also be an affectionate parent. Yet there does seem to be one respect in which different effects are implied. As indicated in the previous chapter, the mother is usually paired with far more reinforcements in the first year or two of life than the father. According to autism theory, children should therefore identify with mothers more than with fathers, boys as well as girls. According to power theory, the father should be the preferred model, since it is the male who usually is the disciplinarian, and hence the controller of punishments, and the money-earner, and hence the controller of reinforcements too. If both implications have some validity, it might be expected that powerful mothers (who are more loving, too) would be imitated more than powerful fathers (who are less loving). A recent study, to be discussed shortly, found exactly these results (Hetherington and Frankie, 1967). It may therefore be concluded that both theories possess some validity.

Direct Control of Habits as a Course of Sex-typing

We now come to a third cause of sex-typing. Stated simply, it is that parents by and large directly reinforce same-sex imitative behavior in their children; that is, both mothers and fathers usually reinforce father imitation in boys and mother imitation in girls. For example, boys are dressed in clothes similar to those worn by the father, e.g., trousers, while girls are clothed in dresses. Such practices begin at birth: boys are clothed in blue, girls in pink. At a less obvious level, parental reinforcement for such characteristics as aggression, independence, non-conformity, and even sexuality are more likely to occur for boys than for girls. As one college girl said:

My mother is very hurt if I don't let her read the letters I receive. After a telephone call she expects me to tell her who called and what was said. My brother could say "a friend" and she would not feel insulted.

Another said:

My brother is fifteen, three years younger than I am. When he goes out after supper mother calls out: "Where are you going, Jimmy?" "Oh, out." Could I get away with this? Not on your life. I would have to tell in detail where to, with whom, and if I am half an hour late mother sits on the edge of the living-room sofa watching the door.

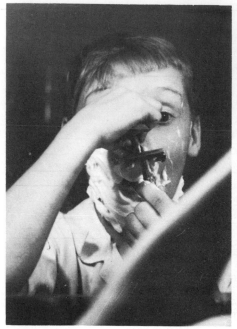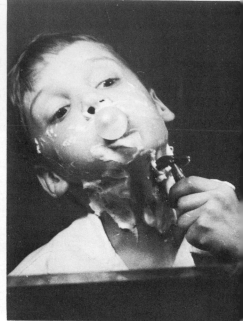

(Wide World Photos)

Successful sex-typing in a boy, garnished with some delicate bubble-gum blowing.

And still another:

I have a brother of twenty-three, and a sister of twenty-two, and a younger brother who is sixteen. My brothers come and go as they please. Even my younger brother feels that his current girl friend is his personal affair. No one knows who she is. But the family wants voluminous files on every boy my sister and I want to date. It is not easy for us to get the complete genealogy of a boy we want to go out with. [Komarovsky, 1950; cited by Krech *et al.*, 1962, p. 501.] *

These retrospective reports are supported by many sources of more objective data (Aberle and Naegele, 1952; Kohn, 1959; Sears *et al.*, 1957). It can be concluded, then, that habits of masculinity and femininity in boys and girls, respectively, are directly reinforced by parental behavior.

* From *Individual in Society* by D. Krech, R. S. Crutchfield, and E. L. Ballachey. Copyright © 1962 McGraw-Hill, Inc. Used by permission of McGraw-Hill Book Company.

uccessful sex-typing, with
an indelicate ending.

(Wide World Photos)

Awareness of Similarity to Same-Sex Parent

A fourth factor that facilitates same-sex identification is the child's discovery and recognition of physical, morphological similarity between himself and his same-sex parent; that is, a boy comes to realize that it is inevitable that he will grow up to be a "daddy" and not a "mommy," and, likewise, a little girl comes to realize her developmental outcome too. It is but a small step for a child to conclude that, if he is going to *look* like one of his parents, he will probably act like him too. Such thought processes would surely push the child toward same-sex identification, thereby facilitating the process of appropriate sex-typing.

Interaction of the Theories: The Hetherington-Frankie Study

A study by Hetherington and Frankie (1967) illustrates how all four of these theories describe processes that interact with each other in the actual home situation. The study is distinguished not only by a careful design but also by the inclusion of information about fathers as well as about mothers, and by the fact that parental behavior was actually observed, as well as obtained from questions addressed to the parents.

Each parent was visited individually in his own home. He was presented with 12 hypothetical problem situations involving child behavior and asked how he would handle them if alone. Two examples are:

"You have friends over in the evening. Your son/daughter keeps getting out of bed to see what's going on."

"You have taken your son/daughter out to dinner in a restaurant as a special treat. He/she is behaving in a generally noisy, ill-mannered way although you have warned him/her to quiet down."

After each parent had answered these problems, they were brought together and asked to arrive at joint solutions to the same problems—solutions agreeable to them both.

All discussions were tape-recorded and analyzed later. One score that was determined for each family was *whether the father or mother was most dominant*. Dominance was rated in terms of which parent changed his mind least from the individual discussion to the joint discussion; who spoke first, last, and longest during the joint discussion; and who was most rejecting of the spouse's solution. A second score, separately determined for each parent, was the *amount of love and affection for the child*. It was rated on a 6-point scale, with *one* representing an ". . . extremely warm, nurturant, and affectionate" parent, "clearly proud of the child, concerned with and enjoys the child as a person; understanding and empathetic," and *six* representing ". . . marked hostility, anger, and punitiveness toward the child; little sympathy or attempt to understand the child's behavior; always interprets the child's behavior in the worst light."

Each child (half of the 160 subjects were boys, half girls) was then tested on imitation tasks after watching each parent alternately perform the tasks four times each. Each parent was preinstructed and trained to behave in certain specific ways; e.g., always selecting a toy of a given color and saying, "_____ is my lucky color"; assuming certain positions in some games, such as squatting and lining up golf shots, sitting sideways in a chair, shooting darts with two hands, etc. Which parent performed first was randomly determined for each child. Then the child's performance was measured, reflecting the amount of imitation of each parent. The parents were not present while the child was tested, and thus the child was under no "pressure" to perform more similarly to one parent than to the other.

The major findings were: (1) mothers were imitated more than fathers (confirming autism theory); (2) warm mothers were imitated more than warm fathers (confirming autism theory); (3) warm parents were imitated more than rejecting parents (confirming autism theory); (4) the dominant parent was imitated more than the non-dominant parent (confirming power theory); (5) if mother was dominant, both boys and girls imitated her more than father; if father was dominant, boys imitated father more than mothers, but girls still imitated mother slightly more than father (indicating that the effect of dominance was greatest for the same-sex parent, thereby confirming awareness of similarity to same-sex parent as well as dominance theory); (6) boys imitated fathers more than mothers, while girls imitated mothers more than fathers (confirming awareness of similarity to same-sex parent, as well as direct reinforcement of appropriate habits).

These differences were large and are quite convincing. Evidence was found that was consistent with all four theories previously discussed. When the results of other studies are combined with these data, the consistency of results from one study to the next is striking. Undoubtedly, all four theories have some validity.

Pathological Sex-typing

In a normal family constellation a little boy finds it natural and easy to follow in his father's footsteps. The father is gratified when he sees "himself" in his son—his attitudes, interests, and masculinity—and he rewards such behavior. The mother, loving the father, is also pleased with this course of development, and she too rewards her son. Occasional deviations of being "like mother," while tolerated, do not meet with enthusiastic approval from either parent, and the boy is thus guided back to his proper destiny. Reverse this description and the psychologically healthy home for feminine sex-typing in girls becomes apparent.

But imagine a different kind of home. Imagine parents who are constantly bickering, who seldom see eye to eye on anything, who would dread seeing their child turn out like the spouse. Now the boy must "take sides," and he is impaled on the horns of a dilemma. If he identifies with his father, it is at the cost of losing his mother's love; she will surely object to seeing her son turn out just like *him*. Siding with the mother, however, loses the love of the father, and the boy encounters all the community pressures associated with being a "momma's boy." In such a household, the boy would have difficulty identifying strongly with either parent, since the reinforcement and love offered by that parent are nullified, at least in part, by the rejection of the other parent.

The picture could be still worse, and is in some families. Imagine that the father is disinterested in the son, offering him little love or reinforcement at any time. He is seldom home anyway, because of the constant friction with his wife, and thus he seldom sees his son. The mother, on the other hand, completely dominates her husband, berating him frequently in the presence of the son. Simultaneously, the son is deeply loved and showered with attention and affection by the mother, approaching the point of overindulgence, especially when he pleases her with his companionship. Imagine, in other words, a home torn by parental dissension, a neglecting father who provides neither modeling cues nor reinforcement for masculine behavior, and a dominant, loving mother who showers affection upon the boy, particularly when he remains proximal to her and does not remind her of "men." Conditions would then appear to be ripe for *cross sex-typing*—sex-typing with the opposite-sex parent. Reverse the description and one has the same pathological situation for girls.

The following excerpt from a therapy session with a young engineer illustrates the identification problems that can arise from such a household. The patient suffered from a congenital testicular atrophy and was supposed to take regular doses of a male hormone preparation. He was disturbed by the fact that he could not bring himself to do so, although he did not know why.

(Patient): I remember that sometimes I was quite confused, bewildered by the fact that my father and mother quarreled, occasionally. It was mostly nagging on the part of my mother, and my father was one of these people who could never remember to be home on time—and would stop to chat with people. He would go out to get a quart of ice cream and arrive home an hour later, having forgotten the ice cream, and so forth. Little squabbles like that. Most of these things we weren't supposed to hear; but I was often a very interested onlooker from the top of the stairs, when I was supposed to be in bed, I think.

I remember one time there was a very considerable "row," with all the attendant tearfulness, and so forth, because my father had been having a small affair with one of the maids we had. Mother had gone through all the business of threatening to go home, and so forth. This I don't think my parents ever knew, that my sister and I knew, but again we heard some commotion and stood at the top of the stairs and listened. It was a very unpleasant experience, hearing parents quarrel.

It's a very funny thing about that incident, that I didn't remember it until years and years and years later—I never consciously remembered it. I don't think I remembered it, perhaps, until four or five years ago. It must have happened fifteen years ago. . . . At one time I wondered if my sister remembered it, a couple of years ago; so I asked her. She said, "Yes," she remembered it. I don't know why I should have wondered if she remembered it or not, unless it might have been of some importance to me.

(Therapist): After that long period of forgetfulness, or repression, it may have been that you were a little distrustful of your memory, perhaps some feeling that you may have just dreamed it up.

(Patient): Yes, that's—I probably might have been, because there's many things I don't know whether I remember or whether I dream them—hazy things. (Pause)

I think perhaps I took my mother's side in a great many of these arguments. Although I said nothing whatsoever, I think probably, in my mind, I took my mother's side, all along realizing that she wasn't blameless either. She nagged pretty thoroughly and pretty hard.

It's unfortunate that she died, because one thinks of a person who is dead in a more respectful way, I think. So I don't know whether I can view my opinions of her objectively or not.

(Therapist): Hmm-uh. But that same subjective distortion would also tend to lessen your opinion of your father, perhaps, in that, saying it very grossly: He killed her!

(Patient) (showing excitement): Which, of course, is nonsense; but I suppose there is some of that attitude. I think my respect for him probably *was* lessened when mother died. Then there may have been to this business, "He killed her," there may have been some connection there also because she died during a double operation, or after a double operation she had for displacement of some organ or other which occurred during childbirth; and so I may have connected that, too. It was a thing they should have had something done about a long time before they did, and didn't.

(Therapist): Well, maybe we're coming back to our old problem, from a new angle here: maybe one of the reasons why you have had difficulty with your medication is that you're not sure you want to be a man, not sure you want to be like father, not sure you want to be—a woman-killer.

(Patient): I don't know; I don't think I've ever had those thoughts. It might be. [Mowrer, 1950, pp. 597–599.]

In this patient, one can clearly see the confusion in sex-typing that might result from a household in which sex roles are not defined or consistently reinforced, because of marital adjustment problems. The clinical literature is full of such evidence, including some that suggests that perversion in men—homosexuality—is associated with family backgrounds that were conducive to cross–sex-typing.

In one study, 106 homosexual men and 100 control men were extensively studied in terms of family background (Bieber *et al.*, 1962). Both groups suffered from adjustment problems, as indicated by the fact that all sought professional help. Concerning mother-son relationships, Table 11.2 presents the percentage of men from these two groups who answered "yes" to the indicated questions. The pattern is clear. Mothers of homosexuals were described as more dominating, discouraging of masculine

TABLE 11.2

Answers of Men to Representative Questions About Mother
(Adapted from Bieber *et al.*, 1962) *

	Percentage Answering "Yes"	
Question	Homosexual	Heterosexual
Was mother dominating?	81	65
What was the amount of contact with mother (time spent)?		
Great deal	56	27
Average	20	53
Did mother encourage masculine activities?	17	47
Did mother try to ally with son against husband?	62	40
Did mother openly prefer son to husband?	58	38
Did mother encourage feminine activities?	35	11

* From *Homosexuality: A Psychoanalytic Study* by Irving Bieber, M.D., and Associates, copyright © 1962 by Society of Medical Psychoanalysts, Basic Books, Inc., Publishers, New York.

attitudes, antagonistic to father, resistant to sons' heterosexual attempts, etc.; i.e., these mothers appear to have created ideal conditions for cross–sex-typing in their sons.

Table 11.3 presents the percentage of the two groups who answered "yes" to questions about the father. Again, the pattern is clear. The fathers of the homosexuals were described as less affectionate and as spending little time with their sons.

TABLE 11.3

Answers of Men to Representative Questions About Father
(Adapted from Bieber *et al.*, 1962) *

| | Percentage Answering "Yes" | |
Question	Homosexual	Heterosexual
Was the son his father's favorite?	7	28
Was the son his father's least-favored child?	44	24
Did the son feel accepted by father?	23	47
Did father spend little time with son?	87	60
Did father express affection for son?	25	51

* From *Homosexuality: A Psychoanalytic Study* by Irving Bieber, M.D., and Associates, copyright © 1962 by Society of Medical Psychoanalysts, Basic Books, Inc., Publishers, New York.

If the percentage of controls answering "yes" to these questions disturbs the reader, it is well to note that these men, as well as the homosexuals, were suffering from adjustment difficulties; *all* these men had sought the services of psychoanalysts. These results merely illustrate that family relationships conducive to pathological sex-typing were not restricted to homosexuality, but to a variety of other symptoms as well.

The following case history illustrates the typical family background of a male homosexual as found by Bieber *et al.*:

The patient, thirty years old, came from a fairly well-to-do background.

The patient's mother was extremely possessive and overprotective. She supervised the play of both the patient and his older sister and chose their playmates. Neither was allowed to play rowdy games, and the boy in particular was constantly cautioned against "rough" boys and "rough" play.

When the patient was six years old, he and his sister were enrolled in a private school close to their home. Since the daughter was excessively shy, the mother decided that something had to be done to ameliorate the child's social backwardness, and she hired an elocution and voice teacher for both children who were tutored after school hours. When the patient was eight years old, the school closed and the children were sent to separate private schools within commuting distance. At the same time, they continued with their elocution and voice lessons and the patient showed unusual vocal ability. Shortly after he was settled at the new school his mother decided that his talent was of professional caliber and she arranged for him to try out for a singing engagement. He soon made his professional debut and received good critical notices. By the time he was nine years old his career was well launched. His mother became deeply involved in all matters affecting his voice and his performance. People who had to deal with her considered her a prime example of the "difficult" mother of a child performer. She was intent on fighting her son's way to the top. She tempered her aggressiveness and single-mindedness with a tendency to be seductive with the men she met in the course of managing her son's career, and some even admired her in a grudging way.

The patient's father was a moderately successful business man before World War II. When the war broke out, he joined the Navy and, except for one short leave, was away from home for almost seven years. Even before this prolonged absence the father had been a shadowy figure who was away on frequent business trips. When home, he was completely dominated and in-timidated by his wife, who showed open preference for her son. When the father rejoined the family late in 1945, he did not return to the business world. The mother, in fact, seemed to discourage him from doing so. The patient's career was running successfully and the financial returns were more than sub-stantial. His father tended to while away his time. "My father was there and there was nothing for him to do; it made me feel guilty." The patient had a vague feeling he had usurped his father's position and felt guilty and uncomfortable with him. He never got to know his father very well. He seemed nice enough, but was no match for his wife. Whenever it appeared that she might not get her way with her husband or with others, as a final resort she would take to her bed. On one occasion she developed hysterical paralysis. The physician who attended her coolly informed her that she was a "hysterical" woman with delusions of grandeur.

The mother's open seductiveness to her son ran parallel with her prudish attitudes concerning heterosexuality, which "disgusted" her. Although she per-mitted some socialization with girls during the patient's adolescence, he was strictly supervised and, in a sexual sense, warned repeatedly against women. Whenever the patient liked a girl, the mother immediately found fault. She encouraged his relationship with a boy with whom the patient had his first homosexual affair.

During the war years the mother often entertained servicemen. She in-vited many young men to stay overnight. If there was only one guest the patient would share his room, otherwise he would sleep in the master bedroom with his mother. He started his homosexual practices when he was twelve years old. Since his mother enjoyed inviting young men to her home, the patient had a number of homosexual partners supplied by his mother. On one occasion she discovered her son in bed with a guest, but she raised no objec-tion and made no comment. The patient concluded that his mother did not object to, or at least could overlook, homosexual activity.

When the patient was nineteen years old he informed his parents that he wanted to be on his own and away from home. This led to a prolonged family quarrel, but the patient was able to break away even though he continued to send most of his earnings home.

The patient was twenty-eight years old when he undertook psychoanalysis with a female analyst. He had been referred by his homosexual partner's psy-choanalyst. The partner was not particularly interested in the patient but stated that he hesitated to terminate the relationship lest the patient "collapse" in the face of rejection. The patient wanted help with two problems: how to free himself of all ties, including financial ones, from his family—especially his mother; and how to cope with his homosexual partner. He did not believe he could give up homosexuality nor did he wish to be "cured" of it.

Treatment was often interrupted by the exigencies of the patient's career and his analysis did not fully develop. When he last saw the responding psychoanalyst he was still concerned about his partner's difficulties, though more as a friend than a lover. He had not given up homosexuality but he was bisexual. He was potent with women, attractive to them, and attracted by them. [Bieber et al., 1962, pp. 54–58.] *

Conditions for mild cross–sex-typing are undoubtedly much more frequent than this extreme example. We might speculate that any mother-father-child triadic relationship that fosters interests and mannerisms particularly characteristic of the opposite sex to the extent that the child is "out of tune" with his peers—i.e., is out of tune with his culture—is likely to lead to adjustment difficulties.

DEPENDENCY AND THE NEED FOR SOCIAL APPROVAL

Now that the fundamental processes of sex-typing and identification have been discussed, more specific personality patterns may be considered. Three such clusters have received enough experimental attention to warrant detailed examination: dependency, aggression, and achievement.

The origins of dependency behavior begin with birth. The infant is totally dependent upon caretaking nurturance; without it, he would die. As was described in the previous chapter, the first year of life, infancy, involves a continuing procession of caretaking responses on the part of the mother that should and does result in a strong emotional bond between mother and child—a *dependency* bond in the sense that the child is dependent upon sights and sounds of the mother for the elicitation of conditioned emotional reactions of well-being and contentment.

In early childhood, however, parents gradually push the child toward more autonomous behavior. He is encouraged to eat by himself, to take care of his toilet needs unassisted, to play by himself for longer and longer periods of time, etc. Such training is not always easy, for there is considerable evidence that, once strong dependency habits have been developed, subsequent deprivation of adult attention temporarily increases attention-seeking.

There are two obvious reasons why this might happen. First, the normal child has learned from past experience, if attention is not forth-

---

* From *Homosexuality: A Psychoanalytic Study* by Irving Bieber, M.D., and Associates, © 1962 by Society of Medical Psychoanalysts, Basic Books, Inc., Publishers, New York.

coming, to "try, try again," until he is reinforced. Deprivation of adult attention would therefore cue off these responses. Second, the child has learned during infancy that absence of adults is likely to be associated with painful events: hunger, soiled diapers, boredom, etc. He has thus had ample opportunity to develop a conditioned anxiety response to isolation. The resulting aversive motivation would activate previously learned responses that would persevere until the anxiety is reduced. As these responses would most likely involve attention-seeking, isolation would be expected to intensify them.

There is experimental support for this prediction. Gewirtz (1954) allowed 56 preschool children to paint at an easel as long as they wanted (an unlimited amount of paint and paper was available). For half the children, an adult sat right next to the child and to his rear, "attending completely to him" (p. 17). For the other half, the adult sat at a desk some 5 to 10 feet away, performing "paper work." Call the former condition the "adult near" condition, and the latter the "adult far" condition. An observer behind a one-way mirror recorded the amount of attention-seeking, as well as the amount of time the child remained in the situation. The major result was that attention-seeking was significantly more frequent under the "adult far" condition.

Waldrop and Bell (1964) carried out a related study that, while not an experiment, was carefully designed. They reasoned that a mother with many children, even though highly affectionate, would be unable to satisfy the dependency needs of any one child as well as a mother with fewer children, particularly if the children were close together in age. It was therefore predicted that children of "high-density" families, i.e., families with many children close together in age, would be more dependent, i.e., more attention-seeking, in a situation where an adult was available than children from less dense families. Forty-four boys attending a summer preschool were rated on a number of scales, one of which was "contact initiations with teachers." A rating of 1 to 11 was possible, with 1 representing no contact initiations at all and 11 defined as follows: "Spends an unusually large amount of time in child-initiated contact with female teachers for warmth, surface stimulation, or security purposes; nuzzles, hugs, curls up in arms; signals for contact either by constantly standing within arm's reach, following closely or using direct gestures."

Each boy was rated five to seven times during his attendance at the preschool, and the average of these ratings constituted his "score." A second score represented the density of his family; the higher the score, the greater the density. The correlation between these two scores was .53, indicating that boys from high-density families exhibited considerably more attention-seeking behavior than boys from low-density families. Presumably, this was because mothers from high-density families spent less time with the boy in question, thus depriving him of needed social approval and attention. In order to actually check this assumption, the investigators sent a "visitor" to each home, who rated the mother on the amount of interaction with the boy. The ratings correlated —.38 with the density score, indicating that the assumption was correct. Mothers in high-density families did indeed spend less time interacting with the boys in question.

Other studies have involved the following reasoning: If deprivation of adult approval causes anxiety, then the child should be more influenced by subsequent approval, since there would be considerable reinforcement (anxiety reduction). Therefore, adult reinforcement following social deprivation should be more effective than adult reinforcement not following social deprivation.

Hartup (1958) tested this prediction. He divided 34 preschoolers into two random groups. A female experimenter played and talked with each of the children of one group, and then asked the child to learn an easy task. When the child made a correct response, the experimenter offered social approval. Rate of learning was measured. Each child in the other group was treated the same except that, while playing and talking with the child during the initial phase, *the experimenter suddenly withdrew her attention and approval, ceasing to play or talk with the child.* The main result was that the second group, from whom the experimenter had withheld her approval, learned the task faster, suggesting that approval for correct responses was more effective in this group than in the non-deprived group. Furthermore, boys who had previously been rated as highly dependent by preschool teachers were more affected by withdrawal of attention than boys rated as independent.

Gewirtz and Baer (1958) found highly similar results using a slightly different procedure. Children were asked to play a game that consisted of putting marbles into one of two holes. The experimenter verbally approved one response but not the other. It was found that children who had been playing alone prior to the marble game (i.e., had been deprived of adult approval) were more influenced by the experimenter's approval than children who had not been deprived of adult attention.

In summary, experiments on dependency behavior during infancy and early childhood show convincingly that it can be manipulated by the behavior of adults. The previous chapter documented the generalization that *dependent responses to adults are learned as a result of the reinforcements provided by normal caretaking activities.* The present chapter suggests two additional generalizations: (1) *deprivation of adult approval temporarily increases attention-seeking,* and (2) *deprivation of adult approval results in greater effectiveness (greater reinforcing value) of subsequent adult approval.*

It should be apparent that learning theory fits these facts reasonably well. The first year or two establishes infantile love for the mother, laying the foundation for later dependency behavior. Once these normal needs have been established, the older child becomes sensitive to variations in adult love in predictable ways. If the love is taken away, the child at first increases his efforts to obtain it. If drastic measures are required to obtain it, the child will learn these drastic measures, for they are reinforced. If no behavior obtains reinforcement from a given adult, attention-seeking toward that adult will extinguish. The underlying anxiety caused by adult deprivation, however, is not weakened, and is revealed in increased attention-seeking toward other people, as well as by greater sensitivity to approval when it is offered.

AGGRESSION

Variations in aggressive behavior during early childhood are clearly apparent: hitting, grabbing toys, biting, pushing, as well as less direct forms, such as shouting, swearing, and threats. What are the determinants of such behavior?

Most forms of physical aggression and some forms of indirect aggression (shouting and swearing) involve *intense* behavior; that is, considerably more pure energy is expended in many types of aggressive behavior than in much non-aggressive behavior. A child wrenching a toy away from a playmate expends more energy than a child who politely says, "May I have the truck now?" Bandura and Walters (1963) have termed this characteristic the "high magnitude" aspect of aggressive behavior.

In Chapter 6, it was observed that *frustration* often produces an increment in the intensity of immediately subsequent responses. A tempting clue is thus provided: perhaps frustration leads to aggression. Such a "frustration-aggression" hypothesis has indeed been proposed as the cause of all aggression (Dollard *et al.*, 1939). It has a certain amount of truth to it; many people tend to get angry and aggressive when frustrated. Yet not everybody does; some simply "give up" and withdraw. The hypothesis thus lacks generality.

A better hypothesis is suggested by the discussion in Chapter 6 to the effect that frustration always produces an aversive emotional response akin to anxiety or tension. This increase in motivation intensifies the occurrence of any subsequent response, aggressive or otherwise. Thus, a "frustration–high motivation" hypothesis is more reasonable than a "frustration-aggression" hypothesis. With this notion in mind, it is instructive to recall the presumed interaction between *motivation* and *habits* in the production of overt *behavior*. As will be recalled from Chapter 6, the effects of increased motivation *depend upon what habits are called forth at that time.* If a child has learned aggressive habits to the extent that they are dominant over other habits, an increase in motivation should result in increased aggressive behavior. If, on the other hand, the child has learned some other type of habit, say withdrawal, then an increase in motivation via frustration should result in more withdrawal behavior. In both cases, the behavior will be intense, but its *form* will be guided by the habits previously learned in that and similar situations. So much for theory. What is the evidence?

Davitz (1952) carried out one of the earliest studies that is directly relevant. Let us obtain an overall view of what he did and then examine the study in more detail. First, he measured how aggressively 10 groups of four children each interacted with each other in a given environmental situation: "room X." Then he reinforced aggressive interactions in half the groups and cooperative interactions in the other half, this training also taking place in room X. Then the children, still in groups of four, were frustrated outside room X, following which they were immediately placed back in the room and allowed to do whatever they wanted to do. Aggressive and cooperative behaviors were carefully measured. The experiment, then, consisted of four main phases: (1) measurement of aggression and cooperation in room X, (2) training in aggression or cooperation in room X, (3) frustration outside room X, and (4) measurement of aggression and cooperation in room X. The main question was concerned with changes in behavior from phase 1 to phase 4 as a function of what happened in phase 2—whether the children were trained to be aggressive or cooperative. Now let us examine the study in more detail.

Room X consisted of a playroom with an array of play materials that remained the same for all 40 children. Each group of four was initially allowed to play together as they pleased in the room for 18 minutes, constituting phase 1. Two hidden cameras recorded their behavior. Then (phase 2) each group was given seven training sessions of 30 minutes each. *Aggressive training* consisted of teaching the children three games and verbally rewarding them for playing "correctly." All three games could be "won" only by engaging in considerable physical aggression against the other children. For example, one game ("cover the spot") required the children to cover an X marked on the floor with their bodies. Whoever was covering the spot when the time ended was the winner. Only one person could cover the spot at a time, and the children were told there were no rules prohibiting any sort of aggression during the game. The second game ("scalp") was played by tieing a cloth around each child's arm and pretending it was his scalp. The object of the game was to "scalp" as many others as possible (i.e., tear the cloth from their arms) while protecting one's own scalp.

Cooperative training was quite different. It consisted of drawing murals and completing jigsaw puzzles. A long sheet of paper was placed on the wall, and the children were told to draw and color a single picture. An integrated picture, necessitating cooperative behavior, was verbally reinforced by the experimenter. A similar procedure was followed with the puzzles. Since all four children worked simultaneously on a single puzzle, its completion (and the subsequent attainment of adult approval) was heavily dependent upon cooperative behavior.

Following training, frustration was introduced (phase 3). Each group of four children was seated on the floor outside the playroom and told they were going to see some movies. A projector was next to them, with five reels of film in boxes, each of which showed a picture of the leading character. The first reel was shown. Then each child was given a bar of candy and the second reel was begun. Just as it reached its climax, the experimenter took the candy bars away from the children and ushered them into the playroom. As he locked the screen door, he said, "You cannot have any more candy or see any more films, but you can play with anything in the room." The same toys were present as during phase 1. The children could see the movie projector as it continued to run but were unable to see the screen. Two hidden cameras photographed the children's behavior for the next 18 minutes, just as in phase 1.

Following the experiment, the films of behavior in phases 1 and 4 were shown to two observers who independently produced a written summary of each child's behavior, one summary for phase 1 and a second summary for phase 4. Not only did the observers work independently of each other, but they were not told whether a given film recording was from phase 1 or phase 4, nor were they given any information about what kind of training the child had experienced in phase 2. The summaries, then, could not possibly have been influenced by knowledge about the experimental conditions. The completed summaries were given to four different judges, doctoral students in psychology, who were experienced in ranking procedures. They were given either the 40 summaries of phase 1 or the 40 summaries of phase 4 and asked to rank them in terms of amount of aggression displayed by each child. Then each of the four judges ranked the other 40 summaries from the other phase. Finally, the four numbers thus assigned to each child for each of the two phases were summed, yielding two aggression scores, one for phase 1 and another for phase 4.

The final step was to compare the rankings of phase 1 with those of phase 4. This comparison indicated that of the 20 children exposed to aggressive training in phase 2, 14 were ranked as more aggressive in phase 4 than in phase 1; of the 20 children exposed to cooperative training, 11 were ranked as less aggressive in phase 4 than in phase 1. Thus, children reinforced for aggressive behavior became more aggressive when frustrated, relative to children who were reinforced for cooperative behavior. These results are precisely as expected from the previous theoretical considerations.

Other experimental studies support Davitz's finding that adult reinforcement is a determinant of aggressive behavior. Walters and his associates have carried out a series of such studies demonstrating not only that aggressive behavior is strengthened by verbal reinforcement but that it generalizes from one situation to another (Cowan and Walters, 1963; Hops and Walters, 1963). Lovaas (1961) showed that reinforcing a preschool child with approval for *verbal* aggression not only resulted in an increase in the amount of verbal aggression but also in a subsequent increase in overt, *physical* aggression. *Talking* tough, it seems, may result in *acting* tough.

It would appear that aggressive responses following frustration are fairly well learned in many children, since they are a common response to frustration in the absence of any specific training. Yarrow, for example, gave three groups of children two doll-play sessions each. Following the first session, two of the groups were frustrated, and the third control group was not. Changes in aggression from the first to the second session were measured. The results are presented in Figure 11.1, where it can be seen that the two frustrated groups showed a greater increase in aggression than the control group. Strong aggressive habits to frustra-

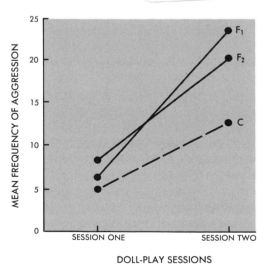

Figure 11.1. Amount of doll-play aggression following frustration (F) and control (C) conditions (Yarrow, 1948).

tion in the absence of specific experimental training are not hard to understand. As previously noted, the frustrated individual is primed for intense activity to begin with, because of his heightened emotionality, and that is half the story. Furthermore, aggressive action against the source of frustration probably is frequently "naturally" reinforced, in that the frustration is removed by such behavior. As noted in Chapter 5, a decrease in frustration-produced anxiety is reinforcing, and thus *successful* aggressive behavior should be strengthened. A more puzzling fact is that often the aggression is not directed against the source of the frustration but is "displaced" toward a different object. In the Yarrow study, for example, the dolls were not the source of frustration, yet it was the dolls which were the recipients of aggression in the second session. The subject of "displaced aggression" is an interesting one, leading to a discussion of punishment for aggression.

Punishment for Aggression and Its Effects

In general, overt, physical aggression toward other people with intent to harm is detrimental in a society as complex as ours, as suggested by laws prohibiting even *threats* of bodily harm. It is therefore natural that many parents, spotting a real or imaginary "aggressive streak" in their child, will attempt to weaken it by punishment. According to avoidance conditioning, once anxiety responses are conditioned to incipient aggressive responses, the child should turn to a non-aggressive behavior pattern, thereby removing the stimuli eliciting the anxiety. The drop in anxiety should strengthen the new behavior, and hence it should become dominant over the previous aggressive responses.

Unfortunately, things are not so simple. The main problem can be introduced with a digression. One way trainers teach a dog to "sit" or "stay" is to punish the dog when he gets up. Often, the trainer will attempt to dissociate himself from the punishment. Thus, he will throw a hard cloth bag at the dog from a distance, or he will jerk the restraining leash from a distance. By maintaining a physical distance between himself and the dog, he attempts to reduce the possibility that anxiety will become conditioned to him rather than to the dog's own behavior of getting up.

Precisely the same possibility exists when a parent punishes a child; the anxiety elicited by the punishment may become conditioned to the parent as well as to the behavior the parent is attempting to weaken. Thus, if a child is punished for aggressive behavior by his parents, incipient aggressive responses may elicit anxiety only when the behavior occurs in the presence of the parents, or only when the behavior occurs in a situation similar to the home situation (stimulus generalization).

Aggressive behavior away from such situations may be influenced only a little or not at all by parental punishment. Such an argument is not new to experienced parents of course; the problem of control is always one of how to maintain it in the absence of the power figure—in the absence of authority.

Another complication is that a parent who punishes a child for aggressive behavior is himself behaving aggressively. He thus provides a model of aggressiveness at the very moment he is attempting to weaken it—surely a self-contradictory situation. If the child is highly identified with the parent, one might even expect punishment for aggression to strengthen aggressive behavior. But the child might be afraid to express it in the home situation out of fear of further punishment. Thus, one might expect him to display it away from home. We thereby arrive at the prediction that *punishment for aggression is likely to result in less aggression at home, but in more aggression away from home.*

This prediction has been investigated in several studies. One of the best known is by Hollenberg and Sperry (1951). In their first study, they set out to determine if punishment for aggressive doll-play would reduce the amount of aggression in the punished situation—in the doll-play situation. Twenty-three children between the ages of three and six participated in four 15-minute doll-play sessions. The sessions were separated by two to five days. An observer behind a one-way screen kept score of the child's behavior. The 23 children were divided into two groups. The control group was presented with a permissive doll-play environment; the experimenter approved almost any activity the child initiated for all four sessions. The experimental group was treated the same except for session two. In this session, the children were verbally scolded for aggressive behavior. Thus, if the child dropped momma doll down the doll-house stairs, the experimenter said something like, "No, Mary, don't you know that nice little girls shouldn't do things like that?"

The behavior of the two groups in all four sessions is summarized in Figures 11.2 and 11.3. Figure 11.2 presents the mean frequency of aggressive acts, and Figure 11.3 presents the mean percentage of intense aggressive acts. (An aggressive act was coded *intense* if it involved physical punishment, physical injury, or destruction of play material. The percentage scores in Figure 11.3 were derived by dividing a child's total number of aggressive acts into the number that were coded as intense. A score of 50 per cent thus means that half of all the aggressive acts were intense.)

Both figures indicate a similar trend. There was little difference between the two groups during the first session, in which the experimenter was equally permissive to both groups. In session 2, the punished group dropped below the control group. This difference was increased in ses-

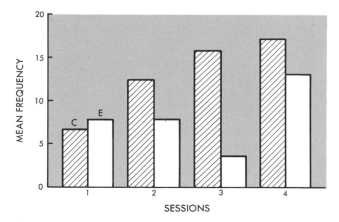

Figure 11.2. Mean frequency of aggressive acts for experimentally punished group (E) and non-punished control group (C). By permission of Grune & Stratton, Inc., from Eleanor Hollenberg and Margaret Sperry (1951), Some antecedents of aggression and effects of frustration in doll play, *Personality*, 1, 32–43.

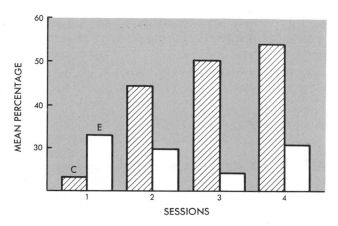

Figure 11.3. Mean percentage of intense aggressive acts for experimentally punished group (E) and non-punished control group (C). By permission of Grune & Stratton, Inc., from Eleanor Hollenberg and Margaret Sperry (1951), Some antecedents of aggression and effects of frustration in doll play, *Personality*, 1, 32–43.

sion 3, even though the experimenter was now permissive again. The fourth session reveals a tendency of the difference to decrease, probably reflecting the child's continued exposure to permissiveness for aggression. The increase for the control group is best explained in a similar manner, with permissiveness for aggression removing the inhibitions (i.e., anxieties) learned at home that affected the early sessions.

Having established that punishment for aggression reduces aggression in the punished situation, Hollenberg and Sperry turned to the effects of home punishment and home frustration on doll-play aggression. The mothers of 30 preschool children were interviewed in their homes concerning child-rearing practices. Included were a number of questions bearing on the amount of frustration at home and the amount of punishment for aggression:

Ratings of degree of frustration were based on the number and kinds of restrictive rules, the lack of responsiveness to the child's needs or requests, and the degree to which the mother forced the child to comply with her own motivations without regard to the child's interests. . . .

Punishment for aggression is broadly defined as inducing pain or discomfort in the child when he acts in an aggressive or asocial manner. The punishment ratings were based on interview reports of the frequency, intensity, and duration of such responses as spanking, threatening, isolating, denying privileges, and derogating. [1951, p. 33.]

On the basis of these ratings, the children were divided into four groups representing all combinations of frustration and punishment for aggression at home: low punishment, low frustration (LP, LF); low punishment, high frustration (LP, HF); and likewise (HP, LF) and (HP, HF). The children then participated in a permissive doll-play session as previously described. Frequency and intensity of aggression were measured as before, and the results are presented in Figures 11.4 and 11.5. The main results are: (1) holding the amount of home frustra-

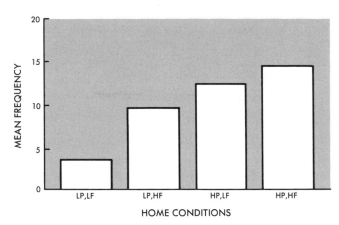

Figure 11.4. Mean frequency of aggressive acts for four groups of children divided on basis of amount of punishment (P) and frustration (F) at home. By permission of Grune & Stratton, Inc., from Eleanor Hollenberg and Margaret Sperry (1951), Some antecedents of aggression and effects of frustration in doll play, *Personality*, 1, 32–43.

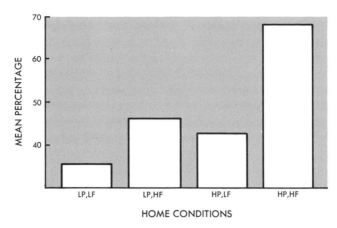

Figure 11.5. Mean percentage of intense aggressive acts for four groups of children divided on basis of amount of punishment (P) and frustration (F) at home. By permission of Grune & Stratton, Inc., from Eleanor Hollenberg and Margaret Sperry (1951), Some antecedents of aggression and effects of frustration in doll play, *Personality,* 1, 32–43.

tion constant (i.e., considering only those two groups where home frustration was high, or the two where it was low), high home punishment for aggression resulted in more doll-play aggression than low home punishment; (2) holding the amount of punishment for aggression constant, high home frustration resulted in more doll-play aggression than low home frustration.

Combining the results of the two Hollenberg and Sperry studies confirms theoretical arguments very well. Punishment for aggression reduced aggression in that (or similar) situation(s) but increased aggression in entirely different situations. Further, the second study showed that high home frustration also resulted in more doll-play aggression, a finding consistent with the frustration-aggression hypothesis.

Studies by Sears, although not experimental, are also relevant here. He also measured punishment for aggression at home by means of interviews and obtained scores of aggression in two situations: ratings of each child's aggressive behavior in the *preschool situation,* the ratings being made by the teachers, and ratings of *doll-play* aggression, the ratings being made by hidden observers. The results are presented in Figure 11.6, which presents the mean aggression scores in preschool and doll-play as a function of maternal punishment for aggression at home. Note that children of parents who were highly punitive of aggression at home manifested considerably more aggression in the doll-play situation than at school. Assuming that the preschool situation is more similar to the

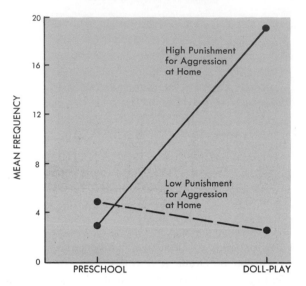

Figure 11.6. Mean frequency of aggressive acts at preschool and doll-play for two groups of children divided on basis of maternal punishment for aggression (Sears, 1951).

home situation than is the doll-play situation, these findings are consistent with those of Hollenberg and Sperry. High punishment for aggression reduced aggression in an environment similar to that of the home (the preschool situation) but increased aggression in a different environment (the doll-play situation).

Levin and Sears (1956) carried out a study that bears upon the identification hypothesis previously discussed—that high home punishment for aggression provides a model for aggression that may increase aggressive responses if the recipient of the punishment is highly identified with the punishing parent. On the basis of this hypothesis, boys highly identified with a punitive father would be expected to manifest more aggression away from home than boys not highly identified with a punitive father. Girls, on the other hand, should be aggressive when highly identified with a punitive mother. They tested these notions by examining interview records of 241 mothers of five-year-old children: 126 boys and 115 girls. On the basis of these records, they secured scores of parental punishment for aggression and the child's identification with each parent as well. Each child then participated in two doll-play sessions in which ratings of his aggression were obtained: the higher the rating, the greater the amount of aggression.

Table 11.4 presents the results of this study. Considering boys first, it can be seen that fathers highly punitive of aggression produced boys who were highly aggressive in doll-play *when identification was high* (23.7 versus 9.1), and that differences in identification with mothers had little effect (17 versus 18), presumably because such cross-sex identification was not strong to begin with. For girls, there is considerably less doll-play aggression than for boys, which is consistent with other studies reporting a similar sex difference in aggression. Further, the effects of identification were about the same regardless of who did the punishing— father or mother. With either parent, high identification resulted in more doll-play aggression than low identification. Thus, the argument that girls should be more influenced by maternal punishment than by paternal punishment was not supported. These results are consistent, however, with a fact previously noted, that girls identify with the same-sexed parent later and less consistently than boys. In other words, since more girls identify with fathers than boys do with mothers, girls should be more influenced by the behavior of either parent, precisely as found.

TABLE 11.4

Mean Percentage of Doll-Play Aggression of Children with High or Low
Identification with Father or Mother
(Adapted from Levin and Sears, 1956)

	Father—Highly Punitive		Mother—Highly Punitive	
	High Identification	Low Identification	High Identification	Low Identification
Boys	23.7	9.1	17.0	18.0
Girls	12.1	6.5	16.7	10.4

The reader must not conclude that one should necessarily condone aggression in order to reduce it away from home—a conclusion that seems to be implied by the preceding studies. Available evidence suggests that both extreme punitiveness and extreme permissiveness of aggression strengthen aggressive behavior. Obviously, the mechanisms are different, but the result is the same. We shall have more to say of this later.

In summary, aggressive behavior is strongly influenced by parental rewards and punishments. Although the frustration-aggression hypothesis implies that an inevitable consequence of frustration is aggression, evidence indicates that parental reinforcement for non-aggressive responses strengthens such responses. A frustration-tension hypothesis better fits the facts. The effects of punishment are particularly complex, partly because punishment of aggression involves parental examples of the very behavior supposedly being discouraged by punishment, and partly because the child may discriminate between the home situation and other situations where punishment is less likely to occur.

ACHIEVEMENT AND RECOGNITION STRIVINGS

"Achievement" is an important, almost sacrosanct, word in modern society. It is doubtful if intellectual achievement, particularly scientific achievement, ever received as much emphasis as it does today. This emphasis is manifested in many ways: the "importance of education," attempts to solve the "dropout problem," environmental enrichment for the "culturally deprived," etc. Teachers and parents attempt to establish a "need for achievement" in children the first day they walk through the school doors, and they succeed to varying degrees. There are five-year-olds so intent on doing well in anything that hints of slow progress elicit strong signs of anxiety and distress. At the other extreme are those who seldom work at anything, and for whom utter failure means nothing—they remain "happy-go-lucky."

What is the experimental evidence concerning the origins of these differences? Unfortunately, there are few data at ages two to five. One possible reason for this dearth is that intellectual achievement does not gain high "visibility" until the school years—until middle childhood. Report cards and parent-teacher conferences then suddenly become regular reminders of achievement behavior. The absence of such signposts during early childhood does not mean, however, that causative factors are not already in operation. For example, Greenberg measured the development of competitive behavior between the ages of two and seven. He asked pairs of Viennese children to sit opposite each other at a table and play with a pile of blocks. After a period of free play, he asked which one could make a "prettier" and "bigger" object. He recorded the amount of competitive, achievement-oriented behavior, such as grabbing of blocks, refusing to help the companion, and making derogatory remarks. The percentage of children showing such competitive behavior increased markedly with age, as shown in Figure 11.7. By the end of early childhood (ages four to five), about 65 per cent of the children made at least some competitive, achievement-oriented responses. Similar findings are reported by Leuba (1933).

Bandura and Kupers (1964) carried out an ingenious experiment showing that achievement standards can be learned by preschoolers as a result of imitation. The children participated in a bowling game with an adult or a peer partner. The scores could range from 5 to 30 and were secretly controlled by the experimenter. In the "high-standard" condition, the partner rewarded himself with candy and self-approval when he obtained a score of 20 or higher; with lower scores, he took no

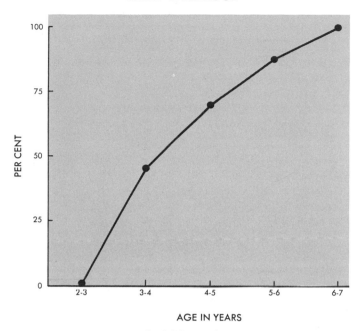

AGE IN YEARS

Figure 11.7. Percentage of children showing competitive responses at different ages (Greenberg, 1932).

candy and verbally berated himself. In the "low-standard" condition, the partner acted the same except that the cutting score was 10 instead of 20; all scores above 10 resulted in self-reward, and all lower scores in self-disapproval. In a third "control" condition, no exposure to a partner was involved. A separate group of children participated in each of these three conditions.

In a subsequent test phase, the children played the game alone, in the absence of the partner. The scores were again secretly manipulated by the experimenter, and the percentage of children who rewarded themselves for different scores was recorded. The results are presented in Figures 11.8 and 11.9, separately for the adult-partner and the peer-partner conditions. The trends are about the same in both figures, indicating that, when scores were low (5–15), children exposed to no partner and children exposed to the "low-standard" partner rewarded themselves more than children exposed to the "high-standard" partner. When scores were high (20-30), however, children exposed to the high-standard condition rewarded themselves most. In other words, the children adopted the standards of their partners to some extent—they imitated them, even in their absence. It is also apparent that more imitation occurred with adult partners than with peer partners.

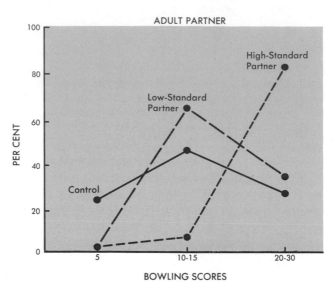

Figure 11.8.   Percentage of children with an adult partner who rewarded themselves for different bowling scores (Bandura and Kupers, 1964). Adapted from Fig. 4–1 from *Social Learning and Personality Development* by A. Bandura and R. H. Walters. Copyright © 1963 by Holt, Rinehart and Winston, Inc. Reprinted by permission of Holt, Rinehart and Winston, Inc.

It would have been most interesting had the standards of these children been measured in a different situation from that involving exposure to the partner. Such a procedure would have revealed if standards of achievement tend to generalize from one situation to another. At the very least, however, the Bandura and Kupers study shows that young children, merely by observing the achievement behavior of others, may develop similar standards of excellence.

Fales (1944) carried out some clever experiments with young preschool children. The measurement of achievement aspirations was one frequently noted by mothers of two- and three-year-olds—the child's wanting to do something alone rather than with mother's help. In a first study, Fales initially recorded such refusals in two- and three-year-olds as they put on and took off their wraps. Then one group was trained until greater skill and confidence had developed. Then the percentage of refusals in this group was compared with that of another group that did not receive the training. More of the trained group showed an increase in refusals, suggesting that training in this type of behavior also increased achievement aspirations. In a second, related study, Fales socially ap-

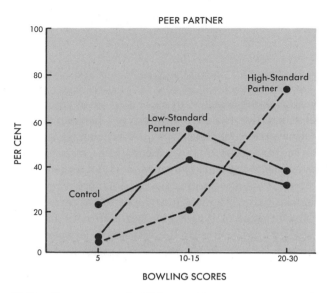

Figure 11.9. Percentage of children with a peer partner who rewarded themselves for different bowling scores (Bandura and Kupers, 1964). Adapted from Fig. 4–2 from *Social Learning and Personality Development* by A. Bandura and R. H. Walters. Copyright © 1963 by Holt, Rinehart and Winston, Inc. Reprinted by permission of Holt, Rinehart and Winston, Inc.

proved such behavior in one group but not in another. Again, the approved group refused help more frequently.

Crandell *et al.* (1964) carried out similar experiments with older children. They found that social approval for high achievement strengthened such behavior. In addition, an interesting "contrast effect" was noted. Social approval followed by no reaction from the adult resulted in extinction of the learned response, whereas no reaction preceded by social disapproval functioned as a reinforcer. Such findings fit learning theory and common sense quite well. The sudden silence of a scolding adult is certainly a welcomed event, in the same sense that termination of a cue previously paired with pain is a "welcomed event" to an animal, as evidenced by avoidance conditioning. Silence can thus function in opposite ways, depending upon preceding behavior. Parents probably unintentionally reinforce many behaviors by their silence and then wonder where the child "picked that up."

In summary, the few experiments concerned with achievement strivings during early childhood show that internal standards of performance can be manipulated by mere exposure to the standards of others, by social approval, and by silence, when the adult had previously been punitive. These results fit well with learning theory.

SUMMARY

During early childhood, a number of personality characteristics emerge. The broadest is that of sex-typing—behavior defined by one's culture as appropriate for one's sex. Sex-typing is probably learned. Identification and imitation are two mechanisms by which such learning occurs. According to these mechanisms, a child imitates the motor and emotional behavior of his same-sex parent. A number of explanations of these mechanisms exist, the most prominent being the autism and power theories. A third mechanism of sex-typing is direct control of habits. A fourth is the child's awareness of the similarity between himself and his same-sex parent. It is through these processes that appropriate sex-typing probably occurs.

Abnormal family situations may result in pathological sex-typing, which in turn may result in a number of secondary adjustment difficulties. A general conclusion is that any family situation that fosters cross–sex-typing to the degree that cultural norms are violated is likely to lead to adjustment problems.

Three specific personality characteristics easily recognizable in early childhood are dependency, aggression, and achievement strivings. The experimental evidence indicates that these behavioral dimensions are manipulatable in ways predicted by learning theory. There are complications. Both adult attention and adult deprivation strengthen dependency behavior in young children, and punishment for aggression actually increases aggression in dissimilar situations. These complications, however, become understandable when the basic drives and habits are carefully analyzed.

BIBLIOGRAPHY

ABERLE, D. F., and NAEGELE, K. D. (1952). Middle class fathers' occupational role and attitudes towards children. *American journal of orthopsychiatry*, 22, 366–378.
APPLEZWEIG, M. H., and MOELLER, G. (1958). Conforming behavior and personality variables. *Technical reports*, No. 8. Contract NONR 997 (02). Connecticut College, New London, Conn.
ASCH, S. E. (1956). Studies of independence and conformity. A minority of one against a unanimous majority. *Psychological monographs*, 70 (9).
BANDURA, A. (1962). Social learning through imitation. In M. R. JONES (Ed.), *Nebraska symposium on motivation*. Lincoln: University of Nebraska Press. Pp. 211–268.
BANDURA, A., and HUSTON, ALETHA C. (1961). Identification as a process of incidental learning. *Journal of abnormal and social psychology*, 63, 311–318.

BANDURA, A., and KUPERS, CAROL J. (1964). Transmission of patterns of self-rein-forcement through modeling. *Journal of abnormal and social psychology,* 69, 1–9.

BANDURA, A., ROSS, DOROTHEA, and ROSS, SHEILA A. (1962). An experimental test of the status envy, social power, and the secondary reinforcement theories of identificatory learning. Unpublished manuscript, Stanford University.

BANDURA, A., and WALTERS, R. H. (1963). *The social learning of deviant behavior: a behavioristic approach to socialization.* New York: Holt, Rinehart & Winston, Inc.

BELOFF, H. (1958). Two forms of social conformity: acquiescence and convention-ality. *Journal of abnormal and social psychology,* 56, 99–104.

BIEBER, I., et al. (1962). *Homosexuality.* New York: Basic Books, Inc.

BROWN, D. G. (1956). Sex-role preference in young children. *Psychological mono-graphs,* 70, (421).

COWAN, P. A., and WALTERS, R. H. (1963). Studies of reinforcement of aggression: I. Effects of scheduling. *Child development,* 34, 543–552.

CRANDELL, VIRGINIA C., GOOD, SUZANNE, and CRANDELL, V. J. (1964). Reinforce-ment effects of adult reactions and nonreactions on children's achievement expec-tations: a replication study. *Child development,* 18, 385–397.

CRUTCHFIELD, R. S. (1955). Conformity and character. *American psychologist,* 10, 191–198.

DAVITZ, J. L. (1952). The effects of previous training on postfrustration behavior. *Journal of abnormal and social psychology,* 47, 309–315.

DOLLARD, J., DOOB, L. W., MILLER, N. E., MOWRER, O. H., and SEARS, R. R. (1939). *Frustration and aggression.* New Haven, Conn.: Yale University Press.

FALES, E. (1944). Genesis of level of aspiration in children from one and one-half to three years of age. Reported in K. LEWIN, TAMARA DEMBO, L. FESTINGER, and PAULINE S. SEARS, Level of aspiration. In J. McV. HUNT (Ed.), *Personality and the behavior disorders.* Vol. 1. New York: The Ronald Press Co. Pp. 333–378.

FAULS, LYDIA, and SMITH, W. D. (1956). Sex-role learning of five-year-olds. *Journal of genetic psychology,* 89, 109–117.

FREUD, S. (1949). *An outline of psychoanalysis.* New York: W. W. Norton & Co., Inc.

GESELL, A., and ILG, FRANCES L. (1937). *Infant and child in the culture of today.* New York: Harper & Row.

GEWIRTZ, J. L. (1954). Three determinants of attention-seeking in young children. *Monographs of the society for research in child development,* 19 (2).

GEWIRTZ, J. L., and BAER, D. M. (1958). Deprivation and satiation of social rein-forcers as drive conditions. *Journal of abnormal and social psychology,* 57, 165–172.

GOODENOUGH, FLORENCE W. (1957). Interests in persons and aspects of sex differ-ences in the early years. *Psychological monographs,* 55, 287–323.

GREENBERG, P. J. (1932). Competition in children: an experimental study. *Amer-ican journal of psychology,* 44, 221–249.

HARTUP, W. W. (1958). Nurturance and nurturance-withdrawal in relation to the dependency behavior of young children. *Child development,* 29, 191–201.

HARTUP, W. W., and ZOOK, ELSIE A. (1960). Sex role preferences in 3 and 4 year old children. *Journal of consulting psychology,* 24, 420–426.

HETHERINGTON, E. MAVIS, and FRANKIE, G. (1967). Effects of parental dominance, warmth, and conflict on imitation in children. *Journal of personality and social psychology,* 6, 119–125.

HILDRETH, G. (1945). The social interests of young adolescents. *Child development,* 16, 119–121.

HOLLENBERG, ELEANOR, and SPERRY, MARGARET (1951). Some antecedents of ag-gression and effects of frustration in doll play. *Personality,* 1, 32–43.

HOPS, H., and WALTERS, R. H. (1963). Studies of reinforcement of aggression: II. Effects of emotionally arousing antecedent conditions. *Child development,* 34, 553–562.

378 PARENTS AND CHILDREN

HOVLAND, C. I., JANIS, I. J., and KELLEY, H. H. (1953). *Communication and persuasion.* New Haven, Conn.: Yale University Press.

KOHN, M. L. (1959). Social class and parental values. *American journal of sociology.* 64, 337–351.

KRECH, D., CRUTCHFIELD, R. S., and BALLACHEY, E. L. (1962). *Individual in society.* New York: McGraw-Hill Book Co.

LANSKY, L. M., CRANDELL, VIRGINIA J., KAGAN, J., and BAKER, C. T. (1961). Sex differences in aggression and its correlates in middle class adolescents. *Child development,* 32, 45–58.

LEUBA, C. (1933). An experimental study of rivalry in young children. *Journal of comparative psychology,* 16, 367–378.

LEVIN, H., and SEARS, R. R. (1956). Identification with parents as a determinant of doll-play aggression. *Child development,* 27, 135–153.

LOVAAS, O. I. (1961). Effect of exposure to symbolic aggression on aggressive behavior. *Child development,* 32, 37–44.

McCANDLESS, B. R., BILOUS, C. B., and BENNETT, H. L. (1961). Peer popularity and dependence on adults in preschool age socialization. *Child development,* 32, 511–518.

MOWRER, O. H. (1950). *Learning theory and personality dynamics—selected papers.* New York: The Ronald Press Co.

MUSSEN, P. H., and DISTLER, L. (1959). Masculinity identification and father-son relationships. *Journal of abnormal and social psychology,* 59, 350–356.

MUSSEN, P. H., and RUTHERFORD, E. (1963). Parent-child relations and parental personality in relation to young children's sex-role preferences. *Child development,* 34, 589–607.

SEARS, R. R. (1951). A theoretical framework for personality and social behavior. *American psychologist,* 6, 476–483.

SEARS, R. R., MACCOBY, ELEANOR E., and LEVIN, H. (1957). *Patterns of child rearing.* New York: Harper & Row.

SEARS, R. R., WHITING, J., NOWLIS, V., and SEARS, PAULINE S. (1953). Some child-rearing antecedents of aggression and dependency in young children. *Genetic psychological monographs,* 47, 135–234.

SIEGEL, A. E., STOLY, L. M., HITCHCOCK, A. E., and ADAMSON, J. (1959). Dependency and independency in the children of working mothers. *Child development,* 30, 533–546.

TERMAN, L. M., and MILES, CATHRINE C. (1936). *Sex and personality. Studies in masculinity and femininity.* New York: McGraw-Hill Book Co.

WALDROP, MARY F., and BELL, R. Q. (1964). Relation of preschool dependency behavior to family size and density. *Child development,* 35, 1187–1195.

WHITEHOUSE, E. (1959). Norms for certain aspects of the Thematic Apperception Test on a group of nine- and ten-year-old children. *Personality,* 1, 12–15.

WINKER, J. B. (1949). Age trends and sex differences in the wishes, identifications, activities and fears of children. *Child development,* 20, 191–200.

YARROW, L. J. (1948). The effect of antecedent frustration on projective play. *Psychological monographs,* 62 (6).

12

Parent-Child Interactions

INTRODUCTION

Chapter 11 summarized a series of experimental laboratory studies indicating that environmental manipulations can strongly affect personality characteristics during early childhood. The present chapter asks if these findings can be generalized to the actual "real-life" situations; i.e., do these findings hold true when they are investigated in the natural setting of the home? We turn, then, from carefully controlled laboratory *experiments* to family *studies* of parental child-rearing practices in early childhood.

We shall use the Fels study as the primary example of such family studies. This choice is based on four considerations: (1) the Fels study is one of the most comprehensive family studies ever reported, (2) the reader is already acquainted with its methodology, (3) it is methodologically "cleaner" than many other studies, and (4) it describes parental relationships to some of the same child behavior patterns we examined in the previous chapter, thus making a comparison of the two sets of findings possible.

The Fels study as summarized in Kagan and Moss (1962) provides information about parent-child interactions, not only during early childhood, but through age ten (child behavior was described through age fourteen, but maternal behavior was not described at ages ten to fourteen because of incompleteness). Such information possesses two unique characteristics: (1) It allows one to determine the *stability of maternal behavior;* i.e., do permissive mothers tend to remain permissive over the years, or do they change in an unsystematic, unorganized fashion? (2) It allows for the determination of relationships between maternal and child behavior *at different ages;* i.e., do the effects of maternal hostility in early childhood leave remnants that are detectable when the child is, say, ten, and does rejection at age ten have the same effect as rejection at age five?

It will be recalled that five general personality patterns were measured in the Fels study: passivity and dependency, aggression, achievement behavior, sexuality, and social interaction anxiety. We shall now proceed to examine the effects of maternal behavior on each of these five patterns. We shall begin by describing what aspects of maternal behavior were measured.

MATERNAL BEHAVIOR

Unfortunately, the Fels study suffers from one important defect—it did not measure paternal behavior, just maternal behavior. However, it did an exceptionally complete job of the latter. Four general dimensions were measured.

Each was defined and rated on a 7-point scale for each of three age periods: zero to three, three to six, and six to ten. As described in Chapter 7, a large amount of information was available on each mother over the years, providing a firm foundation for these ratings.

Maternal protection. This rating reflected the extent to which the mother encouraged and rewarded dependency behavior, by always helping the child when he (she) requested help, and frequently offering help when it was not needed or requested. It also reflected overconcern in times of illness or danger.

Maternal restrictiveness. This rating reflected the extent to which the mother demanded conformity to her wishes, with little consideration of the child's wishes or point of view. Threats and use of punishment were used to back up these demands.

Maternal hostility. This rating reflected the extent to which the mother expressed negative feelings and dissatisfaction about the child, either directly to the child or to other people when talking about him (her).

Maternal acceleration. This rating reflected the extent to which the mother was concerned with all kinds of achievement, such as age of walking, vocabulary, and school grades, and, also, the extent to which she actively encouraged achievement in the child.

Correlations Between the Four Maternal Dimensions

These four dimensions of maternal behavior were not unrelated. Three patterns were found that remained fairly constant throughout the first 10 years of the children's lives. First, overly protective mothers tended to be highly affectionate as well, as indicated by negative correlations between *protectiveness* and *hostility*. These ranged from −.21 to −.52 over the three age ranges for boys, and from −.22 to −.50 for girls. Second, *protectiveness* was also correlated with *acceleration*, but only in the case of boys, not girls. The correlations between protection and acceleration were .28, .46, and .56 for the three age periods involving boys, while for girls they were only −.22, .05, and .13. Third, *restrictive* mothers tended to be *hostile*. The correlations ranged from .08 to .54 for boys, and from .29 to .56 for girls.

Stability of Maternal Behavior

The stability of maternal behavior for the adjacent age periods zero to three, three to six, and six to ten is summarized in Table 12.1, separately for each of the four dimensions and separately for boys and girls.

TABLE 12.1

Stability of Maternal Behavior

| | Age Period | | |
Dimension	0–3 to 3–6	0–3 to 6–10	3–6 to 6–10
Protection			
Boys	.35	.53	.54
Girls	.29	.12	.26
Restrictiveness			
Boys	−.11	.24	.64
Girls	.57	.77	.84
Hostility			
Boys	.36	.11	.64
Girls	.45	.36	.66
Acceleration			
Boys	.49	.27	.49
Girls	.07	.08	.25

Table 12.1 indicates that mothers were not consistent over a 10-year time period on all four dimensions, and that the nature of the consistency-inconsistency pattern varied for boys and girls. Mothers were consistent in terms of *protectiveness* and *acceleration* toward boys, and less consistent in terms of *restrictiveness* and *hostility*. The pattern is exactly the opposite for girls: mothers were more consistent in terms of the latter two dimensions and less consistent in terms of *protectiveness* and *acceleration*.

It is difficult to make much sense out of these differential stability patterns of the sexes except to note the obvious implication that boys and girls may receive entirely different patterns of maternal treatment across the childhood years. On the other hand, it is to be noted that, if the first three years are ignored, the picture is considerably different. Maternal behavior toward sons is stable for all four dimensions, and only slightly less so for girls. *All* the correlations are .25 or higher. The safest conclusion is probably that maternal behavior between ages three and ten was fairly consistent for both sexes except in the areas of *protectiveness* and *acceleration* for girls.

One speculation is in order. Perhaps the instability of maternal behavior during the first three years reflects a learning process on the part of the mother. It probably applies most directly to the firstborn child, when parents must *experiment* to find out what "works." Younger children then tend to be treated in the ways that were most successful with the oldest child. By the time the oldest child is three or four, parents perhaps form some conceptions about the best ways of handling various situations, or perhaps patterns that did not work simply undergo extinction. Either process (or both) would tend to reduce the variability of parental behavior as the child matures, and thus would result in greater stability at later ages.

MATERNAL BEHAVIOR AND CHILD BEHAVIOR

By seeming coincidence, three of the five personality characteristics studied in the Fels investigation are about the same as those experimentally studied in early childhood: dependency, aggression, and achievement behavior. The Fels results can thus profitably be considered in the light of these findings.

Dependency and Passivity

Experimental studies of dependency led to three major conclusions: (1) adult reinforcement for attention-seeking strengthens such behavior, (2) subsequent deprivation of adult approval results in at least a temporary increase in attention-seeking, and (3) deprivation of adult approval results in greater reinforcement value of subsequent adult approval. Consider the first conclusion: adult reinforcement for attention-seeking strengthens such behavior. "Adult reinforcement for attention-seeking" would seem to characterize mothers scoring high on the Fels dimension of *protection:* ". . . the extent to which the mother encouraged and rewarded dependency behavior, by always helping the child when he (she) requested help. . . ." Next, "attention-seeking" in children would seem to characterize children who were rated high in *dependency* by the Fels raters. Thus, the experimentally derived conclusion, "adult reinforcement for attention-seeking strengthens such behavior," may be restated "protective parents tended to instill dependency in their children." Do the Fels data support this prediction?

The correlations between maternal protectiveness at ages zero to three, three to six, and six to ten and dependency at all four periods, ages zero to three to ages ten to fourteen, are presented in Table 12.2.

TABLE 12.2

Relationship Between Maternal Protection and Childhood Dependency

Childhood Dependency at Ages	Maternal Protection at Different Ages of Child					
	0–3		3–6		6–10	
	Boys	Girls	Boys	Girls	Boys	Girls
0–3	.51	.12				
3–6	.45	−.06	.48	.44		
6–10	.35	.11	.22	.04	.37	.17
10–14	.36	.18	−.04	−.25	.36	.36

Table 12.2 indicates that maternal protection was correlated with dependency behavior in boys, but only minimally correlated in girls. For example, maternal protection when boys were three to six years old correlated .45 witIndependency behavior during that age period, .35 with dependency during ages six to ten, and .36 with dependency during ages ten to fourteen. The corresponding correlations for girls are −.06, .11, and .18.

Table 12.3 presents the correlations between maternal protection and childhood independency. According to Table 12.2, these correlations should be negative instead of positive, and should be greater for boys than for girls. Both expectations are confirmed. Of the 16 correlations, 15 are negative, and in every case but one the boys' correlations are higher.

TABLE 12.3

Relationship Between Maternal Protection and Childhood Independency

Childhood Independency at Ages	Maternal Protection at Different Ages of Child					
	0–3		3–6		6–10	
	Boys	Girls	Boys	Girls	Boys	Girls
0–3	*	*				
3–6	−.41	−.24	−.54	−.36		
6–10	−.25	−.02	−.12	−.07	−.32	−.11
10–14	−.49	−.42	.20	−.19	−.34	−.36

* Ratings not made.

Considering both Tables 12.2 and 12.3, it must be concluded that the first generalization derived from experimental studies of dependency is confirmed: protective mothers did tend to instill dependent response patterns in their children, boys more than girls. Perhaps the stronger mother-son relationships are due to the fact that maternal protectiveness was more stable toward boys than toward girls (see Table 12.1).

There is another aspect of these tables that should also be noted. The relationship between maternal protection and childhood dependency was relatively constant during the first 10 years. That is, the relationship held at ages three to six and at ages six to ten too; it was independent of age of the child. Finally, it should be noted that maternal behavior had perseverative effects that were detectable in the child's later behavior. In Table 12.3, for example, maternal protectiveness during the first 3 years of the child's life correlated highly with his dependency in early adolescence: −.49 for boys and −.42 for girls. Part of this relationship is due to the stability of protectiveness, of course, but part of it is also due to the perseverative effects of earlier protectiveness, or else one would expect the correlations to systematically decline as the time between the mothers' behavior and the children's behavior increases. No such systematic decline is evident in Tables 12.2 and 12.3.

The Fels data suggest another determinant of dependency that was not investigated experimentally. Table 12.4 reveals the nature of this finding. It describes the relationships between maternal restrictiveness and dependency. Careful study reveals an interesting pattern; for both sexes, maternal restrictiveness is positively correlated with dependency up to age ten. During ages ten to fourteen, however, this relationship breaks down for boys and, indeed, becomes somewhat negative, while for girls it remains positive. Thus, restrictiveness is associated with dependency up to age ten in both sexes, but then boys tend to free themselves from this influence, while girls do not.

Possibly, the more stable relationship between maternal restrictiveness and dependency in girls is due to the fact that maternal restriction was highly stable toward girls and less so toward boys (see Table 12.1).

Perhaps mothers tended to encourage (or gave way to) "masculine independence" as their sons emerged from babyhood, thus relaxing their restrictions more for boys than for girls. Such behavior would be in line with cultural pressures and thus would not be unexpected.

The restrictiveness-dependency relationship is easily understandable in terms of learning theory. A mother who demands conformity and obedience, who has lots of rules, and who threatens and punishes deviations from her demands (recall that in the Fels study *restrictiveness* included a punishment component) is not likely to foster independent habits in her offspring. Her children have few opportunities for such

TABLE 12.4

Relationship Between Maternal Restrictiveness and Childhood Dependency

| Childhood Dependency at Ages | Maternal Restriction at Different Ages of Child | | | | | |
| | 0–3 | | 3–6 | | 6–10 | |
	Boys	Girls	Boys	Girls	Boys	Girls
0–3	.34	.22				
3–6	−.09	.22	.16	.16	.16	
6–10	.31	.15	.35	.28	.44	.36
10–14 instr.[a]	*	.29	−.38	.45	−.22	.18
10–14 emot.[a]	*	.25	−.15	.25	.02	.46

* Not measured.
[a] Instr. refers to "instrumental" dependency (requesting aid with difficult tasks); emot. refers to "emotional" dependency (attempts to be nourished and comforted).

behavior and are punished when they try it. They are rewarded for obedience, for adherence to her demands, i.e., for dependency and passivity. The following case history illustrates such a process in action.

Case History in Maternal Restrictiveness

Home visit: age twenty months

As soon as the mother brought S in the front door downstairs, she started to cry; a subdued, whining note. The mother carried her up the stairs and held her in her arms for a few minutes.

S wanted to take a doll downstairs with her; she gathered it up in her arms. In so doing, she caught up her dress in front. The mother said, "Put your dress down." S showed no response other than looking at her mother. "I see your stomach. Shame, shame," said the mother. This had no effect, and the mother pulled the dress down herself.

Home visit: three years, one month

The mother told S not to pick the ears off a toy rabbit. S said, "I did pick it off," with some evidence of impudence. Mother said, "What are you doing, defying me or something?" and she struck S two or three light blows with a knitting needle, which brought on a few tears.

Home visit: five years, one month

The mother does not think the nursery school is good for S. After she has been attending, it takes several weeks to cure her of being "fresh." This is definite evidence of a parental attitude that is different from that of the average mother in the sample; she expects her children to obey implicitly; there is no treating them as equals.

Nursery-school summary: five years, eight months

S was not a talkative child. She seemed to be silent most of the time. She played with other children as a follower. She usually cooperated with them and with adults. After her initial shyness, she seemed to enjoy nursery school thoroughly.

S gave the impression of being constantly on the alert for adult interference. She seemed to play most freely when she felt most free from adult scrutiny. She seemed distrustful of any new situation and paused to size it up carefully before entering into it. Her constant companion was Joan, with whom she was previously acquainted. S seemed very dependent on Joan. On one occasion Joan was absent and S was somewhat at a loss. In spite of her dependence on another child, she was at ease in the nursery-school situation and seemed to enjoy it quietly.

Interview notes with the mother at eight years

The mother seems to believe in discipline for children; she thinks the school and the Sisters are too lenient with the children. She contrasted this school with another Catholic school, where strict discipline is maintained. She likened the teachers at S's school to herself, threatening but never carrying out the threats. The mother also seems to take a sheltering or protective attitude toward the children, not allowing or encouraging them to do things for themselves, such as take their baths, comb their hair, or care for themselves at the table. She doesn't allow the children far from home, for she is afraid something will happen to them.

Interview with S at ten years of age.

Seems to be very much afraid of adults. She was extremely shy with me and talked so low that I could hardly understand her even when she was trying to be understood. She was exceedingly inept at verbalization. At the slightest question that had to do with judgment of her position, relevant to someone else, she just would say that she didn't know. She didn't know who she liked or disliked and couldn't describe any aspect of her personality.

Day-camp summary: ten years, three months

Seems to be playing a passive role in relation to her environment. She is nonassertive, nonaggressive, not verbal. She is often dumbly patient and appealing, making silent requests and responses. Her outgoing moments seem to be mainly responses to objects and materials. She drinks in the activity of others and stays parallel, keeping a safe distance.

Interview with mother at eleven years, one month

The mother said, "I have always tried to suppress them (meaning S and her older sister), but I have let the younger one go." The youngest girl, apparently, has a more spirited personality and gets away with so much that it "simple drives the others mad; they would like to kill her." This was said with much humor, as if she finds the rivalry between the girls an amusing spectacle. I had the feeling that she enjoys the youngest girl's spunk, and she is now contemptuous of the mild manner of the suppressed older girls. The oldest one is beginning to come out of it a little bit, but S is rather hopeless.

Home visit: eleven years, ten months

S had a friend visiting, and they sat coyly across the room from me and giggled at whatever was said. S was uncomfortably shy, very uncommunicative and took a long time to warm up. She and her older sister were eating peanuts, and once the mother suggested that she give me some. S came darting across the room at 5-minute intervals, thrusting the dish at me, usually before I had finished my previous handful.

The mother is a tough customer. She continually insulted the girls, managed to toss off a continual string of withering remarks. Her commands to them are of the "get here" and "get there" variety. Their every move is noted and criticized. For example, S and her friend started upstairs, and the mother demanded, "Now what are you going to do?" S mumbled, "going to the bathroom." The mother replied ominously, "Well, mind what you do up there."

Home visit: thirteen years, one month

S seems to grow increasingly dull and solemn; she has lost most of her former winsome attractiveness with developing obesity. The mother now calls her fatty when addressing her. She is more slow moving and heavy-footed than ever, galloping and making funny noises whenever she moves around the house. She rarely does anything at home, seems very lethargic, giving the impression that, in the face of the mother's restricting and interfering policies, it is easier to simply sit than to initiate any activity and have it squelched. S conforms to the mother's orders (e.g., "Get that telephone," or "Go out on the porch and see where your younger sister went to") promptly and methodically. The mother's suggestions arc staged in threatening tones, "If you don't do it, you know what you'll get."

Interview notes with S at fourteen years of age

At the start of the interview S was extremely inhibited. As it progressed, she opened up a little bit, although, for the most part, she answered only in monosyllables and volunteered nothing. She said school was not going too well, although she is passing everything. Throughout the interview S bit nervously on her nails and seemed to finger her mouth considerably. She was dressed well for a girl with such a disadvantageous figure, and her hair was nicely combed. It was apparent that considerable care had gone into her grooming for this occasion. S is socially inhibited and one of the shyest children that I have seen in an interview.

Home visit: fourteen years, two months

The mother ignores S's presence in the room except to tell her to go get something, to stop doing something, or to make some derogatory statement about her appearance. In response to this biting sarcasm, S grins sheepishly. S was readily submissive to the few commands that her mother made this afternoon. For example, her mother told her in stentorian tones to close the garage doors and bring her the keys. S said meekly that she had already done so. The mother then felt called upon to say imperiously, "Well, bring me the keys" and S jumped to do her bidding. [Kagan and Moss, 1962, pp. 215–221.]

This case history clearly demonstrates the meaning of the positive correlations between maternal restrictiveness and childhood dependency and passivity, particularly for girls. One cannot help feeling sorry for this girl, who started life with as good a chance as anybody else for wholesome personality development, but who gradually had her spontaneity, her independence—*her freedom to think and act*—squeezed out and destroyed by the viselike grip of her mother.

Aggression

Experimental studies of aggression led to two major conclusions: (1) While frustration often leads to aggression, presumably because of increased tension (motivation), the relationship is not one to one. Reinforcement for non-aggressive responses, such as withdrawal or cooperation, strengthens such responses, and they may become dominant over aggressive responses. (2) Punishment for aggression introduces complex processes, which lead to less aggression when in the punished situation (i.e., at home), but to more aggression when in different situations, depending upon the magnitude of the difference.

The Fels study provides a number of possibilities in exploring these relationships further. In fact, so many different comparisons invite inspection that one must formulate his hypotheses carefully or he will be lost in a web of data that appears meaningless because of its complexity. For example, it could be hypothesized that restrictive mothers provide many sources of frustration with all their rules and thus create conditions ripe for aggression. But it must be recalled that restrictive mothers were restrictive *in general* and thus tended to not permit aggression any more than they permitted other transgressions. On this basis, one would predict less aggression from children with restrictive mothers, particularly if they are restrictive about aggression. Thus, no clear predictions are possible concerning maternal restriction and aggression at home. However, if we consider aggression away from home, where mothers are not around to restrict aggression, the frustration-aggression hypothesis would lead us to predict a positive relationship.

Fortunately, the Fels study provides indirect indexes of aggression at home and away from home. Since it also provides an index of maternal restrictiveness, the hypothesis can be tested: maternal restrictiveness should not be very predictive of aggression at home, but should be positively correlated with aggression away from home.

One of the aggression scales was *aggression to mother*, providing an obvious measure of aggression in the home. Aggression away from home was not specifically measured, but some indirect indexes are available. If it is assumed that early childhood involves more time at home than middle childhood, then data collected during the years six to ten and ten to fourteen should sample more heavily activities outside the home. In addition, certain types of aggression rated at these later years seem to clearly reflect behavior toward people other than the parents. Thus, *physical aggression to peers, indirect aggression to peers, dominance of peers, and competitiveness* are almost exclusively concerned with aggression to peers, much of which would have occurred outside the home. *Behavioral disorganization* (temper tantrums) also reflects aggression not specifically aimed at parents; a good deal of it must have occurred outside the home in middle childhood. We would thus predict restrictiveness to be weakly and inconsistently related to *aggression to mother*, and more strongly related to these other indexes of aggression. Table 12.5 presents these correlations, separately for boys and girls.

Table 12.5 indicates the hypothesis is supported for boys, but not for girls. Considering the correlations between restrictiveness and aggres-

TABLE 12.5

Relationship Between Maternal Restrictiveness and Various Kinds of Aggression

| Childhood Aggression | Maternal Restrictiveness | | | |
| | 3–6 | | 6–10 | |
	Boys	Girls	Boys	Girls
At Home				
Aggression to mother				
3–6	.21	.35		
6–10	.02	.06	.26	.09
10–14	−.23	.03	.15	−.03
Away from Home				
Physical aggression to peers				
6–10	.17	.00	.11	.01
Indirect aggression to peers				
6–10	.21	−.16	.23	−.16
10–14	.32	−.17	.33	−.18
Dominance of peers				
6–10	.13	−.12	.18	−.07
10–14	.23	−.06	.44	.01
Competitiveness				
6–10	−.03	−.28	.10	−.40
10–14	.43	−.22	.15	−.24
Behavioral disorganization				
6–10	.07	.16	.27	.04
10–14	.23	.24	.30	.23

sion away from home, 17 of 18 are positive for boys, but only 6 of 18 for girls. Aggression at home was unpredictable for both sexes, as expected. Recalling that maternal restrictiveness was correlated with hostility in the Fels study, Table 12.5 suggests the following conclusion: Restrictive mothers who were somewhat punitive reared boys and girls whose home aggression was not related to maternal restrictiveness. Away from home, however, such boys tended to be aggressive and competitive toward peers, while girls tended to be the opposite, i.e., passive. The frustration (displaced) aggression hypothesis is thus supported for boys, but not for girls. Perhaps cultural pressures toward non-aggression tended to mask the relationship for girls. For example, a submissive-aggressive conflict might have been created, producing variable inconsistent behavior from one time to the next, thus lowering the relationships between aggression and other variables. One line of evidence in support of such an interpretation is the fact that aggressive behavior was not highly correlated even with itself in girls; its stability was low in females.

It may be concluded, then, that the frustration-aggression hypothesis, translated into a restriction–aggression away-from-home hypothesis, receives support from the Fels data for boys, but not for girls.

The second experimental conclusion was that punishment causes aggressive reactions, because of imitative or frustrative factors. The aggression is more likely to appear away from the punished situations because of a reduction in fear of punishment.

The clearest measurement of punishment in the Fels study is the *hostility* score. Table 12.6 presents the correlations between maternal hostility and various indexes of aggression, representing aggression at home (to mother) and away from home (to peers). The correlations in this table are remarkable; of 56 correlations, 54 are positive. A positive relationship between maternal hostility and aggression is dramatically confirmed. Furthermore, it holds up at home as well as away from home, since the aggression-to-mother correlations are quite high; 8 out of 10 are above .25. It should also be noted that the relationship is stronger for mothers and sons than it is for mothers and daughters; 19 of 28 correlations for sons are above .25, while only about half this many for girls (10 of 28) reach this magnitude.

Kagan and Moss point out another interesting trend in these data that is likely to escape the untrained eye. Note that the highest correlations tend to occur *when maternal behavior was measured at the same time child behavior was measured.* For example, for aggression-to-mother in boys, maternal hostility, when the boys were three to six years old, correlated .58 *during that same time period,* .27 when they were six to ten years old, and only .06 when they were ten to fourteen. A similar trend is evident for girls: .67, .28, and .01. This trend repeats itself enough times in Table 12.6 that it can hardly be attributed to chance. What does it mean? It means that maternal hostility had transitory effects; aggressive reactions did not necessarily become a permanent characteristic of the child, but were manifested in greatest intensity only while the mother was hostile and rejecting. Such a relationship is exactly what would be expected if maternal hostility is frustrating, since aggressive reactions to frustration are never long-lasting, but short and temporary. On the other hand, this trend could be interpreted as indicating that mothers react with hostility when their children get out of hand, e.g., behave aggressively, and thus the causal relationship is child affecting mother rather than the other way around. It is likely that both processes are involved.

TABLE 12.6

Relationship Between Maternal Hostility and Various Kinds of Aggression

| | Maternal Hostility | | | |
| | 3–6 | | 6–10 | |
	Boys	Girls	Boys	Girls
Aggression to mother				
3–6	.58	.67		
6–10	.27	.28	.70	.68
10–14	.06	.01	.39	.29
Physical aggression to peers				
3–6	.22	.07		
6–10	.26	.06	.46	.35
Indirect aggression to peers				
3–6	.34	.17		
6–10	.35	.08	.65	.39
10–14	.17	.02	.37	.17
Dominance of peers				
3–6	.12	.19		
6–10	.07	.07	.44	.21
10–14	.12	.24	.25	.22
Competitiveness				
3–6	.43	.03		
6–10	.07	−.02	.45	.01
10–14	.13	.18	.29	−.04
Behavioral disorganization				
3–6	.31	.66		
6–10	.25	.37	.45	.34
10–14	.04	.03	.44	.41

In summary, the Fels aggression data suggest the following conclusions: (1) Restrictive, punitive mothers produced aggressive responses in their sons away from home, but not in daughters, who tended to react in an opposite manner. (2) Hostile, rejecting mothers produced aggressive reactions toward themselves in both sons and daughters. (3) Such mothers also produced aggressive responses away from home in their children. (4) These latter two relationships were strongest when maternal and child behavior were correlated from the same time period. Finally, (5) all these relationships held throughout early and middle childhood; they were not unique to a particular age.

Achievement Strivings

It will be recalled that achievement strivings during the early childhood years probably do not have as much "visibility" to the parents as such behavior does during the school years. The children are perhaps affected in a similar manner. The lack of parental orientation toward achievement strivings in the preschool years tends not to elicit such behaviors in the young child. Perhaps for these reasons, there has been little experimental research on determinants of achievement behavior in the preschool years. A summary of the experimental findings can be made in one sentence: Internal standards of performance in young children were successfully manipulated by (1) mere exposure to the standards of friendly others (the Bandura-Kupers "bowling" experiment), (2) social approval (Fales and Crandell), and (3) silence, if previous adult behavior was punitive (Crandell). It would thus seem that imitative and reinforcement variables operate in predictable ways in the determination of achievement strivings.

In the Fels study, achievement and recognition behavior was carefully measured. Furthermore, maternal *acceleration* was specifically measured, in terms of high expectations for achievement, excessive concern for the intellectual development of the child, and "pushing" the child to a level beyond his years. A mother scoring high on this dimension was thus a parent who provided a *model* of achievement as well as rewards and punishments for achieving and non-achieving behavior, respectively. Identification theory and learning theory would thus predict a positive correlation between maternal acceleration and achievement strivings in the children.

Table 12.7 presents these correlations, separately for the three age periods during which maternal behavior was rated.

Ignoring the first three years, these correlations provide strong support for the preceding predictions. Thus, maternal acceleration of boys during years three to six correlated .57 with general achievement during that age period, and .48 during years six to ten. The corresponding correlations for girls are .65 and .14. Intellectual achievement at ages ten to fourteen was predictable not only from maternal acceleration during ages six to ten (correlations of .57 and .49 for boys and girls, respectively) but even from acceleration during the early childhood years (correlations of .57 and .15 for boys and girls, respectively). The same story is true for competitiveness and recognition behavior. Finally, expectancy of task failure and athletic achievement were *negatively* correlated with maternal accelerations; acceleration resulted in a tendency not to expect failure and in little athletic achievement. It may thus be concluded that, from early childhood to adolescence, maternal acceleration was

TABLE 12.7

Relationship Between Maternal Acceleration and Achievement and
Recognition Strivings in Children

| | Maternal Acceleration | | | | | |
| | 0–3 | | 3–6 | | 6–10 | |
	Boys	Girls	Boys	Girls	Boys	Girls
General achievement						
3–6	.35	−.02	.57	.65		
6–10	.10	−.15	.48	.14	.59	.43
Intellectual achievement						
10–14	.34	−.51	.57	.15	.57	.49
Competitiveness						
3–6	−.07	.17	.48	.61		
6–10	−.10	−.22	.30	.37	.12	.39
10–14	*	−.30	.13	.18	.17	.58
Recognition behavior						
6–10	.37	.02	.60	.38	.57	.38
10–14	.23	−.16	.39	.26	.24	.37
Expectancy of task failure						
6–10	.11	.24	−.26	−.26	−.47	−.21
10–14	*	.23	−.23	−.01	−.22	−.22
Athletic achievement						
10–14	.34	−.51	−.47	−.12	−.33	.12

* Not enough data available for a rating.

associated with intellectual achievement, competitiveness, and recognition strivings, and also with expectancies of task success, and with little interest or performance in athletics.

During the first three years, the picture is much the same for boys, but is mysteriously different for girls. For example, maternal acceleration of boys during the first three years was predictive of adolescent intellectual achievement ($r = .34$), but in girls, it was predictive of the opposite ($r = -.51$); such girls tended to be low achievers. Likewise, they were non-competitive (correlations of −.22 and −.30) and had little tendency to engage in recognition behavior (correlations of .02 and −.16). A clue to this reverse effect is suggested by the fact that mothers who attempted to accelerate the behavior of daughters at this age (zero to three) were also hostile (rejecting) toward their daughters; the correlation between maternal acceleration and maternal hostility to daughters during ages zero to three was .47. Such a pattern was not present for boys, where r equaled only $-.11$. Nor was it present for girls at ages three to six or six to ten, the correlations being $-.34$ and $.14$, respectively. Only for girls at ages zero to three, then, were acceleratory mothers also hostile.

Now, what does this mean? One likely possibility is that hostile mothers provided poor conditions for imitation in their daughters. According to data and theory previously discussed, imitation is facilitated by a warm, pleasant relationship between parent and child—hardly to be found in a hostile relationship. It was already noted that maternal hostility was predictive of *aggression toward mother* in both sexes. An aggressive attitude toward one's mother, and a rejecting, hostile mother, would hardly lead to much imitation, except possibly that of aggression. Furthermore, if the bonds of affection between mother and daughter were weak, social approval for achievement strivings might not have as strong a reinforcing effect as social approval from a loving mother. After all, social approval presumably derives its reinforcing power from past pairings with other reinforcers. To the extent that such pairings were minimal, social approval from a hostile mother would have little effect upon the child. From both an imitation point of view and a learning-reinforcement viewpoint, then, one would not expect daughters of rejecting mothers to be as affected by acceleratory pushing as boys of non-rejecting mothers.

This reasoning suggests that maternal hostility might be predictive of non-achievement for both boys and girls, independent of acceleration. Such a possibility is made even more likely by recalling that hostility was correlated with two other dimensions for both boys and girls throughout childhood; hostile mothers tended to be unprotective (i.e., calmly detached) and highly restrictive (i.e., lots of rules). The reader may refer back to page 381 to verify this statement. Consider a mother who is rejecting, unconcerned, and restrictive. Since she is rejecting and hostile, there is not likely to be much reinforcement for achievement behavior or any other behavior unless it has a direct effect upon the mother. Her unconcern would also suggest little interest in the child's achievement behavior (thus, unprotective mothers tended not to be acceleratory, especially toward boys). The effects of restrictiveness are more difficult to predict. If there are rules about study time, for example, restrictiveness might facilitate achievement behavior. On the other hand, if such rules are associated with a negative, uninterested attitude, it is unlikely that much would be accomplished. Such would seem to be the case with hostile mothers. Because of these interrelationships, then, it would not be surprising to find that maternal hostility was negatively correlated with achievement behavior. Table 12.8 presents the relevant correlations.

It can be seen from Table 12.8 that the prediction is generally confirmed, although the age at which mothers' behavior occurred makes a difference for boys and girls. For boys, the prediction is most strongly confirmed when maternal behavior during ages zero to three and three to six is considered. General achievement and intellectual achievement are consistently negatively correlated with hostility when it occurred at these ages, and expectancy of task failure is consistently positively correlated with hostility. For girls, the clearest pattern emerges when maternal behavior at ages three to six and six to ten is considered. These 10 correlations present exactly the same pattern as the previously discussed boys' pattern. Ignoring this dependence upon when the mothers' behavior occurred, the inference is clear. Hostile, unconcerned, restrictive mothers tended to raise children who did rather poorly in terms of general and intellectual achievement. The children were also pessimistic about their own performance; they expected to do poorly.

TABLE 12.8

Correlations Between Maternal Hostility (Plus Detachment and Restrictiveness) and Achievement Strivings in Children

| Child Behavior | Maternal Hostility at Ages | | | | | |
| | 0–3 | | 3–6 | | 6–10 | |
	Boys	Girls	Boys	Girls	Boys	Girls
General achievement strivings						
3–6	−.34	.11	−.04	−.49		
6–10	−.60	.14	−.30	−.04	−.22	−.25
Intellectual achievement strivings						
10–14	−.27	−.19	−.28	−.01	−.02	−.36
Expectancy of task failure						
6–10	.27	−.12	.33	.11	.21	.37
10–14	.37	−.04	.05	.22	−.11	.29

Sexual Behavior

It will be recalled that two quite different types of sexual behavior were measured in the Fels study: *interaction with the opposite sex* and *opposite-sex interests*. It is obvious that the two must be considered separately.

Heterosexual Interactions. Interaction with the opposite sex did not reach an appreciable frequency until the early adolescent years (ten to fourteen). Thus, the present discussion will be restricted exclusively to these years. The maternal antecedents of such behavior were different for boys and girls. The relevant correlations are presented in Table 12.9. Correlations that present a consistent pattern are enclosed in boxes to facilitate interpretation of the table. For boys, interaction with the opposite sex was predictable from maternal behavior on two dimensions: protectiveness and restrictiveness. The negative correlations indicate that protective and restrictive mothers inhibited heterosexual interactions in their sons, and that the opposite maternal behavior, e.g., calm detachment and permissiveness, facilitated heterosexual behavior. For girls, the picture is different. Maternal protection tended to facilitate rather than inhibit heterosexual behavior, restrictiveness had little effect, and hostility had an inhibitory effect.

TABLE 12.9

Relationship Between Various Maternal Behaviors and Interaction
with the Opposite Sex

Maternal Behaviors at Various Ages	Interaction with the Opposite Sex at Ages 10–14	
	Boys	Girls
Protection		
0–3	−.25	.35
3–6	−.37	.25
6–10	−.12	.02
Restriction		
0–3	−.09	.08
3–6	−.58	.04
6–10	−.28	.17
Hostility		
0–3	−.38	−.31
3–6	.14	−.10
6–10	.07	−.10

Considering boys first, one may speculate that, since protective, restrictive mothers were somewhat intolerant of independent behavior in their sons, heterosexual overtures were both restricted and discouraged. After all, protective mothers encouraged and reinforced social behavior *only with themselves*, not with others. And restrictive mothers paid little attention to the child's wishes or point of view. Such processes, operating alone or in combination, would hardly be expected to facilitate outgoing overtures to the opposite sex. Indeed, it will shortly be shown that maternal protectiveness was predictive of social *interaction anxiety* in both boys and girls.

The real mystery concerns girls; here maternal protection was *positively* related to heterosexual interaction. It must be assumed, of course, that protective mothers encouraged dependency in their daughters just as they did in their sons. But perhaps a slightly dependent, retiring adolescent girl is more sexually attractive than one might guess. After all, dependency is a feminine characteristic in our society. Thus, it is possible (remember that these comments are sheer speculation) that dependency in girls was an asset if it was not too severe, while in boys it was a liability. In this respect, it will be shown in the next section that protection served to feminize both boys and girls.

The negative relationship between maternal hostility and heterosexual interaction in girls is more understandable; hostile mothers were also restrictive (see page 381). Thus, a negative mother, perceiving and communicating to her daughter and associates many faults and displeasing characteristics about the daughter, and permitting little independent behavior, would hardly create conditions optimal for heterosexual interaction. Indeed, a boy might be quite reticent in approaching such a household out of fear of the mother, even if the girl herself had survived with an intact and attractive personality. The only surprise is that hostility was not consistently predictive of heterosexual inhibition in boys as it was in girls. The largest correlation, however, is negative (−.38).

In summary, then, maternal protection inhibited heterosexual interactions in adolescent sons and facilitated them in daughters. These opposite effects were possibly due to the feminizing effects of maternal protection in both sexes. In addition, maternal restriction inhibited heterosexual interactions in sons, and hostility inhibited such responses in daughters. Since maternal restrictiveness and hostility were positively correlated with each other, the safest conclusion would seem to be that restrictive, hostile mothers discouraged heterosexual interaction in both sons and daughters.

Opposite-Sex Interests. Opposite-sex interests were predictable from protective mothers, as previously noted. Table 12.10 presents the correlations, separately for boys and girls. All eight correlations for boys are positive, and all eight for girls are negative. Thus, it is clear that protective mothers, overly concerned with helping and nurturing their offspring, tended to feminize them. Both boys and girls developed feminine interests (the latter is indicated by the negative correlations with opposite-sex—masculine—interests).

A similar trend is revealed by examination of the correlations between maternal protection and *passivity*, a feminine characteristic. Table 12.11 indicates that these correlations are positive for both sexes, thus indicat-

TABLE 12.10

Relationship Between Maternal Protection and Opposite-Sex Interests

Opposite-Sex Interests at Ages	Maternal Protection at Ages					
	0–3		3–6		6–10	
	Boys	Girls	Boys	Girls	Boys	Girls
3–6	.48	−.23	.30	−.19		
6–10	.40	−.30	.34	−.21	.38	−.01
10–14	.32	−.67	.32	−.46	.17	−.23

TABLE 12.11

Relationship Between Maternal Protection and Passivity

Passivity at Ages	Maternal Protection at Ages					
	0–3		3–6		6–10	
	Boys	Girls	Boys	Girls	Boys	Girls
3–6	.43	.09	.48	.30		
6–10	.43	.21	.23	.34	.30	.14
10–14	−.09	.15	.39	.13	.29	.20

ing that maternal protection was predictive of this aspect of femininity in both sexes.

A positive relationship between maternal protection and childhood femininity is not entirely unexpected. A mother who is only too anxious to help her child escape from life's little challenges might have at least two general effects upon his behavior. First, the child would have relatively few opportunities to learn that self-help and initiative often work, that they get the job done. Second, the child would have relatively many opportunities to learn that requests for help, dependency upon mother, and a general passive, defenseless attitude often do work; mother comes to the rescue and reinforces these responses. Simultaneously, then, self-assertive, aggressive types of habits have little opportunity to become strong, and dependent, passive responses are systematically strengthened. It is small wonder that such a child appears feminine and passive. Analyzed from a learning point of view, no other conclusion is permitted.

Social Interaction Anxiety

The determinants of social interaction anxiety, the fifth major personality trait measured, are difficult to determine from the Fels data.

During infancy and early childhood (zero to three and three to six), maternal hostility was predictive of a lack of social spontaneity (i.e., inhibition, withdrawal, and uneasiness with peers and adults) in both sexes (see Table 12.12). In middle childhood and early adolescence, however, this relationship broke down. No maternal behavior was predictive of social spontaneity (or a lack thereof) in girls, and boys were now affected by protectiveness rather than by hostility (see Table 12.13).

TABLE 12.12

Relationship Between Maternal Hostility and Social Spontaneity

| | Maternal Hostility at Ages | | | | | |
| Social Spontaneity in Children at Ages | 0–3 | | 3–6 | | 6–10 | |
	Boys	Girls	Boys	Girls	Boys	Girls
0–3	—.25	—.49				
3–6	—.25	—.15	—.28	.19		
6–10	—.15	.25	—.25	—.04	.08	—.16
10–14	.28	.07	—.04	.25	.17	.10

TABLE 12.13

Relationship Between Maternal Protection and Social Interaction Anxiety

| | Maternal Protection at Ages | | | |
| Social Interaction Anxiety in Children at Ages 10–14 | 3–6 | | 6–10 | |
	Boys	Girls	Boys	Girls
Social withdrawal	.13	.22	.37	—.02
Expectancy of peer rejection	.33	.01	.51	.23
Social spontaneity	—.21	—.30	—.22	—.10

Just why these shifts should occur from early years to later years is somewhat of a mystery. In part, it may be due to the instability of this trait through childhood. Social spontaneity did not possess long-term stability, with the correlations between ages three to six and ten to fourteen exactly zero for both boys and girls. One possibility that casts some light on both the instability during childhood and the changing relationships with maternal behavior is that perhaps social interaction anxiety has a lot to do with genetic factors. Popularity in boys is somewhat determined by size and strength; in girls, appearance is more important. All three of these characteristics are heavily determined by heredity, and to this extent maternal behavior would play a minor role.

Finally, the negative correlations between maternal protection and social spontaneity for boys during later years (six to fourteen) may be tentatively interpreted as follows: Recall other effects of protection: such children tended to be feminine and passive. Now, an unassertive, girlish, twelve-year-old boy, not too interested in many boy activities anyway, would hardly impress many of his peers in a favorable light, and hence would make few friends. A similar relationship might not hold for girls because, as previously noted, a passive, feminine girl is not at such a social disadvantage with either boys or girls.

SUMMARY

In general, the Fels data offer few contradictions to the experimentally derived conclusions of the previous chapter; the two sets of data mesh together nicely. Let us recapitulate.

Dependency. There were three conclusions arrived at via the experimental studies. One of these could be checked out in the Fels data—that attention-seeking and dependency are strengthened by reinforcement (overprotection) from adults. The Fels data yielded positive correlations between maternal protection and dependency at all ages (zero to ten), with stronger relationships for boys, thus confirming the conclusion. The lower relationships for girls were not inconsistent with this conclusion either, since maternal protection was not stable toward girls. With little consistent reinforcement for dependency responses, one would not expect high correlations.

A second finding of the Fels study, not investigated experimentally, is that maternal restrictiveness was also predictive of dependency, more so for girls than for boys, where the relationship reversed itself during years ten to fourteen. This finding yields readily to an analysis in learning theory terms. A household with many rules and demands for conformity, with threats and punishments for rule violation, is seen to push in the same direction as overprotection. In the latter case, there is reinforcement for conformity, and in the former case, punishment for non-conformity. Both practices are seen to push in the direction of dependency.

Aggression. Experimental studies led to two conclusions about determinants of aggression: (1) any response to frustration, be it aggressive or otherwise, will be strengthened if it is reinforced; and (2) punishment for aggression reduces it in that situation but increases it in other, different situations. The Fels data allowed for a check on both parts of the second conclusion.

The first part, that punishment for aggression reduces aggression in the punished situation, was tested by studying the correlations between *maternal hostility* (which included punishment for aggression, as well as punishment for other responses) and *aggression to mother*. The correlations were positive, thus contradicting the experimental conclusion: hostile, punitive mothers had children who were highly aggressive toward their mothers. Maternal restriction, on the other hand, which presumably also involved punishment for aggression, was not predictive of aggression to mother, perhaps because of successful maternal enforcement of rules prohibiting aggression. The picture with respect to the first conclusion is thus mixed, and a confident decision is hard to come by. Perhaps, as suggested in this chapter, maternal hostility was positively related to aggression to mother in a *reactionary* sense; it was the child's aggressiveness, perhaps, that was responsible for the mother's hostility. Such an interpretation has the advantage of not contradicting the experimentally acquired conclusion.

The second part of the conclusion, that punishment for aggression increases aggression away from home, was amply confirmed. Both maternal *hostility* and *restriction* were associated with high aggression away from home, as measured by aggression to peers.

Achievement behavior. Experimental studies led to one general conclusion about achievement behavior: a child presented with adult models of achievement orientation, and reinforced for similar behavior himself, is likely to develop strong achievement habits. The Fels data furnished ample confirmation of this conclusion: *maternal acceleration* was highly predictive of achievement strivings in both sexes.

A second finding, not investigated experimentally, was that maternal *hostility* was *negatively* correlated with achievement strivings. Recalling that hostile mothers tended to be detached and restrictive as well, it is not surprising that such a lethal combination would produce a rather negative self-concept in the child, as reflected by general expectations of failure and lack of achievement attempts.

The last two child behavior patterns measured in the Fels study, sexual behavior and social interaction anxiety, were not investigated experimentally, and hence cross-comparisons are not possible. The reader is referred to pages 282 and 293 for summaries of the Fels data in these two areas.

BIBLIOGRAPHY

KAGAN, J., and Moss, H. A. (1962). *Birth to maturity*. New York: John Wiley & Sons, Inc.

13

Dimensions of
Child-Rearing

INTRODUCTION

The Fels study, as intensive as it was, does not quite do justice to all the other family studies of child-rearing effects. There is another approach that begins with a different rationale and analyzes the data in a different, more elaborate way. In this chapter, we shall examine this rationale and investigate some of the better studies that employed the methodology that flows from it.

The problem can be introduced with a question about the Fels study: In measuring maternal behavior, why did the investigators pick the particular dimensions they did pick, and why four? These dimensions were selected primarily because of the investigators' belief that they were important dimensions, from both theoretical and common-sense points of view. But there is no guarantee that they reflected all the important aspects of parental behavior, since theories are always abstractions and simplifications of the data they deal with and usually require change in the face of subsequent data. Common sense is even more fallible, being notorious for its frequent inaccuracy. The variety of parent-child interactions is so multifaceted that a complete description of all the significant interactions between a parent and a child, even over a short duration, is impossible. Even if such a complete description were approached, it would be so long and involved that its very complexity would render it impregnable to analysis and interpretation.

The question is, then, how to pick the most important dimensions and how to reduce the data to manageable proportions. The first part of the chapter describes an answer to this question. In the last part of the chapter, this method is applied in a series of studies initiated by Wesley Becker.

DIMENSIONS OF CHILD-REARING

Suppose it is determined how a particular mother treats her three-year-old daughter in 12 different situations:

1. *Demands for neatness and order.* Does the mother have very high standards—her daughter must always pick up her toys, change her clothes to play, etc.; or moderate standards—she should wash before meals, sometimes pick up her toys; or low standards—mother does not expect any particular behavior of this sort?

2. *Amount of time spent playing with daughter.* Does the mother play with her a great deal, several hours each day, just when the daughter "demands" some attention, or hardly at all?

3. *Deprivation of privileges as a method of control.* To what extent does the mother punish her daughter by such methods as depriving her of a dessert, taking away a favorite doll, not allowing her to watch a favorite TV program, and not allowing her to play with a friend?

4. *Severity of punishment for aggression against herself.* How severely does the mother punish her daughter for striking at her in anger, for screaming at her, for slamming a door in her face—or is she completely tolerant of such responses?

5. *Strictness about household and furniture abuses.* Are there practically no restrictions at all, so that the child might jump on the furniture, mark the walls with crayons, help herself to food in the refrigerator, and eat it where she pleases, or are there many restrictions, such that the child must almost continually be "on guard" while she is inside the home?

6. *Strictness about noise.* Can the daughter yell and scream as she wishes, or is the house a quiet place, where children "speak when spoken to" and otherwise remain quiet?

7. *Affectionate demonstrativeness toward the child.* Does the mother frequently engage in open, overt demonstrations of love, such as hugging and kissing, or is such behavior almost totally lacking, with little expression of affection?

8. *Praise for good table manners.* To what extent does the mother attempt to control table manners by the use of verbal praise, as opposed to scoldings for poor manners?

9. *Standards of obedience.* To what extent is the child expected to promptly obey the mother's requests and instructions? Does the mother

say, "I think they ought to do it right away, whatever you ask," or does she say, "You can't expect too much until he (she) really gets a little older"? (Sears *et al.*, 1957.)

10. *Use of tangible rewards for good behavior.* To what extent does the mother use candy, gold stars, money, favorite foods, etc., as concrete rewards: ". . . teeth, wash their face, dishes, beds, and room, . . . And if they're done well, they get a star. . . ." versus "I haven't done any of that so-called bribing business, or any of that. I don't believe in it"? (Sears *et al.*, 1957.)

11. *Tolerance of aggression toward other children.* To what extent does the mother intervene and attempt to stop quarrels and fights between her child and other children? Is there strict prohibition of all quarrels, or is her daughter allowed, perhaps even encouraged, to "fight it out"?

12. *Encouragement of aggressive behavior toward others.* To what extent does she instigate aggressive reactions from her daughter toward others? Does she preach that one must "fight for what is his" and "stick up for his rights," or is "keeping the peace" the higher principle?

Suppose that a mother is scored "high" or "low" on each of these 12 items. She would thus have a pattern of 12 scores, say $+ + + - - -$ $+ - - - - +$, with $+$ indicating a high score. With 12 items, 2^{12} or 4,096 different patterns are possible. In order to exhaustively investigate the effects of such patterns on child behavior, a minimum of 4,096 mothers would be needed, each representing one of the possible patterns. Many more would actually have to be studied, since the first 4,096 mothers would hardly be cooperative enough so that each mother provided a different pattern. Perhaps 20,000 mothers or more would have to be studied before the desired 4,096 mothers were discovered.

Clearly, such a task is impossible; no study of child-rearing has involved even 4,096 mothers, let alone 20,000. And when it is recognized that these 12 classes of behavior are merely a sample of hundreds of other items, the necessity of economy and simplification becomes overwhelmingly apparent. How is it to be accomplished?

Factor Analysis

The answer lies in the fact that scores on many of the items are related to each other; that is, a mother's answer to one item can be used to predict her answers to certain other items. Considering the 12 items just described, for example, it is plausible to suspect that scores on items 1, 5, and 6 are similar. Most mothers who do not permit the child to jump on the furniture, mark the walls, etc. (item 5), might not permit noise in the house either (item 6), and might have high standards of neatness (item 1).

Common sense would suggest that scores on these 3 items should go together. But common sense need not have the final say. Information about these 3 items could be obtained from a group of mothers, and correlations between the answers to each pair of items easily computed. It could then be determined if the answers go together. If they did, one score could represent all 3 items and economy is achieved. Instead of three scores, there is one score, based upon the knowledge of positive correlations between answers to these 3 items. It is tempting to assume that these items are all related to a general dimension or factor of *permissiveness–non-permissiveness*, since all 3 items are concerned with the amount of freedom the child is allowed in various situations. The single score could thus be called the *permissiveness* score.

By a complex mathematical procedure known as factor analysis, it is possible to actually determine the correlations of the 3 item answers to the factor they are assumed to represent. These correlations are called *factor loadings*, and they describe how accurately each of the items relates to the factor in question.

The 12 items previously described, along with dozens of others, were actually administered to 379 mothers of kindergarten children (Sears *et al.*, 1957); that is, they were interviewed about these 12 items and others. The results of the analysis showed that not only did items 1, 5, and 6 "go together" in the sense previously discussed but so did other groups of the 12 items. As a matter of fact, the 12 items could be formed into four groups of 3 items each, the groupings consisting of items 1, 5, and 6; 2, 7, and 8; 3, 9, and 10; and 4, 11, and 12. Table 13.1 presents the correlations (factor loadings) of these four sets of items to the dimensions they represent. The names of the dimensions are based on the content of the items.

Thus, answers to items 2, 7, and 8 are positively correlated with each other, just as 1, 5, and 6 are, indicating that mothers who spent a lot of time playing with their children (item 2) also were overtly affectionate toward them (item 7) and praised them for good table manners (item 8). All three items obviously reflect the mothers' warmth and affection toward their children, and so were grouped together under such a title. Item 2 correlated .50 with this assumed dimension, and items 7 and 8 correlated .41 and .38, respectively. By the use of factor analysis, it was thus possible to reduce 12 different scores to 4, and at the same time to preserve most of the information contained in all 12 items.

With this introduction, it is now possible to describe in more general terms how economical, yet relatively complete, descriptions of child-rearing can be objectively obtained. One begins by selecting a large pool of

TABLE 13.1

Factor-Analytic Groupings of 12 of the Sears Items

	Factor Loading
I. Permissiveness	
(1) Demands for neatness and order	.35
(5) Freedom of household and furniture uses	.48
(6) Freedom to make noise	.38
II. Warmth and Affection	
(2) Time spent playing with child	.50
(7) Affectionate demonstrativeness	.41
(8) Praise for good table manners	.38
III. Responsible Child-rearing Orientation	
(3) Deprivation as a method of control	.51
(9) High standards of obedience	.45
(10) Use of tangible rewards	.40
IV. Treatment of Aggression	
(4) Punishment for aggression against parents	.41
(11) Tolerance of aggression against others	.42
(12) Encouragement of aggression toward others	.45

specific items (similar to the 12 items considered in Table 13.1) that are representative of parent-child interactions. Usually, somewhere between 100 and 300 such items are used. The investigator's own intuition plays a large role, of course, in the items selected, but there is an attempt to sample those interactions the investigator thinks are significant, i.e., those that strongly affect the behavior of the child. One then describes a large group of mothers with these items. Sears et al., for example, interviewed 379 mothers about each of 188 different child-rearing items. As a third step, one computes the correlations of answers to one item with all other items (electronic computers make this an easy task). In this way, one determines what items go together in the sense of eliciting similar answers. Factor analysis, the fourth step, then determines the correlation (factor loading) of each item within a group with the factor (dimension) assumed to be represented by the group of interrelated items. The final step involves describing each mother in terms of factor scores instead of in terms of item scores. Milton (1958), for example, factor analyzed 44 representative items of the 188 used by Sears et al. Five clear factors were discovered (a "clear" factor is one that is easily named by studying the items that define it; an "unclear" factor is one that is difficult to name). Indeed, Table 13.1 presents four of these factors; the fifth factor, named general family adjustment, reflected how well the parents got along with each other. Thus, 44 item scores were reduced to five factor scores, with very little loss of information.

Results of Factor-Analytic Studies

A number of such factor-analytic studies have been carried out. These studies varied in three major respects. First, each started with a different set of items, thus influencing the factors ultimately discovered. That is, if no items about treatment of aggression are included, one is not going to discover a "treatment of aggression" factor; one can discover only those dimensions that are represented by the original pool of items. The importance of representativeness is thus paramount. Second, the information required by the items was obtained in one of two ways: by direct interviews with the mothers, or by giving the mothers a written copy of the questions and asking them to write their answers. Although these two methods appear comparable, they do not yield identical results. Most experienced investigators agree that the interview yields more valid results, perhaps because it is possible to "probe" the mother with extemporaneous questions when her answers appear vague or contrived. Third, each study used a different sample of mothers from widely scattered parts of the United States. Some studies did not use mothers at all, but rather unmarried women who were asked what they would do if they were mothers.

In spite of these three characteristics, all operating to produce divergent results from one study to another, a remarkably similar set of factors has emerged. It appears that three dimensions are fundamental, i.e., can accurately describe a good share of parent-child interactions. Becker (1964) has named these three dimensions *restrictiveness-permissiveness, hostility-warmth,* and *anxious emotional involvement-calm detachment.* These three dimensions are relatively independent of each other, and therein lies their economy. To the extent dimensions are not independent (that is, to the extent they are correlated with each other), they are redundant, since a score on one dimension implies the value of a score on the other dimension, depending upon the correlation between the two. But with independent (uncorrelated) dimensions, each score provides unique information not predictable from scores on other dimensions. Hence, three scores from uncorrelated dimensions carry more information than three scores from correlated dimensions.

It is possible to reflect this orthogonal relationship geometrically by drawing three lines perpendicular to each other, thus representing the axes of three-dimensional space. Figure 13.1 presents such a drawing, with each axis representing one of the three dimensions. The reader should study this figure carefully, for it summarizes much of what is known of child-rearing dimensions at the present time. A brief description of one end of each dimension is provided to assist in understanding

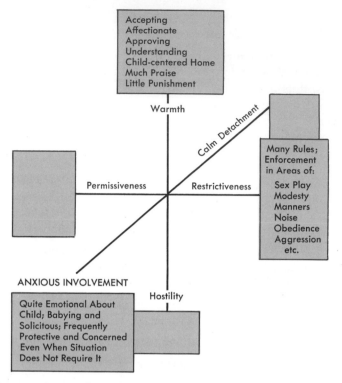

Figure 13.1. Three fundamental dimensions of child-rearing.

the meaning of the dimensions. The other end of each dimension consists simply of the opposite characteristics.

With two ends to each of three independent dimensions, $2^3 = 8$ extreme types of parental behavior can be described. These eight types can be visualized by imagining a cube divided into eight smaller cubes, as in Figure 13.2. Thus, a *warm, permissive, anxiously involved* parent constitutes one of the eight extremes (cube 1); *warm, permissive, calmly detached,* a second (cube 2); *hostile, restrictive, calmly detached,* a third (cube 8); etc.

Most parents, it is important to note, would not approximate one of the eight extremes, but rather would fall near the middle on most of the dimensions; e.g., a more average mother would be neither very restrictive nor very permissive, but somewhere in between. Likewise, she would be neither overpoweringly warm nor completely hostile, but somewhere nearer the middle. Yet it is easier to understand the descriptive implications of these three dimensions by considering extremes.

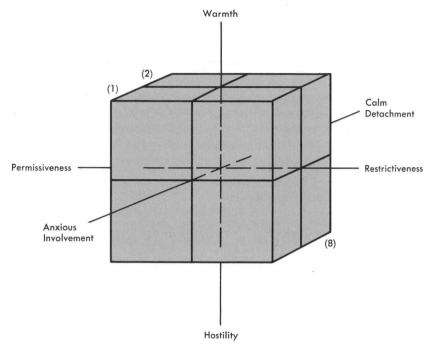

Figure 13.2. Eight extremes of child-rearing.

We shall now attempt to apply what we have just learned to a real-life situation. How should the mother in the following case history be described in terms of these dimensions? The child, a five-year-old, is referred to as "patient" in this excerpt because his behavior problems were sufficient to bring him to the attention of a psychotherapist.

Case History 1

The patient is disobedient, hyperactive, impudent to the parents; calls them names, kicks and scratches when not given his own way, will not come to meals and runs out into the street before he is finished.

Father thinks mother is too much concerned with the patient. Mother says everyone tells her she pays too much attention to patient. Psychiatrist, physician, and social worker indicate an abundant evidence of maternal overprotection.

Patient will not leave his mother, nor will he allow her to go out unless she says she must go to the doctor. At age three he developed independence of the mother in kindergarten, not allowing her to come near him at play. However, after the summer vacation when he was with mother constantly, he refused to leave her side, to return to kindergarten, or to play outside the house alone.

Early psychiatric examinations were made difficult because the patient refused to leave his mother. Later he would run out to his mother in the waiting room.

Patient rules the household by his screaming and imperative voice. Mother will always comply with his demands rather than hear him scream. He comes in for lunch whenever he pleases, and although mother protests, she always feeds him.

When the mother accidentally knocked over his blocks, although he had refused to remove them from under the sink where she was washing dishes, he swore at her and the mother weakly replied, "You mustn't call mamma a bad name." During the patient's psychological tests, the mother, being interviewed in an adjoining office, sat tensely on the edge of her chair, frequently asking, "Is that Johnny? Is that Johnny?" and was sure that he was calling her. After the examination, she had him read aloud nursery tales in the waiting room where children and adults were present.

Observed at a meal, the patient pushed back his plate of potatoes and said, "It stinks." When mother put him back in bed, after his getting out, he kicked at her and struck her in the mouth. [Levy, 1943, pp. 361, 363.]

In terms of the restrictive-permissive dimension, this short description strongly suggests the mother is quite *permissive;* e.g., "Mother will always comply with his demands." It is also apparent that she loves the child, and hence she is *warm.* Finally, she would appear to be *anxiously involved* with him; e.g., "Is that Johnny? Is that Johnny?" It would thus seem reasonable to summarize this mother's behavior as *permissive, warm,* and *anxiously involved.* Depending upon the extremeness of such a constellation, such mothers are often called *indulgent* or *overindulgent.* The behavior in this particular example is extreme enough to merit the latter term.

Three descriptions of parental behavior that are more complete are now provided. Following each is a discussion and a summary in terms of the three-dimensional model previously presented. The student should attempt his own summary before reading the discussion, and then compare his summary with that of the text. In this way, he will tend to extinguish inaccurate summaries and to strengthen accurate ones.

Case History 2

The parents, both graduates of the department of education of a large state university, with training in modern theories of child care, are liberal in their social philosophy and consider it a duty to themselves, to their children, and to society to express their democratic philosophy in the home. Coldly and scientifically, although with unusual insight and intelligence, they have applied the theories of democratic management to the problem of raising Dale. Mrs. Jameson, particularly, in her effort to make each decision the "correct" one has suppressed her natural feelings and spontaneity in dealing with the children. She seldom acts impulsively but instead checks her own policy against the dictates of "the book" before venturing to act. Far brighter, however, and more realistic than the average young mother who relies on scientific testimony, Mrs. J. does maintain a flexible policy and is guided less by specific textbook recommendations than by a broad set of principles.

The particular constellation of forces in Mrs. J.'s personality almost require that she adopt this scientific method of handling Dale. Frustrated in her own desire for prominence, achievement and personal popularity, she simulates the hardboiled intellectual sophisticate. This pose on the one hand protects her from becoming emotionally involved with other people, and on the other hides her feelings of inferiority. When Dale was born, Mrs. J. felt she had been given a second opportunity to achieve her desired goals. She is determined that Dale shall have the assets which she feels are lacking in her own personality. The consequence of such an identification with the child would ordinarily be extreme emotionality and overindulgence. But in the case of Mrs. Jameson this is impossible for three reasons: first, she is unwilling to let herself become so emotionally involved with anybody; second, such behavior would be frowned upon by the other enlightened mothers of her set; and third, she recognizes that such behavior would almost certainly defeat the ends she has in mind. In the light of these factors, her attitude of scientific objectivity is the only workable solution.

The workings of democracy in the Jameson home are quite cleverly adapted to the children's ages and capacities. With children of preschool age, methods which are obviously democratic are difficult to apply. At this level democracy consists of giving the child a choice in all possible situations, allowing him the maximum amount of freedom which is compatible with his safety and the rights of the other members of the household, and, more fundamentally, recognizing and respecting him as an individual even though he is inarticulate, immature, and irrational from the adult's point of view. In these respects, the Jameson home is thoroughly democratic. When he was five, Dale was voicing his opinion as to the menu, whether he should play indoors or out, stay at home or visit the neighbors, have a nap or stay up and play. Beyond the routine schedule, almost every decision during the day relating to immediate issues or plans for activities was child-determined.

Nor were Dale's choices subjected to subtle adult coercion. If Mrs. Jameson wished to influence or modify Dale's activity, she approached the matter directly and openly, rather than by manipulating Dale's decisions into parentally approved channels. If Dale's presence was felt to be an intrusion, for instance, he was not sent away on some conjured up errand which would keep him out of sight and busy for a while but was instead told frankly that this was an adult situation in which he would not be interested. This policy of directness was and is an expression of the Jameson's belief that Dale had a right to know when he was frustrated and why. The same techniques have been used as Dale has become older. In addition, the "family council" method has been adopted to handle Dale's school age adjustments in democratic fashion.

Just as characteristic of the Jameson home as its democracy has been the refusal to baby or protect Dale. Mrs. J., for instance, refrains from pampering the children even when they are ill and tries to make the period in bed as dull and boring as possible so that they will be motivated to get well. When at the age of three Dale retreated to the house scratched and bloody after an encounter with a cat, he met a cool and unsympathetic response from his mother. "You must have been teasing it," was all she would say.

Behind this aloofness there is probably more than a calculated objectivity.

Mrs. Jameson seems psychologically incapable of expressing warmth and affection. Friendly physical contacts have always been predominantly of the rough-house, wrestling type rather than fondling or gentle cuddling. Companionability on an intellectual level, however, between Dale and his mother has never been lacking nor stilted. Mrs. J. can register genuine enthusiasm and interest in Dale's creative efforts and intellectual attainments. She is responsive and stimulating in these areas. It is only when warm, emotional affectionateness is demanded of her that she seems unable to respond; at such moments she is likely to become brusque, clipped in her speech, and inhibited.

To complete the picture of the intellectual *democratic* home, Mrs. Jameson is extremely acceleratory in her treatment of Dale. A policy of providing Dale with every opportunity for experimentation, exploration and drill in useful activities was instituted when he was a baby and has continued unabated. When D. was a small infant just starting to crawl, Mrs. J. would hide toys from him in unlikely places with the idea of training him in the coordination of eye and hand and improving his reasoning ability. When D. was two or three he was taught to use the dial telephone, to answer it, to give and receive messages. When books were read to him, incongruities were pointed out and he was encouraged to comment and criticize. All questions were given grave consideration, answered in language which he could comprehend and the explanation reinforced until he had mastered the point. He was urged to ask about the meanings of words he had heard in conversation or reading and to fit these words into his own vocabulary; language was considered a tool, and he was encouraged to make sharp and precise use of it. In addition to providing this facilitating environment, Mrs. Jameson has been anxious for Dale not only to become competent, but to excel other children in the neighborhood. Finding Dale very responsive to acceleratory measures, Mrs. Jameson has pushed him on to the straining point in her determination that Dale shall reach the heights which she herself has never been able to achieve. Not content with furnishing Dale an accurate speech pattern to copy, Mrs. Jameson has demanded perfection. Dale pronounced his final consonants with a conclusive thud long before other children were out of baby talk. When Dale spontaneously became interested in reading and writing at the age of five, Mrs. Jameson was not content merely to foster the interest by encouragement but set standards of excellence beyond the abilities of the average second grader. Her intellectual ambitions for Dale are so great that the values of the family are centered on rational intelligent behavior. "It's bad and you shouldn't do it" has been entirely replaced by "only *stupid* people behave like that."

It is of interest to note the effect of such child-rearing practices upon the behavior of Dale, since Dale's behavior illustrates a point mentioned . . . : either too much punishment for aggressive behavior, or too much permissiveness, is likely to lead to aggressive behavior away from home. Dale's behavior illustrates the latter case.

Dale is perhaps the most obviously precocious child in the study. The maturity of his speech, as evidenced in pronunciation, content, and manner of expression, has been so strikingly advanced as to focus considerable attention on him. The richness of his imagination and the originality of his play made him stand head and shoulders above other children in the nursery school, and in his grade school group. The tenacity and thoroughness with which he explores an interest is illustrated by these items: interested in baseball, he learned the batting averages of all the important players in the major leagues;

caught in the fervor of war games, he can identify by number all the U. S. plane models.

Even more striking than his precocity, however, has been his violent, uninhibited aggressiveness toward society. Fearing neither man nor beast, he seeks no quarter and gives none. He will kick, bite, and scratch his teachers, his relatives, and even innocent bystanders with the same ferocity that most children reserve for playmates. His over-aggressiveness, particularly its unreasonableness—he is as likely to respond aggressively to a friendly overture as to a disciplinary attempt—seems to indicate a positive need to be defiant and to rebel. This need, born probably of his insecurity and lack of emotional warmth in his relations with his mother and fostered by the permissive atmosphere of the Jameson home, bids fair to lead Dale into seriously antisocial behavior. The prognosis has been much improved, however, since Dale's school entrance by the fact that he wants to be popular and is. Now that he is finding that his nonconformity seriously detracts from his social acceptability, he is beginning to modify his behavior toward a more realistic balance of conformity and freedom. [Baldwin *et al.*, 1945, pp. 46–48.]

It is somewhat difficult to summarize Mrs. Jameson's behavior on the three dimensions and still retain all its richness and subtle shadings. Consider the restrictiveness-permissiveness dimension; where should Mrs. J. be placed? In many, perhaps most, ways, she is quite permissive, yet with respect to pushing Dale toward intellectual achievement, she seems somewhat more directing and restrictive: "Mrs. Jameson has pushed him on to the straining point in her determination that Dale shall reach the heights . . ." The three-dimensional scheme does not allow one to reflect both Mrs. J's general permissiveness and her specific control in the area of intellectual achievement. But even in the latter case, it is not so much that she *forces and restricts* Dale to intellectual activities, but rather that she reinforces such behavior with social approval when it occurs. Thus, all in all, it might be most accurate to place Mrs. J. toward the *permissive* end of this dimension.

In terms of anxious involvement versus calm detachment, it is quite clear that Mrs. J. should be placed toward the *calm detachment* end; she engages in very little babying, solicitous protection, or other behaviors indicating a strong emotional involvement with Dale. On the contrary, she may be described as "calmly determined" rather than "anxiously apprehensive."

Finally, in terms of hostility versus warmth, it seems clear that Mrs. J. is not warm. She is described as "cool and unsympathetic; aloof"; etc. On the other hand, she is also described as enthusiastic and interested, and as providing considerable "companionability" in Dale's creative and more intellectual efforts. Clearly, there is no hostility. Perhaps "somewhat warm" is reasonably accurate.

In summary, then, Mrs. Jameson is most accurately described as *per-*

missive, calmly detached, and somewhat warm in her behavior toward Dale. It is customary to call such a constellation a democratic pattern.

Case History 3

As a mother Mrs. Stone has been from her child's earliest infancy a tense, keyed-up, apprehensive person. While never becoming so disturbed or unhappy as to be forced to seek psychotherapy, she has, through the years, made it clear that her life is unsatisfactory to her and that her only reward is her relationship to her son, now ten years old.

Mr. and Mrs. S., each an only child, were married when they were twenty-five; both are college graduates, Mr. S. having an advanced degree. Mrs. Stone had a professional career before her marriage, did some substitute teaching afterwards which was terminated with pregnancy a year or two later. It was a planned conception.

One of the most salient factors about Mrs. S.'s personality is her inability, even refusal, to form close emotional ties with other people. Significant exceptions to this have been her mother and her son. . . . Once she remarked that "I don't like to get close to people—you get too involved with friends." She is quite aware of the degree of her absorption in her child, has said to the home visitor that no one, even her husband, understood her sincere attempt to make Ted a healthy happy child, adding very emotionally, that she had sacrificed her life for him.

These various factors in her own personality have inevitably been reflected in Mrs. Stone's behavior with Ted. In infancy it was revealed in tremendous rigidity of schedule; in toilet training begun when the baby was three months old, in constant acceleration and overestimates of the child's ability. Having identified herself completely with her product, it was necessary that the child himself be immaculate, perfect in behavior, precocious intellectually. Then and later she was completely unrealistic about him, generously interpreting every squeal, for example, as a meaningful syllable and translating for the benefit of the visitor. Now that he is school age this trait is revealed in her calm assumption that any criticism of Ted, from child or adult, is the product of willful and unjustified malice. When incontrovertible evidence is presented of some mischief he may have done, she is quick to find the scapegoat who "led him into it," though she is on such occasions grievously disappointed with the boy for being amenable to such pressures.

Great solicitude for Ted's moral and physical welfare has been evident from the beginning, but the fact that he early showed himself prone to upper-respiratory infections and was later discovered to have a number of allergies crystallized all the mother's existent anxieties. Despite her acceleration of mental activity, she was babying to the point of being retardatory in other areas—continuing, for example, to feed him part of every meal because he voluntarily finished only those foods he liked and she was fearful of what an inadequate diet might mean; this process was carried on, therefore, until he was six or so.

Standards for Ted's behavior are, and always have been, exceptionally high. The mother's goal has been to produce an adult-child, but a very sober and inhibited kind of adult. A left-handed compliment—"sometimes he's just a perfect little gentleman, so quiet and serious"—was given in apology for some typical small-boy silliness he had shown before the visitor. Another time she was worried because he had started using exaggerated or nonsensical language; "Ted used to be so straightforward and simple, and now he's taken this up from Jerry, and I do think it does cheapen a child so."

The discipline area is conflict-provoking for the mother. On the one hand, she cannot tolerate infractions of her high code for Ted's behavior and is ever watchful to see that he conforms. But when misbehavior does occur, she is loathe to punish because of her devotion to the child. Compromises frequently emerge; for example, on one occasion he was sent to bed an hour early as a punishment, but Mrs. S. decided she'd been overly severe and went to the bedroom and read to him for the extra period. [Baldwin *et al.*, 1949, pp. 29–30.]

Mrs. Stone would seem to be somewhat restrictive toward Ted, as well as highly involved emotionally. ". . . she had sacrificed her life for him." Finally, she obviously feels and acts warmly toward him, even to the extent of being unable to believe that he could occasionally get into mischief. It is fairly easy, then, to summarize Mrs. Stone as *restrictive*, *anxiously involved*, and *warm* in her behavior toward Ted. It is customary to label such a constellation as *protective* or *overprotective*, depending upon the extremeness. This particular example is extreme enough to earn the "overprotective" label.

Case History 4

The Dugan home is soberly industrious, almost puritan in its quality. Married in their teens, both parents have a farm background and setting up as farmers was, for them, a logical and unquestioned step. Both parents are staid, conservative individuals, solemnly intent on life as a business. In their struggles to get ahead both have had to work extremely hard, but their ideology goes beyond this—work is not a means but an end in itself, and most recreation can be chalked off as a frivolous use of time. Both are so firmly entrenched in the pattern of values laid down by generations of industrious forebears, the general "farm culture," that an outsider finds it hard to believe they really are so young—still in their twenties—rather than the settled, middle-aged couple their attitudes would indicate. If there is conflict, restlessness, an urge to see the world in a different perspective than that given by a small Markham County Farm, it is so deeply repressed and hidden as to go unrecognized even by the Dugans themselves.

Their acceptance of the isolation and hard work afforded by the farm life they have chosen is in part a reflection of their own reclusive and rather antisocial temperaments. Mrs. Dugan, in particular, was probably termed shy as a girl. Now a mature woman, she can only be described as cold, hostile, suspicious. Little companionship is evident in the marriage; there is hardly more interaction between husband and wife than between either one and a stranger. Work is divided according to the traditional farm pattern—the man to the barns and fields, the woman to the house and child training—with little mutual interchange of experience beyond routine informational conversation.

In this setting, child bearing is as natural and unquestioned as the farm work itself, a matter not of choice and planning but of custom, even duty. Thus Sam, who was born within a year, was "accepted" as an inevitable part of their marriage, even though the Dugans have no fondness for children as such.

They found little recompense in enjoyment for the burden of fitting his schedule and demands into an already over-crowded work program. Parental policy, therefore, had to set rigid boundaries, require a minimum of contact with the child, and let the parents off in the easiest fashion commensurate with their obligation to the child, so that they could devote themselves to the more important work waiting for them.

This type of handling is evident even in Sam's infancy. Accounts of fondling the baby or playing with him are rare. A visitor reports that, at eleven months, "his mother was dressing him at the kitchen table, holding him on her lap like a small baby and thrusting him into his clothes." No opportunity was given for any degree of self-help because that would have been time-consuming. At the same age, on the other hand, he was already being given sharp slaps to teach him not to get into things. The home has been highly accelerational in those areas where the mother's goal is to be able to leave the child alone without worrying about him; at the same time, more help is given than the child needs if doing so will save time and effort.

Over and above the attempt to conserve time and energy in the handling of the child, Mrs. Dugan is unduly restrictive and autocratic. An example from a time-sample recording made on an early home visit is illustrative: (17 months) "He saw my book and dove for it, jabbering unintelligibly. He slapped at my book and his mother said, 'Don't do that.' He took my ankle in his hand, and his mother told him not to do that. He went over to the couch and pulled at a pillow, to which his mother said, 'Now leave that alone.' He came over to me and pulled at my pen and buttons. His mother pulled him away." Mrs. Dugan's vigilant severity in this instance seems unnecessary, if her only motivation is to conserve energy. Probably it reflects an active resentment and hostility.

As Sam grew older and could more nearly be trusted to conform, the relationship became more inert, with Mrs. D. ignoring his activities until a disciplinary crisis would arise. The fact that Mrs. Dugan rarely forestalls a crisis by acting ahead of time can, in part, be attributed to her lack of attention to the child—there is practically no interaction between her and Sam *except* when he has done something irritating or "wrong." This aloofness is evident in the following anecdote from a report of a visit made when Sam was three: "He had one period of giggling which lasted several minutes and was renewed with a rather forced note once or twice subsequently. His mother did not enter into his giggling, but on the other hand, she made no attempt to stop him and waited until it disappeared . . ."

Lack of interaction is evident in other areas than discipline, too. Sam's speech development was slow, and after he did begin to talk, his language was markedly distorted. Another visitor reports: "Mrs. Dugan said that she and his father could understand him, but that most people could not. They make no attempt to correct his speech." It is as if once bare communication had been established, no matter how faulty, they felt their responsibility was at an end. There is a general disinterest in Sam's inner life, what he thinks, feels, or how he's reacting. One home visitor reports that over a period of two years or so, she had never heard Mrs. Dugan so much as ask Sam what had happened at school that day. In the school area, as in others, Mrs. Dugan's only concern is with success or failure, conforming conduct or troublesome mischief. When Sam was having difficulty with spelling, she dutifully drilled him at home, demonstrating a "What can you expect?" attitude, and some irritation at the extra time entailed.

Again it seems that Mrs. Dugan's behavior is too extreme to be accounted for solely in terms of a minimum expenditure of effort. She now seems unnecessarily aloof and disinterested, just as formerly she seemed unnecessarily vigilant and restrictive. Both probably reflect the same underlying hostility.

Aside from the psychological isolation it provides, the home is not severely restricting at this point. Arbitrary standards for conduct have been laid down, but so long as Sam conforms to those standards, his behavior is not too closely scrutinized—the parents have neither the time nor the interest. The independence this has fostered, plus a desperate seeking for affection and attention and demands for status of one sort or another, have made his school record one of near-delinquency, although at home he is just conforming enough to escape the "problem" classification. By identification with gangs, he has found the affection and status which he misses at home, but there is no reason to suppose that a redirection of his behavior into socially acceptable channels is not possible. So far as Sam himself is concerned, however, help in the redirection of his energies will have to come from teachers or other interested adults—his parents are as unperceptive of his problems now as they were in their own behavior which created the problem. [Baldwin *et al.*, 1945, pp. 20–22).

The Dugans are easy to rate on two dimensions, and somewhat more difficult to rate on a third. They are obviously *calmly detached* from Sam and *somewhat hostile*. But are they restrictive or permissive? Mrs. Dugan seems to be restrictive of bothersome behaviors, but otherwise permissive—a sort of "stay out of my business and I'll stay out of yours" attitude. It is therefore difficult to detect a *general* pattern of restrictiveness or permissiveness. Perhaps it would be more accurate to state that Mrs. Dugan was restrictive during Sam's early childhood, but permissive in his middle childhood. Indeed, the description practically states this trend: ". . . Mrs. Dugan is unduly restrictive and autocratic . . ." (referring to early childhood behavior) and "As Sam grew older and could more nearly be trusted to conform, the relationship became more inert, with Mrs. D. ignoring his activities. . . ." Thus, one may summarize Mrs. Dugan as *restrictive, calmly detached,* and *somewhat hostile* in Sam's early childhood, and *permissive, calmly detached,* and *somewhat hostile* in his middle childhood. The former constellation is often called a *rigid, cold* pattern, and the latter a *neglecting* pattern.

It should now be clear that these dimensions of child-rearing afford an economical yet reasonably accurate method of distilling the complexities of parent-child relationships to manageable summaries. At the same time, it is important to note that a good deal of specificity is lost, and that some types of behavior are not reflected by these dimensions. It was observed in the descriptions of Mrs. Jameson and the Dugans, for example, that certain patterns of behavior were not easily reflected by any of the three dimensions. As a matter of fact, studies of child rearing sometimes turn up an entire dimension that does not appear to be highly related to any of the three main dimensions. More than one study has discovered a dimension of "pushiness" or "demand for achievement." Roff (1949) called it "Activeness of the Home," with one of the specific items defining it stated as follows: "Accelerational Attempt; acceleratory-retardatory." Schaeffer and Bell (1958) found a similar dimension they called "Excessive demand for striving," and it was defined in terms of such specific items as "strictness, acceleration of development," and "demand for activity." On the Fels study, it was called "maternal acceleration." There is no doubt that such parental behavior is most adequately described by a score referring to it and nothing else, even though it may be related, to some extent, to one of the three previously discussed dimensions.

Other intriguing dimensions have appeared only in single studies. Some are of interest because they suggest types of parental behavior that might be expected to have powerful effects on theoretical grounds and do not seem to be clearly reflected in other dimensions. It was previously noted, for example, that Milton's factor analysis of 44 items from the Sears study yielded a dimension describing treatment of aggression (p. 406). Mothers scoring high on this dimension were permissive and even encouraging of aggression toward other children, but were restrictive and punitive of aggression toward themselves. It would be unusual, indeed, if such treatment did not affect the general aggressive behavior of the child. Failure to accurately measure such maternal behavior would leave the child's aggressive behavior unexplained.

In short, the description of parental behavior in terms of broad dimensions has both advantages and disadvantages. Its main advantages are economy and objectivity, and its main disadvantage is incompleteness. One must attempt to arrive at a reasonable compromise between these two consequences. The three dimensions summarized by Becker represent the combined results of many investigations that grappled with this problem. They are encountered again and again in other studies of child rearing. Even the Fels dimensions, selected in an entirely different way, are related to these three dimensions: *maternal protection* is similar to anxious emotional involvement; *restrictiveness* is similar, of course, to the dimension with the same name at one end; and *hostility* relates directly to the third dimension, again with the same name at one end.

A FACTOR-ANALYTIC STUDY OF CHILD-REARING:
THE BECKER STUDIES

Becker and his colleagues intensively studied 71 families, all of which contained a child of kindergarten age. Both the fathers and the mothers furnished two comprehensive sets of information about their own behavior. First, a rating scale consisting of 73 bipolar 7-point rating scales with antonym pairs was filled out by each parent. Each scale reflected a particular component or type of personality characteristic. For example, one of the scales was *objective* 1-2-3-4-5-6-7 *emotional;* another was *boring* 1-2-3-4-5-6-7 *interesting;* etc. The parent circled that number on each scale that was most descriptive of his (her) own behavior in relation to the child. Then each parent filled out all 73 scales again, *but this time describing the behavior of the spouse in relationship to the child.* Thus, each parent "informed" on the other, so to speak. It was then possible to compare a self-description with a description from the other parent, and thus to determine the agreement between self-ratings and ratings by spouse. Presumably, ratings by spouse would be more accurate, since the second party (informant) would be less motivated to "hide" an assumed undesirable trait. Therefore, the greater the correlation between the sets of ratings of a given parent, the greater the presumed validity of either one. It was thus possible to obtain an index of the accuracy of parental self-ratings, an extremely important methodological question. Should such descriptions turn out to be inaccurate, we would have questions about the Fels study, where some of the information was obtained from interviews with mothers.

The second comprehensive set of information about parental behavior was obtained from an hour and a half interview with each parent, following an interview schedule similar to that of the Sears study. All interviews were tape-recorded and subsequently rated on a series of scales reflecting various types of parent-child interactions. At least two investigators independently rated each scale, and those yielding a reliability correlation of less than .50 were abandoned.

Four comprehensive sets of information about each child were also collected. Using the same set of 73 rating scales as previously described, each parent and two different teachers rated each child, thus providing four independent sets of 73 ratings. With this information, several additional methodological questions could be answered; for example: Does a mother's description of her child's behavior correlate with her husband's description of the child's behavior? Do the parents' descriptions correlate with the teachers' descriptions? The answers to these questions allowed the investigators to determine the accuracy of reports from parents and teachers, and to remove sources of bias; that is, instead of using the parent as the source of information both about himself and about the child, it was possible to compare, say, the mother's description of her own behavior with the father's description of the child's behavior, or vice versa. A number of other combinations were possible: mother's self-description with teachers' descriptions of child behavior, father's de-

scription of mother's behavior with teachers' description of child behavior, etc. Each of these methods removes the bias or "confounding,"
which is produced by a parent's tendency to describe his child's behavior
in terms of his own behavior. The Becker studies were the first to
explore this question.

The results of the studies are much too complex to present in their
entirety. Two main kinds of results will be summarized—those pertaining to methodological questions and those pertaining to the main substantive findings.

Methodological Findings

There were four methodological findings of considerable importance.

1. As suspected, there is a measurable contamination factor when a
parent describes his own behavior and his child's behavior too. The
correlations between the parent-child descriptions when both sets of information are supplied by the parent are lowered if the child's behavior
is described by the other parent. A 33 per cent drop in number of significant correlations was found when the other parent served as the
source of information about the child.

2. At the same time, fathers' descriptions of their own behavior did
correlate with mothers' descriptions of fathers' behavior, and vice versa.
The correlation was .40 when the two sets of father descriptions were
correlated, and .46 when the two sets of mother descriptions were correlated. Thus, there was a significant correlation between what a parent
said of his own behavior and what his spouse said of his behavior. Self-
reports of parental behavior possess some validity.

3. It was possible to obtain an evaluation of the accuracy of parental
descriptions of their children's behavior by comparing them not only
with the descriptions obtained from the other parent but also with the
descriptions obtained from the teachers. The 73 ratings of child behavior were reduced to five different dimensions using factor analysis.
The average of these five correlations between fathers and mothers was
.52, indicating reasonably strong agreement between parents concerning
their child's behavior. The average mother-teacher correlation was only
.31, and the average father-teacher correlation, .28. Thus, parents did
not strongly agree with teachers concerning the behavior of their children. And yet this disagreement was not due to unreliable evaluations
by the teachers, since the average correlation between the two teachers'
descriptions was quite high: .76. Thus, the teachers agreed with each
other about the child's behavior, just as the parents agreed with each
other. The lack of high agreement between parents and teachers suggests at least two interpretations: (a) Perhaps parents are simply too

emotionally involved to do a very accurate job of describing their children. This would account for the lower correlations between the two parents than between the two teachers, as well as for the low correlations between parents and teachers; (b) Becker and his associates suggest that children might act quite differently at home and at school—that parents and teachers see different aspects of the child's behavior. The present author would agree with this possibility. There is probably some truth to both interpretations.

4. There was ample evidence that father-child relationships are of considerable importance and that omission of such information is likely to result in an unfinished picture. For example, there were more high correlations between the children's behavior and the fathers' behavior than between children's behavior and mothers' behavior. Of the father-child correlations, 22 per cent were statistically significant, while only 9 per cent of the mother-child correlations were significant. In a second study, a similar picture emerged, but with an interesting twist—father-daughter correlations were higher than mother-daughter correlations, and mother-son correlations were higher than father-son correlations. These differences were substantial and pervasive, and lead to the extremely interesting possibility that cross-sex parent-child relationships are more important than same-sex parent-child relationships. For the moment, however, this must be considered a possibility, not an established fact.

Substantive Findings

The main substantive findings of the Becker studies can be grouped into three natural parts: (a) parental behavior, (b) child behavior, and (c) correlations between parent-child behavior. Although (c) is of primary interest, a rudimentary understanding of (a) and (b) will be of considerable assistance.

Parental Behavior. The ratings of parental behavior obtained from the taped interviews were factor analyzed separately for fathers and mothers. Five factors (dimensions) appeared to be common for both parents. The name of each factor, the four ratings that correlated highest with it (thereby indicating its content), and their factor loadings are presented in Table 13.2. The first three factors are already familiar to the reader. The last two remind the reader that the three main dimensions previously discussed, i.e., the first three factors in Table 13.2, may achieve economy at the cost of too much inaccuracy. Factors 4 and 5 reflect parental behavior that is only imperfectly reflected in the first three factors.

Among the more interesting findings is the difference between factor

2 and factor 5—the difference between restrictiveness and punishment. The fact that the items defining these two factors are not correlated highly with each other means that a restrictive parent was not necessarily a punitive parent, or the two sets of items would have appeared under a single factor.

TABLE 13.2

Dimensions of Parental Behavior Common to Both Parents *
(Adapted from Becker, 1960)

	Factor Loading
Factor 1: *Warmth vs. hostility*	
1. Non-acceptance of child	.79
2. Non-readiness of explanation	.76
3. Not child centered	.73
4. Hostile relationship with child	.68
Factor 2: *Permissiveness vs. restrictiveness (on routines)*	
1. Pressure for conformity—neatness, orderliness	.72
2. Restrictiveness—care of house and furniture	.70
3. High standards—neatness and orderliness	.68
4. Strict in requiring obedience	.59
Factor 3: *Child-rearing anxiety vs. unsolicitousness*	
1. High child-rearing anxiety	−.75
2. Unsolicitousness for child's welfare	.71
3. Little disciplinary friction	.59
4. Maladjustment of mother	−.59
Factor 4: *Low vs. high sex anxiety*	
1. Permissiveness for sex play among children	−.73
2. High sex anxiety	.71
3. Permissiveness for masturbation	−.71
4. Non-protectiveness	−.52
Factor 5: *High vs. low physical punishment*	
1. Frequent use of spankings by mother	−.68
2. Regular use of physical punishment	−.67
3. Mild penalties	.57
4. Frequent use of spankings by father	−.51

* The factor loadings reflect the item correlations with the end of the factor as it is described; thus, non-acceptance of child correlates .79 with the *hostility* end of the factor.

It seems that a parent can be restrictive in two ways: by using severe punishment when the child disobeys (factor 5), or by presenting many demands to the child (factor 2).

It is also important to note that the five factors were not completely independent of each other. In general, factors 1, 3, and 5 were interrelated, as were 2 and 4. Thus, a *warm* parent (1+) tended to be unsolicitous and non-anxious about the child (3−), and also tended not to use physical punishment (5−). The reverse also holds, of course: a hostile parent tended to be anxious and physically punitive. The correlation between factors 2 and 4 means that a parent who was generally *permissive about routines* (2+) tended to be *permissive and calm about sex* (4+), and vice versa. Thus, the five dimensions in Table 13.2 can be further reduced to two "superdimensions," one composed of the items defining factors 1, 3, and 5, and the other composed of items defining factors 2 and 4. Becker and his associates actually carried out such a "second-order" factor analysis, as it is called when factors are factored, and named the former superdimension *warmth vs. hostility*, and the latter, *permissiveness vs. restrictiveness*.

A third interesting finding is that the behavior of fathers and mothers was not independent. In general, there were more similarities than one would expect on the basis of chance. For example, if the husband obtained a high hostility score (factor 1), mother did too, with $r = .37$. If father was rated low in use of physical punishment (factor 5), so was the mother, $r = .35$. If the husband was rated high on sex anxiety (factor 4), so was the mother, $r = .36$, etc. Becker *et al.* concluded: "All in all, these correlations suggest that like begets like or that over the years of a marriage there is a considerable convergence of parental attitudes and behaviors toward the children."

Child Behavior. Description of child behavior is every bit as complex as description of parental behavior. The problems of economy and accuracy remain unchanged. Surely not all the child's behavior can be described, and yet how much can it be "condensed" without losing important parts?

The Fels study employed theoretical assumptions and common sense here too. They measured those aspects of child behavior they *thought* were important for one reason or another. A more objective approach would proceed along the same lines as those used to determine the dimensions of parental behavior; that is, instead of assuming that a particular dimension exists, it is determined whether it exists or not via factor analysis. As applied to child behavior, the procedure would thus involve (1) selection of a large pool of items that are representative of child behavior, (2) description of a representative sample of children on these items, (3) computation of the correlations between items, (4) determination of clusters of interrelated items (i.e., factor analysis), and (5) description of the children on the basis of factor scores instead of in terms of item scores.

Becker carried out this procedure and then elaborated upon it. Recall that there were four sets of 73-item descriptions of each child—one from each parent and one from each of two teachers. Each set was independently factor analyzed. Five factors were discovered that were common to all four sets of information. These five factors, with the 4 items defining them with highest factor loadings, are presented in Table 13.3.

TABLE 13.3

Dimensions of Child Behavior
(Adapted from Becker, 1960)

Factor 1: *Cooperative, responsible vs. defiant, hostile*
1. Kind—cruel
2. Soft-hearted—hard-hearted
3. Easy-going—irritable
4. Not prone to anger—prone to anger

Factor 2: *Happy, optimistic vs. distrusting, depressed*
1. Happy—depressed
2. Loving—not loving
3. Trusting—distrusting
4. Optimistic—pessimistic

Factor 3: *Sociable, interesting vs. withdrawn, boring*
1. Sociable—unsociable
2. Intelligent—dull-minded
3. Quick—slow
4. Curious—uninquiring

Factor 4: *Dominant, tough vs. submissive, sensitive*
1. Active—inactive
2. Extraverted—introverted
3. Dominant—submissive
4. Tough—sensitive

Factor 5: *Emotional, rebellious vs. calm, compliant*
1. Demanding—not demanding
2. Jealous—not jealous
3. Impatient—patient
4. Inconsistent—consistent

These five factors are not completely independent, but are interrelated just as were the five factors of parental behavior. By use of another statistical technique known as *radex theory*, the factors were discovered to be capable of forming what is called a *circumplex model* of behavior. This means that the five dimensions are interrelated to each other in a way that can be described by a circle. If one considers the extremes of the five factors listed in Table 13.3, 10 different personalities result. These 10 extremes form a circumplex in that each of the 10 patterns is most highly correlated with the adjacent one, with the correlation becoming smaller with the next one, and reaching zero with the next, and then becoming negative in sign, until a maximum negative correlation is achieved when the other end of the same dimension is considered. Refer to Table 13.3: Children who were *cooperative and responsible* also tended to be *happy and optimistic,* and showed some tendency to be *sociable and interesting.* It was impossible to predict whether they would be *dominant vs. submissive,* since the correlation with this dimension was near zero. They tended to be the opposite of *emotional and rebellious* and were definitely the opposite of *defiant and hostile.*

All these relationships are neatly summarized by forming the 10 extremes into a circle, as is done in Figure 13.3. The angle between any

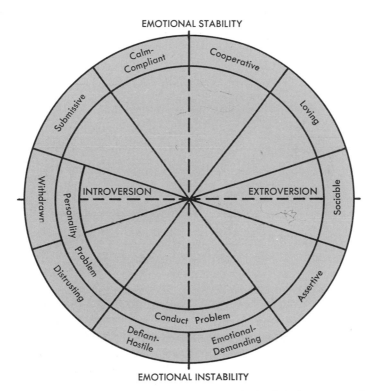

Figure 13.3. Becker's circumplex model of child behavior (Becker and Krug, 1964). Copyright © by The Society for Research in Child Development.

two patterns describes the correlation between them, according to the following rules: the smaller the angle from 90 degrees to 0, the higher the correlation; at 90 degrees, the correlation is zero. From 90 to 180 degrees, the correlation becomes larger and larger with a *negative* sign, reaching a maximum of approximately −1.00 at 180 degrees. The correlation then reduces to zero at 270 degrees, and increases once again to a maximum of +1.00 at 360 degrees (the starting point). For example, using the average of the two teachers' ratings of the children, factor 1 (*cooperative*) correlated .84 with *happy, optimistic;* .56 with *sociable, interesting;* −.14 with *dominant, tough;* and −.74 with *emotional, rebellious.* The advantage of such a model is that an empirically determined order is shown to exist between the various dimensions, and what is said about one pattern is immediately seen to apply, in varying degrees, to other, adjacent patterns as well.

It will be observed that *defiant, hostile,* and *emotional, rebellious* patterns are labeled "conduct problems," and *withdrawn, boring* and *distrusting, depressed* patterns are labeled "personality problems." These are standard labels in common use by clinical and child psychologists and should be understood by the student. Conduct problems consist of behavior patterns where the child's conduct gets him into conflict with others. Such behavior is thus aggressive and emotional. Personality problems refer to withdrawn behavior, which does not lead to conflict with others, but which is assumed to be indicative of inner turmoil. Thus, conduct problems suggest "outer" conflict, and personality problems, "inner" conflict. Some feel that personality problems are more serious, for they suggest the beginning of withdrawal from reality, a symptom of psychosis. There is little evidence to support such an assumption; both can be serious, depending upon their intensity and circumstances.

Notice also that Becker has suggested two more general dimensions that are superimposed on the five dimensions in Figure 13.3: emotional stability–instability and introversion-extraversion. Thus, the calm, compliant, cooperative sort of individual is emotionally stable, while the defiant, hostile, emotional and demanding person is not. Quite independent of stability, the withdrawn person is, of course, introverted, while the sociable person is extraverted.

Parent-Child Relationships. It was previously noted that an important methodological discovery of the Becker investigations is that a spurious correlation results when data about parent and child are both collected from the parent. Becker was able to eliminate this contamination by using a separate source for parent and child information. The present discussion considers only such "clean" correlations.

The most systematic and economical way of reporting the major findings rests upon the facts that (*a*) parental behavior could be reduced to two "superdimensions" of warmth-hostility and permissiveness-restrictiveness, and (*b*) child behavior was describable in terms of a five-factor circumplex model. With this frame of reference, one may summarize the major parent-child relationships by correlating (*a*) with (*b*). Table 13.4 presents these correlations, the top half referring to mother-daughter and father-daughter relationships, and the bottom half to mother-son and father-son relationships. Descriptions of parental behavior were obtained from the parents themselves, and descriptions of child behavior were obtained from the average rating of the two teachers. Since it was previously noted that parent-teacher correlations were quite low, these correlations are underestimates of the population values; i.e. the correlations in Table 13.4 are conservative estimates of what would be found if better measurements were employed with a new sample of families.

TABLE 13.4

Correlations Between Parental and Child Behavior
(Adapted from Becker *et al.*, 1962)

| | Child Behavior | | | | |
| | Conduct Problems | | Personality Problems | | |
	Cooperative, Responsible vs. Defiant, Hostile	Calm, Compliant vs. Emotional, Rebellious	Submissive, Sensitive vs. Dominant, Tough	Withdrawn, Boring vs. Sociable, Interesting	Distrustful, Depressed vs. Happy, Optimistic
Daughters—Mothers					
Warmth	.20	.22	.13	—.12	—.27
Permissiveness	.20	.12	—.10	—.12	—.27
Daughters—Fathers					
Warmth	.47	.32	—.23	—.30	—.53
Permissiveness	.30	.24	.14	—.02	—.21
Sons—Mothers					
Warmth	.42	.41	—.25	—.34	—.45
Permissiveness	—.09	.11	—.09	.01	—.04
Sons—Fathers					
Warmth	.45	.50	.13	—.22	—.30
Permissiveness	—.01	.18	.09	.04	.04

The major findings in Table 13.4 are: (1) Cross-sex parent-child correlations are higher than same-sex parent-child correlations (as previously noted); and (2) in general, warmth and permissiveness are predictive of non-problem behavior, while hostility and restrictiveness are predictive of conduct problems, personality problems, or both. Comments on each of these trends are in order.

The high cross-sex parent-child correlations attest to the importance of studying both parents, not just mothers. For example, if father information had not been collected, it would have been reasonable to conclude that behavior of daughters is only minimally predictable from parental behavior. Such a conclusion would follow from the low mother-daughter correlations, the highest being —.26. Considering the father-daughter relationships, over half the correlations are .26 or higher in absolute magnitude, indicating how false such a conclusion would have been.

Table 13.4 shows particularly strong correlations between parental warmth-hostility and child cooperativeness-defiance. It is clear that hos-

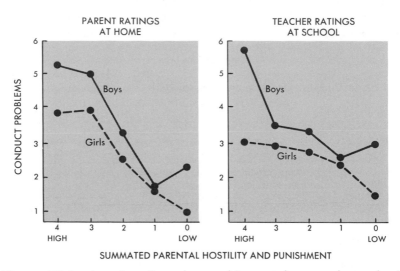

Figure 13.4. Intensity of conduct problems at home and at school as related to parental hostility and punishment (Becker *et al.*, 1962). Copyright © 1962 by The Society for Research in Child Development.

tile, rejecting parents tend to produce hostile, aggressive children, particularly for parents and children of opposite sex. Figure 13.4 describes this relationship more dramatically. Determination of parental scores on hostility and physical punishment are plotted against children's scores on the two factors defining conduct problems: defiant hostility and emotional rebelliousness. The left-hand curves present conduct-problem scores as determined from parental descriptions of their children's behavior at home, while the right-hand curves describe children's behavior at school. These curves clearly show the additive effects of parental hostility and physical punishment; conduct problems regularly diminish as parental scores change from high to low on these dimensions. The relationship tends to be higher for child behavior at home than for behavior at school, suggesting at least two plausible interpretations: (1) Parental hostility and punishment are frustrative, and conduct problems reflect temporary reactions to this frustration. Such behavior does not completely carry over to the school situation because there are fewer such frustrations at school. (2) Having learned to react to the parents with defiance and hostility, the children generalize these responses to the school because of the similarity between home and school (i.e., adult authority figures, etc.). The data are not complete enough to suggest a choice between these two (as well as other) alternatives.

Becker and his associates emphasize that conduct problems did not consist only of defiant hostility and emotional rebelliousness, but had a negative attention-seeking component as well (recall from Table 13.3 that two specific ratings defining emotional rebelliousness were high scores on ratings of "demanding" and "jealous"; high scores on "exhibitionistic" and "attention-seeking" also served to define this end of the factor). Other investigators have also noted this somewhat paradoxical mixture—a positive correlation between hostility and defiance on the one hand, and attention-seeking on the other, as if the child were thinking, "I hate you. . . . I need you." Becker et al. suspect that parents of such children instill a dependency conflict in their children, and in this vein they quote Bandura and Walters:

> While it was assumed that the parents of the aggressive boys had created anxiety by their handling of their sons' dependency, it was not assumed that they had necessarily eradicated the boys' motivation to behave in a dependent manner. They had succeeded, it was presumed, merely in reducing the overt expression of dependency through the conflict that their rejection and punishment of dependency had created. One form of behavior that clearly typifies a dependency-conflict is negative attention-getting. If a child is fearful of dependency on others, he is apt to avoid direct positive requests for attention and to resort instead to disruptive activity as a way of drawing attention to himself. [1959, p. 43.]

Stating it another way, children who are rejected and punished for dependency responses learn a negative approach to save themselves the intolerable anxiety that may come from self-recognition of parental (or adult) rejection. That is to say, instead of recognizing the situation as one describable as, "I need you . . . you don't need me," the negativistic child is able to think, "I don't need you and I know you don't need me." Surely the latter awareness is an easier one to live with.

Personality problems, consisting primarily of withdrawal, are also seen to be produced by parental rejection and restriction. Precisely the same finding appeared in the Fels data. Recall the case history presented in the previous chapter (pp. 385–387). That girl, a representative product of a hostile, restricting mother, was described as *inhibited, lethargic, socially inhibited, dull, solemn, slow moving, dumbly patient, afraid, distrustful, listless.* Compare these adjectives with the items defining personality problems in the Becker studies: *withdrawn, boring, distrustful, depressed* (see Table 13.3), as well as *unsociable, dull-*

minded, slow, uninquiring, fearful, not loving, pessimistic. Clearly, the two sets of descriptions are almost identical, and thus place the Fels girl squarely in the middle of Becker's personality-problem domain. In both studies, rejection and restriction are seen to be the correlated parental behaviors.

It is important to note that two kinds of dependency have appeared in both the Fels and Becker studies. In the Becker studies, it appears both as an emotional, negative, attention-seeking kind of pattern (conduct problem) and as a submissive, withdrawn, distrustful kind of pattern (personality problem). In the Fels study, the passivity-dependency ratings describe the latter, withdrawn, pattern (as illustrated in the case history on pp. 385–387), while the former pattern is suggested by some correlations we noted but did not discuss in detail; on page 251, Table 8.9, it will be seen that aggression correlated .45 with recognition strivings in boys, and .49 in girls. Thus, aggressive children also tended to be dependent. They actively—*aggressively*—sought adult recognition, and thus appear to be similar to, but not as extreme as, Becker's classification of conduct problems. It is tempting to label these two classifications "passive" and "negative-demanding" dependency, and to note their appearance in both studies. It would seem that parental *hostility* is the main determinant of negative-demanding dependency (Becker), and that the addition of parental *restrictiveness* pushes the child toward passive dependency (Fels study).

SUMMARY

We shall summarize this chapter by comparing the results of the different studies. In the summary of the last chapter, we compared the results of experimental studies with the results of the Fels study. We shall now add the results of the Becker studies to the list and see what we have. The main interest, of course, is in findings with *generality,* since these are the ones in which we may have the most confidence. This final summing up will therefore consider results that have appeared in at least two studies; isolated, unreplicated findings will be ignored.

Dependency. The experimental studies of dependency led to three conclusions. The first was that attention-seeking behavior is strengthened by adult reinforcement for such behavior. The Fels finding that dependency is associated with maternal protection strongly supports this conclusion, since protectiveness involves frequent reinforcement for requests of aid. We thus have a confirmation of the experimental finding in the Fels family study.

Some observations common to both the Fels and Becker studies were not investigated experimentally. Both studies found evidence suggesting two kinds of dependency: passive dependency, marked by submission and withdrawal, and a negative-demanding dependency, marked by emotional, aggressive outbursts that attract attention. Becker found that passive dependency (*personality problems* included such behavior) was associated with hostile, restrictive parents, while negative-demanding dependency was associated more exclusively with hostility. The Fels findings are highly similar. Passive dependency, as exemplified in the case history presented in the previous chapter, was strongly associated with maternal hostility and restriction (both of which were measured under the restriction dimension; see p. 381), while aggressive recognition strivings were associated more directly with maternal hostility.

These findings can be summarized in equation-like form as follows. They are grouped together according to their content, which is presented verbally.

Finding 1: *Dependency behavior is strengthened by reinforcing such behavior.*

　　a) Attention seeking $= +f$ (reinforcement for attention seeking).
　　　　　　　　(experimental studies)
　　b) Dependency $= +f$ (maternal protection).
　　　　　　　　(Fels study)

Finding 2: *Submissive, withdrawn dependency is associated with rejecting, restrictive parents.*

　　a) Passive dependency $= +f$ (hostility, rejection).
　　　　　　　　(Becker studies)
　　Passive dependency $= +f$ (hostility, rejection).
　　　　　　　　(Fels study)

Finding 3: *Aggressive emotional dependency is associated with rejecting parents.*

　　a) Aggressive emotional dependency $= +f$ (hostility).
　　　　　　　　(Becker studies)
　　Aggressive emotional dependency $= +f$ (hostility).
　　　　　　　　(Fels study)

Aggression. There were two main experimental conclusions about aggression: (1) any response to frustration, be it aggressive or cooperative, will be strengthened if it is reinforced; and (2) punishment for aggression in a given situation reduces aggression in that situation but increases it in other, different situations.

The first conclusion has little verification from the family studies, simply because it was not investigated. The second experimental conclusion has two parts. The first is that aggression in a given situation will be reduced by punishment in that situation. The Fels and Becker studies found just the opposite: aggression at home was *positively* correlated with punishment for aggression. Becker found that conduct problems at home (consisting of emotional, defiant responses) were positively correlated with parental hostility and punishment. The Fels study found that aggression to mother was positively correlated with maternal hostility. Thus, the two family studies agree with each other in suggesting that hostility and punishment (including punishment for aggression) at home increase aggressive, defiant behavior at home. They disagree with the experimental findings, which suggest the opposite. As previously noted, perhaps the cause-effect direction is reversed in the two family studies; perhaps parental hostility is a *reaction* to aggressiveness, rather than the reverse.

The second part of the second experimental conclusion, that aggression away from the punished situation will be increased, is amply supported by the family studies. Both the Becker and Fels studies found that aggressive responses away from home (at school in the Becker studies, directed toward peers in the Fels study) were positively correlated with hostility and punishment at home.

Finding 1: *While experimental studies suggested that aggression in a given situation is negatively related to punishment for aggression in that same situation, family studies indicated that punishment for aggression at home was positively related to aggression at home.*

   a) Aggression in situation X $= -f$ (punishment for aggression in situation X).

(experimental studies)

   b) Conduct problems at home $= +f$ (hostility and punishment at home).

(Becker studies)

   c) Aggression to mother $= +f$ (hostility of mother).

(Fels study)

Finding 2: *Parental hostility and punishment are positively related to aggressive responses in other situations.*

   a) Aggression away from situation X $= +f$ (punishment for aggression in situation X).

(experimental studies)

   b) Conduct problems at school $= +f$ (hostility and punishment at home).

(Becker studies)

   c) Aggression to peers $= +f$ (hostility and punishment at home).

(Fels study)

Finding 3: *Frustration often leads to aggression.*

  a) Aggression $= +f$ (frustration).
                    (many experimental studies)
  b) Aggression to peers $= +f$ (restrictions at home).
                    (Fels study)
  c) Conduct problems $= +f$ (restrictions at home).
                    (Becker studies)

Achievement behavior. Experimental research led to one general conclusion about the determinants of achievement strivings: a child presented with adult models of achievement orientation, and socially reinforced for similar behavior, is likely to develop strong achievement strivings. Three more specific experimental findings led to this conclusion: (1) standards of excellence were positively correlated with standards of an adult model, (2) achievement strivings were strengthened by social approval, and (3) achievement strivings were strengthened by adult silence if it had been preceded by disapproval.

The Fels study is the only family study that specifically measured such adult behavior. It indicated that maternal acceleration was highly predictive of achievement strivings in both sexes. Since acceleration involved both modeling and reinforcement components, the experimental conclusions are supported by these data.

A second conclusion is suggested by the Becker and Fels data, even though it was not investigated experimentally. It will be recalled from the Fels study that maternal hostility was negatively correlated with achievement strivings. Thus, warmth was *positively* correlated with achievement behavior. In the Becker studies, achievement behavior is somewhat reflected in *sociable, interesting* behavior. It was indicated (p. 424) that three of the four items most clearly defining such behavior were *intelligent, quick,* and *curious*—traits that would appear to be more predictive of achieving than of non-achieving behavior. Thus, positive correlations between scores of *sociable, interesting* and *parental warmth* would support the Fels results (or negative correlations between warmth and the other end of the child-behavior dimension: *withdrawn, boring*). Table 13.4 indicates that the Fels findings are indeed supported; for both mothers and fathers, sons and daughters, the correlations between *withdrawn, boring* and *parental warmth* are negative. It may thus be concluded that considerable evidence exists suggesting that parental warmth is conducive to achievement strivings.

Finding 1: *Parents who themselves strive to achieve, and who reinforce such behavior in their children, are likely to have achieving children.*

a) Performance standards $= +f$ (standards of model).

b) Achievement behavior $= +f$ (reinforcement by others).

c) Achievement behavior $= +f$ (cessation of disapproval for non-achieving behavior).

(experimental findings)

d) Achievement behavior $= +f$ (maternal acceleration).

(Fels study)

Finding 2: *Warm, loving parents are more likely to raise achievement-oriented children than cold, rejecting parents.*

a) Achievement behavior $= +f$ (warmth).

(Becker studies)

b) Achievement behavior $= -f$ (hostility) $= +f$ (warmth).

(Fels study)

Social interaction anxiety. The Fels study found that social interaction anxiety, as measured by a lack of social spontaneity, was predictable in early childhood from maternal hostility (see Table 12.12). The Becker studies confirm this relationship; as pointed out on page 426, children scoring high on personality problems included those with social interaction anxiety. Personality problems were predictable from hostile parents, thereby confirming the Fels finding.

a) Personality problems $= +f$ (hostility).

(Becker studies)

b) Social interaction anxiety $= +f$ (maternal hostility).

(Fels study)

It should be clear by now that personality development is not a mysterious unfolding of traits that inevitably pursue their course to the final product, but is strongly dependent upon the child's *experiences.* Furthermore, these experiences are not a helter-skelter combination of all possible occurrences, but form meaningful patterns that are understandable, by and large, in terms of the principles of learning. The last three chapters have shown what an important role the parents play in such learning during early and middle childhood. If the reader has only become aware of this factor, he has not read in vain.

BIBLIOGRAPHY

BALDWIN, A. L., KALHORN, J., and BREESE, FAY H. (1945). Patterns of parent behavior. *Psychological monographs,* 58, (3).

BALDWIN, A. L., KALHORN, J., and BREESE, FAY H. (1949). The appraisal of parent behavior. *Psychological monographs,* 63, (4).

BANDURA, A., and WALTERS, R. H. (1959). *Adolescent Aggression—a study of the influence of child-training practices and family interrelationships.* New York: The Ronald Press Co.
BECKER, W. C. (1960). The relationship of factors in parental ratings of self and each other to the behavior of kindergarten children as rated by mothers, fathers, and teachers. *Journal of consulting psychology,* 24, 507–527.
BECKER, W. C. (1964). Consequences of different kinds of parental discipline. In M. L. HOFFMAN and LOIS W. HOFFMAN (Eds.), *Review of child development and research.* New York: Russell Sage Foundation. Pp. 169–208.
BECKER, W. C., and KRUG, R. S. (1964). A circumplex model for social behavior in children. *Child development,* 35, 371–396.
BECKER, W. C., PETERSON, D. R., LURIA, ZELLA, SHOEMAKER, D. J., and HELLMER, L. A. (1962). Relations of factors derived from parent-interview ratings to behavior problems of five-year-olds. *Child development,* 33, 509–535.
LEVY, D. M. (1943). *Maternal overprotection.* New York: Columbia University Press.
MILTON, G. A. (1958). A factor analytic study of child-rearing behaviors. *Child development,* 29, 381–392.
ROFF, M. (1949). A factorial study of the Fels Parent Behavior Scales. *Child development,* 20, 29–45.
SCHAEFFER, E. S., and BELL, R. Q. (1958). Development of a parental attitude research instrument. *Child development,* 29, 339–361.
SEARS, R. R., MACCOBY, ELEANOR E., and LEVIN, H. (1957). *Patterns of child rearing.* New York: Harper & Row.

IV

INFLUENCE OF THE COMMUNITY

14

The School

INTRODUCTION

What do children learn at school? Before you answer too readily with "The three R's, of course," consider a question raised by Mill (1960). He asks how most of us were taught to go to church. He says that, during childhood, we were *made* to go to church every Sunday, like it or not; we dressed up, took a nickel for the collection, and sat with Mommy and Daddy while the minister showed us the path. Mill asks, "But did we really learn to go to church?" "No," he says, "in fact, many of us learned just the opposite. We went to church while we were children because we were forced to, but as soon as we became old enough to have some control over our own behavior we stopped going to church. For many of us it was not until much later when we had rethought through the whole matter that we determined for ourselves whether or not we would be regular church goers."

The moral of this story is that adults do not always know what they are teaching their children, and that sometimes just the opposite is taught of that intended. While we think the three R's are learned at school, in *fact* much else is learned besides. The purpose of this chapter is to examine the nature of this learning in some detail. As a matter of fact, we are not interested in the learning of academic subject matter per se; that is the province of educational psychology. Our subject matter is school learning that affects personality. We ask, then, what is the school's role in psychological development?

Next to parents, the school undoubtedly constitutes the most influential determinant of psychological development. From grades 1 through 12, the child attends school 5 hours a day, 5 days a week, 36 weeks a grade—a grand total of 10,800 hours. It is the equivalent of 1,350 8-hour days—5 years' worth of 40-hour weeks, with no vacations. It is instructive to divide this enormous investment of time and energy into the activities that occupy it. Three major types of activities seem to be involved: interactions with teachers, interactions with peers, and independent studying. The third activity is concerned with academic learning and thus does not concern us. The second activity and its result —peer influences—are discussed in the next chapter. We are left, then, with teacher-pupil interactions being the main concern of this chapter. We shall ask two primary questions: How does the child's background and personality affect his adjustment to teachers? How do the teachers' behaviors affect his adjustment?

SCHOOL BOARDS, SCHOOLTEACHERS, AND SCHOOLBOOKS

An examination of the main ingredients of a school system—the school board, the teachers, and the books—can serve as a useful starting point. By determining the characteristics of these components of the school "machinery," we will acquire some understanding of the demands made by the school on its pupils.

School Boards

What members of society become school board members? They usually come from the upper socioeconomic levels. Hollingshead, in his classic study of a midwestern town of 6,000 anonymously named "Elmtown," wrote as follows:

Theoretically, any adult citizen in the district may be a candidate for the school board, and, if he receives enough votes, elected. In practice, the members of the Board of Education come mainly from the two upper classes and have to qualify under informal ground rules. Even to be considered for the Board a person has to be male, Protestant, Republican, a property owner, preferably a Rotarian, or at least approved by the Rotarians. (Rotarians are proud of the way they have controlled the selection of the Board for more than twenty-five years.)

When a vacancy is to occur, the selection of a man for the Board of Education is left to the President of the Board. He discusses possible candidates with his friends on the Board and in the Rotary Club. Generally he invites a fellow Rotarian with whom he believes he can work to become a candidate. The President then files this man's name with the election clerk; nothing is said publicly about the impending vacancy or the forthcoming election until after the last date for filing has passed. Then the Bugle runs a news item stating that the date for filing names for the school election has passed, that such-and-such men have filed as candidates for the Board of Education, and that Mr. X has filed again for President of the Board. Little additional publicity is given to the election until The Bugle carries the necessary legal notices of the polling places and names of candidates. On election day, only a hand-

Much more than the three R's are learned at school. This teacher seems to be teaching her pupils that *school is a pleasant experience.*

ful of voters go to the polls to elect the hand-picked candidates. In 1940, 132 votes were cast; in 1941, 114; and in 1942, 84. This carefully controlled system for the selection of Board members has resulted in the election of conservative men who have represented through the years the political, economic, social, and educational interests of classes I and II rather than the other four-fifths to seven-eighths of the population. [1961, pp. 123–124.]

Data from more recent times, and from a more cosmopolitan environment, is provided by Dejnozka (1963). He sampled school boards in the entire state of New York, obtaining information from all counties except those in New York City: 57 of the 62 counties. The occupations of the 380 board members are presented in Table 14.1. Two out of every four members are from the top of the socioeconomic hierarchy, with about the same number (56 per cent) having at least a college degree (24 per cent have a postgraduate degree). It is clear that these board members do not comprise a representative sampling of the total socioeconomic range, but heavily overrepresent the upper classes.

TABLE 14.1

Socioeconomic Status of School Board Members in the State of New York
(Adapted from Dejnozka, 1963)

Occupation	Per Cent
Professional: doctors, lawyers, pharmacists, etc.	53
Clerical and sales: salesmen, retail clerks, etc.	14
Agriculture, fishing, forestry: farmers, etc.	5
Skilled, semiskilled, unskilled: foremen, pressmen, mechanics, factory workers, etc.	8
Housewives, retired people	9
No response (unknown)	9

Education	Per Cent
Eight years	4
Twelve years	16
College	22
College graduate	21
Postgraduate	11
Postgraduate degree	24

The picture is the same everywhere. It means that a large segment of the population—from the middle class on down—has very little to say about how the schools should be run. Perhaps, of course, this is as it should be—one would hardly want an uneducated person running an educational institution. Still, there is the danger that lack of representation from certain social strata will result in a school system that does not adequately take the special needs of those strata into account. Many authorities, as we shall see, feel that just such a situation exists.

Schoolteachers

With regard to schoolteachers, most studies show a shift downward from the social status of school board members, most teachers having middle-class backgrounds rather than upper-class backgrounds (e.g., Groff, 1962; McGuire and White, 1957). Groff's results are illustrative. He determined the socioeconomic level of parents of 409 student teachers at San Diego State College: every fifth student over a 10-year period. Table 14.2 indicates that more than three out of four came from a middle-class background; their fathers were farmers, skilled laborers, salesmen, public servants (policemen, mail clerks, etc.), small business managers, etc. Only 24 per cent had a college degree, and less than 10 per cent had a postgraduate degree.

TABLE 14.2

Socioeconomic Status of Fathers of 409 Student Teachers at San Diego State College

(Adapted from Groff, 1962)

Socioeconomic Status	Per Cent
(Highest) 1	1
2	11
3	22
4	30
5	26
6	6
(Lowest) 7	4

There is evidence that the picture is gradually changing, with more teachers coming from the upper-lower class—families where the father is a "blue-collar" worker (Campbell, 1967). A recent nationwide survey by Mason (1967) indicates that 36 per cent of the fathers of beginning teachers are blue-collar workers, and an additional 18 per cent are in farming. The pattern depends upon sex to some extent too. While fathers of male teachers are predominantly of the blue-collar variety, fathers of female teachers are predominantly white-collar workers. Of course, most schoolteachers are female: about 88 per cent at the elementary level, and 50 per cent at the high school level (here too the picture is changing, with male teachers increasing in proportion to females—see Table 14.3).

TABLE 14.3

Teacher Trends

(Adapted from Campbell, 1967)

Year	Percentage of Male Teachers	Average Salary	Average Salary, Highest State	Average Salary, Lowest State
1956–1957	26	$4,239	$5,550 (New York)	$2,380 (Arkansas)
1961–1962	30	5,515	6,691 (California)	3,545 (Mississippi)
1966–1967	32	6,821	8,450 (California)	4,650 (Mississippi)

Not only is there a sex difference in the socioeconomic backgrounds of teachers, there is also a big city–small town difference. Campbell reports that more and more of the teachers in big cities come from families where the father is a member of the blue-collar class, whereas in small towns more teachers come from the white-collar class. Campbell feels that, as urbanization continues, it is probable that a greater and greater percentage of teachers will come from the upper lower-class families. Since Negroes comprise a disproportionate share of this class, relatively more Negroes will probably become teachers.

How are teachers perceived by society? Interestingly enough, most people accord them quite high status—just below the professionals, thereby placing them in the lower upper class (Groff, 1962). Thus, teachers are "upwardly mobile"; their own status is higher than that of their parents. Of course, not everyone feels that way. The upper upper class tends to look down on teaching, and few children of upper upper-class families become teachers (see Table 14.2).

Schoolbooks

What do textbooks represent in terms of societal values? Even a math problem can have connotations far beyond its numerical message: "John put $50 into a savings account for one year, at an interest rate of 6 per cent. How much profit did he have at the end of the year?" or "A hand grenade kills an average of 6 per cent of all its victims. If the Communists injure 50 people by throwing a hand grenade into a theatre, how many of them will die?" The mathematics is the same in both problems, but hardly the contexts in which it is embedded.

Is it possible to somehow categorize school textbooks in terms of such "hidden messages," and if so, what is the result? Certain characteristics seem quite evident. For example, in most children's reading books, fathers are Caucasian, well dressed (usually white shirt and tie, even at home in the evenings, at picnics, etc.), perfect linguists, and completely informed—they never say, "I don't know." Mothers are always young and attractive, always wearing a dress or skirt (never slacks), often with a pretty little frilly apron. Children are dressed just as unrealistically, with grade-school boys often wearing white shirts and ties and girls usually wearing brightly colored dresses and white socks, as though they were attending a perpetual birthday party. The houses, too, fit a pattern. They are invariably well painted, with large picture windows presenting a view of the spacious lawn (immaculately clad in a rich green carpet), and a large, climbable tree casting a pleasant shadow over the omnipresent swing set.

Themes are a little harder to classify, but several investigators have made an attempt (see Cronbach, 1963, for a review of these studies). They report the following frequent themes: The central, successful figure in the usual story is so often a *leader* it must become absolutely abhorrent after a few dozen stories. ". . . poor boy to president, laborer to magnate . . . is told over and over. No songs are sung of the office worker or the man who plants 100 acres of soy beans. Where could Mary have read a glamorous, teacher-approved account of the secretary-typist, the vocation her talents suited?" (Cronbach, 1963, pp. 432–433.) Second, life is often extremely *unrealistic*, as previously noted with respect to pictures; life is too pretty, too clean, too orderly—too sugar-coated—to be representative of the lives of many readers. Children, for example, are always rewarded in the end for obedience. They are always *learning* something or *achieving* something, never just "living" for the sheer existential enjoyment of it all. Males are usually described as productive, aggressive, and as "having the answers," while females are portrayed as passive, domestic, and unambitious—and kind.

No wonder children prefer library books and comic books to school-books. They are exciting and non-moralistic (except that the hero always wins), with realistic language—"A-ha! Gotcha this time! Take that (bop) and that (pow)"—physical aggression (the hero is just as aggressive as the villain), and an absence of parents, school, church, and "Mary-Janes," "Johnnies," and "Mr. Jones." Moreover, the vocabulary level is often high—even higher than the child's schoolbooks (Thorndike, 1941), and the child is encouraged to learn new words by the interesting pictorial contexts that accompany every few words.

All in all, then, schoolbooks seem to be quite pollyannish. They seem to inordinantly moralize about the values their authors hold, which are the same as those of the teachers and many members of the school board —the good old upper middle-class values.

One Common Element

It seems clear that school boards, schoolteachers, and schoolbooks are often pulling in the direction of upper middle-class values. We should not overgeneralize this tendency, however; some urban schools in working-class neighborhoods are beginning to use different textbooks that are especially written to take advantage of the backgrounds of the pupils. Nevertheless, any school that has a majority of pupils from middle-class backgrounds is likely to use the more traditional textbooks, with all their middle-class hidden messages. This would seem to be a fortunate state of affairs for middle-class children; they find compatibility between their homelife and their school life. But for children with different values—working-class children—one might expect some adjustment problems. Exposed to contradictory values at home and at school, such as sexual aggression versus sexual inhibition, physical aggression versus verbal aggression, immediate gratification versus delayed gratification, earthy speech versus polite speech, and a *work* orientation versus an *education* orientation, a state of chronic conflict would not be unexpected. Conflict, of course, involves "frustration from within," with accompanying tension, emotionality, and uneasiness. These feelings are aversive, and thus the child is motivationally primed to learn responses to reduce the conflict, such as avoiding school entirely.

ADJUSTMENT TO SCHOOL

Socioeconomic Status

There is abundant evidence supporting the prediction that working-class children might have adjustment difficulties at school. A crude but convincing index of school adjustment is whether the pupil drops out or not prior to obtaining a high school diploma. A breakdown of dropout rates by socioeconomic level shows that the vast majority of dropouts come from the lower classes. Table 14.4, for example, presents the results for "Elmtown," a midwestern community of 6,000 studied intensively by Hollingshead (1961). Eighty-nine per cent of the lowest-class children were not in school.

TABLE 14.4

Dropout Rates in Elmtown According to Socioeconomic Status
(Adapted from Hollingshead, 1961)

Socioeconomic Status	Dropouts	
	Number	Per Cent
I	0	0
II	0	0
III	12	8
IV	129	41
V	204	89

More recent and comprehensive data present a similar picture. For example, in the three high schools within the predominantly Negro area of Los Angeles, the dropout rate was 66 per cent in 1965 (Crump, 1966). In the deep South, characterized by a rural, low-income population, the dropout rate is about 45 per cent, while in the more affluent Midwest and Far West the rate is lower: 17 to 25 per cent (Miller, 1963; Putnam, 1963). With a national average of about 30 per cent, one can see that by any standards school is too bitter a pill to swallow for a large group of youngsters.

The Causative Chain from Socioeconomic Level to Adjustment Problems

Certainly, it is not socioeconomic level per se that produces adjustment difficulties in school, but rather correlated factors that affect the child more directly. We must therefore look beyond socioeconomic level if we are to understand such difficulties. The causative chain would go from socioeconomic level to correlated *parental treatment* of the child at home, which in turn would affect both *intellectual and personality factors*. These, in turn, would affect *teacher reactions* to the child, and on the basis of such treatment, the ultimate result would be obtained: *degrees of school adjustment.*

Figure 14.1 summarizes this complicated causal chain. The dashed arrows indicate the likelihood of "skips" in the hypothesized sequence. The left arrow indicates that socioeconomic level may affect a child's treatment by teachers quite independent of anything else; there may be latent biases that are put into motion by mere knowledge of the child's background alone. The right dashed arrows indicate that school adjust-

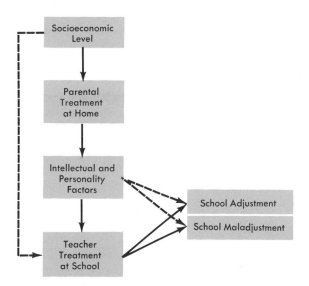

Figure 14.1. The hypothesized causative chain from socioeconomic level to school adjustment behavior.

ment is not solely due to the treatment by teachers either; some children may have intellectual and personality characteristics that doom them to adjustment difficulties regardless of teacher behavior.

With this theoretical overview, let us proceed from socioeconomic status to the other links in the chain.

Home Conditions. Not all working-class children encounter serious adjustment problems at school, nor are all children who do encounter such problems from the working class. Havighurst, in his study of "River City," describes some of the exceptions:

Because of the close relationships between progress in school and social class and intellectual ability, it is interesting to look at the exceptions. For instance, there were two students of high social status who dropped out of high school, one boy and one girl. Both of these students came from families broken by divorce, both had below-average ability, both did below-average work in school, and both had problems of social and personal adjustment. The girl married while still in school and finally dropped out of school to be with her husband who was in service. She intends to finish high school when her husband returns to his college education. The boy disliked school and dropped out to go to work.

There were also two students of the lowest social status, Class D, who went to college, both boys. Both boys come from broken homes. One boy has better than average ability, did good work in high school, won a small scholarship to college, and is doing better than average work in college. The other boy is of the lowest quartile in IQ, did poor work in high school but stayed on because of his interest and skill in athletics. He won an athletic scholarship to college but failed in his freshman year because of poor academic work. Both boys have superior personal and social adjustment and have been quite successful in their summer and part-time employment.

There are more exceptions to the rule that high intellectual ability goes with high-school graduation. The seven students in the top quartile of intellectual ability who dropped out of high school were varied in their school records and personal and social adjustment scores. However, they had one thing in common—they all came from homes which deemphasized education. Only one parent out of 14 of this group had finished high school. [1962, p. 52.]

As Havighurst implies, the home situation is more directly responsible for degree of adjustment to school than socioeconomic level. What are the relevant home conditions? As Havighurst found, the interest or "push" of the parents toward academic achievement is very important. In the Fels study, it was called "maternal acceleration," and it was reliably correlated with achievement strivings in the children. To review those correlations briefly, when the children were six to ten years old, the correlations between achievement strivings and maternal acceleration were .59 for boys and .43 for girls. At early adolescence (ten to fourteen), the correlations were .57 and .49. Even as young adults, intellectual achievement strivings correlated with maternal acceleration at ages six to ten; $r = .32$ for men and .43 for women. There can be little doubt that *cohesion* between home and school, where both are pushing the child in the same direction, has strong beneficial effects.

The Fels and Becker studies also indicated that parental rejection and restriction are likely to lead to school adjustment difficulties; the Fels study found that such maternal practices were associated with aggression to peers, both direct and indirect. Friction with peers within the school environment would hardly be conducive to school adjustment. Rejection was also predictive of low achievement strivings and expectations of failure, both of which would contribute to adjustment problems, most directly in the academic arena. The Becker studies likewise found a direct relationship between parental rejection and school conduct problems (see Figure 13.4 on p. 428).

These findings were generally confirmed in a study carried out by the Youth Studies Center of the University of Southern California (Longstreth and Rice, 1964). Three groups of high school boys were identified: aggressive boys (AGG: nominated by the Dean of Boys as troublemakers), underachieving boys (UA: non-aggressive boys whose grades were below that expected on the basis of IQ), and a comparison group of "well-adjusted" boys (WA: grade average better than C; at least two sociometric nominations as "liked best of all"; not more than two nominations as "not liked"; and above-average scores on teacher ratings of responsibility, ambition, and emotional maturity). The three groups (about 100 in each) were equated on IQ and socioeconomic status.

It may be noted, first of all, that the three groups differed widely. Table 14.5 gives their mean scores on four variables that may be considered indexes of adjustment to school: grades, teacher ratings, per cent dropped out of school, and per cent with police records. On all four indexes, WA presents a significantly more positive picture than AGG or UA.

TABLE 14.5

Four Indexes of Adjustment for Three Groups of High School Boys
(Adapted from Longstreth *et al.*, 1964)

	AGG	UA	WA
Grades *	3.4	3.6	2.1
Teacher ratings †	4.8	4.2	2.0
Per cent dropouts	75	24	13
Per cent with police records	50	26	4

* A = 1, C = 3, F = 5.

† Responsibility, ambition, and emotional maturity combined: high, positive rating = 1, average rating = 4, low rating = 7 (a boy had to average between 1 and 4 in order to qualify for WA).

Information about the parents was obtained from the boys them-selves. They were asked to complete a 20-page document, each page of which showed a teen-age boy interacting with either his father or mother (10 pictures for each parent). At the bottom of each picture were four alternatives describing what the parent might say in that particular situation. The respondent was to pick the alternative most similar to what his real parent would say. The four alternatives had been con-structed to represent the four extreme combinations of the two parental dimensions under study: high love and high restriction (HL, HR), high love and low restriction (HL, LR), low love and high restriction (LL, HR), and low love, low restriction (LL, LR). Figures 14.2 and 14.3 present two of these pictures, along with the alternatives in each (in the actual tests, of course, the alternatives were not labeled).

The main result was that well-adjusted boys described both their mothers and fathers as more loving and more restricting than either AGG or UA boys. Aggressive boys described their parents as slightly (non-significantly) less loving and less restrictive than UA boys. The difference in "love" descriptions appeared on all 20 pictures, and thus was independent of the particular situation described in a given picture. Well-adjusted boys, in other words, described their parents as more af-fectionate in all situations. Differences in restrictiveness, on the other hand, were confined to four pictures (two with father, two with mother) depicting situations in which the son requested permission to leave the house in the evening—"request for freedom" pictures. On all these pic-tures, WA boys described their parents as more likely to attach con-tingencies to giving permission (e.g., "You must be home by ten o'clock") than AGG or UA boys.

The differences in restrictiveness are easy enough to interpret. They suggest that parents of AGG and UA boys were somewhat uninterested in what their sons were doing as long as they, the parents, were not bothered. Going out in the evening, in fact, probably created less bother for the parents than if the boys stayed home. Thus, with little demand to stay home and study, these boys were under little pressure to perform at more than a minimal level. Havighurst reports a similar finding in "River City": 34 per cent of the school dropouts said their parents were indifferent to whether they dropped out or not, while only 7 per cent of the non-dropouts described their parents as indifferent. Havighurst also found that 26 per cent of the dropouts owned cars, as compared to 11 per cent of the non-dropouts.

It should be noted that these findings do not contradict the Fels and Becker results, where restriction apparently worked in the opposite direction, being positively correlated with adjustment difficulties. Re-strictiveness in these studies was more extreme, and correlated with

MOTHER SAYS:

(HL, HC) 1. I want you to tell the policeman just what happened. We'll do everything we can to help you.

(LL, LC) 2. What are you going to tell the policeman? I hope you get what you deserve.

(LL, HC) 3. I want you to tell the policeman just what happened. I hope you get what you deserve.

(HL, LC) 4. What are you going to tell the policeman? We'll do everything we can to help you.

Figure 14.2. Sample item from Perception of Parental Love and Control test (Longstreth and Rice, 1964).

parental rejection, suggesting parental neglect. In the study made by the Youth Studies Center, restrictiveness was indicative of responsible child rearing and occurred in a context of concern rather than of neglect (e.g., "You must be home by ten o'clock").

The differences in love are more difficult to interpret. In discussing

FATHER SAYS:
(LL, HC)   1. It's about time. Making you study evenings has paid off.
(LL, LC)   2. It's about time. Have you been studying more?
(HL, HC)   3. I knew you could do it. Making you study evenings has paid off.
(HL, LC)   4. I knew you could do it. Have you been studying more?

Figure 14.3. Sample item from Perception of Parental Love and Control test (Longstreth and Rice, 1964).

similar findings in the Fels data, it was pointed out that two processes might be involved: (1) a rejecting, hostile parent would provide little reinforcement (e.g., *love*) for any behavior, including achievement strivings; and (2) little identification would occur with such a parent, assuming that such identification would be beneficial if the parent was achievement-oriented.

Personality Factors. Let us now move one step up the hypothesized causative chain, from home conditions to personality characteristics of the children themselves. We assume that these personality characteristics are at least partly a result of the home conditions associated with them.

The study made by the Youth Studies Center indicated three personality differences between WA, AGG, and UA boys. Teachers rated AGG and UA boys as less responsible, less ambitious, and less emotionally mature than WA boys. The positive ends of these scales were described to the teachers as indicated in Table 14.6, which also presents the mean ratings for each group on each scale. The differences between WA and the two problem groups are large and consistent, even though the teachers were not told to which group a given boy "belonged"; the three sets of names were presented to them in a randomly determined order, with no other identifying information.

TABLE 14.6

Teacher Ratings of AGG, UA, and WA High School Boys
on Three Personality Scales
(Adapted from Shanley *et al.*, 1964)

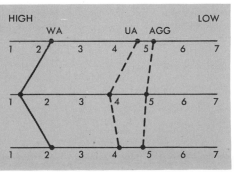

Teachers were not alone in these opinions. Personality tests administered to the students themselves revealed a picture entirely consistent with that provided by the teachers (which speaks well for the accuracy of the teachers). Specifically, the three groups of boys were administered the California Psychological Inventory (CPI), a self-rating personality test of 480 items. The three groups were scored on 10 different scales. Table 14.7 presents their mean scores. On every single scale, the WA scored higher (i.e., toward the "better adjusted" end) than the AGG and UA groups, and on 7 of the scales, the difference is significant. Considering only these 7 scales, AGG and UA boys described themselves as possessing less social initiativeness and leadership (scale 1), as less responsible and dependable (scale 4), less mature socially (scale

5), less reflective and self-controlled (scale 6), less concerned about their impressions on others (scale 7), less motivated to achieve by imitating others (scale 8), and as less efficient intellectually (scale 10). Parenthetically, it may be noted that other investigators using the CPI have found highly similar results. In one study, for example, significant differences between UA's and normal achievers appeared on 5 of the 7 scales in the present study that revealed significant differences (Gawronski and Mathis, 1965).

TABLE 14.7

Mean Scores on 10 Personality Scales of the CPI for Three
Groups of Boys: AGG, UA, and WA
(Adapted from Shanley *et al.*, 1964)

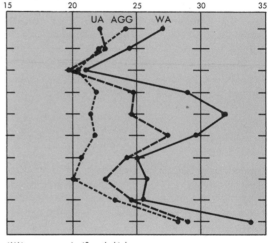

1. Dominance*
2. Sociability
3. Self-Acceptance
4. Responsibility*
5. Socialization*
6. Self-control*,a
7. Good impression*,b
8. Achievement via conformance*
9. Achievement via independenceb
10. Intellectual efficiency*

*WA group was significantly higher.
aFive points were added to each mean.
bTen points were added to each mean.

The "self-concept" has also been found to differ as a function of school adjustment. There is evidence that aggressive and underachieving youngsters think less well of themselves than well-adjusted youngsters. In the study made by the Youth Studies Center, UA's rated themselves as poorer leaders than AGG's or WA's (an opinion that was decidedly accurate), and AGG's rated themselves as receiving poorer grades, doing less well in sports, and as less active in clubs than WA's (again, these opinions were quite accurate). Other investigators have found similar results (Fink, 1962; Jersild, 1952; Reckless *et al.*, 1956, 1957; Reed and Cuadra, 1957; Reeder, 1955).

Just where these self-concepts come from is an open question. Presumably, they are affected by parental treatment, as well as by teacher and peer treatment (we shall see direct evidence of teacher effects shortly), as well as by the youngster's awareness of himself in relation to others. It is assumed that self-concepts act as a determinant of the youngster's overt behavior and are, therefore, important. While there is no direct evidence supporting this assumption, it seems reasonable enough—although one wonders if the opposite could not be the case—the youngster's behavior determines his self-concepts. Perhaps the causative chain works in both directions.

There was one self-concept rating in the study by the Youth Studies Center where WA's rated themselves as worse than UA's or AGG's: they rated themselves as less relaxed and happy. One might be tempted to ignore this finding as a chance one that would not appear again, except that a similar opinion was held by interviewers who held an hour-long interview with each pupil. They rated WA's as less relaxed and less at ease than UA's or AGG's. There appears to be no other study that has found this particular difference, and thus it must be treated with a proper amount of caution. One is tempted to speculate, though, that achievement, academic responsibility, ambition, extracurricular activities, and emotional maturity—all the characteristics that seem to be related to "academic success"—are gained at a subtle price—that of tension and worry. Some educators have wondered if the schools (and parents) do not push too hard, with an implicit motto of "achievement at any price." Some such process probably occurs, particularly with bright, upwardly mobile parents who live in a neighborhood full of other bright, upwardly mobile people. In such neighborhoods, everybody intends to go to college, and everybody knows that school grades have a lot to do with whether one goes to a first-rate or a second-rate college. It would seem that few such parents subscribe to the philosophy suggested by a British schoolteacher: ". . . I would rather see a school produce a happy street cleaner than a neurotic scholar" (Neill, 1960, p. 5).

School adjustment also seems to be related to identification—the extent to which the pupil identifies with parents, teachers, and peers. Peer and parent identification were measured in the Youth Studies Center sample of AGG's, UA's, and WA's. The measuring instrument consisted of 14 simple questions, to each of which the respondent had to pick either "parents" or "peers" as the answer (synonyms of "peer" were used, of course). Two representative questions are as follows:

It is easier to get problems "off your chest" by telling them

(a) to people your own age.
(b) to parents.

A teenager would be very miserable without

(a) parents to look up to.
(b) other teenagers to look up to.

The results were that WA's picked "parents" more often than AGG's or UA's. Thus, WA's tended to identify more with parents than did the two adjustment-problem groups. In terms of *absolute* scores, WA's picked parents and peers about equally often, while AGG's and UA's picked peers more often than parents. Interestingly enough, the greater peer involvement of these two groups was not shared by their peers; they were *less* popular, as judged by sociometric scores. Probably their involvement was with a few other peers like themselves, but since most peers were not like them, their average sociometric score was low.

In this section, a number of personality differences have been observed between children with and without school adjustment problems. Is it the ineptitude of the school that causes these personality differences, or does the student bring them with him to school? It is the author's opinion that one would not expect such dramatic and widespread differences if the adjustment problems were the result of particular idiosyncrasies within particular schools. If the schools were principally to blame, one would expect the dissatisfied students to have specific complaints that distinguish them from adjusted students but to otherwise be similar to them. Yet the facts are quite different. There are pervasive and deep-seated personality differences between adjusted and maladjusted school students that run much deeper than specific complaints about school (Longstreth, 1961). It appears that the student who cannot adjust to school has difficulty adjusting, *period*. Note the police records (Table 14.5) for AGG's and UA's, for example: are the schools to be blamed for these high rates?

Often, the student can verbalize no specific complaint at all, except to say that he does not like school (Dillon, 1949). Although he gives the desire to work as the most frequent reason for quitting school, he is unsuccessful at that, too; dropouts do not distinguish themselves with good work records. (In the Longstreth dropout study, to be discussed shortly, employers kept records of the on-the-job performances of the students; in general, they indicated poor work habits.)

Thus, the author inclines to be in agreement with investigators like Jackson and Getzels (1959), who conclude that:

. . . dissatisfaction with school appears to be part of a larger picture of psychological discontent rather than a direct reflection of inefficient functioning in the classroom. It is almost as if dissatisfaction were a product of a pervasive perceptual set that colors the student's view of himself and his world. [P. 299.]

As we have seen, one determinant of this "set" is the parental treatment the problem student receives at home, which undoubtedly affects the determination of the particular personality characteristics we have observed in the present section.

Classroom and Teacher Effects on Personality. It has already been argued that, at a very general level, the school presents to its students a pervasive set of upper middle-class values. Such a statement, while true, is vague in specifics. To be more articulate, we shall begin our discussion with something just a little less vague than middle-class values —*classroom atmosphere*—and then become more specific as *dimensions of teacher behavior* are considered, and finally we shall become quite specific as *specific teacher behaviors* are considered.

Classrooms vary in terms of the nature of their most typical pupil-pupil and teacher-pupil interactions. In some classrooms, for example, the students and teacher often decide "together" what shall be done (a "democratic" classroom), while in others the teacher usually announces what will be done (an "authoritarian" classroom). In some classrooms (relatively few), the teacher provides practically no hints at all as to what should be done (a laissez-faire classroom), but responds only when requested. Now, what is the effect of such "atmospheres" on the behavior of the children?

The classic study was carried out by Lewin, Lippitt, and White (1939). Four groups of five ten-year-olds, organized for recreational purposes, were guided by leaders who were either authoritarian, democratic, or laissez faire. The leaders, graduate students in psychology, took turns playing the different roles, so that no one person was associated with a single atmosphere. Careful records were kept of group behavior under each type of leadership. Large differences were found. Authoritarian leadership produced either rebellion or passivity, considerable hostility toward fellow members, and a lack of constructive "output" when the leader was absent; laissez-faire leadership produced boredom, disorganization, lack of output, and hostility; democratic leadership produced group cohesion and friendliness, output whether the leader was there or not, and less hostility.

This study is widely cited in educational textbooks as demonstrating the superiority of the "democratic way" (e.g., Cronbach, 1963, pp. 512–513). However, a number of flaws disqualify such a conclusion (McCandless, 1961; Sechrest, 1964). McCandless, who served as one of the leaders, gives this qualification:

Another, but less obvious, flaw in the Lewin, Lippitt, and White study is related to the role-playing done by the four leaders in their three leadership roles. The four leaders were graduate students or postdoctoral fellows in child and clinical psychology. All were convinced and liberal equalitarians, living at a time when Hitler, the arch-authoritarian, was consolidating his power and preparing for world conquest. Each preferred and put his heart into his *democratic* leadership role, becoming perhaps the *warmest* and most dedicated democratic leader in recent history. But, when his turn came to play the authoritarian, he tended to become *cold* and *hard*—a veritable Captain Bligh. In the *laissez-faire* role, detachment of a profound sort became the order of the day. In other words, the crucial variable involved *may* have been warmth. [P. 438.]

McCandless goes on to describe some further studies of his own, substantiating the importance of warmth. He feels that with many groups "benevolent authoritarianism" is the best approach—an atmosphere in which the leader is the "boss," but a warm, understanding boss. He writes:

Fresh from his experience as one of the four group leaders in the Lewin, Lippitt, and White study (and ardent in his convictions concerning democracy, warmth, and child-centeredness), the author went into a situation where he was partially responsible for the conduct of two cottages (residential centers for 30 to 40 boys each) of adolescent, mentally retarded, delinquent and pre-delinquent boys. Under the new regime of sweetness, light, trust in their better nature, and permissiveness, these youngsters went completely to pieces, making life miserable for their cottage personnel, themselves, and the writer. After some months of this nightmare, and after a particularly atrocious betrayal of trust, the author finally took one of the "gang" leaders over his lap and spanked him thoroughly—an embarrassing and temporarily painful experience for the gangling adolescent boy.

Following this incident, the atmosphere of the two cottages changed overnight; these slum youngsters had been talked to in their own language. Only then was it possible to put into action an effective democratic organization of the cottages. The effectiveness of this organization was attested by the fact that, after about two years, one of the cottages—during the acute manpower shortage early in World War II—operated well for some months with no adult living in it. During this time, an adult came in at meal- and bedtimes; but during the rest of the day, the residential group of 13- to 15-year-old low IQ delinquent slum boys managed their own lives. There was no mayhem and there were no runaways, although on the average (under closely supervised conditions) one boy in 30 ran away weekly. [P. 438.]

Thompson (1944) carried out an experiment with much younger children, which seems to confirm McCandless. Two groups of nursery school children were equated on IQ, socioeconomic level, and personality ratings by the teachers. In one group, the teachers were warm and understanding, but aloof, allowing the children to plan their own activities to a considerable extent: "benevolent laissez faire," the atmosphere might be called. In the other group, the teachers were equally warm and understanding, but were also much more directive: a "benevolent authoritarian" atmosphere. The same teachers switched roles in both groups, thus ruling out teacher personality differences. At the end of the school session (eight months later), a number of differences were noted. Children in the benevolent authoritarian atmosphere were more constructive, less destructive, more social with each other, and more ascendant. They also assumed more leadership responsibilities. Thus, authoritarianism, when expressed with warmth, led to positive gains in interpersonal behavior. In learning theory terms, benevolent authoritarianism not only provided ample reinforcement for responses the child was supposed to learn (warmth) but also provided cues (authoritarianism) as to what the correct responses were. In the benevolent laissez-faire atmosphere, the reinforcement was there, but it was applied indiscriminately to "incorrect" as well as to "correct" responses.

It is unlikely that the same classroom atmosphere is maximally beneficial to all children. A child who has experienced complete freedom at home may be expected to have some problems getting used to an authoritarian schoolroom, while a child with more restrictive parents may feel right at home. It must be recognized that the teacher's primary goal is *educational* in nature, not psychological. Authority must be used if these goals are to be shared by the pupils. A teacher cannot walk into a classroom and ask, "What shall we do today?"—unless he wants to lose his job. Most teachers use a considerable amount of authority, and most students expect it. It would seem, therefore, that parents can ease their children's adjustment to school by not being completely permissive at home. *If reasonable restrictions are adopted, the similarity between home and school will probably be maximized, thereby increasing the generalizations between one and the other.*

Dimensions of Teacher Behavior. Just as there are dimensions of child rearing that are useful in summarizing parental behavior, so are there dimensions of teaching. The two sets of dimensions are not always the same, although there is some overlap. The restrictive-permissive dimension of child rearing has its correlate in the authoritarian-democratic dimension of teaching. Usually, however, the dimensions are different, reflecting, no doubt, the fact that the teacher's goal is education, not child rearing, and also reflecting the biases and interests of educationists as compared to psychologists.

Ryans (1961a, b) has reported some interesting research on teacher dimensions. In one study, trained observers rated both teachers and students on a number of dimensions. Specifically, teachers were rated on three broad dimensions: kind and understanding versus aloof and objective, responsible and businesslike versus evasive and planless, and stimulating and imaginative versus dull and routine. Students were rated on seven dimensions: disinterested versus alert, obstructive versus con-

In this photograph, one child is playing with a doll, another is drawing at the blackboard, and the rest are listening to the teacher. Does this classroom seem to be *laissez-faire* or authoritarian?

structive, restrained versus participative, rude versus self-controlled, apathetic versus initiating, dependent and passive versus responsible, and uncertain versus confident. Since ratings on the seven student dimensions tended to be positively correlated with each other, the seven ratings were summed for each student to yield one overall composite score of "goodness" of student behavior. The correlations between this score and each of the three types of teacher behavior are presented in Table 14.8, separately for elementary and secondary school classes.

An interesting pattern is apparent. Teacher and student behaviors are highly related in the elementary classes, but not in secondary classes. The correlations in the elementary classes are very high—about as high as the reliability of the ratings would permit. They arc all positive, indicating that kindly, responsible, and stimulating teachers had stu-

TABLE 14.8

Correlations Between Composite Student Behavior Scores and Teacher Behavior
Scores on Three Dimensions of Teacher Behavior
(Adapted from Ryans, 1961b)

Groups	r_1	r_2	r_3
Elementary school classes			
834 classes, grades 1–6	.82	.80	.75
144 classes, grades 1–6	.83	.78	.80
Secondary school classes			
497 classes, mathematics and science	.20	.18	.21
568 classes, English and social studies	.18	.21	.26
114 classes, mathematics, science, English, and social studies	.07	.11	.14

r_1: correlation between student behavior and teacher ratings on *kindly, understanding* versus *aloof and objective.*

r_2: correlation between student behavior and teacher ratings on *responsible and businesslike* versus *evasive and planless.*

r_3: correlation between student behavior and teacher ratings on *stimulating and imaginative* versus *dull and routine.*

dents who were alert, constructive, participative, self-controlled, etc.—
the seven "good" ends of the student dimensions. With secondary students, however, about the only teacher dimension that showed any relationship at all was the third one: stimulating and imaginative teachers tended to have students with more desirable behavior. One is tempted to speculate that the younger child has not yet developed much emotional independence; he is not emotionally "weaned" from the necessity of an understanding and affectionate relationship with adults—while the older child can more easily stand on his own two feet, without constant assurance of acceptance. Or it could be that the crucial variable is achievement motivation. Perhaps students interested solely in achievement are more affected by the instructional skills of a teacher, while students more interested in simply "passing the time as pleasantly as possible" are more affected by the supportive behavior of the teacher. Assuming that older children are more motivated for achievement, Ryans' results become understandable. There is actually some evidence supporting this interpretation, with Piana *et al.* (1955) and French (1958) both reporting that achievement-oriented students are more affected by teachers' *ability*, while other students are more affected by teachers' *warmth.*

Specific Teacher Behaviors. There are a number of aspects about teacher behavior that are more specific than those reflected in the dimensions previously discussed. Consider the proposition that males are more often dissatisfied with school than females—at least they drop out more frequently. Does the teacher contribute anything to this state of affairs? The author thinks the answer is yes. First of all, teachers are generally biased in favor of girls. Girls get better grades than boys, even when they are not warranted in terms of achievement. Carter (1952) provides representative results. He examined achievement scores and grades in six algebra classes for girls and boys. Achievement scores at the end of the semester indicated that the two groups were equivalent, although boys performed slightly better than girls. Yet girls averaged significantly higher grades.

It is also the case that boys receive more teacher disapproval during the school day than girls (the same is probably true at home, with the parents, too). In one study (Meyer and Thompson, 1956), three sixth-grade teachers and pupils were observed 30 hours per classroom. All teacher-initiated contacts were recorded and scored in terms of whether the teacher was approving or disapproving. In addition, each student was administered a "Guess who?" questionnaire in which the names of four students approved most and four students disapproved most were to be written down.

The main results were (1) the classroom observations showed that boys were disapproved of more than girls, and (2) both boys and girls wrote down the names of boys more frequently than the names of girls when asked to name the disapproved students. It would seem, then, that not only do boys get more blame, but they know they do, and so do girls. Meyer and Thompson speculate as to why this should be so, and as to its possible effects. They argue that, for unknown reasons, possibly genetic as well as learned, boys are more active, outgoing, and aggressive than girls, and female teachers disapprove of such behavior. Since this behavior is normal for boys, they see themselves as being punished for behavior they really do not consider "bad." The incongruity between their positive evaluation of their own behavior and the teachers' negative evaluations leads to anxiety and adjustment problems, which may contribute to a future dropout problem.

Research by Davidson and Lang (1960) suggests that teacher approval-disapproval patterns are directly related to pupils' self-concepts. They found a remarkably high correlation between what junior high school students said about themselves and what they thought their teachers thought of them: $r = .82$. Two other findings are also of interest: (1) the more positive the student's belief about his teacher's evaluation of him, the better was his academic achievement as measured by grades; and (2) children in the upper and middle socioeconomic levels believed their teachers had more positive evaluations of them than did children in the lower socioeconomic levels. They also received higher grades. A related finding by Fink (1962) is that negative self-concepts are correlated with academic underachievement. Children with low evaluations of themselves do worse than would be predicted on the basis of their IQ scores, while children with more positive self-concepts show greater congruity between grades and IQ scores.

Thus, we see a web of intriguing interrelationships between teacher distribution of approval and disapproval and children's beliefs of what teachers think of them, what they think of themselves, their academic achievement, and their general happiness with school. It is tempting to assume that the chain of causation begins with the teacher's behavior, works its way through the child's beliefs about his teacher and himself, and manifests itself finally in academic performance and happiness.

Correlation coefficients alone, however, are not enough. Indeed, there is good reason to believe that at least one causative wave flows in the opposite direction—that children bring certain behavioral tendiencies to school with them that affect their teachers' treatment of them, which in turn affects their subsequent behavior. The cycle, then, is from pupil to teacher to pupil rather than simply from teacher to pupil. Undoubtedly, a teacher-pupil-teacher cycle is also involved, since none of these possibilities necessarily excludes the others. In order to narrow the range of possibilities, *experiments* are needed to clarify the correlational findings.

Staines (1958) reports one such experiment. After students in two junior high schools filled out a series of self-ratings, one of the teachers (Teacher A) studied the self-ratings of each student in his class, noting the pattern of low and high scores. He then tried to raise the low self-ratings, while at the same time maintaining the high self-ratings. The teaching period lasted for 12 weeks. During this period, the teacher carefully monitored his day-to-day comments to each child, tailoring them to his self-concept profile. For example, if a student had an unrealistically negative evaluation of his arithmetic ability, the teacher was careful not to disapprove of his performance in that subject area, but rather to gently praise it with such comments as, "Your score on yesterday's homework was better than the class average, Jack—that's good," instead of, "You got a C, Jack—a lot of people did better than you." If another pupil thought he was too short, the teacher might say, "Bob, you play the part of the father in this skit," instead of, "Bob, you play the part of the little boy in this skit," etc. The other teacher (Teacher B) was not informed of A's project, nor was any mention made of children's self-concepts at all. This teacher had no awareness of the self-concept as an outcome of education; he taught his students as any normal teacher would.

At the end of 12 weeks, pupils in both classes rated their self-concepts again, and changes in the two sets of ratings were examined. A number of changes were found, and all but one indicated greater improvement for A pupils than B pupils. They rated themselves as more fair; better at games; more willing to take a "try at things," regardless of the difficulty; liking hobbies more; and more aware of their own self-directions. They also were more certain of their strengths and weaknesses and judged themselves in less extreme forms than B pupils. The one change that did not suggest improvement was that they described themselves as more willing to cheat than B pupils. But this is irrelevant. The important point is that the Staines experiment shows that the chain of causation can run from teacher to pupil; teachers' behavior *can* affect the self-concepts of pupils. (The changes in self-concepts of A students were not achieved at a cost to academic achievement, either; achievement tests administered before and after the 12-week session indicated that A pupils actually learned a little more than B pupils.)

Flanders and Havumaki (1960) provide evidence of another sort. By an ingenious experiment, they were able to show that teacher approval and attention affect pupils' opinions of each other. They held meetings with 33 groups of 10 tenth-grade students each, all from classes in Minneapolis and St. Paul, Minnesota. Each group believed it had been chosen to appear in a Quiz Kid contest with other schools in the metropolitan area. The ostensive purpose of the meeting was to decide whether the contest should appear on TV or on the radio, either alternative being possible. Elaborate precautions were made to convince the students that the Quiz Kid contest was glamorous and exciting, and it is reported that all of them approached the problem seriously.

The deception in the situation was that, in 17 of the groups (the experimental groups), the adult leader interacted only with students sitting in odd-numbered chairs. Only these students were praised for their participation, and other students had to "interrupt" if they wanted to talk—the leader did not recognize them. In the other 16 (control) groups, all students were allowed to talk, and praise was directed to the group as a whole rather than to specific students.

At the end of the meeting, each group filled out a sociometric questionnaire reflecting peer acceptance within the group. In the experimental groups, students sitting in odd-numbered chairs were chosen significantly more often than students sitting in even-numbered chairs, while in the control groups there was no difference in popularity of students in odd- and even-numbered chairs. The investigators concluded: "The results of this experiment indicate that teacher-pupil interaction involving praise that is supportive and constructive is likely to increase the choice value of a student indicating greater acceptance by his peers" (p. 68).

As a final illustration of teacher effects, a pioneer experiment by Ojemann and Wilkinson (1939) is mentioned. These investigators hypothesized that, if a teacher really knew his students, in terms of their home backgrounds, aspirations, fears, problems, etc., he would interact with them in ways that would reflect this knowledge, which in turn would result in various signs of better student adjustment. Accordingly, two groups of 33 ninth-grade pupils were selected from a larger sample so that they were equal in terms of IQ, age, and academic achievement the previous year. For the experimental group, voluminous records were prepared on each student, including information based on a home visit and personality scores obtained from the pupil. With these data in hand, the investigator prepared a written summary, added his own comments and interpretations, and then discussed the matter in detail with each of the student's teachers for that semester. The control group was not treated this way, but simply as usual, with no special information supplied to the teachers.

At the end of the year, the same measures of adjustment that had been taken at the beginning of the year were taken again. Comparisons of changes revealed a number of positive gains for experimental pupils. Personality scores indicated fewer feelings of inferiority, less need to cheat, and more satisfaction with school; measures of conflict indicated a reduction in school-related conflicts (while the control group showed a slight increase); experimental students also showed better grades than control students, although this may have been a result of bias on the part of the teachers (however, they were not told that grades would be used as a basis for evaluation). The teachers too were visibly affected by the experiment. Following are some representative statements they made about the project:

One teacher:

After your account of L. M. I see her as an unhappy child rather than an insolent one. I find it easier to accept her.

Another teacher:

I was very much interested in the information concerning G. B. I had previously caught myself wishing I knew more about her home life as she always appeared to be under-nourished and inclined to be the "mousy" type. After learning that she received so little encouragement at home I endeavor to praise her school work at every opportunity that arises and I notice she beams at every word.

Another teacher:

After discovering it was shyness and nervousness rather than sulkiness which prevented L. C. from reciting I made a special effort to see what could be done to help him overcome this difficulty. I seated him so he could be centrally located, praised him at every reasonable opportunity, encouraged him not to do things alone but in company with his classmates as asking him along with others to pass paper, and occasionally to read aloud. [Ojemann and Wilkinson, 1939, p. 676.]

The investigators concluded:

These comments show the beginning of more complete understanding of pupil behavior. Shyness, resentment, over-aggression, and indifference are known to be motivated often by conflicts and frustration. They are signals not for neglect or for the drawing of battle lines but for the need of mutual understanding and helpfulness.

The data obtained in this study are consistent in showing that when teachers learn to know their pupils as personalities in their respective environments, teachers tend to become more effective guides for learning—the pupils achieve more in academic areas—and teachers also become more effective personality "developers." [P. 676.]

There is an interesting implication from two of the experiments just considered—the Staines study and the Ojemann and Wilkinson study. Both studies indicate that, if teachers "know" their students better, better student adjustment seems to be the result—an obvious enough conclusion. What school conditions make such personal knowledge possible? Two such conditions would seem to be small classes and teachers who grew up in the area in which they teach. The former condition insures that too heavy a memory burden will not preclude knowledge of each individual pupil, and the latter condition maximizes the probability that the teacher will have had exposure to each child and his family over a long enough period of time to "get acquainted." It appears that current trends are against both of these conditions. The teacher shortage grows worse, and will probably continue to do so until salaries are competitive with other professions. The result is that classes remain large in size, thus making it difficult for the teacher to commit much pupil information to memory. Urbanization continues at a rapid rate, and with it individual mobility, so that the "hometown teacher" grows more and more scarce. Besides, the neighborhood does not remain stable anyway, so even if the teacher did grow up there, he would still be relatively unacquainted with many of his pupils. It would seem that teachers know less about their students today than they did, say, 50 years ago. Perhaps this unfortunate state of affairs is counterbalanced by the better preparation of today's teacher. He may have less information, but he uses what he has to better advantage. One would hope this to be the case, although it is doubtful if it completely makes up for the other conditions.

GRADING AND COMPETITION: A SPECIAL PROBLEM

Are academic grades "good" or "bad"? This question has been discussed a lot in the past few years, although the public schools seem not to have any doubts, since 99 per cent of them do give grades. Yet it is an interesting question, with strong arguments on both sides. Our present interest, as always, is in terms of the possible psychological effects of grading practices.

On the yea side, grades serve as a source of feedback information to the student, telling him how he is doing. They also fulfill the school's responsibility to tell the parents how he is progressing. With such information, the student and his parents are in a position to make realistic decisions about future goals, both short-term ones (what areas need further work) and long-term ones (should he prepare to go to college or not). Grades also serve as a source of guidance for the teachers; they can spot a student's strengths and weaknesses by glancing at his grades and can thus concentrate on those areas where he needs most help.

Grades also serve as a source of motivation; children often work hard to obtain an A, or to go up from a C to a B. No one wants an F, presumably, so there is a source of aversive motivation too, driving the student away from those behaviors that make an F more probable. Grades also serve as rewards and punishments, much as food and shock do to a hungry experimental rat. Thus, teachers can develop good work habits and good school attitudes by reinforcing students with high grades, and can weaken poor work habits and undesirable attitudes by punishing them with low grades.

On the nay side, one argument is that, since grades are usually assigned relative to the class average—"on the curve," so to speak—only a few students have the opportunity of obtaining A's and B's. The remaining students get mostly C's, and a few get D's and an occasional F. Year after year, the student gets the same message: "A" students get A's year after year and "D" students get D's year after year. Now, the question is, what are the effects of being told year after year that you are topnotch, as compared to a yearly message of mediocrity or worse? Grades may be judged as good or bad depending upon the answer to this question. There are two groups of evidence that supply the answer.

First, there is a series of studies concerned with "level of aspiration" (e.g., Lewin, et al., 1944; Sears, 1940) that goes something like this: the subject is confronted with a task and has a "trial"—he performs. Then, according to a prearranged schedule unknown to the subject, he is told, "You didn't do so well that time." Then he is allowed to try again, but first he is asked to state how well he thinks he will do. That defines his level of aspiration (LA) for the next trial. He then tries again, is told again that he did not do so well, is asked to state his LA for the next trial, and so on, for a series of trials. This subject is in the "failure" condition. He is compared with another subject who is treated exactly the same except that he is told, "You did very good that time," after each trial; this subject is in the "success" condition. The question of interest is, what happens to the LA under these two conditions? The answer is, two things happen. First, success tends to raise the LA from what it was on previous trials, while failure tends to lower it. Second, failure produces greater variability between subjects than success; that is, following failure, some subjects will lower their LA a drastic amount, and some will raise it a drastic amount, producing greater differences between subjects than is the case for "success" subjects. Thus, it has been said that LA responses are more "irrational" following failure than following success.

A study by Haas and Maehr (1965) may be used to illustrate the first result, as well as to suggest two other unique findings usually not investigated. A self-rating instrument was administered to eighth-grade boys before and after they were exposed to a "physical development test," in which half were told they had done poorly and half were told they had done well. The self-rating instrument consisted of 30 items that required the subject to rate himself on a 9-point scale from "extremely adequate" to "extremely inadequate." It contained three subparts: (1) 10 items directly related to the behavior that was criticized in the "physical development test"; (2) 10 items related to athletic skills, but not including responses performed in the "test"; and (3) 10 items unrelated to athletic skill at all, but concerned only with general physical fitness.

The self-rating instrument was administered in a different classroom setting than that used in the "test," and by a different experimenter. It was administered one week before the "test," within one hour afterwards, one day later, six days later, and six weeks later (the 10 "unrelated" items were omitted on the one-day and six-day administrations because of practical difficulties).

The mean self-ratings on all three subparts of the instrument are presented in Figure 14.4. Four main results are indicated: (1) if subjects were approved (i.e., "passed") in the "test," their self-ratings improved; (2) if they were disapproved (i.e., "failed"), their self-ratings deteriorated; (3) these changes held up over a six-week period, at least for the criticized items; and (4) approval or disapproval affected not only self-ratings of the specific behaviors occurring in the "test" but also related athletic ratings as well as unrelated general physical fitness ratings.

The *illustrative* findings in this study consist of results (1) and (2); they have been found in many other studies. The *unique* results are (3) and (4). The third result indicates that the effects of approval and

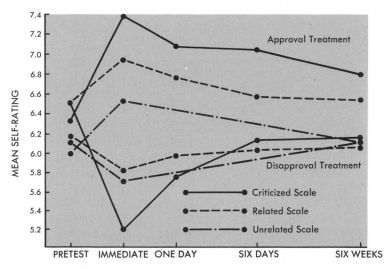

Figure 14.4. Mean self-ratings as a result of approval or disapproval treatment (Haas and Maehr, 1965).

disapproval are not just temporary but have some duration—in this case, extending as far in time as the investigators measured. The fourth result indicates that feelings of self-worth *generalize* to other behaviors, depending upon their similarity to the criticized behavior. As Jersild says:

What often happens is that when a person fails in a given test in life, such as an important assignment at school, it is difficult for him not to view this as a test of him as a person, a total test rather than just a measure of a limited facet of his worth. When a child is deficient in arithmetic or in reading he will have a tendency, at least for the moment, to feel that he is just plain deficient in everything. [1954, pp. 609–610.]

The second group of evidence comes from studies of children who are differentiated by their academic grades. The most extreme comparison involves a group with grades so low it was retained in a grade for a second year and is compared with a group that had been promoted. Goodlad and Anderson (1963) report one such study. They studied two groups of children selected from 23 classrooms who were equated on IQ and achievement and differed only with respect to retention. One group, because of the policies of the particular schools, had not been promoted and remained in the first grade a second year, while the other group had been promoted to the second grade. The children were measured on sociometric ratings, teacher ratings, self-concept ratings, and personality inventories at the beginning and end of the school year. *On all four kinds of measurements, the promoted children outgained the non-promoted children.* They also cheated more, however, apparently feeling under greater pressure to stay up with their classmates.

Similar results have been found in a number of such studies (Goodlad and Anderson review some of them). Many of them show that achievement is affected as well as personality. Retained pupils often achieve less the second time around than their classmates who are in the grade for the first time, even though the retained pupils are a year older.

This second line of evidence—from the schools—supports the first line of evidence—from the psychology laboratory. Both provide the same answer to the question: the effects of low grades and failure are detrimental to both personality development and achievement. The author is thus strongly inclined to conclude that low grades are "bad" more than they are "good," and high grades are "good" more than they are "bad." Grading "on the curve" is thus "good" for above-average pupils, but "bad" for below-average pupils. For these latter pupils, the situation seems to be conducive only to further adjustment problems.

What is the solution? Should academic grades be abandoned entirely? There are those who advocate such a solution. Certainly, the feedback function of grades can be taken care of in other, better ways. Parent-teacher conferences, for example, in which thousands of words are exchanged, are probably much more valuable to both teacher and parent than a few marks on a report card. Let the teacher keep his private marks if he wants to, but do not burden the pupil with them.

The non-graded school seems a promising solution too. Goodlad and Anderson argue that the traditional age-grade school, where six-year-olds are all in the first grade, seven-year-olds all in the second grade, etc., has serious flaws. In the first place, a fifth-grade teacher has some children who perform as third-graders, and some who perform as seventh- or even eighth-graders. Indeed, the same child is a third-grader in some respects, say spelling, and a seventh-grader in other respects, say arithmetic.

> In brief, as extensive data presented . . . clearly reveal, a fifth-grade teacher, in spite of his designation, is not a teacher of fifth-grade children. At a given time, he teaches third, fourth, fifth, sixth, seventh, eighth, and even ninth graders, as far as learner realities are concerned, even though all the pupils in his room may be labeled "fifth grade." Any attempt to deal with these children as fifth graders can only be Procrustean in its ultimate effects. [Goodlad and Anderson, 1963, p. 3.]

The age-grade school refuses to recognize that the average child is not "up to grade" in all areas, but rather "ahead" in some and "behind" in others. The school slows him down if he is too far ahead, resulting in boredom and disinterest, and tries to speed him up if he is behind, resulting in anxiety and a sense of failure. It would make more sense to recognize achievement differences in different areas, and to encourage the pupil to proceed at his own best rate in each area, as is done in the non-graded school. Grades are then assigned, if at all, in terms of each pupil's progress *as compared to his own previous performance*. There is no comparison with the group. Thus, the child who is below average compared to the group can make straight A's if his work shows progress, and if it is representative of his intellectual capacity. Everybody can make A's, since there is no statistical artifact to prevent it. If the parents complain that they cannot tell by such grades whether to send Johnny to college or not, the answer is simple: such information can easily be obtained from intelligence and achievement tests, and it is more reliable than teachers' grades anyway.

A grading system in which the pupils' performance is compared to his own past performance thus gets around the absurdity produced by grading on the curve, where a certain percentage of pupils are foredoomed to low grades regardless of performance. It also has another aspect; it reduces the emphasis on competition. Grading on the curve reinforces competitive behavior because, strictly speaking, that is all a grade may indicate—one's relative standing in the classroom. Since high grades are "good," children are constantly being told to do better than their classmates. Yet they are also told to practice the golden rule—to be kind, considerate, and cooperative. The two principles, competitiveness and cooperativeness, obviously conflict, and thus teachers (and parents) are trapped in an inconsistency. Indeed, the ludicrousness of the situation can be seen by considering a grade in "citizenship," which presumably reflects cooperativeness and deference for others. In order to obtain an A, a pupil would have to compete with his peers for being most non-competitive! A grading system based on competition with *self* would do much to eliminate the inconsistency, and perhaps might even have some ameliorative effect on American competitiveness in general.

DROPOUT PREVENTION

It was previously noted that the dropout problem is a serious one, with almost a third of American youth not graduating from high school. The consequences of dropping out of school are not attractive. The dropout is likely to get into trouble with the law, to have trouble finding and holding a job, and even to have marital problems (Havighurst, 1962; Neumeyer, 1961). But, to these individuals, staying in school is not attractive either. Their school record is one of constant friction, lack of achievement, and frustration. Beginning with little parental help or encouragement, and thereby bringing to school a personality pattern not geared to the school's environment, and facing a school system whose middle-class values are hard to swallow, and which sometimes lead to biased treatment from the teachers, the future dropout is willing to seriously consider any alternative to remaining in school.

What can be done? On the one hand, this chapter has summarized many personality characteristics that differentiate pupils with and without school adjustment problems. Finding these differences so pervasive, the conclusion was considered that the "fault" (*cause*) is not the schools', but the pupils' themselves; it is their own attitudes and values that initiate the trouble. On the other hand, this chapter has also shown that the school can and does influence attitudes and values about the self as well as about others. Perhaps, then, it at least "rubs salt" on the psychic wounds of the potential dropout, even if it does not create the wounds in the first place. Can it not do better? Can it not replace the salt with a healing salve, so that the troubled student becomes less of a problem over the years instead of more of a problem? Havighurst says that society makes the attainment of respectable adulthood for some of its citizens extremely difficult, and challenges the school—*us*—to do something about it:

School provides the only pathway to adolescence in River City, and high school is the only easily travelled route through adolescence to adulthood. For the third of River City youth who do not finish high school the way to adulthood is not an easy one. We see . . . that the dropouts have the greatest difficulty in growing up successfully. They are the most vulnerable to delinquency. They get the poorest jobs, if they get jobs at all. They have the most trouble with marriage. The churches see very little of them.

These boys and girls are somehow alien to the society in which they are trying to live. The evidence is clear that they start school with cultural handicaps, they have inadequate help and encouragement from their parents, and they accumulate a record of failure and frustration in school which drives them out of school at the earliest possible date. Early failure in school starts a process of alienation from society that leads them into delinquency and other forms of adolescent maladjustment.

With its present type of program, the school serves these children poorly. As late as a generation ago this group had the alternative of juvenile work leading to adult competence. Now this alternate pathway has narrowed and seems to be disappearing. The school is challenged to create a new and more satisfactory way to adulthood for a third of our youth. [1962, p. 64.]

Responding to this challenge, as echoed by many educational authorities over the years, schools have developed special programs for the potential dropout. The most widespread practice is the two-curriculum high school, with a "college prep" curriculum for those who are happy in an academic environment, and a "vocational" curriculum for those who do not appreciate "learning for learning's sake" as much as they do preparation for a job. Another widespread solution has been evening classes, so that the student can work on a job in the daytime, thus gaining the money and feeling of manhood he presumably needs, and yet obtaining a high school diploma. Often, the school counselor cooperates in finding a job for these students, although it is not an easy task.

Many related preventive techniques have been developed over the years. In a review of these programs, Kvaraceus (1959) lists 94 specific guidelines that were in use at the time of his survey. The schools are enthusiastic and proud of their special programs, maintaining that they "save" many youths. *Yet this understandable enthusiasm is not based on objective evidence at all,* but mainly on the sayings of the teachers and school administrators, the latter more than the former. Millions of dollars are spent each year on such programs, with practically no evidence as to their effectiveness. What is needed to evaluate such programs is obvious: two groups of students, both consisting solely of potential dropouts, who form the subjects of an experiment. One group must be exposed to a dropout-prevention program that is to be evaluated, and the other to the regular school program. Differences in the academic and social behavior of the two groups would then constitute the basis of evaluation of the special program's effectiveness. The most direct measure of such effectiveness would be the dropout rate. Compared to the control group, would it be reduced in the experimental group or not?

A Dropout-Prevention Experiment

Recognizing the absence of such an experimental evaluation, the Youth Studies Center of the University of Southern California instituted such a study in the fall of 1960, maintained it for three years, and reported the results a year later (Longstreth *et al.*, 1964).

An attempt was made to design a dropout-prevention program that was (1) representative of the presumed most important characteristics of other programs, and (2) financially and practically feasible for other schools, should it prove successful. On the basis of these two requirements, and drawing from the background of a review of other such programs, as well as an exploratory one-semester program of its own, four main characteristics were selected that would define the special program. These are presented as they were in the original report:

Characteristic 1: A Curriculum Designed to Appeal to the Potential Dropout. The rationale underlying the curriculum was simple: academic success requires effort, and effort requires motivation and interest. Therefore, a major goal of the curriculum was to orient the subject matter of each course toward the existing interests of the students. . . . Three courses were ultimately developed: English, practical mathematics, and social studies. All three courses were geared toward practical implications. A second major goal was to individualize academic assignments in order to account for individual differences and maximize the possibility of successful academic performance.

Characteristic 2: A Stable Pupil-Teacher Relationship. There were two experimental classes each year, with about 15 students per class. Not only was the pupil-teacher ratio small, but also all three courses within each class were taught by the same teacher. The rationale was that this small, stable pupil-teacher relationship would facilitate communication and understanding between teachers and students.

In keeping with the requirements of a practical program, work-study teachers were picked from the regular teaching staff of the city school system. They had not had intensive training for the environment they subsequently entered. The primary criterion for selection was a reputation for being a good teacher in general and an expressed interest and some prior experience in working with deviant students. Of the three work-study teachers (one taught for one of the three years of the program, another for two years, and a third for all three years), one had taught mental retardates (IQs from 70 to 90) the previous year, and the other two had a reputation for being unusually successful in working with problem boys at the elementary and secondary school levels.

Characteristic 3: A Counselor Who Was Immediately Available. A counselor was assigned to the experimental program whose main responsibility was to be immediately available for counseling with experimental students. His function was that of a detached, impartial adult to whom the students could communicate their feelings of frustration without fear of reprimands or counteraction.

Characteristic 4: Afternoon Jobs for Pay and School Credit. An attempt was made to obtain employment for all experimental students. These jobs usually were for three hours each weekday afternoon, although some students also worked weekends and evenings on these jobs, as well as during summer vacation. Students were paid by the hour and obtained school credit for their jobs (so they could graduate at the appropriate age). Jobs were obtained by school and by Youth Studies Center personnel in the local community and consisted of such tasks as grocery box boys, employment in city government (electrical tasks, plumbing jobs, street maintenance, park custodian, etc.), grease monkeys in auto agencies, etc. Seventy-seven per cent of the experimental students were employed at one time or another. Some had several consecutive jobs, others lost their jobs and did not obtain others, and some kept their jobs for more than a year. Of those who held jobs, the average number of hours worked was 320.5 and the median, 326. The range was from 13 hours to 840 hours.

It was assumed that employment would serve several goals. First, it would tend to satisfy the vocational goals assumed to be characteristic of potential dropouts. Second, it would show them that the school could actually do something for them that was practical and provided immediate rewards (money in the pocket). Third, the students were given an opportunity to learn good work habits, which perhaps would increase their job potential after leaving school. [Pp. 229–230.]

The school day went as follows: Classes met from 8.30 to 11.30 each day. After lunch, a gym class was held, and then pupils either left campus for afternoon jobs or, if they were not employed, attended a shop course until 2.30, and then were allowed to leave.

Over the three-year course of the experiment, 75 potential dropouts attended the special class, and they were compared with an equal number of potential dropouts who were exposed to the regular school program. The primary criterion for inclusion in the program was a constellation of factors that might be termed the "dropout syndrome." It consisted of a school record of excessive tardinesses and truancy, retardation in basic academic skills, and poor academic grades.

Evaluation was in terms of dropout rates, with secondary information consisting of before-after interviews and police data. The main results of the experiment can be stated simply and quickly: *The special program had practically no effect at all on dropout rates.* Fifty-seven per cent of the experimental students dropped out of school as compared to 60 per cent of the control students. The program was thus an unqualified failure in terms of the primary goal.

Why did it fail? One likely possibility is that any such high school program will fail unless it is so drastic that the child is literally removed completely from the influences of home and peers. Fifteen or sixteen years of age is too late, it could be argued, to affect a basic change in personality with the tools the school has at its disposal. To think that a few hours in school 36 weeks of the year is going to counteract what the child hears and sees every night and all summer at home, and has heard all his life, is perhaps unrealistic, to say the least.

What is the alternative? To begin such programs at an earlier age? Perhaps, except then a difficult practical problem comes up: the younger the age at which prevention is tried, the more difficult it is to spot the potential dropout. Thus, prevention programs at earlier ages would incorrectly diagnose increasing numbers of "potential dropouts." Considering the cost of such programs, taxpayers would be reluctant indeed to see their money "wasted" on individuals who did not desperately need special help. Besides, there is no guarantee that such a program would be effective anyway. Perhaps the influence of home and peers cannot be combated by the school at any age, unless it has recourse to treatment resources it now lacks.

Such an attempt is worth a try, however. Perhaps it should begin in the first grade, the very day the youngster first steps across the threshold. Perhaps all children whose backgrounds form a certain pattern —socioeconomic level, education of parents, etc.—should be exposed to a prevention program. Although it would be "wasted" on some who did not need it, the expense would be worth it many times over if it worked for those who did need it. And a fortune in dividends would be collected a generation later, when the children of these former "potential dropouts" began school. They would not require the program, since their backgrounds would be different—their parents liked school and did not drop out.

SUMMARY

In terms of time expended, the school ranks as the second most important determinant of personality development—second only to the home. What do children learn, personality-wise, from this long exposure?

School boards, schoolteachers, and schoolbooks—the three main ingredients of the school system—seem to have one important characteristic in common: they seem to share the value system of the upper middle class. Thus, from grade 1 through grade 12 for those who last that long, one lesson repeated over and over has to do with the middle-class way of life. To the extent children learn this lesson, they are emotionally "in tune" with the school system; both are working for the same goals. For those who do not learn this lesson, however, there is emotional disharmony with contradictory goals between school and home. For these children, one would expect adjustment problems at school.

Research shows, as common sense would predict, that working-class children are the ones who most frequently have trouble adjusting to school. Dropout rates, grade retention, and underachievement are much more common here than with middle- and upper-class children. Of course, it is not socioeconomic status per se that produces the problem, but the parental behaviors associated with it and their effects on the child.

Probably, the most important aspect of parental behavior determining school adjustment is the parental value for education. Numerous studies show that, where parents value education and expect their children to value it, adjustment problems are rare. Also of importance are the warmth and control of the parents. A child is not likely to adopt the values of an unloved parent, and even so, he needs some direction and encouragement in order to capitalize on his values.

The assumption that personality characteristics are involved in the causal chain is amply confirmed by the facts. Two frequent forms of school maladjustment (most frequent, according to many teachers) are aggressiveness and underachievement. As compared to well-adjusted students, these two groups share many deviant personality characteristics. Teachers rate them as unambitious, irresponsible, and immature, and they describe *themselves* in these terms too. Personality inventories indicate they are also less efficient intellectually, less reflective and self-controlled, and possess less social initiativeness and leadership qualities. They also have relatively negative self-concepts and tend to identify with their peers more frequently than well-adjusted students, who identify more with their parents.

What effect does the teacher have? The data indicate that teacher effects can be quite strong, for making the situation either better or worse. While studies of general teacher behaviors—classroom atmosphere and teacher-behavior dimensions—have not been too informative, careful measurement of more specific behaviors has been illuminating. Teachers often tend to grade girls more favorably than boys, when there is no difference in achievement level, and to disapprove of boys more frequently. Students notice these patterns, and their opinions of themselves are affected, as well as their opinions of each other. There is evidence that their general adjustment is also affected. It is the case, then, that teachers have more pervasive effects on personality development than most of them realize. Parents, of course, have always known this; they see the changes day by day.

Grading practices in general have come in for a good deal of discussion lately. The evidence is overwhelming in showing that low grades are detrimental to personality development as well as to academic achievement. Alternatives to "grading on the curve" should be adopted to correct this state of affairs. The non-graded school system, already in operation in a number of private schools and in some public schools, is one solution. It has the added advantage of de-emphasizing competitive academic behavior and emphasizing self-improvement.

Millions of dollars are spent each year trying to resolve an ultimate symptom of school maladjustment: dropping out of school—the end of the road. Most of these preventive programs are at the high school level. Experimental evaluation of a representative high school program has shown no beneficial effects. It is likely that waiting until the high school years is too late. More attempts should be tried in the elementary grades.

BIBLIOGRAPHY

CAMPBELL, R. F. (1967). Tomorrow's teacher. *Saturday review,* January 14, 60–73.

CARTER, R. S. (1952). How invalid are marks assigned by teachers? *Journal of educational psychology,* 43, 218–228.

CRONBACH, L. J. (1963). *Educational psychology.* New York: Harcourt, Brace & World, Inc.

CRUMP, S. (1966). *Black riot in Los Angeles.* Los Angeles: Trans-Anglo Books.

DAVIDSON, HELEN H., and LANG, G. (1960). Children's perceptions of their teachers' feelings toward them related to self-perception, school achievement, and behavior. *Journal of experimental education,* 29, 107–118.

DEJNOZKA, E. L. (1963). School board members: their opinions, status, and financial willingness. *Journal of educational sociology,* 36, 193–199.

DILLON, H. J. (1949). *Early school leavers—a major educational problem.* National Child Labor Committee.

ELKIN, F. (1961). *The child and society.* New York: Random House, Inc.

FINK, M. B. (1962). Self-concept as it relates to academic underachievement. *California journal of educational research,* 13, (2), 57–62.

FLANDERS, N. H., and HAVUMAKI, S. (1960). The effect of teacher-pupil contacts involving praise on the sociometric choices of students. *Journal of educational psychology,* 51, 65–68.

FRENCH, ELIZABETH G. (1958). Effects of the interaction of motivation and feedback on task performance. In J. W. ATKINSON (Ed.), *Motives in fantasy, action, and society.* Princeton, N.J.: D. Van Nostrand Co., Inc. Pp. 400–408.

GAWRONSKI, D. A., and MATHIS, C. (1965). Differences between over-achieving, normal-achieving, and under-achieving high school students. *Psychology in the schools,* 2, 152–155.

GOODLAD, J. I., and ANDERSON, R. H. (1963). *The nongraded elementary school.* Harcourt, Brace & World, Inc.

GROFF, P. J. (1962). The social status of teachers. *Journal of educational sociology,* 36, 20–25.

HAAS, H. I., and MAEHR, M. L. (1965). Two experiments on the concept of self and the reaction of others. *Journal of personality and social psychology,* 1, 100–105.

HAVIGHURST, R. J., BOWMAN, P. H., LIDDLE, G. P., MATHEWS, C. V., and PIERCE, J. V. (1962). *Growing up in River City.* New York: John Wiley & Sons, Inc.

HOLLINGSHEAD, A. B. (1961). *Elmtown's youth.* New York: John Wiley & Sons, Inc.

JACKSON, P. W., and GETZELS, J. W. (1959). Psychological health and classroom functioning: a study of dissatisfaction with school among adolescents. *Journal of educational psychology,* 50, 295–300.

JERSILD, A. T. (1952). *In search of self.* New York: Columbia University Press.

JERSILD, A. T. (1954). *Child psychology.* Englewood Cliffs, N.J.: Prentice-Hall, Inc.

KVARACEUS, W. C. (1959). *Delinquent behavior: principles and practices.* Washington, D.C.: National Education Association of the United States.

LEWIN, K., DEMBO, TAMARA, FESTINGER, L., and SEARS, PAULINE S. (1944). Level of aspiration. In J. McV. HUNT (Ed.), *Personality and the behavior disorders.* Vol. 1. New York: The Ronald Press Co. Pp. 333–378.

LEWIN, K., LIPPITT, R., and WHITE, R. K. (1939). Patterns of aggressive behavior in experimentally created "social climates." *Journal of social psychology,* 10, 271–299.

LONGSTRETH, L. E. (1961). *School dropouts: a review of recent literature.* Los Angeles: Youth Studies Center, University of Southern California.

LONGSTRETH, L. E., and RICE, R. E. (1964). Perceptions of parental behavior and identification with parents by three groups of boys differing in school adjustment. *Journal of educational psychology,* 55, 144–151.

LONGSTRETH, L. E., SHANLEY, F. J., and RICE, R. E. (1964). Experimental evaluation of a high school program for potential dropouts. *Journal of educational psychology,* 55, 228–236.

McCANDLESS, B. R. (1961). *Children and adolescents.* New York: Holt, Rinehart and Winston, Inc.

McGUIRE, C., and WHITE, G. D. (1957). Social origins of teachers—in Texas. In L. J. STILES (Ed.), *The teacher's role in American society.* New York: Harper & Row. Pp. 23–41.

MASON, W. S. (1967). Cited in *Saturday review,* January 14, 60.

MEYER, W. T., and THOMPSON, G. G. (1956). Sex differences in the distribution of teacher approval and disapproval among ninth-grade children. *Journal of educational psychology,* 47, 385–396.

MILL, C. R. (1960). Attitudes affect pupils' learning. *Educational leadership,* January, 212–216.

MILLER, L. M. (1963). Dropout: schools search for clues to his problem. *School life,* 45, 5–7.

NEILL, A. S. (1960). *Summerhill: a radical approach to child rearing.* New York: Hart Publishing Co., Inc.

NEUMEYER, M. H. (1961). *Juvenile delinquency in modern society.* Princeton, N.J.: D. Van Nostrand Co., Inc.

OJEMANN, R. H., and WILKINSON, F. R. (1939). The effect on pupil growth of an increase in teacher's understanding of pupil behavior. *Journal of experimental education,* 8, 143–147.

PIANA, DELLA, GAGE, G., and GAGE, N. L. (1955). Pupils' values and the validity of the Minnesota Teacher Attitude Inventory. *Journal of educational psychology,* 46, 167–178.

PUTNAM, F. F. (1963). Information about dropouts: terms and computations. *School life,* 45, 24–29.

RECKLESS, W. C., DINITZ, S., and KAY, BARBARA (1956). Self-concept as an insulate against delinquency. *American sociological review,* 21, 744–766.

RECKLESS, W. C., DINITZ, S., and KAY, BARBARA (1957). Self-component in potential delinquency and non-delinquency. *American sociological review,* 22, 566–570.

REED, C. F., and CUADRA, C. A. (1957). The role-taking hypothesis in delinquency. *Journal of consulting psychology,* 21, 386–390.

REEDER, T. A. (1955). A study of some relationships between level of self-concept, academic achievement, and classroom adjustment. *Dissertation abstracts,* 15, 2472.

RYANS, D. G. (1961a). Inventory estimated teacher characteristics as covariants of observer assessed pupil behavior. *Journal of educational psychology,* 52, 91–97.

RYANS, D. G. (1961b). Some relationships between pupil behavior and certain teacher characteristics. *Journal of educational psychology,* 52, 82–90.

SEARS, PAULINE S. (1940). Levels of aspiration in academically successful and unsuccessful children. *Journal of abnormal and social psychology,* 35, 498–536.

SECHREST, L. (1964). Studies of classroom atmosphere. *Psychology in the schools,* 1, 103–118.

SHANLEY, F. J., ALZOBAIE, J., and LeFEVER, D. W. (1964). *Comparative analysis of school record and behavioral data for aggressive, well-adjusted and underachieving students.* Los Angeles: Youth Studies Center, University of Southern California.

STAINES, J. W. (1958). The self-picture as a factor in the classroom. *British journal of education,* 28, 97–111.

THOMPSON, G. G. (1944). The social and emotional development of preschool children under two types of educational programs. *Psychological monographs,* 56, (258).

THORNDIKE, E. L. (1941). Words and the comics. *Journal of experimental education,* 17, 110–113.

15

Peer Influences

INTRODUCTION

There are, presumably, three large categories of environmental events that are the most significant determinants of personality development. Two of them, the home and the school, have been discussed in previous chapters. The third, peers, is discussed in this chapter.

It is conventional to discuss the influence of peers after the influence of the home has been discussed, perhaps because of the chronology of things; the home is experienced first. One should not draw the conclusion, however, that the order of discussion reflects relative importance of the three, for that is unknown. All that will be shown in this chapter is that peer influences have some effect on personality development, and that, in some instances at least, the magnitude of this effect is considerable.

DEVELOPMENTAL CHANGES IN PEER INTERACTIONS

If children's behavior in groups is carefully observed at different ages, various age-related changes become apparent. The best-known age trend is the solitary-play–parallel-play–cooperative-play sequence (Parten and Newhall, 1943). During the first two years of life or so, play is largely in psychological isolation, even when other children are only inches away. The child plays as though he were alone; even imitation is absent at this age. From three to five, roughly, there are indications that the child at least notices and thinks about the behavior of his peers, for he tends to copy them. If they are riding tricycles, he rides his; if they are coloring, he asks for paper and crayons; etc. Yet there is little in the way of interaction; his play is parallel to that of his peers, but still independent. By the time he enters school, however, there is a gradual shift toward cooperative play; hide and seek, dolls, army, and "catch" are examples, as well as such loosely organized activities as wrestling and just talking.

At a later age, another sequence occasionally becomes visible: The loosely organized cooperative play groups of the five- to eight-year-olds sometimes develop into "gangs," beginning at eight years of age and beyond. A gang is distinguished from a play group by its longevity, solidarity, and in-group loyalty. In addition, it is often defined as a competitive organization; it exists to compete with other gangs, illegally as well as legally. A child does not become a member of one gang one day and another gang another day, as he might with play groups, but maintains his gang affiliation for months or years.

Often a clique is joined rather than a gang. A clique is defined as a small, intimate, social group. It is smaller than a gang, less formal (there are no weekly or monthly "meetings," but irregular "parties" or "get-togethers"), and does not exist to compete with other cliques, but exists mainly because of the compatibility of its members—they have a good time together. It often has "snob" characteristics; social class, clothing, and money are important eligibility requirements, as well as desirable personal characteristics. It thus offers prestige for its members as well as companionship.

In general, frequency of peer interactions clearly increases from birth to adolescence. It is fascinating to consider the question of frequency of peer interactions as compared to parent and teacher interactions. Who does a child interact most with at a given age, and how does the hierarchy change with age? Barker and Wright, in a classic study of a midwestern town of 725, "Midwest," came close to answering this question, at least for the children in Midwest (Barker and Wright, 1955; Wright, 1967). Experienced observers followed 16 children during all of their waking hours on certain days, writing down, so far as possible, everything that happened to them and everything they did. These long narrations were then divided into "episodes," each episode describing the beginning and end of a behavioral event, such as playing a game of marbles, talking to a teacher about an arithmetic problem, or looking for a shoe in the morning. It was then possible to determine the percentage of daily episodes occurring with parents, teachers, and peers. The results for eight children, representing an age range from two to eleven, are presented in Figure 15.1. The results are striking. In the first five years or so, almost all social interactions are with the parents (except for some children who had siblings). Then, at age five or six, interactions with teachers and peers begin. By age seven, the number of interactions with teachers and parents is the same but that with

Parallel play: these t[...]
youngsters, although [...]
gaged in the same type [...]
play, are obviously not int[...]
acting with each other.

(Wide World Photos)

peers is way ahead. What the trend would be after age eleven is an open question. Certainly, peer interactions would continue to increase up to the late teens or so, while interactions with teachers would increase at a slower rate, or perhaps remain relatively constant, and interactions with parents would probably continue to decrease. Perhaps, then, the total picture looks something like that in Figure 15.2, which is simply an extension of the Barker and Wright findings through adolescence. Perhaps someone will one day obtain the information necessary to test these guesses.

Another developmental trend in peer interactions is the degree of heterosexuality involved. Although precise normative data are lacking, it seems to be clearly the case that interactions with the opposite sex are related to age in a curvilinear fashion, as indicated in Figure 15.3. In the first year or two, there is no interaction at all, followed by increased interactions with both sexes. With school entrance, a preference for same-sex playmates becomes apparent, with this preference reaching its maximum at around ages seven to ten or so. At this age, a boy would rather "die" than go to a girl's birthday party. From then on, interactions with the opposite sex increase again, culminating in dating behavior a few years later.

There is evidence of more heterosexual interactions now than a generation ago, confirming the fears of some overanxious parents. In 1942 and again in 1963, Kuhlen administered the same sociometric question-

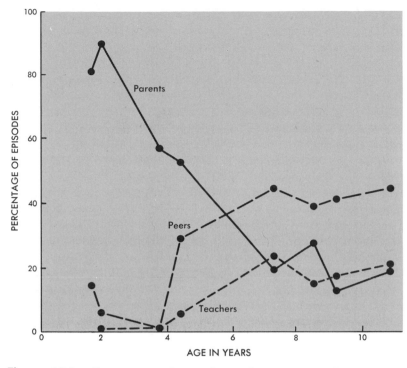

Figure 15.1. Percentage of episodes with parents, teachers, and peers (Wright, 1967).

naire to the same schools in central New York to over 100 girls and 100 boys in each of grades 6, 9, and 12 (Kuhlen and Houlihan, 1965). The questionnaire asked the respondent to make two peer choices for nine different activities, such as going for a walk, occupying an adjacent seat in the classroom, and skating. The results are presented in Figures 15.4 and 15.5 in terms of percentage of boys choosing at least one girl (Figure 15.4) and percentage of girls choosing at least one boy (Figure 15.5). For both sexes, and at all three grades, there is an increase in heterosexual choices from 1942 to 1963, averaging about 12 percentage points. Note also the tendency for the differences to be smallest at grade 6 (averaging about 8 percentage points) and largest at grade 12 (averaging about 18 percentage points). Notice, too, that boys express cross-sex preferences more frequently than girls both in 1942 and 1963. This is not to be interpreted as indicating earlier heterosexual interests by boys than by girls, since the earlier maturation of girls suggests the opposite, but rather the greater tendency for boys to declare such interests, in keeping with the more aggressive and active masculine role.

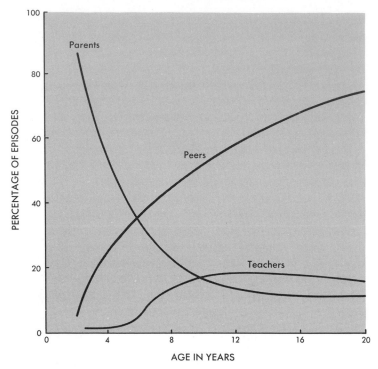

Figure 15.2. Wright's data extrapolated to adulthood.

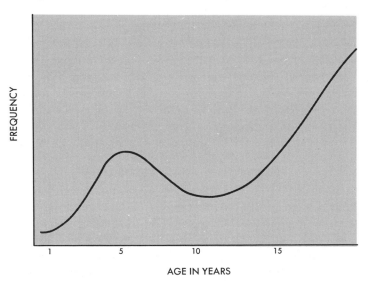

Figure 15.3. Conjectured age norms for frequency of heterosexual interactions.

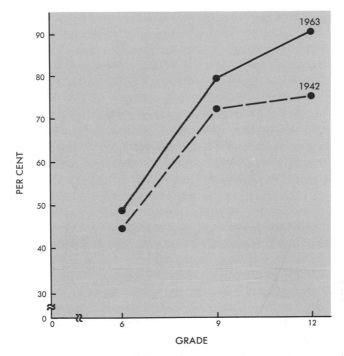

Figure 15.4. Percentage of boys choosing girls as sociometric choices in 1942 and 1963 (Kuhlen and Houlihan, 1965).

NORMS OF PEER SUSCEPTIBILITY

Although the increasing frequency of peer interactions with age is suggestive of the increasing importance of the peer group, more convincing data are desirable. After all, frequency of wearing a watch also increases from ages five to fifteen, but few would argue it is an important determinant of personality at either age. What is needed is a more direct index of the peer group's ability to control behavior—the power of the peer group must be measured.

Berenda (1950) compared the power of peers with the power of a teacher in an interesting experiment. Employing an arrangement similar to Asch's suggestibility experiments (see Chapter 10), children were exposed to lines of different lengths and asked to pick the one that was the same length as a standard. In the first experiment, several children announced their judgments publicly, in the presence of each other. Unknown to one of them, the others were "stooges" who on certain trials purposely picked a line that was too long or too short. Since their judgments were announced first, it was possible to measure the effect of these

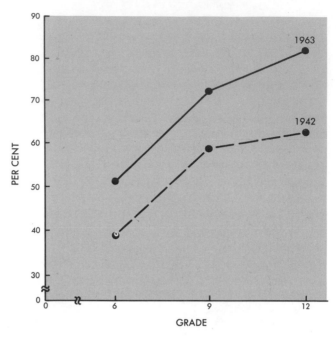

Figure 15.5. Percentage of girls choosing boys as sociometric choices in 1942 and 1963 (Kuhlen and Houlihan, 1965).

peer judgments on the real subject's tendency to pick the same line. The second experiment was exactly the same, except that a teacher was used as the "stooge" instead of peers.

There were seven "test" trials—occasions where the peers or teacher made a wrong judgment prior to the subject's judgment. With either peers or teachers, the subject made more errors, of course, than when he was not exposed at all to an incorrect judgment. But more interesting was the relative power of the peers versus teacher. Table 15.1 presents the percentage of subjects who "followed" zero to seven times on the seven test trials. Thus, 57 per cent of the subjects were not influenced by the teacher on any of the seven test trials, while only 16 per cent remained completely immune to peer influences. Forty-seven per cent followed peers' judgments at least four times, while none followed the teacher's judgments so often. These results clearly indicate that several peers had more influence than one teacher in this situation—a result many teachers would no doubt be willing to generalize to the real classroom.

The author is not aware of any other studies that have matched the influence of peers against the influence of adults, either teachers or parents. Some fascinating possibilities remain to be explored. Much would

TABLE 15.1

Percentage of Subjects Following "Stooges" Zero to Seven Times
on Seven Test Trials
(Adapted from Berenda, 1950)

Stooge	Test Trials							
	0	1	2	3	4	5	6	7
Peers	16	16	13	9	11	9	9	18
Teacher	57	24	13	6	0	0	0	0

depend upon the type of behavior under consideration. Clothing, for example, is probably more under the influence of peers than of parents, at least by age ten or so (perhaps earlier).

With schoolwork, the picture might be different. Suppose a child is doing some arithmetic homework he must hand in the next morning. Suppose he comes across a problem he cannot answer. Who is he more likely to ask for help, his parents or his peers? The parents—unless they had a past history of giving the wrong answers! Or suppose the child is told he may see any movie he wants. Suppose his best friend says he should see movie A, while his mother says he will enjoy movie B most. Here it might be difficult to guess as to whose advice the child would take. The point is, though, that one should not seek a general statement of the sort, "peers (or parents) have more influence," because such generality probably does not exist; it all depends on a given situation.

As an example of the specificity involved, consider a study by Lesser (1959). He asked if it were really true that working-class children exerted more pressure toward "aggressive behavior" than middle-class children. He suspected this was an oversimplification, since there are many kinds of aggression, as the reader will recall from the Fels data. First, he administered a popularity sociometric instrument to 74 working-class fifth-grade boys, asking them to write down the names of the "three boys in your class that you would like to have for your best friends," and the three boys "you wish were not in your class at all." Then the boys were given a booklet describing five kinds of aggression:

1. Provoked physical aggression: to physically attack or injure after provocation. *Example:* Here is a boy who will fight, but only if someone picks on him first.
2. Unprovoked physical aggression: to physically attack or injure without provocation. *Example:* This boy starts a fight over nothing.
3. Outburst aggression: to display uncontrolled, "temper tantrum" aggressive behavior. *Example:* Here is someone who flies off the handle right away and is very hot-headed.

4. Verbal aggression: to verbally attack or injure. *Example:* This boy often threatens other boys.
5. Indirect aggression: to attack or injure indirectly through another person or object. *Example:* This boy tattles to the teacher about what other boys do.

The boys were asked to write down the names of boys who best fit the examples. They could write down as many names as they pleased and could use the same name more than once. The result of major interest is the correlation between a boy's popularity and the frequency of his nomination to each of the five kinds of aggression. If working-class children discriminate among various kinds of aggression, approving some but disapproving others, then positive correlations should appear between popularity and the approved types of aggression, and negative correlations between popularity and the disapproved types of aggression. If, on the other hand, aggression is approved throughout, then all the correlations should be positive.

The results are presented in Table 15.2. Only one type of aggression is approved: provoked physical aggression. Most disapproved are verbal and indirect kinds of aggression. This latter point is of particular interest, since the middle-class teacher often has a reversed set of values about aggression. He often approves of indirect, verbal types of aggression and strongly abhors physical aggression. Thus, the child most popular with the teacher would tend to be least popular with the other children. Knowledge of the students' selectivity about aggression, as well as about other variables, would allow the teacher to take advantage of peer pressures, rather than blindly fighting them.

TABLE 15.2

Correlations Between Kinds of Aggression and Peer Popularity
(Adapted from Lesser, 1959)

Type of Aggression	Correlation
Provoked physical aggression	+.31
Unprovoked physical aggression	—.21
Outburst aggression	—.36
Verbal aggression	—.45
Indirect aggression	—.69

Susceptibility to Peer Influences as a Function of Age

If we were to ignore the niceties of situational specifics, the most prevalent generalization about peer influences would be to the effect that they first increase up to a maximum in early adolescence, and then gradually decline as adulthood is reached. In many neighborhoods, it is the junior high school student whose conformity to peers seems most prevalent. The uniformity of dress is most conspicuous. There is a oneness, a sameness, a repetitiousness so pervasive that one fears he is suffering from multiple vision. By college age, peer conformity seems to diminish a little; dress is more varied, and so is behavior. At the present time, there are quite a few bearded males on campus, and a few "long-hairs" too, serving as reminders that conformity is not yet dead (ironically enough, these conformers maintain they are advertising their non-conformity by their unusual appearance). But by and large, a healthy individuality seems to be the prevalent picture by young adulthood, which, it seems, was totally lacking in a younger age group.

There is recent evidence backing up this assumption of maximum peer conformity during early adolescence. Costanzo and Shaw (1966) carried out a study similar to that of Berenda involving the judgment of lengths of lines after being exposed to the judgments of "stooges." Four different age groups were sampled: seven to nine years, eleven to thirteen, fifteen to seventeen, and nineteen to twenty-one, with 12 males and 12 females at each age level. Each subject was exposed to the (incorrect) judgments of four same-aged peers on certain test trials, and thus a conformity score was derived in terms of the number of "followings." There were 16 such test trials. The results are presented in Figure 15.6, in terms of the average number of conformity responses at each age level, separately for males and females. Conformity is highest during early adolescence (eleven to thirteen), and drops off at both earlier and later ages. Note, too, that females are more conforming than males, a consistent finding in such studies, and one we have discussed previously under the guise of sex-typing.

One should not assume that early adolescence is associated with maximum conformity to all pressures; it is perhaps restricted to only the pressures of peers. McConnell (1963) measured conformity to the adult experimenter in an Asch-like situation, with subjects' ages ranging from six to eighteen, with a minimum of 20 subjects at each age level. Mean conformity scores are presented in Figure 15.7. Conformity from ages six to ten remains steady, shows a slight upward swing from eleven to thirteen, and then decreases at an increasing rate to age eighteen. The upswing during early adolescence is much smaller than in the previous study.

EXPERIMENTAL STUDIES OF PEER INFLUENCES

Now that we have some idea of the frequency of peer interactions as a function of age, and of the relationship between age and conformity to

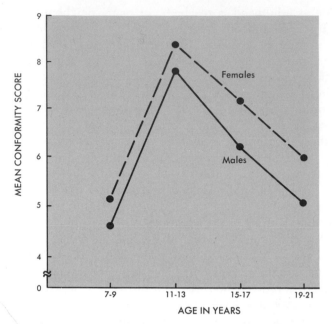

Figure 15.6. Mean conformity scores as a function of age (Costanzo and Shaw, 1966). Copyright © 1966 by The Society for Research in Child Development.

peers, let us consider some concrete, specific illustrations of peer influences. Four recent experiments are described, the first two illustrating peer influences at the preschool ages, the next at the fifth-grade level, and the last at adulthood.

Lever-pushing Influenced by Pictures of Preschool Friends

The first experiment (Horowitz, 1962a) is an ingenious little study, showing that so simple a behavior pattern as pulling a lever is influenced by its social consequences. Preschool children first were shown pictures of their school peers and asked to pick those they liked best and least. Teachers were also questioned about their playmates, in order to confirm their sociometric choices. Then, for a random third of the children, a picture of one of their best friends was selected. For another third, a picture of a "neutral" peer was selected (e.g., a picture of a child who was not picked as either liked or disliked). For the remaining third, a blue light was selected.

The children were then introduced, one at a time, to a lever-pulling apparatus and shown how to work the lever. Then they were told that,

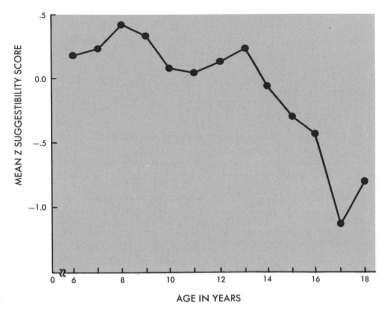

Figure 15.7. Mean conformity scores as a function of age (McConnell, 1963).

if they played the game, they would sometimes see something in a window above the lever. Every third pull, one-third of the children saw the picture of their friend for two seconds, one-third saw the picture of a neutral peer for two seconds, and one-third saw a blue light for two seconds. The children were told they could play as long as they liked, and then the experimenter disappeared behind a screen. Measurements included the total amount of time spent playing, number of lever pulls, and rate of lever pulls.

Rate was not affected by the consequences of lever pulling, but time spent playing and the number of pulls were affected, as indicated in Table 15.3. The top row shows that time spent playing was shortest for the blue light condition (an average of 2.3 minutes) and longest for the best friend condition (an average of 9 minutes). Similarly, the bottom row shows that number of responses was least for the blue light condition (an average of 54.6 responses) and greatest for the best friend condition (an average of 177.3 responses). These results, incidentally, held only for the younger children (average age of three years, ten months), the task apparently being too boring for older children (average age of five years, one month). Restricting generalizations to the younger children, then, it may be concluded that a picture of a friend functioned like a relatively strong reinforcer, maintaining the strength of a preceding response at a high frequency, as compared to a picture of a neutral peer, which, in turn, was more reinforcing than a blue light. The impressive thing about this experiment is that the mere picture of a friend had a reinforcing effect powerful enough to be detected. A picture is certainly more impotent than the real friend, but yet apparently strong enough to exert detectable effects under the right conditions.

TABLE 15.3

Mean Total Time and Mean Number of Responses as a Function of Consequences
(Adapted from Horowitz, 1962a)

Response Measure	Blue Light	Neutral Friend	Best Friend
Total time (minutes)	2.3	4.2	9.0
Number of responses	54.6	89.4	177.3

Weakening a Fear of Dogs by Observing Preschool Peers

The next experiment (Bandura et al., 1967) asks if a child's fear of dogs can be weakened by observing the behavior of a fearless peer. First, parents were asked to rate the magnitude of their children's fear and avoidance of dogs. Those children with high ratings were then given a standardized fear test as follows: They were ushered into a room containing a brown cocker spaniel confined in a playpen. The child was asked to go through a graded series of 14 interactions with the dog, each succeeding step involving greater contact and intimacy with the animal. To begin the series, the child was asked, in the following order, to walk up to the playpen and look at the dog, to touch it, and to pet it. Then the child was asked to open the playpen door, to lead the dog on a leash to a rug, to remove the leash, and to turn the dog over and scratch her stomach. Subsequent steps involved remaining alone in the room with the dog, feeding it biscuits, and, finally, entering the playpen with the dog, with no one else in the room. The child was scored in terms of the number of these steps he could carry out, the highest score reflecting least fear and avoidance.

The children were then divided into four groups of six boys and six girls each, and each group was subjected to a different treatment. In the *model-positive* condition, groups of four subjects went to a "birthday party" twice a day for four consecutive days. Each party involved paper hats, cookies, prizes, balloons, stories, and games. Toward the end of this "positive" experience, a four-year-old child entered, accompanied by an adult and the cocker spaniel. The boy, a "stooge," was unknown to most of the children. He proceeded to play with the dog, ignoring the other children. At first, he played cautiously with the dog, but by the last "party," he was completely casual: hugging her, scratching her stomach, feeding her wieners, and giving her milk from a baby bottle.

Children assigned to the *model-neutral* condition observed the same sequence of model behavior, except that the parties were omitted. Instead, the children, in groups of four, merely sat at a table and watched the model perform. The situation was thus "neutral" rather than "positive."

A third group, assigned to the *exposure-positive* condition, attended the parties, with the dog present as before, except that the model was absent. These children were thus exposed to the dog in a positive context but did not observe a peer fearlessly interacting with the dog. Finally, children in the fourth group were assigned to the *positive* condition. They attended the parties, but there was no model or dog. The inclusion of this control group made it possible to determine if just the parties per se had a fear-reducing influence, even in the absence of the dog.

A day after the treatments just described were finished, the children were given the initial 14-step fear test again. Each child was tested twice, once with the same cocker spaniel and once with a white mongrel. For half the children in each group, the order of testing was reversed, so that half were tested in the order spaniel-mongrel, and half in the order mongrel-spaniel. A month later, a follow-up test was made. Again, each child was tested twice, once with each dog, the same as before. It was thus possible to determine if any ameliorative effects of the treatment conditions generalized to a different dog or not, as well as whether or not they perseverated for a month. To preclude the possibility of experimenter bias affecting the results, the experimenter who administered the post-treatment tests did not know to which of the four treatments a given child had been assigned. Thus, his scoring could not have been influenced by preconceived notions as to how the experiment should come out.

The mean approach scores on the pretest, the post-test, and the one-month follow-up test are presented in Figure 15.8, separately for each of the four treatment conditions. The results are clear-cut. First, all groups showed some improvement, probably as a result of successive exposures to the dogs during the test sessions themselves. Second, children exposed to the model interacting with the dog improved considerably more than children not exposed to the model. Whether the modeling was done in a positive context or not made little difference. If the children were merely exposed to the information that a peer was not harmed by the dog, this was sufficient to reduce their subsequent avoidance be-

Learning by imitation. By observing a peer handling a snake, the girl on the right is probably extinguishing her fear of snakes.

havior a measurable amount. A final point, not indicated by Figure 15.8, is that the fear reduction generalized completely from the cocker spaniel to the white mongrel; there was no difference in test behavior to the two dogs.

The significance of this study is that it shows how powerfully a child's behavior can be affected merely by observing the behavior of a neutral peer, without being exposed to more potent forces, such as talking with the peer or observing a friend rather than a neutral peer. Eight observation sessions, totaling perhaps 30 minutes, were enough to substantially reduce a chronic fear of dogs built up outside the laboratory environment.

Attitudes Toward Teachers Affected by Peers' Behavior

The next study (Gnagey, 1960) illustrates peer influence at an older age (fifth-graders) and shows how attitudes toward a teacher can be

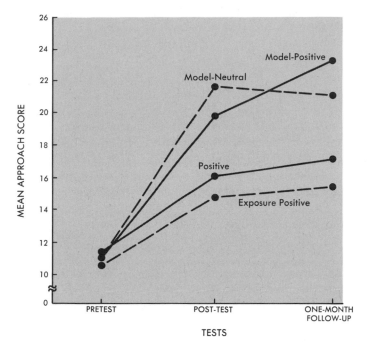

Figure 15.8. Mean approach as a function of four treatment conditions (Bandura et al., 1967).

changed by observing the behavior of other peers toward the teacher. The experimental questions were stated as follows: First, given that a child misbehaves toward the teacher in the presence of peers, does the outcome of the episode, in terms of the student "winning" or the teacher "winning," make any difference upon the attitudes of the audience? Second, does it make any difference whether the misbehaving student is a leader in his classroom or a follower? Presumably, a leader who "wins" should exert the most influence, while a follower who "loses" should exert the least influence.

To test these notions, initial attitudes of four fifth-grade classes toward female teachers in general were assessed, by asking such questions as:

How well can lady teachers handle the kids in this class?
How much do lady teachers know about films?
How well do you like most lady teachers?

Then the peer leaders of the classes were identified, by use of a socio-metric questionnaire that asked such questions as:

When a bunch of kids from this class get together outside of school, which three boys nearly always get the others to do what they want to do?

Some boys are stronger and tougher than others. If it came to a fight, which three boys in this class could win over most of the rest, if they had to?

The next step was to select a "high-powered" leader from two classes, and a "low-powered" follower from the other two classes. Each of these four boys was secretly trained to play a particular role in a misbehavior episode that would take place in front of the rest of the class.

Sometime after the completion of training, the actual misbehavior episode occurred. Each class was taken to a projection room, and the experimenter said, "Yesterday I told you I would bring along a grade-school teacher who would show you a film. This is Miss Robe." (None of the students had seen her before.) The "teacher" introduced the topic of the movie, told the students they would be asked to rate it later, and turned off the lights and began showing the film. About half-way through, the trained "stooge" said in a loud voice, "Hey, is this film about over?" The teacher immediately turned off the projector and said in an irritated voice, "Hey you, I told you not to talk. You leave the room and report to the principal's office." Two of the stooges, one a leader and the other a follower, defied the teacher. They said, "I'll leave the room, but I won't go to the principal's office. The heck with you," as they left the room. The other two, also consisting of a leader and a follower, gave in to the teacher. They hung their heads and said, "Yes ma'am. I'm sorry ma'am," as they left the room. Thus, one class was exposed to a defiant leader, another to a defiant follower, another to a submissive leader, and a fourth to a submissive follower. Following the misbehavior episode, the teacher showed the rest of the film, turned on the lights, and left the room.

Shortly thereafter, the experimenter re-entered the room and passed out a questionnaire that ostensibly allowed the students to rate the movie, but also included a number of questions about female teachers, including the same questions that had been asked at the beginning of the study.

The nature of the results can be summarized by considering the answers to two representative questions that were asked before and after the misbehavior episode. The first question asked the students to comment about how much female teachers knew about showing films. To determine if the misbehavior episode changed their minds, the ratings made after the film were compared to the ratings made beforehand. The number of ratings that did not change or that indicated a higher evaluation of the teacher were lumped together and compared with the number of ratings that showed a shift toward a more negative evaluation. The results for each of the four classrooms are shown in Table 15.4, in terms of percentage of students in each of the two categories. This table indicates that, when the misbehaving student was a leader, his defiance affected his classmates' evaluations of the teacher quite differently than when he was submissive. When he was defiant, about half the class (51 per cent) shifted to a more negative evaluation; when he was submissive, only one student (4 per cent) shifted to a more negative evaluation. The followers' behavior, on the other hand, had no effect at all. Whether they were defiant or submissive, two-thirds of the class did not change their evaluation, or they shifted to a more positive evaluation.

TABLE 15.4

Effects of Deviants' Reactions upon Classmates' Evaluation
of Teacher's Skill: Question 1
(Adapted from Gnagey, 1960)

Classroom	Percentage of No Change or Shift to Improved Evaluation	Percentage of Shift to Negative Evaluation
Leader, defiant	49	51
Leader, submissive	96	4
Follower, defiant	67	33
Follower, submissive	66	34

A second question asked the students how fair it was for a teacher to send a person to the principal's office. Table 15.5 shows the results, again in terms of before-after shifts in evaluation. The picture is almost exactly the same as in Table 15.4. When the misbehaving student was a leader, his defiance or submissiveness had a strong influence; when he was a follower, his reactions to the teacher had no effect at all. Practically no one, in either case, shifted to a more negative evaluation.

TABLE 15.5

Effects of Deviants' Reactions upon Classmates' Evaluation
of Teacher's Control Technique: Question 2
(Adapted from Gnagey, 1960)

Classroom	Percentage of No Change or Shift to Improved Evaluation	Percentage of Shift to Negative Evaluation
Leader, defiant	54	46
Leader, submissive	96	4
Follower, defiant	91	9
Follower, submissive	93	7

The Gnagey experiment clearly indicates that a student's interaction with a teacher not only affects his own behavior but also the behavior of onlookers. Kounin and Kump (1958) called this the "ripple effect" some years previously. The Gnagey experiment also shows that the ripple effect is greater if the model is a leader than if he is a nondescript follower, as one would expect. Teachers, coaches, boy-scout leaders, and other adults who interact with children from a position of authority would do well to realize that their public interactions with a given child have wider ramifications than to just the child himself but affect all observers, depending upon the prestige of the child in question.

Group Pressure Toward Disobedient Adult Behavior

Our last experimental study of peer influences takes place with adult subjects (Milgram, 1965). The setting is as follows: In one situation, single adults are put in a strong conflict situation, where an authoritative scientist says to hurt another human being for the sake of science is permissible, and conscience says not to—for the sake of humanity. In another situation involving exactly the same conflict, the subject first sees two peers defy the scientist and refuse to go along with the experiment, and then his behavior is recorded. By comparing behavior in the two situations, it is possible to assess the effect of peer behavior on resolution of the conflict.

The situation involves shocking another "subject" (really a stooge) who is strapped into an electric chair in an adjoining room. The procedure is exactly as described in Chapter 6 (pp. 209–211), where a previous study by this investigator was discussed in detail (Milgram, 1963). It is suggested that the reader turn back to those pages now and refresh his memory.

The present study can be described very briefly. Half of it is the previous 1963 study, where the subjects performed one at a time and were required to resolve the conflict alone. Under those conditions, 26 out of 40 went all the way; 65 per cent continued to shock the "victim" up to the severest shock—where the sign above the lever read "Danger: Severe shock," with three X's above it and a label reading "450 volts" below. The second half of the experiment involves another 40 subjects exposed to the same situation except that two other subjects (really stooges) were also present. One of them read the stimulus words to the "learner" in the electric chair, and the other recorded his answers. The real subject administered the shock the same as before. When he reached 150 volts, the first stooge protested that the learner was being hurt, and he refused to continue with the study. The scientist insisted that he continue, but the stooge prevailed, left his station and took a chair in another part of the room. The other two participants were then instructed to continue alone. When 210 volts were reached, the second stooge also expressed concern for the learner and refused to continue. The scientist again insisted that he continue, but he replied, "I'm willing to answer any of your questions, but I'm not willing to shock that man against his will; I'll have no part of it."

The naïve subject then found himself seated alone before the shock generator. He had observed two peers refuse to go on with the experiment. The scientist orders him to proceed, stating that it is essential that the study be completed. Nervous symptoms begin to appear. If he continues to 300 volts, the learner pounds on the wall and is heard from no more. If he turns to the scientist, he is goaded on, hearing that the learner will receive "no permanent injury." How does he resolve the conflict?

Four went all the way: 10 per cent, as compared to 65 per cent when there were no peers. Fifty per cent stopped by the time the second stooge had quit, at 210 volts. Only 20 per cent had quit by that point in the first study. The difference is dramatic: peer behavior multiplied by a factor of 2.5 the number of subjects who were "disobedient" to the scientist. And notice that the full potential power of the peers was not utilized. They were not influential friends of the real subject; they did not talk to him and implore him to follow suit; they were not "high-power" peers; etc. They were simply strangers who said nothing to the subject, but merely behaved in his presence. We may conclude with some confidence that the effects of peer pressure are not restricted to childhood, but are operative throughout the life span.

DETERMINANTS OF SUSCEPTIBILITY TO PEER INFLUENCE

Now that the power of the peer group has been experimentally demonstrated, we may ask another question: What are the factors that determine one's susceptibility to peer influence? There are three sets of such factors that would seem to exhaust the list of possibilities: (1) those associated with the *model*, (2) those associated with the *observer*, and (3) those associated with the *situation.*

Bandura (1962) lists the following characteristics as having been demonstrated to be associated with more powerful models: physical attractiveness, rewarding capacity, prestige, competency, status, and power. One addition can be made to the list: friendship (Horowitz, 1962b; Keislar, 1961; Patterson and Anderson, 1964). Thus, a child is most likely to be influenced by a *friend* who is *attractive,* has *status* and *prestige* with other children, is *competent,* has *power,* and has some *control* of *rewards and punishments.*

Characteristics of the observer that have been found to be associated with peer conformity are dependency, low self-esteem, incompetence,

model-observer sex similarity, and a history of reinforcement for conformity behavior (Bandura, 1962). To this list, the author would add
sex (Carlson, 1965: females are generally more conforming than males),
girls with older sisters (Brittain, 1966: perhaps because of "sensitization"
by observing the older sister's orientation to peers), and delinquency
(Bryant et al., 1963: perhaps because delinquents often have hostile, permissive parents, and it was previously noted that such parents have offspring who are highly identified with peers).

Popularity and Peer Influence

There is another whole line of research that is indirectly relevant here
and has to do with the determinants of *popularity*. A popular child is
one who other children want to be with, and who is thus a strong source
of influence. Factors associated with popularity therefore belong to the
first list—characteristics associated with the model. What, then, are the
determinants of popularity? There have been numerous studies that
correlated popularity ratings against a host of scores on personality dimensions, yielding results that are both predictable and not very exciting.
Traits like imaginativeness, intelligence, extraversion, activeness, positive
social aggressiveness, adjustment, attractiveness, etc., have been found
to be associated with popularity (Koch, 1933; Tuddenham, 1951). As
we have seen, sex also makes a difference—in a curvilinear fashion, with
heterosexuality being relatively high in frequency before and after ages
seven to ten or so.

Sheer physical proximity has a sizable effect too. You can hardly become friends with a person who lives so far away you never see him
(Furfey, 1927; Sherif and Sherif, 1953). The Sherifs demonstrated this
point in their famous camping studies with adolescent boys. In one
study, 24 twelve-year-old boys who were away on a summer camping
trip were treated as follows. First, sociometric ratings were obtained
after three days of camping in order to determine friendship patterns.
Then the boys were divided into two cabins, with least popular boys
grouped together. Activities were carried out by each cabin separately
for five days, and then friendship ratings were again secured. In just
five days, the boys' choices of friends went from 33 per cent within the
same cabin to 91 per cent, thereby documenting the importance of
proximity.

In a third phase, of only tangential relevance here, an attempt was
made to develop an active dislike for the former friends in the other
cabin. Competitive "win-lose" activities were arranged between the two
cabins, in which one cabin won while the other cabin lost. The results
were dramatic. Former friendships were distorted into active antago-

nism, as witnessed by name calling (e.g., "Dirty players!" "Cheats!" "Jerks!" "Rotten pukes!" and many other labels too picturesque for the printed page); posters hung up in the common news hall labeling the other cabin boys "pigs," "jackasses," "bums," and "girls"; and actual physical conflict (the throwing of food, sponges, and even saucers and knives at each other, necessitating the intervention of the experimenter). An attempt was finally made to rebuild lost friendships by instituting goals that were common to both cabins, such as a softball game against an outside team. These measures were partially successful in the time that remained, but not completely so. On the last night, the boys refused to join in a common campfire, but built separate ones for each cabin.

Even names affect popularity. McDavid and Harari (1966) carried out an ingenious study to demonstrate this relationship. First, they asked four classes of fourth- and fifth-graders to rate the attractiveness of 75 first names, which included the names of their classmates as well as the names of individuals in the other three classes. Since the classes were in different schools, there was little acquaintance with the children in those classes. Thus, the ratings of names from within their own class (Nw) were affected not only by the names per se but also by the characteristics of the bearers of the names. Ratings of the names in other classrooms (No), however, were a purer measurement of the popularity of the name per se, since the bearers (and their characteristics) were generally unknown. A month or so later, popularity of individuals, not names, within each class was assessed sociometrically (Iw). The final step in the study was then to determine the correlations between two sets of ratings: (1) popularity ratings of individuals by classmates and ratings of their names by the same classmates (i.e., Iw and Nw); and (2) popularity ratings of individuals by classmates and ratings of their names by children in other classrooms (i.e., Iw and No). The former correlation was .63, and the latter, .49. The two are not significantly different from each other. Thus, there is a definite relationship between popularity of names, as rated by peers who do not know people with those names and popularity of the bearers of those names themselves. The popularity of *names alone* presents the same ranking as the popularity of peers with those names! Parents ought to be aware of this fact, for it suggests that children should not be named strange, unusual names, for these are the ones rated low in popularity. As the authors concluded, "A parent might appropriately think twice before naming his offspring for Great Aunt Sophronia!" The best names are the simple, frequent ones: Bob, David, Janet, Mary, etc.

It was previously noted that friendliness is one personality characteristic associated with popularity; friendly children are more popular than aloof children. As with all such correlational studies, the cause-effect direction cannot be determined by the mere relationship. Perhaps popular children are friendly because they are popular, or perhaps they are popular because they are friendly. Keislar (1961), by means of a clever experiment, was able to show that at least part of the causal sequence flows from friendliness to popularity. By a unique arrangement, girls were led to believe that other girls of certain names liked them and others did not. Then they were asked to pick the names of the girls they liked best. There was a decided preference for the names of girls who presumably liked them, indicating that friendliness begets popularity.

Bonney (1943) also obtained some evidence suggesting that a child's popularity is determined by his own behavior, rather than solely by the acceptance or rejection of others. He obtained the sociometric ratings of a group of children before and one year after they had transferred to a new school, where they were generally unknown. Their scores were about the same in both places. Children who had been popular in the old school were popular in the new school and vice-versa. Assuming that their reputations had not followed them, it is difficult to interpret this consistency other than by assuming that the children *behaved in about the same way* in both schools, and their old and new peers did likewise, leading to a similar popularity score in both schools.

Peer Influence as Related to the Situation

There is very little to say about the importance of the situation as a determinant of peer influence, since there are little relevant data. All that need be observed here is a reiteration of the principle previously suggested: conformity may appear in one situation but not in another. Certainly, it is strong with respect to teen-age clothes fashions for girls.

It may be concluded that, although peer behavior may strongly affect a person's behavior, there are important individual differences in susceptibility to such influences. Some of these differences are associated with the model, some with the observer, and some (largely unknown) with the situation. All three sources of individual differences must be taken into consideration in evaluating a given instance of peer conformity.

THE SOCIALIZING INFLUENCE OF PEERS

If one asks what is the most important function of peer interactions, the usual answer is *socialization.* Peer interactions expose the child to the more frequent behavior patterns of his culture, and by this exposure he tends to learn expected modes of interpersonal behavior. Now, of course, such an argument, with qualifications, is reasonable. A child sees that his peers go to school, that boys play baseball in the spring and football in the fall, that girls wear dresses to school and shorts or slacks on weekends, that teen-agers hold hands in public, etc. Yet the very obviousness of the answer leaves it with an empty ring, as though we all know that anyway, and so what else is new? A more interesting question is to ask about the unique functions of the peer group. How do they differ, say, from other socializing influences, such as the home?

One of the obvious differences between the family and the peer group is that a child is *normally* exposed to just one set of parents, while he is exposed to a number of peers. This implies that peer interactions provide a more *representative sampling* of current do's and don'ts within the culture than is provided by the family. Assuming that each peer reflects, to some extent, certain practices and values of his culture, intensive exposure to, say, half-a-dozen peers exposes the child to six "points of view." Presumably, the child somehow "averages" these styles of life, reconciles them with the values of his parents, and thereby creates his own viewpoint, his own hierarchy of response tendencies.

Johnson and Medinnus (1965) have called this process the "normalizing or leveling influence" of the peer group. Interactions with peers tend to counterbalance parental idiosyncrasies, making children more similar than if they were raised in isolation from peers. In a sense, peers may be viewed as forming a protective ring around each other, neutralizing or at least weakening the effects of unusual, culturally infrequent parental pressures. Thus, the ten-year-old girl whose parents are bent upon transforming her into a concert pianist by the age of twenty, and expect her to practice four hours a day on weekdays and eight hours a day on weekends, learns from her friends that some ride horses after school, others play with dolls, others sometimes go ice-skating or roller-skating, others go bike-riding, others read, etc.—and she too learns to value these ways of living. She uses this information to hold her parents "in check." She complains about practicing all the time, saying that "her friends don't"; that she would like a bicycle, "like Susan has," a pair of roller skates, "like June," etc. Her parents are thus exposed to the cultural world in which she, the child, lives, and they are pressured to come to terms with it. They must "take a stand," so to speak, and surely their position will be less extreme than if there were no peer-instigated pressures to contend with in the first place.

What concrete evidence is there for this assumed normalizing influence? Very little—but the author remains convinced of its reality. One is tempted to mention Levy's (1943) studies of overprotected children, a common characteristic of which was active maternal attempts to isolate the children from all but a few carefully chosen and closely supervised playmates. These children showed many dramatic signs of maladjustment, as indicated by the case history reported on page 409. One is tempted to say that they had little opportunity to learn how a normal child should act, and without this guidance they showed numerous manifestations of social deviancy. Later, as adults, many of them returned to comparative normality, presumably as a result of exposure to peers—at school, on the job, and during leisure hours.

One is also tempted to mention studies concerned with adjustment of the "only child," since such children are exposed to less sibling influence than multiple-child families. Although the data are far from consistent (see Schacter, 1959; Spiegel and Bell, 1959, for reviews), there is a tendency for "only" children to contribute disproportionate numbers to the ranks of the deviant. Vogel and Lauterbach (1963), for example, carried out a careful study in which the number of siblings of 79 psychiatric patient-soldiers was compared with the number of siblings of 117 normal soldiers; the two groups matched on age, education, race, marital status, number of children, and years spent living with both of their biological parents. They found that 2 per cent of the normal soldiers were only children as compared to 15 per cent of the patient-soldiers. They also found that of those patient-soldiers who were judged recovered enough to be returned to active duty, 13 per cent had one or no siblings, while of those who were judged unfit for further military service, 35 per cent had one or no siblings.

One is also tempted to mention the fact that one type of psychotherapy with children is group psychotherapy. The idea is that by observing other children with varying degrees of normality, and by their reactions to the patient's social overtures, the patient will be guided back to more acceptable patterns of behavior. Writing of aggressive and passive children, Kessler states:

In a properly balanced group, the aggressive children spur the group to regressive and challenging behavior, and the more stable, socially oriented children serve as group superegos. The therapy lies in the group activity *per se*, which pulls some out of their social isolation, curbs the aggressiveness of others, and gives the more stable children a chance to grow in self-mastery. [1966, p. 398.]

There is no evidence, of course, that group psychotherapy is better than other types of (individual) therapy. It is mentioned here only to indicate that exposure to peers is an acknowledged, customary type of child psychotherapy, based on the belief that such exposure, under the right conditions, has ameliorative effects upon deviant behavior. We must take the word of the practicing psychotherapists—and of the parents of the patients—that the method works.

Finally, Harlow's work with monkeys must be mentioned (Harlow and Harlow, 1962). His work with wire and cloth surrogate mothers was described in Chapter 10, documenting the importance of contact comfort in the development of love for mother. It was also observed, in that chapter, that these monkeys did not develop into normal adult monkeys. Only one, for example, showed normal mating behavior, and the total group had to be written off so far as breeding stock was concerned. They seemed to be unable to develop friendly bonds of affection for each other. What is of interest here is that, in later studies, Harlow investigated the effect of peer interactions as a form of "therapy" for surrogate-raised monkeys. What he found is that opportunity to "play" with other monkeys almost completely prevented the development of social and sexual deviancy found in the previous monkeys, who had been deprived of both real mothers and peers. He concludes:

But at the same time we have found compelling evidence that opportunity for infant-infant interaction under optimal conditions may fully compensate for lack of mothering, at least in so far as infant-infant social and heterosexual relations are concerned. It seems possible—even likely—that the infant-mother affectional system is dispensable, whereas the infant-infant system is the *sine qua non* for later adjustment in all spheres of monkey life. [P. 138.]

Of course, there are peers and there are peers, and there are cultures and subcultures too. Not all peers are the "right" peers, for some represent a dramatic departure from the norms of the larger culture with which a set of parents forms a part. Thus, a child can "pick the wrong friends"—how many times have parents echoed that complaint? They mean that they, the parents, represent the "right" culture, and their child has picked friends who represent other, different cultures. If this can happen, and surely it does happen, it suggests that peer influences are not always normalizing, but are sometimes the opposite—pressuring the child to stray away from the central way of life toward a peripheral, idiosyncratic style. It is said, for example, that juvenile delinquency consists, in the main, of acts committed by groups of boys, not by boys acting alone (Neumeyer, 1961). It is often assumed that, without mutual peer encouragement, much delinquent behavior would never occur.

In such cases, parents sometimes conclude they have moved "into the wrong neighborhood." Perhaps the solution is to move out. Those with the necessary financial resources sometimes adopt this solution. For those who cannot, however, the problem is a difficult one. In this age of mobility and increasing urbanization, parents have less and less control over the associates of their children. It seems that, if the parents are really convinced that their child associates with the "wrong" friends, it is their responsibility to take positive action. They should explain why they feel as they do, and they should take steps to reduce the associations. An effective procedure would be to identify some potential friends acceptable to the parents, and then arrange situations wherein the child comes into contact with these peers. As previously noted, mere exposure is a strong incentive toward the formation of friendships.

SUMMARY

Peer interactions are one of the three large categories of environmental events—home and school being the other two—that are important in personality development. Frequency-wise, a child engages in more interactive episodes with peers than with either parents or teachers by the age of seven or so. Furthermore, it is undoubtedly the case that, at certain ages, and in certain situations, the child is more amenable to the pressure of his friends than to the pressure of parents or teachers. Early adolescence seems to be the age where susceptibility to peer pressure reaches its maximum intensity.

What is the nature of these pressures? Experimental studies have shown powerful effects in such diverse situations as simple lever-pressing, fear of dogs, attitudes toward teachers, and "disobedience." A complete list of specific response patterns affected by peer interactions would be infinitely long; in principle, any response pattern is modifiable by the behavior of peers.

At a more general level, "normalization" or "leveling" seems to be an important function of the peer culture. The argument is that a typical sampling of age-mate friends over the duration of childhood results in exposure to a more representative sampling of the larger culture than is possible by exposure to one set of parents. Thus, idiosyncrasies of the parents tend to be challenged by at least some of the peers, and thus the child brings to bear on his parents a demand of cultural conformity. Although the parents may not always "give in," the effect of the demand serves to dampen parental peculiarities, and thus serves to increase conformity to the larger culture.

Sometimes a group of friends is not representative of the larger culture, but represents, instead, a deviant subculture that holds values that conflict with those of the larger culture. Then, the "normalizing" process does not occur, but rather the opposite. In such cases, it is the responsibility of the parents to counter adverse peer-group influences, although just how this is to be accomplished is not an easy question to answer.

What are the factors that affect one's susceptibility to the group? There are many factors associated with characteristics of the group, of the observer, and of the situation. Powerful peers tend to possess the following characteristics: attractiveness, high rewarding capacity, prestige, competency, status, strong friendships, and the "right" names. The more susceptible children tend to possess the following characteristics: dependency, low self-esteem, same sex as model, a history of reinforcement for conformity, to be females rather than males, to be girls with older sisters, to have records of delinquency, and rejecting, permissive parents. Situational characteristics have not been investigated, but they surely exist. Thus, there are myriad interacting forces that produce individual differences in peer group conformity, so that no two children react the same to all forms of pressure in all situations.

BIBLIOGRAPHY

BANDURA, A. (1962). Social learning through imitation. In M. R. JONES (Ed.), *Nebraska symposium on motivation*. Lincoln: University of Nebraska Press.

BANDURA, A., GRUSEC, JOAN E., and MENLOVE, F. L. (1967). Vicarious extinction of avoidance behavior. *Journal of personality and social psychology*, 5, 16–23.

BARKER, R. G., and WRIGHT, H. F. (1955). *Midwest and its children*. New York: Harper & Row.

BERENDA, RUTH W. (1950). *The influence of the group on the judgments of children*. New York: Columbia University, Kings Crown Press.

BONNEY, M. E. (1943). The constancy of sociometric scores and their relationship to teacher judgments of social success and to personality self-ratings. *Sociometry*, 6, 409–424.

BRITTAIN, C. Y. (1966). Age and sex of siblings and conformity toward parents versus peers in adolescence. *Child development*, 37, 709–714.

BRYANT, H. A., DOBBINS, D. A., and BASS, B. M. (1963). Group effectiveness, coercion, change, and coalescence among delinquents compared to nondelinquents. *Journal of social psychology*, 61, 167–178.

CARLSON, RAE (1965). Stability and change in the adolescent's self-image. *Child development*, 36, 659–666.

COSTANZO, P. R., and SHAW, M. E. (1966). Conformity as a function of age level. *Child development*, 37, 967–975.

FURFEY, P. H. (1927). Some factors influencing the selection of boys' chums. *Journal of applied psychology*, 11, 47–51.

GNAGEY, W. J. (1960). Effects on classmates of a deviant student's power and response to a teacher-exerted control technique. *Journal of educational psychology*, 51, 1–8.

HARLOW, H. F., and HARLOW, MARGARET K. (1962). Social deprivation in monkeys. *Scientific American*, 207, 136–146.

HOROWITZ, FRANCES D. (1962a). Incentive value of social stimuli for preschool children. *Child development*, 33, 111–116.

HOROWITZ, FRANCES D. (1962b). The relationship of anxiety, self-concept, and sociometric status among fourth, fifth, and sixth grade children. *Journal of abnormal and social psychology*, 65, 212–214.

JOHNSON, R. C., and MEDINNUS, G. R. (1965). *Child psychology*. New York: John Wiley & Sons, Inc.

KEISLAR, E. R. (1961). Experimental development of "like" and "dislike" of others among adolescent girls. *Child development*, 32, 59–66.

KESSLER, JANE W. (1966). *Psychopathology of childhood*. Englewood Cliffs, N.J.: Prentice-Hall, Inc.

KOCH, HELEN L. (1933). Popularity in children: some related factors and a technique for its measurement. *Child development*, 5, 164–175.

KOUNIN, J., and GUMP, P. (1958). The ripple effect in discipline. *Elementary school journal*, 59, 158–162.

KUHLEN, R. G., and HOULIHAN, NANCY B. (1965). Adolescent heterosexual interest in 1942 and 1963. *Child development*, 36, 1049–1052.

LESSER, G. S. (1959). The relationship between various forms of aggression and popularity among lower-class children. *Journal of educational psychology*, 50, 20–25.

LEVY, D. M. (1943). *Maternal overprotection*. New York: Columbia University Press.

McCONNELL, T. R. (1963). Suggestibility in children as a function of CA. *Journal of abnormal and social psychology*, 67, 286–289.

McDAVID, J., and HARARI, H. (1966). Stereotyping of names and popularity in grade-school children. *Child development*, 37, 453–460.

MILGRAM, S. (1963). Behavioral study of obedience. *Journal of abnormal and social psychology*, 67, 371–378.

MILGRAM, S. (1965). Liberating effects of group pressure. *Journal of personality and social psychology*, 1, 127–134.

NEUMEYER, M. H. (1961). *Juvenile delinquency in modern society*. Princeton, N.J.: D. Van Nostrand Co., Inc.

PARTEN, MILDRED, and NEWHALL, S. M. (1943). Social behavior of preschool children. In R. G. BARKER, J. S. KOUNIN, and H. F. WRIGHT (Eds.), *Child behavior and development*. New York: McGraw-Hill Book Co. Pp. 509–525.

PATTERSON, G. R., and ANDERSON, D. (1964). Peers and social reinforcers. *Child development*, 35, 951–960.

SCHACTER, S. (1959). *The psychology of affiliation*. Stanford, Calif.: Stanford University Press.

SHERIF, M., and SHERIF, CAROLYN W. (1953). *Groups in harmony and tension*. New York: Harper & Row. Pp. 229–295.

SPIEGEL, J. P., and BELL, N. W. (1959). The family of the psychiatric patient. In S. ARIETE (Ed.), *American handbook of psychiatry*. New York: Basic Books, Inc. Pp. 114–149.

TUDDENHAM, R. D. (1951). Studies in reputation: III. Correlates of popularity among elementary school children. *Journal of educational psychology*, 42, 257–276.

VOGEL, W., and LAUTERBACH, C. G. (1963). Sibling patterns and social adjustment among normal and psychiatrically disturbed soldiers. *Journal of consulting psychology*, 27, 236–242.

WRIGHT, H. F. (1967). *Recording and analyzing child behavior*. New York: Harper & Row.

V

MORAL DEVELOPMENT

16

Morality and Parental Responsibility

Although it may seem a little unusual to devote an entire chapter to morality in a child psychology textbook, there is justification for it. There was a time when morality was the central subject of social learning and development, and the social sciences were termed "the moral sciences" (Kohlberg, 1964). In the 1930's and 1940's, other concepts with less of a value connotation became dominant: "adjustment," "adaptation," and "learning." Recently, however, the study of moral behavior in its own right has come back into prominence, as witnessed by reviews (Kohlberg, 1963, 1964; Pittel and Mendelsohn, 1966) and theoretical articles (e.g., Aronfreed, 1964; Ausubel, 1955; Hill, 1960). Kohlberg points out an interesting reason for the rebirth of interest in morality:

This increased interest . . . seems to be partly the result of recent history, which has sharpened awareness of the distinction between internal moral development and outward socialization and social adjustment. The barbarities of the socially conforming members of the Nazi and Stalinist systems and the hollow lives apparent in our own affluent society have made it painfully evident that adjustment to the group is no substitute for moral maturity. [1964, p. 383.]

Kohlberg is saying there is a distinction between social adjustment and morality, and that a complete study of psychological development must include both.

Morality is a difficult word to define, even with the use of a dictionary. Webster defines it as "the doctrine or practice of the duties of life;

ethics"; etc. Turning to the word *ethics*, one finds "the science that treats of the principles of human morality and duty." Regardless of its dictionary meaning, most of us have an idea of what it means—at least we are continually labeling the behavior of others as moral or immoral, right or wrong, good or bad. It is in part, then, *a value system about behavior.*

The word *value* suggests an emotional component to morality; we feel "good" about some acts and "bad" or "guilty" about others. As we shall see, one line of research is specifically concerned with the emotional aspects of morality. The word *system* implies a set of rules about behavior; we judge behavior to be moral or immoral partly in terms of its "fit" to a system of rules we have about the goodness and badness of behavior in general. A second line of research has been specifically concerned with this cognitive component of morality. Finally, there is behavior itself. One's emotions presumably combine with one's rules according to the specific situation at hand, and out of the emotional-cognitive-situational interaction emerges moral or immoral *behavior.* A third line of research, then, is concerned with overt behavior itself.

We shall begin by discussing the development of cognitive morality—systems of rules for behavior. Jean Piaget is the great pioneer of such research, and thus we will speak of "Genevan morality." Then we will examine the emotional development of morality, using Freud's treatment of "guilt" as the starting point. Finally, we will ask about the development of moral behavior, and will examine the results of "temptation tests"—contrived situations in which the subject is given the opportunity to "cheat," presumably without detection. Then we will consider how the three components interact to form the whole moral system. Finally, we will ask about the environmental determinants of moral development. How are parental practices correlated with moral development?

GENEVAN MORALITY

Piaget discovered a number of ways in which children change in their moral judgments as they get older (Piaget, 1962). We shall sample some of these supposed dimensions to get an idea of what Piaget was talking about. To measure the generality of these dimensions, different contexts in which Piaget studied their development will be considered: marble games, clumsiness, lying, and justice.

Marbles and Moral Realism

According to Piaget, during a child's earliest experience with the game of marbles (ages two to five), there is little awareness of rules.

The child does not try to "win," but plays by himself, enjoying the
sheer muscular-motor sensations associated with all possible maneuvers
with the objects at hand. Toward the end of this period, the child becomes aware of rules by watching older children and by imitating
them. His rule-bound behavior at this age, however, is more in terms
of curiosity and mimicry than in terms of a commitment to a cooperative
agreement as to how to conduct the game.

Beginning at age five or so and extending to age nine or ten, a different type of behavior and a different attitude toward the game become visible. The following interrogation of Pha (age five and a half)
is concerned with the rules of the game: "Do people always play like
that? *Yes, always like that.* Why? *'Cos you couldn't play any other
way*" (Piaget, 1962, p. 58). Geo (age six) told Piaget that the game
of marbles began with:

. . . *people, with the Gentlemen of the Commune.* How was that? *It
came into the gentlemen's head and they made some marbles.* How did they
know how to play? *In their heads. They taught people. Daddies show little
boys how to.* Can one play differently . . . ? *I think you can, but I don't
know how.* Anyhow? *No, there are no games you play anyhow.* Why? *Because God didn't teach them.* [P. 59.]

Beginning at age ten or so, a still different attitude becomes visible.
Ross (age eleven) claims that he often invents new rules:

We make them (up) sometimes. We go up to 200 [instead of to 100]. *We
play about and then hit each other, and then he says to me: "If you go up to
100 I'll give you a marble."* Is this new rule fair like the old ones, or not?
*Perhaps it isn't quite fair, because it isn't very hard to take four marbles that
way!* If everyone does it, will it be a real rule or not? *If they do it often, it
will become a real rule.* Did your father play the way you showed me, or
differently? *Oh, I don't know. It may have been a different game. It
changes. It still changes quite often.* [P. 66.]

Malb (age twelve) thinks the game of marbles began with children
looking for round pebbles.

Later on, boys wanted to play differently and they invented other rules.
. . . Could one change the rules? *Yes.* Could you? *Yes, I could make up
another game. We were playing at home one evening and we found out a
new one* (he shows it to us). Are these new rules as fair as the others? *Yes.*
Which is the fairest, the game you showed me first or the one you invented?
Both the same. If you show this game to the little ones, what will they do?
Perhaps they will play at it. And if they forget the square game and only
play this one, which will be the true game, the new one that will be better
known, or the old one? *The best known one will be the fairest.* [P. 67.]

Now, what is the nature of the differences between, say, the seven-
year-old and the twelve-year-old? Piaget says that younger children act

as though the rules are *sacred and untouchable*, emanating from adults or God in an unchanging form through time, lasting forever, and not to be questioned or changed. Any departure from the sacred rules makes the game unfair, and is unthinkable. There must be implicit *obedience to authority*. Such obedience is always right, and departure is always wrong; a *moral absolutism* thus prevails. It is measured in terms of the child's *objective responsibility* to the rules. Intention is ignored; it is objective conformity that defines rightness.

With older children, these characteristics change. Rules are no longer immutable and sacred, but can be changed at will, the important thing being that whatever the rules are, there must be agreement if they are to be fair. Thus, right and wrong are no longer judged in terms of obedience to authority, but in terms of a subjective, cooperative, *social* thing. Laws do not come from parents or God, but from people themselves, in terms of mutual consent.

The characteristics of the younger child's answer—moral absolutism, obedience to authority, objective responsibility, unchangeability of rules —Piaget calls *moral realism*. The "realism" comes from the child's tendency to confuse the subjective with the objective—to view rules as existing "out there" rather than as psychosocial expectations, to view goodness and badness as existing in the act itself rather than as a subjective evaluation of the observer. It is this tendency to reify the subjective that leads to the label of moral realism.

Clumsiness and Moral Realism

Piaget argues that the moral realism of the younger child pervades all areas of cognition. Consider clumsiness. With his usual brilliant insight, Piaget says that clumsiness plays ". . . however unjustly, an enormously important part in a child's life . . . At every moment, the child arouses the anger of those around him by breaking, soiling, or spoiling some object or other" (p. 121). Parents often react to such accidents in terms of objective responsibility: the greater the material damage, the more scolding and punishment the child receives. "The average housewife . . . will be more angry over 15 [broken] cups than over 1, and independently, up to a point, of the offender's intentions" (p. 133). And even when the parents do react on the basis of the child's presumed intentions, the child is likely to miss the subtle difference between such subjectivism and objective responsibility, and to conclude that it is the consequence of acts that are right or wrong, not their intentions. In other words, through the punishment of the parents (termed "adult constraint" by Piaget), the child learns objective responsibility regarding his own behavior.

Moral subjectivists. According to Piaget, these boys are old enough to know that there is not one game of baseball, but as many as the boys arbitrarily decide to invent.

Piaget came to this conclusion by asking the following kinds of story-questions.

[I.   A.] A little boy who is called John is in his room. He is called to dinner. He goes into the dining room. But behind the door there was a chair, and on the chair there was a tray with 15 cups on it. John couldn't have known that there was all this behind the door. He goes in, the door knocks against the tray, bang go the 15 cups and they all get broken!

[B.] Once there was a little boy whose name was Henry. One day when his mother was out he tried to get some jam out of the cupboard. He climbed up on a chair and stretched out his arm. But the jam was too high up and he couldn't reach it and have any. But while he was trying to get it he knocked over a cup. The cup fell down and broke. [P. 122.]

[II.   A.] There was once a little girl who was called Marie. She wanted to give her mother a nice surprise, and cut out a piece of sewing for her. But she didn't know how to use the scissors properly and cut a big hole in her dress.

[B.] A little girl called Margaret went and took her mother's scissors one day that her mother was out. She played with them for a bit. Then as she didn't know how to use them properly she made a little hole in her dress. [P. 122.]

Piaget asked two kinds of questions about each pair of such stories: (1) Are the children equally guilty? (2) Which of the two is the naughtiest, and why? If A is picked, the child is scored as displaying moral realism, since it is objective responsibility that counts; motives are ignored.

Here are some typical replies. In regard to Story I (broken cups), Geo (age six) is first asked:

Have you understood these stories? *Yes.* What did the first boy do? *He broke 15 cups.* And the second one? *He broke a cup by moving roughly.* Why did the first one break the cups? *Because the door knocked them.* And the second? *He was clumsy. When he was getting the jam the cup fell down.* Is one of the boys naughtier than the other? *The first one is because he knocked over 15 cups.* If you were the daddy, which one would you punish most? *The one who broke 15 cups.* Why did he break them? *The door shut too hard and knocked them over. He didn't do it on purpose.* And why did the other boy break a cup? *He wanted to get the jam. He moved too far. The cup got broken.* Why did he want to get the jam? *Because he was all alone. Because his mother wasn't there.* Have you got a brother? *No, a little sister.* Well, if it was you who had broken the 15 cups when you went into the room and your little sister who had broken one cup while she was trying to get the jam, which of you would be punished more severely? *Me, because I broke more than one cup.* [P. 125.]

Schma (age six) is first asked to retell the story, and then is asked:

Are those children both naughty, or is one not so naughty as the other? *Both just as naughty.* Would you punish them the same? *No. The one who broke fifteen plates.* And would you punish the other one more, or less? *The first one broke lots of things, the other one fewer.* How would you punish them? *The one who broke the 15 cups: two slaps. The other one, one slap.* [P. 125.]

A few years later, a different answer prevails. Corm (age nine) answers:

Well, the one who broke them as he was coming isn't naughty, 'cos he didn't know there was any cups. The other one wanted to take the jam and caught his arm on a cup. Which one is the naughtiest? *The one who wanted to take the jam.* How many cups did he break? *One.* And the other boy? *Fifteen.* Which one would you punish most? *The boy who wanted to take the jam. He knew, he did it on purpose.* [P. 129.]

And Nuss (age ten) says the naughtiest is "*the one who wanted to take the jam.* Does it make any difference the other one having broken more cups? *No, because the one who broke 15 cups didn't do it on purpose"* (p. 130).

The same developmental trend is apparent for Story II (hole in dress). Children six to nine usually answer in terms of objective responsibility; older children answer in terms of intention. Thus, the same moral realism observed in the game of marbles is observed in reactions to these stories of clumsiness.

In asking about the determinants of this developmental trend, Piaget argues, as previously noted, that parents' use of adult constraint is conducive to the younger child's moral realism. What, then, directs the older child toward moral subjectivism? Piaget argues it is the parental and/or peer attitude of *cooperation* that breeds a sensitivity to intentions rather than to consequences. As the child grows older, his parents and peers often draw attention to their own intentions, their own needs, and their own blunders. Thus, the child gradually becomes aware that reciprocity and mutual sympathy are the real determinants of satisfying friendships and social relationships, and not simply the consequences of social acts:

> In this way the child will find himself in the presence, not of a system of commands requiring ritualistic and external obedience, but of a system of social relations such that everyone does his best to obey the same obligations, and does so out of mutual respect. The passage from obedience to cooperation thus marks a progress analogous to that of which we saw the effects in the evolution of the game of marbles: only in the final stage does the morality of intention triumph over the morality of objective responsibility. [P. 138.]

Thus, as adult constraint produces objective responsibility, so peer (and adult) cooperation at a later age produces subjective responsibility.

Lying and Moral Realism

The younger child feels that a *lie is a statement that is untrue*. Thus, a mistake is a lie—intention makes no difference. At a later age, the crucial factor is purposive deception. Referring to Piaget again, Clai (age six) is asked:

> Do you know what a lie is? *It's when you say what isn't true.* Is "2 + 2 = 5" a lie? *Yes, it's a lie.* Why? *Because it isn't right.* Did the boy who said that "2 + 2 = 5" know it wasn't right, or did he make a mistake? *He made a mistake.* Then if he made a mistake, did he tell a lie or not? *Yes, he told a lie.* [P. 144.]

But when Ke (age seven) is asked if 2 + 2 = 5 is a lie, he answers:

> *No, that's not one.* Why did the boy who said it was tell me so? *Perhaps he made a mistake.* What is making a mistake? *When you don't say things right.* Is making a mistake the same thing as telling a lie? *No.* What is the

(Wide World Photos)

A lesson in moral subjectivity. The boy in the photograph at the left is leading his hand-reared Hereford to the beef auction. When the purchaser saw this photograph, the Hereford was returned to the boy, resulting in the photograph at the right, taken two weeks later. Thus the boy learned that adults care about intentions and feelings more than acts, and he was helped along the road to his own moral subjectivism.

difference? *Making a mistake is when you don't say things right; a lie is true, only you don't say it* (you know the truth but do not say it). [P. 146.]

Moral realism in lying is also indicated by attaching overriding importance to the *magnitude of departure from reality*. Consider the following pair of stories:

[A.] A little boy (or a little girl) goes for a walk in the street and meets a big dog who frightens him very much. So then he goes home and tells his mother he has seen a dog that was as big as a cow.

[B.] A child comes home from school and tells his mother that the teacher had given him good marks, but it was not true; the teacher had given him no marks at all, either good or bad. Then his mother was very pleased and rewarded him. [P. 148.]

After making sure that the child understands the stories, he is asked who was the naughtiest, and why. Bug (age six) answers:

The one with the cow. Why is he the naughtiest? *Because it isn't true. And the one of the good marks? He is less naughty.* Why? *Because his mother would have believed, because she believed the lie.* (This is not a slip. We have met with many cases of children 6–7 who, like . . . Bug, measure the naughtiness of a lie by the degree of its incredibility to adults. Consequently the lie about the good marks is not so bad because the mother will be easily taken in by it!) And why did the other child tell the lie about the cow? *Because he was telling his mother a lie.* Which would you punish most? *The one who said he saw a dog as big as a cow.* [P. 151.]

But Kei (age ten) answers:

The lie about the teacher. Why? *Because he deceived his mother.* But so did the other. *But he* (the one of the teacher) *had said something the teacher hadn't said.* The other one too had said something that wasn't true. . . . *He had told a great big lie. The teacher hadn't said he was good.* Why is it naughtier than the lie about the dog? *Because you can see better that it* (the lie about the dog) *is not true. You can't tell with the lie about the teacher.* Why did he say he had seen a dog as big as a cow? *To make them believe he had seen something marvelous.* [P. 158.]

Thus, the younger child observes the greater disparity between the dog and the cow and concludes that it is therefore the naughtier lie, while the older child reasons just the opposite—the more blatant the departure from reality, the *less* serious a lie is. The "smaller" lie is more serious because it is more likely to be believed.

Yet another manifestation of moral realism is the young child's tendency to judge a lie in terms of its *objective consequences to the recipient of the lie.* Thus, a *mistake* that has harmful consequences is more serious than a *lie* that is harmless. The relevant stories concern (A) a boy who purposely shows a man the wrong way, but the man does not get lost; and (B) a boy who mistakenly directs a man in the wrong direction, and the man gets lost. Car (age eight) says the naughtier is:

. . . *the one who made the gentleman lose his way, and the less naughty boy is the one who didn't make the gentleman lose his way.* If you had to punish them, which would you punish most? *The one who didn't know where it was. He made a mistake.* But didn't the other one deceive the gentleman? *Yes, but the gentleman didn't get lost.* And if the gentleman had got lost? *They would have both been equally naughty.* [P. 161.]

But Kei (age ten) says the naughtier is the one *"who did it on purpose. The first one deceived somebody, but he didn't know it"* (p. 162). Thus, we see the younger child thinking in terms of consequences, the older child in terms of intentions.

Justice and Moral Realism

Justice is concerned with rewards and punishments. A reward or punishment is just if we feel it is deserved, unjust if not deserved.

Consider two kinds of punishment: *expiatory* punishment and *reciprocal* punishment. Expiatory punishment is punishment for its own sake, with no concern for its relationship to the nature of the forbidden act, and no concern with its possible effects upon the guilty party. Reciprocal punishment, on the other hand, is based on the principle of cooperation; rules are social agreements—expectations—and are not handed down from an authority figure. As such, violation of an agreement has its own consequences; the person is no longer a part of the social group that subscribes to the agreement. Thus, there need be no punishment at all, or if there is to be punishment, it must have a purpose—to bring the individual back into the circle of society that subscribes to the rule, for the benefit of all. Consider the following two stories:

[A.] One afternoon a little boy was playing in his room. His father had only asked him not to play ball for fear of breaking the windows. His father had hardly gone when the boy got his ball out of the cupboard and began to play with it. And bang goes the ball against a window pane and smashes it! When the father comes home and sees what has happened he thinks of three punishments: (1) To leave the window unmended for several days (and then, as it is winter, the boy will not be able to play in his room). (2) Make the boy pay for having broken the window. (3) Not let him have his toys for a whole week.

[B.] A boy has broken a toy belonging to his little brother. What should be done? Should he (1) give the little fellow one of his own toys? (2) pay for having it mended? (3) not be allowed to play with any of his own toys for a whole week? [P. 203.]

It is easy to see which is the expiatory punishment in these stories—not being allowed to play with his own toys for a week. Here, there is no relationship between the punishment and the act. The other alternatives (1 and 2 in both stories) involve reciprocal punishment. *Restitution* is involved in alternative 2 of each story (as well as in alternative 1 of Story B), while *refusal to help* (letting the child suffer the natural consequences of the act) is involved in alternative 1 of Story A. The reciprocity of this latter situation stems from the fact that the transgressor is forced to recognize that the group approves of the natural consequences of the transgression, and does nothing to stop them.

Now, how do children of different ages respond to stories such as these? Piaget interviewed about 100 children of ages six to twelve and obtained the following results in terms of the percentage of answers that advocated a reciprocal punishment:

	Ages		
	6–7	8–10	11–12
Percentage of reciprocal answers	28	49	82

Thus, a clear trend toward reciprocal punishment is seen to exist.

A second dimension of moral realism in justice is the younger child's subscription to *immanent justice* as compared to the older child's belief in *naturalistic causality.* Consider the following stories:

[A.] Once there were two children who were stealing apples in an orchard. Suddenly a policeman comes along and the two children run away. One of them is caught. The other one, going home by a roundabout way, crosses a river on a rotten bridge and falls into the water. Now what do you think? If he had not stolen the apples and had crossed the river on that rotten bridge all the same, would he also have fallen into the water?

[B.] In a class of very little children the teacher had forbidden them to sharpen their pencils themselves. Once, when the teacher had her back turned, a little boy took the knife and was going to sharpen his pencil. But he cut his finger. If the teacher had allowed him to sharpen his pencil, would he have cut himself just the same? [P. 252.]

The believer in immanent justice believes in automatic, mechanical punishment for all transgressions, in the same way that a dropped object automatically falls to the earth. His objectivism leads him to the belief of moral law as well as physical law, and he treats the two as one. Thus, punishment automatically emanates as a result of the objective transgression per se, quite independent of the intentions and actions of other people. In short, Piaget says the younger child believes in a Great World Order, wherein everything "meshes" according to a grand plan of cause and effect, right and wrong, and everything equalizes in the long run. He is encouraged in this belief by his parents, of course, many of whom themselves have not progressed much beyond this belief. Thus, a parent says, "It serves you right," or "If you hadn't been naughty, you wouldn't have hurt yourself." In later years, experience teaches the child that wickedness often goes unpunished, as well as the reverse; a person often gets punished when innocent of a wrongdoing. Thus, he gradually becomes aware of the *non-universality* of expiation.

Of 167 children questioned on this matter, in terms of the previously described story questions, the percentage answering in terms of automatic expiative punishment was as follows:

	Ages			
	6	7–8	9–10	11–12
Percentage of automatic punishment	86	73	54	34

An example of an automatic punishment answer is provided by Pres (age nine), Story A: "What do you think? *He was punished as much as the other one, and even more.* And if he had not stolen the apples, would he have fallen into the water as he was crossing the river? *No, because he would not have needed to be punished*" (p. 254). Fleu (age twelve) provides an example of subscription to naturalistic causation: "And if he hadn't stolen the apples, would he have fallen in too?—(He laughs). *The bridge isn't supposed to know whether he has stolen the apples*" (p. 255). Thus, Fleu finds Pres's answer so impossible he laughs at the very idea.

A third dimension of moral realism is equating justice with *obedience to authority*, with the other end of the dimension defined by *equalitarianism*. As has been mentioned several times on preceding pages, the younger child equates goodness with obedience to authority. Suppose obedience is opposed to equal treatment, as in the following stories:

[A.] Once there was a camp of Boy Scouts (or Girl Guides). Each one had to do his bit to help with the work and leave things tidy. One had to do the shopping, another washed up, another brought wood or swept the floor. One day there was no bread and the one who did the shopping had already gone. So the Scoutmaster asked one of the Scouts who had already done his job to go and fetch the bread. What did he do?
[B.] One Thursday afternoon, a mother asked her little girl and boy to help her about the house, because she was tired. The girl was to dry the plates and the boy was to fetch in some wood. But the little boy (or girl) went and played in the street. So the mother asked the other one to do all the work. What did he say? [P. 277.]

In these stories, obedience to authority is not correlated with equality, but rather with inequality. How do children of different ages react to this dilemma? Piaget discovered four types of answers, exemplified in the following four replies:

Bar (age six and a half), Story A: "*She ought to have gone to get the bread. Why? Because she had been told to.* Was it fair or not fair to have told her to go? *Yes, it was fair, because she had been told to.*"

Chri (age six), Story A: "Is it fair? *No, the girl does more. She'll be jealous.* Did she go or not? *She went.* Did she think it fair? *No, she'll say, 'It wasn't me was to go and fetch the bread.'* Why did she go? *Because the chief wanted her to.*"

Schu (age twelve), Story B: "*She shouldn't have done it. It's not fair that she should work twice as hard and not the other.* What was to be done? *She should have said to her mother, 'It's not fair. I ought not to do double work.'*"

Balt (age eleven years, nine months), Story B: "*She did it.* What did she think? *That her brother was not very nice.* Was it fair that she should do this? *It wasn't fair, but she did it to help her mother*" (pp. 279–283).

The first answer illustrates complete identification of justice with obedience to authority and is characteristic of the very young child. The second answer illustrates, again, the identification of obedience and justice, but equality is also recognized as something independent and important in its own sense. Authority, however, prevails. The third answer illustrates the evolving supremacy of equality over obedience; for these children, equality outweighs everything, even friendliness with the authority figure. The fourth answer is most interesting of all; it is similar to the second answer in that, although a difference between authoritarianism and equality is recognized, obedience to authority wins out. It is different in that the *reason* for obedience is entirely different; voluntary obedience to an unequalitarian request is seen as superior to equalitarianism at any cost. If the cost is too high, the better choice is seen to involve abandoning equality in order to serve a higher morality—the morality of affection and help to a loved one or to a legitimate authority figure. Equality, then, is no longer seen as an isolated law, but is seen as relative to other factors peculiar to the specific situation, so that it may be *wrong* if, in achieving equality, other people are made to suffer. It is as if the child understands that a responsible involvement with other people requires an occasional sacrifice of one kind or another.

Summary of Genevan Morality

A brief recapitulation of Piaget's theorizing seems to be in order. Piaget saw developmental trends in the understanding of rules and transgressions that have extremely wide generality. They are evident in any activity that involves rules. Consider the dimension of objective responsibility (in the younger child) versus subjective intentionalism (in the older child). In marbles, it is exemplified by the young child's attitude that the rules of the game must be *unquestioned and obeyed,* and the older child's recognition that the essence of the game is not conformity to existing rules, but conformity to *arbitrary agreements the children themselves may make*—and change. With clumsiness, it is exemplified by the *material consequence* of the act (younger child) as opposed to the *intention behind the act* (older child) as the important determinant of "naughtiness." In lying, the young child equates a lie with *any untrue statement,* while the older child defines it in terms of whether it is *intentionally deceptive or not.* Likewise, the younger child measures its seriousness in terms of *magnitude of departure from the truth,* while the older child is more concerned with *the motive behind the lie.* In the area of justice, the younger child equates what

is right with *obedience to authority*, while the older child is more concerned with *equal treatment for all* (equalitarianism). Likewise, the
younger child believes that *all instances of disobedience should be, and
are, automatically punished* (immanent justice), while the older child
believes that such transgressions are *not always wrong, nor are they
always punished* (naturalistic causality). Again, the younger child believes that a *transgression requires punishment, with no necessary relationship between the misdeed and its consequences* (expiatory punishment), while the older child believes the *punishment should be related
to the nature of the crime* (reciprocity), if there is to be any punishment
at all.

In all these cases, a certain common factor is seen to distinguish the
younger and older child: Piaget calls it *moral realism* in the younger
child, which changes to *subjectivism* in the older child. There is a social,
cooperative, logical flavor to the older child's reasoning, as contrasted
to an egocentric, autonomous, authoritarian flavor in the younger child's
thinking. The difference all stems, says Piaget, from two cognitive
defects in the younger child: (1) egocentrism—inability to be aware of
the perspective of others, and (2) realism—the reification of subjective
phenomena (e.g., the confusion of subjective phenomena with exterior,
objective things). Put the two together and you have moral realism.

Piaget's theory of moral development is intimately related to his more
general theory of intellectual development (see Chapter 4). Recall the
first stage of intellectual development: the *sensorimotor* period (ages
zero to two). Recall the discussion of *object constancy:* an adult assumes certain properties of an object—weight, volume, area, etc.—to
remain constant, even though the object produces an ever-changing
panorama of sensations because of changes in position, distance, illumination, etc. The belief in object permanence is not shared by the very
young child. When the three-month-old infant pushes his ball under
the pillow, he does not look for it, but acts as though it no longer exists.
He makes no distinction between the object and the sensations it creates.
The sensations are the object, and when they cease to exist, so does the
object. Thus, the infant, in learning about object permanence, is seen
to suffer from the same cognitive defect—realism—from which the older
child suffers in learning about the subjectivity of morality. In both
cases, there is reification of the subjective into the objective—on the one
hand, sensations, and on the other hand, rules.

There are many other overlaps between Piaget's notions concerning
intelligence and morality. Indeed, the two should not be considered
separate theories at all, but should be considered two aspects of a single,
broad theory of cognitive development. As such, the unity between the
two branches becomes natural and expected, rather than surprising.

It is the generality of Piaget's ideas—the incredibly wide range of events made to bow to a single set of principles—that gives it its power and value.

Evaluation of Genevan Morality

We shall now evaluate Piaget's theory in the light of existing data. Since his methodology has already been discussed, and since it applies to his treatment of morality too, these questions can be dispensed with (the reader is referred to pp. 156–157), and we can proceed directly to the substantive question: How do his notions compare with the facts?

Since the early 1960's, there has been a tremendous awakening of American psychologists to the ideas of Jean Piaget, with a corresponding attempt to verify his conclusions with more adequate methodology and sampling. Restricting ourselves, now, to studies of moral development, we may note two reviews by Kohlberg (1963, 1964). He writes:

A fairly large body of research on Piaget's "stages" of moral judgment has been carried on by other workers. . . . The age trends for several of the Piaget dimensions are consistent enough to warrant the conclusion that they are genuine developmental dimensions in both American [Boehm and Nass, 1962; Johnson, 1962; Kohlberg, 1958; Lerner, 1937; MacRae, 1954] and in French-speaking [Caruso, 1943; Lerner, 1937; Piaget, 1962] cultures. [1963, pp. 316–317.]

Kohlberg means by this that several of the dimensions exhibit an orderly change with age:

. . . regardless of the particular cultural rules or situations which children are questioned about, regardless of the child's cultural milieu, and in which a substantial portion of other favorable social factors which influence the response are expected to influence it in the same way age does; i.e., by stimulating an increase on the dimension. [P. 317.]

For example, Table 16.1 presents the percentage of children in some of these studies (those with a large enough sample at the various ages) who react with the less mature response to Piaget-type story questions. The clear age progressions strongly confirm the findings of Piaget. All his dimensions do not show such a nice age progression, but enough do that no doubt is left about the generality of his findings.

Turning next to the determinants of moral development, recall that Piaget saw three main forces at work: adult constraint, peer group cooperation, and the changing character of the child's mind. Adult constraint restricts the child to egocentric, authoritarian, objective cognitions, while peer group cooperation ". . . delivers the child both from egocentrism and from the results of this constraint." The interaction of

TABLE 16.1

Results of Two Studies Concerned with Piaget's Dimensions of Moral Judgment
(Adapted from Kohlberg, 1963)

Piaget's Dimensions	Percentage of Children of Various Ages Giving Immature Response		
	6–7	9–10	12–13
Moral realism			
Objective responsibility	54	37	28
	60	13	14
Moral absolutism	42	32	7
	60	35	35
Obedience to authority	65	75	50
	50	58	29
Justice			
Immanent justice	60	55	38
	62	29	12

these two forces with each other and with the child's developing cognitive structure produces the observed developmental trends in morality.

Piaget had precious few facts to back up these assumptions. He did not systematically measure parental child-rearing practices, nor did he attempt to measure the influence of the peer group. His assumptions are more in the nature of common-sense guesses than anything else.

A few studies have been concerned with the effects of parental child-rearing factors. Kohlberg reviews these studies and arrives at a generally negative conclusion: democratic and permissive homes are not highly predictive of greater moral maturity, as predicted by Piaget. Some recent studies are more encouraging, however. Hoffman and Saltzstein (1967), in a carefully executed study, found that affectionate, non-punitive parents who explained the consequences of their child's misdemeanor to others had children with greater moral maturity. This finding is consistent with Piaget's common-sense assumption that exposure to the social consequences of acts pushes the child toward moral subjectivism.

Hoffman and Saltzstein, however, offer a somewhat different interpretation of their results, which is penetrating enough to bear repeating. *Affectionate* parents, they argue, produce affectionate offspring, whose affection is then likely to generalize to other people, resulting in a positive emotional attitude toward people in general. There is, of course, plenty of support for this assumption. The reader is reminded of the results of the Fels and Becker studies, both of which found such a relationship. *Non-punitive* parents, according to Hoffman and Saltzstein, serve to underplay and weaken the personal, egocentric considerations of morality.

If the child is not physically punished, he should not learn to worry about the personal consequences of transgressions, since there are none. What should he think about, then? This is where the third factor— *explaining the unfortunate social consequences of the act*—comes in. Such explanations, occurring in a non-punitive context to a child who is generally fond of other people, *capitalize on his positive empathetic tendencies* and make him see that social transgressions contradict his positive orientation toward others. In other words, he learns to feel badly because he feels that his humanistic values are violated, rather than because he might be punished.

The Hoffman and Saltzstein interpretation is not only consistent with the facts but makes good sense in terms of learning theory. To paraphrase this interpretation, first you teach your child to love you, so that he will love others. Then you show him how transgressions against the rules of society hurt others. By loving others, he will feel anxious (guilty) when he realizes that he has hurt them, and thus will be motivated not to repeat the act (i.e., passive avoidance conditioning). Simultaneously, you do not teach him to fear consequences to himself (by punishing him), since the resulting egocentric concerns will only detract from his ability to think of the consequences to others.

This discussion of empathy, anxiety, and guilt brings us quite naturally to the second great theoretical treatment of morality: its *emotional* aspects. It can be seen now, in retrospect, that Piaget's theory is a *cognitive* theory, which concentrates more on what the child thinks than on how he feels. But surely, emotional reactions are intimately tied up with the cognitions of morality. How do these feelings develop? How do they affect moral behavior? These are our next questions.

EMOTIONS AND MORALITY

Assuming that a child has reached a certain level of moral maturity in the cognitive domain, in the Genevan sense, consider this question: If he acts in such a way as to contradict his moral beliefs, and if he is aware of this contradiction, what is the consequence? This question is directed toward a larger question: *What mechanism(s) causes the child to follow his moral beliefs?* To put it another way: *Why are a child's actions usually consistent with his moral beliefs?*

There is a ready-made answer to this question that is so prevalent and widely believed that the question appears rhetorical: *conscience, of course!* Conscience—guilt—is what keeps a person on the path of righteousness. The following quotation is representative of the psychologist's, as well as the layman's, whole-hearted acceptance of this belief:

Guilt is one of the most important psychological mechanisms through which an individual becomes socialized in the ways of his culture. . . . Without the aid rendered by guilt feelings, child-rearing would be a difficult matter indeed. If children felt no sense of accountability or moral obligation to curb their hedonistic and irresponsible impulses, to conform to accepted social norms, or to acquire self-control, the socializing process would be slow, arduous, and incomplete. Sheer physical force, threat of pain, deprivation, and punishment, or withholding of love and approval would be the only available methods—combined with constant surveillance—to exact conformity to cultural standards of acceptable behavior. And since it is plainly evident that the maintenance of perpetual vigilance is impractical, that fear alone is never an effective deterrent against antisocial behavior, and that the interests of personal expediency are not always in agreement with prescribed ethical norms, a social order unbuttressed by a sense of moral obligation in its members would enjoy precious little stability. [Ausubel, 1955, p. 378.]

Thus, we see that it is an emotional response of guilt that is supposed to "monitor" a person's behavior, providing an automatic guide to moral virtue. Freud was the first psychologist to systematically develop such a theory (1927, 1930, 1933). Briefly, according to Freud, when the child identifies with parental figures—usually the same-sex parent—he "introjects" (adopts) the moral system of that parent as well. Thus, the taboos of the parent become his own taboos, providing an "eye from within" to keep watch. This internal standard, corresponding roughly to Freud's "super-ego," produces feelings of guilt when a transgression first becomes conscious. As a result, it is abandoned, lest the resulting emotionality become unbearable.

What does learning theory say about conscience development? A child presumably first learns about non-permissible acts through parental punishment; that is, he performs a response R_x that is followed by punishment, either physical or "psychological." We presume, by definition, that the punishment elicits anxiety. Thus, we have the sequence $R_x \longrightarrow$ punishment $\longrightarrow$ anxiety. We see that such a sequence conforms perfectly to what we previously called classical aversive conditioning: $S_1 \longrightarrow S_2 \longrightarrow R_2$. Therefore, we would expect anxiety to become conditioned to R_x, just as in classical aversive conditioning we saw that R_2 becomes conditioned to S_1. Thus, the child should learn to respond with anxiety to R_x without parental punishment. He then has a "conscience"—at least with respect to R_x. When he begins to make R_x, anxiety is elicited and he feels "guilty."

What happens next? We know that any response that reduces anxiety is likely to be learned. We then ask, what response will reduce the anxiety elicited by the tendency to make R_x? Clearly, one such response is *abandoning* (*inhibiting*) R_x. If the tendency to make R_x is inhibited, then the anxiety that is conditioned to that tendency will subside, and the child will "feel better." The anxiety reduction will reinforce the inhibitory response, and thus the child will learn not to make that response. We have previously called such learning "passive avoidance conditioning" (i.e., by inhibiting a response, the fear stimulus is removed, and thus the inhibition is reinforced by fear reduction).

Fear vs. Guilt: A Problem

Is this, then, all there is to conscience development? Does it consist simply of fear of certain response tendencies that forces the individual to abandon them? Unfortunately, the situation is a good deal more complex. First, it must be recalled that the punishment occurs in the presence of a parent. Thus, the real state of affairs is: R_x, *parent* ——> punishment ——> anxiety. The anxiety should thus become conditioned not only to R_x but also to the presence of the parent. The child, therefore, learns to be afraid of R_x *when mommy is present*. But does this generalize to fear of R_x *when mommy is absent?* That is the crucial question.

How should we proceed to answer it? We may observe that if mommy is not present, the child will often not be punished. Thus, we have two sequences, each occurring with some frequency. In one, R_x and mommy occur together, and the child is punished. In the other, R_x occurs alone, and the child is not punished. It becomes clear that the crucial cue to impending punishment is not R_x at all, but the presence or absence of mommy. What should be the result? Experiments in discrimination learning tell us that *the child should gradually learn to respond to the relevant cues* (i.e., the child should discriminate). Thus, the child will learn to feel anxious about R_x only when a parent is around.

Clearly, this is not "conscience." Ausubel had such an objection in mind when he said, ". . . fear alone is never an effective deterrent against antisocial behavior. . . ." What he meant was that *fear of detection* is not enough; what is required is fear of the *response*—detection or not. He is thus wrong, the author believes, in arguing that *fear* is not enough. What is crucial is the stimulus to which the fear is conditioned. If it is conditioned to the configuration R_x plus parental detection, *that* is not enough. It must be conditioned to R_x alone. Let us call the former "fear" and the latter "guilt." We understand that in both cases the emotional response, anxiety, is the same, but that in one case it is conditioned to two stimuli, the response in the presence of a parent, while in the other case it is conditioned to the response alone.

The difference is an important one, not to be underestimated. Mowrer (1960, 1966) has gone so far as to suggest a new theory of psychoses based on the psychotic's fear of detection. He argues that it is not guilt, as Freud suggested, but fear of detection that drives the individual to maladaptive behavior. Afraid of being "convicted" for the sinner he really is, the psychotic cuts off communication with his "judges" (society), thereby insulating himself against their accusations. He pays a terrible price, of course, for in shutting off society's accusations, he shuts them off entirely and becomes a non-interacting member of society.

Delayed Punishment: A Possible Solution to the Dilemma

The dilemma we face is this: On the one hand, if the child is not punished when parents are absent and R_x occurs, the child is likely to develop "fear" instead of "guilt." On the other hand, it is clearly impossible to punish R_x when parents are absent. What is the solution? One possibility is based on the fact that parents often discover the occurrence of a transgression afterwards: cookie crumbs on the fingers, a report from a neighbor, a missing coin, a crying sibling, etc. In these cases, the parent can punish the child at that time, in which case there is delayed punishment. In this manner, the frequency of R_x occurring in the absence of parents and without punishment is drastically reduced, thus increasing the likelihood of the development of guilt rather than fear.

There are two dangers with this solution—one obvious and one more subtle. The obvious danger is that delayed punishment may be so far removed from R_x that the anxiety it elicits may not become conditioned to R_x. The longer the delay, the more likely this possibility becomes; that is, *the child might not know why he is being punished.* By and large, parents are aware of this possibility and attempt to reduce it by reminding the child of R_x as the punishment is applied; an explanation is offered, consisting, in part, of a verbal description of R_x. Unfortunately, parents are often in a state of anger at such times and fail to offer an articulate explanation. Then, too, the child realizes "what is coming" and is more likely to be thinking about the seat of his pants than about what is being said. The whole situation, then, is not conducive to clear communication.

The other danger is more subtle, but it has experimental support. Delayed punishment occurs at the very end of the forbidden response, not at the beginning. Let us symbolize the durational aspect of the response by indicating an onset and a termination. The delayed punishment sequence then looks as follows:

$$R_x \underset{\text{onset}}{} \longrightarrow R_x \underset{\text{offset}}{} \longrightarrow \text{punishment} \longrightarrow \text{anxiety}$$

In such a case, the stimulus nearest the punishment in time is the one most likely to be conditioned to anxiety. Thus, the child is likely to learn to be anxious after he has completed the forbidden act, but less likely to be anxious at its beginning. By then, it is "too late," of course; the response is over and the damage done. In order for the anxiety to be effective, it must occur at the very beginning of R_x, so that the response is "shut off" (inhibited). Delayed punishment, then, if applied too frequently, might result in an individual who persists in being "naughty," but always feels bad afterwards.

Solomon's Research on Delayed Punishment in Dogs

Solomon carried out a fascinating series of studies with dogs that confirms the preceding reasoning (Mowrer, 1960, pp. 399–404). Dogs were first individually exposed to a *taboo training situation*, in which a hungry puppy was placed in a room containing two trays of food, one with highly preferred boiled horsemeat and the other with less preferred commercial dog chow (Food X). An experimenter was seated in a chair between the two trays. He had a rolled-up newspaper in his hand. After a few seconds of investigation, the dog went for the horsemeat. The experimenter then swatted him until he withdrew from the meat but left him unmolested if he ate Food X. After several such trials, the puppy avoided the horsemeat and ate Food X unmolested.

Then came the *temptation test*. The hungry dog was reintroduced into the room, containing the same two trays—with horsemeat in one and Food X in the other—but with the experimenter absent. Resistance to temptation (conscience?) was measured in terms of the time elapsed before the puppy ate the tabooed horsemeat. Solomon reports that the puppies went through various antics:

All puppies gobbled up the three pellets (Food X) with a short reaction time and then went through various antics in relation to the large dish of horsemeat. Some puppies would circle the dish over and over again. Some puppies walked around the room with their eyes toward the wall, not looking at the dish. Other puppies got down on their bellies and slowly crawled forward, barking and whining. There was a large range of variability in the emotional behavior of the puppies in the presence of the tabooed horsemeat. [From Mowrer, 1960, p. 400.]

One of the variables investigated by Solomon was the *timing of the punishment*. Some dogs were punished just as they began the forbidden response; they were walloped as they *approached* the horsemeat. Others were allowed to approach and *take a few mouthfuls*, and then were walloped. Solomon reports an interesting difference in the behavior of these two groups of dogs in the temptation test. Puppies who were punished at the beginning of the response sequence tended to at first avoid the horsemeat, displaying a good deal of anxiety as they "fought temptation," but if and when they finally succumbed, they did so with *few signs of anxiety:* ". . . when a puppy did kick over the traces and eat the horsemeat, he did so with his tail wagging the whole time; and after he ate the horsemeat, when the experimenter came into the room the puppy greeted him with tail wags, and with no obvious distress" (p. 402). On the other hand, those puppies who were punished later in the response sequence behaved differently; they showed less emotional disturbance when first exposed to the temptation test, but more afterward, after they had succumbed: ". . . in the case of these puppies, there is a lot more emotional disturbance *following* the crime. This could be called a guilt reaction, and the presence of the experimenter is not required to elicit it. The presence of the experimenter seems to intensify it, when he does finally come into the room after the crime is committed" (pp. 402–403).

Solomon's work thus confirms our theoretical fears. Delayed punishment might result in anxiety that is conditioned mainly to the end parts of the forbidden act, and thus occurs too late to choke off the response. Indeed, the picture is even worse than anticipated, since early punishment also has its dangers. The dog then does not feel guilty *later:* ". . . we have yet to see an emotional disturbance following the crime in a puppy whose approach behavior alone has been punished" (p. 403). Thus, we seem to be impaled on the horns of another dilemma. Punish late and you get a happy sinner who suddenly becomes moral afterward; punish early and you get a moralist who feels fine afterward.

Still, the situation is not hopeless, since early punishment should be more effective in suppressing the response than delayed punishment. The fact that there may be little anxiety afterward is really irrelevant so long as the response seldom occurs. Which is more desirable, a person who frequently commits transgressions and then always feels bad, or a person who seldom commits transgressions and does not feel too bad when he does? Clearly, it is the latter person who commits fewer "wrongs." On the other hand, the frequent wrongdoer may make more attempts at restitution, since he is strongly motivated by guilt afterward. The situation is complex indeed.

Follow-up Studies with Children

It was not long before child psychologists repeated Solomon's experiments, using children as subjects (Aronfreed, 1965; Aronfreed and Reber, 1965; Parke and Walters, 1967; Walters and Demkow, 1963; Walters, Parke, and Crane, 1965). Punishment did not, of course, consist of a swat from a rolled-up newspaper, but usually of a loud noise. The general procedure consisted of exposing the child to a set of toys, some attractive, some unattractive. Whenever the child played with an attractive toy, the loud noise was sounded until he replaced it, and the noise was sometimes associated with "No" from the experimenter. Half the children were so punished as they *reached* for the tabooed toys, and half after they had played with them a few seconds. Following such training, a temptation test was introduced, consisting of both sets of toys and the experimenter absent. *In general, these studies report the same effect as Solomon noted with his dogs.* Early punishment resulted in greater resistance to temptation, thus suggesting that the anxiety had indeed become conditioned to the early segments of the response sequence. Early punishment also resulted in fewer manifestations of guilt *after* a transgression. Thus, Parke and Walters found that children who were punished early made fewer transgressions, but when they did transgress, they played with the tabooed material longer than children who were punished late. The interpretation is that, once the children who were punished early began the transgression, there was little anxiety elicited by the remaining segments of the response sequence, and thus there was little reason to quit.

Recapitulation of the Problem

The discussion so far has been concerned with "strategies" whereby a child might be taught to fear a tabooed response rather than to fear detection: "guilt" versus "fear." We started with the general question: *What causes the child to follow a moral system, assuming he has one?* We accepted the popular answer, *guilt.* The child feels anxious when a transgression begins to occur, and therefore he abandons it. Then we asked: *How is such anxiety attached to the tabooed response?* We answered with, *punishment.* Punishment is paired with the tabooed act, and the resulting anxiety soon becomes conditioned to the act itself, making punishment no longer necessary. Then we asked about problems of *discrimination and timing*, and got into all sorts of difficulties. The child may learn to fear detection rather than the act itself, and if delayed punishment is used, he may learn to feel guilty after the act, but not before. We are forced to the conclusion, then, that the simple formula "punish when naughty" is too simple; it does not guarantee that a conscience will develop.

A Different Solution: The Importance of Social Consequences

The trouble lies in what we want to make the child feel guilty about. We have been assuming that we want the child to feel guilty about making certain responses. An alternative is that we want the child to feel guilty about the *consequences* of the response. Perhaps we should

want the child to feel bad when contemplating any response that unnecessarily harms other people; e.g., we want him to feel bad whenever
he sees himself about to violate the Golden Rule. If this is our goal,
then training strategy might be quite different. The major concern
would no longer be on attachment of anxiety to the response itself, but
attachment of anxiety to the child's *understanding of the probable social
consequences of the response*. The emphasis would therefore be on
making the child aware of the social consequences of the act, and then
attempting to attach anxiety to this awareness. Explanations would thus
be of paramount importance, and the relationship of timing between
the act and punishment of secondary importance.

Such an emphasis on understanding of consequences is similar to
Piaget's view that exposure to the social consequences of acts serves to
instill moral subjectivism in the child. There is little difference between
moral subjectivism as used by Piaget and *fear of social consequences*
as used in the present context, except that emotional responses are emphasized in the latter case. Hoffman's work, as described on pages 526–
527, is also seen to be consistent with this point of view. In two separate
studies (Hoffman, 1963; Hoffman and Saltzstein 1967), he has found
that parents who are concerned with the needs of others, and who explain these needs to their children, are parents of children with greater
moral maturity.

According to this point of view, then, *awareness of consequences* and
anxiety over possible negative consequences to others are the important
determinants of moral behavior. Now we return to the question of how
this anxiety is to be instilled. According to Hoffman, punishment is
not necessary at all. If the child likes people in general, his "awareness"
alone will be enough to set off guilt feelings. What is important is to
make sure he likes people. Assuming that loving parents produce such
feelings in their children, and that most parents are loving, it would
seem that one could then forget about how to instill the emotional
component into morality. If the child is aware of the social consequences of an act, he will automatically feel guilty if these consequences
are negative.

Moral Cognition and Moral Behavior

We have now gone full circle, since we have arrived back at the
Genevan premise that the greater the maturity of one's moral understanding, the greater will be the maturity of one's moral behavior. Let
us inquire about the evidence for this Piagetian prediction—a prediction we ourselves have arrived at by a roundabout detour through learning theory with an assist from Hoffman.

The general investigative procedure seems simple enough. Moral understanding would be measured in terms of responses to Piaget-type story questions as previously described. Moral behavior would be measured in some type of "temptation test," where it would be possible for the subject to actually violate his moral rules. A score would be obtained for each set of data, and the test of the hypothesis would consist of measuring the relationship between the two sets of scores.

A number of such studies has been carried out. We may take one by Grinder (1964) as illustrative. The subjects were 106 boys and girls ranging in age from seven to twelve. Four Piaget-type stories were presented to obtain scores of moral understanding. Then a behavior test consisting of a "ray-gun" shooting game where the subject was given the opportunity to cheat was administered. Specifically, as the subject "shot" at a moving target, an automatic recorder indicated the "score" for each shot, ranging from 1 to 5. These scores were prearranged to sum to 32 points by the end of 20 shots. The subject was told he could win a piece of candy for every point over 35, and that he was limited to 20 shots. He was asked to keep his own cumulative score as he proceeded, and the experimenter was out of the room while he played the game. There were two ways he could transgress: (1) he could take more than 20 shots, or (2) he could record the wrong number of points, totaling to more than 32. Both of these indexes were used in arriving at measurements of moral behavior.

The results indicated no relationship between responses to the Piaget stories and the behavioral indexes. Grinder therefore concluded: "The data suggest that, while conscience strength in general appears to increase with age, the behavioral and cognitive dimensions of conscience develop independently" (p. 881). Thus, although both moral understanding and moral behavior increased with age, they were not related to each other.

Kohlberg (1964) and Pittel and Mendelsohn (1966) have reviewed other similar studies. Both arrive at the conclusion suggested by Grinder's data: moral understanding and moral behavior are not highly related. We must therefore conclude that knowledge is not enough. Awareness of the social implications of one's behavior is no guarantee of moral behavior. The emotional component does not seem to be an automatic resultant of moral knowledge.

We come back to the question, then, of how to instill this emotional component. It must be confessed that there is little evidence to guide us. Perhaps Hoffman has part of the answer. Perhaps love and explanation *are* enough, but most parents "score low" on one of these behavioral attributes, thus explaining the low relationship between moral knowledge and behavior. There is an interesting study that supports the assumption that the more a person has positive attitudes about others, the more likely he will be to act morally toward them. Deutsch (1960) presented college students with a "two-person, non-zero-sum" game in which a person's gains or losses (hypothetical amounts of money) depended not only on his own choices but also on those of a partner (stooge). Deutsch found a very strong tendency for people who trusted their partner to also be trustworthy with their partner. Likewise, those who were suspicious of their partner were also untrustworthy with their partner. Confidence and trust in others, then, were associated with trustworthy (moral) behavior, and vice versa.

The Importance of Imitation. Besides love and explanation, *examples* are important. Considering the whole process of identification and imitation, certainly a parent who is himself concerned about the needs and welfare of others is more likely to beget similar concerns in his child. There is direct experimental evidence documenting the importance of this factor. Stein (1967) exposed 84 fourth-grade boys to a temptation situation in which they were asked to monitor a display panel and record occurrences of a certain type (e.g., to press a button whenever a light came on). The light never came on, so there was nothing to do. The subject was told, "The lights probably won't come on very often so you may do whatever you like as long as you stay in your chair. You must stay in your chair, though, so you'll be ready when the lights do come on." Following the instructions, the experimenter left the room. Meanwhile, a film was being shown a few feet away, which the subject could not see without getting up from his chair.

Under one experimental condition, a model, who presumably was working on the same task, parallel with the subject, got up soon after the experimenter left the room and peeked at the film. Under a second condition, the model was obedient and did not look at the film. In a third, control, condition, there was no model present at all. Each subject was scored in terms of the number of times he got up, the time required for the first transgression, and the total time he was out of his chair. *On all three measures, exposure to a transgressing model resulted in more transgressions than exposure to either no model or a "resistant" model.*

Bandura and McDonald (1963) found similar results with respect to imitation of moral *judgment* rather than behavior. Children's responses to Piaget story questions were strongly influenced by exposure to the responses of a model, even though the model's answer was contrary to the usual answer given by the subject. Thus, the evidence is clear and unambiguous concerning the importance of imitation.

Perhaps, then, the important ingredients consist of *loving, affectionate* parents who *explain* to the child the social consequences of behavior that needlessly affects others adversely, and who attempt to *follow their own advice.* Taking the evidence as a whole, such a constellation of parental behavior seems most likely to foster mature morality in children, both in the cognitive domain and in the emotional domain. Hopefully, the interaction of the two will affect the behavioral domain.

BEHAVIOR AND MORALITY

We come now to the third component of morality: overt behavior. It is unquestionably the most important component—who cares how a person *thinks* or *feels*; it is his *behavior* that counts.

We have seen that, in the cognitive domain, there are dimensions of moral maturity that spread out across large areas of intellectual understanding. We now ask if there is a similar generality in moral behavior. If a person behaves morally in one situation, does he tend to behave morally in other situations as well? If he does not lie to his mother, is he equally honest with his father, his teachers, his friends? If he does not cheat in games, does he also not cheat on tests? If he does not steal from his friends' sandpiles, does he also not steal from the cookie jar, his father's wallet, open lockers at school, etc.?

The reference study is a massive investigation carried out in the late 1920's by Hartshorne and May (1928) and their collaborators (Hartshorne, et al., 1929, 1930). Their work (1928) remains the most comprehensive and well known study of moral behavior in existence. They examined some 11,000 school-age children, who were given opportunities to lie, cheat, and steal in a variety of settings: in classrooms, at home, in athletic contests, and in party games. In a scholarly review, Yarrow wrote: "No study of children's values has since been carried out on such an impressive scale, both qualitatively and quantitatively" (1960).

The one central conclusion from this study is that *moral behavior is highly specific to the situation in which it is measured.* This conclusion was based on the correlations between "deceit" scores on the different tests; these correlations were, by and large, quite low.

This conclusion was accepted much at face value for the next 30 years, and is still the prevalent opinion today. Yet it is probably false. In 1963, Burton re-examined the Hartshorne and May data and came to a different conclusion (Burton, 1963). He became doubtful when he noted that many of the tests used were quite unreliable. If a person were to take some of the tests a second time, his score would not correlate highly with the first score. If a test is unreliable, it certainly will not correlate highly with other tests since it does not even correlate with itself. Thus, low correlations between unreliable tests are difficult to interpret. They do not necessarily mean that reliable tests would yield similar low correlations. Burton therefore sorted out the tests that were reliable—those with a reliability of .70 or higher. Six such tests were identified. Since they are of interest in their own right, a brief description of each is provided.

The *Copying* test consisted of intelligence tests in which the individual wrote down his answers, turned them in (where copies were quickly made), and then corrected his own papers when they were returned. The cheating score consisted of the number of changes made on the papers.

The *Speed* test consisted of routine tasks such as number and digit cancellation (e.g., "Cross out as many fives as you can in the next 60 seconds—go!"). Two "practice" sessions were given where subjects had no opportunity to cheat. Then a third "test" session was given and the individual allowed to score his own test. The cheating score was the discrepancy between the second "practice" score and the final "test" score.

The *Peeping* test consisted of first determining how well students could trace mazes or mark X's in circles with their eyes closed. After determining the norms under conditions where peeping did not occur, the children were given the same tests, under conditions where they could peep. The discrepancy from the "honest" norms determined the cheating score.

The *Faking* test involved puzzles that simply could not be solved without cheating. The number of solutions, or approaches to perfect solutions, determined the cheating score.

The *Athletic* tests consisted of a number of physical tests, such as hand dynamometer for measuring strength of grip, a chinning test, and standing broad jump. After three "warm-up" trials in the presence of a tester, who recorded the subject's best performance, the subject was left alone to measure himself on the trials that "counted." Improvements from the best score of the three "warm-up" trials served as the basis for determining the cheating score.

Finally, the *Lying* test was not a test of actual lying at all. College graduate students first attempted to answer honestly a set of questions about whether they did or did not conform to certain prescribed rules of conduct when they were children. These same questions were then presented to the school children, and the discrepancy between their answers and the college norms served as the basis for determining a "lie score."

The intercorrelations between these six scores are presented in Table 16.2. Notice that the correlations do not cluster around zero at all, but around some higher value. Note how well the scores from the four tests that were administered in the classroom correlate with each other (Tests A–D). A factor analysis indicated that there was indeed a single factor that could account for all four of these scores, for all four correlated above .50 with this factor. The Athletic and Lying tests, conducted outside the classroom, did not correlate with this factor ($r = .03$ and $.08$, respectively), nor did they correlate highly with each other (.23).

TABLE 16.2

Intercorrelations Among the Six Tests Factor-analyzed by Burton
(Adapted from Burton, 1963)

Tests	A	B	C	D	E	F
A. Copying (3 tests)	–	.45	.40	.40	.29	.35
B. Speed (6 tests)	.29	–	.37	.43	.35	.25
C. Peeping (3 tests)	.29	.22	–	.30	.10	.11
D. Faking (3 tests)	.29	.26	.20	–	.30	.26
E. Athletic (4 tests)	.20	.19	.06	.18	–	.23
F. Lying (1 test)	.31	.25	.16	.21	.00	–

Burton concluded that Hartshorne and May overstated their case when they concluded moral behavior was situation specific. When unreliable tests are eliminated, a single factor is seen to account for all tests of cheating carried out within the classroom situation. On the other hand, this factor does not account for cheating in the other test situations. Therefore, *both* general tendencies and situations would seem to be important, as suggested by Burton. He offers a theoretical explanation. A child has a certain tendency to behave morally that affects his behavior in many situations. The more similar the situations, the greater the generalization of moral behavior from one to the others. As situations become less similar, generalization of morality drops off, and moral consistency grows weaker.

Although Burton's conclusions go against the prevalent opinion, he cites other data consistent with his conclusions (Barbu, 1951; Brogden, 1940; Maller, 1934). Barbu's results are particularly convincing. He studied 250 fourteen-year-old boys with nine classroom tests of cheating and one questionnaire test of honesty. The average intercorrelation was .46, leading him to conclude that there was strong evidence for a general trait of honesty. Of course, the tests were all similar (excluding the questionnaire), and thus there was not much opportunity to demonstrate situational variability. The only safe conclusion seems to be Burton's: the more similar the situations, the greater is one's moral consistency from one to another.

People are thus not divisible into two groups, the moral and the immoral, the liars and the non-liars, the honest and the dishonest. These groups do not exist as identifiable subgroups. Instead, a person is usually moral or immoral in a given type of situation, and gradually shades off into greater or lesser morality as the situations become non-comparable. Figure 16.1 presents the distribution of behavioral scores from

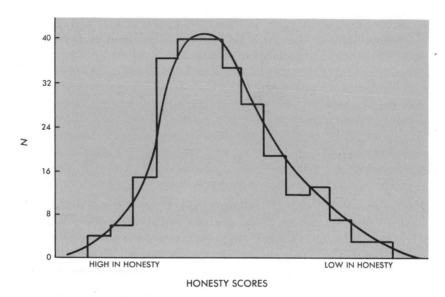

Figure 16.1. The distribution of honesty scores for 265 children, from the mean of 21 tests (from Jones, 1954, p. 788).

21 tests used by Hartshorne and May in school and play situations. This distribution does not show two "humps" at the two extremes, as one would expect if people were either "strong" or "weak." Instead, there is a continuous distribution, much as one finds with IQ, height, or weight. There are *all degrees* of morality and immorality, depending upon a person's "central tendency" plus the specifics of the situation at hand.

The continuity of the distribution is what one would expect when the complexities of morality are considered. Morality is not a simple concept, but an extremely complicated one. It does not consist of an entity that remains clear and unchanged over time, but rather of knowledge, feelings, and behavior that are a product, not only of internal interactive dynamics, but of the times and places in which an individual lives. Different dimensions conflict with each other: truthfulness may conflict with group loyalty ("honor among thieves"), bravery with abhorrence of violence (e.g., conscientious objectors), honesty with good intentions (a "white lie"), etc. Indeed, the more aware a person is of the total situation, the more difficult it becomes to see the moral decision. If the reader has any presumption that the moral choice is always obvious, let him read the following quotation. It makes the subject for a good discussion about morality.

Several years ago in a railroad wreck a lady was imprisoned in the debris in such a way that escape was impossible. Her husband, who might have extricated himself with an effort, deliberately chose to remain and die with her in order that he might give her the support and comfort of his presence in her last moments. She herself, we must suppose, was not aware of the possibility of his escape, otherwise his aim would of course have been defeated. What is to be said of the moral character of his choice in each of the following cases? (a) If he was a clerk with the expectations of the average of his class and had no family ties apart from his wife. (b) Position as in (a), but he had a mother living with him in his home, who was very much devoted to him but not dependent upon him for support. (c) Position again as in (a). He has a distant relative, a lady who was an invalid and absolutely dependent upon him for support. (d) If he had been a clergyman doing a great deal of good. (e) If he had been a Morse, conscious that he was on the eve of the solution of the problem of the electric telegraph. (f) If he had been an artist of very exceptional talents. [Pittel and Mendelsohn, 1966, p. 23.]

RELATIONSHIPS BETWEEN THE THREE FACES OF MORALITY

It is tempting to assume that the three components of morality develop together in a sort of unified fashion, so that a given level of maturity in one area implies a similar maturity in the other two areas. In order to evaluate the tenability of such a "simplistic" notion, let us consider all three possible combinations of the three components.

Moral Judgment and Moral Behavior

We have already anticipated the answer with respect to judgment and behavior. Recall Grinder's study of the relationship between answers to Piaget-type story questions and cheating in the "ray-gun" game. There was no relationship at all. It was noted that reviews by Kohlberg and Pittel and Mendelsohn came to a similar conclusion. Thus, it would seem that the answer is definitely "No" for this combination. But the picture is more complicated than was implied. Consider two qualifications, one suggested by Piaget himself, the other by Kohlberg.

Piaget, with no data to speak of on which to base an evaluation, nevertheless predicted a less than one-to-one correlation between the

542 MORAL DEVELOPMENT

cognitive (judgmental) and behavioral components of morality. He wrote of a "time-lag" between the two, with behavioral morality appearing first. One of his fundamental assumptions is that schemas first develop behaviorally, then verbally: "Conscious realization (verbal comprehension) is a reconstruction and consequently, a new and original construction superimposed upon the constructions already formed by action" (Piaget, 1962, p. 177). He goes on, "If, then, the moral realism we have noted between 6 and 8 on the average . . . corresponds to something present in the moral activity itself, it is not during those years that we must seek for this something, but at a very much earlier period" (p. 177). He gives a charming example of this time-lag in his own daughter's behavior at the age of two and a half:

. . . one evening I find Jacqueline, aged 2; 6 . . . in bed, spoiling a towel by pulling out the threads one by one. Her mother has already often told her that it is a pity to do that, that it makes holes, that you can't mend the holes, etc. So I say to J.: "Oh, but mummy will be sad." J. answers calmly and even with an ill-concealed smile: "Yes. It makes holes. You can't mend" . . . etc. I continue my lecture, but she obviously is not going to take me seriously. Still hiding her amusement with difficulty, she suddenly says to me "Laugh!" in so comic a tone, that in order to keep a straight face I quickly change the subject. J., very conscious of her powers of seduction, then says to me "My little darling Daddy," and the incident ends. The next morning, however, J. wakes up full of it. Her first words refer to what had happened the night before. She thinks about the towel and asks her mother whether she isn't sad. So in spite of the first reaction showing such charming disrespect, my words had told and the command had brought about the usual consequences.
The evening of the same day, J. begins to pull the threads out of the towel again. Her mother repeats that it is a pity. J. listens attentively but says nothing. A moment later she is calling out and cries till someone comes to her: she simply wanted to see her parents again and make sure that they bore her no grudge. [Pp. 178–179.]

Here Jacqueline's overt behavior indicates a clear sensitivity to the harmful effects her thread pulling has on others—she asks her mother if she is sad, and, later, cries. Yet, like any two-and-a-half-year-old, she is unable to verbalize the reasons she feels bad; she cannot say that it was wrong because she did it on purpose rather than accidentally, etc. But at a later age, her verbalizations will "catch up" to her behavior, which, by then, will be still more advanced, thus maintaining the time-lag for some time to come.

Applying the notion of a time-lag to modern studies, one reason for the weak relationship found between the judgmental and behavioral components might be that the verbal index of morality lags behind the behavioral index. A more sensitive procedure might be to make corrections for the lag, and then measure the relationship. One way to automatically make such corrections would be to insure that the behavioral test involves moral principles about which the child can and does verbalize. As far as the author knows, the implications of this time-lag, or ways to minimize it, have not been explicitly considered in current research.

Kohlberg (1964) suggests another possible extenuating factor. He points out that, in the usual "resistance to temptation" situation, moral behavior is in line with known social pressures; that is, the moral response is not to cheat, and the child knows that he is not supposed to cheat, even though he may not know why. Carrying Kohlberg's observation one step further, it may be that the child's awareness of social expectations overrides his own judgmental processes, thus masking the relationship between the two. A more sensitive procedure would therefore separate the two, or even oppose them, so that what is morally right is opposed to group pressure. Perhaps under such circumstances, the relationship between judgmental and behavioral indexes of morality would increase. Kohlberg reports data of his own that support this reasoning: such "moral courage" correlated .44 with maturity of moral judgment (p. 409).

It must be concluded that, although the relationship between moral judgment and moral behavior is usually found to be low, there are extenuating circumstances that leave the matter somewhat undecided. More carefully designed experiments are clearly called for.

Moral Judgment and Guilt

There seems to be only one study that has investigated the possible relationship between Genevan morality and guilt. In this study (Ruma and Mosher, 1967), 36 adolescent delinquent boys were administered Kohlberg's scale of judgmental morality (the scale consists of Piaget story questions). Then, several indexes of guilt were obtained, only one of which we shall consider. For this index, the boys were interviewed about their feelings concerning the delinquent act leading to their incarceration. They were asked such questions as:

What did you do to get in here at J.D.C.?
How did you feel while you were doing this?
How did you feel right afterwards?

Answers were tape-recorded and scored by judges according to the amount of guilt reflected. Thus, responses such as "I felt bad because I knew how much I'd hurt my Ma" or "I felt awful because I knew it was wrong" received high ratings of guilt, while such responses as "I was scared because I knew I was going to get locked up this time" or "I was a little worried that I might get caught" received an intermediate rating (at least emotion was evident, if not guilt), and responses showing no emotion at all, such as "I didn't feel no different," received a rating of zero.

These scores were then correlated against the moral judgment scores to test the hypothesis that the two sets of scores were related. The correlation coefficient was .47, providing reasonably strong support for the hypothesis. As other measures of guilt yielded comparable correlations with moral judgment, the investigators were led to conclude that "The results of this study provide confirming evidence that moral judgment is positively related to guilt over transgression in delinquent boys. This is the first study to examine and demonstrate the presence of such a relationship" (p. 126).

Of course, other studies must be carried out to confirm these findings with normal children. But ignoring this requirement of replication and generality, the author is still hesitant to put much faith in the Ruma and Mosher findings. In the first place, one may question the extent to which these boys really felt guilt, since it did not deter them from a history of chronic delinquency (most had appeared before the courts a number of times prior to the act that led directly to incarceration). If they did feel guilt, it was not *effective* guilt. Then, there is the methodological problem that ratings of guilt may have been influenced by knowledge of moral judgment scores. We are not told of any attempts to eliminate this possibility. In view of these considerations, and in view of the lack of corroborative data, the best conclusion at the present time would seem to be no conclusion at all.

As a final point, it does not seem that verbal responses are the best way to measure guilt. If guilt consists essentially of an emotional response, then why not measure emotional responses? A number of techniques are available: the GSR (galvanic skin response), blood pressure, heart rate, respiration rate, etc. It seems that anyone can *say* he feels guilty, since verbalizations are under voluntary control. Physiological indexes, however, are largely involuntary, and thus less subject to falsification.

Moral Behavior and Guilt

We come, finally, to the relationship between moral behavior and guilt—the final combination. Let us sample a recent study by Rebelski, since it involves the same "ray-gun" game as previously described in Grinder's study (Rebelski *et al.*, 1963). Recall that in this game the child cumulates his own score, but does not score enough points to "win" unless he cheats a little. Rebelski and his colleagues used the "tendency to confess" as an index of guilt. Both before and after the ray-gun game, the subjects (138 sixth-grade children, half of each sex) were presented with four stories that terminated abruptly after the central character had committed a transgression, and then the subjects were asked to finish the story: "Now you finish the story, telling what the people in your story are thinking and feeling, and what happens and how it turns out." The subjects wrote down their story endings and turned them in to the experimenter.

The story completions were scored in terms of whether or not the transgressor confessed. An interesting aspect of the story-stems was that there was little or no possibility that the offender would be detected unless he confessed or gave himself away. A confession, therefore, was not "forced" as a result of detection and thus seems to be a reasonably direct index of guilt tendencies. The judges who scored the story endings did not know the identity of the subjects or their "cheat scores" in the ray-gun game. Thus, experimenter bias was eliminated.

The main finding was clear-cut: *Children who wrote most confessions into their story endings were the ones most likely to be honest in the ray-gun game.* Assuming a relationship between tendency to confess and guilt, the findings can be interpreted to indicate a positive relationship between moral behavior and guilt.

Other studies confirm this conclusion. Kohlberg's review mentions several studies showing a positive relationship between expressions of self-blame and resistance to temptation (Grinder and McMichael, 1963; MacKinnon, 1938), and avoidance of delinquent acts (Bandura and Walters, 1959; McCord and McCord, 1956). Thus, we may take as fairly well established a positive relationship between moral behavior and guilt. Interestingly enough, this is one combination of the three possible ones where learning theory would most directly predict a positive relationship. If one avoids immoral behavior, there must be a reason for it. Avoidance conditioning is usually explained in terms of conditioned fear. Guilt is also assumed to consist of conditioned fear, and hence one would expect the guilt-behavior relationship. It is reassuring to find support for this prediction.

In summary, then, there is little evidence for a "simplistic" view of morality. Moral judgment is only weakly related to moral behavior (and even here intelligence may be a confounded factor, since both components are positively related to intelligence—Unger, 1964), and only one study—with methodological difficulties—has investigated the judgment-guilt relationship. There does seem to be a behavior-guilt relationship, with tendencies to express guilt reactions positively correlated with "resistance" in temptation tests. This relationship is consistent with predictions from learning theory.

CONCLUSIONS

Developmental Norms

What final conclusions can be drawn about moral development in children? Since the three "faces of morality" do not "hang together" in a simplistic sense, concluding remarks must be specific to a particular component. Consider the matter of developmental norms. Cognitive morality, in the Genevan sense, does not attain a very mature level until fairly late in childhood—perhaps not until early adolescence. Kohlberg (1964) has presented the most definitive data on this point. He found three major levels of moral development covering the span from moral realism to moral subjectivism. Following are examples from each level:

Level I.   Premoral: rules are obeyed simply to avoid punishment.
Level II.   Conformity: rules are obeyed to avoid guilt produced by censure from authority.
Level III. Principles: rules are obeyed in terms of individual principles of conscience.

Figure 16.2 presents the percentage of moral statements representative of these three levels at four different ages. Notice that at age seven, responses are primarily at the premoral level—in terms of objective rewards and punishments. At age ten, there is an increase in the number of responses at the conformity-to-authority level, but premoral responses still predominate. By age thirteen, premoral responses have weakened considerably, and conformity to avoid guilt has become very strong. Notice how infrequent Level III responses still are at this age. An individual morality, based on one's awareness of his own moral principles, develops rather late indeed.

Moral *behavior*, on the other hand, appears to develop much earlier, which is consistent with Piaget's hypothesis of a "time-lag" between the verbal and the behavioral. This inference of early development is based on the fact that *behavioral "temptation test" scores are about the same for a seven-year-old as they are for a fourteen-year-old.* The research is quite consistent in showing that behavioral measures of morality do not correlate highly with age. Hartshorne and May, in fact, found a slightly *negative* correlation in their monumental study (although subsequent analyses revealed that high social-class children became more honest with age, while low social-class children became less honest). Other studies find little relationship at all (e.g., Grinder and McMichael, 1963; Rau, 1968; Terman *et al.*, 1925; Tudor-Hart, 1926). Likewise, ratings by adults of such behavioral dimensions as honesty, responsibility, altruism, etc., also fail to show age increases during childhood (Harris and Vala-

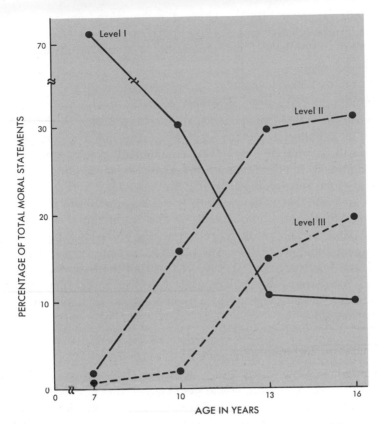

Figure 16.2. Mean percentage of total moral statements (Kohlberg, 1964).

sek, 1954; Hartshorne *et al.*, 1930; Turner, 1952). One is tempted to conclude that *behavioral* morality reaches a fairly mature level rather early, thus explaining the absence of increases at later ages.

Other interpretations are also reasonable. For example, the lack of a later age increase probably is due in part to the extremely simple kinds of moral behavior that have been measured in most of the "temptation tests." Deciding not to cheat on the ray-gun is hardly a very complicated moral decision. If more complicated tests could be devised, where, for example, social pressure conflicts with the moral choice, there would probably be an age progression up to and including adolescence.

Concerning guilt, the third component, there is very little data relating such verbal indexes of guilt as confession to age. What there are suggest that young children, up to the age of eight or so, very rarely assign guilt feelings to the hero, while a majority of older children do so (Aronfreed, 1961; Hoffman, 1963). Thus, a rather slow age progression is suggested, although the data are too spotty to make a confident assessment. With physiological measurements, a more rapid development might be found.

Interactions Between the Components

How do these three components interact to produce all the "real-life" richness of morality at a given age? We have noted a correlation between the behavioral and emotional components that is consistent with a learning-theory interpretation in terms of avoidance conditioning. The lack of a strong relationship between the behavioral and cognitive components suggests that understanding is not a prerequisite for moral behavior—children (and adults) often do the "right thing" without being able to point to a relevant moral principle. Likewise, they often do the immoral thing when they *can* point to a contrary moral principle. Indeed, as Piaget suggested, it may well be that the behavioral responses (schemas) determine the judgmental responses rather than the other way around. Perhaps a child first acts in a certain way, and later figures out a reason why.

Environmental Determinants

According to Piaget, it is adult constraint that encourages the moral realism of the younger child, while peer cooperation at a later age guides him toward considerations of intentionality and equality—moral subjectivism. According to learning theory, it is a matter of attaching anxiety to the right cues, so that guilt is felt in the appropriate circumstances. These cues can consist of either tendencies to make the disapproved responses themselves, or the child's awareness of the social consequences of the responses. Child-rearing data, collected by Hoffman and others, suggest the importance of *affectionate parents* who *explain the social consequences* to their children. The relationship of these findings to learning theory is apparent. Experimental data suggest another factor: the *moral behavior of the parents themselves*, which serves as a model for the child.

Somehow, out of this complicated set of interacting factors, there emerges judgmental, emotional, and overt responses, the aggregate of which we call "morality." It will be a long time before the complete puzzle is assembled.

SUMMARY

Morality can be considered to be an aggregate of cognitive, emotional, and overt response tendencies having to do with "right" and "wrong" behaviors, where "right" and "wrong" are based on value judgments. Research on moral development can be conveniently discussed in terms of what is known about each of these three components.

Piaget is the great pioneer who first laid bare some of the cognitive dimensions of morality. By observing what children do in games of marbles, and by asking questions about hypothetical situations involving clumsiness, stealing, lying, and justice, he perceived a number of dimensions of moral understanding along which the child progresses as he develops. The fundamental core of these dimensions is the progression from moral realism to moral subjectivism, marked by a change from thinking in terms of moral absolutism, objective responsibility, expiatory punishment, obedience to authority, and immanent justice to moral evaluations in terms of relativism, intentionality, reciprocal punishment, cooperation, naturalistic causality, and equalitarianism. More recent research has confirmed the reasonableness of many of these dimensions.

But what motivates a child to follow his judgment? Freud said, ". . . the sense of guilt is the most important problem in the evaluation of culture" (1930). Freud thus stands at the beginning of a second great line of thought concerning the essence of morality—the emotional component. There is a kind of progression here just as there is in the cognitive domain. First there is simple fear of detection, which may or may not be followed by fear ("guilt") of the transgressing response itself. Which of these two responses, "fear" or "guilt," will occur is dependent, among other things, upon intricate timing and situational variables intervening between the response and parental punishment. At a still "higher" level, perhaps, is guilt about the consequences of the act, independent of both detection and the precise nature of the response. A lie can thus be good or bad, depending upon its consequences.

Given the right combination of moral cognition and emotion, appropriate moral *behavior* is presumably the outcome. Evidence suggests that moral behavior is dependent upon both a general tendency to be moral or immoral and the peculiarities of the particular situation at hand. Thus, in similar situations, a person is likely to exhibit similar kinds of morality, and as situations become more disparate, a corresponding variation in moral behavior appears.

Comparing developmental trends of behavioral morality with those of cognitive morality reveals a "time-lag" first suggested by Piaget. Behavioral morality occurs before the child is able to verbalize the principles behind his behavior, but which he nevertheless follows. Therefore, only a weak relationship exists between the cognitive and behavioral domains of morality at a given time. It may also be that emotions must be considered along with cognition before moral behavior becomes predictable. Research indicates that emotions and behavior are related.

Children who more frequently express signs of guilt and self-blame are more honest in "temptation tests" and other situations reflecting behavioral morality.

What are the environmental determinants of morality? Piaget emphasized parental constraint as operating to produce overconcern with rules, authority, and expiatory punishment, thus encouraging the immaturity of moral realism. But social interactions with peers, where the necessity of cooperation is perceived, gradually brings home to the child the importance of agreement, intention, and equality, thus encouraging a higher level of moral cognition.

Learning theory emphasizes the attachment of anxiety and guilt to the appropriate cues in such a way that immoral behavior is avoided because of the negative emotionality it produces. Child-rearing data and experimental investigations of imitation indicate that love, explanation, and example are crucial ingredients. Hoffman suggests that punishment may not be necessary at all, except in the "psychological" sense of pointing out to the child the unfortunate social consequences of immoral behavior.

BIBLIOGRAPHY

ARONFREED, J. (1961). The nature, variety, and social patterning of moral responses to transgression. *Journal of abnormal and social psychology*, 63, 223–241.

ARONFREED, J. (1964). The origin of self-criticism. *Psychological review*, 71, 193–218.

ARONFREED, J. (1965). Punishment learning and internalization: some parameters of reinforcement and cognition. Paper presented at the biennial meeting of the Society for Research in Child Development, Minneapolis, Minn.

ARONFREED, J., and REBER, A. (1965). Internalized behavioral suppression and the timing of social punishment. *Journal of personality and social psychology*, 1, 3–16.

AUSUBEL, D. P. (1955). Relationships between shame and guilt in the socializing process. *Psychological review*, 62, 378–390.

BANDURA, A., and MACDONALD, F. G. (1963). Influence of social reinforcement and the behavior of models in shaping children's moral judgments. *Journal of abnormal and social psychology*, 67, 274–281.

BANDURA, A., and WALTERS, R. H. (1959). *Adolescent aggression—a study of the influence of child-training practices and family interrelationships*. New York: The Ronald Press Co.

BARBU, Z. (1951). Studies in children's honesty. *Quarterly bulletin, British psychological society*, 2, 53–57.

BOEHM, L., and NASS, M. L. (1962). Social class differences in conscience development. *Child development*, 33, 565–575.

BROGDEN, H. E. (1940). A factor analysis of 40 character traits. *Psychological monographs*, 53 (234), 39–55.

BURTON, R. V. (1963). Generality of honesty reconsidered. *Psychological review*, 70, 481–499.

CARUSO, I. H. (1943). La notion de responsibilité et de justice immanente chez l'enfant. *Arch. de psychologie*, 29, (114).

DEUTSCH, M. (1960). Trust, trustworthiness, and the F scale. *Journal of abnormal and social psychology*, 61, 138–140.

FREUD, S. (1927). *The ego and the id*. London: Hogarth Press, Ltd.

FREUD, S. (1930). *Civilization and its discontents*. New York: W. W. Norton & Co., Inc.

FREUD, S. (1933). *New introductory lectures on psychoanalysis*. New York: W. W. Norton & Co., Inc.

GRINDER, R. (1964). Relations between behavioral and cognitive dimensions of conscience in middle childhood. *Child development*, 35, 881–892.

GRINDER, R., and McMICHAEL, R. (1963). Cultural influences on conscience development: resistance to temptation and guilt among Samoans and American Caucasians. *Journal of abnormal and social psychology*, 66, 503–507.

HARRIS, D. B., and VALASEK, F. (1954). The measurement of responsibility in children. *Child development*, 25, 21–28.

HARTSHORNE, H., and MAY, M. A. (1928). *Studies in deceit:* Book I. *General methods and results*. Book II. *Statistical methods and results*. New York: The Macmillan Co.

HARTSHORNE, H., MAY, M. A., and MALLER, J. (1929). *Studies in service and self-control*. New York: The Macmillan Co.

HARTSHORNE, H., MAY, M. A., and SHUTTLEWORTH, F. K. (1930). *Studies in the organization of character*. New York: The Macmillan Co.

HILL, W. F. (1960). Learning theory and the acquisition of values. *Psychological review*, 67, 317–331.

HOFFMAN, M. L. (1963). Parent discipline and the child's consideration for others. *Child development*, 34, 573–588.

HOFFMAN, M. L., and SALTZSTEIN, H. D. (1967). Parent discipline and the child's moral development. *Journal of personality and social psychology*, 5, 45–57.

JOHNSON, R. C. (1962). A study of children's moral judgments. *Child development*, 33, 327–354.

JONES, V. (1954). Character development in children—an objective approach. In L. CARMICHAEL (Ed.), *Manual of child psychology*. (2d ed.) New York: John Wiley & Sons, Inc. Pp. 781–832.

KOHLBERG, L. (1958). The development of modes of moral thinking and choice in the years ten to sixteen. Unpublished doctor's dissertation, University of Chicago.

KOHLBERG, L. (1963). Moral development and identification. In H. W. STEVENSON (Ed.), *Child psychology*. Chicago: University of Chicago Press. Pp. 277–332.

KOHLBERG, L. (1964). Development of moral character and moral ideology. In M. L. HOFFMAN and LOIS W. HOFFMAN (Eds.), *Review of child development research*. New York: Russell Sage Foundation. Pp. 383–432.

LERNER, E. (1937). *Constraint areas and the moral judgment of children*. Menasha, Wis.: George Banta Publishing Co.

McCORD, W., and McCORD, JOAN (1956). *Psychopathy and delinquency*. New York: Grune & Stratton, Inc.

MacKINNON, D. W. (1938). Violation of prohibitions. In H. W. MURRAY (Ed.), *Explorations in personality*. New York: Oxford University Press. Pp. 491–501.

MacRAE, D., JR. (1954). A test of Piaget's theories of moral development. *Journal of abnormal and social psychology*, 49, 14–18.

MALLER, J. B. (1934). General and specific factors in character. *Journal of social psychology*, 5, 97–102.

MOWRER, O. H. (1960). *Learning theory and the symbolic processes*. New York: John Wiley & Sons, Inc.

MOWRER, O. H. (1966). Abnormal reactions or actions? In J. A. VERNON (Ed.), *Introduction to general psychology: a self-selection textbook*. Dubuque, Iowa: W. C. Brown Co.

PARKE, R. D., and WALTERS, R. H. (1967). Some factors influencing the efficacy of punishment training for producing response inhibition. *Monographs of the society for research in child development*, 32 (1).

PIAGET, J. (1962). *The moral judgment of the child.* London: Routledge & Kegan Paul Ltd. New York: Collier Books. (Originally published 1932.)

PITTEL, S. M., and MENDELSOHN, G. A. (1966). Measurement of moral values: a review and critique. *Psychological bulletin,* 66, 22–35.

RAU, L. (1968). Conscience and identification. In R. R. SEARS *et al.* (Eds.), *Identification and child-rearing.* Stanford, Calif.: Stanford University Press.

REBELSKI, FREDA G., ALLINSMITH, W., and GRINDER, R. E. (1963). Resistance to temptation and sex differences in children's use of fantasy confession. *Child development,* 34, 955–962.

RUMA, ELEANOR, H., and MOSHER, D. L. (1967). Relationship between moral judgment and guilt in delinquent boys. *Journal of abnormal psychology,* 72, 122–127.

STEIN, ALTHEA H. (1967). Imitation of resistance to temptation. *Child development,* 38, 157–170.

TERMAN, L. M. *et al.* (1925). *Genetic studies of genius.* Vol. 1: *Mental and physical traits of a thousand gifted children.* Stanford, Calif.: Stanford University Press.

TUDOR-HEART, B. E. (1926). Are there cases in which lies are necessary? *Pediatric seminar,* 33, 586–641.

TURNER, W. (1952). Altruism in children's behavior. In R. KUHLEN and G. THOMPSON (Eds.), *Psychological studies in human development.* New York: Appleton-Century-Crofts, Inc.

UNGER, S. M. (1964). Relation between intelligence and socially-approved behavior: methodological cautionary note. *Child development,* 35, 299–302.

WALTERS, R. H., and DEMKOW, LILLIAN (1963). Timing of punishment as a determinant of response inhibition. *Child development,* 34, 207–214.

WALTERS, R. H., PARKE, R. D., and CRANE, VALERIE A. (1965). Timing of punishment and the observation of consequences to others as determinants of response inhibition. *Journal of experimental child psychology,* 2, 10–30.

YARROW, MARION R. (1960). The measurement of children's attitudes and values. In P. H. MUSSEN (Ed.), *Handbook of research methods in child development.* New York: John Wiley & Sons, Inc. Pp. 643–687.

Epilogue

At this point, the reader might well look back and ask, "What does it all add up to?" Is it possible to formulate a "grand conclusion," and if so, of what does it consist? The author must confess that the great, final insight does not come. What is there, instead, is a feeling that psychological development is incredibly complex, and that we have taken a serious look at the state of knowledge as it exists today. This knowledge does not tell us what parents *should do*, but *what is*, in a factual, scientific sense. What parents should do depends upon what they want of their children—what they want them to become.

Different parents want different things. One parent, himself a product of a poverty-ridden childhood, may want financial security above all for his child. Another, exposed to parental rejection, may value emotional security above all. Another, never having "measured up" to the expectations of parents and/or teachers, may value a "free and happy childhood," devoid of parental pressures. Still another, deprived of a college education, may value a "proper education" above all. Parental values are *determined*, in other words, like everything else, and since the determining factors—genetic and environmental backgrounds—are different for everyone, so are child-rearing goals. Thus, the facts of child development cannot possibly point to "the goal," for the goal varies for each and every parent.

But surely, you say, all parents share *one* goal: *adjustment.* Surely it is the case that, everything else aside, all parents want their children to enter adulthood as *normal, adjusted* adults. While the author shares this belief, it consists of little more than empty words. The simple fact is that "adjustment" is perhaps the most elusive word to define in the English language. The most skilled and gifted psychologists in the world, calling upon all their clinical and experimental knowledge, are not able to agree on what "adjustment" means. This is not the place to summarize the various definitions that have been suggested—any good textbook on personality or abnormal psychology will serve that end. What is important to recognize is that, since definitions of "adjustment" vary, merely to use the label as the major goal of child rearing is to admit the existence of the very problem under discussion—that the goals vary.

Accepting, then, a multitude of possible goals, of what use is the material in this book? The major use, from this "practical" point of view, is to suggest ways of achieving *whatever* goal it is a parent might have in mind. The word "suggest" is used advisedly, for there are no guarantees. The determinants of behavior are too poorly understood to allow anyone to speak with confidence. Yet hints there are, some strong, most weak, and it is on these parents must rely, if they are to rely upon scientific knowledge at all.

The strongest hint of all is that behavior does not just "happen." Whatever our children may become—doctor, lawyer, merchant, thief— one fact stands as clear as the rising sun: *we*, the parents, the contributors to the child's genetic and environmental background, are responsible. We are the ones who mix the genes—*our* genes—to create the living organism, with its host of potentialities—potentialities for environmental selection and development. We are the ones who create the environment, too, not just for our own children, but for all children with whom we come in contact, directly or indirectly. And we should not underestimate the impact of these indirect effects, for they are sizable. The chapter on school influences, for example, documented the effects teachers may have on personality development. Teachers were once children, and some of our children will become teachers. How we treat teachers-to-be thus affects many other children in turn, when our own children grow up and become "surrogate parents." Likewise, the chapter on peer influences documented how powerfully one child can affect the behavior of another child. To the extent that any one child's behavior is affected by the behavior of his parents, and to the extent his behavior affects that of other children, we are as responsible to those other children as to our own.

It would seem that there is little we can do to control our genetic responsibility. Our genes are beyond our control, and we cannot sort out the "good" ones from the "bad" ones (not yet, at least). But even here, we can do more than might be suspected at first blush. We can at least *be aware of both the probable genetic limitations and genetic possibilities of our offspring.* We saw in Chapter 2, for example, that intelligence is strongly affected by heredity. Surely, then, we should accept intellectual behavior in our children that is no greater than our own. While we might expect performance to be up to capacity, to ignore the genetic contribution to that capacity is to invite psychological problems of our own making. We saw in Chapter 15 the harmful effects of continued failure experiences upon level of aspiration.

A second example, closer to home, comes to mind. We have seen that age of physical maturity has a genetic component. Early maturing parents are likely to beget early maturing children, and vice versa. We also saw that age of maturity has certain relationships to interpersonal behavior, particularly for boys. Late maturing boys tend to exhibit more signs of emotional immaturity, as exemplified by silliness, attention-seeking, hyperactivity, lack of heterosexual interests, etc. Now suppose two families living next to each other both have twelve-year-old boys, one early maturing and the other late maturing. There is a noticeable difference in their behavior, of the type just described. Suppose both fathers want their sons to be "men" as soon as possible—to be "chips off the old block," so to speak. The early maturing boy meets this standard more adequately than the late maturing boy, and the difference is noticeable to both fathers. Imagine the different way in which an enlightened father, aware of the indirect genetic contribution of physiological maturity to personality, might react as compared to an unenlightened father— one who sees only that his son is a "sissy" compared to the boy next door, and does not know why. *He* is not a sissy (not anymore)—why should his son be a sissy?

It is not hard to anticipate that such a father, in his blind frustration, might vent his disappointment on his son as though it were the son's fault—after all, who else is responsible? The enlightened father knows that *he* is partly responsible, for he carved the same footsteps a generation earlier, footsteps that in all probability could be traced back another generation or two. Being aware of the genetic factor involved, he can take *informed steps* to soften its impact. He can suggest and encourage activities, for example, in which his son has strengths of his own, in order to strengthen his self-concept. He can treat him as more mature than he is, realizing that his hyperactivity and silliness are reactions, quite likely, to the lack of such recognition to begin with. *He can take advantage, in other words, of the established facts in such a way as to help his son overcome a genetically related liability.* The uninformed father is not likely to do so.

Turning to behavior patterns more directly under the control of environmental influences, parental responsibility becomes even more apparent. The chapters on learning and motivation provided the groundwork. They described the fundamental components that can be seen in every interaction between parents and children. Chapters 11 to 14 documented the extent to which these components affect the personality of the developing child as a result of learning. We saw evidence that, even in the first few days of life, an infant can learn to "reject" its mother

if the mechanics of the feeding situation are such as to produce a conflict between sucking and breathing. The effect on the mother can be
catastrophic: ". . . generally speaking, this is a situation that no mother
can endure" (p. 299). The secondary effects on the infant are not hard
to imagine. The mother loses her enthusiasm and her anticipations of
pleasant interactions with her baby and, in short, begins the long road
that may end in maternal rejection.

In early childhood, learning processes of increased variety occur. Sex-
typing, the accumulation of behavioral repertoires appropriate for one's
sex, was shown in Chapter 11 to be heavily dependent upon learning
experiences with the parents, experiences that affect identification and
imitation. Later in that chapter, the origins of dependency, aggression,
and achievement strivings were considered, and these too were shown
to be affected by learning experiences with the parents. The next two
chapters showed how such experiences continue to mold the child's personality as he develops through middle childhood and into adolescence.
Wherever one looks, the evidence serves as a constant reminder that
those who control the environment of the child—parents, neighbors,
teachers, citizens—are responsible for the behavior of the child to that
same extent.

And behavior has some stability. What is learned in childhood cannot easily be erased at a later age. The Fels data made it abundantly
clear that the child is father to the man. This message was emphasized
again and again as we studied the correlations between behaviors at different ages, describing the stability of passivity and dependency, aggression, achievement striving, sexuality, and social interaction anxiety. Even
when a given bit of behavior was not stable, it was not necessary to
abandon its determinants to the winds of chance and non-causality, but
to look more closely at parental pressures that were linked to the sex of
the child. There we speculated that even instability had its causes,
exemplified, for example, by the changing cultural expectations toward
aggression as girls approach womanhood (the "tomboy"–"sweet sixteen" shift), or expectations toward dependency as boys approach manhood.

It is this stability that most directly implicates the responsibility of
parents. As the child is father to the man, so are the parents father of
the child. By controlling the environment of the child, the parents control the behavior of the man. To the extent the reader recognizes the
role of environmental determinism in personality development, to that
extent will he be prepared to assume his own responsibilities when the
time comes.

Name Index

Aberle, D. F., 350, 376
Adamson, J., 378
Adelman, H. M., 202–204, 218
Allen, Lucile, 334
Allinsmith, W., 552
Alzobaie, J., 479
Ames, R., 56, 73
Anastasi, Anne, 94, 95, 106, 112
Anderson, C. C., 161
Anderson, D., 499, 508
Anderson, J. E., 108, 112
Anderson, L. D., 95, 112
Anderson, R. H., 469, 470, 478
Applezweig, M. H., 339, 376
Ariete, S., 508
Aronfreed, J., 511, 532, 547, 548, 550
Asch, S. E., 339, 376
Asher, E. J., 92, 112
Atkinson, J. W., 478
Ausubel, D. P., 511, 528, 529, 550

Babich, F. R., 113
Baer, D. M., 360, 377
Baker, C. T., 114, 378
Baker, K. E., 126, 161
Baldwin, A., 158, 161, 413, 415, 417, 434
Baldwin, B. T., 93, 112
Ballachey, E. L., 339, 350, 378
Bandura, A., 344, 345, 347, 361, 372–377, 392, 429, 435, 492, 495, 499, 500, 507, 536, 545, 550
Barbu, Z., 539, 550
Barker, R. G., 481, 507, 508
Bass, B. M., 507
Bayley, Nancy, 17, 19, 50, 51, 74, 335
Beaulieu, C., 114
Becker, W. C., 403, 407, 418, 421–434, 435, 449, 450, 526

Bell, N. W., 504, 508
Bell, R. Q., 359, 378, 418, 435
Bellis, C. J., 70, 75
Beloff, H., 339, 377
Benjamin, Lorna, 331, 333
Bennett, E. L., 81, 84, 112, 113, 114
Bennett, H. L., 378
Berenda, Ruth W., 485, 487, 489, 507
Berlyne, D. E., 195, 196, 218
Bernstein, A., 331, 333
Bieber, I., 355, 356, 358, 377
Bilous, C. B., 378
Binet, A., 117, 160, 161
Bird, Grace E., 95, 113
Bloom, B. S., 108, 113
Bloomfield, L., 127, 128, 161
Boardman, W. K., 189, 191
Boehm, L., 525, 550
Bonney, M. E., 502, 507
Boterline, Y. H., 56, 74
Bower, G. H., 82, 113
Bowlby, J., 321, 323, 324, 333
Bowman, P. H., 478
Brackbill, Yvonne, 113
Braine, M. D. S., 131, 161
Breese, Fay H., 434
Brittain, C. Y., 500, 507
Brodbeck, A. J., 331, 333
Brogden, H. E., 539, 550
Brown, A. W., 93, 114
Brown, D. G., 341, 377
Brown, J. S., 212, 218
Brown, P. A., 204–205, 218
Brown, R., 132, 150, 161
Bruner, J. S., 129, 161
Bryant, H. A., 500, 507
Bubash, S., 113
Buck, C., 114
Burgess, M., 218

557

Subject Index

Accommodation, Piaget's theory, 154–156, 160
Acetylcholine (ACH), and intelligence, 82
Achievement behavior
  and intelligence, 266
  as a classification system, 8
  at school; *see* School
  case history, 269–272
  need for, 214–215
  origins of, 372–376, 392–395, 433–434, 448–452
  stability of, 263–273
Acquired characteristics, inheritance of, 34
Acquired distinctiveness of cues, 129–130
Acquired equivalence of cues, 129
Adaptation, and conditioning, 168–169
Adjustment
  and morality, 511
  definition of, 553–554
  peer effects on, 494–498
  school dropouts; *see* School
  sex differences in school, 461–462
  to school, 446–477
Adolescent growth spurt; *see* Growth
Adopted children, and intelligence, 62–63, 106–107
Affection
  and learning, 170–171
  mother and infant, 297–333
Age
  and conformity, 488–489
  and dependency, 358
  and dropout prevention, 475–476
  and heterosexuality, 483–486
  and intelligence, 89–93, 264
  and morality, 546–548
  and motor control, 336–338

  and peer interactions, 480–489
  and play, 480–485
  and vocabulary, 130–131
Aggression
  and dependency, 429, 431
  and dominance, 249–261
  and frustration, 361–362, 388–391
  and identification, 370–372
  and language, 364
  and punishment, 365–372
  and school adjustment, 449–457
  and sex differences, 339–341
  and socioeconomic status, 110, 487–488
  case history, 252–258
  classification of behavior, 8
  correlational study of, 9–11
  experimental study of, 11–12
  genetic determinants in rats, 69–70
  origins of, 361–372, 388–391, 431–433
  stability of, 249–261
Albinism, and heredity, 30
Anemia, and heredity, 30
Anger; *see* Aggression
Anoxia, in infancy, 299–301
Anxiety; *see also* Social interaction anxiety
  and aggression, 365–372
  and avoidance conditioning, 174–177
  and conscience; *see* Morality
  and extinction, 180–189
  and fixations, 177–179
  and genetic determinants, 68–71
  and human motivation, 211–215
  and peers, 492–494
  and punishment, 365–372, 514–517, 520–523
  classification of behavior, 8–9
  conditioning of, 167–171
Aspirations; *see* Level of aspiration

563